The Open Veins of the Postcolonial: Afrodescendants and Racisms

Fall 2020/Spring 2021

Portuguese Literary & Cultural Studies (PLCS) is an interdisciplinary, peer-reviewed hybrid online and print journal that publishes original research related to the literatures and cultures of the diverse communities of the Portuguese-speaking world from a broad range of academic, critical and theoretical approaches. PLCS is published semi-annually by Tagus Press in the Center for Portuguese Studies and Culture at the University of Massachusetts Dartmouth.

Manuscript Policy

Portuguese Literary & Cultural Studies welcomes submission of original and unpublished manuscripts in English or Portuguese appropriate to the goals of the journal. Manuscripts should be between 6,000–8,500 words in length and must be accompanied by an abstract. Manuscripts should be in accordance with the *MLA Style Manual and Guide to Scholarly Publishing* (latest version) or *The Chicago Manual of Style* (latest version) with parenthetical documentation and a list of works cited. The author is responsible for the accuracy of all quotations, titles, names, and dates. Manuscripts should be double-spaced throughout. All of the information must be in the same language (e.g., abstract, body of the article, bio-blurb). Updated guidelines are available at https://ojs.lib.umassd.edu/index.php/plcs/index. PLCS encourages submission of manuscripts in the form of a single attached MS Word document.

Portuguese Literary & Cultural Studies 34/35

The Open Veins of the Postcolonial: Afrodescendants and Racisms

Edited by Inocência Mata & Iolanda Évora

Tagus Press
UMass Dartmouth
Dartmouth, Massachusetts

Portuguese Literary and Cultural Studies 34/35
Center for Portuguese Studies and Culture/Tagus Press
University of Massachusetts Dartmouth

Copy edited by Diana Simões & Grace Holleran
Designed by Richard Hendel
Cover design & typesetting by Inês Sena

For all inquiries, please contact:
Center for Portuguese Studies and Culture/ Tagus Press
University of Massachusetts Dartmouth
285 Old Westport Road
North Dartmouth MA 02747–2300
Tel. 508–999–8255 / Fax 508–999–9272
https://www.umassd.edu/portuguese-studies-center/

Cover Image: Januario Jano. *Puzzle. The Begin.*
"memories are the most insightful things that can take backward or forward,
it gives a real perspective of who you are."—Januario Jano.
Reproduced with permission of the artist.

Publicado com o apoio do Centro de Estudos sobre África
e Desenvolvimento (CEsA) do Instituto Superior de Economia e Gestão
(ISEG) da Universidade de Lisboa (ULisboa).

ISSN: 1521-804X (print)
ISSN: 2573-1432 (online)
ISBN: 978-1-933227-96-2 (pbk.: alk. paper)
ISBN: 978-1-951470-18-0 (Ebook)

Library of Congress Control Number: 2022937243

5 4 3 2 1

Contents

The Open Veins
of the Postcolonial:
Afrodescendants
and Racisms

Apresentação: As veias abertas do pós-colonial: Afrodescendências e racismos

A Fernando Arenas
In memoriam

1. A motivação: A *Década Internacional de Afrodescendentes*

O tema deste número da revista *Portuguese Literary & Cultural Studies* (PLCS) surge num momento – e por causa dele – em que vai a meio o que se pretende que seja um amplo debate proposto pela ONU sobre a condição dos afrodescendentes no mundo, através da declaração da *Década Internacional de Afrodescendentes*, 2015-2024 (resolução 68/237). A proposta da ONU visa(va) alertar para a precariedade desses segmentos, em vários espaços do mundo, em termos de "reconhecimento, justiça e desenvolvimento".

Neste contexto, com este título, As Veias Abertas do Pós-colonial: Afrodescendência e Racismos,[i] que é uma ostensiva apropriação do livro de Eduardo Galeano, *As Veias Abertas da América Latina*, publicado há mais de 40 anos, pretendemos rastrear as heranças coloniais que têm vindo a prolongar-se e a reproduzir-se ao longo de décadas após a queda dos mais recentes impérios coloniais. Esse momento colonial imperial mantém-se nas sociedades contemporâneas das antigas metrópoles marcadas por uma matriz racial que participa ativamente da regulação das relações sociais pós-coloniais, hierárquicas e assimétricas. E é sobre essas heranças – e a sua normalização – que pretendemos reflectir, convocando diferentes perspectivas disciplinares e de enunciação, também impulsionadas pela investigação que estamos a desenvolver no âmbito do projecto AFRO-PORT - *Afro descendência em Portugal: sociabilidades, representações e dinâmicas sociopolíticas e culturais. Um estudo na Área Metropolitana de Lisboa* / *Afro-descendance in Portugal: Sociability, Representations and Sociopolitical and Cultural Dynamics. A Study in the Lisbon Metropolitan Area*, financiado pela Fundação para a Ciência e Tecnologia (FCT). Foi, pois, muito oportuno o convite (que muito agradecemos) que nos chegou da Direcção de *Portuguese Literary & Cultural Studies* para sermos "editoras convidadas" de um número da revista.

2. De *Afrodescendentes* e suas categorias: as diferentes abordagens

Para cumprir o desiderato de desconstrução de expressões normalizadas que "criam" falsas realidades, propusemos, através das linhas temáticas enunciadas na chamada de trabalhos, reunir ensaios que contribuam para a discussão e a compreensão da forma como se articula o lugar de pertença com a identidade étnico-racial neste século XXI, revendo e propondo algumas categorizações e conceitos aparentemente estabilizados (populações racializadas, afrodescendente...). Fazêmo-lo na medida em que vão surgindo categorias epistemológicas e temáticas da análise de diferenças raciais e étnicas bem assim como decorrentes da sociabilidade, representações e dinâmicas sociopolíticas e culturais. O que se pretende, igualmente, é que se possa desvelar a discursividade naturalizante da ideologia da subalternidade e a discriminação institucionalizada por várias "crenças" e práticas tácitas (por exemplo, o pressuposto de que a criança africana ou afrodescendente tem mais dificuldade na disciplina de Português). Pretende-se, enfim, encontrar estratégias, discursivas e de acção, que possibilitem que essas veias abertas possam ser "cosidas" para que não sangrem até a uma crónica invisibilidade. E estas são as propostas para esta discussão, reunidas neste *dossier* em cinco partes.

A primeira parte, denominada "As veias abertas do pós-colonial: a contemporaneidade," abre com um tema que aborda um assunto caro a quem hoje, em Portugal, pugna pelo reconhecimento e inclusão do segmento negro na nação portuguesa. Em "Black Europe and a Contested European Union," Kwame Nimako fala da posição, do estatuto e da condição dos negros no projecto europeu. Referindo-se a diferentes "estádios" da questão nos diferentes países europeus, e diferentes experiências negras também nesses países, Nimako realça, no entanto, que existem pontos comuns entre essas experiências decorrentes da relação histórica com o colonialismo e os arranjos constitucionais prevalecentes em cada Estado-nação. Partindo da relação entre o nacionalismo na Europa, o surgimento, a consolidação e a expansão da União Europeia e as implicações das relações raciais e étnicas na Europa actualmente, Nimako destaca a ambiguidade da condição do negro europeu, entre a visibilidade e a invisibilidade, que se tornou uma parte importante do quadro de análises da posição e do status dos europeus negros, realçando a investigação sobre o assunto de negros europeus. No segundo artigo, "Ninguém imagina de verdade um português negro," Miguel Vale de Almeida, "partindo da [sua] posição social como branco, não-racializado e com consciência política disso mesmo," interroga-se sobre a "confusão" que em Portugal, ainda dimensionado num discurso sobre descobrimentos e o *aggiornamento* lusotropicalista, se faz entre cidadania e a pertença étnica/nacional. Daí resulta um estado de negação que permeia e reforça o racismo nas suas diferentes modalidades: interpessoal, institucional e estrutural, sendo este "o mais complexo de identificar e que é o que efetivamente reproduz o racismo." O último artigo deste segmento, da autoria das organizadoras deste *dossier*, intitula-se "As Veias Abertas da Afrodescendência: Herança Colonial e Contemporaneidade" e propõe-se a uma reflexão sobre esta categoria que entrou na terminologia dos estudos sociais e que nem sempre significa e nomeia o mesmo referente, havendo, por isso, alguma ambiguidade no seu uso em Portugal, onde há "afrodescendentes" que não o aceitam como auto-identificação.

Na segunda parte do *dossier*, em "Histórias imperiais e estruturações políticas," percorre-se a história de africanos e afrodescendentes na metrópole imperial, desde o século XVI ao século XX. No texto "Africanos em Portugal: uma dialéctica de integração e de exclusão (séculos XV- XX)," Isabel Castro Henriques rastreia o processo fundador da presença dos africanos em Portugal, e como intervieram na estruturação da sociedade portuguesa dos séculos XVI a XX através de um riquíssimo e variado suporte iconográfico. Henriques estuda o processo de resistência e mestiçagens culturais, através dos africanos (escravizados e livres) que intervieram na estruturação da sociedade portuguesa dos séculos XVI a XX. O ensaio mostra como todo esse processo de reconstrução identitária se organizou em torno de um jogo inclusivo e integrador nas práticas sociais portuguesas, e exclusivo e discriminatório pela força do preconceito anti-negro e anti-escravo construído e consolidado pelos portugueses, revelando as manifestações silenciosas mas interventivas de uma comunidade secular na organização, na história e na memória portuguesas, o que gerou patrimónios culturais sincréticos que permaneceram no país. Na mesma linha, Cláudia Castelo, preocupada com uma ausência existente na historiografia no que respeita aos estudos disponíveis sobre a história contemporânea dos africanos e afrodescendentes em Portugal – que, no entanto, quase não abordam o período posterior à abolição da escravatura ou fazem-no de forma insuficiente – propõe um regresso ao "arquivo imperial." Por isso, o título "Africanos e afrodescendentes na metrópole imperial (século XX): um regresso ao 'arquivo imperial'" propõe uma "reconversão do ângulo de análise" através de uma prática historiográfica eticamente e civicamente empenhada, não sem antes fazer um "estado da arte" sobre este assunto, estabelecendo um quadro mais abrangente e comparativo sobre os africanos e afrodescendentes nas metrópoles europeias – a "Londres negra" e a "Paris negra." A autora conclui que continua a "invisibilização dos africanos e afrodescendentes, negros e mestiços, portugueses (assim autoidentificados ou não) na metrópole imperial" e que esta se articula "com a persistência do racismo e da discriminação racial na sociedade portuguesa contemporânea." O terceiro artigo deste segmento, "The relationship between the formation of Cape Verdean society and Upper Guinea," de Paulino de Oliveira do Canto, persegue ainda o viés histórico para perceber o projecto de expansão do imperialismo e a consequente institucionalização da escravidão em outras partes do mundo, particularmente no Atlântico e nas "Américas." No entanto, diferentemente dos dois primeiros, afasta-se das premissas da presença africana em Portugal, optando por se interrogar sobre o quão o passado da formação da sociedade cabo-verdiana e as suas relações (socioculturais, políticas e económicas) com a (Alta) Guiné tem influenciado os processos migratórios entre os países da Comunidade Económica dos Estados da África Ocidental (CEDEAO).

A terceira parte do *dossier* inclui igualmente três ensaios que incidem sobre "Identidades afro-diaspóricas: entre a herança colonial e a afirmação identitária" e têm o Brasil como "lugar de fala," buscando compreender a contemporaneidade do racismo antinegro. Lia Vainer Schucman reflecte, em "Entre o Branco e a Branquitude: letramento racial e formas de desconstrução do racismo," sobre ideia de raça e os significados acerca da branquitude apropriados e construídos por sujeitos brancos. A autora concentra-se, principalmente, na análise sobre possíveis formas de desconstrução do racismo nas identidades raciais brancas, o que tem sido nomeado no Brasil como Branquitude. Esta abordagem é complementada com as reflexões de Ana Flauzina e Thula Pires em "Por formas *amefricanas* de autoinscrição": a partir das noções de antinegritude, genocídio e amefricanidade, as autoras desvelam os processos de assalto à vida negra como o grande sustentáculo do pacto social e político no Brasil, propondo o neologismo "*amefricana*" para referir "sobrevivências" da cultura africana no continente americano. Por seu lado, Aristeu Portela traça uma periodização analítica desses discursos, por meio do que denomina "ordens de discurso" de raça e identidade nacional em "Relações raciais e identidade nacional no Brasil: da nação (ambiguamente) mestiça à nação multicultural e pluriétnica."

Seguem-se dois segmentos sobre a produção cultural de afrodescendentes, com dez ensaios, "Afrodescendência e a Afro-diáspora: representações e produções culturais e Afrodescendência e enunciação literária." O primeiro segmento, a quarta parte do volume, inclui três ensaios. O de Fernando Arenas – a quem homenageamos, dedicando-lhe este número de *PLCS*, e que muito o enriquece – intitula-se "Africanos e afrodescendentes no cinema português contemporâneo: imigrantes, cidadãos, humanos"; Ana Cristina Pereira é autora de "O peso do passado em conversas sobre *Cavalo Dinheiro* (2014) de Pedro Costa: (re)formulação e (re)produção do discurso racista e colonialista através de 'novas' estratégias discursivas"; e Kaian Lam (aka Cindy Lam) apresenta "Stomach Thoughts: A Socio-Cultural Study of Indirect Afro-Representations in Popular Portuguese Imageries of 'African' Food as Compared to 'Asian' Food and the Implications." O artigo de Fernando Arenas traça uma panorâmica crítica de filmes (longas-metragens e documentários) de Pedro Costa, Inês Oliveira, Leonel Vieira, Joaquim Leitão, e o coletivo composto por Kiluanje Liberdade, Inês Gonçalves e Vasco Pimentel, ligados às experiências de africanos e afrodescendentes no Portugal contemporâneo; aí discute como essa produção cultural reflecte uma nação portuguesa em plena mutação, quando estão a ser (re)definidas as percepções do que é "ser africano" ou "ser europeu"; Ana Cristina Pereira continua na senda de pensar a produção cultural afrodescendente através da linguagem fílmica, elaborando o seu artigo a partir de duas questões epistemológicas, tentando perceber como dialogam jovens portugueses com as representações identitárias do "outro" africano propostas no filme *Cavalo Dinheiro* e como analisar um filme que questiona discursos vigentes sobre a história, as expressões simbólicas e a identidade portuguesa. Kaian Lam, no entanto, aborda outro tipo de produção cultural: a comida (ou, se quiserem, a gastronomia), através de uma proposta (original) de politização dos "pensamentos do estômago" e de uma maneira criativa de compreender os desafios e oportunidades para os afrodescendentes em Portugal. Lam propõe uma reflexão sobre a comunicação intercultural (interétnica também) a partir das representações africanas no mundo imaginário português acerca de alimentação "africana," contrapondo esse imaginário com a alimentação "asiática" (que é apenas referida, diz a autora, para ilustrar o caso africano).

O quinto segmento do *dossier*, "Afrodescendência e enunciação literária," concentra-se na literatura de autoria afrodescendente portuguesa e brasileira, o que constitui um momento interessante para comparar duas realidades literárias – a brasileira e a portuguesa –, em que a autoria negra e afrodescendente é sempre remetida ou para as margens do cânone literário (no caso brasileiro) ou, no caso português, para as literaturas dos países de que são originários os autores. Emerson Inácio, Margarida Calafate Ribeiro e Erin Rossnan McCombe abordam a dicção portuguesa de autoria negra, enquanto Rosangela Sarteschi fala de "literatura negra brasileira." Com efeito, Emerson Inácio, em "'Língua de preto' e dicção negra: do dialeto barroco à veiculação identitária," fala de *Açafate de Floremas* (1971), de António (de Brito Oliveira e) Cruz, uma cartografia descritiva da autoria negra em Portugal num momento em que uma produção literária vem consolidando as suas particularidades discursiva e estética no campo que o autor designa como "Literatura Afroportuguesa," num gesto de reconhecimento das particularidades discursivas dessas produções. Enquanto isso, Margarida Calafate Ribeiro situa a sua análise num tempo mais recente, o da pós-colonialidade; em "*O Sentimento de um(a) Ocidental* declinado no feminino," a autora aborda a literatura recentemente produzida por mulheres afrodescendentes Negras, a saber: Djaimilia Pereira de Almeida, *Esse Cabelo*; Tvon (pseudónimo de Telma Escórcio da Silva), *Um Preto Muito Português*; e Yara Monteiro, *Essa Dama Bate Bué*; porém não sem antes fazer uma breve apresentação sobre o "estado da arte" da produção cultural afrodescendente em Portugal, no campo das artes visuais e performativas. Finalmente, Erin Mccombe, partindo do quadro metodológico para os estudos de intermedialidade, analisa, em "The right to represent, reproduce and refuse: Memory, Photography and Postcolonial ekphrasis in the work of Djaimilia Pereira de Almeida," dois textos de Djaimilia Pereira de Almeida – o romance *Esse Cabelo* (2015) e a crónica "Pérola sem rapariga" – através do diálogo entre a memória, a fotografia e a écfrase pós-colonial no contexto lusófono. Já no quadro brasileiro, Rosangela Sarteschi aborda, numa perspectiva histórica (desde o grupo *Quilombhoje* e dos *Cadernos Negros*), a trajectória de resistência na poesia de autoria negra (Miriam Alves, Cuti, Éle Semog, Jônatas Conceição, Salgado Maranhão e Sacolinha, pertencentes a gerações diferentes). Em "Literatura negra brasileira e os diálogos com o cânone: outros olhares, outras histórias," a autora analisa a representação desses sujeitos numa escrita orientada pelos valores éticos e estéticos fundamentalmente brancos mas que buscam construir um horizonte utópico em que o negro surge como voz essencial no âmbito do sistema literário nacional.

A revista inclui também uma parte dedicada a "Recensões" de obras que versam sobre a produção intelectual, cultural e artística de africanos e afrodescendentes, publicadas a partir de 2018, quando este *dossier* começou a ser organizado. Quatro recensões compõem esta parte, em resenhas feitas por Maria Paula Meneses (*Mahanyela: a vida na periferia da grande cidade*, de Nely Nyaka e Gita

Honwana), Sheila Khan (*Descolonizações. Reler Amílcar Cabral, Césaire e Du Bois no Séc. XXI*, livro organizado por Manuela Ribeiro Sanches), Simone Amorim (*História e Cultura Afrodescendente*, publicação organizada por Elio Ferreira de Souza, Iraneide Soares da Silva, José Bispo de Miranda, Cláudio Rodrigues de Melo) e Luca Fazzini (*Quem tem medo do feminismo negro?*, de Djamila Ribeiro).

Esperamos que este *dossier* da revista *Portuguese Literary & Cultural Studies* possa vir a constituir-se como uma "obra" de referência para o estudo da afrodescendência em Portugal, na sua perspectiva diacrónica e contemporânea – em Portugal sobretudo, onde o tema ainda é visto como disruptivo.

Lisboa, Dezembro de 2020

NOTA

1. Começamos por referir um aspecto deste dossier que nos parece importante e tem a ver com a grafia: o segundo aspecto, que parece ser de ordem ortográfica, é, na verdade, de ordem epistemológica – e ideológica: a grafia de *Afrodescendência/Afrodescendente*. Talvez tivéssemos preferido a grafia com hífen precisamente porque gostaríamos que as palavras não designassem um "simples" nome ou adjectivo relacional, mas que as duas identidades associadas aos termos funcionassem como identidades **sumativas (sim, sumativas, não somativas)** – cumulativas, se quisermos. Porém, neste momento em que a discussão tem estado na ordem do dia em Portugal, não quisemos polemizar por causa de algo formal: com efeito, preferimos uma polémica sobre a substância. E também para alinharmos com outras geografias linguísticas que nos servem de termo de comparação.

INOCÊNCIA MATA é Professora do Departamento de Literaturas Românicas, na Área de Literaturas, Artes e Culturas da Faculdade de Letras da Universidade de Lisboa (FLUL/ULisboa), directora do Doutoramento em Língua e Cultura Portuguesa (Português Língua Estrangeira-Língua Segunda), membro integrado do Centro de Estudos Comparatistas da ULisboa. E Co-Investigadora Responsável do Projecto AFRO-PORT. Afrodescendência em Portugal: sociabilidades, representações e dinâmicas sociopolíticas e culturais. Um estudo na Área Metropolitana de Lisboa."

IOLANDA ÉVORA é Investigadora Associada do Centro de Estudos sobre África e o Desenvolvimento (CEsA) e Professora Auxiliar do Mestrado em Desenvolvimento e Cooperação Internacional do Instituto Superior de Economia e Gestão da Universidade de Lisboa (ISEG/ULisboa). Investigadora Responsável do Projecto AFRO-PORT. Afrodescendência em Portugal: sociabilidades, representações e dinâmicas sociopolíticas e culturais. Um estudo na Área Metropolitana de Lisboa."

I. As veias abertas do pós-colonial: a contemporaneidade

KWAME NIMAKO

Black Europe and a Contested European Union

ABSTRACT: European nations have several things in common, such as notions of geography, religion and race, they also have differences, such as their historical relationship to colonialism, and the constitutional arrangements prevalent in each nation-state. Each of these differences in turn can have a significant impact on the possibilities and the constraints for political mobilization and social mobility of Black Europeans within member states. The European Union (EU) is also a contested project in which multiple 'stakeholders' compete or cooperate to defend or advance their position and status within it. The stakeholders include nations, states, political parties, ethnic groups, religious groups, and social and civil movements, each of which has differential access to political power, and to economic and cultural resources.

KEYWORDS: Black Europe, European Union, Populism, Nativism, Social movements

Introduction and Context

The European Union (EU) is a contested project in which multiple "stakeholders" compete or cooperate to defend or advance their position and status within it. The stakeholders include nations, states, political parties, ethnic groups, religious groups, and social and civil movements, each of which has differential access to political power and to economic and cultural resources. The EU is contested in part because although those with vested interests in the project have a relatively clear idea about when it was set in motion, it is not clear that they know where it is heading and when it will end. This uncertainty—and ambivalence—regarding the EU likewise characterizes the position, status, and condition of Black Europeans within the EU. In this article I seek to shed some light on the place of Black Europeans in the EU project. Even mentioning the issue of Black Europeans evokes strong emotions among those who equate "Europeanness" with "race" or whiteness. It can also evoke equally strong and ambivalent emotions among some Black people who question whether they will be allowed to be fully European—to feel European and be treated as European—beyond the status of possessing formal citizenship in one of the European states. This is all the more so since the notion of Black Europe implies an implicit knowledge and acknowledgement of the existence of an Other Europe of color.

It has become common in academic research and publications, in conferences and in various social media, to speak of Black Europeans (Small; Hine et al.; Pitts; Afroeuropeans 7th annual conference, 2019). This common language recognizes that there are national differences in the Black experience across European nations, but it highlights that there are also some important common dimensions to these experiences (Small 2018). It is important to note that although people speak of Black Europeans, there is in fact no European citizenship. Instead, there are Black people possessing the citizenship of different European nations. In addition, European nations have several things in common, such as notions of geography, religion, and race, while they also have differences, such as their historical relationship to colonialism and the constitutional arrangements in each nation-state. Each of these differences in turn can have a significant impact on the possibilities and constraints for political mobilization and social mobility of Black Europeans within member states.

The first section of this article examines the relationship between nationalism in Europe, the emergence, consolidation, and expansion of the EU, and the implications of both for race and ethnic relations in Europe at present, with a particular focus on Black Europeans. This is followed by an analysis of the relation between populism and nativism. I explore these two important phenomena by raising issues that revolve around notions regarding claims, citizenship, class, gender, and "race." In the third section, I reflect on the notion of visibility/invisibility that has become an important part of the frame of analyses of the position and status of Black Europeans in some of the literature by Black European scholars and activists (Essed and Hoving; Keaton et al.; McEachrane).

I conclude by arguing that what tends to be classified as populism today may more usefully be considered as a form of nativism. This is all the more so since the conditions that nurtured European nationalism—of which colonialism was a major and consequential component—no longer operate in the same way, and they cannot be reversed. Sovereign nations in Africa and Asia today cannot be recolonized. Nevertheless, the rise of populist movements has put left-leaning political groupings on the defensive, partly because their intellectual tradition tends overwhelmingly to subsume race under class; this, in turn, has directly affected their current assessment of right-wing politics. The right-leaning political groupings tend to adopt the language of the nativist and "dog whistle" to hold on to what they believe can be salvaged from what is left of their pre–World War II power. The inclusion of race and ethnic relations into political-economic analysis will enhance our knowledge on the making of the European Union.

On Nationalism and the Emergence of the EU

It can be stated that the European Union, as a formal organization, emerged out of the ashes of World War II and formed part of an attempt to deal with some of the challenges that revolved around nationalism, communism, and decolonization. This included key concerns about both European and global security. The creation of the EU was also motivated by important economic goals and interests. With regard to nationalism, Jerry Muller noted about a decade ago that:

> A familiar and influential narrative of the twentieth-century European history argues that nationalism twice led to war, in 1914 and then again in 1939. Therefore, the story goes, Europeans concluded that nationalism was a danger and gradually abandoned it. In the post-war decades, *western Europeans* enmeshed themselves in a web of transnational institutions, culminating in the European Union (EU). (2008: 19; my emphasis)

Muller's observation strongly suggests that the end of World War II is a useful date for periodization to analyze and discuss the *formation, consolidation, and expansion* of the EU. Like all periodization, a narrative can be built backward or forward. This is all the more so since nationalism does not stand on its own; it stands for something or against something. At a certain time in history it stood for notions of European expansion and colonization of non-European territories, while at another time it stood for the containment of communism.

If we take a backward look, it can be argued that nation-states, as we understand them today, emerged after the conclusion of the Peace of Westphalia of 1648 (Nimako and Willemsen 2011). The treaty that underpinned the Peace of Westphalia occurred in the context of thirty years of religious wars between different factions of the Christian religious faith in Europe and its conclusion gave rise to Catholic-led nations and monarchs and Protestant-led nations and monarchs. These developments not only established the basis of what we refer to as nation-states, but it can also be argued that the movement toward secularization accelerated after the religious wars and the recognition of national sovereignties under the treaty. This affected the organization of knowledge in the

13

arena of "secular science" and "secular philosophy," and both in turn challenged and undermined the authority of European Christian theology. But the moral basis that Christian theology established lingered and it should not be overlooked, though this tends to be denied publicly by those who consider themselves as rational and reasonable, including those who describe themselves atheist.

In addition to containing nationalism, the new security and economic project that was initiated was designed to contain communism and foster economic recovery. Thus, in a quick succession, a political union was formed between Belgium, Luxemburg, and the Netherlands that became known as the Benelux Union in 1948. The relevant documents were initially signed in 1944 by the exiled representatives from Belgium, the Netherlands, and Luxemburg at the London Customs Convention as a customs agreement, and they were later ratified as the Benelux Customs Union in 1947, which became a political-economic union in 1948 (Nimako and Small 2009). The Benelux, together with West Germany, France, and Italy formed the European Coal and Steel Community in 1951. All of the objectives described above from this union of nations were relevant, but the economic motivation seemed at first glance to be the most important, especially because of the explicit attention to coal and steel.

In 1957, these six countries signed the Treaty of Rome and were renamed the European Economic Community (EEC), a regional organization designed to foster economic integration among its members. In addition to the concerns about keeping communism at bay and facilitating new economic arrangements, these developments also set new parameters for the geography of Europe. These parameters had important dimensions on both sides of the Atlantic. On the European side of the Atlantic, this gave rise to the notions of Western Europe and Eastern Europe; thus, geographically, what had for a long time been widely known as Central Europe, became politically Eastern Europe. At another level, communism, and its containment, served as the demarcation of Europe, and the post-war economic recovery project at home became an all-hands-on-deck project to keep class struggle in check through the welfare state.

In the background of what appeared to be an exclusively Pan-European project, we can identify the interests of those across the Atlantic seeking to develop a robust American military shield, as well as those within Europe seeking to develop a German economic shield. Changes across the Atlantic likewise affected the geography of Europe due to the territories located outside of its immediate physical geography that are either officially component parts of nation-states in

Europe (such as Martinique and Guadeloupe; Sharpley-Whiting 2009) or that are claimed by European countries, such as the Dutch Antilles. Though these territories are often represented as integral and essential parts of European states, they are, in fact, highly racialized in ways that have significant consequences. These issues affect not only nations across the Atlantic in the Americas, but also nations in Africa, because of the widespread and enduring impact of colonialism across that continent. The legacy of these developments can be seen today in the geographic areas referred to as Anglophone Africa, Francophone Africa, and Lusophone Africa.

In the long historical processes described above, it is often overlooked that as European nations met with one another to formalize and operationalize their sovereign nations, they also failed to recognize the sovereignties and humanities of other people (Nimako and Willemsen 2011). One consequence of this is that while nation-state formation on first appearance seems to be exclusively about the physical geography of Europe, it is, in fact, highly implicated in the extension of nation-states' sovereignty beyond the physical geographic location that we currently refer to as Europe.

Of the six countries that formed the EEC, two (Germany and Italy) had lost their colonies as a consequence of the First and Second World Wars; three (Belgium, France, and the Netherlands) were still colonial powers and they took their colonies into account. In fact, Articles 131 through 136 of the European Economic Community Treaty of 1957 provided for "association" with its colonies and opened up the territories to member states that did not have colonies. But the political irony is that it referred to the colonies as non-European countries and territories with which EEC member states had "special relations." This culminated in the signing of the first Yaoundé Convention on 20 July 1963 between eighteen African states (Association of African States and Madagascar—AASM) and six EEC member states and overseas departments and territories (ODTs), namely, the Dutch Antilles and Suriname and the French overseas departments and territories (Nimako and Small 2009: 217).

In 2019, we are currently dealing with the consequence of these processes, one of the most important aspects of which is that we now have European citizens whose genealogy is located outside the geographic location we call Europe. These Europeans carry nation-state passports, they have many of the rights of Europeans within geographical Europe, they speak the languages of these nations, and they are socialized in the culture of these nations. But they are racialized in ways that mean that their rights are in practice constrained. One constraint is that they are regarded as permanent strangers (Sivanandan 1982). They carry the burden of the history of non-recognition. Some refer to them now as migrants even if they hold citizenship of European nations, but I refer to them as Black Europeans. We will return to this below. For the moment, suffice it to say that the EEC was further consolidated between 1957 and 1972; its membership expanded to nine when the UK, Ireland, and Norway joined in 1973, followed by Greece in 1981 and Portugal and Spain in 1986. This increased the EEC membership to twelve. In 1995, after the EEC was renamed the EU in 1993, Austria, Finland and Sweden joined and brought its membership to fifteen.

As a result of the end of the Cold War, and by implication the end of the threat of communism, Cyprus, Czech Republic, Estonia, Hungary, Latvia, Lithuania, Malta, Poland, Slovakia, and Slovenia became members in 2004, Bulgaria and Romania in 2007, and Croatia in 2013. At the time of writing—2019—there were twenty-eight members.

As the number of member nations increased, some key elements of the motivating forces were modified or changed. For example, the renaming of the EEC as the EU in 1993 indicated that economics was no longer the only, or primary, reason for European integration. By 1995, EU leaders were confident enough to enact the Schengen Agreement to regulate free movement of people across EU member states. This, in turn, accelerated the four constituent conditions of EU membership, namely, freedom of movement of goods, capital, service, and labor.

The Schengen agreement was followed by the Dublin Agreement, signed in the Republic of Ireland in 1997. Apparently, the Dublin agreement is a EU Regulation designed to determine which EU member state is responsible for the examination of an application for asylum, submitted by people who seek asylum. Thus, in a way, if the EEC became a shield against communism, Dublin became a shield against decolonization, hence, Fortress Europe. This is all the more so since it made it almost impossible for people outside the borders of the EU to seek asylum through EU airports, and it pushed the boundaries of the EU to the countries that border non-EU countries by land or sea.

The end of the Cold War revealed some of the contradictions in the EU model. After framing the EEC as a security and economic arrangement to withstand nationalism, communism, and decolonization, and building intellectual and state propaganda to underpin it, the EU found that a number of the nations that had been politically labelled as East European countries, formally referred to as "communist regimes" because they were under Russian occupation, were now knocking on the door of freedom. In fact, this new love of freedom occurred after the nations in question were free already from Russian nationalist or Soviet communist control. All of these developments had implications for the core of what defines Europe, namely, geography, race, religion, and citizenship. For example, after joining the EU, the nations of East and Central Europe, such as Hungary and Poland, complained that there were too many EU rules, including those governing asylum-seeking and refugees. When they were behind the iron curtain, they had sought asylum, but others, it would seem, should not seek asylum in their territories. At the same time, nations under the Federation of Yugoslavia imploded in the process of transition from command economy to deregulated economy.

Reflecting on the social dislocation and human displacement that accompanied such an implosion, *The Economist* noted that:

> From 1992 to 1995 Bosnia was the Syria of its day. Some 100,000 people died in the three-way war between the country's communities: its Orthodox Serbs, its Catholic Croats and its Muslims (often referred to as Bosnians). Unlike in Syria, though, Western powers intervened and eventually ended the shooting. (*The Economist*, 22)

This has given a new meaning to European geography and boundaries. Countries such as Greece, Italy, Hungary, and Poland have now found themselves with the new frontiers of Europe. This, in turn, has bolstered far right and new nationalist movements, such as in Iraq, Libya, and Syria, depending on the geographic location of human displacement due to wars and the role of EU member states therein. These developments all have profound implications for Black Europe, some of which I discuss below.

Populism, Nativism or Racialized Europe?

The recent (2019) losses in parliamentary elections by Christian Democrats and Labour Parties in favor of anti-refugee groups have brought notions of populism to the fore. Underlying these notions is intellectual bankruptcy and ideological dishonesty. This is all the more so since the issues of immigration, asylum-seekers, and refugees have been conflated. As we noted above, the enactment of the Schengen Agreement increased labor movement within the EU and generated a backlash in some countries, including the UK. This was compounded by the increased flow of asylum-seekers occasioned by human displacement associated with wars initiated by the US under George Bush in Afghanistan (2001) and Iraq (2003), and by France under Nicholas Sarkozy in Libya (2011) and Syria (2014).

The anti-refugee groups and the political parties that have consequently emerged from this situation are referred to as populists on two grounds. First, because they were considered marginal but have now found a strong voice as a result of the refugee crisis. Second, because they want to reverse the gains of transnationalism and return to nationalism. In fact, the left likened the right--wing populist parties originating from Conservative and Liberal parties to Nazis and Fascists. The Conservative and Liberal parties adopted the populist language of being tough on immigration. This conflated the issue of immigration with asylum-seekers and refugees, and it is not clear which one they want to address: immigration or human displacement to avoid asylum-seeking or refuse refugee status to those who apply. What is clear is that the language is xenophobic.

This is compounded by claims made by citizens on the state, as well as claims among citizens. Claims also make the distinction between the economic and social issues a false dichotomy because the economic affects the social.

In political campaigns, what matters is who is on the offensive and who is on the defensive. Both the far-left and far-right have now found a new enemy called Brussels; they do not express that capitalism is the enemy, because nobody knows what capitalism is. Left-leaning politicians and intellectuals tend to attribute the rise of the far-right to economic crisis.

It should be noted that many of the individuals who lead the far-right movements and political parties were at a given moment part of the center-right and liberal political parties. But their followers come from all walks of life. What they and their followers have in common is an imaginary notion of who should or should not belong to the "ideal nation."

Why claims? Because claims are central to social and political change; claims also test the limits of race and citizenship. The claims of citizens tend to be different from non-citizens. The non-citizens at this point in time are largely represented by asylum-seekers. There is also the issue of hierarchy of claims. Whose claim has urgency and priority? Let me explain. Long before the current economic crisis became a household topic, there were sections of the citizenry who were living in perpetual crisis. Governments knew it; trade unions knew it; "civil society" knew it; but those affected did not take to the streets to demand jobs; neither did people take to the street on their behalf. In fact, very many of those affected by unemployment have even resigned to their fate and have stopped looking for jobs. Again, governments knew it, and still know it, but did not call it a crisis; instead, the order of the day is the criminalization of the Black communities that depend on state safety, also called social welfare.

So, we are back to the issue of the hierarchy of claims. Whose claims have urgency and priority? When the popular image equates citizenship with race, we get nativism. What is nativism? Nativism serves as a powerful force in policing and the regulating of race and ethnic relations. Whereas citizenship "guarantees" equal legal rights in relation to nationality within the state, nativism becomes a conscious or unconscious attempt by groups and individuals considered to be native Europeans to replace overt rights derived from citizenship by covert rights derived from history and skin color. Thus, nativism becomes the structural and ideological attempt by individuals and/or groups to enforce subordination by emphasizing difference and ethnic hierarchy or *ethnarchy* where biology--informed racism, culture-informed ethnicism, and legal-informed citizenship for the same have failed.

This can be clarified further by making clear what nativism is not. Unlike racism, nativism is not based on notions of superiority and inferiority; thus, nativism cannot be legislated for or against. Nativism is based on notions of presumed inherent historical rights, national identity, and national interest. While under certain conditions class can neutralize racism, class cannot neutralize nativism because nativism appeals to deeply embedded notions and beliefs about history, belonging, national identity, and national interest. That said, even those Blacks who are able to find jobs tend to be blamed by others for taking jobs from "natives." This is what we have elsewhere called nativism (Nimako and Small 2009).

However, from the point of view of nativism, as well as of racism, equality poses more problems than inequality. In other words, both racism and nativism thrive on inequality. But the world has changed. Thus, unlike racism, which can no longer be defended formally, nativism can be defended formally, in the name of "national identity" and "national interest" in response to a changing world. This partly explains why mainstream political parties resort to the dog whistle. For a case in point we can look to the recent (2019) political developments in the Social Democratic Party of Denmark. These changes will affect our notions of citizenship, race, and our claims as citizens to each other and to our institutions. Take a look at the demography of the ethnic composition of some, if not most, of the prison populations in Europe and you will notice that any talk of color blindness is a delusion at best and a lie at worst.

We can conclude this section with the following: if we operationalize European nationalism to include factors such as wars, national economic interest and development, and colonialism, then many of the current populist parties do not qualify as nationalist. This is all the more so since the international environment is different. Decolonization is complete and will not and cannot be revisited. The EU governments that engaged in wars in Iraq, Libya, and Syria, that opened the floodgates of asylum-seekers to Europe and elsewhere were not populist right-wing extremist parties; they were mainstream governments. The problem is that the populists turn the other way when it comes to mainstream governments waging wars that give rise to asylum-seekers. What populist groupings have in common is nativism.

This raises the question of what should be done? To which my response is the following: democracy and politics as we know them in the EU depend on those who vote and those who do not vote. Politics also depends on who is on the offensive and who is on the defensive. At the moment, the nativists are on the offensive, but it does not mean they are in the majority.

Black Europe, the Public Square, and the Boardroom

Race and inequalities find their expression in notions of visibility and invisibility, and these notions have become recurring themes in Black Europe (Hine et al. 2009). These notions and their many variants have been used for conferences, workshops, and publications. Underlying or hidden in this "now you see, now you don't" phenomenon are fundamental questions concerning citizenship, the public square, and the boardroom (Simon 2008). At one level of visibility, it is common to observe Black Europeans during major entertainment events, like the Eurovision contest, and at major sports events such as football and athletics.

In fact, Stephen Small correctly speaks of ambiguous hyper-visibility. In his words:

Black people are hyper-visible in a range of highly stereotypical arenas. This includes those at the very bottom—unskilled, low-paid workers, street vendors and beggars, sex workers, the unemployed and homeless, as well as criminals and prisoners. Images of illegal immigrants, and Africans suffering and dying in the Mediterranean are ubiquitous. It also includes hyper-visible images—so-called positive images—in the music, television and entertainment, and in sport such as soccer and athletics. Some images are of black Europeans—Patricia Mamona, Kaddi Sagnia, Nafissatou Thiam and Katarina Johnson-Thompson. But many of the most popular images are of Black Americans, for example, Oprah Winfrey, Barak Obama, Beyonce and Nicki Minaj, Serena and Venus Williams, and Naomi Osaka. And there are some others too—Bob Marley and Usain Bolt. (2018)

He goes on to note that:

These images are meant to suggest black people are a success, but it's simply not true. They are entirely unrepresentative of black people as a whole; any success that has been achieved is largely limited to a minuscule number of black people; most black people in these industries occupy subordinate roles. And there are also highly sexualized images of half-naked black women athletes. (2018)

What underlines these ambiguous visibilities is that they are based on competitions whose ultimate judges are the broader public. On the other hand, there is invisibility at play that reflects the widespread exclusion of Black Europeans from essential networks that propel social mobility. Again, in the words of Stephen Small:

At the same time, Black people are also subject to hyper-invisibility in the upper echelons of wealth, status and power. No one is surprised when a black woman sings, dances, performs. That's what black women are supposed to do. But a black woman who is CEO of pharmaceutical company, an IT company, a surgeon or Lawyer, and then its WOW? How the hell on earth did she do that? (2018)

As the European Union election of 23 May 2019 approached, the April 2019 edition of *The Economist* gave a quick tour of the major issues under discussion in the election. Under the title "Votes without frontiers," *The Economist* noted that:

The unprecedented wave of crisis and change over the 2014 to 2019 parliamentary term has emphasized Europe's interdependence and with it the role of pan-European politics. The migration surge of 2015 was a European drama, not just a Greek or Hungarian or German one. Terror networks have crossed

> borders and attack cities in various European countries. Brexit, Donald Trump's presidency and the rise of China threaten Europe as a whole. The crowd scene have been continental, not national refugees trudging along motorways, pro- and anti-migration demonstrations, the anti-establishment *gilets jaunes* protests and, most recently, environmentalist school strikes. (*The Economist*, 25)

Now that the election has come to pass, I think we can test some of the consequences of the observations by *The Economist*. As the table below indicates, the tra itional political parties, namely Christian Democrats and Social Democrats, lost some ground to liberal and green parties, but the gains of the right-wing populists were not as large. Together with the Liberal Conservatives, the Christian Democrats lost 32 seats in 2019. But this was less than the Social Democrats, who lost 39 seats. Some of those losses became gains for the Social Liberals and Conservative Liberals who gained 41 seats in 2019.

Table 1

Preliminary 2019 Results by Political Group

Political Group	Name	Seats	
		2014	2019
Christian democrats and Liberal Conservatives	EPP	221	179
Social Democrats	S & D	191	152
Social Liberals and Conservative Liberals	ALDE	69	110
Ecologists and Regionalists	Greens/EFA	50	75
National Conservatives and Sovereignists	ECR	70	73
Far-right and hard Eurosceptics	ENF	36	61
Right-wing populists and hard Eurosceptics	EFDD	48	44
Democratic Socialists and Communists	GUE/NGL	52	41
Non-Inscrits	Non-Inscrits	52	10
Others and new parties	N/A	-	6
Total		751	751

If we do some permutations and combinations, we will notice that the vote increase of the far-right is not as great as it appears. Given the history of European politics, if you group into five on a continuum, namely, Right-wing and Left-wing, we get the following outcome.

At the European Union parliament level, the five right-wing political groupings are EPP, ALDE, ECR, ENF, and EFDD, and they remain the majority of the 751-seat parliament. The left-wing political groupings are S&D, EFA, GUE, and NGL. During the 2014 European Union election the right-wing grouping gained 444 seats (59%); and this increased to 485 (65%) in the 2019 election. This is an increase of 41 seats, and the far-right took eleven of these. On the contrary, the share of the four left-wing political groupings, namely, S&D, EFA, GUE and NGL, decreased from 293 (39%) in 2014 to 268 (36%) in 2019. This represents a loss of 25 seats, of which the far-left lost eleven seats.

What is the relevance of these ideological groupings for Black Europe? In theory, the Right and far-right political grouping is closed to Black Europe (largely because they refuse to discuss race or racism, and they are often directly involved in, or closely associated with, policies that are harmful to Black people's lives and interests). Black people tend to vote for Social Democratic parties. I have heard about Black complaints about Black invisibility in national parliaments; in fact, some of these border on conspiracy theories. A closer inspection reveals that the constitutional arrangements of various European countries can also highlight important sources of such invisibility.

The issue of a race and ethnic relations policy was an object of discussion in the UK far earlier than in other European nations and culminated in a series of laws and policies, along with the establishment of institutions and organizations designed to control immigration as well as promote "good race relations" (Small and Solomos 2006). This includes the 1962 Commonwealth Immigrants Act, the 1971 Immigration Act, the 1981 Nationality Act, and the 2000 Race Relations (Amendment) Act. It also includes the Race Relations Act of 1976, the Macpherson Report of 1999, and the Parekh Report of 2000 (Small and Solomos 2006). But this type of legislation is far less common across mainland continental Europe.

The Case of the Netherlands

Examples abound across Europe on the issue of Black invisibility (Hawthorne 2019; Small 2018); given limitations of space I will discuss the specific case of the Netherlands. In the early 1980s the Netherlands attempted to follow the UK example by enacting what it called Minorities Policy. The assumption behind the Minorities Policy is demographic in the sense that the policy target was considered a small group of people in a larger society. However, Dutch demographers observed that by the mid-1980s, for the first time since the end of World War II, immigration was greater than emigration; fewer people were leaving the Netherlands than arriving for settlement (Mullard et. al 1991). As a result, in the tradition of dog whistle tactics, the concept of "minorities" was taken out of the lexicon and was replaced with the concepts of *autochthone* (natives) and *allochthone* (aliens, but not necessarily strangers) (Haney-Lopez 2014). This was followed by a policy to restrict immigration and reduce the budget for the "minorities organizations" that benefited from the policy. But as a result of protests from Black groups, the government replaced the word *allochthone* with the phrase "people with immigration background" in 2016; however, it still has racial connotations and serves as a code word for non-white people.

After the revolt against Minorities Policy, and its replacement with "aliens' policy," the groups that formed the background of the Minorities Policy went their separate ways. The colonial subjects from East Asia (or Moluccans) were offered a job project and a museum; the Muslims became the object of multicultural discourse and ridicule, and later Islamophobia. The welfare organizations of the colonial subjects from Suriname and the Antilles were gradually dismantled, of which more below. For the moment, suffice it to say that in response to vicious Islamophobia and far-right agitation, a new political party called DENK (Think) has emerged among the ranks of people of Turkish descent and Dutch constitutional and proportional representation electoral arrangements facilitated it.

The political party DENK originates with two Turkish members of parliament for the Labour Party. They were sacked from the party and decided not to go quietly. The reader should be reminded that like Wilders (now leader of a far-right political party, Party for Freedom or PVV), the DENK members were sacked on the basis of their party's top objection to matters related to politics in Turkey; Wilders was sacked from the People's Party of Freedom and Democracy (VVD) political party for being anti-Turkey, and DENK for being pro-Turkey. They had the choice to vacate the parliament and hand over their parliamentary seats to the Labour Party or remain in the parliament with their seats under a new party. They decided to form their own political party (DENK) and took parliamentary votes from the Labour Party, the very political party that brought them to the parliament. Thus, three decades later, the Labour Party, the political party that had initiated the Minorities Policy in the name of emancipation, has been revolted against by some of the very "ethnic minorities" who benefited from that policy. In fact, from the perspective of race and ethnic relations, the recent Dutch general election of 17 March 2017 produced three contradictions.

First, DENK (Think) was able to gain an extra seat and thus has three seats in the parliament, two of Turkish background and one of Moroccan background. DENK is a "secular political party" but it draws its support predominantly from Turks and Moroccans. But given the circumstances (among them Islamophobia) in which it emerged, irrespective of its intentions, DENK would be viewed by some people as a Turkish and Moroccan political party; this places limits on its capacity to grow, as well as on its capacity to make coalitions with other political parties and, thus, influence policy in the parliament (Nimako 2018). Thus, in the short term these parliamentary gains may generate incomes for DENK members of parliament but the chances of the party winning more seats in the parliament in the future is doubtful. This goes some way to explain why DENK ran in the European Union election but did not meet the threshold for a seat.

Second, before the election, some of the people who declared their intention to vote for DENK said they had not previously voted. Thus, DENK also appealed to those who did not normally vote but who have experienced racism and Islamophobia; their thinking was that finally someone is defending them against Islamophobia, racist bullies, and institutional racism. This in itself is contradictory because the people who have anti-racist campaign track records in Dutch history are Dutch citizens of African descent, especially those of Surinamese and Antillean origin. But irrespective of what one adds or subtracts, as of July 2019 when this article was written, there is no Antillean or Surinamese (regardless of ethnicity) in the Dutch parliament.

Third, there had previously been Surinamese and Antillean members of parliament; but the 2017 election eliminated Surinamese and Antilleans from the parliament. This is partly because Surinamese and Antilleans tend to vote for the Labour Party, and when the Labour Party lost nearly 75% of its 38 parliamentary seats, it worked to the disadvantage of Black representation in the parliament. It now has nine seats, but it received more votes from Amsterdam Southeast, where the majority of the population that can be classified as Black lives, than from other districts. But due to the constitutional arrangement and electoral system, no Surinamese or Antillean was among the first nine people on the parliamentary list. Thus, thirty years after the Minorities Policy was initiated and abandoned, no Moluccan, Surinamese, or Antillean, some of the former colonial subjects on whose name the policy was initiated, can be found in parliament at present. Rather, the right-wing People's Party for Freedom and Democracy (VVD), the political party that gave the world Ayaan Hirsi Ali and Geert Wilders, and indirectly Pim Fortuyn, and that cut funding for the Institute for the Study of Dutch Slavery and its Legacy (NiNsee), is now back in control at a time when people of African descent had been negotiating with the Labour Party Minister to release funds for the events around the United Nations Decade of People of African Descent project.

It should be recalled that the revolt against the Dutch state by Moluccans in the 1970s gave rise to the Minorities Policy. Since the 1990s the social mobilization and demands of some Surinamese and Antilleans of African descent have actively drawn public attention to Dutch slavery and its legacies. Similar developments across the African diaspora took place at the international level and culminated in the United Nations World Conference against Racism in Durban, South Africa, in 2001. Both developments converged and it prompted the Dutch government to respond. The Dutch Minister responsible for Minorities and Integration Affairs announced at the 2001 UN Durban World Conference against Racism that the Dutch state would erect a monument to commemorate Dutch involvement in Atlantic slavery. The monument became a reality in 2002 and, as demanded by Black activists, it was followed by the establishment of NiNsee in 2003.

But NiNsee did not receive structural funding from the state. Thus, like the Minorities Policy of the 1980s against which there was a revolt after five years, funding for NiNsee was cut eight years after it was founded. As a result, NiNsee lost its research and public history education capacity and, consequently, its institutional capacity to produce knowledge.

Although it was short-lived, NiNsee has played an important role because it created an institutional space for many Black people to meet, discuss, and share knowledge. It also raised a number of enduring issues that resonated with issues of memory and museums—issues to do with past and current racism, inequality, and opportunity, with racial discrimination and lack of political representation. And it began a momentum that continues today, that seems to be growing in strength, and that has actively linked Black people campaigning for equality in the Netherlands with Black people fighting for equality and social justice in other nations across Western Europe (Small 2018). For instance, at the annual commemoration of abolition of Dutch slavery held in Amsterdam on 1 July 2011, Quinsy Gario produced T-shirts with the inscription "Zwarte Piet is Racism" (Black Piet is Racism) and circulated them to raise awareness about the racist character of the Zwarte Piet figure in the Dutch Sinterklaas.

In the early phase of public manifestations of Black opposition to Zwarte Piet, Quinsy Gario and Jeffrey Afriyie were arrested in November 2011 at a Sinterklaas event at the city of Dortrecht for wearing the T-shirt that Gario had developed. In the process of their arrest, they were physically assaulted. But a woman of Antillean descent recorded the arrests and assault and posted the video on the Internet; it went viral. These developments have thrown the legitimacy of Zwarte Piet into crisis. But there are some Dutch people, including intellectuals, who still strongly believe that the Black people who oppose Zwarte Piet are strangers who do not understand Dutch society and its traditions.

Yet in recognition of the protests against Zwarte Piet, on 16 December 2014, the European Network Against Racism (ENAR) and Malin Björk, a Swedish Member of the European Parliament of the Democratic Socialist and Communist grouping (GUE/NGL, Sweden), organized a debate on "Afrophobic stereotypes vs. tradition: the case of Zwarte Piet in the Netherland" in the European Parliament in Strasbourg.

Some Dutch right-wing MEPs (Members of the European Parliament) were dismissive of the event. At the end of the presentations, one Dutch MEP of the far-right populists and hard Eurosceptics, Olaf Stuger (PVV), became irritated and expressed his feelings in the following terms to journalist Kevin P. Roberson:

> I am very disappointed by the debate. The discussion takes the joy out the Sinterlaas holiday for children. I do not think Europe should be having debates about Zwarte Piet. *I think we have a lot more important issues to discuss, in the world.* And also, in the Netherlands. For me, Zwarte Piet is a Dutch tradition. I think that not a lot of people are bothered by Zwarte Piet. There is a small group of activists, which you saw at this meeting. They're really mad and bitter. I notice this, because the holiday is very joyful and its joyful for me. (my emphasis)

He went on to state that:

> When I am in Curacao or in Suriname, where my ancestors come from, I don't see anyone protesting and everyone thinks it is a nice holiday. There is a small

group, that has problem with this. They are venting their frustration, with the hope that it will get them publicity. This is unfortunate for the children who do enjoy the holiday (Kevin P. Roberson; *The Roberson Report Medea Media* 2014; ENAR and MEP Malin Björk discuss Afrophobia in the European Parliament)

Apparently, the PVV MEP has revealed that he and his colleagues have other priorities, and that racial equality and the emancipation of Black people is not one of them. The idea that the European parliament has important things to do should not be taken lightly. Here the Dutch MEP was ignoring the fact that the protesters were Dutch citizens (Nimako 2013). It should be added that the PVV lost their four seats in the European Parliament during the election of 23 May 2019; three of the seats went to a newly formed far-right political party, the Forum for Democracy.

But there is more to this than meets the eye, and that is why Black mobilization continues. For example, in response to the UN declaration of the Decade of People of African Descent (2015-2024), which is an extension of the 2011 Durban Conference, the Dutch state responded and allocated some resources that raise awareness about the conditions of people of African Descent in the Netherlands. A number of Black organizations sought funding for their projects, but it is likely that most will return home empty-handed because like NiNsee, there is no space in the Dutch bureaucratic tradition for a project like the Decade. This is all the more so since the Decade is not being treated as an emancipation issue, but rather a social cohesion issue and thus calls for progressive control, namely, managing change without sharing power. Like the Minorities Policy of the 1980s, there is no structural space for state fiscal policy arrangements for Black emancipation projects. Thus, those who would benefit from the Decade funding would likely be established Dutch groups and mainstream institutions that would receive funding to organize conferences and exhibitions in the name of Black people or the Decade.

Suffice it to say that the Netherlands is not alone in its failure—and indeed in its refusal—to prioritize, or even address, the needs of its Black citizens. Other nations across Europe are equally dismissive (Keaton et al. 2014). To the extent that they pay any attention to Black people at all, it is only to those who are immigrants and refugees—sometimes to Black women who are the victims of so-called sex trafficking—and the attention is mainly to continue to exclude them from Europe. And although the UK has some race and ethnic relations policies, as I mentioned above, they are largely being dismantled. Thus, on matters related to the boardroom, Black Europe remains invisible.

Conclusion: More to this than meets the eye!

The formation and evolution of nation-states in Europe after the end of World War II and the particular configuration of the European Union as it exists today have involved a range of economic, political, and nationalist elements that on first inspection appear to have little or nothing to do with Black people, either those in the colonies or those resident in Europe. They also appear to have had nothing to do with the long history of colonial expansion and imperial domination across Africa and the Americas. However, a closer inspection reveals that during this entire process, confronting the presence—and implications—of Black European citizens, both in the colonies and in continental Europe, became major issues. And they remain major issues today. Many of the issues that the EU is facing in terms of economic and political crises also appear to have little or nothing to do with colonialism or Black people in Europe, but again closer inspection reveals this too is an error. Today, we can find a complex interaction of national identity, nativism, and populism, and it is important to distinguish what each of these ideologies actually means in practice. And we have the permanent presence of Black European citizens, who are mainly regarded by white Europeans as permanent strangers. Black Europeans have mobilized in a number of ways to reject this non-recognition. And they continue to do so today. This is the crux of the conundrum that confronts Europe with regard to its Black citizens. And these are the challenges that Black Europeans face in terms of full citizenship rights, belonging and recognition, especially with regard to resentment, discrimination, and inequality.

Acknowledgement

I thank my friend and colleague Stephen Small for his feedback on drafts of this paper. I appreciate it very much.

WORKS CITED

Essed, Philomena and Isabel Hoving. *Dutch Racism.* Thamyris, 2014.

Haney-Lopez, Ian. *Dog Whistle Politics: How Coded Racial Appeals Have Reinvented Racism, and Wrecked the Middle Class.* Oxford UP, 2014.

Hawthorne, Camilla. "Making Italy: Afro-Italian Entrepreneurs and the Racial Boundaries of Citizenship." *Social & Cultural Geography,* 2019.

Hine, Darlene Clark, et al. *Black Europe and the African Diaspora.* U of Illinois P, 2009.

Keaton, Trica Danielle. "The Politics of Race-Blindness (Anti) Blackness and Category-blindness in Contemporary France." *Dubois Review: Social Science and Research on Race,* vol. 7, no. 1, 2010, pp. 103-31.

Keaton, Trica Danielle et al. *Black France/France, Noire: The History and Politics of Blackness.* Duke UP, 2012.

Nimako, Kwame. "Layers of Emancipation Struggles: Some Reflections on the Dutch Case." *Smash the Pillars,* Lexington Books, 2018, pp 97-112.

———. "Let Citizenship Blossom." *Letters to the Europeans,* ALICE ERC Project, 2014, pp. 218-233.

———. "Location and Social Thought in the Black: A Testimony of Africana Intellectual Tradition." *Postcoloniality – Decoloniality - Black Critique: Joints and Fissures,* Campus Verlag, 2014.

Nimako, Kwame and Stephen Small. "Theorizing Black Europe and African Diaspora: Implications for Citizenship, Nativism and Xenophobia." *Black Europe and the African Diaspora,* U of Illinois P, 2009.

Nimako, Kwame and Glenn Willemsen. *The Dutch Atlantic: Slavery, Abolition and Emancipation.* Pluto Press, 2011.

McEachrane, Michael. *Afro-Nordic Landscapes: Equality and Race in Northern Europe.* Routledge Press, 2014.

Muller, Jerry Z. "Us and Them: The Enduring Power of Ethnic Nationalism." *Foreign Affairs,* March/April 2008.

Roberson, Kevin P. *The Roberson Report Medea Media.* 2014.

Sharpley-Whiting, T. and Tiffany Ruby Patterson. "The Conundrum of Geography, Europe d'outre mer, and Transcontinental Diasporic Identity." *Black Europe and the African Diaspora,* U of Illinois P, 2009, pp. 84-94.

Simon, Patrick. "The Choice of Ignorance: The Debate on Ethnic and Racial Statistics in France." *French Politics, Culture & Society,* vol. 26, no. 1, 2008, pp. 7-31.

Sivanandan, A. *A Different Hunger.* Pluto Press, 1982.

Small, Stephen. *20 Questions and Answers on Black Europe.* Amrit Publishers, 2018.

KWAME NIMAKO is the founder and director of the Black Europe Summer School (BESS) based in Amsterdam since 2007. He lectured International Relations in the Department of Political Sciences at the Universiteit van Amsterdam (1991-2013). He was also a fellow in the Faculty of Economics at the Tinbergen Institute (1989-1991), and he taught Race and Ethnic Relations in the Department of Education (1986- 1991) at the University of Amsterdam. He held visiting professor positions in the Department of African American Studies at the University of California at Berkeley (Spring 2018 and 2012-2015) and at the University of Suriname (2011). Dr. Nimako is the author or co-author of more than thirty books, reports and guidebooks on economic development, ethnic relations, social policy, urban renewal, and migration.

MIGUEL VALE DE ALMEIDA

Ninguém imagina de verdade um português negro

RESUMO: Este texto assenta na transcrição de uma entrevista concedida em 2018 ao site *QI News* sobre continuidades e articulações entre as classificações e representações coloniais e a negação do racismo no Portugal de hoje. Esse processo é visto como constitutivo das representações de nacionalidade que são, assim, racializadas e não permitindo o reconhecimento das pessoas negras e afrodescendentes como portuguesas cultural e socialmente legítimas.

PALAVRAS-CHAVE: Racismo, negação, identidade nacional, contínuo colonial-póscolonial

ABSTRACT: The following is the edited transcription of a 2018 interview to the Internet site *QI News*. It focuses on continuities and articulations between colonial classifications and representations, on the one hand, and the denial of racism in contemporary Portugal, on the other. It is argued that this process is part of the constitution of representations of national identity, which are racialized and therefore preclude Black and Afrodescendant persons from being recognized as legitimately Portuguese in cultural and social terms.

KEYWORDS: Racism, denial, national identity, colonial-postcolonial continuum

Em 2018 dei uma entrevista ao site de informação QI News que viria a ter um impacto significativo nos meios preocupados com o combate ao racismo em Portugal, redes sociais, estudantes universitários, e mesmo no campo político. Ao longo dos anos tenho verificado que este modelo de intervenção – no fundo, divulgação ou extensão em linguagem acessível do conhecimento científico politicamente comprometido – exerce uma maior influência transformadora do que o trabalho estritamente académico ou do que a intervenção opinativa e beligerante da política organizada ou da participação em redes sociais. Essa é a razão para a escolha do modelo pouco ortodoxo para este texto: trata-se da transcrição (por mim feita e posteriormente editada para os efeitos desta publicação) dos conteúdos fundamentais daquela entrevista.

A entrevista original pode ser ouvida e vista em https://qinews.pt/entrevista-qi-miguel-vale-de-almeida-ninguem-imagina-de-verdade-um-portugues-negro/, e foi conduzida por António Castelo.

Vivemos com a ideia e a crença hegemónica de que algumas pessoas têm um direito a serem cidadãs de Portugal em virtude duma inerência genealógica, e essas pessoas-cidadãs são os portugueses auto-classificados como brancos. A sua pertença, por via desse direito, sustenta-se na representação de pessoas, outras, que são vistas como não podendo pertencer pela sua própria natureza, entendidas como sendo duma humanidade diferente, como tendo uma ontologia diferente – os *indígenas*, por assim dizer, africanos ou outros. Além delas, haveria uma categoria de/em trânsito e intermédia, correspondente aos *assimilados*, pessoas que conseguiriam transitar do estatuto de indígena para o estatuto de cidadão, através de um conjunto de provas que teriam de demonstrar e que teriam de performatizar. Essas provas eram – e o tempo verbal é agora propositado, já que estas ideias e crenças remetem para o passado colonial – civilizacionais, culturais, linguísticas, religiosas, indo ao pormenor da definição do modo de vestir ou do modo de comer.

Ora, estas exigências de demonstração de assimilação são, curiosamente, as que se pede hoje aos não-cidadãos que queiram aceder à nacionalidade.[1] O que se pede não são as competências do exercício da cidadania – trabalhar, pagar impostos, descontar para a segurança social, votar, participar nas decisões – ou, pelo menos, não todas elas, já que os deveres, esses sim, são exigidos, mas não os direitos. O que se pede, o que se espera e o que em última instância, social e politicamente, se exige é de ordem cultural.

Enquanto não-afrodescendente e pessoa não-racializada, e enquanto pessoa que reconhece o privilégio branco e se debruça sobre a organização racializada da sociedade portuguesa, tenho noção do esforço que é necessário da parte dos não-racializados que desejam eticamente outro tipo de país. A própria definição de "tipo de país" escapa ao nosso controlo, já que as definições legais sobre a pertença têm sido mudadas constantemente, o que não deixa de ser fonte de estranheza, pois normalmente imaginar-se-ia que um país definiria muito claramente a escolha entre direito de solo ou direito de sangue como princípio organizador dum modelo de cidadania e sociedade, assente numa filosofia política sobre quem considera ser incluível na comunidade política ou não. Mesmo uma visão rápida permite entender que se muda *mais para o sangue* ou *mais para o solo* consoante pressões políticas internas mais ou menos nacionalistas, mas sobretudo em conexão com a regulação dos fluxos migratórios. Tal facto tem sido evidente em Portugal: como a própria economia portuguesa vive de solavancos, de *puxa-arranca*, de pequenos impulsos seguidos de recessões – em Portugal está-se sempre à espera da próxima crise – a eles correspondem diferentes pressões ou alívios regulatórios em relação aos fluxos migratórios. Parece, pois – e esta é uma hipótese a ser verificada por quem no assunto se especializa – haver uma gestão, pelo estado, da articulação entre política migratória e política da nacionalidade. Dizer isto aproxima-se da banalidade, mas o que suspeito é que essa gestão seja em grande medida feita a montante, através das leis da nacionalidade, da naturalização e da residência, com o apoio ideológico das noções hegemónicas de pertença e competência culturais.

A partir dum ângulo mais antropológico, a questão principal talvez seja, portanto, outra, de cariz cultural-político profundo, a saber: "quem é que é considerado português?" Em Portugal verifica-se uma confusão significativa – como, aliás, em muitos países, uma vez que todos os estados-nação foram feitos dessa maneira – entre a cidadania, que em princípio é o usufruto e exercício de direitos e deveres numa comunidade política, e a pertença étnica/nacional, assente numa metáfora da família e da genealogia. "Somos todos uma grande família, a nação é uma grande família," diz a metáfora, na medida em que as pessoas se veem como descendentes de gerações de antepassados recuando até um princípio dos tempos, inclusive pré-nacionais (vide "os Lusitanos"). Trata-se evidentemente (o uso da expressão deveria ser seguido do complemento "para a minoria de pessoas com literacia das ciências sociais") duma construção mi(s)tificada, uma vez que no decurso histórico se verificaram inúmeras misturas, branqueamentos, limpezas étnicas, alteração de fronteiras e, sobretudo, formas de estado intrinsecamente diferentes do atual modelo do estado-nação.

Essa ideia da nação como família e genealogia, baseada na metáfora do sangue, exatamente a mesma que se usa na linguagem do parentesco, é politicamente perigosa porque ela traz implícita a ideia de que se acede à cidadania apenas, sobretudo ou preferencialmente através desse laço de sangue. Isso já está "na cabeça das pessoas" (uma forma pedestre de dizer "mentalidades"), mas que a lei o possa dizer exponencia os efeitos. Ao consenso generalizado, automático, que gera a confusão quotidiana, do "homem ou mulher da rua," em torno do sangue, não corresponde, portanto, um consenso social em torno da ideia de que quem aqui viva, trabalhe, e pague impostos seja cidadão e, logo, usufrutuário dos direitos correspondentes. Na discussão em torno desse dissenso, trocam-se avaliações, opiniões e juízos de valor sobre quem tem mais e menos direito aos direitos. O problema histórico e cultural português profundo é que certas categorias de pessoas são vistas como pertencendo *ainda menos*, por causa da História de expansão e colonialismo.

A questão racial coloca-se como um marcador imediato de não-pertença. Ou seja, Portugal construiu-se como um país branco. A noção de nação que vigora em Portugal foi construída também enquanto noção de branquitude. E o principal mecanismo para construir essa branquitude, ainda por cima por um país que não era visto pelos seus parceiros regionais como sendo duma Europa do norte de branquitude hegemónica, foi o colonialismo e, ainda antes do colonialismo enquanto modelo moderno dos séculos XIX e XX, através do comércio de pessoas escravizadas, que contribuiu para a construção das ideias racistas sobre as divisões da humanidade. Muito da branquitude portuguesa foi construído sobre a distinção entre um Portugal, aqui, na Europa, e branco, e algo de outro, as colónias nossas subalternas – conquistadas, pacificadas, dominadas, civilizadas, cuidadas, portugalizadas – e onde vive um *certo tipo* de pessoas que são imediatamente visíveis como pertencendo ao mundo colonial (e independentemente de nos estarmos a referir a temporalidades colonial ou pós-colonial). Isso continua a existir como um traço de suspeita sobre a não-pertença verdadeira das pessoas, mesmo quando elas pertencem legal e formalmente. A nação ter-se construído como branca é um facto com vários significados e consequências. "Branco" não se reduz à cor da pele, mas inclui sim os significados comportados pelo significante *branco*: um conjunto de estatutos de superioridade que, para existirem, têm de criar uma ideia de inferioridade, marcada dicotomicamente como *negra*, oriunda do mundo colonial.

As Américas, em geral, têm, desde que se deram as independências, primeiro nos casos dos EUA e do Haiti e, no século XIX nos outros países, direito de solo. Na Europa é exatamente o contrário. Esta dicotomia é muito interessante: por um lado, porque essa figura do estado-nação – misturar a unidade política com a unidade étnica (inventando assim esta, aliás) – é de facto uma invenção europeia e está na base duma miríade de conflitos e dramas sobejamente conhecidos; por outro, porque as Américas como que levaram mais a sério os ideais universalistas e republicanos da Revolução Francesa. Não que estes fossem perfeitos (conhecemos a história das suas exclusões implícitas), mas levaram-nos a sério. Viveram e vivem igualmente processos racistas, escravatura, colonialismo interno, predomínio dos descendentes de europeus, mitologias sobre miscigenação e ausência de racismo, imigração seletiva, eugenia; mas pelo menos fizeram-no com um contrato social assente no direito de solo. Porque o sinal que o estado dá é relevante para a legitimação das reivindicações de inclusão cidadã, o que se viria a verificar na maior incidência de demandas de reconhecimento de categorias historicamente discriminadas. No caso da Europa, pelo contrário, verificou-se uma obsessão com a noção de integração, com a noção de assimilação, com a adequação religiosa mesmo quando os estados são laicos, com o comportamento cultural *adequado* e fazendo as vezes de cidadania. E o que muitos de nós temos visto é que as exigências impostas – e em Portugal isso é mais evidente ainda – por essas ideias de assimilação e integração são patentemente semelhantes ao que eu chamo de *Constituição Colonial*: a forma como se organizavam diferencialmente e desigualmente as populações coloniais.

As *mentalidades* não são exclusivas do homem ou mulher da rua, são partilhadas pelo deputado, pelo legislador, pelo governante, pelo burocarata, que participam do mesmo quadro cultural. Um dos impedimentos à mudança das mentalidades é não termos feito, na sociedade portuguesa, o que poderíamos chamar – e recorrendo ao exemplo sul-africano com as devidas ressalvas diferenciadoras – um processo de Verdade e Reconciliação sobre a questão colonial. Fizemos o 25 de abril, que foi em grande medida resultado dos movimentos de libertação em África e nem isso foi reconhecido com a devida propriedade. É comum ouvir-se que "nós descolonizámos" ou "demos a independência," colocando a agência do lado do ex-colonizador, quando, na realidade, os movimentos de libertação e a guerra colonial provocaram a queda do regime ditatorial, permitindo o estabelecimento da democracia. Além disso, no 25 de abril (no período do processo revolucionário e, depois, na chamada "normalização") preocupámo-nos com dois tipos de questões que eram de facto urgentes: a reconstrução completa do sistema político, de ditadura para democracia, e a implantação de formas de igualdade de oportunidades ou de redistribuição de tipo social-democrata. O que aconteceu foi que, no plano da reflexão sobre o tipo de cidadania e de sociedade que queremos ter, o máximo que se fez foi (como não podia deixar de ser, obviamente) mudar algumas questões de género, repondo a igualdade formal. Todas as questões que não fossem relacionadas com as classes sociais e a desigualdade socio-económica, além da questão da igualdade formal de género, ficaram suspensas até muito tarde, em rigor até ao século XXI.

As questões racial e do passado colonial não foram tratadas de todo. O que a democracia fez, e animemo-la como se de uma pessoa se tratasse, foi dizer: "já que o colonialismo foi uma coisa feia, já que houve a descolonização e já que nós queremos e gostamos que Portugal torne a ser um país europeu, apenas o retângulo e ilhas, então subscrevamos as coisas bonitas, as coisas tal como elas *devem* ser: não há raça e não há colonialismo e, portanto, o nosso país é um país pós-racial, é um país onde *essas questões* não existem." Isto aproxima-se, naturalmente, de um tomar o desejo pela realidade, quando a realidade continua a reproduzir um esquema colonial. Mudou-se de um discurso glorificador dos Descobrimentos, da expansão e do colonialismo para um discurso glorificador dum *wishful thinking*, feito duma retórica de universalismo, contacto de culturas, interculturalidade, e mesmo *lusofonia*. Se atentarmos à linguagem usada pelo estado português democrático para falar de questões raciais e migratórias, ela é humanista e positiva. Só que isso fez com que a História fosse revisitada desse ponto de vista, acabando por dar continuidade, ou um novo fôlego *aggiornato*, ao discurso lusotropicalista. Os manuais de História, por exemplo, referem o "contacto," mas um contacto em que "nós" oferecemos algo, não interessando muito o que veio de lá para cá. Dom sem contra-dom. Isso permite a omissão das fontes de vergonha e embaraço, como a escravatura e o comércio de pessoas escravizadas, o trabalho forçado e obrigatório, o código do indigenato, as guerras de pacificação, a violência colonial, a desigualdade de poder no campo do género na própria miscigenação que tenha factualmente ocorrido. Em suma, em vez de "Verdade e Reconciliação" especializámo-nos na Negação: nega-se algo porque dói, mas ao ser negado esse algo é reprimido e vai manifestar-se em sintomas paralelos, na reprodução do racismo institucional e estrutural, que é o mais difícil de identificar.

Não é o racismo das relações entre as pessoas, mais identificável (ainda que, e este é apenas um exemplo, seja preciso muito trabalho pedagógico para as pessoas perceberem não só que as anedotas racistas não devem ser contadas mas que, sobretudo, não se deve achar que têm graça). Além desse racismo interpessoal, dos insultos, das anedotas, da recusa em alugar a casa a um negro, da surpresa por ver alguém negro quando se presumia que aquele cargo seria ocupado por um branco, etc., temos os racismos institucional e estrutural. O institucional é o que ocorre em sede de instituições do estado que são supostas gerir de forma igual a cidadania, mas que o fazem efetivamente de forma discriminatória, sendo os casos mais flagrantes os da Justiça e das Polícias, mas também na Educação (nos manuais, na educação diferenciada, na expectativa de que os alunos negros são mais fracos e, portanto, investindo-se menos neles) e também na Saúde. O estrutural, que é o mais complexo de identificar e o que efetivamente reproduz o racismo, é uma estrutura de economia política e de biopoder que garante que as pessoas racializadas cumprem os piores trabalhos, assim reproduzindo o ciclo de pobreza e de exclusão (e de revolta também); que garante que a geografia urbana seja *apartheidizada*, onde aquilo que é definido como bairro social é sobremaneira um bairro negro e/ou cigano. É esse tipo de estrutura material que reproduz o racismo e que ao mesmo tempo não é reconhecida como sendo racista, sendo comum o desvio explicativo para categorias como pobreza, classe ou imigração.

Todas as sociedades são racistas. Sobretudo todas as que participaram na construção duma modernidade cujos alicerces foram a maior migração de todas, a migração forçada de africanos para as Américas. A modernidade construiu-se assim, e "O Ocidente" é feito disso. Casos há em que, por força dos movimentos sociais, se fez de facto algum processo de verdade e reconciliação. Nos Estados Unidos, e apesar de tudo, a discussão é grande e generalizada; o Canadá tem feito esse trabalho insistentemente, sobretudo com a população indígena; e até na Austrália, onde as coisas foram e são muito graves no plano colonial, tem havido políticas oficiais de reposição da verdade. Isso vai acontecendo nalguns locais, quase todos *settler societies* ou onde a população negra tem um peso forte, como é o caso do Brasil. Mas na Europa está tudo largamente por fazer, com a exceção de alguns países que, por razões de filosofia política liberal ou social-democrata já muito estabelecida, por aí enveredaram. Portugal foi o principal traficante de pessoas escravizadas, teve um colonialismo mais longo e duradouro e, no entanto – ou talvez por isso mesmo? – não fez esse processo de revisitação do passado e de identificação dos legados no presente. A consequência é que a nossa noção de cidadania é mais baseada em ideias de nação e de sangue do que em ideais de comunidade política organizada em torno de um projeto de cidadania. Um projeto que ao mesmo tempo valorize a cidadania universal e reconheça que no seu passado houve um processo iníquo, e que assuma que isso resultou em categorias sociais historicamente discriminadas e necessitadas de políticas de igualdade de oportunidades, quando não mesmo de reparação.

Como podemos agora mudar alguma coisa? Em primeiro lugar, nos últimos cinco ou seis anos, verificou-se um crescimento de grupos e protagonistas que resultam em grande parte da criação dum capital cultural por movimentos anti-racistas anteriores; resulta também do facto de algumas pessoas terem conseguido furar a barreira da desigualdade racial na educação; e vemos o surgimento duma geração que se considera portuguesa de direito pleno e que é confrontada, normalmente através da ação policial, com o não reconhecimento desse estatuto pelos representantes da hegemonia cultural.[2] Começa a haver – e por esforço próprio das pessoas racializadas e não por incentivo do estado ou dos partidos – brechas e fendas no cerco, e vozes que se ouvem. Multiplicam-se em várias plataformas, desde rádios *online*, a canais no *Youtube*, passando por associativismos vários. E, dentro do associativismo, até com a riqueza de diversidade ideológica ou de atenção à interseccionalidade.

No plano político e legislativo discute-se finalmente a questão da inclusão de categorias etno-raciais nos Censos e estatísticas, de modo a haver uma base para o desenho e a promoção de políticas de ação afirmativa e igualdade de oportunidades. Os detratores, muitas vezes vindos do campo da defesa do universalismo republicano, temem pelo crescimento do racismo por causa da simples enunciação da racialização na sociedade – o que nos leva a pensar em como a ideologia liberal do universalismo não é necessariamente um antídoto aos processos da Negação, podendo perpetuá-la. Qualquer antropólogo sabe que a raça não existe biologicamente e que é uma construção social. Sabemos, todavia, que ela existe no sentido sociológico, que a crença racial tem efeito sobre a vida das pessoas racializadas – e efeito de privilégio sobre quem construiu a branquitude como não-racialidade. É sobre essa realidade factual, substantiva, que temos de trabalhar, e não sobre a questão "intelectual." Temporariamente tem de haver a construção de identidades negras e afrodescendentes para que elas possam ter presença como atores sociais e sujeitos da História, de modo a poderem usufruir de políticas de ação afirmativa.

Mas, a montante disso, a questão educativa é fundamental. O papel que os historiadores, cientistas sociais, académicos, e decisores têm é uma obrigação enorme de transformar a forma como o processo educativo é feito com as nossas crianças, todas, para que ele seja mais inclusivo no falar sobre a nossa História – *nossa* no sentido de todos os antepassados de todos nós que estamos aqui e agora –, e abordando o modo como a modernidade e o eurocentrismo se construíram na base da racialização. O estado-nação constrói-se com uma narrativa única, mas hoje temos obrigação de propor que os manuais e as aulas apresentem narrativas contraditórias e conflituantes. Isso daria mais autonomia às pessoas, afastá-las-ia mais duma ideia unívoca de identidade nacional.

O estado-nação, aliás, já não tem autonomia verdadeira, soberania plena – económica, militar, etc. – e por isso mesmo vastos segmentos sociais agarram-se ao reduto da identidade nacional mi(s)tificada, como vemos acontecer em vários contextos europeus e não só. Políticas em torno das categorias etno-raciais, das ações afirmativas e da igualdade de oportunidades, da plurivocalidade narrativa no sistema educativo, são fundamentais, junto com políticas de nacionalidade, naturalização e imigração que privilegiem a cidadania sobre a pertença e competência culturais, o solo sobre o sangue e, por fim, a vigilância na aplicação dos princípios anti-racistas já existentes, no que às instituições do estado e aos serviços diz respeito.

No entanto, o que se tem verificado é a ausência de investimento político. De 1974 até hoje nunca se ouviu ou leu um programa político, uma campanha eleitoral, um discurso de órgão de soberania, que afirmasse uma prioridade política no combate aos racismos estrutural e institucional.[3] Pelo contrário, o que surge, sim, ainda que timidamente, são tentativas de transformação dos discursos populistas das redes sociais em programas políticos de cariz racista. Evidentemente parte do problema reside na ausência de representatividade política das pessoas racializadas. O papel de aliados que alguns não-racializados jogam é sem dúvida importante, mas não poderá nunca substituir o verdadeiro lugar da fala. Por vezes, quando participo em eventos com pessoas dos movimentos afrodescendentes, digo, como *disclaimer*, que estou "partindo da minha posição social como branco, não-racializado e com consciência política disso mesmo," e perguntando-me o que me compete fazer. Não me compete "fingir" que sou negro, nem absorver negritude, no que seria um convoluto processo com matizes coloniais, mas sim pensar em discursos que sejam convincentes para a maioria branca. Como é que eu posso convencer a maioria branca de que é possível e desejável mudar alguma coisa? Esse, sim, é o meu lugar da (necessidade da) fala: num desafio parecido com o que tivemos nas lutas pelo casamento igualitário, ou pelo aborto, por exemplo, em que apostámos em estratégias de convencimento, em transformar o que parece ser só de alguns numa questão que seja de todos. Como é que convencemos a maioria de que a questão do racismo não é só uma questão dos negros e dos ciganos, mas que afeta a comunidade inteira na forma como ela se representa a si própria? Esse é o grande esforço de pedagogia política. O esforço de muitas e diversificadas pessoas e grupos surtirá efeito, mas a questão só estará ganha quando uma parte do centro do poder, um partido político forte e da área da governação, assumir a causa, colocando no seu programa, na sua estratégia, e de uma forma absolutamente clara, o reconhecimento do problema estrutural do racismo, do problema de que a narrativa nacional que andamos a usar é a mesma, em versão envernizada, que a anterior ao 25 de abril – e que, portanto, não de(s)colonizámos –, e que tudo isto tem consequências nas vidas das pessoas, havendo políticas concretas que podem e devem ser implementadas para efetivar mudança.

NOTAS

1. As que se pedem culturalmente, nas expectativas sociais, não necessariamente na lei, embora por vezes coincidindo. Uma mudança recente importante foi o fim da exigência de provas linguísticas.

2. O caso da manifestação espontânea de jovens na Avenida da Liberdade em fevereiro de 2019 é um exemplo fulcral. Não ligados a partidos ou movimentos anti-racistas, crentes na sua pertença à sociedade, foram subitamente politizados pelo seu confronto com uma ação policial violenta no bairro Jamaica, no Seixal. Indiciados e julgados a partir da queixa policial contra a sua participação na manifestação e reação à polícia, foram acusados judicialmente de *motim*, uma figura com conotações que dispenso explicar.

3. Em março de 2019, no entanto, a deputada do PS Isabel Moreira usou o seu direito a uma declaração política ao assunto, sustentando análises muito próximas das que este texto transmite. E o partido político Livre anunciou a ativista afrodescendente Joacine Katar Moreira como cabeça de lista por Lisboa nas eleições legislativas e segunda nas eleições europeias, ambas em 2019. (À data da publicação deste texto, muito mudou. A deputada seria desvinculada do partido Livre e seria alvo de insultos racistas no próprio Parlamento por parte da extrema-direita, além de perseguições várias nos media e nas redes sociais. Deixou de ser deputada nas eleições de 2021.)

MIGUEL VALE DE ALMEIDA (Lisboa, 1960) é professor catedrático de antropologia no Iscte – Instituto Universitário de Lisboa e investigador no CRIA – Centro em rede de Investigação em Antropologia.

As Veias Abertas da Afrodescendência:
Herança Colonial e Contemporaneidade[1]

Neutral is white. The default is white . . . Blackness, however, is considered the "other" and therefore to be suspected.
Reni Eddo-Lodge

RESUMO: A partir de uma reflexão que percorre os elementos principais dos meandros das conceptualizações que caracterizam a Afrodescendência, o artigo ressalta a experiência actual dos afrodescendentes em Portugal, marcada pelas especificidades dos modos de incorporação dos ex-colonizados no país e pelos esforços de delimitação da identidade nacional nas fronteiras da branquitude, mesmo perante pessoas cuja existência não permite mais duvidar de que há negros portugueses. Apontando para a relevância dos modos pelos quais os portugueses não-brancos (e afrodescendentes) buscam uma designação de/para si actualmente, ousando afastar-se (e/ou contrapor-se) à estigmatização de que são alvo, o artigo busca inventariar e questionar conceitos que são adoptados e vulgarizados em torno da Afrodescendência que, na actualidade, vão mais além do desvelamento da estigmatização, da presença e existência de afrodescendentes no espaço social português.

PALAVRAS-CHAVE: Afrodescendência; Portugal; diásporas africanas; herança colonial; Projecto Afro-Port

ABSTRACT: On the basis of a reflection that identifies the main elements of the intricacies of conceptualizations that characterize Afrodescendence, the article highlights the current experience of Afro-descendants in Portugal, which is distinguished by the specificities of the ways the ex-colonized are incorporated into the country and by the efforts of delimitating national identity in terms of whiteness, despite the presence of people whose existence leaves no room for doubt that there is a Black Portuguese population. Indicating the relevance of the ways in which non-white Portuguese (and Afro-descendants) seek a designation of/for themselves today, daring to distance themselves from (and/ or counteract) the stigmatization that targets them, the article seeks to inventory and question concepts that are adopted and vulgarized around Afrodescendence that, at present, extend beyond the unveiling of stigmatization, the presence and existence of Afro-descendants in the Portuguese social space.

KEYWORDS: Afrodescendence; Portugal; African diaspora; colonial heritage; Projecto Afro-Port

1. *Afrodescendência*:
história e meandros epistemológicos de uma categoria

O conceito "afrodescendente" foi sugerido em 2000, com um forte enfoque político, quando organizações sociais das Américas e Caraíbas se mobilizaram em torno da preparação da Conferência de Durban e, na Conferência Preparatória das Américas, simbolizaram uma ruptura epistemológica ao declarar, nas palavras de Romero Rodriguez: "Entramos negros e saímos afrodescendentes."[2] Esta afirmação tem um grande significado estratégico na medida em que muda o tradicional conceito de "negro" para o de "afrodescendente," no interior de um modelo complexo que ultrapassa a "raça" para reconhecer-se a si próprio como uma comunidade étnica. Embora não se possa indicar uma expansão universal linear das caracterizações sobre a *Afrodescendência* a partir das Américas e Caraíbas,[3] a partir das últimas décadas, os movimentos afrodescendentes que se constituíram, com base em dinâmicos actores, têm procurado posicionar suas reivindicações nas agendas nacionais e internacionais.[4] Assim como os seus antepassados escravizados e migrantes que engendraram (e inventaram) formas de vencer a subalternidade, o contínuo processo de subalternização e de exclusão, primeiro nas colónias, depois nas nações emergentes das Américas e, ainda, nos países colonizadores, os afrodescendentes procuram defender a sua representatividade e as suas agendas como sociedade civil. Sob esta perspectiva, procuramos trazer para este número especial uma reflexao que deveria percorrer os elementos principais dos meandros das conceptualizações que caracterizam a Afrodescendência e os afrodescendentes. Identificaremos distintos momentos históricos da sua presença, ressaltando as dinâmicas de actuação política na sociedade civil e destacando as suas experiências sociais, os desafios internos e externos que enfrentam e os desdobramentos de uma categoria que, no caso de Portugal, parece estar a gerar um efeito disruptivo nos estudos das chamadas "minorias étnicas" na diversa paisagem humana portuguesa e, mesmo encontrando muita relutância, tem-se imposto como realidade histórica e sociocultural da nação portuguesa.

O que parece acontecer é que, para enfrentar essa nova situação de intensa reivindicação do reconhecimento de uma realidade histórica, os afrodescendentes têm procurado actuar colectivamente, exigindo o respeito aos seus direitos e o cumprimento dos compromissos adquiridos em conferências mundiais que obrigam os Estados a reduzir a exclusão, a discriminação e a pobreza em que vive a maioria do segmento afrodescendente. Tal se deve também – ou para esse gesto parece contribuir – o facto de que, como representante da comunidade internacional, a Organização das Nações Unidas (ONU) tenha proclamado 2015-2024 como a *Década Internacional dos Afrodescendentes*,[5] por considerar que as pessoas de ascendência africana ainda têm acesso limitado à educação de qualidade, serviços de saúde, habitação e segurança social, permanecendo a sua situação em grande parte invisível e insuficiente o reconhecimento do esforço em busca de reparação para a sua condição actual. Além disso, a ONU afirma que estas pessoas são discriminadas no acesso à justiça e apresentam taxas alarmantes de violência policial associada a perfis raciais.

As orientações da ONU para a *Década Internacional dos Afrodescendentes* têm particular significado no caso dos países europeus cujos processos de descolonização exponenciaram a reconfiguração das suas sociedades e engendraram tentativas mais ou menos peculiares de delimitação da identidade nacional, sempre dentro das fronteiras da branquitude, tanto no sentido de "White mythologies" (Robert Young), quanto no de "White people," que indica um dos termos como "two macro-level, socially recognized divisions of the social hierarchy" (DiAngelo 2008, xi). Em Portugal, traduziu-se num esforço de consolidação da tese de um "nós" nacional, português e implicitamente branco, por oposição a um "eles," africanos e implicitamente negros (Araújo e Maeso 2016, 311). De um modo geral, e em linha com as abordagens dominantes, os afrodescendentes, negros nascidos na Europa, desafiam os sistemas já instalados que procuram lidar com as consequências decorrentes da colonização – neste caso da deslocação das populações colonizadas para a "metrópole," que foram transformadas em questões migratórias. Os afrodescendentes não parecem caber no figurino ainda em vigor aplicado aos sujeitos anteriormente colonizados, entretanto transformados em imigrantes, e que estariam prontos para serem "assimilados no rebanho nacional" (Hesse e Sayyid 2006, 23).

Este contexto de normalizada perversa associação entre *afrodescendentes e imigrantes* concebe determinados sujeitos – portadores de certos traços culturais e étnicos – como dissociados e não constituintes da "nação imaginada": nos discursos e práticas de representação política hegemónicas são definidos por uma alteridade radical, como uma "ameaça" interna que convém conter ou erradicar. Não admira que, assim, esse contexto determine que questões de racismo são tuteladas por instituições relacionadas com políticas de migração (em Portugal, o Alto Comissariado para as Migrações) e justifique expressões como "primeira e segunda gerações de imigrantes" referentes a não-brancos quando, na verdade, estamos diante de (apenas) portugueses negros, de origem africana – afinal europeus afrodescendentes. Daí a "novidade" de três deputadas negras, na XIV Legislatura (2019-2023), como se fosse uma anomalia numa sociedade em que a presença de negros é uma realidade desde há pelo menos 500 anos, embora para esse segmento ainda funcione o pêndulo da visibilidade/invisibilidade. É por isso produtivo falar também a partir de outros *lugares* da ex-metrópole, como a França, em que ninguém vê como menos francês Nicolas Paul Stéphane Sárközy de Nagy-Bocsa, aliás, Nicolas Sárkozy, ex-presidente da França, da primeira geração de imigrantes húngaros no país; ou espaços emblemáticos que funcionem como metrópoles pós-coloniais dado o seu lugar na reconfiguração do mundo moderno porque foram destinos de homens escravizados, através de "um rio chamado Atlântico" (Alberto da Costa e Silva),[6] como o Brasil ou os Estados Unidos. Neste caso, nunca se referiu a John F. Kennedy, ou a seus irmãos Robert e Edward, como segunda ou terceira geração de imigrantes irlandeses – embora essa "naturalização" da nacionalidade norte-americana não tenha acontecido de forma pacífica com Barack Obama (por motivos que talvez não caibam neste artigo). É então que a questão da representatividade do segmento afrodescendente em instâncias da "comunidade imaginada" se cruza com a do racismo como ideologia de deslegitimização que visa a exclusão desse segmento e o circunscreve à problemática da (i)migração, para que não se interroguem os fundamentos imaginários e onto-políticos dos discursos e práticas hegemónicas da "nação imaginada."

No entanto, convém assinalar as diferentes perspectivas epistemológicas e abordagens teóricas desta categoria em outras geografias, que dizem respeito a ligações da Afrodescendência às diásporas africanas que, nas Américas, Caraíbas ou na Europa, respondem a regimes distintos de historicidade. Para as Américas e Caraíbas, o foco recai sobre a história da escravatura e do tráfico atlântico de pessoas escravizadas a partir de África, enquanto na Europa são apontadas, em primeiro lugar, as relações com a herança colonial e a transformação das populações colonizadas nos migrantes das ex-metrópoles. Neste último caso, especificamente em Portugal e Espanha, a presença africana antes da invasão e ocupação de África é mencionada mas, em geral, ainda na actualidade, mantém--se como um dado muito encoberto e pouco referenciado.

Não ignorando tal diversidade, importa sublinhar que os percursos de representações e construções em torno da Afrodescendência exigem o aprofundamento de pressupostos teóricos e críticos (por exemplo, no interior dos Estudos Culturais, *Estudos Subalternos* ou Estudos Pós-coloniais) para continuarmos a abordar a presença e a história negra no mundo, interrogando as representações subalternizantes dos afrodescendentes nas narrativas nacionais, nomeadamente na Europa, nas Américas e Caraíbas e, por fim, em África. Mais especificamente, procura-se compreender as relações que os imaginários coletivos dessas "regiões do Mundo" (Édouard Glissant) mantêm, apesar das incontestáveis mutações verificadas nas últimas décadas, no que se refere às culturas, línguas, religiões, identidades cromáticas e ao combate pelo acesso efectivo à cidadania política – portanto, não apenas da "cidadania multicultural," proposta como teoria para o reconhecimento de direitos das minorias (Kymlicka 1995). Verifica-se, ainda, que a África do nosso tempo – como aliás, o "resto do mundo" (aqui no sentido literal da expressão e não na versão ideológica de Stuart Hall) – é culturalmente mestiça (Glissant teria dito que ela se crioulizou) pois, ao contrário do que se pensa, as culturas africanas não permaneceram as mesmas depois da colonização (já nem falando das dinâmicas migratórias internas que levaram a dinâmicas culturais). E é isso que os negros portugueses, afroeuropeus, americanos ou afroamericanos devem tomar em conta na sua apreciação do que têm em comum com os africanos, principalmente da África subsaariana.

É por isso que, embora possa parecer inadequada a paráfrase que fazemos do livro de Eduardo Galeano, tendo em conta que o seu autor "renegou" o livro e considerou a época a que ele se reporta como "uma etapa superada," o certo é que essas cicatrizes são as veias do rio colonial que vêm desaguar num delta pós-colonial, banhando as múltiplas margens das diferentes realidades de portadores da herança colonial – seja as dos ex-colonizados que vivem em seus países, seja as daqueles que vivem nas ex-metrópoles coloniais e seus descendentes, a que temos vindo a designar como *afrodescendentes*: estes vivem este momento com as veias abertas, um estado que, note-se, é também partilhado pelos ex-colonizadores e seus descendentes. Desconcertados quando as velhas narrativas colonialistas e esclavagistas são postas em causa, para estes últimos trata-se de admitir que há significados histórico-culturais construídos sobre o fenótipo branco, pois, na actualidade, o desafio às suas concepções (raciais, ocidentais) é vivido como um desafio à sua própria identidade e ao seu imaginário histórico. Em geral, entendem qualquer tentativa de mostrar o seu segmento conectado à herança colonial ou ao sistema do racismo como uma ofensa moral inquietante e injusta (DiAngelo 2018).

Com efeito, o segmento afrodescendente é, nos espaços que habita nas Américas e na Europa particularmente (embora não apenas), bastante fustigado por uma série de bloqueios, que vão desde bloqueios endógenos (mesmo que impulsionados por factores exógenos) a bloqueios que (lhes) são impostos por uma sociedade cuja visão identitária de "comunidade imaginada" teima em reproduzir modelos essencialistas, que não incentivam uma visão plural, em termos identitários e de paisagem humana, do país. Referimo-nos a Portugal, que é indubitavelmente feito hoje, no século XXI, de várias pertenças, realidade não exclusiva de qualquer país de imigração mas também de países que foram potência – e Portugal foi potência colonial, portanto, um *Próspero*, mesmo que concordemos que tenha sido, também, um *Caliban*, como propõe Boaventura Sousa Santos na análise de relações de poder colonial na Europa (no caso, entre as potências coloniais).[7]

Um dos elementos centrais desse processo de questionamento das narrativas históricas prevalecentes é a possibilidade que a sociedade oferece a um dos seus segmentos de ocupar um lugar confortável, a partir do qual pode olhar os outros através da lente pela qual não olha a si mesmo.[8] Essa lente – a raça – é aplicada a negros ou indígenas, enquanto os brancos são identificados como indivíduos neutros do ponto de vista da racialidade, numa normalização também assumida pelos não-brancos, muitos dos quais se referem a si próprios e aos segmentos a que pertencem como "grupos racializados". Portanto, assim laboram na manutenção do estatuto de *Outro* na sociedade em que se inserem e na qual pugnam pelo reconhecimento da sua plena pertença (mesmo que eventualmente reivindicando outras), como bem lembra Reni Eddo-Lodge, em afirmação que resgatamos da epígrafe e expandimos:

> Neutral is white. The default is white. Because we are born into an already written script that tells us what to expect from strangers due to their skin colour, accents and social status, the whole of humanity is coded as white. Blackness, however, is considered the "other" and therefore to be suspected. (Eddo-Lodge 2018, 85)

E, embora proclamando uma histórica multiculturalidade (como se esta fosse uma especificidade portuguesa!), esse não-reconhecimento do *Outro* como o *Mesmo*, *diverso* apenas e não *diferente*, causa tanta perplexidade quando esta ex-potência colonial – Portugal, nosso lugar de enunciação – se vangloria da sua herança atlântica ao mesmo tempo que continua a perpetuar a *racialização* do *Outro*, que, curiosamente a aceita e a internaliza, o que nos parece mais problemático, como atrás já referimos. Isso demonstra o não reconhecimento de que a heterogeneidade não é apenas constitutiva mas fundadora da sociedade pós-colonial, com traços perceptíveis na paisagem humana, de que a geografia e a arquitectura urbanas deixam visíveis, mas também nas produções culturais, artísticas, nas práticas religiosas, nas identidades cromáticas, nas práticas culinárias, musicais, nas disjunções em certas onomásticas imaginadas e nas regiões ou sujeitos que os trazem.

É ainda essa não-consciência que conduz ao não reconhecimento da realidade pós-colonial, na ex-metrópole, que normaliza a invisibilidade – real, física – do não-branco em instituições da sociedade civil, nos partidos, nas instituições do Estado ou do outro tipo, enfim nos lugares da supersestrutura da sociedade. E essa invisibilidade é reforçada, porque omissa enquanto problema, quando artistas africanos ou afrodescendentes que conseguem romper as barreiras do silêncio e conquistar um espaço na cena social, cultural e artística omitem do seu discurso questões como a do racismo ("racismo epidérmico ou naturalmente espontâneo,"[9] estrutural ou institucional) ou a da representatividade – mais preocupados em buscar o "reconhecimento" daqueles que sempre os discrimina(ra)m do que em buscar uma emancipação e afirmação identitária, individual ou colectiva. Em *Pele Negra, Máscaras Brancas* (1952), Frantz Fanon ajudar-nos-ia a compreender essa busca de reconhecimento precisamente por aqueles que antes lhes bloqueavam a caminhada.

No debate sempre presente entre continuidade, ruptura e transformações, o ponto da discussão mantém o *Calling at Africa* (Glissant, 2005), fortemente associado às lutas políticas dos afrodescendentes nos nossos dias. De acordo com Jésus Chucho Garcia (2005), nas Américas, os afrodescendentes resultam de um amplo processo de conservação-recriação e transformação ligado às condições sócio-históricas e económicas que viveram. Neste sentido, a cultura afrodescendente enquadra-se em fenómenos históricos de longa duração, caracterizados por momentos de ruptura, continuidades, desconstrução e reconstrução. Neste processo, considera o autor, a *africanía*[10] resistiu e, por mecanismos de sobrevivência, lançou as sementes para a revalorização cultural, a busca da liberdade, a conquista da cidadania, a politização da identidade e, também, a luta frontal contra o racismo e a pobreza. Ao contrário da presunção de um exclusivo *continuum* cultural, ou mesmo da presença de "bolsões de africanidade" relacionados diretamente às suas origens africanas, Édouard Glissant sublinha que as experiências dão espaço ao imprevisto, à aleatoriedade, às metamorfoses e transformações, às resignificações ou reapropriações históricas e políticas nos contextos específicos em questão. É neste âmbito que devem ser interpretadas, enquadradas e reconhecidas as reivindicações de representatividade equitativa, assim como a aspiração ao controle das representações oficiais e populares de aspectos da denominada herança cultural, que Glissant prefere descrever como diversidades realizadas do *Tout-Monde* que interrogam o universalismo abstracto.

2. Afrodescendência e narrativa nacional em Portugal

Nesta reflexão, tomamos como referência o processo, a organização e as condições em que vivem os portugueses de ascendência africana, pessoas que não são mais os que transitam, como se fossem "estranhos em permanência" (Mata 2006), cuja existência não mais permite duvidar-se de que há negros portugueses que não são brancos, nomeadamente, portugueses negros. E mesmo que o país ainda esteja relutante em dizer que são imigrantes (de segunda, terceira, quarta gerações!), a sua presença tornou-se um objecto permanente de discussão e de impossibilidade de recusar o reconhecimento das mestiçagens, deslocamentos e dinâmicas de enraizamentos que caracterizam a presente realidade do mundo global. Mesmo que, buscando-se negá-la, se encontre definitivamente colocada a reivindicação da unipertença ("Sou português") ou de múltiplas pertenças ("Sou português de origem X ou Y"), essa multipertença não tem de descrever o habitar a fronteira, enfim, uma identidade de fronteira que recusa a obrigatoriedade de se ter de escolher uma das pertenças e renunciar à outra (Miano 2012).

Trata-se, para nós, de uma presença existência que tem as suas possibilidades fortemente associadas aos modos de relação da sociedade portuguesa contemporânea com a alteridade. Contudo, suscita igualmente novas e necessárias leituras e apropriações, porque se refere a representações hegemónicas dos afrodescendentes presentes nas narrativas pedagógicas nacionais: literaturas, discursos, manuais escolares ou discursos essencialistas sobre as identidades nacionais "imaginadas." Com efeito, são essas narrativas hegemónicas que recusam as reivindicações dos excluídos quando afirmam que certas culturas subsaarianas trazem, em si, elementos definitivamente incompatíveis com a cultura portuguesa;[11] é também frequentemente dessa exclusão que se trata quando se fustigam as *leis memoriais* ou se propõe o "lapso" (recusa) da nacionalidade aos que, aqui nascidos, não são jogadores de futebol ou de (reconhecido e imediato) prestígio e interesse nacionais; e é, em grande parte, por causa dessa recusa que se celebra a recente alteração da monocor do Parlamento como afirmação de "democracia racial"[12] em Portugal. Porém, o facto de esse sujeito se ter tornado, nos últimos tempos, fortemente presente, não quer dizer que os negros acabaram de chegar a este país, como vem afirmando, em inúmeros estudos, com suporte iconográfico, a historiadora Isabel Castro Henriques.[13]

Muitos são os estudos que nos dizem ter sido o número de pessoas negras e de origem africana certamente muito inferior ao atual, embora essas já fizessem parte da paisagem portuguesa desde o século XVI. E, no entanto, de forma suficientemente inexplicável, não figuram como portugueses de tão longa data, e relatos sobre a sua presença são marcados pela excepcionalidade. Historiadores, romancistas, escritores, artistas plásticos, cineastas, assim como os cientistas sociais, parecem ter interiorizado a ideia segundo a qual um negro só poderia ser um imigrante – de preferência, indocumentado. Portugueses negros não aparecem na narrativa nacional, de qualquer modalidade discursiva (artística, política ou referencial) na história que Portugal conta sobre si mesmo, depois aos seus filhos e, por fim, ao mundo, há tantas gerações. Essa narrativa inventou uma memória branca, e isso, evidentemente, coloca um problema, se se considerar que dominou numerosos povos não brancos, e se estendeu para além-mar, para a África, a América do Sul e o Oceano Índico. No aspecto cultural, um dos elementos mais importantes da mitologia nacional apresenta a República como uma ideia que se sobrepõe ao real em lugar de se juntar a ele. Não é temerário pensar-se que essa "entidade" (a III República, como sucedânea do Estado Novo colonial) continua a ser assimilacionista e centralizadora, embora se diga cega à cor, às diferenças de todo o tipo, exigindo apenas uma coisa: a conformidade aos seus princípios. Todavia, e de modo similar ao que aconteceu em França, como descreve Léonora Miano em *Habiter la frontière* (2012), os adversários da República não são, contemporaneamente (o tempo do português negro), os que, sem ver a cor dos *Outros*, recusam categoricamente contratá-los ou alugar-lhes apartamentos decentes, os que procuram não inscrever os seus filhos em escolas com forte população não branca, ou os que propõem programas escolares, sobretudo livros de História, nos quais nenhum português não branco reconhece a sua face nem reconhece as razões pelas quais ele é, tanto quanto qualquer outro, legítimo na sua reivindicação de Portugal como sendo o seu país. E, no entanto, tal como a situação do Negro francês referida por Miano (2012), neste início do século XXI, muito além da inserção de secções sobre os impérios subsaarianos nos programas escolares, que ainda tarda, estamos convencidas de que é o ensino de todos os detalhes da história dos Negros em Portugal (e na Europa) que lhes permitirá aceitar naturalmente a sua identidade portuguesa.

Na análise sobre as possibilidades de pertença dos afrodescendentes à comunidade imaginada, o destino que o país oferecer às suas minorias será revelador das suas capacidades de se mostrar à altura do desafio, e isso é importante na medida em que se trata de saber se Portugal pode realmente ser o território da Igualdade e dos Direitos Humanos.[14] Do ponto de vista interno, as definições identitárias associadas à Afrodescendência – as que não desvinculam a reivindicação do *ser português* da sua herança africana – têm trazido fortes reações no espaço público. Estes actos afirmativos deviam tornar necessárias operações de uniformização, similares, em certa medida, àquela que a acção colonial fez quando promoveu a assimilação dos colonizados à cultura portuguesa. De facto, tais actos contrariam a aceitação de que *ser português* não é uma questão de origem, uma vez que há portugueses que são originários de outros lugares – ironicamente, dos lugares onde, por séculos, Portugal tentou impor a ideia de pertença a uma mesma unidade política e nacional, através de ideologia de uma "nação multirracial, multicultural e pluricontinental." Todavia, desta vez, o facto de os afrodescendentes e negros portugueses reivindicarem a pertença à comunidade imaginada (através da sua inclusão na narrativa nacional) tem suscitado um tipo de sentimento de memória ferida, de perigo de subjugação e da construção do *Outro* (que, em todo o caso, deveria ser visto apenas como *Diverso*) como portador de uma cultura fechada ao diálogo,[15] ameaçando o que, até agora, cada região de Portugal sempre pôde contar: uma história monocolorida e monolítica que, certamente, facilitou o embranquecimento da memória portuguesa.

As reacções e agressões explícitas que esta exigência vem provocando parecem evidenciar que, se os afrodescendentes e portugueses negros não podem ancorar e relacionar as suas reivindicações a uma longa ancestralidade e à possessão da terra (na ex-metrópole) ao longo de gerações, a sua presença é embaraçosa porque carrega reminiscências do encontro brutal entre povos. De facto, essa existência torna presente a memória dos crimes que não prescrevem, mas que se sabe que, em grande parte, foram os que permitiram a Portugal apresentar-se como uma grande potência. O Negro de Portugal lembra constantemente o passado colonial do país (como o do Brasil e dos Estados Unidos lembram o passado escravocrata) e se não se despe daquilo que o liga ao solo dos seus ancestrais, ele confronta a sociedade portuguesa na ideia da sua "estrangeiridade," alteridade e exterioridade.

Em conjunto com aquilo para o que o tema remete relativamente à constituição da narrativa nacional e da comunidade imaginada portuguesa contemporânea, como mostram os resultados obtidos até ao momento (Dezembro de 2020) no Projecto AFRO-PORT,[16] outras operações de compreensão e clarificação acerca do alcance de conceito são realizadas. Mais do que um termo, estas correspondem à busca de um modo de designar os portugueses de outra origem (afrodescendentes e negros) que não os confunda com imigrantes, porque esta forma de os caracterizar não corresponde à realidade histórica, política e cultural e tem apenas em conta a ideologia essencialista sobre o *ser português*.

Em primeiro lugar, a consideração sobre se é a homogeneidade da cor necessária à categorização e aproximação ainda se mostra insuficiente para afirmar que o debate sobre a Afrodescendência se confunde com as questões de pertença do Negro português, cujas constituintes mantêm relações entre si, sem que uma das constituintes sufoque a(s) outra(s) – abrindo-se ao Outro sem asfixiar o Mesmo, como diria Édouard Glissant, em *Introduction à une poétique du divers* (1996), nas suas (re)interpretações sobre as dinâmicas identitárias caribenhas – ainda que, no caso de Portugal, a constituinte africana possa ser fundamental pelo facto de, por ela, começar o processo de auto-reconhecimento identitário. Este facto é relevante, no caso de Portugal, pois, tal como mostram as primeiras informações recolhidas no projecto AFRO-PORT, as autodefinições ou definições colectivamente articuladas em torno do *ser afrodescendente* destacam dois elementos: por um lado, a origem que remete à África e, por outro, a reivindicação de direitos de cidadania plena em Portugal, lugar de nascimento, de vivência e de existência (Évora, 2020b). A questão da Afrodescendência tem de se traduzir numa discussão sobre o reconhecimento dessa identidade no espaço público – que se tem mostrado resiliente em relação a isso, pois, para os detentores históricos do *poder da fala*, "[o] acesso ao espaço público de novas personagens, portadoras de culturas e de reivindicações diversas, desagrega a homogeneidade do espaço e coloca o problema da preservação da continuidade deste, ao mesmo tempo em que aceita sua crescente heterogeneidade" (Semprini 1999, 131).

É que hoje a questão da Afrodescendência em Portugal remete, em primeiro lugar, ao tema da presença do português de origem subsaariana e à existência de uma *comunidade negra* (a par de uma comunidade crioula) que se propõe actuante no espaço público. E exige maior aprofundamento sobre a diferença entre origem territorial e cultural e ascendência, na medida em que grande parte dos que chamamos de Negros partilham uma ancestralidade subsaariana. Mas será possível afirmar que, em Portugal, Negros formam um grupo homogéneo no plano cultural e mesmo de experiência histórica? O facto de essa comunidade ser percebida como tendo a mesma cor de pele será suficiente para categorizar ou aproximar pessoas ou, pelo contrário, o que pode uni-la deveria ser procurado muito mais em outros *lugares*?

A existência de uma comunidade negra em Portugal remete, ainda, para a grande diversidade cultural interna dos países africanos de origem e entre si, mesmo os de língua portuguesa, vistos como um grupo político homogéneo. Por outro lado, os africanos que diversificaram a migração em Portugal nas últimas décadas confirmam que a África subsaariana, frequentemente percebida como um bloco monolítico, abriga, no entanto, poderosas heterogeneidades. Não se vive da mesma maneira no Sahel como na África Ocidental, África Central, na África Austral ou no Corno de África e, na medida em que os migrantes subsaarianos transportam consigo a sua bagagem identitária quando chegam à Europa, essas diferenças persistem. E quanto mais numerosa for a comunidade, maior a tendência de os portugueses de origem subsaariana se reagruparem no seio de colectivos mais ligados ao lugar geocultural da sua ancestralidade do que ao continente. Existem associações de guineenses, cabo-verdianos, angolanos, são-tomenses, moçambicanos, senegaleses, mas também existem associações de principenses, balantas, mandingas, cabindas... E têm a particularidade de serem abertas, ao mesmo tempo, aos que têm uma (auto)-identificação portuguesa e aos *Outros*. A única condição que parece ser necessária para se fazer parte é reconhecer uma filiação à referida entidade (país ou região), o que pode levar, por vezes, a uma fragmentação e à criação de estruturas ligadas, não a um país, mas a uma região desse país, preservando as suas particularidades, uma vez que, na África subsaariana, cada país é composto por territórios multiculturais onde as etnias têm tradições diferentes e co-habitam[17]. Em Portugal, não existem antagonismos entre as diferentes populações de origem africana, portuguesas ou com estatuto de imigrantes, e essas pessoas consideram-se como uma comunidade, reconhecendo as suas proximidades, mesmo se, do ponto de vista político, isso não se opere no espaço público. Em certa medida, esta condição parece indicar a existência, nessas populações, de um sentimento panafricano não ideológico, natural e espontâneo – cuja compreensão deveria ser aprofundada para se pensar as suas pertenças identitárias num mundo em que certas identidades *hifenizadas* são celebradas.

O segundo facto a tomar-se em consideração para compreender a ausência (ou o tipo de presença) da comunidade negra em Portugal está relacionado com a História. No Portugal colonial do Estado Novo, embora não fosse legal a segregação racial – nos moldes sul-africanos ou norte-americanos, determinando, por exemplo, a existência de escolas e igrejas reservadas aos negro-africanos –, cumpria essa função o *Estatuto dos Indígenas Portugueses das Províncias da Guiné, Angola e Moçambique* (1957).[18] Através deste estatuto, os africanos não eram considerados *cidadãos*, mas *indígenas* sem quaisquer direitos civis ou jurídicos, e a sua vida tinha de ser regulada, a não ser que se dispusessem a assimilar a cultura portuguesa, renegando a sua para integrar a categoria dos "assimilados," isto é, portugueses de pele negra. Assim, ainda que o racismo não estivesse explicitamente inscrito na lei, aos Negros não era permitido formularem as suas reivindicações como Negros. Por esse motivo, o racismo ainda prospera na actualidade, de forma menos espectacular, mas as suas manifestações são mais perniciosas e, assim como a condição do Negro em França, os que actualmente reivindicam são bastante incompreendidos, na medida em que essa prática não cabe nos hábitos portugueses. Estes sustentam fortemente a recusa em avaliar o número de pessoas que se consideram negras, em contraste, por exemplo, com a facilidade em defini-las como imigrantes, não originárias, portanto, do país onde se encontram. O que se evidencia é a facilidade com que se considera que essas pessoas, se desejarem, podem voltar para os espaços (em África) nos quais a sua presença é maioritária e podem reivindicá-lo como constituindo a principal parte da sua identidade.

Além disso, o tratamento do tema da Afrodescendência coloca em pauta os efeitos da colonização dentro e fora do continente, pois, o processo colonizatório fez desaparecer o mundo conhecido, precipitando os povos da África subsaariana num universo do qual não tiveram controlo do desenho dos contornos do seu destino que, com dificuldade, ainda estão a tentar habitar. Questiona-se, assim, se Portugal permitiu o aparecimento de *lugares* de debate entre os Negros sobre esses assuntos, para além de algumas associações militantes do Movimento Negro em Portugal, frequentemente afrocentradas, sempre forjadas a contrapelo da política colonial, tanto do regime militar da I República quanto a do Estado Novo. De notar que se é incontestável, no contexto da imigração, a invenção de uma nova cultura a partir de influências diversas, também na África subsaariana a colonização levou à mutilação de identidades, redefinição de espaços de pertenças, pressionando as populações que, também ali, tiveram de assimilar novos modos de vida e, portanto, de recriar o seu quotidiano.

Consideramos que esses *lugares* de que falamos acima têm estatutos diferentes na relação que Portugal estabelece com as suas antigas colónias de África. Apesar do marco forte das independências, é necessário considerar (e estudar com maior profundidade, para além de abordagens ensaísticas) as especificidades dos modos de incorporação dos ex-colonizados em Portugal, em grande parte articulados com o grau de proximidade ao colonizador. Em contexto da ex-metrópole, esse processo resulta em classificações (implícitas) das culturas de acordo com o grau de visibilidade do "selo africano," por exemplo, na música e nas línguas de socialização (com destaque para as línguas crioulas), nas práticas quotidianas e na alimentação, nos rituais de socialização e nas crenças religiosas.

A título ilustrativo, note-se que, por razões históricas, em muitos casos, há os que se beneficiaram de uma condição social mais vantajosa como resultado das posições ocupadas nas colónias, como é o caso dos cabo-verdianos que pertenciam às administrações coloniais em todos os países africanos de ocupação portuguesa. Todavia, logo a seguir, as condições económicas ditaram a consolidação de um segmento ligado à construção civil cuja face mais visível é descrita, sobretudo, pela presença de migrantes cabo-verdianos pobres e seus descendentes, enquanto que, nas últimas décadas, constrói-se uma imagem dos angolanos em Portugal muito mais associada às parcerias económicas entre os dois países. Pretende-se aqui ilustrar que, em Portugal, houve diferenças nessas migrações organizadas, em termos de quais poderiam ser consideradas definitivas, essencialmente femininas ou masculinas, de agrupamento familiar ou as que se esperava que seriam concluídas com o retorno. É preciso mesmo notar que os grupos foram sempre vistos como maleáveis e adaptáveis às perspectivas originais de Portugal, tendo sido, ao longo do tempo, concentrados na Área Metropolitana de Lisboa onde, actualmente, os Negros ainda se encontram em maior número.

3. Âmbitos da articulação Afrodescendência /cor da pele

O termo *Afrodescendência* ganha destaque numa altura em que os privilégios e as desvantagens ligadas à cor da pele (não descartando, aqui, o colorismo),[19] ainda são inegáveis, apesar das (acreditamos) bem-intencionadas afirmações que mais apontam para *colour blindness* do que para uma incidência sem valor associado, considerando que, nos últimos tempos, tem havido uma preocupação maior em ocupar o espaço público para a problematização dessas afirmações. Os esforços em retirar esta componente do seu substrato existencial atesta um truque de memória e de excisão de um passado que, no entanto, continua a colocar problemas.

Muito além de questionar a adequação (e a justeza) de um ou outro termo que possa ser adotado (português, imigrante de segunda geração, africano em Portugal, afroportuguês, etc), é mais pertinente compreender se os portugueses negros buscam uma designação de/para si atualmente, ousando afastar-se (e ou contrapor-se) à estigmatização de que são alvo.

Os resultados obtidos, até ao momento, no âmbito do Projecto AFRO-PORT sobre a Afrodescendência em Portugal, confirmam que o sujeito enuncia-se aqui, pois é precisamente a denúncia que lhe confere o lugar de enunciação. A referência à Afrodescendência evidencia, por um lado, que *português* mantém-se como sinónimo de *branco* e, ao mesmo tempo, confirma a complexidade que é para os negros reivindicarem-se como portugueses (Évora 2020a). A introdução atual do conceito de Afrodescendência como dispositivo (e recurso) identitário mostra-se esclarecedora do grau de identificação das pessoas com as definições que o país, inconscientemente, sempre lhes atribuiu, bem como a extensão com que se deixam modelar e respondem, performativamente, às palavras que os têm nomeado no espaço público (e pensamos que a auto-referência *racializadas/os* é um dos resultados desse gesto performativo). Como afirma Léonora Miano, na obra acima citada a propósito dos Negros em França ou na Grã-Bretanha, na medida em que é também o olhar do *Outro* que nos faz existir, não é de se estranhar que os Negros europeus sejam associados à visão que os seus países têm deles, mesmo que isso não seja satisfatório e tenha como efeito acentuar as tensões internas e um sentimento de estranheza no lugar ao qual pertencem.

Ainda sobre a comunidade negra e a forma como a dinâmica da sua presença se articula com a emergência de reivindicações em torno da categoria *afrodescendente*, é possível que o aprofundamento de medidas de maior representatividade desse segmento, em Portugal, evidencie a complexidade existencial e as tensões que definem e formatam as relações dos negro-africanos entre si e entre diferentes segmentos da diversa sociedade portuguesa. Este elemento é, de *per si*, suficiente para compreender que a experiência de uns e outros não é idêntica entre si, em todos os aspectos. Contudo, tem sido sugerido na pesquisa de terreno do

Projecto AFRO-PORT que aqueles que se afirmam africanos ou afrodescenden-tes – porque estão ligados ao continente africano (e não porque nasceram em Portugal), mesmo que nunca tenham lá ido – privilegiam as suas origens negro--africanas e atribuem prioridade aos valores comuns (distância do *ser português* e dificuldades ou desinteresse em exprimi-lo) (Évora 2020b).

Num outro sentido, há grupos e pessoas que consideram que encontraram um meio de marcar a sua especificidade identitária – negro europeu – e explorar as possibilidades de um continente de contornos fictícios que Byrne baptizou de *Afropea* (Miano 2012) para simbolizar a *longue durée* da influência das culturas sub-saarianas na Europa. Outros, ainda, enfatizam a sua pertença, em simultâneo, a dois mundos e recusam a possibilidade de serem associados a apenas um deles. Sob o argumento de que não podem ser confrontadas com uma escolha que exi-giria que se divorciassem de uma parte de si mesmas, estas pessoas reivindicam as suas pertenças múltiplas e recusam a alegação feita a uma só e única *nação*, por conseguinte, colocando diretamente em causa o Estado-nação.

Em referência ao Negro português, podemos experimentar uma classificação em duas grandes categorias, em que os primeiros resultam do tráfico transatlân-tico e da escravatura colonial e já foram desligados da sua genealogia africana; em relação aos segundos, que vêm de países da África subsaariana anteriormente colonizados por Portugal, trazem os patrimónios subsaarianos e, na maior parte do tempo, conservam as ligações com os países onde nasceram os seus pais e avós. Estas ligações são mais ou menos fortes conforme os casos e, por exem-plo, nem todos falam a língua dos pais ou vão a África com regularidade, mas em geral, o património está lá para marcar a origem.

Através de movimentos como os da Negritude e *lugares* como Casa dos Estudantes do Império, os subsaarianos das ex-colónias portuguesas encontra-ram-se enquanto colonizados e negros. E, nos nossos dias, um número cres-cente de jovens têm escolhido, também eles, ligar-se a essas semelhanças entre si, para fazerem entender que as suas vozes não serão as de subsaarianos (ou latino americanos-brasileiros) em Portugal mas de *portugueses negros*. Entre estes e os subsaarianos ex-colonizados, encontram-se os colectivos que reivindicam a herança africana e adoptam uma argumentação panafricanista revolucionária no modo de estar e viver em Portugal, denunciando o racismo e as desigualdades de que os africanos e seus descendentes são as principais vítimas.

Mais recentemente, os jovens portugueses negros chamam a atenção pelos seus posicionamentos – por exemplo, mulheres negras, jovens, com formação superior ou especializada, que se organizam em torno da produção/reivindicação cultural e política, ligadas a movimentos negros na Europa e utilizando recursos e ferramentas a partir da sua articulação com outras afrodescendentes negras europeias. Ou os colectivos que se articulam com movimentos europeus de jovens negros da diáspora africana e criam formas de ligação e cooperação entre si e, juntos, com o continente africano. Trata-se de dinâmicas relevantes para a conceptualização da Afrodescendência na Europa, não apenas em razão da radicalidade que podem trazer, mas no que isso diz de uma cultura em provável gestação, a definição e a afirmação de um *ser português* que se constitui no território físico e da tensão que interpõe os que são considerados legítimos ou não (ou mais ou menos legítimos).

Em síntese, são identificadas nas actuações desses segmentos tanto as críticas ao facto de que nenhuma instância parece capaz de fazer os protestos serem ouvidos, como também as dificuldades em trazer o contraditório quando os africanos ou portugueses negros são sistematicamente associados à malfeitoria. De formas diversas, os colectivos propõem que a sua acção procure contrariar a ausência de Poder desses segmentos no espaço público, a falta de controle da sua imagem (em contraste com a imagem estereotipada, e geralmente deturpada, que é veiculada pelos *media*, em geral) ou uma descrição inferiorizante daquilo que podia ser considerado como sua participação na produção social portuguesa. O que consiste, neste caso, numa forma de indicar ao Negro que, não sendo branco, não pode representar ou produzir o seu país e não está em condições de dizer a si mesmo o que é. Neste sentido, a forte disseminação (e apropriação) do conceito de "lugar de fala" entre esses colectivos tem servido para contrariar a perspectiva de que é mais pertinente um não-negro produzir um discurso sobre estas populações.

No caso contrário, várias experiências e reacções no espaço público demonstram que *ser negro* em Portugal e falar de Negros é constituir uma ameaça, qualquer que seja o objectivo que se tem (como acontece amiúde quando um não-branco com algum capital social toma a palavra para denunciar alguma iniquidade decorrente das relações racializadas de Poder e lhe lembram que ela/ele até é um privilegiado). No século XXI, a presença de portugueses negros ainda reatualiza a ideia de que ao Negro no espaço público atribui-se um favor e, por isso, por diversos meios, é-lhe lembrado que deve *manter-se no seu lugar*, como um *bom negro*. As produções consagradas através dos afrodescendentes de Portugal recebem um acolhimento morno por parte dos *media*, e obras que tocam fortemente esse segmento praticamente não são comentadas nos noticiários ou indicadas como tendências no âmbito nacional. No caso da música produzida pelos afrodescendentes, as plataformas digitais asseguram a sua difusão e o nascimento de verdadeiras estrelas, fenómenos de público com forte penetração entre a juventude, mas a maior parte desses casos continua a ser ignorada pelos decisores do meio e *opinion makers* da indústria musical portuguesa. Em suma, a estes artistas de portugueses negros do século XXI não se lhes reconhece o direito de se exprimirem sobre questões da sociedade portuguesa. As suas temáticas somente são identificadas pelo *mainstream* se se confirma que são estrangeiros e em dificuldade ou se estiverem relacionadas com África, lugar que lhes foi atribuído para sempre e que parece não permitir outra composição no vasto campo de articulações e sobreposições entre as diásporas africanas e as ex-metrópoles.

O que a sociedade diz de si mesma é o que está escrito nos seus livros e nos anais da sua História – por isso Ki-Zerbo proclamava, em *Para Quando a África?*, que "a acumulação dos conhecimentos se faz na Europa" (2006, 94), e V-Y. Mudimbe fala em "biblioteca colonial" (1988), acervo de enunciados produzidos por grupos externos de "africanistas" que se imbuem de uma "razão etnológica" para a interpretação das realidades africanas e constroem "regimes de verdade" (sobre a África), que acabam por ser vistos como verdades científicas até por africanos. Pretende-se acreditar que o que não é mencionado é porque não existe no país e, portanto, assegura-se o regresso à identidade nacional mais essencializada, como se isso fosse possível, como se isso tivesse existido alguma vez (paradoxalmente enquanto se proclama a vocação atlântica e se celebra a história da Expansão). Numa atitude que ignora o seu poder de radicalizar as minorias e acentuar as clivagens, o país que redefiniu o destino de tantos povos procura impedir a descendência dos colonizados de lhe imprimir a sua contribuição e a sua marca – contrariamente ao que se passa no espaço africano, em que o segmento de origem europeia goza de todos os direitos, erigindo-se, até, a uma etnia nacional, como os africâneres/*afrikaners*/*afrikaanders* na África do Sul, ou os pretensos "crioulos" em Angola.

Por isso pensamos ser necessário aprofundar, a partir das pesquisas realizadas no âmbito do Projecto AFRO-PORT os seguintes aspetos: movimentos mais ou menos conscientes para tentar encaixar-se num molde que se formata sobre Afrodescendência; grau de consciência e perceção sobre a utilidade do esforço para serem reconhecidos como herdeiros legítimos do espaço nacional que habitam e das linhagens que prevalecem apesar de todos os discursos; diferentes formas e graus de equilíbrio e de apropriação como Europeus negros; a escolha entre a sua constituinte subsaariana e o seu lado europeu; diferentes distâncias e posições sobre habitar (em) ambos os lados, transitar entre eles, misturá-los sem hierarquizar. E nesse *entre-dois*, sentirem-se confortáveis, completos, florescentes, como artesãos de um lugar outrora sempre descrito como de rutura (em relação ao de seus pais) e, agora, num espaço de acolhimento onde os dois mundos que os constituem se tocam sem se afrontar.

4. Considerações (por enquanto) finais: alargar o âmbito da discussão em Portugal

Laboramos segundo uma perspectiva heurística. Neste contexto, incluir os grupos afrodescendentes como parte de uma comunidade imaginada pressuporia a implementação de "políticas de identidade" que contrastariam com as identidades imaginadas do passado, introduzindo "novas políticas" que visariam, também, limitar um pouco as disfunções e restrições impostas aos Negros e Negras, de um modo geral, as primeiras vítimas e alvo do desprezo da sociedade. Os discursos racistas contemporâneos, ao abandonarem as noções biológicas de raça e superioridade racial, centraram-se, sobretudo, no estabelecimento de relações implícitas entre raça, nacionalidade, patriotismo e homogeneidade cultural. No caso de Portugal, isso dificulta uma ação sistemática, por exemplo, em torno de modificações nas leis gerais do Estado (tal como a lei da nacionalidade), a criminalização do racismo, uma política de quotas, ações afirmativas, reformas educativas que visem a educação para a cidadania numa perspectiva intercultural, defesa e promoção de um programa político de gestão da multiculturalidade e revisão crítica das histórias locais, regionais e nacional.

O que tem sido amplamente confirmado no contexto da investigação no âmbito do Projecto AFRO-PORT é o caráter incipiente de uma Academia que vê o termo *afrodescendente* como uma forma de apaziguamento, pois para ela as questões de raça e de memória (sobretudo a dos negros na ex-metrópole e descendentes de ex-colonizados) não se colocam no espaço português. É surpreendente que não tenham nada a dizer sobre aqueles que não são imigrantes, mas seus compatriotas.

Por todas estas razões, pensamos que este tema da Afrodescendência tem o potencial de expor uma forma mais profunda do esvaziamento da retórica da unidade definida pela cor da pele que serve para identificar cada segmento da sociedade, mas que, até ao momento, mantém as pessoas brancas neutras no quesito cromático. A categorização tem a vantagem de se tornar útil e interessante para pontuar o facto de que Portugal – e a Europa, *grosso modo* – não (re)conhecem comunidades negras ou brancas homogéneas. Possibilidade de abordagens ao mesmo tempo sensíveis e subjectivas e objectivas admitem a Afrodescendência quer nas suas produções afrodiaspóricas que abraçam populações de origem africana, quer, também, como a face mais actual da Europa globalizada e do século XXI. Colectivos afrodescendentes em Portugal atuam em torno do reconhecimento e valorização de uma sororidade, embora, na nossa perspectiva, ainda sejam incipientes as diligências objetivas e claramente apontadas em torno de tópicos como o apaziguamento, o abandono do ressentimento, a capacidade de se projectar de forma válida no futuro, o que exige, antes de tudo, a cicatrização das feridas íntimas ligadas a uma história dolorosa.

Porém, falta ainda realizar a recolha exaustiva dos conceitos que são adotados e vulgarizados em torno da Afrodescendência que, na atualidade, busca ir mais além do desvelamento da estigmatização da sua presença e existência no espaço social português. Seria, no entanto, importante não desconsiderar uma abordagem contemporânea à Afrodescendência e às reivindicações dos afrodescendentes na Europa, Américas e Caraíbas, assim como compreender o significado atribuído à Afrodescendência em diferentes países africanos e a forma como esta categorização está articulada como a noção da presença africana no mundo, da *África-Mundo*, de que fala Achille Mbembe.

NOTAS

1. Este artigo é parte dos resultados da investigação realizada pelas autoras no âmbito do Projecto Afro-Port. Afrodescendência em Portugal: sociabilidades, representações e dinâmicas sociopolíticas e culturais. Um estudo na Área Metropolitana de Lisboa", com financiamento da Fundação para a Ciência e Tecnologia de Portugal (PTDC/SOC-ANT/2017) e a ser realizado no período 2018-2022.

2. Romero Rodriguez, "Entramos Negros y Salimos Afrodescendientes: breve evaluación de los resultados de la III Cumbre Mundial contra el Racismo en América del Sur," *Revista Futuros*, Nº5, Vol.II (2004).

3. Cerca de 200 milhões de pessoas autoidentificadas como afrodescendentes vivem nas Américas. Muitos outros milhões vivem em outras partes do mundo, fora do continente africano (fonte: https://nacoesunidas.org/tema/decada-afro/) e, na Europa, é de cerca de 15 milhões o número indicado pela União Europeia para descendentes de Africanos ou Afro-caribenhos.

4. Jean-Arsène Yao, *Afrodescendientes en America. De Esclavos a Ciudadanos* (Madrid: Editorial Mundo Negro, 2014).

5. Embora este tema não caiba no âmbito desta reflexão, vale assinalar que esta não é uma questão linear, no sentido da celebração acrítica dessa efeméride. Com efeito, as intenções da ONU ao indicar a Década foram alvo de muita crítica, por exemplo, pelos que consideram que esta é uma forma de manter as distinções entre negros e brancos, num tempo em que a longa presença na Europa já devia ter operado a diluição do que se possa considerar das particularidades de africanidade e europeidade. Essa crítica ganha sustentação quando se pensa que foram os países ex-metrópoles coloniais que insistiram nessa Década, não representando o que as Américas e as Caraíbas discutem sobre a Afrodescendência.

6. Ver: Alberto da Costa e Silva, Um Rio Chamado Atlântico: *A África no Brasil e o Brasil na África* (Rio de Janeiro: Nova Fronteira, 2003).

7. Boaventura Sousa Santos, "Entre Próspero e Caliban: Colonialismo, Pós-Colonialismo e Interidentidade," *Novos Estudos* 66 (Julho de 2003): 23-52.

8. Ruth Frankenberg, *White Women, Race Matters: The Social Construction of Whiteness* (Minneapolis: University of Minnesota Press/Routledge, 1993).

9. Isabel Castro Henriques, *De Escravos a Indígenas: O Longo Processo de Instrumentalização dos Africanos (séculos XV - XX)* (Lisboa: Caleidoscópio, 2019): 376.

10. Jésus Chucho Garcia usa o termo *africanía*, cunhado por volta dos anos 1980-90, e surgido, possivelmente, na cátedra de africania de Alcalá de Henares (UNESCO). *Africanía* pretende reafirmar os laços históricos culturais e espirituais na África (negra) e nas suas diásporas, no *Tout-Monde*, como diria Glissant. Enquanto o termo *africanidade* tem a África como berço e referência direta, *africanía*, mais do que um conceito, é uma

reivindicação de co-pertença imaginária e onto-política entre África negra e Américas e Caraíbas. Nestas regiões, muitos negros consideram-se africanos, mas *africanía* indica crioulização, hibridismo e temporalidades e historicidades singulares como componentes do imaginário das diásporas.

11. Recorde-se, a título de exemplo, o polémico artigo da historiadora portuguesa Maria de Fátima Bonifácio, "Podemos? Não, não Podemos?" (*Público*, 6 de Julho de 2019), em que a autora afirma que os negros e os ciganos não partilham "as mesmas crenças religiosas e os mesmos valores morais" (que os portugueses, obviamente) e não "fazem parte de uma entidade civilizacional e cultural milenária que dá pelo nome de Cristandade," pois "[n]em uns nem outros descendem dos Direitos Universais do Homem decretados pela Grande Revolução Francesa de 1789. Uns e outros possuem os seus códigos de honra, as suas crenças, cultos e liturgias próprios," para concluir que "[o]s ciganos, sobretudo, são inassimiláveis."

12. Embora o significado moderno da expressão "democracia racial" tenha sido gerado a partir das ideias de Gilberto Freyre, a quem se atribui a sua autoria (e que, na verdade, usou uma expressão sinónima em 1944, "democracia étnica e social," nas conferências na Universidade de Indiana, EUA), os primeiros registos desta expressão já se encontravam difundidos na década de 30 do século XX, para ganhar lugar sistémico nos estudos de relações raciais no Brasil na obra de Arthur Ramos (1941) e Roger Bastide (1944). Segundo Aristeu Portela Júnior, Gilberto Freyre só começaria a utilizar a expressão a partir da década de 60, depois da sua utilização por Abdias de Nascimento, na sua conferência inaugural do I Congresso do Negro Brasileiro, em Agosto de 1950 (sobre o assunto, ver: Antônio Sérgio Guimarães, "Democracia Racial: O Ideal, o Pacto e o Mito," *Novos Estudos Cebrap* 61 (2001): 147-162; Antônio Sérgio Guimarães, *Classes, Raças e Democracia* (São Paulo: Editora 34, 2012); e Aristeu Portela, *A Nação em Disputa: Ações Afirmativas com Recorte Racial no Ensino Superior e Controvérsias em Torno da Identidade Nacional no Brasil* (Recife: Editora UFPE, 2020).

13. Citamos apenas os mais recentes livros de Isabel Castro Henriques sobre esta questão: A Herança Africana em Portugal (Lisboa: CTT, 2007); *Mulheres Africanas em Portugal: O Discurso das Imagens (séculos XV-XX)* (Lisboa: Secretaria de Estado para a Cidadania e Igualdade, 2019); *Roteiro Histórico de uma Lisboa Africana (séculos XV-XXI)* (Lisboa: Alto Comissariado para as Migrações, 2019); *Os "Pretos do Sado": História e Memória de uma Comunidade Alentejana de Origem Africana* (Lisboa: Edições Colibri, 2020); *De Escravos a Indígenas: O Longo Processo de Instrumentalização dos Africanos* (Lisboa: Caleidoscópio, 2020). A autora também comissariou inúmeras exposições sobre este tema.

14. Isso nos pressionaria a examinar diversas questões associadas, entre outras, às suas complexas relações com a África onde, frequentemente, forjou o neocolonialismo e a dependência, além de continuar a explorar os seus recursos, apresentando-se como

a parceira por excelência e transmutando a colonização para uma união privilegiada suportada pelo argumento dos laços históricos.

15. Um dos casos mais ostensivos desse gesto de discriminatória exclusão é o artigo "Podemos? Não, Não Podemos," da historiadora Maria de Fátima Bonifácio, para quem negros e ciganos não "fazem parte de uma entidade civilizacional e cultural milenária que dá pelo nome de Cristandade," *Público*, 6 de Julho, 2019.

16. AFRO-PORT. *Afro-Descendência em Portugal: Sociabilidades, Representações e Dinâmicas Sociopolíticas e Culturais. Um Estudo na Área Metropolitana de Lisboa* (FCT/ PTDC/ SOC-ANT/30651/2017).

17. Quando há conflitos, o critério da etnicidade pode ser instrumentalizado pelos políticos ou chefes da guerra, mas a natureza do contencioso tem a ver, em geral, com a conquista do poder ou o acesso aos recursos.

18. Este Estatuto é uma reformulação do *Estatuto Político, Civil e Criminal dos Indígenas de Angola e Moçambique*", Decreto-Lei 12.533, de 23 de Outubro de 1926, reformulado em 1954 com a designação *Estatuto dos Indígenas Portugueses das Províncias da Guiné, Angola e Moçambique*. Este *Estatuto* é referido muitas vezes como sendo de 1957 por causa da sua segunda edição anotada acompanhada de *Legislação Complementar*, por José Carlos Ney Ferreira e Vasco Soares da Veiga. Este Estatuto viria a ser revogado em 1961, com o início da luta armada em Angola, durante o consulado de Adriano Moreira como ministro do Ultramar.

19. Termo da lavra da escritora norte-americana Alice Walker no ensaio "If the Present Looks Like the Past, What Does the Future Look Like?," que foi publicado no livro *In Search of Our Mothers' Garden*, em 1982.

REFERÊNCIAS BIBLIOGRÁFICAS

Araújo, Marta e Silvia R Maeso. 2016. *Os Contornos do Eurocentrismo – Raça, história e textos políticos*. Coimbra: Almedina.

Diangelo, Robin. 2018. *White Fragility. Why It's So Hard for White People to Talk About Racism*. Boston: Beacon Press.

Eddo-Lodge, Reni. 2018. *Why I'm No Longer Talking To White People About Race*. London: Bloombury Publishing.

Évora, Iolanda. 2020a. "As (Im)Pertinências do Método. Metodologia Participativa e o Estudo sobre a Afrodescendência em Portugal." In *Representations Collectives Croisées: Afriques, Amériques et Caraibes. XIX-XXI Siècles*, edição de Jean-Arséne Yao, Victorien Lavou Zoungbo e Luis Mancha San Esteban. III GRELAT. Actas do Colóquio, 167-176. Madrid: UAH Editora, por publicar.

Évora, Iolanda. 2020b. "Afrodescendência em Portugal e a Construção de um Campo de Conhecimento." *Mundo Crítico. Revista de Desenvolvimento e Cooperação* 5 (outubro): 117-125.

García, Jésus Chucho. 2005. "Desconstrucción, Transformación y Construcción de Nuevos Escenarios de las Práticas de la Afroamericanidad." *Estudios Latinoamericanos sobre Cultura y Transformaciones Sociales en Tiempos de Globalización 2*, edição de Daniel Mato. Buenos Aires: CLACSO.

Gilroy, Paul. 1993. *The Black Atlantic: Modernity and Double Consciousness*. Cambridge: Harvard University Press.

Glissant, Édouard. 2005. Introdução a uma Poética da Diversidade. Juiz de Fora: Editora UFJF.

Hesse, Barnor e S. Sayyid. 2006. *Narrating the Postcolonial Political and the Immigrant Imaginary*. London: C. Hurst & Publishers.

Ki-Zerbo, Joseph. 2006. *Para Quando África?* (Entrevista de René Holenstein). Tradução de Carlos Aboim de Brito. Porto: Campo das Letras.

Kymlicka, Will. 1995. *Multicultural Citizenship: A Liberal Theory of Minority Rights*. Oxford: Oxford University Press.

Mata, Inocência. 2006. "Estranhos em Permanência: A Negociação da Identidade Portuguesa na Pós-Colonialidade." In *"Portugal não é um país pequeno." Contar o império na pós-colonialidade*, organização de Manuela Ribeiro Sanches, 285-315. Lisboa: Cotovia.

Miano, Léonora. 2012. "Les Noires Réalités de la France." In *Habiter la Frontière. Conférences*, edição de Léonora Miano, 59-88. Paris: L´Arche Éditeur.

Mudimbe, Valentin-Yves. 1988. *The Invention of Africa: Gnosis, Philosophy, and the Order of Knowledge*. Bloomington: Indiana University Press.

Semprini, Andrea. 1999. *Multiculturalismo*. Tradução de Laureano Pelegrin. Bauru. São Paulo: EDUSC.

IOLANDA ÉVORA é Investigadora Associada do Centro de Estudos sobre África e o Desenvolvimento (CEsA) e Professora Auxiliar do Mestrado em Desenvolvimento e Cooperação Internacional do Instituto Superior de Economia e Gestão da Universidade de Lisboa (ISEG/ULisboa). Investigadora Responsável do Projecto AFRO-PORT. Afrodescendência em Portugal: sociabilidades, representações e dinâmicas sociopolíticas e culturais. Um estudo na Área Metropolitana de Lisboa."

INOCÊNCIA MATA é Professora do Departamento de Literaturas Românicas, na Área de Literaturas, Artes e Culturas da Faculdade de Letras da Universidade de Lisboa (FLUL/ ULisboa), directora do Doutoramento em Língua e Cultura Portuguesa (Português Língua Estrangeira-Língua Segunda), membro integrado do Centro de Estudos Comparatistas da ULisboa. E Co-Investigadora Responsável do Projecto AFRO-PORT. Afrodescendência em Portugal: sociabilidades, representações e dinâmicas sociopolíticas e culturais. Um estudo na Área Metropolitana de Lisboa."

II. Histórias imperiais e estruturações políticas

ISABEL CASTRO HENRIQUES

Africanos em Portugal: Uma dialética de integração e de exclusão (séculos XV-XX)

RESUMO: A presença africana em Portugal, que se estendeu por vários séculos até aos dias de hoje, procurou integrar-se criando formas de convivência e de participação nas mais diferentes esferas da vida portuguesa. As muitas operações, resultantes das imposições e dos projectos portugueses, não foram aceites passivamente pelos Africanos, limitando as suas reacções ao primarismo da fuga ou da violência, mas, perante a inevitabilidade da situação de dominação, elaboraram estratégias de adesão destinadas a preservar, numa dinâmica de mudança, as suas raízes culturais e a inventar situações inovadoras de africanidade. Esse esforço permitiu-lhes uma reconstrução identitária autónoma, associando práticas culturais portuguesas a valores civilizacionais africanos, profundamente dependentes da sua própria singularidade histórica, criando formas culturais inéditas, e marcando um património português fortemente sincrético que permaneceu até à contemporaneidade.

PALAVRAS-CHAVE: Presença Africana em Portugal, diáspora, integração/exclusão, estratégias de resistência, africanidade, formas sincréticas, cultura, identidade.

ABSTRACT: The African presence in Portugal, which has continued for several centuries until the present, has sought to integrate itself by creating forms of coexistence and participation in the most varied spheres of Portuguese life. The many operations resulting from Portuguese impositions and projects were not passively accepted by the Africans, limiting their reactions to the flight or fight response; but rather, faced with the inevitability of the situation of domination, they developed adhesion strategies aimed at preserving in a dynamic of change their cultural roots and inventing innovative situations of Africanity. This effort enabled them to reconstruct an autonomous identity, associating Portuguese cultural practices with African civilizational values, deeply dependent on their own historical singularity, creating unprecedented cultural forms and marking a strongly syncretic Portuguese heritage that has remained until the present.

KEYWORDS: African presence in Portugal, diaspora, integration/exclusion, resistance strategies, Africanity, syncretic forms, culture, identity.

A longa duração da diáspora africana em Portugal caracteriza-se por um conjunto de operações de integração e de exclusão que se desenvolvem num processo marcado por uma alternância ou uma concomitância de movimentos opostos, levados a cabo quer pelos Africanos, quer pelos Portugueses, de forma continuada durante séculos, marcados por conjunturas e ideologias que se vão transformando e sucedendo no tempo.

Transportados pelas forças esclavagistas portuguesas e desembarcados como escravos no país entre os séculos XV e XIX, os Africanos desenvolveram estratégias destinadas a garantir a sua sobrevivência num território desconhecido, hostil, controlado e sem espaços abertos à fuga libertadora, aceitando e adaptando-se às propostas portuguesas e construindo uma identidade inédita, marcada pela preservação da sua africanidade e simultaneamente integradora das realidades teóricas e práticas portuguesas.

Todo este processo de reconstrução identitária dos Africanos organizou-se em torno de um jogo inclusivo e integrador nas práticas sociais portuguesas, e exclusivo e discriminatório pela força do preconceito anti-negro e anti-escravo construído e consolidado pelos Portugueses, gerando patrimónios culturais sincréticos que permaneceram no país, revelando as manifestações silenciosas mas interventivas de uma comunidade secular na organização, na história e na memória portuguesas.

I. A Instalação dos Africanos em Portugal e a Construção e o Reforço do Preconceito Anti-Negro (Séculos XV-XX)

Se, historicamente, a memória da presença africana terá começado a organizar-se no século XIII, foi sobretudo a partir do século XV que a chegada massiva de homens e mulheres africanos, introduzidos em Portugal como escravos, conduziu à criação portuguesa de formas de rejeição física e social desses Outros diferentes nos corpos e nos comportamentos.

Tratou-se do início de um longo processo de construção e de afirmação de um preconceito que desvalorizou a humanidade dos Africanos, marcado pelos diferentes contextos históricos que se foram sucedendo, refazendo e reforçando a sua inferiorização, numa linha de continuidade que permite compreender a eficácia e a durabilidade deste fenómeno português. Até quase aos nossos dias, a identificação imediata entre *Preto* ou *Negro* = *Escravo* marcava ainda o nosso imaginário: a discriminação racial e social articulava-se para construir uma imagem negativa do Africano.

As primeiras referências a populações negras na Península Ibérica, e mais particularmente no território galego, encontram-se registadas numa memória escrita e iconográfica, que possui a qualidade de definir as condições em que nasceram alguns preconceitos que tanto evocam a estrutura física dos Africanos. Os seus corpos são desvalorizados devido, primeiro, à côr, e, depois, aos outros caracteres somáticos considerados negativos – o cabelo, a boca, o nariz, o cheiro –, que os aproximam dos animais, opondo-os à superioridade do corpo da norma que só pode ser branco.[1] Esta lógica do corpo e da côr, se permite que os Africanos organizem as suas vidas, não deixa por isso de constituir um obstáculo à sua plena integração na sociedade dos homens, isto é, dos "Brancos."

No quadro histórico das populações que chegaram à Península Ibérica, por terra ou por mar, como foi o caso de duas das mais significativas colonizações – a romana e a árabe, em períodos diferentes e relativamente curtos – que deixaram inúmeras marcas no país, a matriz, a longa duração e a natureza da presença de Africanos em Portugal constituem um elemento diferenciador fundamental, que se inscreve numa outra lógica civilizacional, iniciada pelos Europeus a partir do século XV. A maioria dos homens, mulheres e crianças de África não vieram de livre vontade, mas foram capturados ou comprados no litoral do continente africano, para serem desembarcados como escravos no extremo ocidental do fragmento ibérico da Europa.[2]

Séculos de escravização em Portugal e no Brasil e de conflitos em África, marcados pelo tráfico negreiro, conduziram a um contínuo reforço da inferiorização do Africano, que as teorias e a ciência oitocentista e novecentista, aliadas às práticas portuguesas no quadro da colonização e às operações de dominação e de guerra coloniais de Portugal em África, legitimaram de forma científica e histórica. O reforço de um preconceito robusto, gerador das operações classificatórias que marcaram e hierarquizaram as humanidades, traduzindo-se na consolidação e banalização de imagens e de estereótipos que foram organizando o imaginário português, marcou as relações dos Portugueses com as populações de origem africana.

II. Modelos e Estratégias de Integração dos Africanos na Sociedade Portuguesa (Séculos XV-XIX)

Despojados de tudo, milhares de africanos, oriundos de regiões e de culturas diversas, integraram-se no país, entre os séculos XV e XIX, tornando-se uma presença estruturante da sociedade, deixando sinais diretos ou indiretos nas memórias e nos imaginários portugueses. Se a visibilidade dessa presença é pouco consistente, uma análise atenta e sistemática revela a densidade de uma herança africana silenciosa, frequentemente assinalada para registar fenómenos negativos, na organização do país: no trabalho, na produção, na religião, na magia, na festa, na música, na dança, no corpo, na sexualidade, na língua, ou na toponímia.

A Organização do Espaço Urbano: O Bairro do Mocambo em Lisboa

De entre os lugares cuja forte marca africana foi revelada pela toponímia oitocentista, salienta-se pelo seu carácter inédito e único na Europa o *Mocambo* de Lisboa, hoje a Madragoa. Bairro da cidade, por alvará régio de 1593, cujo nome *mocambo* em umbundo, sinónimo de *quilombo,* em quimbundo – ambas línguas de Angola –, designa "lugar de refúgio," "local de instalação," "pequena aldeia." O *Mocambo* era, desde os finais de Quinhentos, um espaço urbano onde os Africanos, sobretudo os livres, se instalaram ou eram instalados, coabitando, a partir do século XVII, com Portugueses, principalmente gente ligada às atividades do mar. A partir do século XVIII, o Africanos foram abandonando o bairro e a desaparição do *Mocambo* de Lisboa foi-se acentuando, transformando-se em *Rua do Mocambo* e depois em Travessa, e desaparecendo na segunda metade do século XIX.

Registe-se a singularidade deste facto: por um lado, a argúcia das autoridades portuguesas que se traduz na aceitação/utilização de um termo africano (que conheciam, desde 1530, como lugar de refúgio dos escravos fugidos dos engenhos de açúcar da ilha de São Tomé) para identificar o bairro dos "pretos" ou "negros" que, à semelhança da "mouraria" e da "judiaria," poderia ter sido designado de "pretaria" ou "negraria"; por outro lado, sublinha também o engenho africano capaz de criar um território próprio, permitindo travar a pulverização da presença africana e estruturar uma comunidade integradora de formas culturais diversas, portuguesas e africanas.

Para além de um espaço de habitação, o bairro do Mocambo era um lugar essencial de práticas e de memórias africanas, pois permitia manter as formas mínimas de parentesco e contribuía para a preservação de certas práticas sociais africanas, pondo em evidência uma capacidade de definir estratégias de não dissolução total no espaço português, criando assim um espaço próprio. O Mocambo, ou outros espaços urbanos concentrando Africanos, garantiam uma certa discrição e ocultação de factos aos olhos dos Portugueses, como a sua organização face aos nascimentos, aos casamentos, à morte, dado que as regras africanas impunham rituais que divergiam das práticas portuguesas.

Não devemos esquecer também a poligamia africana que, a ter-se mantido no Mocambo, terá juntado esposas de várias origens e falando diferentes línguas, como era corrente em África. Dado o quadro do parentesco classificatório, cada mulher do patriarca era a mãe dos seus próprios filhos, sendo-o também dos outros filhos do patriarca. As mulheres, mais do que os homens, agiam como guardiãs dos valores culturais, da sua tradição naturalmente contrariada pelas condições do funcionamento da sociedade portuguesa, mas de que as estratégias religiosas africanas permitiam conservar amplos fragmentos.

A Integração Africana nos Quotidianos Portugueses: O Trabalho

Presentes de norte a sul, do litoral ao interior do país, os Africanos desempenharam um número amplo de tarefas indispensáveis ao funcionamento da sociedade portuguesa, quer nos campos, quer nas cidades, quer ainda nos empreendimentos marítimos, como marinheiros nas caravelas portuguesas. Se a maioria das atividades domésticas lhes era atribuída, também os trabalhos agrícolas e piscatórios, as práticas artesanais e as tarefas comerciais, como a venda dos produtos essenciais às populações, caracterizavam as suas esferas de ação e de participação na vida das comunidades. Registe-se a sua intervenção na manutenção das estruturas urbanas – o fornecimento de água, a recolha e despejo dos detritos, a limpeza das ruas, o transporte de pessoas e mercadorias, a circulação da informação –, da qual dependiam muitos Portugueses.

Mais do que nos espaços rurais, onde trabalhavam sobretudo na agricultura e na pastorícia, era nas cidades que os Africanos, em particular os forros e livres, dispunham de um vasto leque de tarefas que, pela sua importância social, lhes permitiam uma certa autonomia. As tarefas associadas à gestão e higiene urbanas – varredores, caiadores, calhandreiras –, mas também de serviços tão indispensáveis como o abastecimento de água (que levou as autoridades a construir chafarizes e a gerir e controlar a utilização das bicas), estavam a cargo sobretudo das mulheres. Para além disso, estas dedicavam-se também a outras tarefas de natureza doméstica e social, como lavadeiras, domésticas, amas de crianças e ainda à atividade comercial centrada nos bens alimentares, como os produtos agrícolas, o peixe e produtos de fabrico doméstico, não esquecendo a venda de outros bens de consumo, como o carvão. Muitas mulheres tinham clientes portuguesas certas, as *freguesas*, que nelas confiavam, esperando-as quotidianamente e comprando os seus produtos indispensáveis à alimentação e à vida familiar. Aos homens, que também podiam transportar água, cabiam tarefas mais pesadas como a caiação das casas e outros trabalhos na construção e manutenção de edifícios, o transporte de pessoas e mercadorias, a circulação de informações e mensagens, as produções artesanais, como a olaria, a carpintaria, o trabalho do ferro e do couro, a ourivesaria, a tecelagem, e ainda as atividades ligadas à construção naval, à marinha, ou à pesca.[3] Registe-se ainda a especialização do trabalho dos Africanos livres que, integrados na sociedade, tendo aprendido o lucro, impunham regras, preços, formas de relacionamento, conseguindo a adesão dos Portugueses. Inseridos em todos os setores criadores de riqueza, os Africanos foram um elemento estruturante da vida urbana do país.

Mas o trabalho dos escravos africanos ficou também marcado por uma situação degradante, desumana e dolorosa da qual se conhecem poucas informações. Nem todos os escravos se integraram na sociedade portuguesa, pois uma provável minoria sofreu um processo de "animalização" durante séculos, silenciados pelas autoridades, pelos documentos, pelo conhecimento. Trata-se da "criação de escravos," como se de animais se tratasse, referida num documento de finais do século XVI,[4] que seria uma prática de grande violência, corrente em diversas regiões do país, traduzindo-se numa produção e comercialização de homens e de mulheres, que permitia aos proprietários a realização de lucros importantes.

Se no último quartel do século XVIII, após a abolição pombalina da escravatura em Portugal (1761-1773), o número de escravos negros continuava elevado, não só porque os filhos de pais escravos herdavam o mesmo estatuto, mas também porque se mantinha a criação de escravos denunciada em documentos oficiais, o século XIX deixou vestígios perturbadores dessa violência no património português. Esta zoomorfização dos homens é revelada pela existência de coleiras identificando o proprietário, colocadas no pescoço do escravo, pondo em evidência a condição animalizada dos "pretos." Leite de Vasconcelos, que recolheu duas coleiras em latão, em finais do século XIX, integrando-as nas coleções do Museu Nacional de Arqueologia, em Lisboa, traduz essa violência num texto de 1915: "Como este objeto escalda as mãos quando se lhe toca! Que vilipêndios não traduz! A que lágrimas não deu origem!"[5]

A Participação dos Africanos nos Espaços Religiosos e Lúdicos Portugueses

Se a atividade económica marcava a participação dos Africanos nos quotidianos portugueses, estes organizavam-se igualmente em torno dos mais diferentes acontecimentos de natureza social, sobretudo cerimónias festivas lúdico-religiosas onde encontravam um espaço privilegiado de integração. Africanos de estatutos sociais diversos – se a maioria eram escravos ou forros, é importante sublinhar a presença de outras figuras africanas como representantes diplomáticos ou altos dignitários religiosos – participavam intensamente na vida pública e privada portuguesa. Procissões, touradas, espetáculos coletivos, celebrações associando o religioso e o profano, punham em evidência a forte intervenção africana, através da dança, da música e das suas manifestações religiosas,[6] conduzindo à criação e consolidação de formas religiosas e culturais sincréticas que persistiram nos imaginários e nas práticas portuguesas.

Aceitando as iniciativas portuguesas, os Africanos aderiram desde muito cedo às confrarias, participando nas muitas organizações e atividades da Igreja, criando assim um espaço velado de preservação dos seus valores especificamente africanos, levando o clero mais conservador a denunciar a existência de práticas religiosas onde a estrutura africana procurava dissolver as regras europeias.

De entre as confrarias, instituições de natureza religiosa que tinham como objetivo proteger os seus membros, organizar convívios e ações de apoio e de solidariedade, consagrando-se ao culto de uma figura religiosa do Catolicismo, a Confraria de Nossa Senhora do Rosário dos Homens Pretos, fundada por volta de 1520 na Igreja de São Domingos em Lisboa, situada no Largo do mesmo nome, junto ao Rossio, reunia homens e mulheres negros e mestiços, escravos, forros e livres, bem como todos aqueles que o desejassem, desempenhando uma função social, económica, familiar, moral, religiosa, fundamental na vida dos Africanos.[7] Se a memória da importância religiosa deste espaço urbano na vida dos Africanos se perdeu, podemos contudo aceitar que, hoje como ontem, o Largo de S. Domingos e o Rossio que o ladeia, constituem o "lugar do encontro," símbolo de um "território africanizado," secular, transmitido de geração em geração.

Primeiro em Lisboa, depois em Évora, as confrarias foram-se multiplicando por todo o país, reunindo frequentemente Africanos oriundos da mesma "nação" – Mina, Congo, Angola, Benim –, fixando-se nos locais onde a densidade populacional africana era mais significativa para gerar uma comunidade de interesses e de práticas coincidentes. Se as confrarias não provavam a cristianização dos Africanos, punham em evidência a maneira como estes utilizaram uma associação de raíz portuguesa que lhes permitia organizar sistemas de defesa e de proteção, dando-lhes a possibilidade de recuperar dinheiro para assegurar a alforria dos seus membros e de desenvolver estratégias de integração social e de preservação cultural. Participando nas muitas cerimónias religiosas, os Africanos introduziram práticas consideradas profanas, como as suas danças, muito apreciadas pela população portuguesa, e censuradas (mas não proibidas) pelos poderes político e eclesiástico.

Até ao início de novecentos, as confrarias participavam nas numerosas procissões – acontecimentos religiosos, lúdicos, coletivos reveladores das hierarquias sociais e do poder económico –, que se organizavam em honra de figuras dos cultos católicos, como Nossa Senhora do Rosário ou o Corpo de Deus, e que marcavam o calendário católico. Mas a presença dos Africanos nestes eventos não se enquadrava num único registo: se alguns participavam como membros das confrarias, outros integravam-se no corpo das procissões com os seus instrumentos e os seus ritmos, com os seus comportamentos e com as suas oferendas, contando sempre com o acordo dos organizadores. Estamos perante um dos aspetos mais característicos desta situação que confiava aos Africanos a produção festiva e musical, criando espaços de diversão de rua e de espetáculo, indispensáveis ao bom êxito da iniciativa. Estes evidenciavam um processo de africanização de um ritual católico, pois a música e a dança não eram apenas manifestações lúdicas africanas, mas faziam parte da relação social entre os homens, organizando também as relações com as divindades.[8]

Na dança, música, nas mais diversas atividades festivas – das touradas aos carnavais, a concertos e bailes espontâneos nos espaços públicos e privados, a espectáculos de rua variados –, a participação dos Africanos era constante, ativa e apreciada por todos, em particular, pelos próprios Portugueses.

III. Os "Africanos-Portugueses": A Reinvenção de uma Identidade Nova (Séculos XV-XIX)

Integrados na sociedade portuguesa, os Africanos organizaram as condições para assegurar a preservação da sua africanidade, adaptando-a às novas realidades com que se confrontavam e renovando os seus valores culturais e as suas formas identitárias, deixando, através das suas práticas sociais, marcas estruturantes no tecido cultural português.

O conhecimento deste processo de reinvenção identitária obriga ao estudo das estratégias pensadas e utilizadas por estes homens e mulheres, brutalmente retirados do seu espaço geográfico e familiar, social e cultural, para assegurar naturalmente a sua sobrevivência física, mas também cultural. As formas de adesão às práticas portuguesas, as cumplicidades, as criações sincréticas, devem ser consideradas em duas perspetivas: por um lado, traduzem uma maneira inteligente de responder à violência, integrando-se, reconstituindo a sua identidade

e preservando valores fundamentais das suas culturas ancestrais; por outro, permitiram a fixação de marcas culturais africanas na sociedade portuguesa, por
vezes sob a forma de sincretismos, em particular nos espaços lúdicos, mágico-
-religiosos, linguísticos, toponímicos,[9] constituindo, hoje como ontem, heranças sobretudo imateriais existentes em Portugal.

Um Outro Nome, um Novo Corpo, uma Língua Diferente

Uma das primeiras tarefas dos Africanos transferidos para Portugal como escravos consistiu na necessidade de se despojarem da dimensão visível da identidade
africana, que deixara de se adaptar às condições de funcionamento da sociedade
portuguesa. Estavam eles obrigados a resolver o problema fundamental da identidade: tendo sido retirados pela força do seu território e da sua família africana,
forçados a renunciar à sua língua materna e a falar português, a cobrir o corpo
e a praticar outra religião, os Africanos foram levados a reinventar-se sem perder a sua originalidade. Os Portugueses multiplicaram os obstáculos, desquali-
ficaram-nos, recusaram-lhes autonomia. Os Africanos, culturalmente heterogé-
neos, mantendo a memória do país de origem, viram-se obrigados a organizar
estratégias de sobrevivência, começando por inventar uma outra personalidade,
mais próxima dos valores e das práticas portuguesas.

Registe-se uma questão importante, reconhecida e realçada nos textos portugueses: estes Africanos pertenciam a sociedades e culturas africanas diferentes. Se, para a maioria dos Portugueses, os Africanos apareciam como um bloco
homogéneo, pela cor e pelas suas práticas sociais, eram eles culturalmente distintos, carregando memórias históricas muito diferenciadas. Portadores de uma
identidade inscrita no corpo e no espírito, foram submetidos pelos Portugueses
a rituais diversos destinados a afastá-los dos seus valores e práticas culturais e
a integrá-los na norma portuguesa. Aderindo às novas formas sociais e religiosas, os Africanos aceitaram o batismo e o nome cristão, a rejeição da nudez com
o corpo vestido, o casamento cristão, as relações afetivas, aderindo também às
organizações, práticas e festas católicas, aos eventos lúdicos, políticos e militares, introduzindo marcas da sua singularidade cultural na vida portuguesa.

Um aspeto essencial à consolidação da sua nova identidade não podia deixar
de ser a aprendizagem e o uso da língua portuguesa. Desvalorizada e ridicula-
rizada, apareceu desde o século XV, sobretudo nas cidades, a "língua de preto,"
ou seja, uma língua portuguesa onde se multiplicavam os particularismos foné-
ticos, sintáxicos e semânticos introduzidos pelos Africanos. A fixação desta

"língua de preto" deveu-se à sua utilização na esfera teatral quinhentista,[10] tendo-se consolidado ao longo dos séculos, e traduzindo a forma como a sociedade portuguesa classificava os Africanos de forma redutora e inferiorizante.[11]

Africanização de Práticas Religiosas Portuguesas

Desembarcados como escravos de forma continuada, em Portugal, durante três séculos, os Africanos procuraram aderir às formas sociais e religiosas portuguesas. O comércio negreiro tinha-os transformado em mercadoria e a sociedade portuguesa organizado as operações destinadas a reforçar a sua despersonalização e des-socialização, de modo a eliminar a sua africanidade. Assim, os Africanos, que tinham perdido o território, a linhagem, a língua, o nome, procuraram reconstruir uma identidade nova e autónoma, associando práticas culturais portuguesas a valores civilizacionais africanos, profundamente marcados pela sua própria singularidade histórica, criando formas socioculturais inéditas.

Constituindo o parentesco, a religião e a música os alicerces das formas existenciais dos Africanos, compreende-se que as condições em que foram transferidos para a Europa, como aliás também para as colónias americanas, se revelassem manifestamente contrárias à manutenção de tais estruturas. Na ausência do parentesco – isto é, da família alargada, que inclui tanto os vivos como os mortos que ficaram em África –, os Africanos, culturalmente muito diversos, aderiram aos espaços de culto portugueses, associando-se através da religião, que pela sua natureza invisível se podia manter no quadro apertado das suas vivências, não esquecendo o facto de que as religiões são quase sempre marcadas pela mestiçagem de crenças.

Se os territórios do sagrado português e do africano não coincidiam e se é fácil perceber que as autoridades, os senhores e o clero tivessem procurado desmantelar as religiões africanas, demasiado dependentes dos "feitiços" ou "ídolos" – designação dos objetos de culto africanos –,[12] é também certo que os Africanos procuraram encontrar no Catolicismo os nichos sociais capazes de lhes assegurar uma certa autonomia religiosa. Saliente-se o modo como os Africanos procuraram transplantar para a Europa, assim como para o Brasil, a organização das festas destinadas a homenagear os espíritos dos antepassados que, do Além, deviam assegurar a sua protecção. Encontramos aqui o vigor das religiões africanas, que se mostraram capazes de, por um lado, integrar um certo número de práticas cristãs, tendo ao mesmo tempo a argúcia necessária para impor as suas práticas religiosas, caracterizadas pela conjunção do discurso teológico, da música e da dança.

A regulação do facto religioso revelou-se fundamental pois, por um lado, permitia recuperar a ordem organizada em África e, pelo outro, dava conta dos sincretismos que se registaram em Portugal e que, se não criaram religiões novas, obrigaram a modificar alguns códigos religiosos, tanto europeus como africanos, levando o clero mais conservador a denunciar a existência de práticas religiosas onde a estrutura africana procurava dissolver as regras europeias.

A profunda dissociação religiosa entre Africanos e Portugueses não impediu a aparição das formas religiosas sincréticas, bem visível através da presença de figuras religiosas negras nas Igrejas – o que permite dar conta da dispersão dos Africanos por todo o país –, assim como das confrarias e das muitas festas religiosas católicas que se iam desenrolando, segundo o calendário religioso, nas cidades, nas vilas e nas aldeias portuguesas. Afastados dos seus chefes religiosos, os Africanos viram-se na necessidade de inventar outras formas de autoridade religiosa, como as figuras santas negras, veneradas por Africanos e Portugueses, que põem em evidência não só a capacidade de integração da comunidade africana no país, mas também um aspeto particular do sincretismo religioso resultante da construção de um cristianismo "africanizado."[13]

Festas, Memória Histórica e Reinvenção da Africanidade

Danças, músicas e personagens africanas marcavam as cerimónias religiosas católicas, onde as festas das confrarias ocupavam lugar privilegiado, integrando os Africanos no espaço português, mas permitindo-lhes recuperar e viver algumas das suas práticas culturais que assentavam em pilares fundamentais da sua memória histórica.

Sendo a Confraria de Nossa Senhora do Rosário dos Homens Pretos a mais relevante para a comunidade africana, as festas consagradas a esta Virgem assumiam uma importância particular, pois, para todas as confrarias, a festa anual do seu santo era o momento mais importante da vida da instituição. Por todo o país, se assistia às populares festas das confrarias negras da Senhora do Rosário, que, como acontece ainda hoje no Brasil, elegiam um negro da sua "nação," a quem davam o título honorífico de rei.

Os Congo e os Angola eram os mais agarrados a essa tradição, o que evidencia a sua importância demográfica, organizando as festas, fazendo convites a personalidades importantes para as cerimónias, elegendo os reis, procurando ocupar uma posição privilegiada face aos outros Africanos, fixando uma secular história de relações entre os reis de Portugal, do Congo e o N'gola, tradição essa que marcou de forma profunda e duradoura a conservação de memória histórica. O exemplo dos reis e das rainhas do Congo era singular pela sua longa duração, mas também pelas muitas situações criadas em torno destas figuras reais africanas na sociedade portuguesa.[14]

A eleição de um rei ou rainha africanos no quadro das cerimónias religiosas portuguesas revelava uma estratégia de revitalização histórica, cultural e identitária africanas: a importância destas figuras reais, que possuíam um poder restrito e abstrato, limitado pelas fronteiras dos seus espaços e práticas, assentava na evocação do passado e salientava a existência de uma história que assegurava a longa autonomia e hegemonia dos Africanos. Todavia a manutenção destes reis e destas rainhas, chefes políticos, mas sobretudo elos de ligação com a sua história e com a sua religião, se lembrava o passado, não perdia de vista nem o presente, nem o futuro: os atos "reais," acompanhados da presença constante da música e da dança, aparecem como meios de garantir a integração dos Africanos nas práticas culturais portuguesas.

Uma longa descrição de 1731, intitulada " Bayle dos Negros," que se realizava na cidade de Braga, no norte de Portugal, relatada por um eclesiástico, põe em evidência a complexidade da articulação das vertentes cultural e identitária africanas, em eventos religiosos portugueses, reveladores também da integração de outras comunidades instaladas em Portugal. A descrição desta procissão particular, desfile profano que se segue ao recolhimento religioso, dá conta do lugar de destaque dado ao rei e à rainha de Angola, acompanhados de muitos participantes que apresentam as suas danças e cantam o seu juramento de fidelidade simultaneamente à Igreja e aos seus soberanos angolanos. Canto, dança, memória histórica e sentimento identitário africanos caracterizam este baile, associados à "língua de preto" e à organização religiosa portuguesa, pondo em evidência as formas sincréticas festivas que marcavam a sociedade.[15]

Também as festas e os bailes públicos e privados centrados na personagem do rei e no reino do Congo eram frequentes no século XIX e noticiados nos periódicos portugueses. Desta tradição dava conta o *Jornal do Comércio* (1860), que assinalava um baile de

> O Congo em Lisboa . . ., dado pela princesa Sebastiana Júlia, regente do império do Congo . . . muito concorrido dos brancos . . . Depois da meia-noite, saíram os convidados, que haviam pago os seus bilhetes de entrada, e ficaram só a princesa e a sua corte . . . e alguns brancos. A pretaria dançou a sua dança do Congo e outras danças da Europa.

Sublinhe-se a importância africana da relação festa/história/religião, a reconstrução de uma nova identidade africana baseada no passado mas inserida no presente português, como revela a adesão a elementos da cultura e da modernidade portuguesa – como as iguarias das festas, as danças e as formas de vestir portuguesas, bem como o elemento financeiro ou a proteção policial de que estas festas dispunham –, resultando na criação de operações sincréticas inéditas.

Festas, danças, músicas, mas também trabalhos, preços, negócios, e ainda as praticas de "feitiçaria," muito concorridas e apreciadas pelos Portugueses,[16] permitiram aos Africanos integrar-se na sociedade portuguesa, mas também o "regresso a África," a recuperação da memória e do passado e a reconstrução de novas identidades, introduzindo marcas da sua singularidade cultural na vida portuguesa.

Os "Mulatos": Uma Integração Inédita

Um dos problemas menos estudado, mas muito significativo, reside na aparição, desde finais do século XV, de um forte número de populações mestiças, que causou grande perplexidade na sociedade portuguesa, traduzindo-se na organização de uma estrutura classificatória zoomorfizante destinada a acrescentar estes homens e mulheres designados de "Mulatos" ao vasto catálogo dos muares, recusando aceitá-los como Portugueses que eram. A essa maneira de os classificar, deve somar-se a ideia da sua hiperactividade sexual – sobretudo das "Mulatas" – atribuída ao seu sangue africano, que marcou a construção de um arquétipo duradouro e desvalorizante que ainda não se extinguiu completamente.

Alguns Portugueses mestiços se tinham imposto na sociedade – pela via do casamento com Portugueses de estatuto social elevado, como foi o caso de D. Simoa Godinho, de origem santomense (XVI); pelo prestígio da profissão desempenhada, como foram exemplos o dramaturgo Afonso Álvares e o pintor Domingos Lourenço Pardo (XVII), ou ainda pelo estatuto religioso, como a Madre Cecília de Jesus (XVII). Mas foi nas décadas finais do século XVIII que se assistiu a duas operações cuja complementaridade antagonista merece ser referida. Vencendo pouco a pouco a dureza dos preconceitos, muitos mestiços, filhos de pais brancos e socialmente reconhecidos, conseguiram apoios sociais e financeiros para ingressar nas universidades ou no clero portugueses. Se a protecção familiar, o dinheiro e o prestígio literário e profissional ou as carreiras na administração pública constituíram factores de alguma diluição do estigma somático, estes mestiços provocaram também dores de cabeça aos dirigentes políticos dos séculos seguintes, na medida em que conseguiram adquirir posições de arbitragem na trama relacional portuguesa. Muito criticados por diferentes setores e personalidades da sociedade portuguesa,[17] os "Mulatos," considerados mais pretos que brancos, puderam reforçar a sua posição, nos séculos XIX e XX, apesar da emergência e da consolidação das teorias científicas que legitimavam a hierarquização das raças, das geografias, das civilizações. Do Pai Paulino a Fernanda do Vale (a "Preta Fernanda"), Honório Barreto, Sousa Martins, Gonçalves Crespo, Costa Alegre, Virgínia Quaresma e a outros muitos intelectuais e grandes profissionais de Novecentos, podemos verificar, observando as suas práticas e as suas reflexões, quão importante foi a sua intensa participação na vida coletiva portuguesa.

Tal, porém, não eliminou da sociedade a ferocidade dos juízos de valor relativos aos mestiços. Em 1925, o poeta Mário Saa sublinhava que a "influência do sangue negro em Portugal, transparece em numerosíssimas pessoas, . . . os mestiços dominam em Portugal por elemento de população mais que em outra qualquer nação da Europa, com incremento de boçalidade e redução do índice encefálico."[18] Este juízo de valor muito popularizado serviu para alimentar os princípios fundamentais do racismo, apresentando os Africanos como uma teratologia: os "mulatos" estariam inscritos no quadro das monstruosidades capazes de macular a espécie humana, pois, apesar de terem pai ou mãe brancos, reflectiam a inferioridade estrutural africana.

IV. As Representações Coloniais e o Reforço Ideológico da Desvalorização dos Africanos (Séculos XIX e XX)

Os Processos de Legitimação Colonial: Ideologia e Ciência

A revisão político-ideológica do império começou a desenhar-se após a independência do Brasil (1822), a abolição (legal) da escravatura nos espaços africanos controlados pelos portugueses (1836-1869) e no contexto internacional da Conferência de Berlim (1884-1885), levando as autoridades portuguesas a apostar, entre os anos 1880 e 1910, na construção de uma mitologia colonial. Esta destinava-se a envolver a sociedade portuguesa na "questão africana," que devia adquirir uma dimensão nacional – o Estado português procurando apresentar Portugal como vítima dos ilegítimos apetites das grandes potências europeias. Tal estrutura ideológica fornecia os instrumentos capazes de fundamentar as pretensões portuguesas, de apelar a um esforço nacional integrador da noção de "pátria una e grandiosa," de reforçar as ideias de "prioridade" e "especificidade" portuguesas nas relações com os Outros, de legitimar as escolhas coloniais, a violência dos confrontos em África e a concretização da "missão civilizadora."

Esta situação traduziu-se no reforço de ideias e de preconceitos já enraizados na sociedade portuguesa, em que o somático, "o preto," e o social, "o escravo," se articulavam para definir o Africano. Se a legislação portuguesa reconhecia aos Africanos – libertos da escravatura pelas medidas pombalinas de 1761 e 1773 – a liberdade e, teoricamente, a sua "portugalidade,"[19] a consolidação secular da imagem do Africano como ser *naturalmente* escravo dificilmente permitia encarar a alteração do seu estatuto. Esta desvalorização encontrou uma nova legitimidade, nas décadas finais de Oitocentos, no quadro da construção de uma ciência colonial, onde se cruzavam várias dimensões do conhecimento das humanidades, das sociedades, das geografias, traduzida numa produção científica que os políticos e os ideólogos viam com grande interesse, pois permitia justificar os projetos coloniais.

Coube a Oliveira Martins (1880) fornecer o registo científico da "inferioridade congénita dos negros e o absurdo da sua educação," pois "abunda[va]m os documentos que nos mostra[va]m no negro um tipo antropologicamente inferior, não raro próximo do antropóide, e bem pouco digno do nome de homem." Contudo, foi António Ennes (1899), figura central do pensamento e dos projetos coloniais, que pôs em evidência a dicotomia primitivo/civilizado, considerando os Europeus como os "filhos apurados das raças policiadas" e os Africanos como "broncos," "entes quase impensantes e impulsivos," "rudes" e "vadios ociosos." Ennes completou, com a solidez e a densidade das suas experiências vividas em África, as provas teóricas de Oliveira Martins.

Registe-se outro fator que desempenhou um papel relevante neste processo de desvalorização do africano: as "campanhas militares" em África mostraram a "natureza feroz e bárbara" da guerra praticada pelos Africanos, assegurando a "produção" de heróis portugueses. Exemplo significativo, pela sua banalização na sociedade, pelo lugar que ocupou na história e pela persistência no tempo, foi o episódio que, em Moçambique, opôs Mouzinho de Albuquerque à figura do chefe nguni Gungunhana, transformando-o no símbolo da selvajaria africana.

A articulação destes três registos da inferiorização do negro – o científico, resultante do avanço teórico do conhecimento; o político, decorrente das experiências vividas no terreno; e o militar, apoiado nos conflitos reais – não só permitiu salientar a proximidade das populações africanas com a natureza e a animalidade, mas forneceu o fôlego ideológico que faltava para reforçar ou reatualizar arquétipos seculares, como a preguiça, a antropofagia, a brutalidade, a força física e a ausência de inteligência, a sexualidade desmedida, a feitiçaria e a idolatria, cuja difusão viria a assegurar a fixação de uma cultura colonial no espaço português.

A Banalização do "Selvagem" no Portugal Colonial (Século XX)

Se a proclamação da República (1910) deu lugar a uma revisão das políticas coloniais, sob a pressão das duras críticas provenientes dos circuitos económicos europeus em relação à legislação do trabalho indígena, o quadro ideológico manteve-se fiel à mesma perspetiva mitológica. Acrescente-se o reforço paradoxal resultante das ideias do pensamento republicano – liberdade, progresso, educação, trabalho –, que legitimavam as duras operações de modernização das economias coloniais e a violência do trabalho imposto aos colonizados, como mecanismo civilizador absoluto. A operacionalidade desta estrutura ideológica, após a criação do Estado Novo (1933), que aderiu aos projetos coloniais republicanos, resultou de um trabalho de consolidação de um *corpus* teórico organizado, de ideias, de mitos, de representações, centrado nos "direitos históricos" de Portugal em África, na inferioridade incontestável do "preto" e na superioridade inequívoca do "branco," na fragilidade civilizacional do assimilado e na excelência da missão civilizadora portuguesa.

Novas formulações foram sendo introduzidas para reforçar a desvalorização do "preto" e do "mulato," mas o essencial da ideologia colonial manteve a sua densidade teórica e uma vitalidade interventora, orientando as muitas operações de propaganda organizadas pelo Estado Novo para mostrar o império aos Portugueses. Grandes manifestações patrióticas, como foi o caso da *Exposição Colonial Portuguesa*, no Porto (1934), e da *Exposição do Mundo Português*, em Lisboa (1940), convidavam os portugueses a olhar o conjunto das "suas" colónias, incluindo também "amostras" das diferentes populações do Império.

Estas exposições, verdadeiros "jardins zoológicos humanos," recordavam as grandes datas e os heróis portugueses, servindo também para pôr em evidência as diferenças físicas e culturais dos Outros, utilizando algumas das máscaras da negatividade das regiões e das populações africanas, há muito enraizadas no imaginário português. Homens, mulheres e crianças foram apresentados "ao vivo," precariamente instalados em mini-aldeias e mini-paisagens, que procuravam refazer o *habitat* dos Africanos, onde "morriam como tordos de pneumonia."[20] A população portuguesa foi assim colocada perante os comportamentos, atitudes e costumes "primitivos" dos Africanos, que impunham e justificavam a colonização.

As diferentes maneiras de inferiorizar e ridicularizar o Africano – negro ou mestiço – multiplicaram-se até ao último quartel do século XX: jornais, bandas desenhadas, anúncios, uma vasta produção iconográfica destinada às crianças, aos jovens e aos adultos, aos letrados e aos analfabetos, ou seja uma significativa parcela da população portuguesa.

Tendo já uma intimidade secular com os Africanos, marcada pelo preconceito somático e social, os Portugueses foram confrontados com uma nova visão destes homens e mulheres, cuja negatividade era legitimada pelo poder político, pelas ideias científicas e pela denúncia das práticas monstruosas que lhes eram atribuídas.

O "preto-antropófago" constituiu uma das mais perturbadoras representações do Africano que o imaginário português ainda não eliminou completamente. Sublinhando uma natureza selvagem, desprovida da humanidade mais elementar, a imagem do canibal impôs-se a partir dos finais de Oitocentos. Numa espécie de delírio antropofágico, a sociedade portuguesa foi sacudida por um terramoto de imagens, de informações e de "provas" – como aquelas fornecidas por Henrique Galvão no seu livro *Antropófagos*[21] –, que a tornavam incapaz de qualquer atitude crítica e racional. Estamos perante um dos paradoxos das relações intercivilizacionais: os Portugueses, que acreditavam e denunciavam as práticas canibalescas dos "pretos," eram também aqueles que, sem o menor receio do seu pendor antropofágico, lhes confiavam a guarda das suas próprias crianças!

Colonialismo, Guerra Colonial e Reforço do Racismo

Nos anos 1950-1960, marcados pela nova realidade internacional de apoio ao fim do colonialismo ditado pela Conferência de Bandung (1955), pela independência das colónias africanas e asiáticas, e também pela recusa portuguesa em abandonar o império, o sistema ideológico português registou um "refrescamento" teórico, graças à recuperação das propostas lusotropicalistas do sociólogo brasileiro Gilberto Freyre, que permitiram reforçar a ideia de um vasto mundo português, harmonioso e homogéneo, do Minho a Timor, isento da mancha do racismo. Registe-se o apoio da oposição ao regime em matéria colonial – Cunha Leal afirmava, em 1961, que só a intervenção dos portugueses, "os únicos capazes de bem civilizar," podia eliminar a "selvajaria," o "canibalismo," a "nudez,"

85

a "preguiça," a "doença do sono," os "feiticeiros" –, seguido de uma produção legislativa que, sublinhando a grandeza da Nação e valorizando os particularismos civilizacionais dos Portugueses, devia permitir maquilhar a persistência das formas de dominação colonial.

Acrescente-se mais um paradoxo: por um lado, usava-se o lusotropicalismo para justificar as escolhas e as soluções do Estado e a igualdade dos portugueses "de cá" e "de lá"; pelo outro, multiplicavam-se as regras discriminatórias nas colónias (transformadas em províncias ultramarinas), que viriam mais tarde a provocar conflitos armados. Estas regras devem também ser compreendidas no âmbito de um fortíssimo projeto de branqueamento das colónias, criando os mecanismos necessários para incentivar e apoiar a emigração dos Portugueses para a África, sobretudo para Angola. Esta opção reforçava o carácter obstinado do colonialismo português, apoiado por uma massa cada vez mais significativa de colonos, na sua grande maioria analfabetos e sem competências técnicas, provenientes dos espaços rurais portugueses, que no Ultramar podiam obter uma promoção social impossível em Portugal: "superiores" aos Africanos "indígenas" ou "assimilados," estes Portugueses, também desprezados pela população metropolitana, encontravam nos "pretos" os trabalhadores indispensáveis à melhoria das suas condições de vida.

As respostas africanas à violência da situação colonial passaram primeiro pela criação de movimentos de libertação, que vieram a liderar e a organizar as populações das colónias para combater o colonizador e alcançar a independência nacional. Vários acontecimentos trágicos – a "guerra do Batepá" em São Tomé (1953), o "massacre de Pidjiguiti" no porto de Bissau (1959), a tentativa angolana, em 4 de Fevereiro de 1961, de libertar os presos políticos detidos na prisão de S. Paulo, em Luanda, a que se seguiram os ataques aos Europeus e aos seus bens – reforçaram substancialmente o juízo dos Portugueses a respeito dos Africanos e deram início à guerra colonial/luta de libertação nacional. Os Portugueses procederam quase de imediato à invenção de um termo, os "turras," abreviação de "terroristas," que, descaracterizando e desvalorizando os combatentes africanos, punha também em evidência a barbárie das suas práticas antropofágicas, de que eram vítimas os militares portugueses. Mau grado os famosos cinco séculos de colonização, que fazem parte ainda hoje das relações míticas entre Portugal e as Áfricas, os Portugueses conservaram, até muito tarde no século XX, o fantasma da antropofagia, empurrando os Africanos para uma constante desqualificação.

Durante mais de 13 anos, a guerra colonial, que se estendeu a Angola, à Guiné e a Moçambique, consagrou uma imagem negativa do Africano, consolidando as formas mais duras do preconceito e da discriminação, traduzindo-se na fixação de uma visão racista dos "pretos," fossem eles Portugueses ou Africanos.

O engenheiro agrónomo Daniel Nunes, cabo-verdiano, instalado algures na Beira para proceder à instalação da cultura da beterraba açucareira, saiu de casa, ao lusco-fusco, e cruzou-se com uma empregada que, esbaforida, fugiu aos berros, gritando "É o diabo, o diabo, o diabo...!" Também Paulo António dos Anjos, jornalista lisboeta, mestiço, foi abordado na rua por uma senhora carregada de embrulhos que lhos estendeu dizendo: "leva-me isto até casa." Francisco Tenreiro, geógrafo, poeta e professor universitário santomense, ia sentado num eléctrico quando se deu conta de que uma mãe insistia com a filha: "vai lá... e toca," pois tocar na carapinha de um preto dava sorte, segundo uma convicção lisboeta. A hesitação da criança foi desfeita pela réplica de Tenreiro: "ela toca, minha senhora, mas eu como-a!" Registe-se o facto dos três protagonistas mestiços destas histórias, contadas e vividas em Lisboa, nos anos sessenta, por Alfredo Margarido, terem um estatuto social reconhecido na sociedade portuguesa: mesmo assim, a cor da pele era um marcador absoluto.[22] Podíamos certamente contar muitas outras histórias que mostram a dificuldade portuguesa em reconhecer a igualdade do Africano ou do Português de pele negra ou mestiça.

Da Visibilidade/Invisibilidade dos Africanos em Portugal

A presença de Africanos na sociedade portuguesa nos vinte anos que decorreram entre 1955 (Bandoung) e 1975 (África "lusófona"), período marcado pelas independências africanas e pelas guerras coloniais, não tem suscitado um interesse significativo da comunidade académica,[23] capaz de permitir eliminar a escassez e a fragilidade dos conhecimentos relativos aos fluxos migratórios, às formas de instalação e de integração verificados então em Portugal.

Comecemos por registar a instalação de Portugueses ou Africanos brancos, mestiços ou negros, vindos das colónias para estudar nas universidades portuguesas. Em número escasso, estes estudantes instalados na Casa dos Estudantes do Império (CEI), criada em 1944, em Lisboa, pela Mocidade Portuguesa – órgão do regime que geria as juventudes nacionais –, procuraram denunciar o colonialismo português.[24] Durante a década de 1950, a CEI, que se tinha vindo a organizar como espaço associativo de debate político e cultural anti-salazarista e anti--colonialista, publicando textos, poemas, depoimentos, ensaios na *Mensagem* (órgão de informação e publicação da CEI desde 1948), cria entre 1951 e 1953 o Centro de Estudos Africanos, onde viriam a colaborar muitas das figuras fundadoras dos movimentos independentistas. A partir de 1961, o reforço da adesão de vários estudantes das colónias a organizações anti-regime como o MUD Juvenil e o PCP, a dureza da vigilância e da censura política, as prisões e a repressão da PIDE, a fuga de parte significativa dos dirigentes nacionalistas – como Amílcar Cabral, Agostinho Neto, Mário de Andrade, Eduardo Mondlane, Vasco Cabral, entre outros –, ou a luta independentista que exigia outro tipo de acções no terreno e de formação de quadros para assegurar a libertação das colónias constituem factores que levaram ao fim da CEI, encerrada pelo governo português em 1965. Importante pelo papel que desempenhou na formação de elites africanas, a sua influência foi muito reduzida na sociedade portuguesa, que não soube (não pôde ou não quis) construir qualquer movimento social de cariz anticolonial.

Diga-se, no entanto, que, apesar da guerra colonial que mobilizou centenas de milhares de Portugueses e condicionou a vida nacional, não se verificaram, em Portugal, assomos de violência explícita – o que não elimina a violência silenciosa do preconceito – contra os Africanos que aqui viviam e trabalhavam. As comunidades africanas ou portuguesas de origem africana, fosse qual fosse o seu nível social, puderam viver entre os Portugueses sem recear ataques racistas dos extremistas. A frágil (e arcaica) extrema-direita que apoiava incondicionalmente as opções colonialistas, a incipiente economia, a rígida estrutura social portuguesa – "cada um no seu lugar" –, mantiveram a "paz," que se apoiava naturalmente na repressão política. Nunca nenhum aluno negro ou mestiço, na escola, recusou a autoridade do professor branco, tal como os alunos brancos não repeliram a autoridade de qualquer professor não branco (situação rara). Devemos acrescentar a este conjunto de elementos que explicam as relações sociais na sociedade portuguesa de então, as muitas formas de intimidade e de cumplicidade que marcaram o relacionamento secular entre Portugueses e Africanos em Portugal. Tal facto não eliminava os juízos de valor negativos dos Portugueses sobre o "preto" ou "negro," mas permitia integrá-lo com naturalidade e de forma quase invisível, porque desprezível, na paisagem portuguesa. Por outro lado, numa sociedade como a portuguesa, em que imperava o analfabetismo e a ausência de reflexão teórica e de conhecimentos científicos, agravados pela censura do regime salazarista, o "racismo epidérmico" ou naturalmente "espontâneo" – adoptando a maneira de dizer de Paul Mercier[25] para definir um certo discurso antropológico anterior à criação da disciplina –, era o único capaz de ser praticado e entendido pela população portuguesa.[26]

Em 1971, um historiador português afirmava num texto consagrado à *Escravatura*:

Qual foi a consequência para o País desta abundância de escravos? O abastardamento dos costumes . . . a falta de disciplina moral . . . não se desenvolveu no País o gosto pelo trabalho e pelo progresso . . . Os métodos de produção nunca avançaram e a dependência da indústria estrangeira acentuou-se. A ociosidade foi outra consequência. As tarefas mais duras foram abandonadas e os homens livres procuraram a grande aventura do mar . . . os escravos . . . transformavam-se em vagabundos e ladrões e . . . as escravas . . . passaram a mulheres fáceis.[27]

A violência deste juízo, na segunda metade do século XX, põe-nos perante a necessidade de refletirmos sobre a maneira portuguesa de inferiorizar o Outro, que "não pode senão ser a causa de todas as desgraças vividas no país!"

A situação da imigração de Africanos até 1974, que eram Portugueses na lógica aparente do regime, manteve-se quase sem alterações. A chegada de imigrantes africanos sem qualificação, um terço dos quais proveniente de Cabo Verde, só começa a ter algum significado a partir de 1973.[28] Como refere Pena Pires, até "1960, a maioria dos cerca de 30000 estrangeiros residentes em Portugal era composta por europeus (67%) e brasileiros (22%)," a imigração tendo aumentado ligeiramente a partir de meados de sessenta e inícios de setenta, graças a uma ligeira aceleração da economia, da construção civil e do turismo, em particular. Acrescenta que é nas primeiras décadas de setenta " que têm início alguns dos fluxos migratórios com origem nas então colónias africanas [sendo] difícil contabilizá-los . . . [pois] eram considerados migrações inter-regionais . . . que vinham colmatar a escassez de mão-de-obra em setores de trabalho mais afetados pela emigração para a Europa e pelo recrutamento militar para as colónias."[29]

Pena Pires sublinha ainda que a "imigração africana que se seguiu à descolonização foi, durante alguns anos, relativamente invisível, quer para as autoridades políticas, quer para os cientistas sociais," sendo apenas assinalada ocasionalmente pela opinião pública e pelos *media*, o Africano tornando-se sinónimo de Cabo-verdiano. Pires acrescenta que "essa primeira vaga migratória" envolveu "nacionais de todas as ex-colónias – cerca de 45000 segundo os dados do Censo de 1981," sendo "muito difícil determinar o número preciso de africanos imigrados em Portugal no início da década de oitenta."[30] Este primeiro grupo integrava naturalmente trabalhadores sem quaisquer competências técnicas, mas também estudantes e sobretudo "os retornados não brancos . . . [que] possuíam . . .

nacionalidade portuguesa, alguma qualificação profissional e grau de instrução, o que tornou possível uma inserção mais rápida . . . na sociedade portuguesa, já que preenchiam os requisitos de 'civilidade' necessários para o bom convívio social."[31] A sua posição social e económica marcou o seu auto-afastamento em relação não só às comunidades "negras" ou "mulatas" já instaladas em bairros periféricos de Lisboa, mas também aos imigrantes africanos, que vieram depois, de vários países de África,[32] fornecendo uma mão de obra não qualificada, absorvida pela construção civil. Pires vê nesta "primeira fase da imigração africana pós-1974 . . . [a coexistência de] uma *migração de refugiados*, protagonizada por angolanos e moçambicanos e uma *migração laboral*" sobretudo cabo-verdiana.

É este significativo aumento de imigrantes a partir de 1980, visível no espaço laboral português e nos "bairros de lata," que "permite [à sociedade portuguesa] perceber que a imigração africana era um processo mais vasto, heterogéneo e dinâmico do que a imagem que então dela se tinha construído."[33] Esta constatação, que reforça a *invisibilidade* do Africano até 1980, é certamente um dos elementos mais perturbadores da sociedade portuguesa do século XX, pois a invisibilidade é a negação do Outro.

Conclusão

A diáspora africana em Portugal, que se estendeu por vários séculos, procurou integrar-se criando formas de convivência e de participação nas mais diferentes esferas da vida portuguesa. As muitas operações, resultantes das imposições e dos projetos portugueses, não foram aceites passivamente pelos Africanos, limitando as suas reacções ao primarismo da fuga ou da violência. Estes, perante a inevitabilidade da situação de dominação, elaboraram estratégias de adesão destinadas a preservar, numa dinâmica de mudança, as suas raízes culturais e a inventar situações inovadoras de africanidade. Esse esforço permitiu-lhes uma reconstrução identitária autónoma, associando práticas culturais portuguesas a valores civilizacionais africanos, profundamente dependentes da sua própria singularidade histórica, criando formas culturais inéditas, e marcando um património português fortemente sincrético que permaneceu até à contemporaneidade.

O 25 de abril de 1974, que liquidou a guerra colonial, abriu também as portas para essa revisão – é verdade que ainda modesta – da história das relações dos Portugueses com a África, assim como dos conceitos e preconceitos que as sedimentaram, exigindo leituras rigorosas dos documentos que revelam justamente a contribuição multissecular dos Africanos para a construção da sociedade portuguesa. O fim do processo colonial português, por via das independências das colónias africanas, que tinham começado a balbuciar em português há já alguns séculos, permitiu que estes novos países de África integrassem a língua portuguesa na sua escarcela teórica. A inquietação portuguesa revelou-se então na tentativa de assegurar o controlo da língua portuguesa, suporte por assim dizer único da "lusofonia,"[34] que, alguns ainda marcados pelo espectro do Império, o fantasma do (nosso) castelo de Elsenor, pretendiam transformar em espaço isolado do mundo, representando o génio português, especialmente adaptado às estruturas tropicais.

Os últimos vinte anos têm vindo a mostrar uma (lenta) eliminação de estereótipos que desvalorizavam o Africano. Mas a força do preconceito secular, marcado pelas características somáticas, emerge através da recuperação de fórmulas e representações negativas, que reforçam, no quadro das novas regras e dos novos problemas inerentes à globalização, as formas de discriminação racial e social com que ainda se confrontam hoje muitos Africanos imigrantes – e Portugueses de origem africana "denunciados" pela côr da pele –, que procuram na Europa novas formas de vida coletiva.

O Discurso da Imagem: Representações dos Africanos no Espaço Português (XV-XX)

Pequenas esculturas de prata representando duas **escravas africanas**, produzidas no México no final do século XVIII. Museu da Quinta das Cruzes, Funchal.

Se as imagens, escritas, iconográficas, materiais construídas durante séculos nem sempre representam a realidade, exprimem sim fórmulas metafóricas, visões fantasmagóricas e juízos de valor dos Africanos, revelam não os Outros mas nós próprios, os Europeus. O problema crucial da interpretação das representações dos Africanos elaboradas pelos Portugueses, sobretudo nos séculos XIX e XX marcados por uma panóplia eficaz de instrumentos técnicos e conceptuais ao serviço da fabricação da figura do Outro, é certamente o de desmontar o discurso paradigmático ocidental/ europeu/ português, compreender o olhar que foi sendo organizado sobre o "preto" e o "mulato" e utilizar/filtrar/ reinterpretar toda a documentação produzida – textos, fotografias, publicidades, pinturas, cerâmicas, desenhos, gravuras, filmes…. – para encontrar no emaranhado dos preconceitos a realidade do Outro africano.

Litografia de Macphail, de 1842 representando dois **caiadores com os seus instrumentos de trabalho**. Estas representações centradas nesta actividade masculina africana percorrem a produção gráfica até hoje, de tal maneira esta tarefa simbolizou o trabalho preferencial dos Africanos em Portugal. *Trajos dos Habitantes de Lisboa*…, Museu da Cidade-CML, Lisboa. Fotografia de Júlio Marques.

Discursos Fundadores do Preconceito Anti-Negro (séculos XIII-XV)

«Non quer' eu donzela fea
Que ant' a mia porta pea.
Non quer' eu donzela fea
E nega como carvon,
Que ant' mia porta pea
Nen faça como sison.[…]
Non quer' eu donzela fea
E velosa come can,[…]
Nem faça como alermã. […]
Non quer' eu donzela fea,
Velha de máa coor.
Que ant' mia porta pea
Nen me faça i peior.[…]»

Cantiga de escárnio e maldizer de Afonso X, o
Sábio, rei de Leão e Castela, integrada na sua
obra *Cantigas de Santa Maria*, 1252-1284, que
descreve com grande crueldade uma mulher
negra identificável através dos caracteres físicos
apresentados de forma negativa e repugnante.
Velha e donzela, feia e negra de má cor, peluda
como um cão, mal cheirosa como sison (ave
pernalta) e alermã (planta da família da
arruda que cheira mal quando queimada
e pertence ao mundo da feitiçaria), que
ninguém pode tolerar à porta de sua
casa. O lugar destinado aos Africanos
está fixado: à margem da sociedade da
norma, os seus caracteres somáticos
transportam-nos para o mundo animal e
vegetal, retirando-lhes a humanidade.

**Caneca de Vinho representando uma
mulher negra**, associada como era comum
ao consumo excessivo de vinho e marcada
pelas características físicas que alimentavam
o preconceito português. Cerâmica de Barcelos,
início do século XX. Colecção Particular.
Fotografia de Júlio Marques.

Pormenor de Iluminura do século XII
representando cristãos e mouros face a face.
Afonso X, Cantigas de Santa Maria, século
XII. Patrimonio Nacional - Real Monastério.
Biblioteca del Escorial, Espanha.

«No outro dia, que eram VIII dias do mês de Agosto, muito
cedo pela manhã por razão da calma, começaram os mareantes
de correger seus batéis e tirar aqueles cativos, para os levarem
segundo lhes fora mandado: os quaes postos juntamente
naquele campo, eram uma maravilhosa coisa de se ver, que
entre eles havia alguns de razoada brancura, formosos e
apostos; outros menos brancos, que queriam semelhar pardos;
outros tão negros como etíopes, tão desafeiçoados assim nas
caras como nos corpos, que quasi parecia, aos homens que os
esguardavam, que viam as imagens do hemisfério mais baixo.»

Em meados do século XV, o cronista Gomes Eanes
de Zurara descreve o desembarque e a partilha do
primeiro grande carregamento de escravos
africanos na cidade de Lagos, em 1444,
na presença do Infante D. Henrique.
Acontecimento marcante porque
fundador de uma prática cruel que
viria a durar séculos, permitindo a
introdução massiva de Africanos
no espaço português. Zurara
organiza o seu discurso em
torno das características
somáticas, sublinhando
a heterogeneidade física
destes Africanos – os mais
negros, tão feios que pareciam
«imagens do hemisfério mais
baixo», ou seja, do inferno
- e propondo uma grelha
classificatória e hierarquizadora
dos homens, que os séculos
irão reforçar.

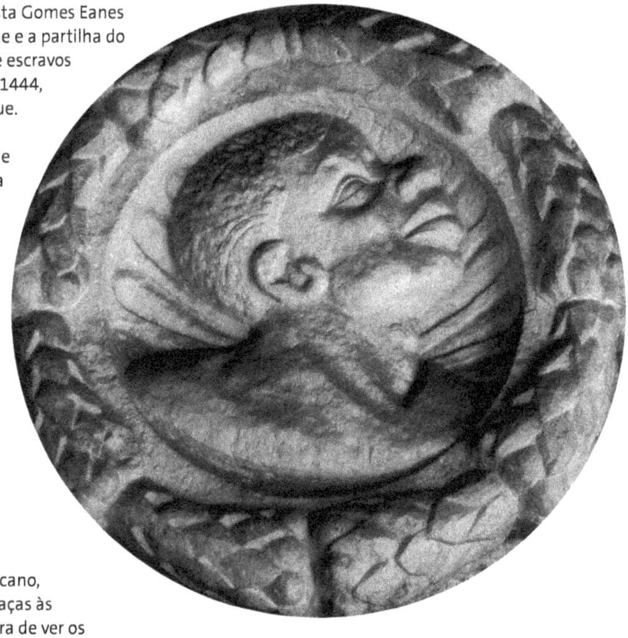

Escultura em pedra quinhentista,
representando o perfil de um Africano,
permitindo a sua identificação graças às
características físicas. Esta maneira de ver os
Africanos, centrada na leitura fisiognómica do
rosto, começou a organizar-se no século XIII,
consolidando-se durante séculos. Claustro do
Mosteiro dos Jerónimos, Lisboa. Fotografia: Luís
Pavão. IGESPAR DIDA AF.

Espaços Africanos e Integração na Lisboa dos Séculos XVI a XVIII

O Chafariz d'El Rei no século XVI

Pintura de autor desconhecido, datada de c.1570- c.1580, representando uma cena urbana lisboeta junto ao Chafariz d'El Rei. A imagem concentra uma multidão misturando vários grupos sociais, onde se destaca uma grande quantidade de Africanos, homens e mulheres, desempenhando as mais diversas tarefas, vendendo produtos, transportando água ou calhandras cheias de detritos, descarregando as embarcações, acompanhando os senhores ou sendo levados bêbados para a cadeia. Mas algumas cenas são inusitadas e surpreendentes: um Africano ao leme de uma pequena embarcação, enquanto o colega toca pandeireta para tornar mais doce a relação amorosa dos dois passageiros brancos; à esquerda, na "pista de dança" onde se desenrola um baile, emerge a figura de um escravo negro carregando uma bilha na cabeça e preso por uma corrente de ferro que liga o pescoço aos pés; um outro Africano a cavalo envergando o hábito da Ordem de Santiago, situa-se no primeiro plano; e, no baile, podemos ver um par dançante formado por um homem negro, aparentemente calçado, e uma mulher branca, descalça! Às janelas, as Portuguesas contemplam o espectáculo, certamente barulhento, marcado pela música e pela dança. Saliente-se ainda que o uso das bicas dos diferentes chafarizes urbanos foi rigorosamente regulamentado no século XVI, segundo a côr da pele e o estatuto social dos utilizadores (Postura Municipal de 1551). Colecção Berardo, Lisboa.

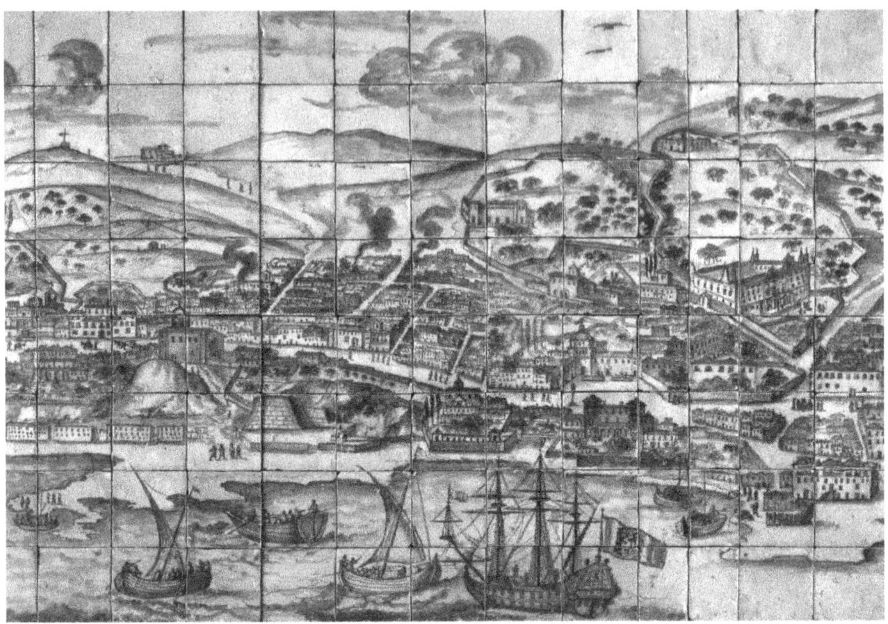

**O Bairro do Mocambo no século XVIII
e o 'Poço dos Negros', em Lisboa**

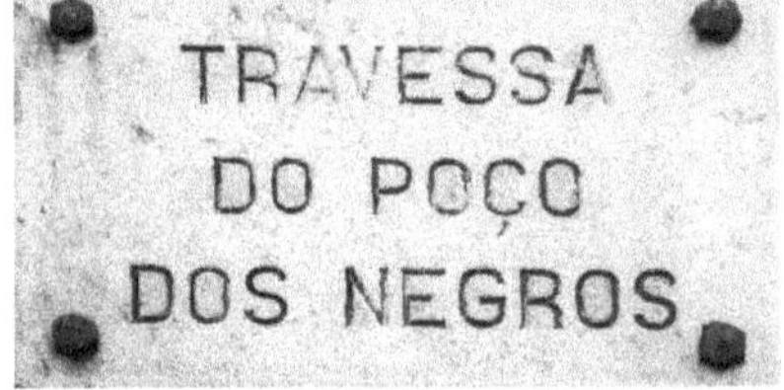

Painel de azulejos pertencente à Grande Vista de Lisboa,
de barro vidrado, fabricada entre 1700 e 1725 e atribuída a
Gabriel del Barco, que representa a cidade antes do terramoto
de 1755. Este pormenor assinala a maneira como o Bairro do
Mocambo se integrava no espaço urbano ocidental de Lisboa
– fora de portas mas permitindo a proximidade necessária
para o desempenho fácil das diferentes actividades urbanas
das populações africanas aí residentes -, assinalado pelas
colunas de fumo das olarias que ali teriam funcionado.
Museu Nacional do Azulejo, Lisboa. Fotografia de Carlos
Monteiro, DDF-IMC,IP. Entre Santa Catarina e o Mocambo,
a rua e a travessa Poço dos Negros assinalam hoje um lugar
onde teria existido um poço que a história fixou com duas
origens possíveis: o Poço dos Negros que D. Manuel I teria
ordenado construir, por carta régia de 1515, para aí serem
lançados os escravos negros mortos, ou o poço de águas
límpidas erigido pelos 'Negros', isto é, os padres de hábito
negro instalados naquela zona da cidade. Uma questão é,
no entanto, certa: o rei mandou edificar um poço para esse
fim na parte ocidental da cidade, para evitar que os corpos
dos escravos fossem lançados do alto de Santa Catarina,
ficando a descoberto e criando situações malsãs na cidade.
Fotografia de Júlio Marques.

O Trabalho e a sua Função Integradora e Excludente

Actividades africanas urbanas masculinas e femininas
Durante séculos, os Africanos levaram a cabo as tarefas mais duras
mas indispensáveis à vida urbana, que não só diziam respeito à gestão
e limpeza da cidade, mas garantiam o transporte, a produção e o
comércio de bens destinados às populações.

Em cima: **Mulher provavelmente doméstica amanhando peixe**. Painel
de azulejos do século XVIII, Museu da Cidade - CML, Lisboa.

Homens e mulher africanos pescando no rio. Azulejos seiscentistas,
Palácio Fronteira, Fundação das Casas de Fronteira e Alorna, Lisboa.

Vendedeiras negras ou mestiças ocupando-se do pequeno comércio de rua, assegurando o abastecimento dos bens necessários ao quotidiano dos Portugueses, sobretudo destinados à alimentação, como tremoços, fava rica, peixe. Litografia colorida, Museu da Cidade – CML, Lisboa.

Fotografia de **vendedeira de mexilhão**. Museu da Cidade – CML, Lisboa.

p. 99, em cima, esquerda: **Caiador** – a tarefa masculina mais corrente que perdurou ao longo dos séculos – e vendedeira de mexilhão.

p. 99, em cima, direita: **Calhandreira africana**, figura típica que assegurava a recolha dos detritos das casas lisboetas. Representações oitocentistas: vendedeiras de tremoços e de fava-rica, gravuras aguareladas de Manuel S. Godinho, Colecção de Estampas intitulada Ruas de Lisboa..., 1826;

p. 99, em baixo: Esta imagem põe em evidência dois pólos da actividade dos Africanos: enquanto os homens se empenham na descarga do barco ancorado na areia, as mulheres procedem ao despejo das calhandras; uma delas descansa depois de efectuado o despejo, a outra executa a operação. Este gesto durou séculos, só tendo terminado no final do século XIX. Litografia colorida, *Sketches of Portuguese Life* ..., Londres, 1826. Biblioteca Nacional de Portugal, Lisboa. Fotografias do Museu da Cidade: Júlio Marques

LA NEGRESSE ALLANT JETTER LES ORDURES

STRAW BOAT UNLOADING. BLACK WOMEN EMPTYING THEIR POTS.

«Há uma raça de escravos negros, alguns dos quais são reservados somente para emprenhadores de muitas mulheres, como garanhões, fazendo-se exactamente com eles, como com as raças de cavalos em Itália. Deixam-se cavalgar estas mulheres para que possam parir, porque o produto é sempre do patrão destas escravas, e digo, que são servas prenhas. Não é permitido aos garanhões negros cavalgar as prenhas sob pena de 50 chicotadas, mas cavalgar somente as não prenhas, porque se vendem as crias a 30 ou 40 escudos cada uma; e destes rebanhos de fêmeas há muitos em Portugal e nas Índias, só para venderem as crias...»

A 'criação' de escravos nas terras do interior e a 'animalização' dos homens
A violência desta descrição de Giovanni Venturino em 1571, põe em evidência a desumanização dos escravos africanos, situação que se terá mantido até finais do século XVIII. Um documento de 1773 denuncia a existência de proprietários de escravos que possuem «escravas reprodutoras.....para perpetuarem os cativeiros»

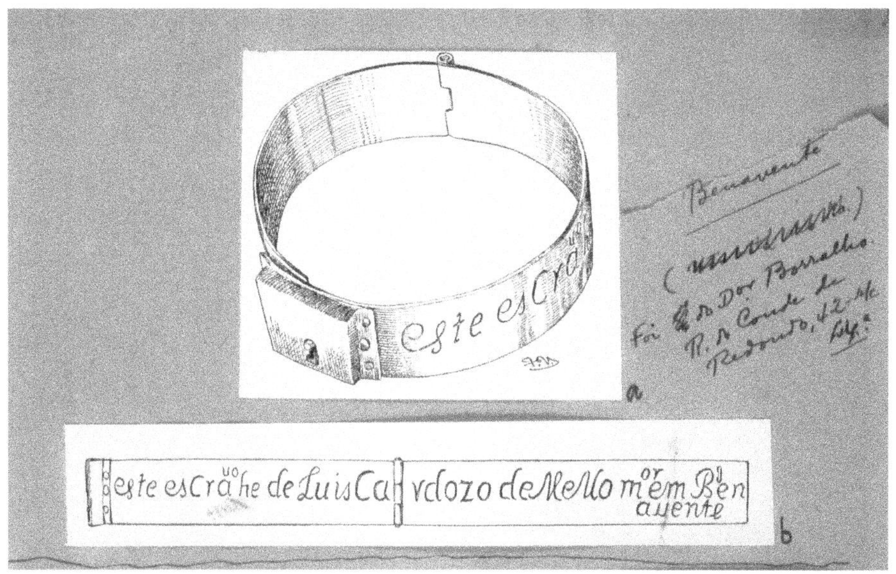

Coleiras de escravos e algemas de ferro
destinadas a assegurar a prisão dos escravos – como
se de animais se tratasse –, sem impedir o trabalho.
Museu Nacional de Arqueologia, Lisboa. Fotografias:
Luísa Oliveira, DDF-IMC, I.P.

A Adesão Africana ao Espaço Religioso Português

Manifestações de uma religiosidade africana no quadro do catolicismo

Em cima, à esquerda: **Casal rezando a Nossa Senhora do Rosário**. Pintura de autor desconhecido, datado dos finais do século XVI, representando um casal de Africanos com o vestuário da época – a mulher com a cabeça tapada –, provavelmente casados segundo os rituais católicos, a orar à Santa. Se o casamento era um fortíssimo marcador social e religioso nas sociedades africanas, o matrimónio católico permitia aos Africanos adquirir estatuto social e lugar nos rituais sagrados da sociedade portuguesa. Igreja de Santa Catarina, Lisboa. FOotografia de Júlio Marques.

Em cima, à direita: **«Altar da Irmandade de Nossa Senhora do Rosário dos Homens Pretos»**. Este altar consagrado a Nossa Senhora do Rosário, instalado na Igreja setecentista da Graça, em Lisboa, sublinha a relação desta Santa com a população em geral, mas com os Africanos em particular. A Santa está ladeada por quatro santos negros, Santo António de Noto e São Benedito, ambos quinhentistas vivendo em Palermo, descendentes de escravos africanos, Santo Elesbão, imperador da Etiópia no século VI e Santa Ifigénia, princesa da Nubia no século I, venerados na Andaluzia, de onde o seu culto foi introduzido em Portugal, no século XVIII. Fotografia de Júlio Marques.

Africana rezando na Igreja. Intitulada «Atitude das Portuguesas na Igreja», esta litografia francesa de Zacharie-Félix Doumet, de 1806, condena as práticas femininas portuguesas nos cultos católicos, mostrando o interior de uma capela, aparentemente particular, e integrando uma mulher negra, ajoelhada e rezando, não se sabendo o seu estatuto, mas sendo provavelmente doméstica das damas brancas. Museu da Cidade, Lisboa. Fotografia: Júlio Marques.

Compromisso de Nossa Senhora do Rosário dos Homens Pretos. Datado de 2 de Dezembro de 1565, este Compromisso é um dos muitos documentos desta natureza que revelam a preocupação da Igreja em multiplicar, por todo o país, confrarias e irmandades, que permitiam a participação de Africanos nas diferentes actividades religiosas. Biblioteca Nacional de Portugal, Lisboa. damas brancas. Museu da Cidade, Lisboa. Fotografia: Júlio Marques.

LE MENINO JESUS.
L'Agoadeiro et Le Dragon Portugnis

BEGGING FOR THE FESTIVAL OF N.S. D'ATALAYA.

Festas e práticas religiosas e participação africana

Pág. 104, em cima: **Africano usando a imagem do menino-Jesus para obter esmolas**. Trata-se de uma figura repetidamente apresentada na iconografia dos séculos XVII, XVIII e XIX, em que são representadas diversas personagens mais ou menos populares da sociedade portuguesa, como acontece nesta pintura de Zacharie-Félix Doumet, de 1806, intitulada « O menino-Jesus, o Aguadeiro e o Dragão Português», em que o Africano pede esmola, vendo-se uma figura militar, uma devota ajoelhada e um aguadeiro galego. Museu da Cidade – CML, Lisboa. Fotografia de Júlio Marques.

Pág. 104, em baixo: **A dança, a música e o peditório**. Litografia colorida oitocentista, intitulada «Peditório de Nossa Senhora da Atalaya», representando um peditório levado a cabo por Africanos vestidos segundo as normas das confrarias, acompanhados de músicos e de bailarinos africanos dançando o lundum, dança africana comum nestas cerimónias públicas, apreciada pelos Portugueses e condenada pelos autores estrangeiros. *Sketches of Portuguese Life*, Londres, 1826. Biblioteca Nacional de Portugal, Lisboa.

Pequenas esculturas representando a presença africana nas procissões portuguesas

Em cima: As **«Figurinhas da Procissão do Corpo de Cristo»** representam os irmãos africanos das confrarias portuguesas, identificáveis pela côr das capas, que participavam nas grandes procissões, cortejos, festas católicas nacionais. Moldadas em pasta de argila com orifício para vela, da autoria do escultor miniaturista Vasco Pereira Conceição, pintadas por António Soares, integram um vasto conjunto de objectos semelhantes fabricados entre 1936 e 1938.

Os **«Os Pretos de São Jorge»** é a designação dada a esta orquestra dos cinco músicos negros, talhados em madeira, vestindo trajes exuberantes e associando instrumentos de rufo e de sopro, que integravam (e integraram ainda no século XX) a Procissão do Corpo de Cristo, a mais importante festividade religiosa católica, que obrigava à participação de todas as Confrarias. Saliente-se o apreço da população lisboeta pela presença deste grupo africano, que dava côr e música muito apreciadas ao evento religioso. Museu da Cidade - CML, Lisboa. Fotografias: Júlio Marques.

Os Espaços Lúdicos: Dança, Música, Festa

A participação africana nos mais diversos espectáculos de natureza lúdica organizados pelos Portugueses ou pelos próprios africanos, ou simplesmente em manifestações espontâneas de alegria e festa, era constante nos quotidianos de Lisboa.

Em cima: **'Concerto' espontâneo no Cais do Sodré**, onde uma pequena orquestra de Africanos toca tambor, viola e pandeireta, vendo-se também um dos muitos portadores da imagem do menino-jesus procurando obter esmola e ainda duas mulheres africanas, provavelmente vendedeiras, uma delas carregando um cesto na cabeça. «O Cais do Sodré em 1785», pintura de Joaquim Marques, Museu Nacional de Arte Antiga, Lisboa.

«Os pretos em cavalinhos de pasta» mostra a participação, muito apreciada pelos próprios africanos e pelos outros, de «fusca e encarapinhada gente», montados em cavalos de pasta, facilmente varridos pela força do touro, que alegravam os intervalos das touradas. Litografia oitocentista de Legrand, integrada no *Album Touradas*, Museu da Cidade – CML, Lisboa

«O Carnaval de Lisboa», festa culturalmente mestiça,
onde brancos, negros e mulatos participam em conjunto
na possibilidade de infringir, sem castigo, a rigidez
da norma social. Litografia de Canongia de 1875, Museu
da Cidade – CML, Lisboa.

**Representação de um marinheiro mestiço tocando uma
guitarra portuguesa**, função muito estimada pela sociedade
portuguesa, onde se crê que o fado foi introduzido, sobretudo
nos meios aristocráticos, por personagens de origem
africana. Desenho a aguarela e tinta-da-china sobre papel,
de E. J. Maia, Typos e Trajos de Lisboa, 1845, Museu da Cidade
– CML -, Lisboa. Fotografias: Júlio Marques

107

História, Memória, Identidade

BAYLE DOS NEGROS.

Rey.   *Rainha.*
Seis negros.   *Quatro negras.*
Dois Titeres.   *Acompanhamento,*
e Muſicos inſtrumentos da meſma naçaõ.

ORMARSE-HA hum viſtozo Carro, ou Carroça, pela qual hiraõ puxando dous Leões, no fronteſpicio, do Carro ſe veraõ duas Aguias, e no fim ſe levantarà huma gruta, dentro da qual hiràõ ſentados Rey, Rainha, ſobre a gruta ſe verà hum pavilhaõ, ou guardaſol de penas, o qual ſuſtentarà hum Negro veſtido à Ethiopeza, hiraõ cobrindo à ſuperficie deſte Carro variedades de paſſaros, como Araras, Papagayos, como tambem Bugios; ſobre os Leoens hiraõ os Titeres, & finalmente ſe ſatisfarà tudo à propriedade da Naçaõ.

BAYLE.

Introdu. TOro os pleto ḡ ha em Blaga
N   aos feſſa vem com plimor,
que ſà huns feſſa que alegla
plo ſer feſſa do Sior.
    Vaya vaya ri ſorſa,
    que os blanco paſma
    ver que toca os pletio,
    e as neglas baya.
Rey. Ah reſſos grutas!
Rainha. Ah reſſos mattos.
Negros. Vozo que manda?
Rey.Ray. Que oy toro os pleto ri Angora
    faſſa feſſa, canta, y toca.
Negros. Toro os pletio ſiolo
    que he teu Vaſſaro
    baya, canta, toca, y ſarta,
    que he ſeu regáro,

Titer. E voſo pletia canta,
    vozo faça cabriola,
    e vozo ſiolo Monarca,
    manda que eſtos neglos toca?
Rey.Rai. Si ſi ſi ſi ſi,
    plo que os blanco oya,
    que ri Angora os pleto
    cantar ſabe os ſorta.
Todos a 4. Si ſi ſi. ſi ſi, &c.   *Volta.*
    Vem decendo.
Rey.Rai. Quello al Pan glaciozo
    fazer huns dança
    Vozo neglo bliozo   (ta
    huns baya, outro toca, vozo cã-
Tit. 1. Ea ſióro Rey
    vozo me mandà
    plo que eu ſa ſeus ſervo
      A 3   gaſta

Festas, bailes, cortejos africanos, por vezes sabiamente integrados nas festas religiosas ou profanas portuguesas constituíam uma estratégia de preservação de formas culturais e históricas africanas, revelando também a compreensão da natureza dinâmica da identidade e da necessidade constante da sua renovação. Ligados à música e à dança, estes outros ritmos festivos, organizados em torno de figuras nacionais africanas – particularmente sob a forma política que é sempre religiosa na lógica civilizacional africana – asseguravam a autonomia dos Africanos na sociedade portuguesa, cuja identidade africana se consolidava também em lugares de encontros ritualizados, que permaneceram até aos dias de hoje.

O «Bayle dos Negros» de Braga. Esta longa descrição de 1731, dançada e acompanhada por um cântico que alude às relações de dependência e respeito dos participantes para com os seus reis angolanos, põe em evidência a complexa associação entre canto, dança, 'língua de preto', memória histórica e sentimento identitário africanos e a organização religiosa portuguesa, dando conta do sincretismo festivo que marcava a sociedade portuguesa. Biblioteca Nacional de Portugal, Lisboa.

21 DE SETEMBRO DE 1882   O ANTONIO MARIA   311

GRANDE SUCCESSO

Domingo 17 de Setembro de 1882

ASSOMBROSA FESTA

Na Travessa do Outeiro á Rua da Bella Vista á Lapa

ACCLAMAÇÃO E COROAÇÃO

DA NOVA RAINHA DO CONGO, MARIA AMALIA 1.ª

Grande festa da côrte do Congo

Para solemnisar tão fausto e grandioso dia

A côrte procurando dar a esta festa o explendor que requerem taes actos, não se tem poupado, pelo que haverá salvas de morteiros, ascenção de balões, beija-mão, concessão de mercês honorificas, commendas, titulos, etc. terminando por explendido baile.

Convidam-se todos os portuguezes e os que o não sejam a tomarem parte n'esta festa, estreitando assim os laços de amisade e fraternidade com os vassallos da nova rainha.

PRINCIPIA A'S 8 E MEIA

EM PRETO OU EM BRANCO
TODAS AS CÔRTES SE PARECEM

Carta de Calixto Moreira
a Antonio Maria

Senhor Antonio Maria,
Disse Vossa Senhoria
Que o artista confeiteiro,
Que ao paladar dá consolos,
Não tinha amor pelos bolos
Por enjoado do cheiro.

Saiba que se enganou n'isto.
Pois cá 'stou eu, o Calixto,
O irmão do 103,
Que, sério, lhe certifico
Ser dos bolos que fabrico
O mais guloso freguez.

A SUA MAGESTADE A NOVA RAINHA DO CONGO

Rainha do Congo,
Com todo o respeito
Te offreço o meu preito
De branco leal :
O teres o rosto
Da côr do coquilho,
Não tira o aureo brilho
Da c'rôa real.

Que seja ditoso,
Que seja mui longo,
Rainha do Congo,
Teu justo reinar.
Se posso em governos
Metter o bedelho,
Lá vae um conselho
Que vem a *calhar*

Se queres do povo
As lôas e os hymnos,
A dedo os *Paulinos*
Vae prompta escolher ;
E dá-lhes as pastas
Da guerra e justiça,
E a feia preguiça
Castiga a valer.

Se achares um rombo
Nas tuas finanças,
Não sejas das *tanças,*
Não faças *banxé.*
— P'ra males tamanhos,
Remedios bem promptos :
Deixa-te de contos,
E chama o Burnay.

Verás syndicatos
Salvando a futrica,
Render fava rica
Luzento metal ;
Terás, rodeada
De condes e duques,
Festanças, batuques
E coisas e tal.

Do frontão eu muito pasmo,
Mas vejo ali pleonasmo.
— Onde o vês ?... debalde scismo.
— Olha, bruto, faz favor,
Pois não vês da Patria o Amôr
Ao lado do *patriotismo !*

Se a primeira imagem anuncia **«Grande Sucesso»** e mais uma **«Assombrosa Festa»**, onde se procederá à aclamação e coroação da nova Rainha do Congo, Maria Amália I, a segunda imagem, que ridiculariza particularmente os Africanos, consagra um poema à nova soberana, homenageada e respeitada tanto por Brancos como por Pretos. Documentos publicados em *O António Maria*, de 21 a 28 de Setembro de 1882. Hemeroteca Municipal – CML, Lisboa.

109

O «lugar do encontro»: o Rossio e o Largo de São Domingos. Nesta representação setecentista da Praça do Rossio — lugar de muitas festas e cerimónias religiosas ou punitivas (como as da Inquisição) portuguesas - com o Hospital de Todos-os-Santos, onde na imponente escadaria se sentavam vendedeiras africanas, descansando ou esperando fregueses, podemos também ver o Largo e a Igreja de São Domingos, lugar da primeira confraria quinhentista de Nossa Senhora do Rosário dos Homens Pretos. Este amplo espaço lisboeta continua a acolher o encontro de todos os Africanos, qualquer que seja a origem, o sexo, a idade, a profissão, a religião, onde conversas, negócios, feitiçarias se cruzam marcando a singularidade do local.

Em cima: **O Rossio antes do terramoto de 1755**, desenho de Zuzarte de 1757, Arquivo CTT. Fotografia: Júlio Marques.

«O Preto caiador no Rocio à espera dos Freguezes», figura que pode integrar o 'preto do ganho', comum no século XIX. Litografia de Joaquim Pedro Aragão, 1835, Museu da Cidade — CML, Lisboa. Fotografia: Júlio Marques. 6c-3. Da feitiçaria do passado à astrologia de hoje, as práticas africanas de adivinhação do futuro prosseguem e são anunciadas no «lugar do encontro» lisboeta.

Da feitiçaria do passado à astrologia de hoje, as práticas africanas de adivinhação do futuro prosseguem e são anunciadas no «lugar do encontro» lisboeta.

Personalidades Mestiças Relevantes na Sociedade Portuguesa

Pai Paulino, Fernanda do Valle, pejorativamente designada
'Preta Fernanda', Sousa Martins, Virgínia Quaresma, são algumas
das figuras oitocentistas com origem africana, conhecida ou
longínqua, que se destacaram, nas suas áreas de trabalho,
na sociedade portuguesa.

Se o **Pai Paulino**, Paulino José da Conceição, nascido no Brasil, figura típica de
Lisboa, caiador, gaiteiro na procissão do Corpo de Cristo, membro de diferentes
confrarias, combatente liberal condecorado, defensor dos direitos dos
Africanos, desempenhou um papel relevante na resolução de conflitos que os
envolviam, participando em diferentes actividades religiosas, culturais, lúdicas
portuguesas. Busto de faiança de Rafael Bordalo Pinheiro 1894, Museu Bordalo
Pinheiro   CML, Lisboa.

Sousa Martins, médico português de renome, professor da Escola Médico-
Cirúrgica de Lisboa ficou conhecido pelas suas práticas curativas, sendo até hoje
venerado em vários lugares do país. Escultura de Costa Mota (tio), Estátua no
Campo de Santana, Lisboa. Fotografia: Júlio Marques.

Fernanda do Valle, pseudónimo literária da cabo-verdiana Andrêsa do Nascimento, foi escritora e toureira destacando-se sobretudo pela sua participação em festas públicas e privadas lisboetas. Aguarela de Alberto Sousa, capa do livro *Recordações de uma Colonial – Memórias da Preta Fernanda*, de que foi co-autora com A. Totta e F. Machado, Lisboa, 1912.

Virgínia Quaresma, nascida em Elvas e 1882, foi a primeira mulher jornalista portuguesa, licenciada pela Universidade de Lisboa num tempo em que o acesso das mulheres ao ensino superior era muito reduzido, tendo desempenhado um papel pioneiro interventivo na protecção dos direitos das mulheres. Fotografia do Arquivo Nacional da Torre do Tombo, Lisboa.

A Desvalorização do Africano nos Séculos XIX e XX

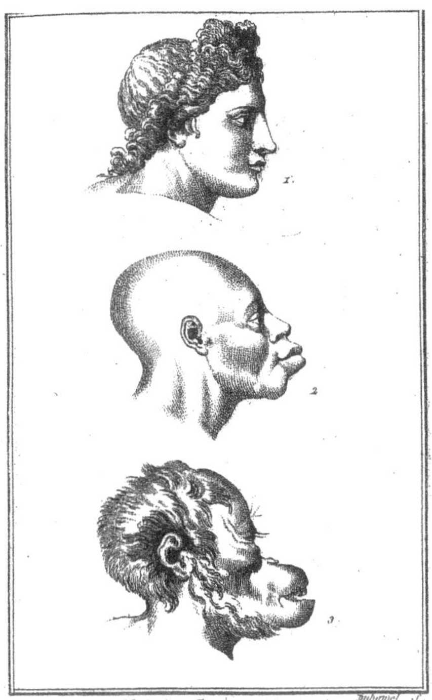

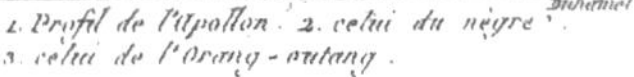

1. Profil de l'Apollon. 2. celui du nègre. 3. celui de l'Orang-outang.

Selvagem, antropófago, primitivo são algumas das categorias classificatórias oitocentistas banalizadas no vocabulário europeu e português para definir os Africanos, com o apoio e a legitimação da história e da ciência. Se estas classificações se baseiam nas leituras europeias dos Africanos em África, não deixam de marcar o imaginário português relativo à totalidade desses homens e mulheres de pele não branca. O fenómeno do racismo, aliando raça e cultura, marca as relações entre os Portugueses e os Outros e reforça preconceitos e formas redutoras e discriminatórias agravadas pelo colonialismo do século XX, assegurando a desvalorização dos Africanos na sociedade portuguesa.

Classificações, representações e preconceitos oitocentistas

As raças humanas, segundo Virey (1801). Desenho de Duhamel, integrado na obra de Virey *Histoire Naturel du Genre Humain*, Paris, 1801, onde o autor, professor de medicina, naturalista e antropólogo, recorre ao critério craniométrico do 'ângulo facial' para classificar e hierarquizar as raças humanas, distanciando o perfil do negro do perfil branco, clássico, do Apolo de Belvedere, e aproximando-o do perfil do orangotango. Em Portugal, Oliveira Martins chamou a si o papel de representar e banalizar estas teorias europeias. Muitos foram os primatas, sobretudo macacos, produzidos em cerâmica europeia em finais do século XIX, como aconteceu em Portugal com Rafael Bordalo Pinheiro. Estes primatas estudados já pelos anatomistas setecentistas confortavam a ideia do parentesco com os homens africanos, banalizando essa semelhança no mundo ocidental.

Gungunhana. Figura maior da selvajaria africana no imaginário português, o chefe nguni aqui representado numa gravura de Rafael Bordalo Pinheiro, de 1878, intitulada "O Entrudo que não se viu", de forma caricatural, bebendo, descalço, com ornamentos ridicularizados ridicularizantes, acompanhado por uma das suas muitas mulheres, sinal também da sua selvajaria, e pondo em evidência a manutenção dos preconceitos reformulados a partir dos conhecimentos científicos estabelecidos no século XIX. Museu Bordalo Pinheiro – CML, Lisboa.

113

A HERANÇA HISTORICA
Banquete de antropophagos

PORTUGAL E AS COLONIAS
AS MENINAS

Pág. 114, em cima: **«A Herança Histórica – Banquete de antropophagos»**.
Sob este título, esta gravura de Rafael Bordalo Pinheiro, publicada
em 1900 no periódico *A Paródia*, que regista o sarcasmo político dos
Ingleses perante as atitudes portuguesas relativas à África, dá conta da
banalização da ideia do preto-antropófago que marcava a sociedade
portuguesa, fornecendo um espectáculo singular em que os estereótipos
desvalorizadores dos Africanos são amplamente utilizados: nudez,
caveiras, bananeiras, cubatas e naturalmente a saborosa refeição
antropofágica. Museu Bordalo Pinheiro – CML, Lisboa.

Pág. 114, em baixo: **As Meninas» ou as Mulatas**. Gravura de Rafael
Bordalo Pinheiro, intitulada "Portugal e as Colónias", publicada no
periódico *A Paródia*, em 1902, que pretende mostrar Portugal e as
colónias portuguesas a braços com as potências europeias, que não
reconhecem os argumentos históricos portugueses para justificar as
pretensões portuguesas em África. As "Meninas" que representam
as colónias portuguesas recusam o "velho e trôpego' Portugal
fazendo a corte, como 'boas mulatas' – preconceito da época – aos
colonialistas europeus, mais jovens e mais dinâmicos. Museu Bordalo
Pinheiro – CML, Lisboa.

As 'novidades' do século XX : manifestações do colonialismo português e práticas de inferiorização dos Africanos em Portugal

As Exposições Coloniais Portuguesas
(1934 e 1940). Convidando os
Portugueses a olhar o conjunto das
suas colónias, incluindo 'amostras ao
vivo' das populações apresentadas
como animais exóticos de um
qualquer jardim zoológico, o Estado
Novo preparou duas grandes
Exposições, a primeira, no Porto
em 1934, intitulada *Exposição
Colonial Portuguesa*, e a segunda,
em 1940, em Lisboa, a *Exposição
do Mundo Português*. Estes dois
cartazes dão conta do exotismo das
populações e das naturezas, ambas
marcadas pela selvajaria africana
e pela desvalorização cultural
dos povos africanos, perante o
esforço civilizador português, cujas
acções foram igualmente postas
em evidência nestes dois grandes
eventos nacionais.

 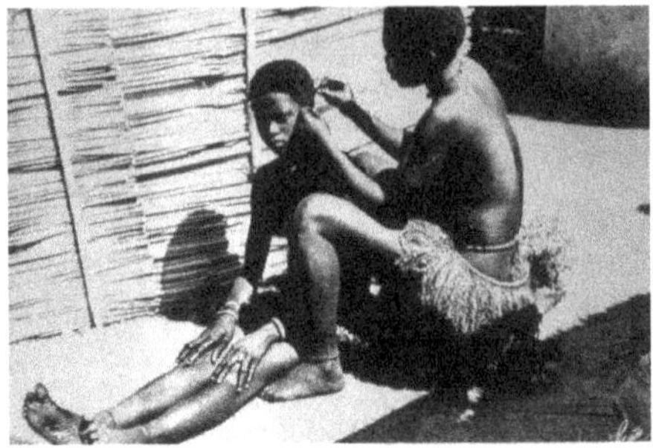

« Jardins zoológicos humanos»

Registos gráficos e escultóricos das Exposições coloniais.
As Exposições coloniais procederam à organização de aldeias africanas,
onde foram expostos muitos Africanos trazidos expressamente para ser
mostrados aos Portugueses e legitimar a acção colonizadora em curso,
em África. Nus ou semi-vestidos, os seus quotidianos, comportamentos e
práticas foram registados graficamente no *Album Fotográfico da Exposição
Colonial Portuguesa*, Porto, 1934, e no jornal *O Primeiro de Janeiro* de 2 de
Julho de 1940. Biblioteca Nacional de Portugal, Lisboa, tendo-se também
procedido a uma produção escultórica para sublinhar as características
físicas destas populações: cabeças africanas modeladas em cimento
pintado de negro, existentes no Jardim Botânico Tropical, em Lisboa, onde
teve lugar a Exposição de 1940. Fotografias de Júlio Marques.

Os Africanos, objectos da publicidade portuguesa.

Se o Cartaz publicitário do "Sabonete Arêgos" (1917) põe em
evidência o choque somático entre as peles' brancas e belas' e as
'negras e sujas', revelando o forte preconceito racial português, a
publicidade do «rhum velho» como de outras bebidas alcoólicas
não podia deixar de recorrer às representações de Africanos
considerados adeptos das bebedeiras desenfreadas, reveladoras
da sua natureza selvagem e irracional. Acrescente-se ainda o
"Preto da Casa Africana", representado no papel de carregador,
simbolizando a força física dos Africanos, que só pode opor-
se à natural inteligência dos Europeus. *Cartaz publicitário*,
Biblioteca Nacional de Portugal, Lisboa. Outros documentos:
Colecção Particular.

PIM★PAM★PUM

O SOL E A NOITE

Por VIRGINIA LOPES DE MENDONÇA

OI no princípio do mundo que êste caso sucedeu.

A noite, uma velha muito preta, muito feia, de grande beiçola grossa, carapinha desgrenhada, ares carrañeudos de meter mêdo, tinha uma raiva, um rancor sem limites, ao louro sol, risonho, brilhante, resplandecente, que espalhava o seu brilho sôbre tôdas as coisas.

E tanto a negra noite barafustou, na maneira de fazer desaparecer do firmamento aquele doirado e lindo rival, que pôs em acção uma ideia estranha, diabólica.

Tempos e tempos, andou numa labuta, arrecadando farrapinhos de nuvens, das mais pesadas, das mais pretas.

Calculem lá para o que queria ela tantos farrapinhos de nuvens?!

Eram retalhinhos que ia juntando uns aos outros, para fazer um saco, grande, muito grande, enorme, formidavel!

Depois, veio de mansinho, desatando logo a encher de sombras o céu e a terra, tal era o seu negrume, a sua pretidão!

Ao chegar perto do sol, fez uma carantonha horrenda e zás! deitou-lhe por cima o tal saco, feito de nuvens muito grossas, muito escuras e, assim, conseguiu escondê-lo.

Já se vê, a escuridão foi tão grande no mundo que tudo deixou de ser lindo, para se tornar horroroso, pois o reino das sombras substituíra o reino da luz.

Mas o sol é que não estava pelos ajustes... Nascera para ser visto, admirado, e cheio de furia com o procedimento da maldosa noite, muito zangado, à fôrça de calor, rebentou o grosso tecido do enorme saco, aonde estava metido.

Então, por êsses buracos, uns bocadinhos de sol foram saindo...

A sua beleza não era exactamente a da luz, que brilhava de dia, não tinha o seu calor intenso, nem o seu brilho estonteante, mas era uma beleza suave e linda que enfeitava o céu em pedacinhos muito pequeninos, dando-lhe uma poesia admiravel.

E o céu, a-pesar da sua escuridão, ficou uma formosura!

A noite, furiosa, o que fez?

Pôs-se a remendar o saco com remendos de mais nuvens e de vez em quando consegue continuar a escurecer de todo o firmamento, porque o sol, dentro do saco remendado, não pode brilhar, nem mesmo aos pedacinhos.

Esta luta, sem treguas, nunca mais parou!

A's vezes, o sol, com os seus ataques de furia, rebenta todos os dias o seu saco-prisão e, até brilha no céu não só aos pedacinhos — que são as estrêlas, como já perceberam — como também num astro maior e ainda mais poético: a linda lua!

Outras vezes, a noite horrenda consegue os seus fins, tem tais artes de o esconder, que êle fica dentro do saco e pelo céu e pela terra só ela reina, como senhora absoluta, com a sua pretidão e fealdade.

Eis aqui uma fantasia que talvez os tenha divertido, meus queridos amiguinhos. Mas, não passa de fantasia, que também tem o seu lugar nos contos para entreter.

★ Fim ★

«O Sol e a Noite». Conto para crianças, de Virgínia Lopes de Mendonça, datado de 1940, que opõe um branco sereno, "risonho e brilhante" a "uma velha muito preta, muito feia,...beiçola grossa, carapinha desgrenhada, ... de meter medo". A escritora mobilizou todos os lugares-comuns negativos que marcavam os Africanos, opondo o negro retinto ao louro solar, repetindo os estereótipos que os definiam. Suplemento infantil Pim-pam-pum do jornal O Século (05.09.1940), Biblioteca Nacional de Portugal, Lisboa.

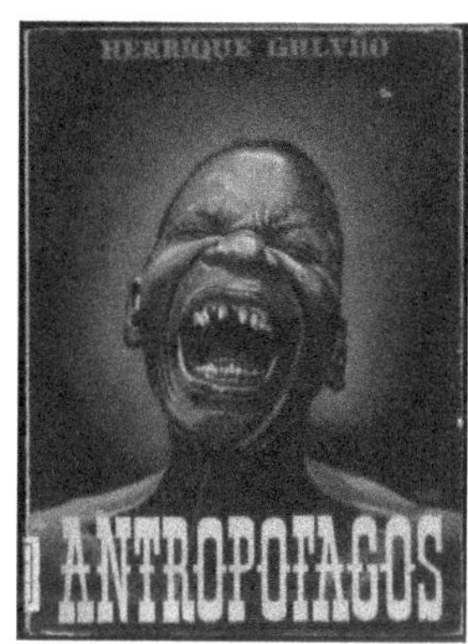

«O Preto-Antropófago»

Histórias para crianças e adolescentes, anedotas para adultos, textos de natureza antropológica, todos se concentram em sublinhar o canibalismo congénito dos Africanos, remetidos assim para a selvajaria mais violenta que impõe a intervenção da missão civilizadora portuguesa.

"O Almoço do Antropófago", banda desenhada inserida em *O Senhor Doutor*, 46, de 27 de Janeiro de 1934

"Aventuras de Valentim", banda desenhada publicada no periódico *O Mosquito* de 3 de Abril de 1946;

"O Preto-Papusse-Papão", poema ilustrado para assustar crianças malcomportadas, de Augusto de Santa-Ritta, *O Mundo dos meus Bonitos: Poemas*, Rio de Janeiro, 1920 (1ª edição)

Capa da obra de Henrique Galvão intitulada *Antropófagos*, datada de 1947. Biblioteca Nacional de Portugal, Lisboa.

RUA
RAINHA
DO CONGO
(FIGURA POPULAR)

RUA
DA PRETA
CONSTANCA
(FIGURA POPULAR DA AJUDA)

RUA
DAS
PRETAS

RUA
DO
POÇO DOS NEGROS

RUA
CIDADE DE BAFATÁ

RUA
DA ILHA
DE SÁO TOMÉ

RUA
CIDADE DE
MALANJE

RUA
DA ILHA
DO PRÍNCIPE

RUA
DE
CABO VERDE

RUA
DE
ANGOLA

**As colónias e as suas independências fixadas
na toponímia portuguesa**

A toponímia portuguesa é bem reveladora do processo
relacional de Portugal com a África e da constante presença
africana no país, dando conta dos espaços do império colonial
português e ainda evidenciando a força da leitura física do
Africano: a sua instalação em cidades, aldeias, sítios e ruas
originou designações, por todo o país, que remetem para
o aspecto físico, em particular a côr e a pele, dos Africanos.
Registem-se três blocos de imagens: figuras africanas, poucas e
quase sempre sem nome, o 'urbanismo colonial' e a renovação
político-ideológica do país pós-1974 que presta homenagem
aos heróis africanos das independências das colónias,
designados de 'terroristas/turras' no passado colonial.
Fotografias: Júlio Marques.

Afro-Portugueses, Afro-Descendentes, Africanos Imigrantes: Vivências, Práticas Sociais e Formas Sincréticas no Portugal Democrático

Se hoje todo o país reconhece a presença de muitos Africanos e descendentes de Africanos, são sobretudo os espaços das periferias urbanas que acolhem os lugares onde se encontram ainda diversos bairros africanos, com uma habitação degradada, pobreza, más condições de vida, onde vivem Africanos-imigrantes, Afro-descendentes, Portugueses de origem e cultura histórica africana, que articulam as práticas europeias com as singularidades culturais africanas, criando formas culturais e sociais inovadoras, resultado de sincretismos e de cruzamentos da África e do Mundo.

Em cima, esquerda: **«Habitante de São Romão»**, uma comunidade inédita em Portugal. «Os Mulatos do Sado» foram revelados por Leite de Vasconcelos nos finais de Oitocentos, princípios de Novecentos, constituem uma população portuguesa de origem africana que continua a ter nos dias de hoje uma história secular obscura, que urge esclarecer. *Boletim de Etnografia*, nº 1, Lisboa, Imprensa Nacional, 1920.

Em cima, direita: Do **Bairro da Cova da Moura** aos novos espaços de habitação: permanências e mudanças. Fotografias: Ricardo Pereira (Batoto Yetu Portugal).

P. 123, em cima: Práticas africanas num bairro de Lisboa, num registo sincrético afro-português: das brincadeiras na rua, às formas sociais e aos bailes cruzando ritmos africanos e formas de dança portuguesas. Fotografias: Joost de Raeymaeker

p. 123, em baixo: O «lugar do encontro», permanece o espaço urbano entre o Rossio e o Largo de São Domingos, em Lisboa. Se a memória antiga da importância social e religiosa deste lugar na vida dos Africanos se perdeu certamente, podemos contudo aceitar que o sítio constitui um símbolo dessa presença secular, transmitida de geração em geração, ao longo de séculos de história. Fotografias: Júlio Marques.

NOTAS

1. Intitulada *Cantigas de Santa Maria*, a obra mandada organizar por Afonso X, o Sábio, rei de Leão e Castela, reúne cantigas em honra da Virgem, entre 1252 e 1284, servindo o texto de suporte a ilustrações executadas em Castela por artistas locais. Madrid, Biblioteca del Escorial. Refira-se uma "Cantiga de Maldizer" do mesmo rei, estudada por Margarido 2003, que é provavelmente a primeira referência a uma Africana "negra como o carvão," retratada com a violência somática que vai perdurar durante séculos no vasto mundo ocidental.

2. As primeiras referências à presença significativa de populações oriundas de África em Portugal, e provavelmente na Europa, pertencem ao cronista Gomes Eanes de Zurara (1453), que descreve a chegada do primeiro grande carregamento, desembarque e partilha de cativos, que se haviam de transformar em escravos. Este acontecimento, que envolveu mais de duzentos homens, mulheres e crianças africanas, registou-se na cidade de Lagos, no sul de Portugal, em 5 de Agosto de 1444, na presença do Infante D. Henrique. O cronista organiza o seu discurso em torno das características somáticas, sublinhando a heterogeneidade física destes Africanos, propondo a primeira hierarquização dos corpos e das raças e definindo uma grelha classificatória que os séculos seguintes irão reforçar (Zurara 1453, 1973).

3. Homens e mulheres africanos, escravos ou forros, asseguravam as tarefas do quotidiano respeitando uma divisão sexual do trabalho que as regras portuguesas definiam com rigor, quer nos campos, quer sobretudo nas cidades.

4. Descrição de Giovanni Battista Venturino, enviado do Papa Pio V à Corte portuguesa em 1571, que vê e relata uma "indústria" de produção de escravos em Vila Viçosa, nas propriedades reais. Biblioteca da Ajuda, Lisboa.

5. Vasconcelos 1915.

6. As práticas religiosas africanas eram consideradas negativamente como atos de feitiçaria ou bruxaria, os seus praticantes sendo perseguidos e duramente punidos. Estas práticas, que suscitavam a adesão e o entusiasmo da população portuguesa, constituíam um espaço de convergência e de complementaridade onde as formas de magia "branca" e "negra" se associavam com harmonia, integrando práticas cristãs.

7. Em 1533, esta Confraria estava em plena atividade no Mosteiro de São Domingos, em Lisboa, dispondo de todas as estruturas indispensáveis ao seu funcionamento normal, os Africanos desempenhando diversos cargos ao lado de "irmãos brancos," pois esta Confraria – contrariamente a muitas outras que excluíam os negros e mestiços – estava aberta a todos aqueles que nela se quisessem integrar.

8. Embora a informação anterior ao século XVII seja escassa sobre as práticas rituais africanas organizadas no quadro das festas religiosas católicas, podemos referir uma interessante descrição de 1633, fornecida por um missionário capuchinho castelhano

que dá conta da africanização de um ritual católico aceite pelas autoridades religiosas portuguesas, a propósito "do modo como os negros lisboetas celebravam o dia de Nª Sª ad Nives [o 5 de Agosto]: . . . os negros vestiam-se à moda da sua terra, muitos nus com faixa da cabeça a um braço ao peito, e pano de cores para esconder o traseiro e assim adornados, andaram e bailaram pelas ruas, alguns ao jeito de África, ao som de castanholas, violas, tambores, flautas e instrumentos africanos. . . . Sempre a cantar e a dançar, entraram na Igreja do Convento de S. Francisco da Cidade e aí desfilaram duas ou três vezes, até que pararam e assistiram à missa. Deixaram então as oferendas e retiraram-se a dançar." Ver: Saunders 1994.

9. Uma rápida leitura da toponímia portuguesa revela a força da presença africana em todo o país, os aspetos somáticos constituindo preferencialmente as referências das designações utilizadas. Em Lisboa, como em outros lugares, a toponímia evoluiu em função das conjunturas, muitas das designações mantendo-se até à atualidade e permitindo proceder à elaboração de uma cartografia rigorosa dos lugares de memória da diáspora africana em Portugal. Ver: Costa 1947.

10. No seu Auto *Frágua de Amor*, Gil Vicente explicita o seu juízo dramatúrgico, pondo em cena um negro que pede ao ferreiro que o torne branco. A operação resulta, mas o africano lamenta-se: a branquização do corpo não alterou a sua fala.

11. Se a dramaturgia portuguesa, em particular a vicentina, fixou a variedade dos falares do português e a riqueza dos seus vocabulários, de onde sobressaía o "português dos negros da Guiné," refira-se também o facto de, multiplicando o recurso a personagens africanas marcadas pelas características somáticas, dar conta da importância assumida pelos Africanos na organização da vida portuguesa.

12. Os preconceitos europeus que até meados do século XX repudiavam, com uma violência reforçada pelos missionários, os objectos de culto africanos, conduziram ao desaparecimento de parte substancial do património religioso e estético dos Africanos em Portugal, como aconteceu nos outros espaços da colonização europeia.

13. Entre as personagens negras, que incluem santos mas também outras figuras religiosas do Catolicismo, como os anjos, presentes nas igrejas portuguesas, multiplicam-se as representações escultóricas setecentistas de São Benedicto de Palermo e Santo António de Noto, venerados desde o século XVI, e ainda Santa Ifigénia e Santo Elesbão, ambos originários da Etiópia, cujo culto terá sido introduzido da Andaluzia no século XVIII.

14. A coroação solene, sob a forma teatral, dos reis do Congo nas igrejas portuguesas, como a de São Domingos em Lisboa, desde o século XVI, era uma cerimónia frequente, levada a cabo pelos confrades africanos da Confraria da Senhora do Rosário dos Homens Pretos, que procediam igualmente à organização de Congadas e de danças do rei do Congo.

15. Este "Bayle dos Negros" é acompanhado por um cântico cujo texto faz frequentes alusões à relação de "vassalagem" dos participantes, designados de súbditos, para com

os seus reis angolanos; canta também a nostalgia da terra longínqua – "a pátria onde nasci" –, sublinhando ainda a ligação com os Portugueses que "pasmam ver que tocam os pretos e as negras bailam." *Breve Extracto do Augustíssimo Triunfo, que a Augusta Braga Prepara em Obséquio do Santíssimo Sacramento* (Coimbra, 1773).

16. A feitiçaria constituía crime de que eram frequentemente acusados e condenados à morte pelo fogo ou ao degredo, pelo Tribunal da Inquisição, homens e mulheres africanos. Este foi o caso de Maria Ortega, solteira, "parda," forra, rica, feiticeira de renome em Lisboa, com clientes portugueses de estatuto elevado, que foi denunciada em 1637 por um rico cliente da Corte e degredada para Angola. Arquivo Nacional da Torre do Tombo, Lisboa.

17. De entre as mais variadas personagens portuguesas destaca-se o poeta setecentista Bocage, que muito contribuíu para estabilizar os estereótipos negativos que pesavam sobre os Africanos.

18. Saa 1948, 155.

19. Sublinhe-se a dificuldade em reconhecer o Outro, porque é negro ou mestiço, como Português, situação que ainda se mantém nos dias de hoje, onde o reconhecimento da cidadania portuguesa aos Portugueses de origem africana ou Afrodescendentes é uma questão não resolvida.

20. Óscar Lopes 2007.

21. Galvão 1947.

22. Ambas as histórias foram contadas pelos próprios a Alfredo Margarido, por volta de 1962.

23. Ver: Pires 1999 e Gusmão 2004.

24. Ver os textos e as diversas perspetivas sobre a CEI, na publicação relativa ao cinquentenário da sua fundação (*Mensagem*, 1997).

25. Mercier 1966, 15.

26. Sobre a questão do "conhecimento português" relativo à África e aos Africanos, ver: Henriques 1997, 40-56.

27. Miguel 1981, 423.

28. Ver: Pires 1999, Gráfico sobre a "Evolução da população estrangeira em situação regular, segundo a origem, 1960-1997," publicado em *Estatísticas Demográficas, Estatísticas e Relatórios Anuais* (Lisboa: Instituto Nacional de Estatística, 1997).

29. Pires 1999, 198-199.

30. Pires 1999, 199-200.

31. Gusmão 2004, 136-137.

32. Desde os anos 1975 e sobretudo 1980, a periferia de Lisboa – que já na década anterior crescera desordenadamente em consequência das migrações internas (do campo para a cidade) – foi progressivamente ocupada por "bairros de lata" ou "barracas"

que acolheram os imigrantes africanos, de início frequentemente organizados por nacionalidade de origem, mas que o tempo acabou por eliminar, mantendo-se apenas alguns núcleos cabo-verdianos. Ver: Gusmão 2004, cap. III.

33. Pires 1999, 199.

34. Ver: Margarido 2000.

REFERÊNCIAS BIBLIOGRÁFICAS

Acciaiuoli, Margarida. 1998. *Exposições do Estado Novo – 1934 – 1940*. Lisboa: Livros Horizonte.

Alexandre, Valentim. 1995."A África no Imaginário Político Português, Séculos XIX-XX." *Penélope* 15: 39-52.

Ameal, João, 1959, *Obreiros do Império*, Direcção-Geral do Ensino Primário, série D, nº5, Lisboa.

Bastide, Roger. 1971. *Anthropologie Appliquée*. Paris: Payot.

Brásio, António. 1944. *Os Pretos em Portugal*. Lisboa: Agência Geral das Colónias.

Costa, Américo. 1929-1949. *Diccionário Corográfico de Portugal Continental e Insular*, 12 vols. Porto: Livraria Civilização.

Devisse, Jean e Michel Mollat. 1979. *L'Image du Noir dans l'Art Occidental*, 2 vols. Paris: Office du Livre.

Ferreira, Vicente. 1946. "Alguns Aspectos da Política Indígena de Angola." *Antologia Colonial Portuguesa* I. Lisboa: Agência Geral das Colónias.

Fonseca, Jorge. 2010. *Escravos e Senhores na Lisboa Quinhentista*. Lisboa: Colibri.

Freyre, Gilberto. 1933. *Casa Grande e Senzala*. Lisboa: Livros do Brasil.

Freyre, Gilberto. 1940. *O Mundo que o Português Criou. Aspectos das Relações Sociais e de Cultura do Brasil com Portugal e as Colónias Portuguesas*. Rio de Janeiro: Livraria José Olympio.

Freyre, Gilberto. 1961. *O Luso e o Trópico*. Lisboa: Comemoração do V Centenário da Morte do Infante D. Henrique.

Freyre, Gilberto. 1963. *O Brasil em Face das Áfricas Negra e Mestiça*. Lisboa: Edição particular de um grupo de Amigos.

Galvão, Henrique. 1947. *Antropófagos*. Lisboa: Editorial Jornal de Notícias.

Gusmão, Neuza M. Mendes. 2004. *Os Filhos da África em Portugal. Antropologia, Multiculturalidade e Educação*. Lisboa: Imprensa de Ciências Sociais.

Henriques, Isabel Castro. 1993. "L'Afrique dans l'Iconographie Coloniale Portugaise." In *Images et Colonies*, edição de P. Blanchard e A. Chatelier. Paris: SYROS/ACHAC – Association pour la connaissance de l'Afrique contemporaine.

Henriques, Isabel Castro. 1997. *Percursos da Modernidade em Angola. Dinâmicas Comerciais e Transformações Sociais no Século XIX*. Lisboa: Instituto de Investigação Científica Tropical e Instituto da Cooperação Portuguesa.

Henriques, Isabel Castro. 1999. "A Sociedade Colonial em África. Ideologias, Hierarquias, Quotidianos." In *História da Expansão Portuguesa*, vol. 5, edição de F. Bethencourt e K. Chaudury, 216-274. Lisboa: Círculo de Leitores.

Henriques, Isabel Castro. 2004. *Os Pilares da Diferença. Relações Portugal-África (Séculos XV-XX)*. Lisboa: Caleidoscópio.

Henriques, Isabel Castro. 2009. *A Herança Africana em Portugal – séculos XV-XX*. Lisboa: Correios de Portugal.

João, Maria Isabel. 2003. *Memória e Império. Comemorações em Portugal 1880-1960*. Lisboa: Ed. Gulbenkian.

Lahon, Didier. 1999. *O Negro no Coração do Império – Uma Memória a Resgatar. Séc. XV-XIX*. Lisboa: Ministério da Educação.

Lahon, Didier e Maria Cristina Neto, eds. 1999. *Os Negros em Portugal – Sécs. XV a XI*. Lisboa: Catálogo da Exposição, Comissão Nacional de Comemorações das Descobertas Portuguesas.

Leal, Cunha. 1961. *O Colonialismo dos Anticolonialistas*. Lisboa: Ed. do Autor.

Lopes, Óscar. 2007. *As Mãos e o Espírito*. Lisboa: Campo das Letras.

Margarido, Alfredo. 1984. *La Vision de l'Autre (Africain et Indien d'Amérique) dans la Renaissance Portugaise*. Paris: Fundação Calouste Gulbenkian.

Margarido, Alfredo. 2000. *A Lusofonia e os Lusófonos. Novos Mitos Portugueses*. Lisboa: Edições Universitárias Lusófonas.

Margarido, Alfredo. 2003. "As Normas Somáticas de Duas Cantigas de Maldizer." *Revista de Humanidades e Tecnologias* 9: 138-142. Lisboa: Edições Universitárias Lusófonas.

Martins, J. P. de Oliveira. 1953. *O Brasil e as Colónias Portuguesas*. Lisboa: Guimarães Editora [1ª edição: 1880].

Matos, Patrícia Ferraz. 2006. *As Cores do Império. Representações Raciais no Império Colonial Português*. Lisboa: Instituto de Ciências Sociais.

Mensagem – Cinquentenário da fundação da Casa dos Estudantes do Império – 1944-1994. 1997. Lisboa: Associação Casa dos Estudantes do Império.

Miguel, Carlos F. Montenegro Sousa. 1981. "Escravatura." In *Dicionário de História de Portugal*, edição de Joel Serrão, 2ª edição, vol. 2. Lisboa: Iniciativas Editoriais.

Monteiro, Armindo. 1933. *Para uma Política Imperial. Alguns Discursos do Ministro das Colónias*. Lisboa: Agência Geral do Ultramar.

Moutinho, Mário. 2000. *O Indígena no Pensamento Colonial Português*. Lisboa: Edições Universitárias Lusófonas.

Nogueira, Franco. 1967. *The Third World*. Londres: Johnson.

Pantoja, Selma. 2011. *Negras em Terras de Brancas: As Africanas na Rede da Inquisição*. Brasília: Ed. Universidade de Brasília.

Pimentel, Maria do Rosário. 1995. *Viagem ao Fundo das Consciências. A Escravatura na Época Moderna*. Lisboa: Colibri.

Pimentel, Maria do Rosário. 2010. *Chão de Sombras – Estudos sobe a Escravatura*. Lisboa: Colibri.

Pinto, A. Costa. 1999. "A Guerra Colonial e o Fim do Império Português." in *História da Expansão Portuguesa*, vol. 5, edição de F. Bethencourt e K. Chaudury, 65-101. Lisboa: Círculo de Leitores.

Pires, R. Pena. 1999. "A Imigração." In *História da Expansão Portuguesa*, vol. 5, edição de F. Bethencourt e K. Chaudury, 197-213. Lisboa: Círculo de Leitores.

Saa, Mário. 1925. *A Invasão dos Judeus*. Porto: Edição do Autor.

Salazar, A. Oliveira. 1957. *A Atmosfera Mundial e os Problemas Nacionais*. Lisboa: Serviço Nacional de Informação.

Salazar, A. Oliveira. 1963. *Temos Também o Dever de Ser Orgulhosos dos Vivos*. Lisboa: Serviço Nacional de Informação.

Santa-Rita, A. 1951. *O Mundo dos meus Bonitos. Poemas*. Lisboa: Livraria Didáctica [1ª edição, 1920, Rio de Janeiro].

Saunders, A. C. C. M. 1994. *História Social dos Escravos e Libertos Negros em Portugal (1441-1555)*. Lisboa: Imprensa Nacional-Casa da Moeda [1ª edição 1982].

Tinhorão, José Ramos. 1988. *Os Negros em Portugal. Uma Presença Silenciosa*. Lisboa: Caminho.

Vasconcelos, J. Leite de. 1915. *De Campolide a Melrose. Relação de uma Viagem de Estudo (Filologia, Etnografia, Arqueologia)*. Lisboa: Imprensa Nacional.

Vasconcelos, J. Leite de. 1942. *Etnografia Portuguesa*, vol. III. Lisboa: Imprensa Nacional.

Vincke, Edouard. 1995. "L'Image du Noir dans les Espaces Publics." In *L'Autre et Nous. "Scènes et Types"*, edição de Pascal Blanchard, Stéphane Blanchoin, Nicolas Bancel, Gilles Boëtsch e Hubert Gerbeau, 253-259. Paris: ACHAC – Association pour la Connaissance de l'Afrique Contemporaine e Syros.

Zurara, Gomes Eanes de. 1973. *Crónica de Guiné (1453)*. Lisboa: Livraria Civilização Editora.

ISABEL CASTRO HENRIQUES nasceu em Lisboa em 1946, tendo-se licenciado em História em 1974, na Universidade de Paris I – Panthéon-Sorbonne. Em 1993, doutorou-se em História de África na mesma universidade francesa, com uma tese consagrada ao estudo da Angola oitocentista, publicada em francês (*Commerce et Changement en Angola au XIXe siècle*, Paris, L'Harmattan, 2 volumes, 1995) e posteriormente em português sob o título *Percursos da Modernidade em Angola. Dinâmicas Comerciais e Transformações Sociais no século XIX*, Lisboa, IICT, 1997. É Professora Associada com Agregação, Aposentada, do Departamento de História da Faculdade de Letras da Universidade de Lisboa, onde introduziu os estudos de História de África em 1974, ensinando História de África, História do Colonialismo Português e História das Relações afro-portuguesas entre 1974 e 2010. Além de participar/dirigir projectos de investigação histórica sobre África, colóquios, exposições, orientou (e orienta) dissertações de mestrado e de doutoramento nestas áreas do conhecimento, continuando a desenvolver a sua pesquisa histórica sobre África e sobre os Africanos no Centro de Estudos sobre África (CEsA) / ISEG-Universidade de Lisboa, onde é investigadora. Algumas das últimas publicações: *A Herança Africana em Portugal (séculos XV-XX)*, Lisboa, CTT- Correios de Portugal, 2009; *Roteiro Histórico de uma Lisboa Africana*, Lisboa, Alto Comissariado para a Imigração (ACM), 2019. Re-edição revista e aumentada, Lisboa, Colibri, 2021; *A Presença Africana em Portugal, uma História Secular. Preconceito, Integração, Reconhecimento (Séculos XV-XX)*, Lisboa, Alto Comissariado para a Imigração (ACM), 2019; *De Escravos a Indígenas. O longo Processo de Instrumentalização dos Africanos (Séculos XV-XX)*, Lisboa, Caleidoscópio, 2019; *A Descolonização da História. Portugal, a África e a desconstrução de mitos historiográficos*, Lisboa, Caleidoscópio, 2020; *A África e o Mundo: circulação, apropriação e cruzamento de conhecimentos, séculos XV-XX"*, Lisboa, Caleidoscópio, 2021; "Os Africanos em Portugal: integração e africanidade (séculos XV-XIX)" e " Modalidades da 'escravatura' no centro-sul de África (séculos XVIII-XIX)", in *História Geral da África da* UNESCO, volume 9, Paris, UNESCO, no prelo.

CLÁUDIA CASTELO

Africanos e afrodescendentes na metrópole portuguesa (século XX): regresso ao "arquivo imperial"

RESUMO: Pouco se sabe sobre os africanos e afrodescendentes que viviam em Portugal no período que medeia entre o fim da escravatura e a independência das colónias portuguesas em África. Nestas notas de pesquisa, apresento um breve balanço da produção científica sobre a presença africana em Portugal em perspetiva histórica, para evidenciar o hiato que subsiste relativamente àquele período. Depois, identifico fontes impressas que podemos mobilizar e caminhos imprevistos no "arquivo imperial" que podemos seguir, para dar visibilidade aos habitantes, naturais e nacionais de origem africana no país e, em particular, em Lisboa. Concluo que uma história social das pessoas negras na metrópole imperial está ainda por fazer e exige criatividade heurística e metodológica, mas poderá também contribuir para desmistificar a homologia equívoca entre africano/negro e imigrante/estrangeiro na sociedade portuguesa.

PALAVRAS-CHAVE: Africanos; afrodescendentes; arquivo imperial; história contemporânea; Portugal.

ABSTRACT: Little is known about Africans and Afro-descendants who lived in Portugal in the period between the end of slavery and the independence of Portuguese colonies in Africa. In this research notes, I present a brief overview of the scholarship on the African presence in Portugal in historical perspective, to highlight the gap that remains in relation to the abovementioned period. Then, I identify printed sources and unforeseen paths on the "imperial archive" to shed light on the inhabitants, naturals and nationals of African origin in the country and, in particular, in Lisbon. I conclude that a social history of Black lives in the imperial metropolis is not yet written and requires heuristic and methodological creativity. It may also contribute to demystify the equivocal homology between African/Black and immigrant/foreigner in Portuguese society.

KEYWORDS: Africans; Afro-descendents; imperial archive; modern history; Portugal.

Introdução

O que sabemos e o que falta saber sobre a história contemporânea dos africanos e afrodescendentes em Portugal?[1] Este texto não dá conta de resultados de uma pesquisa já concluída; assume-se antes como um conjunto de notas exploratórias e programáticas, fruto de algumas perplexidades e de encontros fortuitos no "arquivo imperial."[2] Aponta e discute propostas metodológicas capazes de dar maior visibilidade e inteligibilidade à presença de africanos e afrodescendentes em Portugal, quando o país possuía um império centrado sobretudo em África e havia procedido à ocupação efetiva dos territórios africanos.[3] O que se pretende evidenciar e vir a conhecer melhor são os naturais das colónias portuguesas no continente africano (Angola, Cabo Verde, Guiné "portuguesa," Moçambique e São Tomé e Príncipe) sem ascendência europeia estabelecidos na metrópole; e os seus descendentes que nasceram ou viveram a sua primeira fase de socialização no Portugal metropolitano.[4]

Estas notas de pesquisa visam contribuir para que a breve prazo se venha a colmatar uma ausência, ou melhor, um hiato existente na historiografia: os estudos disponíveis, embora apostados em resgatar uma história silenciada, quase não abordam o período posterior à abolição da escravatura ou fazem-no de forma insuficiente. As dinâmicas africanas no Portugal novecentista, quando aparecem, são quase sempre reduzidas às decorrentes do movimento migratório da descolonização, como se africanos e afrodescendentes tivessem estado ausentes do espaço europeu, reemergindo apenas após 1974/75 e sobretudo nas décadas de 1980 e 1990, período de crescimento e diversificação da imigração africana em Portugal.

O texto está estruturado em três partes. Na primeira parte, procede-se ao levantamento dos principais trabalhos de cariz historiográfico já realizados sobre a presença africana em Portugal e das lacunas que subsistem.[5] De seguida, identificam-se as pesquisas que, embora tenham outros propósitos, nos podem ajudar a mapear os africanos e os afrodescendentes na metrópole imperial no século XX. Por fim, apontam-se fontes primárias e metodologias que podemos mobilizar para inscrever no espaço metropolitano e na história do último império os africanos e os afrodescendentes que habitaram no país e, em particular, em Lisboa. A história destes residentes e naturais foi descurada e ignorada por demasiado tempo, seja por conta do colonialismo e dos preconceitos raciais, pelas "armadilhas" da ideologia do Estado Novo e das categorias coloniais, pela menor dimensão do fenómeno face a épocas anteriores e posteriores, e ainda pela aparente escassez de fontes documentais.

Os estudos sobre a "Londres negra" e a "Paris negra" ou sobre os colonizados no coração do império britânico e do império francês, ao longo do século XX, constituem desde já excelentes referências para se estabelecer um quadro mais abrangente e comparativo sobre os africanos e afrodescendentes nas metrópoles europeias (ver, por exemplo: Blanchard 2012; Gilroy 2007; Goebel 2015; Matera 2015).

1. O Conhecimento Disponível

Durante o Estado Novo, António Brásio, padre da Congregação do Espírito Santo e historiador, debruçou-se sobre a presença secular de negros na então metrópole, num livro publicado pela Agência Geral das Colónias, na Colecção Pelo Império (Brásio 1944). Abordou os traços que deles permaneciam na etnografia, no folclore, na antroponímia e na lenda, bem como as confrarias "para pretos" em Lisboa e na província. O livro veiculava a posição ideológica do autor, comprometido com o regime nacionalista e colonialista e defensor de uma suposta missão evangelizadora e civilizadora dos portugueses.

Já em plena vigência do regime democrático em Portugal, é publicada uma investigação liberta do viés ideológico da anterior, da autoria de José Ramos Tinhorão (1988). O pesquisador brasileiro, especialista em musicologia, inscreveu a "presença silenciosa" dos negros na longa duração, e estudou os seus reflexos no teatro, na literatura de cordel, no fado-canção, no vocabulário e na devoção religiosa. O último capítulo do livro, sobre o "branqueamento dos negros em Portugal," tratava da presença de descendentes de escravos em diversos pontos do sul do país, sobretudo com base nos trabalhos do etnólogo José Leite de Vasconcelos na transição do século XIX para o século XX. O livro, reeditado em 2019, só indiretamente nos traz a dimensão experiencial dos sujeitos africanos na vida social portuguesa (Martins 2019).

No final do século XX, o Ministério da Educação de Portugal publicou um livro do historiador e antropólogo francês Didier Lahon, dedicado à memória da escravidão negra em Portugal entre os séculos XV e XIX (Lahon 1999), e a Comissão Nacional para as Comemorações dos Descobrimentos Portugueses (CNCDP) patrocinou a exposição "Os Negros em Portugal – Sécs. XV-XIX," patente ao público no Mosteiro dos Jerónimos até Janeiro de 2000, cujo catálogo teve coordenação científica de Maria Cristina Neto (investigadora do Centro de Antropobiologia do Instituto de Investigação Científica Tropical, de Lisboa) e Didier Lahon, que também assinaram vários textos. Algumas "Personagens importantes," como o poeta Caetano da Costa Alegre, oriundo de uma família crioula cabo-verdiana e nascido em São Tomé, e o médico mestiço Sousa Martins, foram alvo de apontamentos biográficos (Rodrigues 1999, 217-237). Num e noutro caso, o século XX não foi abordado.

Nos últimos doze anos, Isabel de Castro Henriques tem contribuído de forma consistente e continuada para a divulgação junto do grande público da história da herança africana em Portugal.[6] Depois da publicação do livro *A Herança Africana em Portugal – Séculos XV-XX*, pelos Correios de Portugal (2009), organizou a exposição "Os Africanos em Portugal: História e Memória, Século XV-XXI," realizada na Torre de Belém, acompanhada de catálogo (2011), que também foi apresentada em Coimbra, em 2012, e as brochuras *A Presença Africana em Portugal, uma História Secular: Preconceito, Integração, Reconhecimento (Séculos XV-XX)* (Henriques 2019a) e *Mulheres Africanas: O Discurso das Imagens (Sécs. XV-XX)* (Henriques 2019b), ambas patrocinadas pelo Alto Comissariado para as Migrações, no contexto da Década Internacional de Afrodescendentes. Nestes trabalhos há uma tentativa de alargamento do âmbito cronológico de análise ao período pós-abolição da escravatura no império português. Contudo, a presença africana no Portugal colonial novecentista é sobretudo remetida para o domínio do imaginário, dos modos de ver o "Outro." Aborda-se a desvalorização e a ridicularização dos africanos em diversos *media*, as leis que instituem estatutos diferentes e os registos científicos, a imagem do "preto antropófago," a promoção dos "zoos humanos" nas exposições coloniais ou as representações femininas na publicidade. Fernanda do Valle (pseudónimo literário da escritora e toureira cabo-verdiana Andrêsa do Nascimento) ou Virgínia Quaresma, a primeira jornalista portuguesa, mestiça, natural de Évora (Henriques 2019b, 47) aparecem como percursos singulares. Fica, porém, por conhecer a história social, as experiências de vida, as práticas profissionais, as subjetividades dos africanos e das africanas no coração do império.

Isabel de Castro Henriques é responsável por dois roteiros de percursos e lugares da memória africana na cidade de Lisboa (Henriques e Leite 2013; Henriques 2019c). O seu objetivo é dar "a ver a africanidade de Lisboa, dispersa numa pluralidade de memórias e de vestígios imateriais," mas a presença de residentes africanos e afrodescendentes na cidade, no período da Primeira República e do Estado Novo acaba ficando obscurecida pelas representações (Henriques 2019c, 9). A autora analisa as construções da ideologia e da propaganda nacionalista e colonialista, fazendo-nos olhar para a reorganização imperial do espaço urbano, para os grandes eventos comemorativos (como a Exposição do Mundo

Português e a sua secção colonial), e inadvertidamente desvia-se e desvia-nos da procura dos africanos e dos afrodescendentes, sujeitos e agentes da história, que dia-a-dia – como começa por reconhecer – habitavam e construíam a cidade (Henriques 2019c, 8, 80-85).

A não inscrição das pessoas negras na história do século XX português anterior ao advento da democracia decorre da ideia que, na primeira metade do século, "as populações africanas introduzidas em Portugal através da escravatura desde meados do século XV tinham praticamente desaparecido," salvo um pequeno contingente, onde se destacavam os jovens associados na Casa dos Estudantes do Império (Loude 2005, 11; Peralta e Domingos 2019). Vale a pena reequacionar esta ausência (eventualmente relativa, mas seguramente não absoluta) e olhar para além da imaginação imperial e das suas geografias, até porque Brásio escrevia no ano em que foi fundada a Casa dos Estudantes do Império:

> Embora muito menos avultada do que em tempos idos, a população de cor é ainda hoje bastante numerosa em Portugal. . . .
> São bastante numerosos, presentemente, os indivíduos de raça preta em Lisboa, uns de arribação e outros, os mais deles, nados e criados em Portugal. Quantos? Não nos é possível sabê-lo. Infelizmente o censo de 1940, não curou de raças, omissão tão lamentável como incompreensível, pois já se fazia em pleno século XVI. (Brásio 1944, 120-121)[7]

Num artigo intitulado "O Triunfo da Raça Negra – Como Vivem os Pretos de Lisboa?," publicado em 1931 na ABC: *Revista Portuguesa*, encontram-se alguns dados concretos.[8] No entanto, desconhecendo em que fontes o articulista se baseou, não conseguimos assegurar se as informações que veicula são fidedignas. O artigo, que não está assinado (mas provavelmente é da responsabilidade do editor), faz um elogio das "virtudes e qualidades da raça negra" e reconhece a sua capacidade para "dominar todas as funções sociais que o branco tinha como privilégio" (Anónimo 1931, [14]). Depois procura mostrar como vivia "A colónia africana em Lisboa," que, "segundo uma recente estatística, revela uns cinco mil negros," sendo que a maioria, "mais de dois mil e quinhentos, aproximadamente, está a estudar" (Anónimo 1931, [15]). Além dos estudantes, que frequentavam o ensino superior, mas também os liceus e o ensino particular, o artigo destaca alguns negros ilustres nas respetivas áreas profissionais, como o político José de Magalhães, os jornalistas e escritores João de Castro e Mário Domingues, ou o general Viriato Gomes da Fonseca, diretor do Instituto Geográfico Cadastral.

Não deixa também de mencionar que havia mais de mil operários negros no cais e nas oficinas lisboetas, e ainda *manicures*, datilógrafas, barbeiros, massagistas, criados de restaurantes, cauteleiros e engraxadores. Finalmente, afirma que "Só um por cento da população negra da capital cai no vício e no crime" e, na maioria das vezes, arrastada por brancos (Anónimo 1931, [15]).

2. Reconversão do Ângulo de Análise

Dificilmente conseguiremos apurar com precisão a dimensão quantitativa da presença africana em Portugal ao longo do século XX até 1974, mas há formas de nos aproximarmos da dimensão qualitativa. É possível começar a carrear elementos para uma cartografia do quotidiano, das vivências, das sociabilidades de africanos e afrodescendentes na capital imperial, desde logo em trabalhos elaborados com outros objetivos. Sugiro que se revisitem, por um lado, estudos que focam a emergência do movimento negro em Portugal, nas suas dimensões política e cultural (associações, imprensa, produção jornalística, literatura); por outro, estudos sobre as migrações e os imigrantes africanos em Portugal.

José Castro e José Luís Garcia (1995) estabeleceram o pano de fundo da contestação anticolonial na metrópole, no período republicano. A sua análise centrou-se nas posições anticoloniais veiculadas pelo jornal operário *A Batalha*, em particular os artigos do jovem jornalista afro-português Mário Domingues, na criação do Partido Nacional Africano, na polémica entre este e a Liga Africana, e nas divergências patentes no Congresso Pan-Africano.

Mário Pinto de Andrade (1997), embora interessado em estabelecer uma genealogia do nacionalismo africano, procedeu ao levantamento da imprensa e associações criadas em Lisboa por africanos e afrodescendentes (no livro este conceito não é usado) nas primeiras décadas do século XX. Refere-se, designadamente a: *O Negro: Órgão dos Estudantes Negros*, criado no mesmo ano em que foi criada a Universidade de Lisboa (1911); à primeira organização pan-africana portuguesa, a Junta de Defesa dos Direitos d'África (1912), cujo órgão oficial era *A Voz d'África*; à Liga Africana, fundada em 1920, apoiada pelo *Correio de África*; ao Partido Nacional Africano (1921); e a personalidades como António Rebelo Cabral, João de Castro, José António de Magalhães, Martinho Nobre de Mello ou Ayres do Sacramento Menezes, entre outros.

Pedro Aires Oliveira (2017) examinou a iniciativa de ativistas pan-africanistas em Portugal, muitos deles crioulos ou africanos "assimilados" originários das colónias portuguesas, e as ambiguidades do seu relacionamento com as autoridades coloniais na metrópole no período entre-guerras, concretamente face às crescentes pressões internacionais para que o domínio imperial português fosse mais "esclarecido."

Recentemente, Pedro Varela e José Pereira (2019 e 2020), na senda do trabalho de Mário Pinto de Andrade, mas propondo interpretações distintas, analisaram as origens do movimento negro e da contestação antirracista em Portugal no século XX, focando a geração de 1911-1933, cuja atividade decorreu em associações e jornais de Lisboa e se integrou no movimento pan-africano internacional. Também Cristina Rodão (2019), num artigo de divulgação sobre o movimento feminista negro em Portugal, nos reenvia para o seu surgimento no contexto da Primeira República em Lisboa.

A imprensa do movimento negro ou pan-africano das primeiras décadas do século XX, já analisada para o apuramento das ideias políticas, seja "protonacionalistas," seja mais ou menos abertamente anticoloniais, antirracistas ou feministas, pode também ser um ponto de entrada nas questões sociais e nas vivências urbanas das populações africanas e afrodescendentes.

José Luís Garcia (2012 e 2017) voltou a examinar o percurso singular de Mário Domingues e o seu papel na emergência de um discurso anticolonial e antirracista. A biografia do jornalista e escritor nascido no Príncipe também nos permite refletir sobre a sua história de vida enquanto afrodescendente em Lisboa na primeira metade do século XX. Nascido numa roça, em 1899, filho de um funcionário de uma empresa portuguesa e de uma serviçal de Angola que ali trabalhava como contratada, foi levado para Lisboa com apenas 18 meses. Na capital, foi criado por parentes paternos num ambiente de classe média, sem qualquer contacto com a mãe que, durante anos, julgou morta. O seu romance autobiográfico *O Menino entre Gigantes* (Domingos 1960) é raro e valioso enquanto fonte histórica. Dá-nos conta das vivências e emoções – mormente decorrentes da discriminação racial de que foi alvo e da descoberta da verdade sobre a mãe angolana – experienciadas durante a infância por um mulato na Lisboa africanista dos anos que medeiam entre o *Ultimatum* e a instauração da Primeira República (Grossegesse e Thorau 2009, 25).

O poeta e geógrafo Francisco José Tenreiro, intelectual de "múltiplas faces," "insigne figura da são-tomensidade" (Mata 2010, 9), tem sido estudado sobretudo pela sua obra literária no contexto da emergência das literaturas africanas de língua portuguesa, mas enquadra-se numa situação semelhante à de Mário Domingues e de tantos outros indivíduos, nascidos nas colónias, filhos de pais brancos e mães negras, subtraídos à envolvente materna e enviados para a metrópole para serem criados pelas famílias paternas.[9]

No contexto da guerra colonial, houve vários casos (quantos, falta apurar) de crianças africanas "perfilhadas" por soldados portugueses. Catarina Gomes escreveu um conjunto de reportagens no jornal *Público* (2013-2015) e um livro (2018) sobre os filhos que os militares portugueses tiveram com mulheres africanas e deixaram em África. Falta um estudo sobre os filhos de África, retirados do seu meio, e levados para Portugal. Numa crónica publicada na revista *Permanência*, da Agência Geral do Ultramar, depois de narrar um episódio passado em Dezembro de 1961, em que, perante dois meninos encontrados numa sanzala destruída pelos "bandos de Holden Roberto," dois soldados se ofereceram para "tomar conta deles" e "tratá-los como filhos," o cronista afirma:

> é um episódio entre milhares análogos. Sempre que encontraram – ou encontram – crianças abandonadas, durante as operações em Angola (e estamos certos de que sucede o mesmo em Moçambique e na Guiné) os militares portugueses recolhem-nas, cuidam delas e, em muitas ocasiões, levam-nas para junto das suas famílias, na Metrópole, educam-nas como filhos. Nenhuma que avistem ficará "entregue aos bichos..." (Reed 1971, 20)

Apresentados como ilustração do suposto humanismo português, estes casos envolveram uma grande dose de ambiguidade e de violência explícita e simbólica, e podemos encará-los como tentativas de aliviar a consciência, já que, muitas vezes, os pais, as famílias, as aldeias dessas crianças foram dizimadas pela tropa portuguesa. Este assunto, de enorme melindre ético, foi tratado com mestria literária por António Lobo Antunes, no romance *Até que as Pedras se Tornem mais Leves que a Água* (2017).

Embora o foco não seja a presença dos africanos em Lisboa, os trabalhos sobre a Casa dos Estudantes do Império (1944-1965), associação de enquadramento e assistência aos estudantes oriundos das colónias portuguesas a estudar na metrópole, com sede na Avenida Duque d'Ávila, e com um primeiro lar na Rua Carlos Barreiros, também fornecem elementos que nos podem ajudar a mapear locais e circuitos para uma cartografia social africana em/de Lisboa (nomeadamente, Borges et al. 1995; Sanches 2013; Castelo e Jerónimo 2017). Esse trabalho terá igualmente que ter em conta a presença dos profissionais de origem africana da marinha mercante portuguesa, associados no Clube Marítimo Africano (1955-1961). Esta agremiação desportiva, lúdica e cultural, com sede na Calçada de São Vicente à Graça e depois na Rua Augusto Rosa, junto à Sé Catedral de Lisboa, dispunha de um posto médico e uma escola para a comunidade africana (Rocha 1998; Zau 2005). Por ambas as associações e pelo Centro de Estudos Africanos, reunido na rua Actor Vale, passaram futuros militantes e líderes dos movimentos de libertação das colónias portuguesas.[10] De igual forma, as memórias e as entrevistas de antigos sócios da Casa dos Estudantes do Império e militantes dos movimentos anticoloniais e de libertação africana poderão conter dados úteis sobre a experiência de vida desses indivíduos na metrópole (Chabal 1994; Chissano 2011, entre outros).

Finalmente, uma história dos africanos e afrodescendentes em Lisboa antes da descolonização não poderá ignorar a chegada a Portugal da primeira vaga de migração laboral de Cabo Verde, no final da década de 1960 (Carreira 1977; Lopes Filho 2007; Góis 2008; Machado 2009; Vasconcelos 2012). Fomentada pelos poderes públicos, esta migração respondia a carências de mão-de-obra em diversos setores da economia portuguesa, devido à mobilização dos jovens para a guerra colonial e ao crescimento da emigração para França e Alemanha, a partir de 1963. A maioria dos trabalhadores cabo-verdianos concentrou-se na região metropolitana de Lisboa e trabalhava na construção civil e nas obras públicas (nomeadamente nas obras do metro) no centro do império. Sabe-se pouco sobre estes migrantes, desde logo não se sabe a real dimensão do fenómeno porque, tratando-se de uma migração "interna" (no seio da autoproclamada nação pluricontinental), não havia registo desse movimento (Machado 2009, 135). Uma aproximação através dos dados do censo de 1981 ao número de nacionais dos Países Africanos de Língua Oficial Portuguesa que tinham chegado a Portugal antes de 1974 revela que em 12112 indivíduos, 8055 (47%) eram de Cabo Verde (Pires 2003, 120 e 123). Seria útil proceder ao apuramento, no *Anuário Estatístico do Ultramar*, do movimento de passageiros entre Cabo Verde e Portugal (e vice-versa) nos anos anteriores à independência daquele país africano. Procurando ir além da questão numérica, poderá ser útil consultar: o inquérito promovido em 1972 pela Casa de Cabo Verde junto dos trabalhadores cabo-verdianos residentes em Lisboa e arredores;[11] o arquivo do Centro de Apoio aos Trabalhadores Ultramarinos – CATU, criado "durante a fase de maior carência de mão-de-obre em Portugal" e "encarregado de receber os trabalhadores cabo-verdianos e encaminhá-los para os locais onde a falta de braços se fazia sentir mais" (Lopes Filho 2007, 84);[12] e a imprensa e outros órgãos de comunicação social. Esta última sugestão também resulta do que nos diz João Lopes Filho:

> Eram, então, "desejados," e as suas reuniões dominicais na Praça Luís de Camões e no Jardim da Estrela (a fim de permutarem notícias da terra, ler e escrever cartas e enviar encomendas a familiares e fornecer informações aos patrícios recém-chegados), dado o seu "exotismo" face aos hábitos citadinos, foram tema de desenvolvidas reportagens por parte de vários órgãos da comunicação social. (Lopes Filho 2007, 84)

3. Revisitando o "Arquivo Imperial"

Quando, em 2000, iniciei no Arquivo Histórico Ultramarino (Lisboa, Portugal) a pesquisa para a elaboração do meu projeto de tese de doutoramento sobre a migração de portugueses da metrópole para Angola e Moçambique, comecei por consultar o ficheiro topográfico que existia na sala de referência e leitura daquele arquivo. Nesse ficheiro, constituído por fichas que reproduziam os elementos constantes nas guias de remessa da documentação do Ministério das Colónias/ do Ultramar para o Arquivo Histórico Ultramarino, percebi que poderia dispor de um conjunto de maços com "processos de colonos," "passagens de colonos," mas também "processos de colonos e repatriados" e "passagens de colonos e repatriados" referente grosso modo à primeira metade do século XX.[13] Devido ao meu tema de investigação optei por me focar apenas nos processos de colonos (a parte mais significativa da série documental), deixando para outra ocasião os "repatriados," que também apareciam na documentação de arquivo (embora em muito menor número). Inicialmente pensei que se tratava de portugueses instalados nas colónias que pediam para regressar à metrópole (provavelmente assim seria se estivesse a consultar os arquivos dos governos coloniais). Porém, logo que requisitei o primeiro maço, percebi que eram pessoas naturais das colónias que viviam em Portugal e pediam "passagem de repatriado" para regressar à terra da sua naturalidade, alegando carência de meios para pagar o transporte; eram africanos na sua esmagadora maioria. Foram as suas fotografias, fotos tipo passe apensas aos processos, que o evidenciaram. Mulheres, homens e crianças, negros e mestiços, originários das colónias, habitando no centro do império. Não se tratava dos africanos trazidos para serem exibidos nas exposições coloniais, mas de uma presença quotidiana na metrópole.

A análise daqueles processos em agregado remete-nos para a questão da gestão e controlo dos movimentos populacionais no seio do império colonial português (só em Fevereiro de 1962 seria decretada a livre circulação de pessoas no seio do então criado "espaço económico português").[14] Ajuda-nos a perceber as expectativas e ansiedades estatais relativas à fixação de metropolitanos em África e de africanos na metrópole, sobretudo a preocupação com sinais de pobreza de brancos em África e de africanos na metrópole. Uns e outros tinham de provar ter colocação garantida ou alguém que assegurasse o seu sustento no destino. A gestão (e o controlo) dos fluxos populacionais no império é um tema que merece um estudo específico. Mas aqui quero refletir sobre o contributo desta documentação para uma história social dos africanos em Portugal após a abolição da escravatura e ao longo da primeira metade de novecentos.

Os processos eram instruídos a partir da apresentação de um requerimento dirigido ao ministro das Colónias pelo interessado, por alguém em sua representação (no caso de o requerente ser analfabeto), pela Polícia de Segurança Pública – PSP ou pela polícia política (no caso de ilegais e indigentes), ou pelo governador civil (relativamente a pessoas que se encontravam na cidade sem recursos), acompanhado de duas ou três fotografias, certidão de nascimento, certificado do registo criminal e atestado de pobreza passado pelo regedor da freguesia. Pontualmente eram anexados outros documentos, como atestados de óbito de progenitor do requerente ou cartas. Os processos permitem-nos conhecer os que foram autorizados a embarcar na condição de repatriados (a favor dos quais eram emitidas guias de embarque), os que não foram autorizados a embarcar e os que faltaram ao embarque.

Embora aqueles processos sejam de indivíduos que queriam deixar a metrópole e voltar a África, e enquanto não localizamos outras fontes documentais relativas à presença na metrópole imperial de africanos e descendentes de africanos livres originários das colónias portuguesas, gostaria de argumentar que os processos de repatriados nos ajudam a compor um panorama (parcial, com falhas e imprecisões) de quem eram, como e porquê se encontravam em Portugal, onde moravam, que profissão tinham, que dificuldades enfrentavam. Os processos deixam entrever aspectos demográficos, sociais, económicos e culturais que se prendem com a situação colonial, mas também remetem para o contexto nacional e internacional. Como se percebe, não estamos perante uma ausência no arquivo, mas de uma presença que ainda não mereceu a devida atenção. Desde logo a não existência de uma descrição do âmbito e conteúdo da série documental fornecida pelo AHU compromete a sua apreensão (o leitor apenas tem acesso ao título).

É meu propósito analisar aqueles processos no âmbito da minha participação no projecto AFRO-PORT (Afro-Descendance in Portugal: Sociability,

141

Representations and Sociopolitical and Cultural Dynamics. A Study in the Lisbon Metropolitan Area).[15] De momento, posso afirmar que entre os africanos em Portugal se encontravam naturais de várias colónias, homens e mulheres, solteiros e casados, sem e com filhos, adultos, jovens e crianças, motoristas, criadas de servir, mulheres a dias, trabalhadores manuais, estudantes de diferentes graus de ensino, desempregados, indigentes, indivíduos que chegaram ilegalmente escondidos em navios, indivíduos repatriados dos EUA e de França. A partir de uma amostragem aleatória de processos de repatriados foi possível identificar cinco modalidades de entrada de africanos na metrópole, na primeira metade do século XX. Apresento em baixo exemplos ilustrativos de cada uma delas.

1. Contratados nas colónias por portugueses, como serviçais domésticos, criadas, motoristas (inclui menores contratados para serviços domésticos).

1.1. Joaquim Domingos André, natural de Luanda, descreve-se como "um pobre preto . . . vítima da crise que arrasta por Lisboa uma vida de quase vagabundo, sofrendo todas as inclemências da maior miséria agravada por ser casado e para cúmulo da desdita [ter] uma filha recém-nascida." Em Outubro de 1934, "suplica" passagem gratuita para a terra da sua naturalidade, apenas para si, pois seria "um transtorno" levar naquele momento a família, e porque tem "cá uma alma caridosa que recolhe a mulher," que vai trabalhando "a dias." Vivia na Avenida João Crisóstomo.[16]

1.2. Irene Júlia da Conceição, que havia trazido "na sua companhia, de Angola para a Metrópole, a indígena Cristina de Jesus, de 50 anos de idade provável, natural daquela Colónia, que não deseja aqui continuar," solicita ao ministro das Colónias que "mande conceder passagem à dita indígena," em Janeiro de 1935. A patroa havia depositado o valor da passagem de regresso na Direcção de Serviços de Negócios Indígenas, em Julho de 1932. Não junta a certidão de idade da "indígena" "por não a possuir."[17]

1.3. Maria de Lourdes, de 42 anos, filha de pais incógnitos, natural de Benguela, foi levada com cerca de 12 anos para Portugal por um casal, em casa de quem serviu como criada. Deixou essa casa devido aos maus tratos dos patrões, tendo servido depois noutras casas. Nos últimos tempos não consegue trabalho, nem mesmo "a dias." Pede para ser repatriada em Março de 1940.[18]

1.4. Maria Simões, de 16 anos, natural de Bissau, Guiné, viera em 1945 (com 13 anos) para a metrópole como criada, trazida pela Senhora D. Leopoldina Pontes Hugh, casada com um senhor de nacionalidade alemã. Os patrões separaram-se e a antiga patroa ficou sem meios de continuar com a criada, pois também ela se viu na circunstância de ir servir para se sustentar a si e aos filhos. Neste caso, passagem paga pelo fundo de colonização, porque o vapor da Companhia Nacional de Navegação, em que o Ministério das Colónias tinha direito a cinco passagens gratuitas para Cabo Verde e Guiné, estava em reparação.[19]

2. Menores trazidos pelo pai português/branco ou enviados por este para casa de familiares paternos.

2.1. Filipe Dias Martins, de 26 anos, natural do Chindambo, Lubango (Angola), filho de José Dias Martins e de Mariana, fora levado pelo pai para a Maia, aos 9 anos. O pai regressou pouco depois a África "sem nunca mais se interessar pelo filho, que não voltou a ter notícias dele." "O rapaz é de cor," "vive em precárias condições" e deseja voltar "à terra da sua naturalidade para se juntar a seu pai," segundo informa o delegado policial do Concelho do Porto, em Novembro de 1939.[20]

2.2. Domingos Tavares, 18 anos, do Amboim, "filho de Domingos Faztudo falecido e de Julieta Faztudo, tendo vindo para Portugal para se educar, encontra-se impossibilitado de continuar esta [educação] devido às precárias condições em que se encontra, desde o falecimento de seu pai." Vivia no Porto, mas "Exausto de procurar um emprego cá," a 6 de Novembro de 1934, solicita "a sua repatriação para a terra da sua naturalidade."[21]

3. Jovens que vinham frequentar estabelecimentos de ensino.

3.1 Três irmãos de 17, 14 e 12 anos, naturais de Benguela, Ambriz e Luanda, estudantes num liceu da capital, viviam com o pai, oficial da fazenda da Colónia de Angola, em Lisboa, para onde este tinha vindo para se tratar de uma "grave enfermidade." Este facto remete-nos para a falta de investimento no domínio da saúde nas colónias portuguesas. Com a morte do pai, as crianças ficaram "por caridade" em "casa de umas senhoras que por serem também bastante pobres não [podiam] por mais tempo mantê-los." Daí que a viúva, residente em Luanda, requeria ao ministro das Colónias passagens para os filhos e a enteada como repatriados, em Julho de 1941.[22]

3.2. Vito José de Sousa, estudante, natural de Bolama, faltou ao embarque que lhe tinha sido marcado no vapor Guiné, saído de Lisboa a 16 de Fevereiro de 1937, por motivo de doença. Depois de restabelecido, volta a requerer "passagem de repatriação" no vapor de 23 de Março de 1937, sendo-lhe concedida.[23]

4. Migrantes oriundos de colónias onde não se aplicava o estatuto do indígena (Cabo Verde e São Tomé e Príncipe).

    4.1 Gabriel Jorge Silveira, de 20 anos, solteiro, serralheiro, natural de São Tomé, "veio para o Continente para se empregar, não o tendo conseguido," pediu "alimentação e guarida" na Polícia, que o internou no Albergue da Mendicidade da Mitra. Em Agosto de 1942, o segundo comandante da PSP, de Lisboa, requer passagem gratuita para o referido "indigente."[24]

5. Clandestinos

    5.1 Indivíduo cabo-verdiano, preso nas instalações da Polícia de Vigilância e Defesa do Estado, havia embarcado ilegalmente no porto da cidade da Praia com destino a Lisboa. Aquela polícia pede ao Ministério das Colónias a sua repatriação, em Fevereiro de 1940.[25]

As situações de maus tratos, trabalho infantil, desemprego, e falta de perspetivas na metrópole, mesmo quando se trata de indivíduos com estudos, não podem deixar de ser equacionadas num contexto marcado pela subalternização dos africanos, pelos entraves à sua promoção social e pela discriminação racial. São frequentes os casos de filhos ilegítimos ou de pais incógnitos, o que nos remete para a miscigenação fora de relações legalmente constituídas e para a violência sexual. Está por fazer uma história da miscigenação forçada e das crianças mestiças e negras retirados às mães.

Isabel de Castro Henriques, numa entrevista recente sobre o seu percurso pioneiro na história de África em Portugal, referiu-se à modalidade identificada acima (ponto 1.), ao abordar um episódio da sua vida que a marcou muito como pessoa.

A minha família tinha uma quinta na zona do Ribatejo onde passava sempre, com os meus pais e os meus irmãos, uns largos dias no Verão: a velha cozinheira da casa, a senhora Maria, era negra e conversava comigo. Contou-me que era de Angola e que tinha sido vendida como escrava em São Tomé quando era criança. Como é que era possível que uma pessoa que eu conheci com 10, 12, 14 anos tivesse sido vendida como escrava? Já não havia escravos... A escravatura tinha sido abolida, mas na sua memória persistia esse facto doloroso da infância: tinha sido vendida como escrava. Não sei se de facto foi ou não vendida, mas, para ela, essa era uma situação real. Na altura eu nada sabia nem de história, nem de África, mas hoje penso que ela terá sido levada criança para São Tomé, acompanhando a mãe angolana e serviçal para as roças de cacau, e depois entregue provavelmente a uma família de roceiros portugueses, separada da mãe e acabando por vir parar a Portugal. Bem tratada na quinta como doméstica da altura, nunca perdeu a memória terrível de uma suposta escravização em São Tomé. (Silva e Direito 2019, 223)

Esta memória de infância de Isabel Castro Henriques parece ter escapado ao seu exame crítico enquanto historiadora. O estudo de Inês Brasão (2012) sobre a condição servil em Portugal durante o Estado Novo foi feito com base em entrevistas a antigas criadas. Importa prossegui-lo e alargá-lo, incluindo na análise as criadas trazidas de África e procurando averiguar como se jogou a questão racial na construção social da trabalhadora servil doméstica na metrópole imperial.

Os casos referidos acima fornecem-nos pistas para um alargamento e aprofundamento do trabalho heurístico. Algumas sugestões por onde prosseguir: no fundo da Procuradoria dos Estudantes Ultramarinos (no Arquivo Histórico Ultramarino), no fundo da Junta Nacional da Marinha Mercante (no Arquivo Histórico da Marinha), nos fundos dos Governos Civis (nos Arquivos Distritais e no caso do Arquivo Distrital de Lisboa, na Torre do Tombo), nos arquivos dos estabelecimentos de ensino secundário e superior, do Porto de Lisboa, da PSP, da PVDE/PIDE, em espólios pessoais.

Em articulação com a localização e análise de fontes de arquivo, de carácter institucional e pessoal, da imprensa e da literatura da época, urge mobilizar a metodologia da história oral, mais capaz de nos transportar para o domínio das identidades e das subjetividades. Importa entrevistar os cabo-verdianos e cabo-verdianas que ainda possam dar o seu testemunho pessoal sobre as suas vivências da grande Lisboa nos anos 60-inícios dos anos 70, solicitar-lhes o acesso a fotografias, correspondência e outros documentos de carácter particular que tenham conservado.[26] Para além daqueles depoentes, há um amplo universo de potenciais entrevistados entre naturais de África em Portugal e, tirando partido dos processos de constituição de pós-memória (Hirsch 2008, 103), entre portuguesas e portugueses de origem africana.

Conclusão Provisória

Este texto identifica lacunas que subsistem no nosso conhecimento sobre a história social dos africanos e afrodescendentes no centro do império português e aponta caminhos de pesquisa em duas direções que se podem complementar. Por um lado, propõe uma releitura de trabalhos já realizados com outros enfoques, mas que incluem elementos úteis sobre a presença africana em Portugal, ao longo do século XX. Por outro, sugere que se estude, de forma sistemática e exaustiva, as fontes aqui referenciadas, e se procure ativamente localizar outros vestígios documentais da presença africana contemporânea no país. A pesquisa em fontes escritas deverá ser, sempre que possível, cruzada com fontes visuais e fontes orais. Os historiadores da época contemporânea não devem continuar a passar ao lado desta história. A ocultação das pessoas africanas e afrodescendentes, negras e mestiças, portuguesas (assim autoidentificadas ou não) na metrópole imperial articula-se com a persistência do racismo e da discriminação racial na sociedade portuguesa contemporânea. Cabe aos que se reveem numa prática historiográfica eticamente e civicamente empenhada arranjar maneiras de pensar e escrever uma história com gente africana e afrodescendentes dentro (também do que era o centro metropolitano), na sua pluralidade social e cultural, e desmistificar a homologia equívoca entre africano/negro e imigrante/estrangeiro.

NOTAS

1. A revista *Cadernos de Estudos Africanos* dedicou um número especial aos "Africanos e Afrodescendentes no Portugal Contemporâneo." Aí "as populações naturais ou provenientes de África estabelecidas em Portugal, incluindo os respetivos descendentes," foram sobretudo tratadas do ponto de vista das ciências sociais (Vasconcelos 2012, 16).

2. Como Reid e Paisley (2017), encaro o "arquivo imperial" enquanto recurso e objecto de investigação, onde se joga a relação dinâmica entre produção do conhecimento, processos de registo (envolvendo inscrição e esquecimento) e poder colonial.

3. Em Angola, na Guiné e em Moçambique, só depois de concluídas as campanhas militares de ocupação, iniciadas na década de 1890, foi possível proceder à implementação efetiva da administração portuguesa em toda a extensão dos territórios. Reportamo-nos, portanto, ao período do século XX até 1974-75 (aquando das independências das colónias portuguesas em África).

4. No período colonial, as categorias usadas eram sobretudo raciais ou relativas ao estatuto jurídico das populações colonizadas (indígena e assimilado), refletindo o próprio estatuto as políticas de diferença racial. A Organização das Nações Unidas, que estabeleceu 2011 como o Ano Internacional de Povos Afrodescendentes e proclamou depois a Década Internacional de Afrodescendentes (2015-2024), não explicita o papel do colonialismo moderno na construção desta categoria. Nela engloba os povos de ascendência africana que vivem fora do continente africano, "Seja como descendentes das vítimas do tráfico transatlântico de escravos ou como migrantes mais recentemente . . . Todos eles

são, com frequência, vítimas de discriminação perante a justiça, enfrentam alarmantes índices de violência policial e discriminação racial" (ONU, "Década Internacional de Afro-descendentes," *Contexto*. Disponível em: http://decada-afro-onu.org/background.shtml).

5. Não farei referência aos trabalhos exclusivamente sobre escravos e/ou libertos negros em Portugal na época moderna.

6. Sobre o percurso académico desta historiadora portuguesa e o seu contributo para a história de África, veja-se a entrevista concedida a Silva e Direito, 2019.

7. A população negra de Lisboa na época moderna era cerca de 10% da população total. A inexistência de informação sobre origem étnico-racial é uma constante nos censos gerais da população portuguesa e tem sido muito debatida nos últimos anos, após uma reco-mendação da ONU para o apuramento censitário da diversidade étnica (nomeadamente, Martins). No recenseamento geral da população de 1940 e 1950, dispomos apenas do total de portugueses naturais das colónias portuguesas com residência habitual em Portugal. Eram 5487 (sendo 2448 homens) e 8361 (sendo 3873 homens), respetivamente, os naturais das colónias portuguesas residentes na capital, em 1940 e 1950 (Portugal, Instituto Nacio-nal de Estatística 1945, 49; e Portugal, Instituto Nacional de Estatística 1952, 567). Estas cifras, além de nada nos dizerem sobre os afrodescendentes (já nascidos na metrópole), agregam os naturais de todas as colónias portuguesas e de qualquer origem étnica.

8. Foi Rodão (2019) que nos alertou para este artigo. Refira-se que a *ABC foi fundada por Mimon Anahory e Rocha Martins; Herculano Pereira assegurava o cargo de diretor substituto e Carlos Ferrão era o editor.*

9. Nalguns casos, de relações mistas assumidas, as mães acompanharam os filhos, enviados para estudar na metrópole, dada a escassez de liceus e escolas técnicas nas colónias e a ausência de ensino superior até muito tarde (em Angola e Moçambique, os Estudos Gerais Universitários só seriam criados em 1962).

10. Sobre as elites fundadoras dos movimentos de libertação africanos (MPLA, PAIGC e FRELIMO) que se formaram no centro metropolitano (Mateus 1999).

11. Maria Margarida Mascarenhas, "A Mão-de-Obra Cabo-Verdiana," *Presença Crioula* 3 (Março 1973), cit. in Lopes Filho 2007, 57-58.

12. Segundo Monteiro (1995, 87), o CATU foi criado por despacho conjunto dos titula-res do Ministério do Ultramar e do Ministério das Corporações e entregue ao Secretariado Nacional da Emigração (SNE). Há cerca de 20 anos, o Arquivo do SNE estava à guarda do centro de documentação da Direção-Geral dos Assuntos Consulares e das Comunidades Portuguesas. Recentemente contactei essa Direção-Geral para saber se podia consultar a documentação produzida pelo CATU. Fui, então, informada de que o arquivo da SNE tinha sido integrado no Arquivo Histórico-Diplomático (AHD). No Arquivo Histórico Ultra-marino (AHU), entre a documentação da Repartição de Povoamento e Assuntos Demo-gráficos, da Direcção-Geral de Economia, do Ministério do Ultramar, encontram-se

documentos produzidos pelo Núcleo de Apoio aos Trabalhadores Migrantes Cabo-verdianos, serviço destinado a enquadrar estes migrantes, e que antecedeu a criação do CATU.

13. Processos produzidos pelo Ministério dos Negócios da Marinha e Ultramar e, a partir de 1911, pelo Ministério das Colónias, especificamente pela Direção-Geral de Administração Política e Civil. A concessão de passagens de colonos foi regulada inicialmente pelo decreto de 27.11.1907.

14. Decreto n.º 44171, *Diário do Governo*, n.º 22/1962, Série I, 1.2.1962.

15. Projecto financiado pela Fundação para a Ciência e a Tecnologia, de Portugal, coordenado por Iolanda Évora, do CEsA, ISEG, Universidade de Lisboa, e co-coordenado por Inocência Mata, Centro de Estudos Comparatistas, Faculdade de Letras, Universidade de Lisboa.

16. AHU, MU, DGAPC, RNPAC, cx. 4.

17. AHU, MU, DGAPC, RNPAC, cx. 4.

18. AHU, MU, DGAPC, RNPAC, cx. 1, 2.

19. AHU, MU, DGAPC, RNPAC, cx. 5.

20. AHU, MU, DGAPC, RNPAC, cx. 4.

21. AHU, MU, DGAPC, RNPAC, cx. 4.

22. AHU, MU, DGAPC, RNPAC, cx. 23, 1.

23. AHU, MU, DGAPC, RNPAC, cx. 23, 1.

24. AHU, MU, DGAPC, RNPAC, cx. 23, 1.

25. AHU, MU, DGAPC, RNPAC, cx. 4. No Arquivo Histórico da Marinha há documentação relativa à presença de passageiros clandestinos de origem africana nos navios que faziam a ligação entre os territórios coloniais e Portugal. Informação prestada à autora pela historiadora Yvette dos Santos, email, 18 de Março de 2021.

26. Este trabalho de registo de histórias de vida começou a ser feito no âmbito do já referido projeto de investigação AFRO-PORT.

FONTES MANUSCRITAS

Arquivo Histórico Ultramarino

Ministério das Colónias, Direcção-Geral de Administração Política e Civil, Repartição de Negócios Políticos e Administração Civil, Processos de passagens de colonos e repatriados.

Ministério do Ultramar, Direcção-Geral de Economia, Repartição de Povoamento e Assuntos Demográficos, Núcleo de Apoio aos Trabalhadores Migrantes Cabo-Verdianos.

REFERÊNCIAS BIBLIOGRÁFICAS

Andrade, Mário Pinto de. 1997. *Origens do Nacionalismo Africano: Continuidade e Ruptura nos Movimentos Unitários Emergentes da Luta contra a Dominação Colonial Portuguesa 1911-1961.* Lisboa: Dom Quixote.

Anónimo. 1931. "O Triunfo da Raça Negra – Como Vivem os Pretos de Lisboa?" *ABC: Revista Portuguesa* 551 (5 de Março): 14-15.

Antunes, António Lobo. 2017. *Até que as Pedras se Tornem mais Leves que a Água.* Lisboa: Dom Quixote.

Batalha, Luís. 2004. *The Cape Verdean Diaspora in Portugal: Colonial Subjects in a Postcolonial World.* Lanham: Lexington Books.

Blanchard, Pascal, dir. 2012. *La France Noire: Présence et Migrations des Afriques, des Amériques et de l'OCÉAN Indien en France.* Paris: La Découverte.

Borges, Pedro, Aida Freudenthal, e Tomás Medeiros, org. 1995. *Mensagem: Número Especial do Cinquentenário da Casa dos Estudantes do Império.* Lisboa: ACEI.

Brasão, Inês. 2012. *O Tempo das Criadas: a Condição Servil em Portugal (1940-1970).* Lisboa: Tinta-da-China.

Brásio, António. 1944. *Os Pretos em Portugal.* Lisboa: Agência Geral das Colónias.

Carreira, António. 1977. *Migrações nas Ilhas de Cabo Verde.* Lisboa: Universidade Nova de Lisboa.

Castelo, Cláudia, e Miguel Bandeira Jerónimo, org. 2017. *Casa dos Estudantes do Império: Dinâmicas Coloniais, Conexões Transnacionais.* Lisboa: Edições 70.

Castro, José, e José Luís Garcia. 1995. "'A Batalha' e a Questão Colonial." *Ler História* 27-28: 125-146.

Chabal, Patrick. 1994. *Vozes Moçambicanas.* Lisboa: Vega.

Chissano, Joaquim. 2011. *Vidas, Lugares e Tempos.* Alfragide: Texto.

Domingos, Mário. 1960. *Menino entre Gigantes.* Lisboa: Prelo.

Garcia, José Luís. 2012. "Um Mulato contra o Império Português. Descobrir Mário Domingues no Século XXI." In *Estado, Regimes e Revoluções: Estudos em Homenagem a Manuel de Lucena,* editado por Carlos Gaspar, Fátima Patriarca, e Luís Salgado de Matos, 457-483. Lisboa: Imprensa de Ciências Sociais.

Garcia, José Luís. 2017. "The First Stirrings of Anti-Colonial Discourse in the Portuguese Press." In *Media and the Portuguese Empire*, editado por José Luís Garcia, Chandrika Kaul, Filipa Subtil, e Alexandra Santos, 125-143. Cham: Palgrave Macmillan.

Gilroy, Paul. 2007. *Black Britain: A Photographic History*. Londres: Saqi.

Goebel, Michael. 2015. *Anti-Imperial Metropolis: Interwar Paris and the Seeds of Third-World Nationalism*. Nova Iorque: Cambridge University Press.

Góis, Pedro, org. 2008. *Comunidade(s) Cabo-Verdiana(s): As Múltiplas Faces da Imigração Cabo-Verdiana*. Lisboa: ACIDI.

Gomes, Catarina. 2018. *Furriel Não É Nome de Pai. Os Filhos que os Militares Portugueses Deixaram na Guerra Colonial*. Lisboa: Tinta-da-China.

Grossegesse, Orlando, e Henry Thorau, org. 2009. À Procura da Lisboa Africana: Da Encenação do Império Ultramarino às Realidades Suburbanas. [Braga]: Universidade do Minho. Centro de Estudos Humanísticos.

Henriques, Isabel Castro. 2009. *A Herança Africana em Portugal*. Lisboa: Clube do Coleccionador dos Correios.

Henriques, Isabel de Castro. 2011. *Os Africanos em Portugal: História e Memória, Séc. XV-XXI*. Lisboa: Comité Português Projecto UNESCO Rota dos Escravos.

Henriques, Isabel de Castro. 2019a. *A PresençA Africana em Portugal, uma História Secular: Preconceito, IntegraçÃo, Reconhecimento (Séculos XV-XX)*. Lisboa: Alto Comissariado para as Migrações.

Henriques, Isabel de Castro. 2019b. *Mulheres Africanas: O Discurso das Imagens (Sécs. XV-XX)*. Lisboa: Alto Comissariado para as Migrações.

Henriques, Isabel de Castro. 2019c. *Roteiro Histórico de uma Lisboa Africana, Séculos XV-XXI*. Lisboa: Alto Comissariado para as Migrações.

Henriques, Isabel Castro, e Pedro Pereira Leite. 2013. Lisboa, Cidade Africana: Percursos e Lugares de Memória da Presença Africana, Séculos XV-XXI. Lisboa/Ilha de Moçambique: Marca d'Água – Publicações e Projetos.

Hirsch, Marianne. 2008. "The Generation of Postmemory." Poetics Today 29 (1): 103-128.

Lahon, Didier. 1999. O Negro no Coração do Império. Uma Memória a Resgatar: Séculos XV a XIX. Lisboa: Ministério da Educação.

Lopes, Alexandra. 2017. "Invisible Man: Sketches for a Portrait of Mário Domingues, Intellectual and (Pseudo)Translator." In *Authorizing Translation*, editado por Michelle Woods, 61-79. Londres e Nova Iorque: Routledge.

Lopes Filho, João. 2007. Imigrantes em Terra de Emigrantes. CV: Instituto da Biblioteca Nacional e do Livro.

Loude, Jean-Yves. 2005. *Lisboa, na Cidade Negra*. Lisboa: Dom Quixote.

Machado, Fernando Luís. 2009. "Quarenta Anos de Imigração Africana: Um Balanço." *Ler História* 56: 135-165.

Martins, Bruno Sena. 2019. "Os Negros em Portugal." *Buala*, 26 de Maio. Disponível em: https://www.buala.org/pt/a-ler/os-negros-em-portugal

Mata, Inocência, org. 2010. *Francisco José Tenreiro: As Múltiplas Faces de um Intelectual.* Lisboa: Colibri.

Matara, Marc. 2015. *Black London: The Imperial Metropolis and Decolonization in the Twentieth Century.* Oakland: University of California Press.

Mateus, Dalila Cabrita. 1999. *A Luta pela Independência: A Formação das Elites Fundadoras da FRELIMO, MPLA e PAIGC.* Lisboa: Editorial Inquérito.

Mateus, Dalila Cabrita. 2006. *Memórias do Colonialismo e da Guerra.* Lisboa: Edições Asa.

Monteiro, Vladimir Nobre. 1995. *Portugal Crioulo.* Lisboa: Instituto da Cultura e da Língua.

Oliveira, Jorge Eduardo da Costa. 1993. *A Economia de São Tomé e Príncipe.* Lisboa: IICT e ICE.

Oliveira, Pedro Aires. 2017. "Portugal's Empire in the Wake of WWI: Coping with the Challenges of Pan-Africanism and the League of Nations." *E-Journal of Portuguese History* 15 (1): 129-152.

Peralta, Elsa, e Nuno Domingos. 2019. "Lisbon: Reading the (Post-)Colonial City from the Nineteenth to the Twenty-First Century." *Urban History* 46 (2): 246-265.

Pires, Rui Pena. 2003. Migrações e Integração: Teoria e Aplicações à Sociedade Portuguesa. Oeiras: Celta Editora.

Portugal. Instituto Nacional de Estatística. 1945. *VIII Recenseamento Geral da População no Continente e Ilhas Adjacentes em 12 de Dezembro de 1940. Volume XII – Distrito de Lisboa.* Lisboa: Soc. Tipográfica.

Portugal. Instituto Nacional de Estatística. 1952. *IX Recenseamento Geral da População no Continente e Ilhas Adjacentes em 15 de Dezembro de 1950. Tomo I – População residente e presente.* Lisboa: Tipografia Portuguesa.

Reed, Robert. 1971. "Os 'Meninos Lobos' e os Meninos Salvos." *Permanência: Revista mensal de actualidades ultramarinas* 2 (14): 20-22.

Reid, Kirsty, and Fiona Paisley, eds. 2017. *Sources and Methods in Histories of Colonialism Approaching the Imperial Archive.* Abingdon: Routledge.

Rocha, Edmundo. 1998. *O Clube Marítimo Africano: A sua Contribuição para a Luta pela Independência Nacional dos Países sob Domínio Colonial Português, 1955-1961.* Lisboa: Biblioteca Museu República e Resistência.

Rodrigues, Ana Maria, coord. geral. 1999. *Os Negros em Portugal, Séc. XV a XIX.* Lisboa: CNCDP.

Roldão, Cristina. 2019. "Feminismo Negro em Portugal: Falta Contar-nos." *Público*, 18 de Janeiro. Disponível em: https://www.publico.pt/2019/01/18/culturaipsilon/noticia/feminismo-negro-portugal-falta-contarnos-1857501

Sanches, Manuela Ribeiro. 2013. "Lisboa, Capital do Império. Trânsitos, Afiliações, Transnacionalismos." In *Cidades e Império Dinâmicas Coloniais e Reconfigurações Pós-Coloniais,* editado por Elsa Peralta e Nuno Domingos, 279-318. Lisboa: Edições 70.

Silva, Elisa Lopes da Silva e Bárbara Direito. 2019. "As Histórias da História de África. Entrevista a Isabel de Castro Henriques." *Práticas da História* 8: 221-257.

Tinhorão, José Ramos. 1988. *Os Negros em Portugal: Uma Presença Silenciosa*. 1.ª edição. Lisboa: Caminho.

Varela, Pedro, e José Pereira. 2019. "As Origens do Movimento Negro e da Luta Antirracista em Portugal no Século XX: A Geração de 1911-1933." *Buala*, 8 de Janeiro. Disponível em: https://www.buala.org/pt/mukanda/as-origens-do-movimento-negro-e-da-luta-antirracista-em-portugal-no-seculo-xx-a-geracao-de-1

Varela, Pedro, e José Pereira. 2020. "As Origens do Movimento Negro em Portugal (1911-1933): Uma Geração Pan-Africanista e Antirracista." *Revista de História* 179: 1-36.

Vasconcelos, João. 2012. "Africanos e Afrodescendentes no Portugal Contemporâneo: Redefinindo Práticas, Projetos e Identidades." *Cadernos de Estudos Africanos* 24: 15-23.

Zau, Filipe. 2005. *Marítimos Africanos e um Clube com História*. Lisboa: Universitária Editora.

CLÁUDIA CASTELO é atualmente investigadora contratada no Centro de Estudos Sociais da Universidade de Coimbra e membro do projecto AFRO-PORT. Doutorada em Ciências Sociais (Universidade de Lisboa), tem-se dedicado à história da circulação de pessoas, ideias e conhecimento científico no império colonial português nos séculos XIX e XX.

PAULINO OLIVEIRA DO CANTO

The Relationship Between the Formation of Cabo Verdean Society and Upper Guinea

ABSTRACT: The historical narratives in the context of colonial exploitation generally seek to show that the (re)configuration of national identities—and consequently the formation of societies in the region formerly called Upper Guinea—has resulted from sociocultural interactions of different ethnic groups that are characterized by their fluidity and, at the same time, ambiguity of belonging. This article uses a sociohistorical approach to understand narratives of the role of the institutionalization of slavery in the process of the formation of Cabo Verdean society, highlighting sociocultural, political, and economic influences in its relationship with Upper Guinea. The article also critically explores the historical factors or milestones of, perhaps, a colonial "modernity" of Upper Guinea, which effectively succeeded in pursuing its own expansion project of imperialism and institutionalization of slavery in other parts of the world, particularly in the Atlantic and in the "Americas." In this sense, the main research question becomes: How was the institutionalization of slavery in Cabo Verde and its relationship with the Upper Guinea triggered for the configuration of Cabo Verdean society? After a systematic analysis of the available data, the results show that the configuration of Cabo Verdean society, marked by its specific identity, resulted from slavery and, of course, from resistance to it, and from a common history, correlated by sociocultural and linguistic phenomena and processes of this region.

KEYWORDS: Sociohistorical approach; institutionalization of Slavery; Upper Guinea; formation of Cabo Verdean society.

RESUMO: As narrativas históricas existentes no contexto da exploração colonial procuram geralmente mostrar que a (re)configuração das identidades nacionais e - consequentemente a formação das sociedades na região, outrora designada de Alta Guiné - resultaram das interações socioculturais de diferentes grupos étnicos caraterizados pela sua fluidez e, ao mesmo tempo, ambiguidade de pertença. O estudo emprega uma abordagem sócio-histórica para compreender as narrativas do papel da institucionalização da escravidão no processo da formação da sociedade cabo-verdiana, destacando as influências socioculturais, políticas e económicas na sua relação com a Alta Guiné. O estudo também explora criticamente os fatores ou marcos históricos de, quiçá, uma "modernidade" colonial a partir da Alta Guiné que, efetivamente conseguiu imprimir um projeto próprio de expansão do imperialismo e institucionalização da escravidão nas outras partes do mundo, em particular no Atlântico e nas "Américas". Neste sentido, procura-se questionar como a institucionalização da escravatura em Cabo Verde e a sua relação com a Alta Guiné despoletou-se numa identidade própria para a configuração da sociedade cabo-verdiana? Após uma análise sistemática dos dados disponíveis, os resultados mostram que a configuração da formação da sociedade cabo-verdiana marcada pela sua especificidade identitária resultou graças à escravatura e naturalmente à sua resistência, de uma história comum correlacionada por fenómenos e processos socioculturais e linguísticos desta região.

PALAVRAS-CHAVE: colonização, institucionalização da escravidão, Alta Guiné e a formação da sociedade cabo-verdiana.

Introduction

Understanding the formation of Creole society from the institutionalization of slavery is a pertinent topic in African studies. The formation of Cabo Verdean society is closely related to the process of the institutionalization of slavery in the Upper Guinea region where the Portuguese slave trade occurred, and this trade played an important role in increasing cycles of violence and political instability. This process had already begun with the expansion of the Mandinka, which is considered one of the first steps toward establishing the inseparable link between creolization and slavery. The continuities between intra-regional long-distance slave trade routes contributed significantly to the large-scale political and social changes that culminated in the formation of Cabo Verdean Creole society (Green 2012).

The article aims, therefore, to understand how the institutionalization of slavery in Cabo Verde and its relationship with Upper Guinea was triggered, shaping the identity of Cabo Verdean society. Consequently, this document raises the following research question: Are ECOWAS (Economic Community of West African States) member countries opposed to the migration of people from other member states? To explore this issue, the article uses a sociohistorical analysis to understand the narratives of the role of the institutionalization of slavery in the process of the formation of Cabo Verdean society, highlighting sociocultural, political, and economic influences in its relationship with Upper Guinea through a qualitative methodology and a comprehensive case study.

Brief Overview of the Role of the Institutionalization of Slavery in Upper Guinea

In the fifteenth century, the Portuguese arrived in the region of Senegambia, which at the time included the Senegal and Gambia river basins, and this gave great geopolitical importance to Europe. The Senegambia then became a point of entry and axis of economic and political domination, which would later have a strong influence on the (re)definition of the slave trade policy on the African Coast (Silvério 2013).

The history of Cabo Verde's relationship with Upper Guinea falls within the context of Portuguese colonial exploration. The Portuguese primarily managed trade from the islands, the interregional trade of the region from the Southern rivers to Gambia and the diverting of trade to the Atlantic, and the trade of Sudan and Senegambia, which was traditionally directed to the north by the Saharan route (Silvério 2013). Besides the commercialization of products such as gold, ivory, hides, spices, slaves, wax, iron, and leather, which were diverted to the trade in the Atlantic, the settling of the Portuguese on the Cabo Verde islands allowed slaves to be brought there from the African Coast in order to develop a plantation economy based on sugar, salt, cotton, and indigo fabrics (Carreira 2000).

The cycle of exploration and the diverting of trade to the Atlantic strengthened the Portuguese crown's economy, but it also weakened the economic dynamics of the region. Consequently, after the sixteenth century, profound social, economic, and, above all, political changes had, on the one hand, resulted in the collapse of the Jolof confederation and, on the other hand, favored the strengthening of the power of Kabuu to control the entire territory between the Gambia River and the Futa-Djalon. In addition, the Bijagos started to play an important role in the slave trade between the Gambia and Senegal Rivers (Lopes 2003; Silvério 2013).

However, the Portuguese monopoly would begin to decline in the seventeenth century with the successive arrival of the Dutch, British, and French (Rodney 1965; Carreira 2000). Other European powers invaded the region and through the slave trade they heightened the political, economic, and social crisis in the region known as Upper Guinea of Cabo Verde.

Theoretical Framework and Research Methodology

The theoretical framework guiding this article is based on a sociohistorical approach. The focus is on the relationship between the formation of Cabo Verdean society and the Upper Guinea region of West Africa. The approach adopted is essential to analyze the relationship between the configuration of Cabo Verdean and Guinean societies in the context of colonial exploration. The study shows that the formation of Cabo Verdean society is marked by its specific Creole identity (re)produced from the narratives of institutionalized slavery in the region.

Although economic motives were the principal factor for the expansion of colonization in the African countries belonging to Upper Guinea, the complexity of factors present in their evolution and the resistance and variety of operational fields of trade or slave trade involved sociocultural and political interactions and other forms of sociability in a mobility network that later resulted in the formation of Creole society in Cabo Verde. Hence, the factors and mutual influences that led to the formation of Creole society were correlated to geography and history (Teye et al. 2015).

Although the idea of a metropolis was of colonial interest, the evolution of this context tended to widen other ties that allowed the strengthening of the (re) negotiation of cultural identities through exogenous and endogenous factors (Diallo 2016).

The concept of identity in general is quite problematic. However, in this article, cultural identity is understood to refer to the result of a set of sociocultural, political, and economic factors tied to slavery to a shared history with the region of Upper Guinea (Hall 2003). It should be noted that although Western nations have exercised cultural hegemony over colonized Africans, there are neo-imperial spheres which have also been influenced by the colonized, that is, "modern nations are all cultural hybrids" (Hall 2003, 62). Therefore, Cabo Verdean society and Creole identity emerged in the context of institutionalized slavery, marked by the strong cultural interaction that took place in the Upper Guinea region. Thanks to a set of sociocultural representations, (re)produced by different peoples as an effect of resistance and political friction, structures of social organization were built, linked to the action and conception of the Creole being (Hall 2003).

This work is defined by the qualitative methodology supported systematically by the documentary analysis necessary to understand the main factors intrinsic to the Portuguese slave trade in the Upper Guinea region, which later resulted in the formation of Cabo Verdean society. The study employs a comprehensive analysis approach, critically exploring the historical factors or milestones of, perhaps, a colonial "modernity" from Upper Guinea that effectively succeeded in establishing a project of imperial expansion and institutionalization of slavery in other parts of the world, in particular in the Atlantic and the "Americas."

The main method used to collect secondary data was the analysis of documents, books, and academic journals that discussed in some way the institutionalization of slavery in the context of Portuguese colonization in the Upper Guinea region, with a focus on the formation of Cabo Verdean society as a result of its relationship with Upper Guinea.

The Formation of Cabo Verdean Society and the Relationship with Upper Guinea

In the context of European maritime expansion, especially that of the Portuguese, Cabo Verde, due to its strategic position, was "founded" in the fifteenth century, but was colonized only after an arduous process of the institutionalization of slavery. This process was potentially favored by the depopulated setting in which these islands were found. This factor, which is seen as having significantly enabled the establishment of Portuguese sovereignty, helped the development of a mercantile class under the unstable political situation of the kingdoms of the coast and rivers of Guinea or Upper Guinea (Horta 2002; Ribeiro 2011).

Ribeira Grande de Santiago played a fundamental role in this process because it was endowed with a port with sheltered areas where ships could anchor. It was there that colonization began. The first settlers were attracted by favorable conditions, such as the proximity to land where the foundations for the development of profitable agriculture would be laid (Carreira 2000). Over time, the village of Ribeira Grande grew considerably, and in 1533 it was upgraded to the status of a city and became the seat of the first bishopric of Africa (Rodney 1965; Carreira 2000).

This situation was relevant for the development of Cabo Verde's relationship with Upper Guinea. This relationship was further strengthened in 1466 with the signing of the "Letter of Privileges" by the crown, which granted the residents of Santiago the right to practice the slave trade in all regions of the so-called Coast of Guinea (that extended from the Senegal river to Sierra Leone), with the exception of the Arguim trading post, which was reserved for the crown (Carreira 2000; Jesus 2010; Ribeiro 2011).

The signing of the "Letter of Privileges" of 1466 allowed many slaves and merchants to come to the island of Santiago, which helped contribute to the increase in population, especially in the coastal areas. Within this framework of greater flexibility for the movement of people, goods, and services, there were free Blacks, namely *banhuns*, *cassangas*, and *brâmes*, who, because they spoke Portuguese, accompanied the merchants, mercenaries, and captains of ships and who would also become Christianized (Rodney 1965; Jesus 2010).

Likewise, the presence of *reinóis*—gentlemen who came from Portugal to assume administative positions in the colonies and to invest in the construction of ships for trade with the Coast of Guinea—contributed to the expansion of the administration and its occupation of the interior of the Santiago island. This kind of expansion also contributed to the occupation of the other islands, such as the island of Fogo, and enabled a diversification of the economy, including the breeding of horse and the cultivation of cotton—the most coveted commodity of trade on the Guinea Coast along with cloth made in Santiago (Carreira 2000).

In this sense, the law of 1466, which, however, was restricted in 1472, is understood as marking the beginning of the (re)configuration of the national identity, as well as favoring a change in the organization of Cabo Verde society, since the inhabitants felt obliged to pursue effective settlement on the islands and to strengthen productive activities through the exploitation of land (Carreira 2000; Pereira 2006).

The context inherent to the commercialization of slaves reinforced Cabo Verde's relations with Upper Guinea, as did the decision of the Portuguese crown to expel from Cabo Verde anyone who tried to operate outside of its control (Lopes 2003). Moreover, since the environment was unfavorable to the slave trade and the interests of the first elites that emerged in Cabo Verde diverged from those of the crown, which restricted the trade with the African Coast,[1] many Cabo Verdeans in general began to (e)migrate to other places within the region of Upper Guinea. This, consequently, led to a decrease in the number of white people, specifically Europeans, on the Cabo Verde Islands, which contributed to a change in the structure of Cabo Verdean society. This can be seen, for example, in the fact that mestiços began to hold public offices (Cabral 2000; Cabral 2012; Carreira 2000).

In addition, successive droughts and famines on the archipelago caused the emigration of some royal administrators, including Crioulos and Europeans who no longer had sufficient resources to maintain their servants/slaves and, as a result, had to migrate to the West African Coast, namely, to Cachéu and Guinala (Carreira 2000). This was because migration/mobility provided an interaction between networks that transformed ideological structures and structural conceptualizations into forms of organization (Green 2011; Horta 2014).

In fact, migration played an essential role in the reconfiguration of national identities and in the formation of societies, by promoting the transfer of ideals or forms of organization of social entities not only to the African coast, but also to the Americas and Europe (Grenn 2011; Horta 2014). In this sense, we highlight the privileged position the island. of Ribeira Grande de Santiago in internal and external economic activities that connected the African, American, and European continents, known as triangular trade, which allowed it to play a important role in Cabo Verde's identity formation and society-building.

Therefore, the relationships built were not restricted to economic ties (by the area of commerce connected to the archipelago and its "head" island, Santiago), which was all inseparable from the familial and personal ties that established the connection between the islands and the coast; but it also included political ties (by the jurisdiction that the representatives of the crown had on the islands) and religious ties (by the area of influence of the episcopal power) (Horta 2002; Pereira 2006).

The relationship with the African coast, which was initially connected more to the economic interests of the metropolis, was nevertheless acquiring a socio-cultural dimension, with the formation of its own identity and specific lifestyles. As a result of miscegenation,[2] the geostrategic and economic interests of the metropolis, and the forms of resistance, the modus operandi and modus vivendi of the African slaves from a number of diferente areas, the distinct Creole Cabo Verdean identity was born.

The limitation of the commercialization of various products, guaranteed by the charter "limiting the privileges of the residents of Santiago" in 1472, to the African coast led to the formation of an intermediate mercantile class that played an important role in shaping the formation of the first Cabo Verdean elite called "White, Honorable and Powerful Men" (Cabral 2012, 1; Carreira 2000).

The contours of the institutionalization of slavery that served the Atlantic contributed to the (re)construction of the infrastructures leading to the formation of Cabo Verdean society. In the wake of these changes, Cabo Verdean identity gained a new dimension, along with new ideological and cultural influences. It is important to note that it was thanks to the resistance to social, cultural, political, and economic changes in Upper Guinea that the the internal social dynamics on Cabo Verde were transformed. With its inhabitants opposing the oppressive action of the Portuguese crown, the settlement of the archipelago gained its own dynamics for the construction of Cabo Verdean society (Carreira 2000).

This is why the early modern histories of the Atlantic and the West African Coast cannot be studied in isolation from one another. The different contexts of Cabo Verde's relationship with Upper Guinea have shaped to some extent the very project of the institutionalization of slavery and, consequently, "the initial phase of the colonial period in Cabo Verde of the 16th century as the reference point for what would follow" (Green 2011, 232). In any case, the interests of the emerging Creole society prevailed, bringing a new order to the world that had formed on both sides of the Atlantic.

Therefore, these new cultural, economic, and geographical spaces of the Atlantic were fundamental to help transform existing ideologies and structures into something new (Green 2011). Barros refers to this new development as "colonial modernity," which consists of the transformation of men (i.e., slaves) into a marketable product, and then, through the process of *laidinização*, they became more highly valued and were taken to the Americas, Brazil, Spain, and the West Indies/Antilles (Carreira 2000; Green 2011). For Barros, it is important to question the universality of the theory of modernity, if, after all, it had begun in the Americas in 1492 or with the institutionalization of slaves in Ribeira Grande of Santiago between 1461 and 1462 with the process of Portuguese colonization in Cabo Verde (Barros 2017).

Generally, the scholarship of Atlantic history does not seem to be aware that "the Atlantic world has begun in West Africa" (Green 2012, 69). Specifically, there is a need for deconstruction, that is, a new perspective on the beginning of the Atlantic world in the phase before Spanish expeditions to America. Even though "neither Africans nor Europeans saw this world as being revolutionarily new … effectively elements of continuity enabled the first steps towards the creation of a mixed society to be taken on the coast of West Africa" (Green 2012, 70).

It turns out that the role of slavery, or its institutionalization and mutual influence on trade in the region, has been vital to the development of the Atlantic and of European, American, and African societies. The pre-existing political formation on the African continent per se constitutes extremely relevant data for understanding the influences that played a role in the design of the new Atlantic trade (Green 2012).

Slavery in this sense is a product of colonization, and it exerted an influence both on the functioning of the colonized, in this case Africans, and on the colonizer. In other words, it is a deeply interdependent relationship that has significantly influenced the formation of Creole society and the way it was structured. One cannot deny, much less hide, the Black-African influences on Caboe Verdean culture. There were many different ethnicities that participated in this process. The identity configuration and formation of Cabo Verdean society results from slavery and, of course, resistance (Carreira 2000).

The (De)Construction of Historical Narratives on Slavery

The structure of scholarly knowledge necessarily passes through the process of the (de)construction of historical narratives. Reflecting on the formation of Cabo Verdean society and its relationship with Upper Guinea requires, at a minimum, a questioning of the (re)production of the history of this society and, of course, of the Upper Guinea region. In the context of colonization, in which the European continent appears as the holder of power and knowledge, it becomes imperative to "distrust" scholarly history itself.

The debate around the history of Cabo Verde itself is important and relevant to questioning the power of science in the context of colonization and the effect that the production of the history of a certain reality had and has in the extension of the relations between the ex-colonized and former colonizer. The official documents point to the "discovery" of Cabo Verde by the Portuguese. However, historians have consistently questioned this "discovery," and prefer a hypothesis of "finding." This is because Cabo Verdean history is significantly limited by official written documents and has been given little importance because of its oral tradition.

Certain scholars, such as Carreira (2000), have shown that the Black Jolofs had already set foot on the island of Santiago and defend the thesis that Cabo Verde had been "discovered" by Black Africans who were possibly escaping from the persecution of the Falupos when storm currents or strong winds pushed their vessels to this island's shore. According to Carreira:

In any case, although the old documentation presents the islands as deserted at the arrival of the discoverers, it should not at all be excluded that Santiago was a refuge for a small group of shipwrecked Jolofs or other inhabitants of Cabo Verde (Lêbus or Sèrère, etc.), before the arrival of the Portuguese. But this would have occurred by purely accidental circumstances with no deliberate purpose or continuity of settlement—they had no living conditions, no other contacts[3] (Carreira 2000, 297, my trans.)

Therefore, this hypothesis can only be accepted if, at some point, the Black Jolofs landed on the islands by accidental causes. Because the islands lacked conditions for survival, and without other types of contacts, it would be impossible for them (Jolofs, Lebus, Sèrères or others) to have developed the process of organized settlement before the arrival of the Portuguese (Carreira 2000).

Another important factor for the (de)construction of historical narratives is the way in which Eurocentric readings of slavery make reference to historical milestones from Europe. It is understood that, in fact, "modernity" in colonial times may have its beginning in Africa, more concretely in Cabo Verde, between 1461 and 1462, with the process of *laidinização* of slaves from Ribeira Grande de Santiago—much earlier than beginning in 1492 in the Americas, which has been the conventional historical reference point (Varela 2017). For "there is not enough reason to assume that modernization, an addition of Western society, is only an 'original' variant of the West" (Højbjerg et al. 2012, 3). Therefore, it is still necessary to work hard to deconstruct academic thought, not least because "the first slave societies of the Atlantic world existed in the African Atlantic, and not in the Caribbean or in the Americas" (Green 2011, 228).

Cabo Verdean identity was formed in a process of miscegenation, the result of physical and symbolic violence that was an inherent part of this process, involving the region in a cycle of internal instabilities driven by the exploitation and trade of slaves and other goods used in commercial exchange on the coast of the Upper Guinea region (Anjos 2003; Green 2011). The lack of official records does not allow for full knowledge of the ethnic origins of slaves who came from the African coast since they were treated as commercial products. However, it is thought that the majority of the slaves came from Guinea from a plurality of ethnic identities, such as Pepel, Manjacos, Mancanha, Beafada, and Balanta (Højbjerg et al. 2012). In other words, they came from the area formerly known as the Upper Guinea Coast, which stretched from the southern Senegal River to the Orange River, to the northern border of Sierra Leone. They came from several ethnicities such as Banhus, Cassangas, Jabundos, Manjacos, Felupes, Ariantas, Balantas, Papéis, Naluns, Bijagós, and Burames (Rodney 1965; Carreira 2000; Green 2011 and Silva 2014).

In this sense, perhaps the history itself needs studies that demonstrate the controversy of slavery's influences in Africa, that is to say, from the great works made by the hands of slaves, from the linguistic and ideological influences that circulated through migration and that were carried by the Europeans themselves, in addition to the large numbers of slaves who moved to Europe as well as to the Americas for several reasons: "the importance of these early slave societies and the early transatlantic slave trade was underestimated by historians" (Green 2011, 228).

Another striking event was the treaty of Guinea, signed on October 24, 1512, which stipulated that all slaves from Guinea territory should be taken directly to Lisbon and settled in Portugal (Carreira 2000). These events show that slaves were traded to Europe and to America, notably the "Creoles and Creolities in the region who have played and still play an important role in building the postcolonial nation on different continents because they symbolize modernity, civilization and education—all of which are conceptually linked to the construction of national identity and the configuration of society itself in this region" (Højbjerg et al. 2012, 17).

Likewise, there is a certain tendency toward the universalization of perspectives on African culture and, in this case, Creole culture as a process of assimilation with predominantly European elements of analysis. In fact, the nomenclature "Africa" is a European product (Varela 2017). However, the mutual influences demonstrate the reflected historical ambiguity.

Although several of the studies cited in this article focus (Anjos 2003; Cabral 2012; Carreira, 2000) on the reflections on institutional analytical aspects inherited or imported from the metropolis, we believe it is essential to highlight some elements in order to complement this analysis, focusing on African sociocultural aspects present in Cabo Verdean daily life: in gastronomy, we emphasize Kachupa, a typical Cabo Verdean dish that uses corn and that is also prepared in Guinea-Bissau; in music, we emphasize Tabanca, which resisted the harsh repressive measures exercised by the slave regime and which is currently celebrated in the capital of the country, constituting an element of national immaterial patrimony. Tabanca is also a cultural event celebrated in Cabo Verde where it arrived with the first Black people from Guinea. Likewise, Batuque has a strong presence, especially on Santiago Island. In addition, the Creole language itself, which is spoken by almost all the regions that were part of Upper Guinea (Senegal, Guinea Bissau, Sierra Leone, and Cabo Verde), is the most pervasive element inherited from slavery.

In addition, in daily practices, there is the custom of women carrying children on their back. Moreover, there is a rich oral tradition, embodied in myths, stories, riddles, and proverbs, which were brought by the slaves who were came from the coast of Africa. Therefore, "Cabo Verde was the first place in the Atlantic where slavery adopted an exclusively racial character, with all the slaves of Saharan Africa" (Green 2012, 227 apud Silva 2014, 265).

Final Considerations

This article has argued that the (re)configuration of national identity and the formation of Cabo Verdean society emerged in a context of permanent (re)negotiation between the Portuguese crown and the colonized societies, among which we highlight the relationship between Cabo Verde and the Upper Guinea Coast and also with other continents, namely America and Europe. These relations implied matrices of diverse economic and political relations and new social orders whose influence was crucial in the formation of Cabo Verdean identity and society.

In the context of the slave trade, which enabled both the passage and the permanence of African slaves, a number of important heritages have endured and these should not be reduced to insignificant phenotypic aspects. Nevertheless, despite all forms of violence resulting from the practice of slavery, which for centuries entailed the subjugation of African cultural values by the colonial powers, there is a set of sociocultural traits that reveals its distant African origin, especially from the so-called Upper Guinea of Cabo Verde. They are cultural manifestations that have significantly influenced Creole identity and the construction of Cabo Verdean society.

Therefore, Cabo Verdean national identity is formed in a context of sociocultural diversities built in the Upper Guinea Coast region and which over time asserted itself through the Creole language, as one of the greatest "heritages" of the slavery process. It is a heterogeneous process, in which power relations remain present to this day.

NOTES

1. The restrictions stated that they could only bring slaves to work on the islands but not sell them and they could only trade goods produced on the islands. These restrictions were motivated, in part, by the successive damages caused to the Portuguese Crown due to disobedience in relation to the area demarcated by free trade and the competition they had with the Crown at the African coast (Pereira 2006).

2. Understood in this article as a result of "physical and symbolic violence that destroyed a large part of the ethnic memory of the enslaved", but which, in the reading of most Cabo Verdeans, restricts to the simplistic idea of a "cultural fusion of Europeans and Africans" (Anjos 2003, 581).

3. See the original quote: "em qualquer caso, embora a documentação antiga apresente as ilhas como desertas à chegada dos descobridores, não se deve excluir de todo, a hipótese de, Santiago, ter sido refúgio de um pequeno grupo de náufragos Jalofos ou outros habitantes do Cabo Verde (Lêbus ou Sèrère, etc.), antes da chegada dos portugueses. Mas, isso ter-se-ia dado, por circunstâncias puramente acidentais, sem propósito deliberado, nem continuidade de povoamento - não tinham condições de vida, sem outros contatos" (Carreira 2000, 297).

WORKS CITED

Anjos, José Carlos Gomes dos. 2003. "Elites intelectuais e a conformação da identidade nacional em Cabo Verde." *Estudos Afro-Asiáticos* 3, 2003: 579-96.

Cabral, Iva Maria. 2012. "Origem e evolução da elite cabo-verdiana: terras, gentes e mestiçagens." *Portal do Conhecimento*. 23 March 2012. https://core.ac.uk/display/38680205/.

Cabral, Iva Maria. 2000. "Dos povoadores aos 'filhos da terra': a dinâmica da sociedade cabo-verdiana." *Studia* 56-57: 279-300.

Carreira, António. 2000. *Formação e extinção de uma sociedade escravocrata (1460-1878)*. 3rd ed. Praia: IPC.

Diallo, Mamadou Alpha. 2016. "A integração regional na África ocidental (1960-2015): Balanço e Perspectivas." *Revista brasileira de estudos africanos* 1, no. 1: 243-263.

Horta, José Silva da. 2008. "'O nosso Guiné': representações luso-Africanas do espaço guineense (sécs. XVI-XVII)." *Actas do Congresso Internacional Espaço Atlântico de Antigo Regime: poderes e sociedades*. Instituto Camões. http://cvc.instituto-camoes.pt/eaar/coloquio/comunicacoes/jose_silva_horta.pdf.

Horta, José Silva da. 2014. "Trânsito de africanos: Circulação de pessoas, de saberes e experiências religiosas entre os rios de Guiné e o arquipélago de Cabo Verde (séculos XV-XVII)." *Porto Alegre: Anos 90* 21, no. 40: 23-49.

Hall, Stuart. 2003. *A identidade cultural na pós-modernidade*. Rio de Janeiro: DP&A Editora.

Højbjerg, Christian, et al. 2012. "National, Ethnic, and Creole Identities in Contemporary Upper Guinea Coast Societies." *Max Planck Institute for Social Anthropology Working Papers* 135:1-30.

Jesus, Nilton Jorge Mendes. 2010. "Impacto socioeconómico da abolição da escravatura na sociedade cabo-verdiana." Graduation diss., Universidade de Cabo Verde.

Lopes, Carlos. 2003. "Construção da identidade nos rios da Guiné do Cabo Verde." *Africa studia* 6: 45-64.

Green, Toby. 2011. "Building Slavery in the Atlantic World: Atlantic Connections and the Changing Institution of Slavery in Cabo Verde, Fifteenth–Sixteenth Centuries." *Slavery & Abolition: A Journal of Slave and Post-Slave Studies* 32, no. 2: 227-45.

Green, Toby. 2012. *African Studies: The Rise of the Trans-Atlantic Slave Trade in Western Africa, 1300-1589*. Cambridge: Cambridge University Press.

Pereira, Camilo Eduardo Adilson. 2006. *"Os caminhos da revolta em Cabo Verde e a cultura da resistência: as Revoltas dos Engenhos (1822) e de Achada Falcão (1841)"*. Master Diss., Universidade de São Paulo.

Ribeiro, Francisco A. Carvalho. 2011. "Cabo Verde e 'os Rios da Guiné' na formação do mundo Atlântico, sécs. XV-XVI." *Anais do XXVI Simpósio Nacional de História*. July 2011. http://www.snh2011.anpuh.org/resources/anais/14/1300678108_ARQUIVO_TextoAnpuh-FranciscoAimara.pdf.

Rodney, Walter. 1965. "Portuguese Attempts at Monopoly on the Upper Guinea Coast, 1580-1650. " *Journal of African History* 6, no. 3: 307-22.

Silva, Daniel B. Domingues da. 2014. "África: um continente crioulo?" *Afro-Ásia* 50: 263-67.

Silvério, Valter Roberto, ed. 2013. *Síntese da coleção história geral da África: século XVI ao século XX*. UNESCO / MEC / UFSCar, 65-93.

Teye, Joseph Kofi, Mariama Awumbila, and Yaw Benneh. 2015. "Intraregional Migration in the ECOWAS Region: Trends and Emerging Challenges." Edited by Ablam Benjamin Akoutou, Sohn Rike, and Yeboah Daniel. *WAI-ZEI Paper* 23: 103-30.

Varela, Odair Barros. 2017. "África: o berço da 'modernidade.' Por uma visão pós-colonial da modernidade e do território." Edited by Andreia Moassab and Berthet Marina. *Cidades e globalização*. São Paulo: Casa das Áfricas (in press).

PAULINO OLIVEIRA DO CANTO holds a Master's Degree in African Regional Integration and a Bachelor's Degree in Social Science (Political Science) from the University of Cabo Verde. He is a researcher and consultant for the project "Recognize and Change" (EuropeAid CSO-LA/2017/388-053), supported by the European Union with partnership the Praia City Council, and a Land Monitor / Analyst for the ECOWAR platform—ECOWAS Early Warning and Prevention System. He is currently a researcher at the Center for Research and Training in Gender and Family (CIGEF) at the University of Cabo Verde and project coordinator at the Cape Verdean Institute for Gender Equality and Equity (ICIEG).

III. Identidades afro-diaspóricas: entre a herança colonial e a afirmação identitária

LIA VAINER SCHUCMAN

O Branco e a Branquitude: Letramento Racial e Formas de Desconstrução do Racismo[1]

RESUMO: O objetivo deste artigo é compreender e analisar como a ideia de raça e os significados acerca da branquitude são apropriados e construídos por sujeitos brancos, e principalmente focar-se na análise sobre possíveis formas de desconstrução do racismo nas identidades raciais brancas, o que tem sido designado no Brasil como Branquitude. A branquitude é entendida aqui como uma construção sócio-histórica produzida pela ideia falaciosa de superioridade racial branca, e que resulta, nas sociedades estruturadas pelo racismo, em uma posição em que os sujeitos identificados como brancos adquirem privilégios simbólicos e materiais em relação aos não brancos. A pesquisa de campo foi desenvolvida por meio da realização de entrevistas e conversas informais com sujeitos que se auto-identificaram como brancos de diferentes classes sociais, idade e sexo. As análises demonstraram que há, por parte destes sujeitos, a insistência em discursos biológicos e culturais hierárquicos do branco sobre outras construções racializadas, e, portanto, o racismo ainda faz parte de um dos traços unificadores da identidade racial branca paulistana. Percebemos também que os significados construídos sobre a branquitude exercem poder sobre o próprio grupo de indivíduos brancos, marcando diferenças e hierarquias internas. Assim, a branquitude é deslocada dentro das diferenças de origem, regionalidade, gênero, fenótipo e classe, o que demonstra que a categoria "branco" é uma questão internamente controversa e que alguns tipos de branquitude são marcadores de hierarquias da própria categoria. E ainda compreendemos que há, por parte de alguns sujeitos, um distanciamento entre a brancura da pele e o poder da branquitude, abrindo espaço para possíveis formas de desconstrução do racismo nas identidades raciais brancas.

PALAVRAS-CHAVE: Branquitude, Racismo, Antirracismo, Psicologia Social.

ABTRACT: The goal of this paper is to understand and analyze how the ideas of race and whiteness are constructed and given meaning by white inhabitants in the city of São Paulo. Whiteness is understood as a socio-historical construction produced by the deceptive notion of white racial supremacy. In societies that are structured by racism,

171

whiteness generates a situation in which individuals that are identified as white are given symbolic and material privilege in relation to those individuals considered not white. Field research was conducted through interviews and informal conversation with individuals from diverse social classes, ages and genders that self-identified as white. Our aim was to understand the heterogeneous character of whiteness in São Paulo. Analyses demonstrated that, for these individuals, biological and hierarchical cultural discourses remain as explanation to racial differences, and racism is still a structural element of the paulistano white racial identity. We also noticed that the social meaning that derives from the notion of whiteness operates in white individuals, indicating internal hierarchical differences. Whiteness is therefore dislocated and relocated in relation to social origin and class, regional, gender and phenotypical differences, which demonstrates that the category "white" is internally controversial, and that some kinds of whiteness are indicative of hierarchical power within it. And we also understand that for some individuals there is a distinction between the whiteness of their skin and the power of whiteness in itself, which opens up possibilities of deconstructing racism in the realm of white racial identities.

KEYWORDS: Whiteness, Racism, Anti-racism, Social Psychology.

---

1. Branquitude

O objetivo deste artigo é discutir como a ideia de raça construída ao longo do século XIX ainda é apropriada e estabelece sentidos e significados na produção de identidades raciais brancas na contemporaneidade brasileira. Este olhar sobre a categoria racial branca nos estudos de relações raciais se insere no que foi chamado nos Estados Unidos de estudos críticos sobre a branquitude (*critical whiteness studies*). Partindo do pressuposto que a categoria "raça" é necessariamente relacional, os estudos da branquitude[2] passam também a estudar e colocar o branco em questão, retirando, assim, o negro do foco problemático no qual recaem os estudos sobre as desigualdades de raça. A lógica aqui segue duas formulações: a primeira é desviar o olhar das identidades consideradas de margem e voltá-lo para a autoconstrução do centro com o intuito de observar, revelar e denunciar também o seu conteúdo, que tem sido privado de uma análise crítica. Concentrar-se apenas nos grupos minoritários contribui para a ideia de norma dos grupos hegemônicos, ou seja, olhar apenas para o negro[3] nos estudos de relações raciais ajuda a contribuir para a ideia de um branco em que a identidade racial é a norma. A segunda formulação se prende com pensar que, se podemos admitir a problemática pós-colonial para os negros, é porque estamos todos inseridos em uma sociedade pós-colonial, logo não podemos localizar apenas um estrato da sociedade nesta posição. Assim, se os negros são pós-coloniais, os brancos também o são. E se o são, de que forma? Como constroem suas identidades racializadas? São estas perguntas a que procuro responder neste artigo.

Neste sentido, este trabalho situa-se dentro do campo de estudos pós-coloniais sobre branquitude, que têm como objetivo central colocar o branco em questão com a perspectiva de compreender como o racismo sustenta as construções identitárias de sujeitos considerados socialmente brancos. Entendemos, neste estudo, que a branquitude se caracteriza nas sociedades que foram estruturadas pelo colonialismo como lugar de privilégios materiais e simbólicos. Ruth Frankenberg (2004) aponta que a branquitude é produto da história e é uma categoria relacional. Como outras localizações raciais, não tem significado intrínseco, mas apenas significados socialmente construídos. Nessas condições, os significados da branquitude têm camadas complexas e variam localmente; contudo, são construções baseadas na ideia falaciosa de "superioridade branca."

Outra consideração fundamental para se pensar a branquitude é que esta identidade racial no Brasil, para além de criar uma divisão externa entre brancos, negros e indígenas, tem fronteiras e distinções internas que hierarquizam os brancos através de outros marcadores sociais, como classe social, gênero, origem, regionalidade e fenótipo.

Aqui é relevante compreender o conceito de identidade não como semelhança entre sujeitos, mas sim como um processo histórico aberto e inacabado que se caracteriza pela unificação de histórias, projetos e significados comuns, construídos socialmente e compartilhados em contraposição a outros grupos (Maheirie 2002). Assim, ao falar em identidade racial branca – branquitude – entendemos que ela se constrói a partir de movimentos dialéticos que articulam semelhanças e diferenças, permanência e transformação, raízes e opções (Santos 1995). Sob esta ótica, o conceito se apropria da noção de diferença e o incorpora na sua interioridade: identidade é semelhança e diferença ao mesmo tempo. Ou seja, ela se constrói como semelhante em oposição à diferença de outros grupos.

Estes estudos sobre branquitude se formaram como um campo de estudo transnacional e de intercâmbio entre ex-colônias e colonizadores: isto corresponde à cadeia de fatos históricos que começou com o projeto moderno de colonização. Este desencadeou a escravidão, o tráfico de africanos para o Novo Mundo, a colonização, as formações e construções de novas nações e nacionalidades em toda a América e a colonização da África. Portanto, é nestes processos históricos que a branquitude se construiu como posição ideológica de poder em que os brancos tomam sua identidade racial como norma e padrão, e, dessa forma, outros grupos aparecem, ora como margem, ora como desviantes, ora como inferiores. Neste sentido, é importante pensar que as culturas nacionais e as identidades brancas e não brancas têm sido historicamente criadas, recriadas, significadas e redefinidas através das trocas circulares de símbolos, ideias e populações entre a África, a Europa e as Américas. Assim, este campo de estudo também aparece como trocas de pesquisas e ideias entre estes continentes.

A investigação que deu origem a este artigo parte de minha pesquisa de doutorado (Schucman 2014) e se deu a partir de entrevistas[4] realizadas com pessoas de variadas classes sociais, idade e sexo, sendo que os diferentes sujeitos se auto-identificaram como brancos. A partir das falas transcritas, procuramos compreender como o significado de raça se inscreve no corpo, através das representações que os sujeitos têm sobre ele e, a partir disso, sobre si próprios como brancos e sobre *os outros*. Assim, nas análises que fiz, procurei compreender como estes privilégios são apropriados, legitimados e construídos pelos sujeitos brancos em um cenário urbano específico, a cidade de São Paulo. O enfoque se deu, portanto, na compreensão daquilo que define "quem somos nós" e "quem são os outros," o que nos permite construir, ainda, as fronteiras externas entre brancos e não brancos.

2. A Geografia da Raça

O primeiro elemento demarcador apontado por mim como parte do que caracteriza as divisões entre "nós brancos" e "outros não brancos" em São Paulo são os marcadores espaciais simbolizados como "lugar de branco," que estão associados diretamente a bairros, ambientes e lugares onde se acumula riqueza. Esses lugares simbolizam, também, a ideia de progresso paulista. Mostram que a construção da branquitude e da identidade paulistana associada à ideia de civilização, progresso, e riqueza – anunciada na estrofe "São Paulo engrandece a nossa terra," da música *Aquarela do Brasil* –, entrecruzam-se e constroem-se mutuamente.

Neste sentido, é preciso entender que a branquitude se objetifica e materializa em um espaço e localização, como podemos ver nas falas abaixo:

Sabe, ontem eu fui na sala São Paulo, tinha um espetáculo lindo, mas fiquei surpresa com o tipo de pessoas que estavam lá. Antigamente só tinha gente bonita, europeus, gente fina mesmo. Agora dá todo o tipo de gente (fala de uma conhecida em um almoço).
Só por curiosidade, o que é todo tipo de gente? (Lia)
Ah, gente sem classe, brasileiros em geral, essa mistura.

Esta fala de uma conhecida me fez pensar que há, na cidade de São Paulo, lugares que são marcados e representados como espaços onde brancos circulam, e que, caso não brancos venham a circular neles, é como se estes tivessem fora do lugar, pois são locais que demarcam espacialmente os brancos. Fernanda e Vanessa deixam isto ainda mais explícito quando descrevem áreas nobres da cidade:

Ah, por exemplo, quando eu ando na Oscar Freire, na Paulista, no Itaim eu acho estranho quando vejo um negro, a não ser quando ele está trabalhando, porque para mim é lugar de branco, é difícil mesmo ver um negro que não seja zelador, ou empregado (Fernanda).

Eu sou representante de venda nos bairros nobres da cidade, aí eu até entendo que não tenha nenhum vendedor negro, é um lugar onde precisa ter boa aparência para vender (Vanessa).

A exclusão sócio-espacial da população negra observada nas falas apresentadas funciona como materialização de outros inúmeros tipos de marginalizações a que os negros estão submetidos na cidade – nas áreas de moradia, emprego, saúde, educação e representação política. Estas falas sugerem que, em São Paulo, não há somente padrões de ocupação urbana que formatam a distribuição racial. Há, também, conceituações sobre raça que derivam das várias formas de como o espaço urbano é compreendido. Existem, por assim dizer, padrões de diferenciação social e de separação, que variam na cidade e estruturam a vida pública e o relacionamento dos grupos no espaço social.

3. A Apropriação da Ideia de Superioridade Racial

Sobre as características demarcadoras entre brancos e não brancos, compreendi que os indivíduos, querendo ou não, são classificados racialmente logo ao nascerem: àqueles classificados socialmente como brancos recaem atributos e significados positivos ligados à identidade racial a que pertencem, tais como inteligência, beleza, educação, progresso, moralidade etc. Este traço de falsa superioridade contido na construção social da branquitude produz significados compartilhados, dos quais os sujeitos se apropriam, singularizam, produzem sentidos e sobre os quais atuam, de alguma forma, reproduzindo-os. Assim, os conteúdos racistas de nossa linguagem, bem como a ideia de superioridade racial, são ainda apropriados pelos sujeitos.

Você se dá conta, no seu dia a dia, de que é branca? Pensa sobre isso? Em que situações? Sim, principalmente quando as pessoas chegam e dizem: "Ah, meu cabelo hoje tá horrível!" Tem um amigo meu, ele é moreno e reclama muito do cabelo, aí ele faz assim: "Ah, hoje meu cabelo tá horrível!"... E eu lembro, meu cabelo nunca tá ruim; e nesse momento eu me dou conta, eu sou branca, e ele não (Isabela).

Sim, quando eu tô no meio de outras muitas pessoas que não são brancas. Por exemplo, quando você tá num lugar em que a predominância é negra. Você pega um transporte público, você vai pra periferia e aí você vê que não tem gente branca ali. Você é um cara meio isolado naquele micro-universo ali, mas ainda assim não é nem a cor que chama atenção, é mais a feiura da situação toda, das pessoas, das construções, da pobreza (Marcelo).

Nos dois casos, os entrevistados dizem apenas lembrar que são brancos quando percebem a diferença em relação a outra identidade racial. Podemos então pensar que toda e qualquer identidade singular e coletiva só se constrói em relação a uma outra, ou seja, só aparece quando há uma contraposição. A diferença, no caso desta identidade racial branca, surge nas duas falas associadas a aspectos que são significados negativamente em relação à alteridade. A identidade é sempre algo que define fronteiras entre quem somos nós e quem são os outros; portanto, só existe em relação a uma alteridade. Deste modo, a beleza – associada nas falas ao cabelo que não é ruim, ou a beleza que se contrapõe à feiura, que lembra Marcelo de ser "um cara meio isolado" no território da periferia nomeada por ele como feia – aparece como um marco estético de igualar-se e diferenciar-se entre "nós/brancos" e "outros/negros."

A concepção estética e subjetiva construída diariamente acerca da branquitude é, em nossa sociedade, supervalorizada em relação às identidades raciais não brancas. Isso implica que a crença na superioridade moral, intelectual e estética construída pelo racismo científico dos cientistas em fins do século XIX constitua um dos traços característicos da branquitude paulistana contemporânea, como vemos nas falas seguintes:

> São Paulo só é tão desenvolvida graças à cultura de trabalho dos imigrantes europeus, eles chegaram aqui e trouxeram a ética do trabalho e a religião católica, que tem como princípio o bem . . . Você pode perceber como o Sul é melhor, é mais educado, tem mais gente trabalhadora. Isto é coisa da imigração, da cultura Alemã, Italiana, etc. (Marcelo)

Aqui é preciso considerar que o discurso baseado em processos históricos e inclinações culturais apresentado pelos entrevistados pode ser, ao mesmo tempo, mais flexível, durável, com maior convencimento e mais difícil de desconstruir do que o discurso biologicista, pois aquele oculta a discriminação racial pela justificativa cultural e mantém a ideia de superioridade moral, ética e intelectual que havia no discurso do racismo biológico do século XIX.

4. As Hierarquias entre Nós

Entre as diferenças internas do grupo, a primeira divisão que chamou minha atenção foi a dos significados sociais inscritos sobre o corpo, ou seja, o corpo branco também está imerso em um campo de significados construído por uma ideologia racista. Portanto, ao ser percebido socialmente, esse corpo emerge do campo ideológico marcado, investido e fabricado por significados inscritos na sua própria corporeidade, com uma heterogeneidade que corresponde a uma escala de valores raciais. Segundo estes valores, o corpo branco – ou melhor, alguns sinais/marcas físicas atribuídos à brancura – baliza uma hierarquia, na qual alguns brancos conseguem ter mais estatuto e valor do que outros. O fenótipo dos brancos ainda aparece, sobretudo, como marcador de regionalidade e falsas ideias sobre origem que se sobrepõem uma à outra para hierarquizar internamente os brancos.

> **Quando você acha que a pessoas deixam de ser brancas, qual é essa fronteira? (Lia)** É a cor. Tem beiço, tem a cor das mucosas, é ter um pé na cozinha, né, essa famosa frase, "ah, aquela família tem pé na cozinha. **E você acha que tem diferença entre os brancos? Há um branco que é mais branco?(Lia)** O meu privilégio, eu diria que foi muito mais internacional, eu não fui discriminada fora, nos EUA. Hotel... teve brasileiro branco que chegou em hotel e foi posto para fora. Você sabe disso. Eu não corri riscos sendo branca tipo

européia. Branca, branca, risco de ser tomada por mestiça... qual é a fronteira que separa? A mestiçagem. (Fernanda)

Quem é branco para você? Quanto mais limpa a genética vinda da Europa, você tem o branco mais puro, tipo propaganda de sabão em pó. Que vem do norte da Europa e Rússia, aquela região. Eu sou bem branco, deve ser a descendência russa, norte da Europa é diferente do sul, norte e sul da Itália, por exemplo, no sul as pessoas são mais morenas, cabelo mais enrolado. Por exemplo, tem gente misturada da invasão dos otomanos. No norte já são mais "suíças" por exemplo, no sul as pessoas são mais morenas, e já é tudo mais bagunçado, mais desorganizado. Você pode ver, da Suíça para cima, onde não teve mistura é tudo melhor. O branco brasileiro não é tão branco, não é branco puramente branco. Mesmo porque o branco brasileiro descende de Portugal e o português é misturado, sempre foi colônia de férias de outros povos, da África, dos árabes. (Marcelo)

Nas falas de Marcelo e Fernanda é possível perceber que os paulistanos descendentes de imigrantes europeus não se consideram como misturados, ou como não brancos, como propaga o discurso sobre mestiçagem no Brasil tão bem enunciado na música "Olhos Coloridos" de Sandra de Sá:

A verdade é que você
todo brasileiro tem!
tem sangue crioulo
tem cabelo duro
sarará, sarará
sarará, sarará
sarará crioulo.

Num discurso contrário, os entrevistados afirmam uma branquitude sem misturas, e ainda uma branquitude "melhor," pois vêm de etnias que, diferentes da portuguesa, não se misturaram com outras. E assim, apesar de brasileiros, os entrevistados apontam que há um branco que é branco só no Brasil, mas fora não é. Não à toa, Fernanda e Denise apontam que tiveram facilidades para circular na Europa que outros brancos brasileiros não tiveram. Aqui, percebemos a fluidez da raça na própria fala dos sujeitos. E cabe perguntar: Qual é a fronteira que faz com que os entrevistados percebam que alguns fazem parte da branquitude brasileira, mas não fariam parte da branquitude de países Europeus ou dos Estados Unidos?

Marcelo responde a isto definindo que há uma hierarquia nas nacionalidades europeias. Esta hierarquia está relacionada às nacionalidades que, em seu imaginário, tiveram misturas e a outras que não tiveram. Aquelas que não sofreram misturas demonstraram, para ele, melhor organização e uma "superioridade cultural."

O estudo sobre a branquitude paulista também demonstrou que há demarcações internas de gênero entre os brancos que diferenciam o valor da branquitude para homens e mulheres. Podemos perceber, então, que há uma fronteira interna ao grupo que modula a questão de gênero e, portanto, marca significados diferentes aos homens e mulheres brancas. Há, também, a fronteira externa à branquitude, que marca os significados da sexualidade, matrimônio e afetividade para os não brancos.

Existem diversas fronteiras internas neste grupo, em que a classe social e as condições de vida foram tomadas por todos os sujeitos como um divisor da categoria "branco," não apenas em relação ao diferencial de poder entre brancos pobres, classe média e ricos, mas, principalmente, como experiência que aproximaria os brancos pobres de outros grupos explorados e aviltados. Ser branco e pobre, nessa interpretação, seria estar sujeito à mesma opressão sofrida por outros pobres, independente das divisões de gênero, regionalidade e raça contida na pobreza. Contudo, quando comparamos brancos pobres com negros pobres, percebemos que os significados construídos em torno da pertença racial branca asseguram a eles privilégios e vantagens em diversos setores sociais.

Além dessa transversalidade heterogênea, estrategicamente dispersiva e constitutiva, este trabalho caracteriza-se, ainda, como uma síntese de diversas análises que poderiam ser aprofundadas em novos estudos que priorizassem pensar qual o papel do branco nas relações raciais brasileiras. Neste sentido, este artigo é uma abertura para outras pesquisas, pois acredito que cada questão aqui colocada poderia ser investigada separadamente, contribuindo para responder a Ware, a saber, quais seriam as estratégias antirracistas apropriadas para subverter as forças da branquitude?

Como tímida resposta à pergunta de Ware (2002), neste artigo me focarei com mais atenção nas análises onde sujeitos brancos perfazem uma fissura entre a brancura do corpo e o poder identitário da branquitude.

5. Fissuras entre a Brancura e a Branquitude: Possibilidades para a Desconstrução do Racismo

> *Aprendemos a ser racistas, logo podemos também aprender a não ser. Racismo não é genético. Tem tudo a ver com poder.*
> Jane Elliot

Como apontado na literatura sobre o tema, a branquitude se refere a um lugar de poder, de vantagem sistêmica nas sociedades estruturadas pela dominação racial. Este lugar é, na maioria das vezes, ocupado por sujeitos considerados brancos. No entanto, a auto-inclusão na categoria "branco" é uma questão controversa e pode diferir entre os sujeitos, dependendo do lugar e do contexto histórico. Portanto, é importante perceber que brancura difere de branquitude. A brancura são as características fenotípicas que se referem à cor da pele clara, traços finos e cabelos lisos de sujeitos que, na maioria dos casos, são europeus ou euro-descendentes. Posto isso, é importante pensar que os sujeitos brancos não têm em sua essência uma identificação com a branquitude, mas, sim, processos psicossociais de identificação.

É interessante observar que cada sujeito produz sentidos para a sua brancura através de identificações diversas, na sociedade em que estão inseridos, com seus conteúdos e significados. Significados e sentidos são entendidos aqui tal como propõe a psicologia de Vigotsky (1999). Na concepção de Vygotsky (1999) sobre os significados atribuídos a cada conceito, há uma nítida relação entre aspectos cognitivos e afetivos do funcionamento psíquico. Isso se verifica porque este funcionamento estabeleceu uma distinção entre os dois componentes de um conceito: o significado propriamente dito e o *sentido*.

O primeiro consistiria em um núcleo relativamente estável de compreensão da palavra (o signo), compartilhado pelos sujeitos que a utilizam, referindo-se, então, ao sistema de relações objetivas, formado no processo de desenvolvimento do conceito (significado). "O sentido, por sua vez, refere-se ao significado da palavra (signo) para cada indivíduo, composto por relações que dizem respeito ao contexto de uso da palavra e às vivências afetivas do indivíduo" (Oliveira 1992, 81). O sentido atribuído à brancura será, então, constituído por cada sujeito de forma dinâmica, fluida e complexa. Ele é a unificação de todos os fatos psicossociais que despertam na consciência de cada sujeito, estando, portanto, entrelaçado de conteúdos intelectuais, vivenciais e afetivos. Assim, os significados de branquitude na constituição dos sujeitos são aqueles em que o sujeito se apossa da cultura, e o sentido de ser branco é o que cada um produz através das apropriações dos significados culturais mediados por suas vivências e afetos.

Para compreender o processo de como um sujeito se torna racista é preciso entender que este é constituído e constituinte nas e pelas relações sociais; é o sujeito que se relaciona na e pela linguagem no campo das intersubjetividades (Vigotsky 1999). O sujeito, desta forma, se constrói e se realiza pela apropriação dos significados socioculturais onde está inserido e, portanto, para se compreender como alguém, se auto-identifica e identifica o "outro." É preciso perguntar – e se perguntar – pelas suas relações sociais, que são significadas sempre na relação eu-outro.

A partir deste enfoque, podemos dizer que sujeitos considerados brancos em nossa sociedade passam por um processo psicossocial resultante das mediações que experienciam durante a vida de identificação com a branquitude. Portanto, podemos pensar que eles também podem, por diversas questões, não se identificar com o lugar simbólico da branquitude, e construir fissuras entre a brancura e a branquitude, proporcionando-nos, desta forma, algumas indicações para pensarmos em propostas sobre a desconstrução do racismo na identidade racial branca.

A branquitude, como visto anteriormente, tem um significado construído sócio-historicamente dentro da cultura ocidental. Ela carrega significados de norma, de beleza, de civilização, etc. Porém, estes significados podem ser desconstruídos através de vivências e afetos diversos, que irão produzir sentidos e tramas de significações não necessariamente coincidentes com aqueles construídos em nossa sociedade de maneira supostamente objetiva, desvinculando e separando a brancura da pele do lugar de poder dado à branquitude.

Para compreendermos as formas como a brancura pode ser desvinculada da branquitude, invoco os estudos da antropóloga afro-americana France Winddance Twine (2004, 2006, 2007), que cunhou o conceito de "Racial Literacy"[5] para ser usado na compreensão de como os sujeitos brancos adquirem consciência dos privilégios da branquitude, da estrutura racista da sociedade e como negoceiam sua branquitude. Portanto, sujeitos brancos agem em seu cotidiano para desconstruir o racismo de suas identidades raciais brancas, abrem novos lugares, produzem novos sentidos ao ser branco, desidentificando a brancura da branquitude. Twine propõe que, para que haja uma real desconstrução do racismo nas identidades raciais brancas, é preciso que os sujeitos brancos se percebam racializados e adquiram o que ela irá chamar de *Racial Literacy*,[6] que descreve como um conjunto de práticas que pode ser melhor caracterizado como uma "prática de leitura" – uma forma de perceber e responder individualmente às tensões das hierarquias raciais da estrutura social. Esta prática inclui:

> (1) um reconhecimento do valor simbólico e material da branquitude; (2) a definição do racismo como um problema social atual, em vez de um legado histórico; (3) um entendimento de que as identidades raciais são aprendidas e um resultado de práticas sociais; (4) a posse de gramática e um vocabulário racial que facilita a discussão de raça, racismo e antirracismo; (5) a capacidade de traduzir e interpretar os códigos e práticas racializadas de nossa sociedade e (6) uma análise das formas em que o racismo é mediado por desigualdades de classe, hierarquias de gênero e heteronormatividade. (Twine 2006, 344, tradução minha)[7]

Para cunhar este conceito, Twine realizou um trabalho etnográfico de aproximadamente sete anos, que incluiu tanto entrevistas como também a permanência nas casas dos sujeitos. A pesquisa foi realizada com 121 casais interraciais na Inglaterra e nos Estados Unidos. Um dos resultados encontrados na pesquisa foi que a convivência nas relações íntimas interraciais pode aparecer como um microssistema político onde o sujeito branco pode construir uma crítica à própria branquitude, fazer uma análise das configurações racistas da sociedade, assim como perceber-se como racializado e, portanto, produzir novos sentidos para as identidades raciais brancas e negras.

Na pesquisa realizada por mim na cidade de São Paulo, as relações amorosas interraciais não apareceram como condição para que os sujeitos brancos destes relacionamentos adquirissem *racial literacy*, pois a grande parte dos sujeitos entrevistados que se relacionaram amorosamente com negros tinham uma percepção neutralizada de sua racialidade. Em algumas vezes, exaltavam até a máxima de que, no Brasil, somos todos iguais e todos mestiços e que, portanto, não haveria diferenças entre eles e os parceiros. Os entrevistados que tiveram estas relações, em sua maioria, não se relacionaram como os entrevistados de Twine (2006), com negros que possuíam identidades negras afirmativas e/ou em comunidades de maioria negra. Ao contrário disto, os parceiros destes entrevistados eram uma minoria negra em um mundo de brancos.

No entanto, assim como na pesquisa de Twine, alguns de meus entrevistados, Lilian, Pedro e Tadeu, pareceram ter adquirido, durante suas vidas, a *Racial Literacy*. Portanto, pensar nestes três sujeitos pode ser uma forma de produzir conhecimento para criarmos possibilidades de mediações, a fim de que haja a construção de identidades raciais brancas, não mais como dominação, supremacia, e normatividade, mas sim como diferenças. E para isto é necessário que a sociedade produza novos significados para os lugares racializados de brancos e negros, e que os sujeitos produzam novos sentidos, assim como Pedro e Tadeu.

Os entrevistados apresentaram características parecidas no modo como pensam, sentem e vivenciam a experiência da raça. Estes reconhecem os privilégios materiais e simbólicos que a brancura lhes concede; reconhecem o racismo na sociedade brasileira; percebem que não há diferenças biológicas entre brancos e negros, mas reconhecem que há desigualdades sociais entre os grupos, percebem que já tiveram sentimentos racistas involuntários e fizeram uma análise crítica nestas situações. Todos apoiavam, ainda, ações afirmativas para a população negra como proposta para reparação do racismo.

Na tentativa de compreender quais foram as mediações destes sujeitos que possibilitaram suas constituições como brancos não racistas, pude perceber que diversos fatores e vivências contribuíram para tal, porém uma delas me pareceu fundamental: estes tiveram relações de afetos não hierarquizadas com não brancos. Pedro cresceu em um bairro onde grande parte da população é negra, estudou, teve professores e amigos negros desde pequeno. Tadeu convive e tem relações de amizade com uma maioria negra. Aqui é importante perceber que a chave não está na convivência com os negros, nem na convivência pacífica, mas sim na convivência não hierarquizada com estes.

Foi exatamente a convivência não hierarquizada que permitiu a estes sujeitos se deslocarem de si, se colocarem no lugar deste outro e voltarem a olhar para si. Nas descrições e falas destes sujeitos, é como se os olhos dos afetos negros fossem emprestados aos brancos para que estes olhassem de volta para si, mas agora com um saber outro *e do* outro. Esta experiência de olhar para si com os olhos de outros só foi possível porque, para cada um destes, o "outro" era alguém com quem se tinha uma relação de proximidade. Aqui é importante frisar que o que possibilita esta vivência não é a experiência positiva com o outro, mas sim o deslocamento de si para uma outra posição subjetiva, a de perceber a alteridade nem como inferior, nem como superior, ou com qualquer conteúdo *a priori*, mas apenas como alteridade. Lilian nos apresenta este olhar quando diz que:

Eu tenho uma colega que também é doméstica, ela é negra, e um dia fiquei conversando com ela e ela dizia de algumas situações racistas que passava, fiquei ouvindo e de repente não escutei mais nada, pois fiquei me imaginando na mesma situação que ela estava, fiquei pensando como seria se eu fosse ela, fiquei imaginando aquilo de não conseguir o emprego pela cor da pele, e depois pensei na mesma situação sendo eu mesma. É estranho porque imaginei que deve ser difícil ela saber se não conseguiu o emprego porque é negra, ou por outro motivo, eu quando não consigo não preciso pensar que é a cor da minha pele. Isto me faz pensar como a vida do meu pai e minha irmã é mais difícil que a minha.

Este saber olhar para o mundo e para si mesmo com a experiência do outro já foi teorizado por W.E.B. Du Bois para pensar a condição dos negros em diáspora, se referindo à consciência do negro na América do Norte como clivada entre duas experiências: a identificação com sua raça pela opressão comum e a identificação com valores construídos pelo opressor de origem europeia, ou seja, pela branquitude. Esta posição de sempre olhar para si através dos olhos dos outros foi chamada por ele de dupla consciência (Du Bois 2003, 9).

Inspirados no conceito de Du Bois, Winant (1997) e Twine (2006) conferem esta dupla consciência também aos brancos que conseguiram se olhar como socialmente racializados e adquiriram uma crítica à branquitude. Twine demonstra em sua pesquisa que esta consciência foi adquirida através dos relacionamentos interpessoais com sujeitos negros. Winant (1997) considera que esta foi uma conquista dos movimentos por direitos civis da década de 60 nos Estados Unidos. Para ele:

> Não apenas os negros, mas também os brancos agora experimentam uma divisão em suas identidades raciais. Por um lado, os brancos herdam o legado da supremacia branca, a partir da qual continuam a se beneficiar, mas por outro lado eles estão sujeitos à moral, e politicamente aos desafios colocados pelo parcial êxito do movimento negro e movimentos afiliados. (Winant 1997, 4, tradução minha)[8]

No Brasil, o movimento negro, apesar de ter conseguido algumas conquistas, ainda não teve o mesmo êxito que na América do Norte. No entanto, podemos pensar que alguns movimentos estéticos de negritude também possibilitaram a alguns brancos esta dupla consciência. É o caso de Pedro: ele relata que sua grande tomada de consciência foi escutar o rap de Mano Brown. Foi a música que fez ele se deslocar de sua posição racial e olhar para sua vida e a dos negros através da poesia do rap. Pedro sabe que é impossível vestir a pele do outro – dilema da raça. O que difere Pedro de seu vizinho não é a forma de vida, o tipo de comida, a religião que frequenta, nem tampouco as condições socioeconômicas, já que estes são traços, por assim dizer, "experimentáveis." Neste sentido, foram a sensibilidade e a identificação estética que fizeram com que ele se deslocasse sem trocar a pele. Nas palavras de Pedro:

> O momento fundamental para a consciência ficar mais solidificada foi começar a escutar muito rap. Desde 14 anos ouço. E boa parte das temáticas das letras é sobre racismo. Não sei por quê, mas me identifiquei e comecei a me revoltar com a condição dos negros contida nas letras. O rap trazia um discurso que eu, sendo branco ainda não tinha criado. Depois, aos poucos, comecei a conversar com negros sobre isto, mas de uma forma ainda tímida. Teve uma vez que disse que queria ser negro, pois eu já tinha o olhar. E eu queria ser negro porque aí eu poderia brigar de fato contra o racismo. Na minha cabeça havia esta contradição, de ter uma revolta de "uma causa que não era minha." Mas, ao mesmo tempo, e sei que posso falar isso pra você, eu via os negros de forma diferente. Sabia que eles não eram eu, pois mesmo que eu tivesse o olhar sabia que pelo racismo eles tinham vivido a vida toda coisas diferentes de mim. E sempre me senti estranho de ter essa visão sobre eles.

Algo fundamental no depoimento de Pedro o faz, por sua vez, diferir de um determinado senso comum brasileiro, em que "somos todos iguais." Pedro reconhece o outro e identifica neste outro as vivências diferentes das suas em função do racismo. No entanto, entende que estas diferenças não são imanentes, mas sim resultado de uma condição de dominação. Ao mesmo tempo, ele se sente estranho. Pode-se dizer, aqui, que esta estranheza é o principal fator que caracteriza a dupla consciência. Sabe-se do outro, mas não se é o outro. Mais um fator importante é perceber que os brancos não têm a possibilidade de compreender sozinhos o que é a branquitude. Foi necessário o rap para que isto afetasse Pedro, demonstrando, mais uma vez, como apontam Winant e Twine, que são as relações com os significados construídos, ora por sujeitos negros, ora pela estética negra ou pelo esforço das organizações negras, que determinam as percepções e sensibilidades sociais acerca da ideia de raça negra. Ainda caracterizando esta dupla consciência, Pedro afirma e reconhece o que Winant caracteriza como um dos traços dos brancos de dupla consciência: o benefício do privilégio.

> Apesar de eu ser branco, tenho uma consciência que o grupo de brancos na humanidade como um todo foram aqueles que destruíram boa parte do mundo, e também propagaram grandes guerras e violência. É estranho que este grupo é considerado o avanço, o civilizado. Eu não me identifico com esta ideia de brancos, e não gosto do grupo branco nem de lugares que só tem brancos, me sinto mal, mas ao mesmo tempo tenho amigos brancos, sei que cada pessoa é cada pessoa. E também pessoas como eu e meus amigos não têm culpa de terem nascidos brancos. A gente teria culpa se continuasse legitimando e aprovando isto, é horrível quando eu percebo que tenho vantagens por ser branco, porque nesta hora eu não posso fazer nada. É para além de mim se o cara do banco acha que eu posso entrar, que sou confiável e meu amigo não (Pedro).

Este depoimento permite observar que há, na luta antirracista, diversas frentes a serem atingidas. Uma delas é o processo de identificação social – de sua responsabilidade e participação – em que o ator social pode e deve ser agente de mudanças, que está ligado a uma tomada de posição sobre seu racismo latente, sobre perceber seus privilégios e, portanto, sobre um trabalho para desconstruir o racismo e os significados racistas apropriados por cada sujeito, produzindo, assim, novos sentidos para o que significa ser branco e o que significa ser negro. Tanto Pedro quanto Lilian tiveram vivências que lhes possibilitaram desconstruir muitos dos significados racistas de suas respectivas culturas. No entanto, ambos admitem que, mesmo sem intenção, usufruem de privilégios em relação aos negros, ou seja, são, dentre os entrevistados, dos poucos que já refletiram sobre o assunto, além de lutarem contra uma identificação inercial com a branquitude. Contudo, apesar de continuarem obtendo benefício de suas posições raciais, Lilian e Pedro adquiriram *Racial Literacy*, o que caracteriza uma mudança no espaço social em que atuam.

É impossível afirmar, no entanto, que estes sujeitos tenham adquirido uma vida completamente não racista: os depoimentos não são suficientes para mensurar uma tomada de posição desta natureza. Não acredito, ainda, que exista em qualquer sujeito racismo *on*, ou racismo *off*, mas que há pessoas que passam a adquirir uma conscientização da questão e outras não. Lembremos que há o caráter de ambivalência e contradição em todo sujeito. De qualquer modo, podemos afirmar que, tanto em Pedro como em Lilian, há uma posição de não legitimação do racismo, bem como uma movimentação para mudanças no cotidiano deles e de quem está próximo.

Para uma real transformação no tecido social brasileiro nesse sentido, precisamos que haja – além dos sujeitos brancos adquirirem *racial literacy* e serem precursores de mudanças em seus micro-lugares de poder e atuação – uma mudança estrutural nos valores culturais da sociedade como um todo: é necessário que a branquitude como lugar de normatividade e poder se transforme em identidades étnico-raciais brancas onde o racismo não seja o pilar de sua sustentação. Para isto, além da psicologia e da constituição dos sujeitos enquanto atores sociais, é preciso alterar as relações socioeconômicas, os padrões culturais e as formas de produzir e reproduzir a história brasileira. Assim, as políticas públicas voltadas para a igualdade racial como as cotas, o reconhecimento da história, do espaço e a ação do movimento negro, são essenciais para que os brancos consigam se deslocar da posição de norma e hegemonia cultural.

NOTAS

1. Este artigo é um resumo de minha tese de doutorado que já foi publicada no livro *Entre o Encardido, o Branco e o Branquíssimo: Branquitude, Hierarquia e Poder na Cidade de São Paulo* (Annablume, 2014).

2. A eleição do termo *Branquitude* ao invés de *Branquidade* deve-se à opção de seguir a escolha de Maria Aparecida Silva Bento (2002), primeira a trazer o termo para o Brasil. Segundo Lourenço Cardoso, a relação entre os dois termos tem a ver com o processo de tradução do conceito em inglês, em que, de acordo com sua revisão literária, no Brasil, ambos têm o mesmo significado. Sendo assim, a utilização dos termos encaixa-se em critérios opcionais (Cardoso 2008).

3. No Brasil, de maneira geral, a questão da negritude tem sido mais investigada do que a do indígena e dos orientais, e estes estudos mostram que o contraponto do branco no imaginário coletivo tem sido o negro.

4. Todos os nomes são fictícios.

5. Os trabalhos de France Winddance Twine não foram traduzidos para o português. As traduções a seguir são de minha responsabilidade.

6. *Racial Literacy* significa literalmente alfabetização racial. Penso que a melhor tradução para o conceito seria letramento racial, pois a ideia de letramento está mais ligada à ideia de conhecimento do saber, da cultura envolvida. Seria, portanto, a competência de utilizar a linguagem adequada para cada situação social necessária. Optei, no entanto, por deixar o conceito em sua forma original e traduzir apenas o seu significado.

7. No original: "Racial literacy is a set of practices. It can best be characterized as a 'reading practice' – a way of perceiving and responding to the racial climate and racial structures individuals encounter and include the following: 1) a recognition of the

symbolic and material value of Whiteness; 2) the definition of racism as a current social problem rather than a historical legacy; 3) an understanding that racial identities are learned and an outcome of social practices; 4) the possession of racial grammar and a vocabulary that facilitates a discussion of race, racism, and antiracism; 5) the ability to translate (interpret) racial codes and racialized practices; and 6) an analysis of the ways that racism is mediated by class inequalities, gender hierarchies, and heteronormativity" (Twine 2006, 344).

8. Retirado da página do autor Howard Winant, em 28 setembro 2011 (http://www.soc.ucsb.edu/faculty/winant/whitness.html). Artigo publicado em *New Left Review* 225 (Set-Out. 1997). No original: "Therefore, not only blacks, but also whites, now experience a division in their racial identities. On the one hand, whites inherit the legacy of white supremacy, from which they continue to benefit. But on the other hand, they are subject to the moral and political challenges posed to that inheritance by the partial but real successes of the black movement (and affiliated movements)" (Winant 1997, 4).

REFERÊNCIAS BIBLIOGRÁFICAS

Bento, M. A. da S. 2002. *Pactos Narcísicos no Racismo: Branquitude e Poder nas Organizações Empresariais e no Poder Público*. Tese de doutorado. São Paulo: Instituto de Psicologia da Universidade de São Paulo.

Britzman, D. P. 2004. "A Diferença e Tom Menor: Algumas Modulações da História, da Memória e da Comunidade." In *Branquidade, Identidade Branca e Multiculturalismo*, organização de V. Ware. Rio de Janeiro: Garamond.

Cardoso, L. 2008. *O Branco "Invisível": Um Estudo sobre a Emergência da Branquitude nas Pesquisas sobre as Relações Raciais no Brasil (Período: 1957-2007)*. Dissertação de Mestrado. Coimbra: Faculdade de Economia e Centro de Estudos Sociais da Universidade de Coimbra.

Carone, I. 2007. "Breve Histórico de uma Pesquisa Psicossocial sobre a Questão Racial Brasileira." In *Psicologia Social do Racismo*, organização de I. Carone e M. A.Bento, 13-24. Petrópolis: Vozes.

Du Bois, W. E. B. 2003. *The Souls of Black Folk*. Nova Iorque: Barnes & Noble.

Frankenberg, R. 1999. *White Women, Race Masters: The Social Construction of Whiteness*. Minneapolis: University of Minnesota Press.

Frankenberg, R. 2004. "A Miragem de uma Branquitude não Marcada." In *Branquidade, Identidade Branca e Multiculturalismo*, organização de V. Ware, 307-338. Rio de Janeiro: Garamond.

Piza, E. 2002. "Porta de Vidro: Uma Entrada para Branquitude." In *Psicologia Social do Racismo: Estudos sobre Branquitude e Branqueamento no Brasil*, organização de I. Carone, e M. A. Bento, 59-90. Petrópolis: Vozes.

Schucman, L. V. 2014. *Entre o Encardido, o Branco e o Branquíssimo: Branquitude, Hierarquia, e Poder na Cidade de São Paulo*. São Paulo: Annablume.

Spink, P. 2003. *Pesquisa de Campo em Psicologia Social: Uma Perspectiva Pós-construcionista*. Texto organizado por Spink e membros do Núcleo de Organização e Ação Social. São Paulo: Programa de Pós-graduação em Psicologia Social da Puc-SP.

Steyn, M. 2004. "Novos Matizes da 'Branquitude': A Identidade Branca numa África do Sul Multicultural e Democrática." In *Branquidade, Identidade Branca e Multiculturalismo*, organização de V. Ware, 115-137. Rio de Janeiro: Garamond.

Sovik, L. 2009. *Aqui Ninguém É Branco*. Rio de Janeiro: Aeroplano Editora.

Twine, F. W. 2004. "A White Side of Black Britain: The Concept of Racial Literacy." *Ethnic and Racial Studies* 27 (6): 878-907.

Twine, F. W. e A. Steinbugler. 2006. "The Gap Between Whites and Whiteness: Interracial Intimacy and Racial Literacy." *Du Bois Review* 3 (2): 341-363.

Twine, F. W. e C. Gallagher. 2007. "The Future of Whiteness: A Map of the 'Third Wave'." *Ethnic and Racial Studies* 31 (1): 1-21.

Vygotsky, L. S. 2001. *A Construção do Pensamento e da Linguagem*. São Paulo: Martins Fontes.

Ware, V. 2004. "O Poder Duradouro da Branquidade: 'Um Problema a Solucionar.' Introdução." In *Branquidade, Identidade Branca e Multiculturalismo*, organização de V. Ware, 7-40. Rio de Janeiro: Garamond.

Winant, H. 2001. *The World Is a Ghetto: Race and Democracy Since World War II*. Nova Iorque: Basic Books.

Winant, H. 1997. "Behind Blue Eyes: Whiteness and Contemporary U.S. Racial Politics." *New Left Review* 225: 73-88.

LIA VAINER SCHUCMAN é Doutora em Psicologia Social pela Universidade de São Paulo com estágio de Doutoramento no Centro de Novos Estudos Raciais pela Universidade da Califórnia. Professora do Departamento de Psicologia da Universidade Federal de Santa Catarina (UFSC) e pesquisadora de Psicologia e Relações étnico-raciais. Autora dos livros "Entre o Encardido, o Branco e o Branquíssimo: Branquitude, Hierarquia e Poder na Cidade de São Paulo" (Veneta 2020) e Famílias Interraciais: tensões entre cor e amor (EDUFBA, 2018)

ANA FLAUZINA & THULA PIRES

Por Formas *Amefricanas* de Autoinscrição

RESUMO: O artigo discute, a partir das noções de racismo antinegro, genocídio e amefricanidade, os processos de assalto à vida negra como o grande sustentáculo do pacto social e político no Brasil. Sustenta que a fragilidade da existência social negra, pertencente à zona do não ser, é condição historicamente delineada pelos processo coloniais. Nesse processo de expropriação, sublinha que há um posicionamento compulsório dos sujeitos negros como os receptores de uma violência gratuita e naturalizada nas órbitas do Estado e da sociedade civil. Destaca ainda que esse padrão perverso tem sido aprofundado no atual contexto político do Brasil, em que se observa um alinhamento institucional com as demandas históricas de produção de extermínios fundamentados pelo racismo. Convoca, por fim, a um tipo de reação que passe pelo reconhecimento de privilégios nos setores ditos progressistas, a fim de que se possa superar as condicionantes do racismo que tem estruturado a tragédia social brasileira.

PALAVRAS-CHAVE: Genocídio, Amefricanidade, Racismo antinegro

ABSTRACT: The article discusses, from the notions of antiblackness, genocide, and amefricanity, the processes of assault on the black life as the great support of the social and political pact in Brazil. It maintains that the fragility of black social existence, belonging to the zone of non-being, is a condition historically delineated by colonial processes. In this process of expropriation, there is a compulsory positioning of black subjects as the recipients of gratuitous and naturalized violence in the orbits of the state and civil society. It also highlights that this perverse pattern has been deepened in the current political context of Brazil, in which an institutional alignment with the historical demands of production of exterminations based on racism is observed. Finally, it calls for a kind of reaction based on the recognition of privileges in the so-called progressive sectors, in order to overcome the determinants of racism that has shaped the Brazilian social tragedy.

KEYWORDS: Genocide, Amefricanity, Antiblackness racism

A partir da provocação da Revista *Portuguese Literary & Cultural Studies* e aceitando o desafio que Mbembe (2001) nos faz no texto As *Formas Africanas de Autoinscrição*, optamos por nos inserir no debate sobre afrodescendências e racismos a partir do nosso lugar de enunciação, tanto epistêmico quanto político. Nesse sentido, tomamos a categoria político-cultural da *amefricanidade* desenvolvida por Lélia Gonzalez (1988) para, a partir do encontro colonial produzido no Brasil, oferecer chaves de interpretação sobre a colonialidade centradas nas ideias de racismo antinegro e genocídio (Flauzina 2008; Vargas 2010).

Parece-nos que as dinâmicas de violência que o racismo engendrou na realidade brasileira, bem como as experiências de reexistência que por aqui se desenvolveram, podem subsidiar não apenas discussões relacionadas aos seus efeitos por aqui. Assumir o compromisso de tomar as referidas violências em contexto e de considerar as reexistências nos termos em que foram produzidas pode informar realidades distintas da brasileira, mas marcadas pela diáspora africana e pela colonialidade.

Nesse sentido, pretendemos inaugurar a conversa a partir de duas questões, que entendemos serem eixos centrais das violências a que os afrodescendentes estão submetidos no contexto brasileiro: racismo antinegro e genocídio. Em seguida, passamos a apresentar as matrizes a partir das quais a categoria político-cultural da *amefricanidade* foi construída e a apontar os caminhos que ela apresenta para o enfrentamento dos problemas anteriormente destacados. Por fim, buscaremos analisar, no atual contexto de supressão do Estado Democrático de Direito e do acirramento do racismo no Brasil, as implicações desse cenário nos processos de violência sobre o povo negro.

1. Racismo Antinegro e Genocídio

Quando falamos de racismo no Brasil, estamos nos referindo a uma dinâmica violenta de hierarquização de humanidade com base na raça, que opera, de acordo com Lélia Gonzalez, através da ideia de denegação (Gonzalez 1984). Resgatando a categoria freudiana de denegação, Lélia Gonzalez caracteriza o racismo no Brasil como um processo através do qual o indivíduo, embora formulando um de seus desejos, pensamentos ou sentimentos, até aí recalcado, continua a defender-se dele, negando que lhe pertença.

Em bom pretuguês,[1] a manutenção e o acirramento da estratificação social entre brancos e negros no Brasil – representada pela despossessão, violência gratuita e morte prematura evitável (Vargas 2017) – se dá, entre outros aspectos, pela negação da existência do racismo, camuflado através do mito da democracia racial.[2]

Nesse sentido, o racismo "à brasileira" se volta contra aqueles e aquelas que são o testemunho vivo de nossa ladinoamefricanidade (os/as negros/as),[3] ao mesmo tempo que diz não o fazer. Lélia Gonzalez classifica o racismo como a "neurose cultural da sociedade brasileira" (Gonzalez 1984), que, enquanto dinâmica de denegação, explicita processos de desumanização que convivem com institutos de igualdade jurídico-formal positivada e práticas institucionais e intersubjetivas de violência como norma para corpos negros.

Tomando por influência o pensamento de Frantz Fanon (2008), mobilizamos os conceitos de *zona do ser* e *zona do não ser* para pensarmos o racismo a partir da colonialidade. O projeto moderno/colonial mobilizou a categoria *raça* para instituir uma linha que separa de forma incomensurável duas zonas: a do humano (*zona do ser*) e a do não humano (*zona do não ser*). Ser negro no Brasil "significa ser, desde sempre, excluído das esferas de cidadania, do consumo, de pertencimento político. Da humanidade. Ser negro significa não ser; significa ser, desde sempre, socialmente morto" (Vargas 2017, 85).

Tomamos a concepção de antinegritude[4] desenvolvida por João Vargas para configurarmos aspectos centrais do funcionamento estrutural do racismo. Isso significa que, na análise que se segue, as intenções de quem violenta importam tão pouco quanto as intenções de quem é violentado pelo racismo. Este facto não retira de cada sujeito a responsabilidade que possui pelas ações e omissões que desencadeia, mas nos permite perceber que são as posicionalidades sociais que irão definir a atuação de cada sujeito dentro da engrenagem do extermínio:

> Uma pessoa é branca ou negra antes de nascer, ou seja, essa pessoa habitará necessariamente um campo semântico estruturado a partir de qualidades atribuídas a sua epiderme, sua cor. Não se trata, então, de qualidades intrínsecas a esses sujeitos, as quais lhes definem sua posição nesse campo, mas como cada sujeito, por causa de suas características físicas – por causa do significado social de suas características físicas – ganha sua posição relativa ao conjunto de sujeitos contidos nesse campo. (Vargas 2017, 92)

Na experiência colonial em Abya Yala, a ideia de raça exerceu um papel definitivo na determinação das hierarquias entre cada grupo: "O negro é o não-sujeito com posicionalidade a partir da qual todos os sujeitos não-negros se definem" (Vargas 2017, 92). Foi sobre os africanos escravizados e seus descendentes[5] que recaiu desproporcionalmente os ônus de sustentar a legalidade e a liberdade como atributos exclusivos da *zona do ser*: "o sujeito negro, num mundo antinegro, é tanto irrelevante quanto fundamental na formação do ser não-negro, incluindo o ser branco" (Vargas 2017, 92).

Sem a noção de antinegritude não teria sido possível manter o tráfico atlântico, forjar as engrenagens do capitalismo e subsidiar a consolidação do sistema mundo moderno colonial e suas atualizações contemporâneas. Nas palavras de João Vargas:

> A perspectiva que proponho é que a gramática da antinegritude e seu campo assimétrico de posicionalidades são normativos, subliminares, ubíquos, transhistóricos e, assim, efetivamente imunes à contestação.
>
> . . . No campo semântico planetário, as pessoas negras ocupam uma posição única e incomunicável porque a escravidão póstuma faz com que elas convivam com a violência estrutural e gratuita continuamente. Trata-se de uma violência estrutural porque, de acordo com a perspectiva de Fanon, a pessoa negra está posicionada fora dos âmbitos da sociedade civil e da Humanidade. E a violência antinegra é gratuita porque, ao contrário do que o não-negro vivencia, a violência não depende de a pessoa negra transgredir a hegemonia da sociedade civil. Ou seja, negros vivenciam violência não por causa do que fazem, mas por causa de quem são, ou melhor, de quem não são. A violência gratuita equivale a um estado de terror que é independente de leis, direitos e cidadania. A violência gratuita é terror porque é imprevisível na sua previsibilidade, ou previsível na sua imprevisibilidade. Da perspectiva de uma pessoa negra, não se trata de perguntar se ela será brutalizada a esmo, mas quando. (Vargas 2017, 93)

É a partir dessa gramática desagregadora da antinegritude que os processos que culminam no cerceamento das possibilidades de sustentação da vida consubstanciam o que sustentamos ser um genocídio dirigido ao povo negro na Diáspora.

De fato, desde que a *Convenção do Genocídio* emerge no cenário internacional em 1948, há uma tentativa de se qualificar os atos de brutalização e extermínio na direção dos corpos negros diaspóricos como partes de ataques de perfil genocida. Já em 1951, na histórica petição *We Charge Genocide* (1970), dirigida à Assembleia Geral da ONU sob a liderança de William Patterson, há a formalização da denúncia da existência do genocídio como a categoria mais bem acabada para descrever a condição social e política do povo negro nos Estados Unidos.

No Brasil, a denúncia do genocídio também tem um longo lastro histórico nos esforços da resistência negra. Em 1978, Abdias do Nascimento publica *O Genocídio do Negro Brasileiro: Processo de um Racismo Mascarado* (1978), ecoando os preceitos fundamentais que reivindicam o racismo como uma fonte de destruição que nega o direito de existência de grupos humanos.

Em comum, essas duas importantes referências históricas agregam o que está no centro do entendimento contemporâneo do que vem a ser genocídio no contexto da Diáspora Africana. Trata-se de uma noção que situa o sufocamento das comunidades negras por amplos processos de vilipêndio e expropriação, que tem a morte física como uma de suas balizas estruturantes (James 1996; Vargas 2010; Flauzina 2008).

Na análise específica da realidade brasileira, entendemos que o genocídio se materializa nas mais diversas atuações e omissões institucionais que fragilizam as chances de vida do segmento negro da população. Essas práticas podem ser encontradas na negação ao direito pleno à educação, nos processos de aniquilamentos de vida, que se perfaz pelas condições do atendimento de saúde, chegando às práticas naturalizadas de extermínio da juventude negra pelas ações de agentes do Estado que produziram dados alarmantes nas últimas décadas.

É importante situar que a noção de genocídio com a qual trabalhamos está vinculada aos efeitos do racismo antinegro com suas correlatas dimensões de gênero e sexualidade. Com isso, visibilizamos o fato de que a denúncia do sofrimento imposto aos corpos negros tem sido, em grande medida, pautada pela dor imposta aos homens e meninos negros nos processos de execuções em curso no país. Importa-nos assegurar, entretanto, que a denúncia do extermínio não seja silenciadora das demais práticas de vulnerabilização da vida, que tem encontrado as mulheres e a comunidade LGBT como alvos fáceis do apetite genocida. Portanto, as práticas sexistas e LGBTfóbicas, que animam a performance brutalizada de agrupamentos de homens negros vulnerabilizados pelo racismo, têm de ser computadas no espectro do genocídio, sob o risco de haver uma hierarquização da dor negra.

Considerando essas condicionantes, entendemos o uso da categoria *genocídio* como útil para iluminar os contextos de fragilização das comunidades negras no Brasil, tanto do ponto de vista dos ataques institucionais à vida, como também para refletir a forma como os parâmetros da antinegritude têm sido capazes de se infiltrar nas próprias comunidades, produzindo lógicas autofágicas de desagregação social.

Nesse contexto, recuperando a noção da *zona do não ser*, representada por uma constelação de corpos abjetos marcados pelo racismo antinegro, entendemos que a vitimização genocida se converteu no destino natural reservado ao povo negro no país. A normalização da *zona do ser* como representativa do pleno, autônomo e centrado gera processos de violência que estruturam e condicionam a própria percepção sobre o que pode ser entendido como violência. Nesse sentido, é fundamental que possamos pensá-la a partir de chaves analíticas que nos digam respeito e que sejam capazes de posicionar os diagnósticos e agenciamentos desse mesmo lugar.

A seguir, passaremos a apresentar a categoria político-cultural da amefricanidade como forma de oferecer uma interpretação sobre a realidade radicada na *zona do não ser* e comprometida com a afirmação incondicional de nossas humanidades.

2. Os Aportes Político-Epistêmicos da Amefricanidade

A categoria desenvolvida por Lélia Gonzalez nos permite levar a sério os desafios de autoinscrição *amefricana* e enfrentar os mecanismos de reprodução do racismo e de suas imbricações com outras formas de opressão. Trata-se de uma epistemologia que "carrega na tinta," que busca racializar para politizar, de modo a oferecer formas encarnadas de exercício de liberdade e de limitação de poder no mundo que herdamos. Possibilita uma *práxis* apta a produzir respostas para as questões que se colocam em relação à população negra em Abya Ayla,[6] como o genocídio nas suas mais variadas formas de execução: o encarceramento em massa, o epistemicídio, o feminicídio, entre outros.

Confrontando o modelo moderno/colonial centrado na experiência europeia e comprometido com a ideologia do branqueamento, a *amefricanidade* propõe uma leitura da realidade e uma produção de conhecimento construída a partir da experiência compartilhada por negros em diáspora, submetidos ao legado da colonialidade na *Améfrica Ladina*.

A *amefricanidade* designa a experiência histórica comum de luta promovida por africanos e seus descendentes e pelos povos originários em Abya Yala. Seu valor metodológico, segundo Lélia Gonzalez, radica na possibilidade de resgatar uma unidade específica, forjada pela violência do racismo e pela resistência contra medidas seculares de espoliação, expropriação e apagamento da memória e das contribuições científicas, históricas e políticas de povos negros.

Lélia Gonzalez reforça a importância de se reconhecer um fazer próprio da experiência *amefricana*. Para ela, tentar achar as "sobrevivências" da cultura africana no continente americano, atribuindo à África aquilo que aqui é produzido, é um equívoco que pode encobrir as resistências e a criatividade da luta contra a escravidão, contra o genocídio e a exploração que por aqui se desenvolveram. A *amefricanidade* carrega um sentido positivo, "de explosão criadora," de reinvenção afrocentrada da vida na diáspora, afinal, "foi dentro da comunidade escravizada que se desenvolveram formas político-culturais de resistência que hoje nos permitem continuar uma luta plurissecular de liberação" (Gonzalez 1988, 78).

Trata-se de uma proposta epistêmico-metodológica que leva a sério os desafios de autoinscrição e oferece a possibilidade de revisitarmos o encontro colonial, atribuindo centralidade à experiência amefricana, denunciando o racismo e o sexismo das sociedades coloniais e mobilizando o protagonismo da resistência à opressão desencadeada, notadamente, por mulheres como inspiração para enfrentarmos os legados que a colonialidade nos impõe.

Em atenção ao alerta de Achille Mbembe sobre a necessidade de elaboração de uma autoinscrição que não nos encerre em uma identidade limitada e essencializada, nem reafirme leituras de nós criadas pelo opressor (Mbembe 2001), nossas formas de autoinscrição não se dão nos mesmos termos que no continente africano. Ao mesmo tempo, rompem radicalmente com descrições hierarquizadas que a colonialidade fez de nós.

Não disputamos a possibilidade de sermos incluídos (sempre de maneira controlada) na noção de sujeito de direito e de sujeito político que está posta. Disputamos a possibilidade de produzir o Direito, o Estado e a política de nosso lugar e nos nossos termos.

A *amefricanidade* busca, na experiência daqueles que sofreram a dominação colonial em Abya Yala, as respostas para os problemas estruturais que nos afligem. Não é sobredeterminada pelo continente africano, tampouco pela hegemonia eurocêntrica. Produz-se com base na resistência e criatividade que a luta negra em diáspora, protagonizada por mulheres, conduziu a partir do encontro colonial que por aqui se forjou; no enfrentamento direto, concreto e permanente ao genocídio, em todas as suas dimensões.

Lélia Gonzalez (1988) afirma que negros em diáspora não podem atingir uma consciência efetiva de si, enquanto descendentes de africanos, se permanecerem prisioneiros de uma linguagem racista. Por isso, compromete-se com a assunção de uma linguagem própria (o *pretuguês*), propõe o termo *amefricanos* para designar a todos nós e rompe com a linguagem imperialista que define o mundo e os "outros" a partir da autoimagem de sua supremacia.

Falar *pretuguês* não é falar um dialeto, é colocar-se politicamente como alguém que reconhece e assume que a linguagem culta falada no Brasil é resultado dos processos de assimilação, aculturação e violência de povos indígenas e africanos. Interpelar a realidade em *pretuguês* é pôr em questão as categorias de estratificação de humanidade que relaciona a *zona do ser* ao sujeito branco, masculino, cisheteronormativo, proprietário, cristão, sem deficiência e de origem norte-atlântica. É perceber que o indivíduo abstrato, sobre o qual a ordem da legalidade se constitui, é da ordem da branquitude como uma racialidade não-nomeada. Ao contrário, como nos ensina Fanon, os negros têm sua subjetividade deslocada através de olhares alheios que não os reconhecem em seus próprios termos (Fanon 2008). Apreender a realidade em *pretuguês* nos capacita a lidar com as implicações de estar na *zona do não ser*, de enfrentar o secular processo de desumanização que se impôs a nós, por processos de extermínio permanente ou pelas mais variadas práticas de morte em vida que marcam nossas trajetórias.

A experiência *amefricana* tem, com a teimosia e criatividade que permitiu a subsistência do povo negro em diáspora por séculos de opressão, muito a contribuir para a redefinição das teias de violência a que estamos submetidos, bem como as redes de reexistência que forjamos para garantir-nos como possibilidade. Essas reorientações têm por objetivo responder ao mundo herdado, e não ao mundo idealizado pelas leituras hierarquizadas que foram produzidas sobre nossa história, memória, agência e epistemes.

A categoria da *amefricanidade*, informada pela denúncia do mito da democracia racial e das políticas públicas de branqueamento, aporta um sofisticado letramento racial para pensar o contexto de disputa política a que estamos submetidos.

3. Matrizes Contemporâneas do Extermínio no Brasil

Fazer uma leitura da realidade brasileira na atual conjuntura é, fundamentalmente, iluminar aquilo que não se altera no percurso histórico do país. Na contramão de uma tendência esquerdista que aposta na *exceção* como categoria analítica, há uma perspectiva negra que entende a continuidade das estruturas políticas e sociais como a melhor forma de compreensão dos fatos (Wilderson III 2003). A assunção desse tipo de postura crítica requer que, de partida, explicitemos as premissas que orientam nosso olhar. Aqui, assinamos um contrato com o direito à vida como a métrica a pautar a temperatura da ação do Estado. Trazendo a condição específica do povo negro para o centro do debate, sustentamos que o recrudescimento da agenda governista no Brasil está assentado na ampliação da chancela social para o aniquilamento de corpos negros. Ou seja, a nova capangagem institucional, que se reveza na alta patente do governo desde o *impeachment* da ex-presidenta Dilma Rousseff (em 2016), tem no aprofundamento do genocídio negro um dos pilares essenciais de sua atuação.

Tomando essa perspectiva como acertada, pode-se sustentar que o sofrimento impingido aos corpos negros constitui o Brasil. Conforme disse o então Prefeito do Município do Rio de Janeiro, o bispo Marcelo Crivella, em 07 de março de 2018: "Tudo na vida pode ser perigoso. . . . É impossível também você fazer uma incursão na comunidade carente sem que haja uma certa ação de violência porque a criminalidade ali é muito grande, é muito forte."[7] No mesmo dia, o General Augusto Heleno (ex-comandante das tropas brasileiras no Haiti e atual Ministro-Chefe do Gabinete de Segurança Institucional da Presidência da República no governo de Jair Bolsonaro), falou na Escola Superior de Guerra: "O verbo da missão é eliminar. Ou bota na cadeia ou mata. . . . A Colômbia ficou 50 anos em guerra civil porque não fizeram o que fizemos no Araguaia."[8] No dia 1 de novembro de 2018, o governador do Estado do Rio Janeiro, Wilson Witzel, em entrevista ao jornal *Estado de São Paulo*, disse: "a polícia vai fazer o correto: vai mirar na cabecinha e... fogo! Para não ter erro."[9] Em entrevista concedida ao *Jornal Nacional* no dia 28 de agosto de 2018, o então candidato à Presidência da República Jair Bolsonaro declarou "que criminoso não pode ser tratado como 'um ser humano normal' e, por isso, se um policial 'matar 10, 15 ou 20 com 10 ou 30 tiros cada um' deve ser condecorado e não processado."[10]

A autorização pública para relativizar o valor da vida e da humanidade de boa parte da população brasileira é tão expressiva que trechos como esses são repetidos sem nenhum constrangimento por pessoas que ocupam diferentes posições institucionais. São governadores, prefeitos, comandantes, desembargadores e parlamentares, irmanados na enunciação de agressões amplamente veiculadas. As violências a que estamos submetidos/as se perpetua através de crimes contra nós, contra a possibilidade de sermos vidas viáveis, de construirmos relações e instituições respeitosas. Ao nos violarem, violam a Democracia, o Estado de Direito e o projeto constitucional que construímos a muitas mãos em 1987/88.

A maneira pela qual essas violências (não) são registradas pela população brasileira demonstra o quão frágil são os pactos políticos que fomos capazes de construir. Trata-se de arranjos políticos frágeis, porque incapazes de nos reconhecer em nossa igual humanidade, frágeis porque acumpliciados com o racismo, com o sexismo, com a LGBTfobia, com o encarceramento em massa e com todas as formas de hierarquização da vida.

Os tiros que executaram Marielle Franco e Anderson Gomes em 14 de março de 2018,[11] os pneus que arrastaram Claudia da Silva Ferreira em 2014,[12] as fardas que impediram que a marcha contra a farsa da abolição em 1988 alcançasse o monumento a Zumbi,[13] as togas que condenaram Rafael Braga (2017/2018) contrariando ou impedindo a constituição de provas periciais,[14] ou a subnotificação dos assassinatos contra a população transvestigênero[15] são exemplos dos processos de hierarquização entre humanos e das (im)possibilidades de seguir sendo,[16] que não são exclusivas daqui, não se constituem como eventos isolados e continuam a marcar o que vem pela frente.

Cada faceta dessa realidade permite mostrar uma parte do que nos constitui como sociedade. Elas mostram o racismo que se manifesta nas nossas instituições públicas e nas nossas relações sociais, dimensões muito pouco visíveis nas imagens que se (re)produzem sobre o Brasil. Mostram que o ódio que mata e que se multiplica decorre daqueles que determinam o padrão do humano a partir de si, daqueles que têm o poder de definir as vidas que importam.

4. Dos Passos da Resistência

Se, até aqui, consideramos importante destacar a crueza do terror no Brasil, uma leitura amefricana da realidade nos impele a tomar como igualmente prementes as perspectivas de resistência ensejadas a confrontar esse estado de coisas. Nesse sentido, é sempre oportuno lembrar que, no amálgama político que conforma as estruturas sociais no país, o forjamento de "alianças progressistas" é testado pelos limites impostos pelo racismo.

Por isso, quando Iya N'la Beata de Yemonja disse, em 2015, "vamos mulheres, me dêem a mão que vocês estão seguras. Não solte a minha mão que eu não soltarei a de vocês,"[17] o fez imbuída de sua matripotência para conclamar o Brasil para a luta. Uma luta de todas e todos, tecida na união que permitiu a nossa sobrevivência a despeito da escravidão colonial e de suas manifestações contemporâneas. Nos conclamou a uma luta sem armas, com palavras e com dignidade. Nos conclamou a lutar pela vida, assim como ela fez durante toda sua passagem física por aqui, representando uma longa e linda linhagem de mulheres negras comprometida com a continuidade de seu povo, com a preservação de nossa memória, com a conquista de direitos e de condições materiais e simbólicas de dignidade e respeito.

O que disse Iya N'la Beata de Yemonja e o que reivindicava Marielle Franco quando mobilizava a expressão "eu sou porque nós somos" é diferente do que tem virado a utilização – como *slogan* – da ideia "ninguém solta a mão de ninguém."[18] Para que faça sentido eu pedir que alguém não solte a minha mão, é preciso que estejamos de mãos dadas e que essa relação seja uma relação segura. Através do conceito de racismo antinegro, percebemos que não estamos juntos e juntas. Na melhor das hipóteses, podemos agir de forma coordenada quando efetivamente partilharmos o desejo de viver em uma sociedade antirracista. Não estamos irmanados/as, nem do ponto de vista do vilipêndio e nem do ponto de vista das responsabilidades para a construção de uma sociedade efetivamente democrática. Para que possamos agir de forma coordenada, é preciso que cada um e cada uma, do seu lugar, trabalhe na mesma direção.

A responsabilidade dos corpos privilegiados é de implosão, por dentro. Porque é a *zona do ser* que faz parte das engrenagens de controle. A responsabilidade de quem é alvo do genocídio é outra. Não podemos implodir por dentro algo do qual não fazemos parte. Não seremos eternamente a mãe preta a acalentar o sono intranquilo dos meninos e meninas de engenho que enunciam discursos de liberdade e democracia, sem se implicarem radicalmente com a sua realização. É preciso que a *zona do ser* aprenda a se colocar "na reta,"[19] não no centro. É preciso que ofereçam seus privilégios para que se convertam em políticas de reparação.

A nossa responsabilidade é de outra natureza e repousa numa generosidade incapaz de ser compreendida por muitos. Fomos e somos pilhadas, descontinuadas, mutiladas em nossas potencialidades, mas historicamente oferecemos projetos políticos de liberdade capazes de congregar todas as formas de ser e estar na natureza, pautadas no acordo mútuo sobre nossa igual humanidade. Nossa responsabilidade é sobreviver! Sobreviver a despeito e apesar do racismo antinegro, em todas as suas formas de manifestação. E faremos isso não porque somos mais fortes, mas porque não nos condicionaremos aos vocabulários de luta, nem aos caminhos de resistência que são considerados válidos. Sobreviveremos porque nossa humanidade não está reduzida à versão depreciativa que projetam sobre nós, e porque temos uma ancestral caminhada de ampliação de estratégias de liberdade, de luta por democracia e por respeito.

Resistiremos porque há muita gente que enfrenta a morte e os processos de morte em vida não como algo que eventualmente pode acontecer, mas como presença cotidiana, que tem muito a ensinar. Mães, familiares de vítimas de violência do Estado, jovens e velhas mulheres cis e transvestigêneres, mesmo cotidianamente lembradas/os da vulnerabilidade de seus corpos nos apresentam caminhos alternativos de reexistência.

Marielle Franco escreveu em sua conta no Twitter, dias antes de sua execução: "Quantos mais precisarão morrer?"[20] O que mais precisa acontecer para que os defensores das armas sejam confrontados com as mortes em série que produzem com dinheiro público (nos quartéis, nas delegacias, nos hospitais públicos, nas escolas públicas, nos gabinetes do executivo, legislativo, judiciário e órgãos do sistema de justiça) ou com sua cumplicidade?

Conversando recentemente com Edson Cardoso, ouvimos que até hoje, no Brasil, nenhuma força política pôde prescindir da imagem do negro submisso. Nenhuma. Se, nas narrativas autoritárias, nossas mortes são defendidas ostensivamente, é também sobre a nossa carne que repousam os efeitos desproporcionais do que precisa ser negociado, nas narrativas mais democráticas.

Nesse sentido, é importante dar visibilidade ao fato de que o aprofundamento dos termos do racismo no Brasil não é apenas a consequência mais tangível dessa guinada conservadora em curso no país. A plataforma do racismo é, antes de tudo, o pressuposto que permite a própria consolidação desse projeto político. É em torno do racismo que se forma o consenso necessário para sustentar dinâmicas políticas impopulares. A promessa de que haverá derramamento de sangue negro no "reestabelecimento da ordem" é um dos *slogans* mais poderosos para garantir a adesão social aos arranjos dos novos tempos.

Diante disso, nos perguntamos: o que falta para que sejamos capazes de construir um pacto de civilidade ancorado na defesa de nossa igual humanidade? Não há democracia onde os privilégios permanecem intocados. Não há justiça onde o sistema de justiça opera com o objetivo de garantir a legalidade para a zona do ser e perpetuar a violência, como norma, na zona do não ser.

Cientes dessas desigualdades fundantes, calibramos o sentido da resistência negra como artefato político fundamental não só para a sobrevivência das comunidades negras, mas para o forjamento de arranjos sociais verdadeiramente democráticos no Brasil. Nesse horizonte, a denúncia da atual conjuntura social brasileira é tão importante quanto o estabelecimento de parcerias em África e na Diáspora, para que se milite a favor de uma ruptura das dinâmicas da antinegritude que assaltam os corpos negros em seus mais variados contextos.

É a partir de um reclame que se inicia nas batalhas locais e supera as fronteiras artificiais criadas pelos muros da dominação que seremos capazes de enfrentar os processos de expropriação, que têm sentenciado de forma desproporcional as pessoas negras em toda parte. Por isso, escolhemos fechar esta reflexão com um convite à partilha de nossos dilemas e estratégias. Fazemos isso por acreditar que um encontro nas águas que nos apartaram, nos perversos processos da colonização, pode servir como fonte de fortalecimento dos passos da resistência ao racismo.

Sigamos então, no tempo das travessias oceânicas que nos irmanam, nos termos dos compromissos que nos convocam e nos horizontes que enunciam o amor como o cais seguro, a aportar o destino final de nossa navegação.

NOTAS

1. Lélia Gonzalez (1988) chama pretuguês ou pretoguês à língua culta falada no Brasil, significativamente distinta do português falado em Portugal, exatamente pelo aspecto (tão) constitutivo (quanto negado) das línguas africanas e indígenas na sua conformação: "chamo de 'pretoguês' e que nada mais é do que marca de africanização do português falado no Brasil, facilmente constatável sobretudo no espanhol da região caribenha" (Gonzalez 1988, 70).

2. Sobre o significado do mito da democracia racial, recorremos à contribuição que Sueli Carneiro levou ao Supremo Tribunal Federal Brasileiro quando da audiência pública no âmbito da Arguição de Descumprimento de Preceito Fundamental 186, que julgava a constitucionalidade da adoção de ações afirmativas de corte étnico-racial para os processos seletivos das universidades públicas. Ao longo de sua contribuição, Sueli Carneiro destaca a pergunta feita pelo psicanalista Contardo Calligaris: "De onde surge, em tantos brasileiros brancos bem intencionados, a convicção de viver em uma democracia racial? Qual é a origem desse mito?" Para Sueli e para Calligaris, a resposta não é difícil, o mito da democracia racial é fundado em uma sensação unilateral e branca de conforto nas relações inter-raciais. Esse conforto não é uma invenção, ele existe de fato, ele é efeito de uma posição dominante incontestada. Quando Calligaris faz referência à ideia de incontestada no contexto da sociedade brasileira, quer dizer que não é só uma posição dominante de fato – mais riqueza, mais poder –, é mais do que isso, é sim uma posição dominante de fato, mas que vale como uma posição de direito, ou seja, como efeito não da riqueza, mas de uma espécie de hierarquia de castas. A desigualdade no Brasil, segundo o psicanalista, é a expressão material de uma organização hierárquica, ou seja, é a continuação da escravatura. Neste sentido, Calligaris conclui que: "Sonhar com a continuação da pretensa democracia racial brasileira é aqui a expressão da nostalgia de uma estrutura social que assegura, a tal ponto, o conforto de uma posição branca dominante, que o branco e só ele pode se dar ao luxo de afirmar que a raça não importa" (Pires 2016, 142).

3. No texto *A Categoria Político-Cultural de Amefricanidade*, Lélia Gonzalez (1988) propõe uma maneira alternativa de compreender o processo histórico de formação do Brasil e da América. Ao eleger a noção de *Améfrica Ladina* como representativa das experiências que

aqui se conformaram, Gonzalez redimensiona a importância da influência da cultura ameríndia e africana para produção e compreensão da realidade. Além da afirmação dessas pertenças, o termo *ladino* desessencializa essas matrizes culturais, ao pressupor um processo de aculturação e os desafios do "não lugar" que se apresentam na dificuldade de integração dessas heranças e sujeitos à sociedade colonial.

4. Se tomamos a díade branco vs. não-branco para pensar as estruturas racialmente hierarquizadas, entenderemos o branco (o representativo do ocidental, cisheteronormativo, patriarcal, proprietário, cristão, sem deficiência) como modelo de humanidade sustentado pela supremacia branca. No contexto das relações raciais estadunidenses, por exemplo, estão excluídos da categoria "branco" os asiáticos, indígenas e latinos. Nesse sentido, ser humano – ter a sua humanidade reconhecida – é ser não-negro, mais do que não-branco (Vargas 2017). No Brasil, o mesmo raciocínio pode ser feito em relação a Asiáticos e outros grupos "não brancos" (pela lógica da supremacia branca), mas que são lidos socialmente como brancos na dinâmica de relações raciais que por aqui se desenvolveu. Em relação aos povos indígenas, a questão de vinculá-los à *zona do ser* ou à *zona do não ser* ganha complexidade. A proximidade que existe entre o genocídio negro e indígena no Brasil não se reflete em outras manifestações de violência e resistência. Como o objetivo central deste volume da revista é discutir o racismo referenciado aos afrodescendentes, tomaremos como premissa o conceito de racismo antinegro, sem explorar as especificidades da questão indígena sobre os processos de violência que serão trabalhados.

5. No contexto brasileiro, apelar para a ideia de mestiçagem/miscigenação para explicar as relações raciais significa mascarar e amplificar as hierarquias de humanidade que a colonialidade constituiu sobre a população afrodescendente. O cenário que temos por aqui posiciona os negros (pretos e pardos) de forma sobrerrepresentada nas estatísticas de extermínio e dos processos de morte em vida desencadeados pelo encarceramento em massa, falta de acesso à saúde, educação, trabalho, previdência social, lazer, segurança alimentar e moradia, e sub-representados nos indicadores que refletem o bem viver. A noção de mestiçagem que por aqui se desenvolveu está intrinsecamente vinculada com a ideia de branqueamento da população e de reprodução de violências materiais e simbólicas sobre negros e negras. Por esses motivos, só faz sentido para nós pautar o racismo a partir da noção de antinegritude.

6. De acordo com Yuderkys Espinosa-Miñoso, *Abya Yala* é o nome em língua Kuna para designar "terra em plena maturidade" ou "terra de sangue vital," ou seja, o território que representa o continente que os colonizadores espanhóis passaram a denominar América. Nesse sentido, ver: Yuderkys Espinosa Miñoso, Diana Gómez Correal e Karina Ochoa Muñoz, eds., *Tejiendo de Otro Modo: Feminismo, Epistemología y Apuestas Descoloniales en Abya Yala* (Popayán: Editorial Universidad del Cauca, 2014), 15.

7. Disponível em https://oglobo.globo.com/rio/crivella-diz-que-impossivel-entrar-em-comunidade-carente-sem-violencia-22465721, acesso em 15 de março de 2019.

8. De acordo com matéria de Marco Aurélio Canônico: "Rio, Haiti, Araguaia." Disponível em https://www1.folha.uol.com.br/colunas/marco-aurelio-canonico/2018/03/rio-haiti-araguaia.shtml, acesso em 08 de março de 2018.

9. Disponível em https://veja.abril.com.br/politica/wilson-witzel-a-policia-vai-mirar-na-cabecinha-e-fogo/, acesso em 15 de março de 2019.

10. Disponível em https://g1.globo.com/politica/eleicoes/2018/noticia/2018/08/28/bolsonaro-diz-ao-jn-que-criminoso-nao-e-ser-humano-normal-e-defende-policial-que-matar-10-15-ou-20.ghtml, acesso em 15 de março de 2019.

11. Para mais Informações sobre o desdobramento do caso, ver https://www.bbc.com/portuguese/brasil-47530611, acesso em 15 de março de 2019.

12. Notícia sobre o caso disponível em http://g1.globo.com/rio-de-janeiro/noticia203/2014/ 03/arrastada-por-carro-da-pm-do-rio-foi-morta-por-tiro-diz-atestado.html, acesso em 15 de março de 2019.

13. Informações sobre a marcha disponível em https://mamapress.wordpress.com/2014/10/25/a-marcha-que-mudou-o-movimento-negro/, acesso em 15 de março de 2019.

14. Informações sobre o caso Rafael Braga disponíveis em http://www.justificando.com/2018/06/27/rafael-braga-5-anos-de-injustica/, acesso em 15 de março de 2019.

15. Os índices de assassinatos e violências contra travestis e transexuais no Brasil são escandalosos. Para maiores informações, ver o "Dossiê: Assassinatos e Violência contra Travestis e Transexuais no Brasil em 2018," desenvolvido por Bruna G. Benevides e Sayonara Naider Bonfim Nogueira. Documento disponível em https://antrabrasil.files.wordpress.com/2019/01/dossie-dos-assassinatos-e-violencia-contra-pessoas-trans-em-2018.pdf, acesso em 04 de maio de 2019.

16. Cada vida perdida representa os limites de uma sociedade forjada na manutenção de privilégios para poucos e na violência permanente sobre a maior parte de sua gente: a subjugação da vida ao poder da morte, o signo da necropolítica explicado por Mbembe (2018), é entendido por nós a cada corpo que tomba. Esses crimes representam as fraturas expostas do modelo de moer gente negra sobre o qual se construiu o Brasil e que continua a ditar o funcionamento de nossas instituições, principalmente as de (in)segurança pública.

17. Fala de Iya Nla Beata de Yemonja. Disponível no vídeo "Feminismo Ancestral," em https://www.youtube.com/watch?v=KoxLn49af2A, acesso em 20 de março de 2019.

18. Sobre o sentido que a expressão vem ganhando, ver: https://g1.globo.com/mg/minas-gerais/eleicoes/2018/noticia/2018/10/29/ninguem-solta-a-mao-de-ninguem-desenho-que-viralizou-no-pais-e-criacao-de-mineira.ghtml, acesso em 19 de março de 2019.

19. Mobilizamos a expressão "colocar-se na reta" por representar o oposto do comportamento que entendemos caracterizar os corpos privilegiados em relação aos privilégios

que possuem, resumido na expressão "tirar da reta," que significaria: 1) Tomar providências para evitar ser responsabilizado por algo que provavelmente dará errado; 2) Atitude da pessoa que, ao surgirem problemas graves com seus subordinados ou sistemas gerenciados por ela, mostra argumentos que podem convencer outros de que é inocente apesar de ter parte da culpa.

20. Nesse sentido, ver: https://g1.globo.com/rj/rio-de-janeiro/noticia/quantos-mais-precisarao-morrer-postou-vereadora-um-dia-antes-de-ser-assassinada-no-rj.ghtml, acesso em 25 de março de 2021.

REFERÊNCIAS BIBLIOGRÁFICAS

Fanon, Frantz. 2008. *Pele Negra, Máscaras Brancas.* Tradução de Renato da Silveira. Salvador: EDUFBA.

Flauzina, Ana Luiza Pinheiro. 2008. *Corpo Negro Caído no Chão. O Sistema Penal e o Projeto Genocida do Estado Brasileiro.* Rio de Janeiro: Contraponto.

Gonzalez, Lélia. 1988. "A Categoria Político-Cultural de Amefricanidade." *Tempo Brasileiro* 92 (93): 69-82.

James, Joy. 1996. *Resisting State Violence. Radicalism, Gender and Race in U.S. Culture.* Minneapolis: University of Minnesota Press.

Mbembe, Achille. 2001. "As Formas Africanas de Auto-Inscrição." *Estudos Afro-Asiáticos* 23 (1): 171-209.

Mbembe, Achille. 2018. *Necropolítica: Biopoder, Soberania, Estado de Exceção, Política da Morte.* Tradução de Renata Santini. São Paulo: N-1 Edições.

Nascimento, Abdias do. 1978. *O Genocídio do Negro Brasileiro: Processo de um Racismo Mascarado.* Rio de Janeiro: Editora Paz e Terra.

Patterson, William L. et al. 1970. *We Charge Genocide: The Historic Petition to the United Nations for Relief from a Crime of the United States Government against the Negro People.* 2ª edição. Nova Iorque: International Publishers.

Pires, Thula. 2016. *Criminalização do Racismo: Entre Política de Reconhecimento e Meio de Legitimação do Controle Social sobre os Negros.* Brasília: Brado Negro.

Vargas, João Costa. 2010. "A Diáspora Negra como Genocídio." *Revista da ABPN* 2 (Jun.- Out.): 31-56.

Vargas, João Costa. 2017. "Por uma Mudança de Paradigma: Antinegritude e Antagonismo Estrutural." *Revista de Ciências Sociais: RCS* 48 (2): 83-105.

ANA FLAUZINA é mulher preta que aposta nos movimentos da vida, do amor e das batalhas. É professora adjunta da Faculdade de Educação da Universidade Federal da Bahia, Brasil.

THULA PIRES é mulher preta de axé, mãe da Dandara e bailarina. Professora adjunta de Direito Constitucional Pontifícia Universidade Católica do Rio de Janeiro (PUC-Rio, Brasil) e coordenadora do NIREMA (Núcleo Interdisciplinar de Reflexão e Memória Afrodescendente) na mesma Instituição.

Relações Raciais e Identidade Nacional no Brasil: da Nação (ambiguamente) Mestiça à Nação Multicultural e Pluriétnica[1]

RESUMO: Discursos de identidade nacional no Brasil foram construídos vinculados à problemática das relações raciais. O presente trabalho elabora uma periodização analítica desses discursos, por meio do que denominamos "ordens de discurso" de raça e identidade nacional. Atentando para como o Estado se articula com intelectuais na construção de narrativas sobre a nação, delineamos três ordens de discurso hegemônicas em contextos históricos particulares. A primeira consolida-se entre as décadas de 1870 e 1930, período em que a incorporação de teorias racistas pela elite política subsidiou o estabelecimento de critérios diferenciados de cidadania, com a mestiçagem considerada um obstáculo para a construção da nação. A segunda ordem, cuja hegemonia seguiu até fins dos anos 1970, consolida a "fábula das três raças" como mito fundador da nação – o discurso da "mestiçagem harmoniosa" construiu uma identidade nacional homogeneizante que negava as desigualdades raciais. A terceira ordem de discurso começa a tomar corpo no final da ditadura militar e segue até os anos 2010. Essa narrativa de nação insurge-se contra a anterior e se fundamenta na crítica da "democracia racial" e na valorização da raça enquanto elemento identitário e definidor de direitos. O Estado incorpora então, de forma circunscrita e conflituosa, o discurso da nação multicultural e pluriétnica. O delineamento dessas ordens de discurso auxilia na compreensão dos fundamentos teóricos de debates atuais sobre políticas de promoção da igualdade racial no Brasil, em particular das ações afirmativas.

PALAVRAS-CHAVE: Brasil; Identidade nacional; Mestiçagem; Relações raciais.

ABSTRACT: Discourses of national identity in Brazil were built linked to the problem of race relations. This paper elaborates an analytical periodization of these discourses, through what we denominate "orders of discourse" of race and national identity. It pays attention to how the State articulates with intellectuals in the construction of national narratives, and delineates three orders of hegemonic discourses in particular historical contexts.

The first order was consolidated between the years of 1870 and 1930, the period in which the incorporation of racist theories by the political elite subsidized the creation of differentiated criteria of citizenship, and the miscegenation of the population was considered an obstacle to the nation's construction. The second order was hegemonic until the late 1970s, and consolidated the "fable of the three races" as a founding myth of the nation. The discourse of "harmonic miscegenation" constructed an homogeneous national identity that denied the existence of racial inequalities. The third order of discourse began to take shape at the end of the military dictatorship and continued until the years 2010. This narrative of the nation insisted against the previous one and was/is based on the critique of "racial democracy" and on the valorization of race as an element of identity. The State then incorporates, in a circumscribed and conflicted way, the discourse of the multicultural and multiethnic nation. The delineation of these orders of discourse assists in understanding the theoretical foundations of current debates on policies to promote racial equality in Brazil, in particular affirmative action.

KEYWORDS: Brazil; National identity; Miscegenation; Race relations.

Introdução

É usual reconhecer como estão incrustadas, na história da política e da intelectualidade brasileiras, as reflexões sobre identidade nacional. Pelo menos desde que o país conquista a independência jurídico-política, no início do século XIX, suas elites dirigentes buscam delinear os traços identitários que seriam característicos do Brasil – seu povo, sua história, seus símbolos – para, assim, descortinar os caminhos a serem seguidos no processo de constituição da nação que se almeja. Mesmo hoje, os debates sobre identidade nacional continuam politicamente importantes – seja em nível global, especialmente no que diz respeito à situação dos refugiados e à perseguição a "minorias" étnicas, raciais e religiosas (McCrone e Bechhofer 2015, 196e 199); seja, no caso brasileiro, via o reconhecimento de que estamos, há algum tempo, colocando em xeque os padrões e modelos consolidados de se delinear a identidade nacional, vivenciando agora processos de reconfiguração que não ocorrem desprovidos de conflitos e problematizações (Soares 2011; Guimarães 2012).

Seria difícil ignorar o fato de que, no Brasil, as reflexões (e as políticas de Estado) em torno da identidade nacional carregam, desde o início, uma vinculação com modos específicos de se compreender as relações raciais no país.

Veremos mais adiante que a "raça" foi, e continua sendo, um elemento chave para se entender as narrativas de nação em torno do Brasil – seja em fins do século XIX, quando as teorias e práticas de "branqueamento" mobilizavam o projeto de nação concebido por nossas elites; em meados do século XX, em que se estabelece institucionalmente a imagem do Brasil como um paraíso das relações raciais; ou neste início do século XXI, em que "novas etnicidades negras" (Costa 2006a) e políticas de ação afirmativa com recorte racial colocam em xeque as noções consolidadas acerca da nacionalidade.

O objetivo do presente trabalho é construir uma periodização analítica desses diferentes modos de se compreender a identidade nacional no Brasil – e, no processo, mostrar a conformação de interpretações hegemônicas acerca das relações raciais no país. Recorremos, para tanto, à noção de "ordem de discurso," visando dar conta dos modos como a reflexão teórica se articula à ação do Estado para elaborar, discursivamente, imagens do Brasil enquanto nação. Apresentamos, de início, a concepção de identidade nacional que orienta nossas reflexões, e em seguida abordamos três ordens de discurso distintas, terminando enfim por refletir sobre como essa sistematização auxilia na compreensão dos fundamentos teóricos dos debates atuais sobre políticas de ação afirmativa com recorte racial no Brasil.

Discurso e Identidade Nacional

De pouca serventia seriam, para os nossos fins, as antigas abordagens de nação e identidade nacional que tendem a vê-las como realidades dotadas de características unívocas e imutáveis. Ao invés disso, partimos aqui das chamadas "interpretações construtivistas" no estudo das nações (Costa 2006b, 133), que têm em Benedict Anderson sua referência principal, e das implicações que Stuart Hall desenvolve, no seio dessa perspectiva teórica, para uma definição "discursiva" de identidade nacional.

Talvez uma das principais contribuições de Hall, nesse aspecto, esteja em entender a nação não apenas como uma entidade política, "mas algo que produz sentidos – *um sistema de representação cultural*. As pessoas não são apenas cidadãos legais de uma nação; elas participam na *ideia* de nação como representada na sua cultura nacional" (Hall 1996, 612;[2] itálico no original). O autor argumenta que a identidade nacional consiste num conjunto de "significados sobre 'a nação' com os quais nós podemos nos *identificar*" (Hall 1996, 613; itálico no original). Significados contingentes, historicamente particulares, que estariam contidos nas histórias e memórias que conectam o presente e o passado da nação, nas imagens que são construídas sobre ela.

A identidade nacional pode, assim, ser concebida como um *discurso*. "Discurso," aqui, precisa ser entendido como a prática a partir da qual os indivíduos dotam a realidade de significado (Ruiz Ruiz 2009, 3). Como afirma Hall (1992, 201): "Um discurso é um grupo de enunciados que fornece uma linguagem para falar sobre – isto é, um modo de representar – um tipo particular de conhecimento sobre um tópico."

A "comunidade imaginada" que é a nação (Anderson 2008) é, assim, construída discursivamente, através de narrativas que contêm os elementos definidores de unidade e igualdade coletivas, de fronteiras e autonomia – e que são continuamente lançadas por políticos, intelectuais, mídia etc. Tais discursos, segundo Hall, fornecem uma série de imagens, panoramas, cenários, eventos históricos, símbolos que representam as experiências partilhadas que dão significado à nação: "Como membros de tal 'comunidade imaginada,' nós nos vemos partilhando desta narrativa" (Hall 1996, 614).

Essa interpretação, que aponta para a possibilidade de conceber a identidade nacional como construção discursiva, é fecunda por nos possibilitar perceber que não existe *uma* identidade nacional, num sentido essencialista (Wodak *et al.* 2009, 186-187). Diferentes identidades são discursivamente construídas de acordo com os atores sociais envolvidos, as conjunturas sociais e os contextos históricos. O que significa dizer que ideias sobre a nação são elementos pertinentes nas lutas políticas das sociedades.

Por ser esse grande construto disputado por diferentes grupos que manobram para se apoderar da sua definição e efeitos legitimadores, "a nação tende a converter-se num símbolo manipulável e a ser disputado em grau, profundidade e resultados diferentes pelos indivíduos e grupos em interação" (Fernandes 2006, 47-48). A luta pela definição de uma identidade é uma forma de delimitar as fronteiras de uma política que procura se impor como legítima. Nesse sentido, a pergunta fundamental seria: quem são os artífices "desta identidade e desta memória que se querem nacionais? A que grupos sociais elas se vinculam e a que interesses elas servem?" (Ortiz 2006, 139).

A análise dos discursos de identidade nacional historicamente construídos na sociedade brasileira envolve, assim, considerações dessa dimensão política. E é justamente para melhor compreendê-la que iremos empregar o conceito de "ordem de discurso," como trabalhado por Fairclough (2001). O autor o utiliza para designar as convenções e normas discursivas subjacentes a todo evento discursivo. Para os fins deste trabalho, tratam-se de convenções e normas acerca do modo particular de construir determinado "assunto" ou "tópico" (Fairclough 2001, 164) – no caso, a identidade nacional. Os "elementos" das ordens de discurso são, aqui, acessados a partir dos conceitos e os sentidos particulares que assumem em determinado contexto histórico-social.

A principal riqueza desse conceito está no reconhecimento da constituição iminentemente histórica e social do discurso. Segundo Fairclough (2001, 99), as ordens de discurso podem ser consideradas facetas discursivas das ordens sociais – facetas discursivas do "equilíbrio instável e contraditório que constitui uma hegemonia" (Fairclough 2001, 123-124). As ordens de discurso, portanto, são parte das disputas políticas e culturais para a constituição de hegemonias em contextos histórico-sociais particulares, podendo ser desarticuladas e rearticuladas nesse processo.

Isso significa que, no processo de sistematização de tais ordens de discurso, precisamos estar atentos às lutas e aos atores sociais envolvidos na sua construção. Especificamente no caso brasileiro, seguiremos a trilha aberta por Ortiz (2006, 140-141) e levaremos em conta dois pontos: a relação do Estado brasileiro com o processo de elaboração de narrativas sobre a nação; e o papel dos "intelectuais"[3] enquanto "mediadores simbólicos" na construção da identidade nacional.

Assentados nesses critérios, e com base num exame da literatura pertinente, delineamos três momentos históricos em que ordens de discurso específicas estabeleceram uma hegemonia política e cultural no Brasil. Um primeiro período que segue da década de 1870 até a década de 1930; outro que vai dos anos 1930 até fins da década de 1970; e um terceiro que segue daí até a década de 2010. Esses períodos delineiam os contextos em que se constituem padrões discursivos acerca da identidade nacional no Brasil. Iremos, a seguir, abordar cada uma dessas ordens de discurso, verificando como os projetos de nação e as concepções de identidade nacional estiveram vinculados com uma problematização das relações raciais na sociedade brasileira.

Brasil, Nação Branca?

É no final do século XIX, particularmente após a década de 1870, que podemos localizar a conformação de uma primeira ordem de discurso de raça e identidade nacional no Brasil. Tanto o fim do sistema escravista quanto a proclamação da República colocaram às camadas dirigentes o desafio de pensar e construir uma nação adequada aos padrões civilizatórios então considerados essenciais – não só no que diz respeito às configurações jurídico-políticas de cidadania e de trabalho, mas também (e talvez sobretudo) no que se refere à configuração racial da população.

Tendo a abolição da escravatura, em 1888, estabelecido, ao menos juridicamente, a população negra como detentora do rótulo de cidadã, ela não podia ser desconsiderada do projeto de nação que então se buscava forjar. E, no entanto, na perspectiva das elites – na medida em que não se alteraram os padrões culturais racistas característicos do período escravocrata –, era justamente esse grande contingente populacional não branco que dificultava a incorporação dos padrões civilizatórios de inspiração europeia, considerados superiores (Costa 2010, 1). Como afirma Munanga (1999, 52), o que estava em jogo, para muitos intelectuais nas décadas seguintes à Abolição, era a questão de como transformar a pluralidade de raças, culturas e valores civilizatórios tão diferentes, de identidades tão diversas, numa única coletividade de cidadãos, numa só nação. "A pluralidade racial nascida do processo colonial representava, na cabeça dessa elite, uma ameaça e um grande obstáculo no caminho da construção de uma nação que se pensava branca" (Munanga 1999, 51).

Desse modo, a reflexão sobre raça no Brasil (ou sobre as *diferenças* e as *relações* raciais, num viés escancaradamente desfavorável à população negra) começa a se desenvolver de forma articulada a uma reflexão sobre o caráter e os destinos da nação. Os dois aspectos evidenciam desde esse período sua profunda vinculação: as relações raciais se tornam, nesse momento (e posteriormente), objeto de detida reflexão intelectual e, *simultânea e articuladamente*, de políticas estatais. É no inter-relacionamento dessas duas dimensões que podemos perceber a conformação da ordem de discurso a que nos referimos, na qual a ideia de *mestiçagem* desenvolve um papel central.

Hoje já são relativamente bem conhecidos os meandros da reflexão sobre a "questão racial" nesse período, seus principais expoentes e as instituições que lhe deram guarida e divulgação, como os museus etnográficos, os institutos históricos e geográficos e as faculdades de direito e medicina (Skidmore 2012; Schwarcz 1993). Para o que nos interessa neste trabalho, cabe atentar para o modo paradoxal com que a mestiçagem foi concebida pela elite nacional detentora das posições institucionais que lhe permitiam ditar os rumos do país – paradoxo que nasce, em certo sentido, da influência de teorias raciais europeias, especialmente as de Arthur de Gobineau, Friedrich Ratzel e Thomas Buckle (Schwarcz 1993; Costa 2006a).

De um lado, a mestiçagem vai ser vista, por intelectuais como Silvio Romero e Nina Rodrigues, como crucial para explicar o atraso ou uma possível inviabilidade da nação no Brasil. As teorias europeias, que enfatizavam a pureza e a hierarquia racial, ajudarão a conformar uma interpretação da sociedade brasileira que destacava a inviabilidade, a degenerescência de uma nação composta por raças mistas; em outras palavras, a composição étnica e racial do Brasil, distante do modelo branco então valorizado, tornava-o um "modelo da falta e do atraso" (Schwarcz 1993, 48). A mestiçagem é, assim, vista sob um prisma essencialmente negativo, uma espécie de patologia incurável da sociedade brasileira que impossibilitava a construção de uma identidade nacional edificante: "A presença majoritária de povos/raças considerados inferiores e a indesejável mestiçagem transformavam o Brasil, na visão da intelectualidade do século XIX, em uma nação condenada ao fracasso, impossibilitada, pela sua composição étnico-racial, de alcançar o estatuto de nação civilizada" (Soares 2011, 101).

De outro lado, além dessa chave de leitura, digamos "pessimista," ela será lida, simultânea e paradoxalmente, numa outra chave, se não "positiva" ao menos "esperançosa." A incorporação de ideias eugenistas – especificamente neo-lamarckianas (Telles 2003, 45) – pelas camadas dirigentes fará com que a mestiçagem seja vista como um *meio*, uma espécie de *instrumento* para a construção da nação branca que, esperava-se, o Brasil ainda poderia se tornar.

Grosso modo, essas concepções eugenistas apontavam que as deficiências genéticas das raças consideradas inferiores poderiam ser superadas nas gerações seguintes via o cruzamento com as raças ditas superiores – entendendo-se, nesse contexto, as "deficiências" como a não adequação ao padrão racial branco. Sendo assim, tais pensadores aceitavam as previsões racistas de inferioridade do negro e do mulato, mas acreditavam que essa inferioridade poderia ser suplantada através da miscigenação. Conforme apontam Skidmore (2012, 111-112) e Telles (2003, 45-46), a partir da taxa mais alta de fecundidade entre os brancos e da crença de que os genes brancos eram dominantes, os eugenistas concluíram que a mistura de raças eliminaria a população negra e conduziria, gradualmente, a uma população brasileira completamente branca.

Evidentemente que a mestiçagem, posta nestes termos, carrega em si o pressuposto da superioridade de uma nação formada majoritariamente por uma população branca. Era nesse ideal nacional que repousavam as esperanças das elites políticas e intelectuais da época, em completo contraste com a realidade racialmente diversa do Brasil – e daí podermos chamar de "branqueamento" o ideal e as políticas de Estado que buscaram concretizá-lo então. Esse conjunto de noções vai orientar a ação do Estado brasileiro na direção do estabelecimento de uma nação completamente branca, em que a superioridade numérica da população negra seja superada (Munanga 1999, 52-53).

É esse "branqueamento," prescrito pelos eugenistas, que vai se tornar a principal sustentação da política de imigração do Brasil. Como afirma Telles (2003, 46), a elite brasileira trouxe e subsidiou imigrantes europeus para "melhorar a qualidade" de sua força de trabalho e substituir os ex-escravizados negros. Reafirmando, nesse processo, um conjunto de estereótipos negativos com relação à população negra, e tornando explícita sua inadequação, sua ausência de lugar no projeto de nação que se construía – pois, fundamentalmente, o que se pretendia a longo prazo era o desaparecimento da população negra, seja via mestiçagem, seja via imigração de europeus.

Em resposta ao "racismo científico" do século XIX, a elite brasileira decidiu promover maior miscigenação, mas com a infusão maciça de sangue branco, de milhões de imigrantes europeus. Eles buscaram planejar uma nação branca, através da imigração europeia e das previsões otimistas de que os genes determinantes de traços brancos predominariam na mistura racial, eventualmente branqueando os elementos negros de sua população. (Telles 2003, 315)

Mesmo que esse processo de branqueamento físico da sociedade tenha fracassado – em parte devido aos seus problemáticos e hoje desacreditados pressupostos "científicos" –, seu ideal de nação "ficou intacto no inconsciente coletivo brasileiro" (Munanga 1999, 16). Foi o ideal de branqueamento que orientou, segundo Ricardo Costa (2010, 6-7), a construção de uma identidade nacional baseada na herança cultural europeia, que nega qualquer possibilidade de se pensar em alguma identidade alternativa, fundamentada, por exemplo, em heranças culturais de origem africana ou mesmo indígenas. E daí termos não só um ideal de modernização, levado a cabo na Primeira República, calcado na "europeização" dos costumes (Guimarães 2012, 117), como também a naturalização das desigualdades raciais no período pós-escravização da população negra (Jaccoud 2009, 21).

De fato, a construção dessas ideologias raciais, e a sua incorporação via políticas de Estado, reafirma noções de inferioridade da população negra e, consequentemente, contribui para manter as posições hierárquicas estabelecidas no período anterior. O que mostra que, no fundo, a reflexão e as políticas raciais atuaram, no período pós-escravização, como os pilares da construção de critérios diferenciados de cidadania – pois, na medida em que excluídos do projeto de nação que então se forjava, à população negra restava apenas a integração (política, social) nos padrões dominantes, ou o desaparecimento (resultado esperado pelas políticas de branqueamento).

Nessa primeira ordem de discurso, podemos identificar alguns pontos que permanecerão característicos da forma como o Brasil busca construir seus discursos de identidade nacional. Antes de tudo, a própria preocupação, já anotada, das relações raciais como elemento fundamental para se pensar o passado, o presente e o futuro da nação brasileira. Mas talvez o legado mais duradouro dessa ordem de discurso esteja na sua valorização do "branqueamento" enquanto ideal a ser buscado. Ainda que, nesse período, ela esteja associada com uma total desvalorização da mestiçagem (e consequentemente da população negra), é possível argumentar que o ideal do "branqueamento" permanece mesmo quando a intelectualidade e o Estado brasileiro passam a reconhecer o valor da mestiçagem, e a caracterizar o Brasil enquanto país eminentemente mestiço, como veremos a seguir.

Brasil, Nação Mestiça?

Os anos 1930 no Brasil foram marcados pelo questionamento dos padrões identitários anteriormente construídos acerca da nação, e pela paulatina construção de uma nova ordem de discurso. Progressivamente, as teorias e as políticas de "branqueamento," com a perspectiva do "racismo científico" que as acompanhava, foram postas em causa, e formulou-se um novo modo de compreender a identidade nacional que estendeu sua hegemonia, nas ciências, nas artes e na política, até mais ou menos o fim da década de 1970 (embora sua influência permaneça ainda hoje, como veremos).

Assim como na ordem de discurso anterior, a noção de mestiçagem constitui a chave de leitura essencial para compreendermos as rotações teóricas e políticas efetuadas nesse período. Então, de elemento que singulariza negativamente a sociedade brasileira, e que deve ser buscado apenas na medida em que funciona como caminho para se atingir o ideal de branqueamento, a mistura racial passa a ser vista como o grande trunfo civilizacional do Brasil.

Segundo Guimarães (2012, 120), os principais responsáveis pela construção dessa nova visão da "questão racial" e, consequentemente, da identidade nacional, foram sobretudo Getúlio Vargas, na política, e Gilberto Freyre, nas ciências sociais, mas também os artistas e literatos modernistas e regionalistas, nas artes.

A figura de Gilberto Freyre, em particular, é de importância inescapável no nosso rol de discussões, ainda que fuja do escopo deste trabalho fazer uma leitura detida do seu pensamento.[4] Para os nossos propósitos, cabe, essencialmente, observar os elementos que ajudaram na conformação de uma nova ideia de nação, ainda bastante influente. Nesse sentido, considero que são dois os principais pontos da reflexão de Freyre que dizem respeito à relação entre raça e identidade nacional.

O primeiro deles reside na sua valorização do papel das populações negra e indígena para a formação do Brasil. Evidentemente que essa afirmação precisa ser acompanhada de todas as precauções possíveis. Pois, por um lado, em sua crítica aos pressupostos do "racismo científico" então prevalecente nos meios intelectuais e políticos, Freyre reconhece, de fato, não apenas no elemento branco português, mas também no negro e no índio, elementos formadores que contribuíram para a constituição da cultura e da sociedade brasileiras. É ao escritor pernambucano que se costuma associar essa redefinição positiva do fenômeno da mestiçagem, e a consequente fundamentação de uma nova leitura da identidade nacional, que enfatiza a proeminência do "Brasil mestiço." Ele teria sido um dos primeiros (e certamente o mais influente) a, frente à ideia da degenerescência da nação mestiça brasileira, valorizar as contribuições culturais das diferentes raças para a constituição do Brasil. E, ao fazer isso, "Gilberto Freyre oferece ao brasileiro [sic] uma carteira de identidade" (Ortiz 2006, 42).

Por outro lado, no entanto, esse reconhecimento da constituição "mestiça" da nação brasileira não supera as concepções hierarquizantes relativas às categorias étnico-raciais em contato, características ainda do "racismo científico." O processo formativo narrado nas suas obras clássicas – *Casa-Grande e Senzala* (1933) e *Sobrados e Mucambos* (1936) –, o é a partir ainda de um olhar que concede a primazia da ação constitutiva da nação ao elemento português. Assim, por exemplo, mesmo que Freyre (2006a, 367-368) critique aqueles que não reconhecem o papel dos "escravos negros" na formação econômica e social do Brasil, o seu próprio reconhecimento positivo da "influência negra" é feito a partir da contribuição dos escravizados para a vida cotidiana dos filhos dos senhores de engenho, na sua criação, nos hábitos de lazer, na vida sexual.

A primazia do elemento português na constituição da nação brasileira, mesmo se levando em conta as contribuições de negros e indígenas, é ainda mais evidente quando se examinam as formulações da teoria do lusotropicalismo, que Freyre constrói ao longo da década de 1950. Teoria elaborada no esteio da tentativa do autor de caracterizar "aquele tipo de civilização lusitana que, vitoriosa nos trópicos, constitui hoje toda uma civilização em fase ainda de expansão" – e que ele chama de "lusotropical," em referência "ao fato de vir a expansão lusitana na África, na Ásia, na América, manifestando evidente pendor, da parte do português, pela aclimação como que voluptuosa e não apenas interessada em áreas tropicais ou em terras quentes" (Freyre 2010b, 172).

Conforme mostra Cláudia Castelo (2011), a teoria do lusotropicalismo serviu aos interesses político-ideológicos conjunturais do Estado Novo português, ajudando a perpetuar uma imagem mítica da identidade cultural portuguesa – e alcançou grande reputação e influência na época, mesmo com seus problemáticos pressupostos científicos. Ainda conforme a autora, é interessante observar como as ideias-chave dessa teoria – sobretudo a questão da mestiçagem, da interpenetração de culturas como elemento fundador de um novo tipo de nação – estavam já presentes nas obras-mestre de Freyre, no seu processo de caracterização da colonização portuguesa no Brasil e do encontro e "amalgamento" de raças que se deu nessas terras.

Para caracterizar esse novo tipo de civilização que surge do encontro da cultura e dos padrões civilizacionais portugueses com outros povos originários da América, da Ásia e da África, é que Freyre recorre à ideia do "lusotropical." Há, segundo ele, uma "unidade transnacional de cultura" que perpassa todas essas experiências coloniais e as caracteriza, em conjunto, como uma grande civilização lusotropical. O fundamento dessa unidade, segundo Freyre (2010a, 130), reside na "capacidade, única no português, para confraternizar lírica e franciscamente com os povos dos trópicos, para amar a natureza e os valores tropicais, para dissolver-se amorosamente neles sem perder a alma ou o sentido cristão de vida."

Toda a reflexão do autor referente ao lusotropicalismo tem por base essa presumida peculiaridade do povo português e dos processos de colonização que ele ensejou nos "trópicos" – ou, conforme Castelo (2011, 14), o pressuposto de uma "imagem essencialista da personalidade do povo português." Essa singularidade diz respeito à capacidade do português de construir toda uma civilização, no contato com outros povos e culturas, antes através da confraternização do que da dominação propriamente dita. Nas palavras do próprio Freyre (2010b, 175-176):

do português pode-se com exatidão dizer que cedo deixou de ser na cultura um povo exclusivamente europeu para tornar-se a gente lusotropical que continua a ser e que encontrou nos trópicos zonas naturais e congeniais de expansão, ao motivo econômico e ao motivo religioso e político de expansão tendo-se juntando sempre o gosto, ausente noutros europeus expansionistas, de viver, amar, procriar e criar filhos nos trópicos, confraternizando com mulheres, homens e valores tropicais e não apenas explorando os homens, devastando os valores, violando as mulheres das terras conquistadas.

Os portugueses, assim, possuem uma "maior aptidão para confraternizarem com a gente tropical" (Freyre 2010b, 177). Como fruto dessa confraternização capitaneada por eles, existiriam culturas e civilizações "mestiças," como a brasileira, mas ainda "lusas," no fundo – justamente porque a colonização portuguesa na América, na Ásia e na África não teria se dado por meio da supressão cultural dos povos subjugados, mas por meio da sua incorporação num todo global – na sua "confraternização" com os valores lusos, portanto. Em outras palavras, sua suposta valorização das várias contribuições étnico-raciais para a constituição da nação brasileira não se desvincula dos pressupostos etnocêntricos da hierarquização entre povos e culturas distintas.

O segundo aspecto das reflexões de Freyre pertinente para nossa discussão em torno dos discursos de identidade nacional no Brasil consiste na sua caracterização das relações raciais no país como apresentando uma dimensão harmoniosa, não conflituosa. Gilberto Freyre considera a ampla e disseminada miscigenação ocorrida no Brasil como um indício, ou mesmo comprovação, da harmonia que marca nossas relações raciais. Essa leitura já está presente desde *Casa-Grande e Senzala*, quando o autor afirma que a miscigenação teria contribuído para uma "democratização social do Brasil" (Freyre 2006a, 33), além de ser um dos fatores que contribuiu para harmonizar os polos antagônicos dos senhores e dos escravos, seguindo o princípio mesmo do "equilíbrio de antagonismos," processo que marcaria a sociedade brasileira desde sua constituição (Freyre 2006a, 116-117).

O Brasil é visto, assim, como uma nação, simultânea e inter-relacionadamente, *mestiça* e *harmoniosa*. Referindo-se ao papel dos povos indígenas na formação social do país, Freyre (2006a, 160) o caracteriza do seguinte modo:

Híbrida desde o início, a sociedade brasileira é de todas da América a que se constituiu mais harmoniosamente quanto às relações de raça: dentro de um ambiente de quase reciprocidade cultural que resultou no máximo de aproveitamento dos valores e experiências dos povos atrasados pelo adiantado; no máximo de contemporização da cultura adventícia com a nativa, da do conquistador com a do conquistado.

A dimensão "harmoniosa," "recíproca," de "complementaridade" das relações entre as raças se constituiria ainda quando da formação da sociedade patriarcal no Brasil colonial. Na perspectiva de Freyre (2006b, 475), as formas mais rígidas da "organização patriarcal de família, de economia e de cultura" – isto é, o que ela continha "de mais renitentemente aristocrático" – foram atingidas, inquietadas, pelo "amalgamento de raças e culturas," que sempre conteve algo de "contagiosamente democrático ou democratizante e até anarquizante."

Seguindo essa linha de raciocínio, acerca das distâncias sociais que a mestiçagem teria contribuído para amenizar ou suprimir, Freyre (2006b, 530, nota 23) argumenta que o sistema patriarcal no Brasil teria criado, entre senhores e escravos, sentimentos de solidariedade, e que eles não eram elementos antagônicos, mas, sim, simbióticos, dada a tendência dominante de o escravo sentir-se membro da família. Freyre (2006b, 402-403) critica explicitamente a ideia de que o escravo foi sempre um "mártir" ou um "sofredor," já que ele possuía um padrão de vida relativamente bom na sociedade colonial, em termos de formas de tratamento e de alimentação. Em suma, conforme afirmou ainda em *Casa-Grande e Senzala*, na perspectiva do autor os males do sistema da escravidão foram atenuados pela "doçura nas relações de senhores com escravos domésticos" (Freyre 2006a, 435).

Eis assim presente, já no nascedouro da sociedade brasileira, sua característica definidora como nação: relações raciais não conflituosas, observáveis através da sua ampla mestiçagem. Tanto em termos culturais quanto físicos: as "manifestações híbridas não só de cultura como de tipo físico" mostrariam, nessa perspectiva, que o sistema patriarcal brasileiro foi marcado por mútua comunicação e "complementação afetiva," e não apenas por "diversificação antagônica," entre casa-grande e senzala, sobrado e mucambo – e, deduz-se, entre brancos e negros (Freyre 2006b, 55). À nova configuração de cultura e sociedade que surge desse encontro, o autor concede o qualificativo de "democrática."

Nessa perspectiva, Freyre faz da mestiçagem uma dimensão singular do Brasil, tomando-a praticamente como um sinônimo de tolerância. E, conforme Schwarcz (2012, 58), no discurso oficial ocorre um processo paralelo em que "o mestiço vira nacional," o que implica, no fim das contas, "um processo de desafricanização de vários elementos culturais, simbolicamente clareados" – elementos como a feijoada, a capoeira e o samba vão virando símbolos mestiços, para indicar nossa nacionalidade e harmonia racial.

É então a partir da atuação político-intelectual de Freyre que a mestiçagem será entendida, não apenas do ponto de vista biológico, mas também (e talvez sobretudo) cultural: o Brasil é uma "nação mestiça," no sentido de ser um todo singular formado a partir da união de matrizes culturais distintas, em particular as europeias (portuguesas), africanas e indígenas. "A partir desse período histórico, o povo brasileiro é definido não como branco, negro ou indígena. Nem mesmo como uma raça, mas como um 'povo mestiço'" (Goss 2008, 86). Ou, nas palavras do próprio Freyre (2006b, 811): "uma sociedade ao mesmo tempo mestiça e vária na sua composição étnica e cultural."

Evidentemente que a mestiçagem, nessa perspectiva, é mais do que uma assertiva acerca das raízes étnico-raciais de um suposto povo brasileiro. Ela começa a se tornar, a partir desse período, a via de manifestação de um conjunto de predicados associados à nação, e que apenas muito dificilmente serão contestados décadas depois – é à noção de mestiçagem que são associadas ideias relativas à harmonia das relações raciais, à ausência de conflitos no passado e no presente, à formação de um povo único que transcende as particularidades raciais e não pode mais ser identificado pelas pertenças raciais específicas.

O cerne dessa "ideologia da mestiçagem," como a chama Costa (2001), está, portanto, na imagem da nação como um amálgama exemplar de culturas e raças em plena sintonia e interpenetração. Ela introduz, no debate político e intelectual, um aspecto desconhecido da ordem de discurso anterior, que diz respeito ao reconhecimento das diferentes contribuições étnico-raciais para a formação da sociedade brasileira, não mais apenas da matriz que remete à civilização branca de origem europeia.

Embora suas origens remetam a Von Martius,[5] ainda no século XIX, é apenas nessa primeira metade do século XX que se consolida aquilo que DaMatta (1987, 58) denomina de "fábula das três raças." Essa construção discursiva se tornaria, progressivamente, o "mito originário da sociedade brasileira" (Munanga 1999, 79), que apresenta a formação da nação como marcada pelo encontro harmonioso de brancos, índios e negros, a partir do qual cada um teria contribuído com seu "cadinho" para a formação desse todo cultural sincrético que é o Brasil.

Tais formulações aproximam-se do que ficou conhecido posteriormente como a noção de "democracia racial." Embora usualmente atribuída a Freyre, ele não pode ser responsabilizado integralmente nem pelas ideias associadas a ela, nem pelo rótulo em si (Guimarães 2012, 139). Mas ele, certamente, foi tanto seu principal inspirador quanto um dos propagadores fundamentais da associação do Brasil com tais ideias. Ainda que amplamente conhecida, a expressão "democracia racial" é menos clara do que aparenta: Guimarães (2012, 137-177), por exemplo, conseguiu registrar cerca de sete usos diferentes dela, ao longo do século XX. No entanto, no que diz respeito à sua vinculação com discursos de identidade nacional, ela remete justamente aos aspectos já abordados da suposta ausência de conflitos e desigualdades raciais no Brasil.

Talvez a melhor tradução político-institucional dessa nova concepção de nação esteja nas políticas desenvolvidas pelo governo Vargas ainda na década de 1930, mas sobretudo durante o período do Estado Novo (1937-1946). De acordo com Sérgio Costa (2001, 147-148), a noção de "brasilidade" conforme concebida por Freyre encontrou uma correspondência política perfeita nas ações do governo Vargas. Para compreender as razões dessa correspondência, é preciso ter em mente que o projeto de modernização levado a cabo após a Revolução de 1930 envolvia a unificação econômica, política e cultural do país, necessária para o desenvolvimento do capitalismo industrial – e para o que a integração do povo em torno de uma identidade nacional englobadora funcionava como esteio social (ainda que essa integração fosse sobretudo simbólica, e apenas parcialmente englobasse direitos e bens materiais).

A construção discursiva de uma identidade nacional aparece, novamente, como elemento essencial no processo de definição dos rumos políticos da nação. Acontece que, agora, esse discurso identitário buscará integrar todas as parcelas da população em torno de um projeto unívoco, que não deixa margens para dissidências. E a imagem do Brasil como nação harmoniosamente mestiça tem afinidades evidentes com esse projeto, contribuindo para apaziguar, ao menos simbolicamente, a exclusão a que a ordem de discurso anterior relegava a população negra. Daí que as concepções freyreanas acerca da mestiçagem – como apontando para o caráter harmonioso e desprovido de conflitos das nossas relações raciais – tenham sido adotadas pelo Estado como o conjunto de ideais que, imaginava-se, produziria o nacionalismo necessário ao processo de modernização (Telles 2003, 63).

Essa correspondência entre uma "brasileiridade" freyreana – "monocultural em sua mesticidade," como diz Costa (2001, 147) – e a política varguista pode ser evidenciada na Campanha de nacionalização levada a efeito a partir de 1937:

Com efeito, não parece exagerado traduzir o objetivo declarado da campanha de integrar culturalmente os imigrantes e seus descendentes como um esforço de abrasileiramento dos recém-chegados, a partir da concepção de brasilidade sintetizada por Freyre, àquela altura já dominante. Uma gama infindável de pronunciamentos e declarações esboçadas no âmbito da campanha de nacionalização varguista atesta a indignação contra os imigrantes e sobretudo seus descendentes que, supunha-se, descaracterizavam o direito de nacionalidade brasileiro, ao merecer o mesmo *status* de cidadania concernente aos demais brasileiros, sem se desfazer dos vínculos emocionais e culturais que os ligavam à pátria de seus antepassados (Costa 2001, 147-148).

Mas não apenas nessa Campanha fica evidente essa correspondência. Na verdade, todo o período compreendido entre a década de 1930 e a instauração do golpe civil-militar envolve a construção de um tipo de "pacto social" em que, conforme Guimarães (2012, 174), a população negra seria integrada à nação brasileira – não em termos materiais, o que se dá apenas parcialmente (através da regulamentação do mercado de trabalho e da seguridade social urbanos), mas em termos simbólicos, através da ação de uma cultura nacional mestiça ou sincrética.

De fato, segundo Telles (2003, 53-55), Vargas iniciou uma série de reformas para proteger os trabalhadores locais da competição com os imigrantes, assegurando assim que um grande número de negros e mestiços ingressasse na crescente força de trabalho pela primeira vez. E, ao mesmo tempo, integrou-os de modo simbólico à cultura nacional brasileira, promovendo de forma ativa a glorificação nacional nos brasileiros de todas as classes e fazendo do carnaval e do futebol símbolos proeminentes da identidade nacional (na medida em que representam a autoimagem de harmonia multirracial e o espírito festivo do Brasil).

São extremamente evidentes os limites desse projeto de integração, pois ele se dá sem que se reconheçam as desigualdades raciais, que são subsumidas, sobretudo, em desigualdades econômicas, e sem que se considere a raça um elemento pertinente às disputas políticas. Não só os próprios discursos da identidade nacional mestiça, mas também a sua tradução político-institucional, contribuem, assim, para a não tematização do racismo na sociedade brasileira, na medida em que a discriminação racial não fazia parte do seu leque de questões.

Não havia, nesse "pacto social," espaço para o reconhecimento de especificidades étnico-raciais: os negros entravam nesse processo como povo, como trabalhadores e, eventualmente, como intelectuais (Guimarães 2006, 270-271).

Não havia abertura para a problematização dos preconceitos e discriminações a que estão sujeitos, já que a raça era desconsiderada enquanto elemento pertinente à sociabilidade. Na medida em que o Brasil se percebia como país harmonioso, porque integrado cultural e etnicamente, a abordagem política de questões raciais era desencorajada e, no limite, combatida.

Com a instauração do regime civil-militar em 1964, esse "pacto," que já era incerto no que diz respeito à dimensão material, é completamente deixado de lado, ao mesmo tempo em que se reforça a adesão do Estado ao discurso do Brasil enquanto racialmente harmonioso. Nessa época, conforme Guimarães (2012, 98-99), a "democracia racial" é transformada em "dogma de governo."

> Nos anos duros do regime militar, especialmente entre 1967 e 1974, a ideologia da democracia racial havia se firmado e era amplamente compreendida. A mera menção de raça ou racismo resultava em sanções sociais, e, frequentemente, qualquer um que mencionasse a questão seria rotulado de racista. Se as sanções não fossem o bastante, havia sempre o poder de repressão e a vontade do governo militar de utilizá-lo. No contexto dos protestos dos negros nos Estados Unidos, o governo militar do Brasil via no movimento negro uma ameaça de peso à segurança nacional. Para limitar ou evitar seu crescimento, os militares promoveram ainda mais a ideologia da democracia racial, enquanto reprimiam qualquer sinal do movimento negro e exilavam os principais acadêmicos brasileiros da área das relações raciais, que se tornavam cada vez mais críticos da ideologia de democracia racial. (Telles 2003, 57)

Essas políticas de silenciamento da questão racial e de valorização de um ideal mestiço de nação, levadas a cabo pelo regime ditatorial, podem ser observadas em várias instâncias: a exclusão do quesito "cor" no Censo de 1970; a consideração dos estudos sobre discriminação racial como "subversivos"; a expulsão da universidade de pesquisadores com perspectivas mais críticas sobre a situação do "negro" na sociedade brasileira; e a proibição de veiculação do tema da discriminação racial pela imprensa (Anjos 2013, 110).

Tais políticas foram desenvolvidas a despeito de já virem se formando, desde os anos 1950, na academia e na militância política, vozes discordantes dessa visão de identidade nacional. Talvez a mais famosa provenha de Florestan Fernandes (2008; 2007), um dos primeiros a criticar o que chamou de "mito da democracia racial," e a mostrar como a ideia da mestiçagem podia ser utilizada para fundar e legitimar um certo "padrão de brasilidade" excludente e, no limite, extremamente perverso. Mas também as atividades do Teatro Experimental do Negro (TEN), fundado em 1944, apontavam nesse sentido de problematização dos modos usuais de se compreender a nacionalidade:

> A postura do TEN colidia frontalmente com o *mainstream* da intelectualidade brasileira, tanto na interpretação sociológica, quanto no plano ideológico. No plano sociológico, o pensamento negro pressupunha a existência de formação racial e não apenas de classe; no plano ideológico, reivindicava a identidade negra e não apenas mestiça, que constituiria o âmago da identidade nacional brasileira. Era desse modo que os líderes dos anos 1950 procuravam equacionar o nacionalismo e a negritude. Isso os afastava do modo como os demais intelectuais, principalmente os nordestinos, entendiam a democracia racial então vigente, que se sustentava sobre a negação dos negros, *qua* raça ou grupo social, e na afirmação de um ideal – que na verdade era tido como uma realidade concreta – de mestiçagem racial e sincretismo cultural. (Guimarães 2012, 94)

No entanto, por importantes e vigorosas que tenham sido essas vozes, a concepção harmoniosa da nação brasileira é a que se sagra hegemônica ao longo desse período. A tal ponto que, a partir dos anos 1940, a constituição de uma nação brasileira unitária, acima das diferenças étnicas, que ainda na política getulista representava um *objetivo a ser alcançado*, torna-se uma *descrição da nação*, que passa a ser tratada como o amálgama exemplar de culturas e raças em plena sintonia e interpenetração (Costa 2001). A "ideologia da mestiçagem" converte-se assim em "ideologia de Estado," passando a orientar as intervenções estatais no sentido da criação e do reforço de uma "brasilidade" enquanto identidade mestiça não étnica, capaz de assimilar todas as outras representações étnicas (Costa 2001). E, na medida em que a própria noção de raça é desqualificada enquanto instrumento analítico e político, contribui para a não tematização do racismo e das desigualdades raciais, com as consequências conhecidas de aprofundamento dessas mesmas desigualdades.

Brasil, Nação Multicultural?

Novos discursos de identidade nacional são lançados ao debate público, a partir do fim dos anos 1970, afetando sobremaneira os modos arraigados de compreender a nação no Brasil. Eles foram encabeçados sobretudo pelo movimento negro[6] – seja atuando "de costas para o Estado," a partir da iniciativa de ONGs e outras entidades da sociedade civil, seja pela incrustação de seus militantes no interior de esferas governamentais em nível municipal e estadual (Ribeiro 2014) –, e por setores das ciências sociais cujas pesquisas ajudaram a redefinir o modo de se entender as desigualdades raciais no país. É por essa dupla e quase simultânea origem que podemos começar a perscrutar o surgimento de uma nova ordem de discurso de identidade nacional no Brasil.

Como afirmam Jesus e Gomes (2014, 91), ao longo do processo de redemocratização, os militantes e pensadores sociais vinculados ao movimento negro passaram a apresentar uma contundente contestação à imagem de nação que se consolidou ao longo do século XX, alicerçada tanto no orgulho de ser uma nação na qual a convivência harmônica entre as três matrizes raciais seria predominante, quanto no inconfessável desejo de se tornar uma nação branca. Nesse processo, o discurso da "mestiçagem," enquanto discurso sobre a nação no Brasil, "é virado ao avesso pela emergência de novas formas de representação da nação" (Costa 2006a, 149).

É na luta pela redemocratização da sociedade brasileira, nos anos finais do regime civil-militar, que o ativismo negro se reorganiza, depois de décadas de repressão, em torno do Movimento Negro Unificado (MNU). Nesse processo, o tema da identidade negra assume uma grande importância, praticamente inédita: "A denúncia do racismo vinha associada à demanda por respeito à cultura dos descendentes de africanos e da afirmação de sua identidade específica" (Jaccoud 2009, 25). Trata-se de uma novidade histórica extremamente significativa, porque, como aponta Guimarães (2006, 277), gesta-se a fusão de duas tendências que, no Brasil, pareciam opostas: a busca de uma maior integração e participação na vida social, por parte da população negra, e a construção de um sentimento étnico, baseado na identidade racial.

Influenciados sobretudo pelos movimentos norte-americanos e os processos de independência das colônias africanas, os militantes negros começaram a construir a noção de uma cultura negra, *afrodescendente*, diferenciada do todo englobante que vinha sendo construído pelo Estado brasileiro desde os anos 1930. Desse modo, a noção de uma identidade nacional sincrética, incorporadora das diferenças numa síntese original, começou a perder terreno em prol da valorização de pertenças e identidades étnico-raciais específicas. Essa busca de construção de uma "cultura negra" sinaliza, consequentemente, uma tentativa de ruptura da "homogeneidade construída simbolicamente pela política da mestiçagem, como se se tratasse de dissociar os grupos socioculturais fundidos na simbologia da nação mestiça" (Costa 2001, 150).

Ao contrário dos períodos históricos anteriores, em que a luta política da população negra visou a integração social por meio da assimilação numa identidade nacional englobante, o que implicava a dissolução das particularidades étnico-raciais, o movimento negro atual acentua sua referência cultural de raízes africanas e busca valorizar identidades étnicas particulares em detrimento da pertença "nacional." Ou seja,

> os processos que ocorrem no contexto brasileiro contemporâneo são antes caracterizados pelo esforço de diferenciação e afirmação das particularidades culturais que pela fusão cultural. Trata-se do esforço político de separar as diversas partes daquilo que, na esteira da constituição da nação, se construiu como cultura nacional mestiça. (Costa 2001, 154)

Nesse processo de reconstrução, o movimento negro elegeu a crítica ao "mito da democracia racial" como uma de suas principais bandeiras políticas (Costa 2006a, 144). E, desse modo, começou a elaborar as bases de uma nova narrativa da constituição do Brasil como nação. Os discursos então emergentes destacaram a condição estrutural do racismo na sociedade brasileira, bem como a persistência de mecanismos que buscam negar a sua existência – entre os quais desempenham papel central os discursos baseados nas ideias de "democracia racial," "encontro das três raças," "mestiçagem," etc.

Paralelamente, os trabalhos sociológicos de Carlos Hasenbalg e Nelson do Valle e Silva, na década de 1970, começaram a dar o tom do modo como as desigualdades raciais passariam a ser enxergadas pelo Estado e a sociedade brasileira nas décadas seguintes. Partindo de um contexto em que a própria existência dessas desigualdades era negada, os autores demonstraram as diferenças entre brancos e "não-brancos" no que diz respeito ao acesso à educação, à saúde, ao emprego etc. Subjacente a seus argumentos, estava a ideia de que tais desigualdades não podem ser explicadas pela herança do passado escravagista ou pela pertença de negros e brancos a classes sociais distintas, mas sim que resultam de diferenças de oportunidades de vida e formas de tratamento peculiares a esses grupos raciais.

Em outras palavras, ao mesmo tempo em que o movimento negro buscava politizar a ideia de "raça," mostrando a sua importância para a afirmação identitária e a luta por direitos, os trabalhos de Hasenbalg (2005) demonstraram a pertinência sociológica da noção, enquanto indicador de desigualdades sociais. E tais trabalhos contribuíram justamente para a crescente visibilidade da questão racial no Brasil, sobretudo a partir do final dos anos 1990. Eles ajudaram a consolidar o debate sobre as iniquidades raciais no Brasil, tanto do ponto de vista da construção de uma agenda de reivindicações pelo movimento negro desde os anos 1980, quanto na receptividade dessas demandas pelos governos de Fernando Henrique Cardoso e de Luís Inácio Lula da Silva (Feres Jr., Daflon e Campos 2012; Portela Jr. 2018).

As mudanças conceituais e políticas provocadas por essas duas frentes de atuação não poderiam deixar de afetar a ordem de discurso já consolidada de identidade nacional. Conforme sugere Guimarães (2012, 124), a identidade nacional do Brasil está se movendo do paradigma da "nação mestiça," advinda principalmente das ideias freyreanas, para um outro, internacionalista, de "nação multicultural." Intelectuais brasileiros e internacionais tendem cada vez mais a ver o Brasil como uma nação multirracial, em vez de uma nação mestiça.

> O que está acontecendo no Brasil é a perda de consenso de uma visão praticamente hegemônica a respeito da sociedade brasileira – como não preconceituosa e não-discriminatória –, para outra que identifica profundas desigualdades, não apenas decorrentes de diferenças de classe mas também em função de pertencimentos distintos, sejam eles étnicos, culturais e/ou sociais. (Goss 2008, 89)

Talvez a grande força que esses discursos vêm obtendo, no sentido de alterarem os marcos centrais em torno dos quais a identidade nacional é concebida no Brasil, se deva ao processo praticamente inédito de sua penetração no Estado brasileiro. O que por vezes implicou, desde os anos 1980 e progressivamente a partir de então, a inserção dos próprios militantes do movimento negro em âmbitos institucionais capazes de orientar a construção de políticas públicas que tematizam o racismo e as desigualdades raciais.

Com efeito, como resposta às proposições articuladas pelo movimento negro, é possível observar, desde a Constituição de 1988 – que criminaliza o racismo e aponta para a demarcação de terras quilombolas – até os dias atuais – quando se estabelecem políticas de ação afirmativa para afrodescendentes e se valorizam, em editais públicos, expressões culturais consideradas "afro-brasileiras" –, a operação de "uma política oficial de reconhecimento e mesmo promoção das diferenças culturais," em lugar de uma estratégia de assimilação pura e simples (Costa 2001, 150). E não se deve perder de vista a novidade histórica que isso representa em termos de discursos de identidade nacional:

> As reformas constitucionais recentes na América Latina [na transição para regimes democráticos], . . . no que toca às identidades raciais, trouxeram como novidade a concepção de sociedades e nações pluriétnicas e multiculturais. Tais constituições submergiram, assim, o ideal fundador de nações mestiças e culturalmente homogêneas, vistas como produto da miscigenação biológica e cultural entre europeus, indígenas americanos e africanos, ideal cuidadosa e trabalhosamente gestado desde as guerras de independência do século XIX. (Guimarães 2006, 273)

É justamente sob a chave conceitual do "multiculturalismo" que as políticas de igualdade racial começaram a ser mais sistematicamente debatidas na sociedade brasileira, a partir de um diálogo (tenso e desigual) entre o Estado e representantes do movimento negro (Portela Jr. 2018, 156-180). E apesar de a abertura do governo federal para a tematização das políticas de ação afirmativa com recorte racial remeter ao final da década de 1990, foi somente em 2001 que o Brasil assumiu o compromisso efetivo de implementar políticas de Estado de combate ao racismo e de redução das desigualdades raciais (Jaccoud 2009, 34).

2001 é um ano-chave para esse debate em virtude da realização, em Durban, na África do Sul, da III Conferência Mundial contra Racismo, Discriminação Racial, Xenofobia e Intolerância Correlata. Uma vasta mobilização nacional consolidou-se, contando com iniciativas, tanto do Estado quanto de organizações do movimento negro, que fomentaram o debate nacional em torno das questões relacionadas ao racismo e às desigualdades raciais (Jaccoud 2009, 36).

Em virtude da contínua e sistemática pressão do movimento negro, várias medidas começaram a ser implementadas pelo governo federal. Ainda em 2001, foi criado o Conselho Nacional de Combate à Discriminação Racial (CNCDR), ligado à Secretaria de Estado de Direitos Humanos, tendo como objetivo incentivar a criação de políticas públicas afirmativas e a proteção dos direitos de indivíduos e de grupos sociais sujeitos à discriminação racial. Em 2003, já no governo Lula, é criada a Secretaria Especial de Políticas de Promoção da Igualdade Racial (Seppir), com *status* de ministério e tendo como objetivo formular e coordenar as políticas para a promoção da igualdade racial, e articular as ações do governo federal de combate à discriminação racial (Jaccoud 2009, 37). Essas novas configurações institucionais vão fornecer o arcabouço para a incorporação, em setores específicos do Estado brasileiro, de agentes sociais oriundos do movimento negro.

Considerações Finais

Tendo em vista a progressiva interpenetração institucional das demandas do movimento negro no Estado brasileiro, aliada a outros indicadores, Sérgio Costa (2001, 149) afirma que "a mestiçagem, como ideologia de Estado, deixa de existir no Brasil contemporâneo, verificando-se que elementos essenciais desse construto político são crescentemente colocados em questão" (Costa 2001, 149). E é certo que as transformações discursivas e institucionais, no que diz respeito à identidade nacional no Brasil, vêm-se processando segundo as linhas gerais que delineamos acima. No entanto, é preciso cautela no diagnóstico, pois todo esse processo permanece carregado de resistências, de movimentos contrários que buscam combater quer os pressupostos teóricos e políticos desse discurso, quer a sua institucionalização no Estado brasileiro.

Isso fica bastante evidente quando observamos o debate em torno das ações afirmativas que se desenvolveu na mídia e no judiciário brasileiro desde o final dos anos 1990. Segundo apontam diversos estudos (Moya e Silvério 2009; Feres Jr. e Campos 2013; Jesus e Gomes 2014; Portela Jr. 2018), os argumentos levantados contra essas políticas têm resgatado valores associados com a antiga "ideologia da mestiçagem," buscando mostrar que o Brasil possui uma história de assimilação de todos os grupos culturais e raciais, assim como uma cultura inclusiva que não admite representações e afirmações de identidades étnico-raciais específicas (como "branco," "negro," "indígena," etc.). Trata-se de um discurso que busca não só ressignificar o sentido preferencial de "democracia racial" enquanto mito, levantado pelo movimento negro desde os anos 1980, considerando-o elemento essencial da nacionalidade brasileira (Maggie e Fry 2002), mas também questionar a própria validade da ideia de "raça" enquanto elemento delimitador de desigualdades sociais.

No sentido contrário, as ações afirmativas com recorte racial foram usualmente defendidas recorrendo-se a elementos característicos da terceira ordem de discurso aqui apontada. Em outras palavras, enfatizando o reconhecimento do racismo e das desigualdades raciais no país e contestando o ideário impregnado na ideia de "democracia racial" (Portela Jr. 2018). Ou seja, no discurso dos seus defensores, tais políticas confrontariam diretamente o discurso da mestiçagem harmoniosa, integracionista e mistificadora.

O que fica evidente nesse debate é como a identidade nacional persiste enquanto construto discursivo em disputa no Brasil contemporâneo. As ordens de discurso aqui sistematizadas, mais do que configurações estanques no tempo e no espaço, mostram a sua vitalidade e atualidade, na medida em que embasaram e embasam os argumentos contrários e favoráveis ao estabelecimento das políticas de ação afirmativa com recorte racial no país. Reforçam, ainda, como a afirmação e a institucionalização de discursos de identidade nacional são sempre dependentes de disputas por hegemonia política e cultural em contextos histórico-sociais específicos. Trata-se, esse, de um lembrete fundamental, ainda mais no atual cenário político brasileiro, quando "novos (velhos?) discursos de nação entram em cena para disputar o sentido legítimo dos caminhos a serem traçados pelo país, nem sempre favoráveis para aqueles que historicamente são colocados nas franjas dos direitos sociais" (Portela Jr. 2018, 308). Essa reflexão, portanto, nos sugere a importância de compreender os fundamentos históricos, conceituais e políticos de tais discursos de identidade nacional, bem como as suas consequências do ponto de vista do enfrentamento das desigualdades sociais – para o que este trabalho procurou dar uma contribuição inicial.

NOTAS

1. Este trabalho toma por base minha Tese de Doutorado (Portela Jr. 2018), em particular uma parte do Capítulo 5. Por sua vez, as reflexões desenvolvidas aqui tiveram uma versão preliminar apresentada no 18º Congresso Brasileiro de Sociologia, ocorrido em Brasília em julho de 2017 (agradeço os comentários feitos na ocasião, em especial às professoras Eliane Veras Soares e Adélia Miglievich Ribeiro). A pesquisa que originou este trabalho foi orientada pela Doutora Eliane Veras Soares e contou com o apoio de bolsa do Conselho Nacional de Desenvolvimento Científico e Tecnológico (CNPq).

2. As traduções de textos estrangeiros para a língua portuguesa são da responsabilidade do autor.

3. A categoria de "intelectual" aqui utilizada "une não apenas ideólogos e filósofos, mas ativistas políticos, técnicos industriais, economistas políticos, especialistas jurídicos, etc. Tal figura é menos um pensador contemplativo, no velho estilo idealista da *intelligentsia*, que um organizador, construtor, 'persuasor permanente,' que participa ativamente da vida social e ajuda a trazer para a articulação teórica correntes políticas positivas já contidas nela" (Eagleton 1997, 110).

4. Para análises do pensamento e da vida de Gilberto Freyre, cf. Bastos (2006), Pallares-Burke (2005), Pallares-Burke e Burke (2009).

5. Trata-se do naturalista alemão e sócio correspondente do Instituto Histórico e Geográfico Brasileiro que venceu o concurso, promovido em 1844 pela instituição, que buscava premiar o melhor projeto sobre "Como escrever a história do Brasil." De acordo com Schwarcz (1993, 146-147), a tese vencedora de Von Martius centrava-se na especificidade da trajetória do Brasil, que seria composta por três raças mescladas e formadoras. Segundo a autora: "O projeto vencedor propunha, portanto, uma 'fórmula,' uma maneira de entender o Brasil. A ideia era correlacionar o desenvolvimento do país com o aperfeiçoamento específico das três raças que o compunham. Estas, por sua vez, segundo Von Martius, possuíam características absolutamente variadas. Ao branco, cabia representar o papel de elemento civilizador. Ao índio, era necessário restituir sua dignidade original ajudando-o a galgar os degraus da civilização. Ao negro, por fim, restava o espaço da detração, uma vez que era entendido como fator de impedimento ao progresso da nação" (Schwarcz 1993, 146-147).

6. Conforme Domingues (2007, 101-102): "Movimento negro é a luta dos negros na perspectiva de resolver seus problemas na sociedade abrangente, em particular os provenientes dos preconceitos e das discriminações raciais, que os marginalizam no mercado de trabalho, no sistema educacional, político, social e cultural. Para o movimento negro, a 'raça,' e, por conseguinte, a identidade racial, é utilizada não só como elemento de mobilização, mas também de mediação das reivindicações políticas. Em outras palavras, para o movimento negro, a 'raça' é o fator determinante de organização dos negros em torno de um projeto comum de ação."

REFERÊNCIAS BIBLIOGRÁFICAS

Anderson, B. 2008. *Comunidades Imaginadas*. São Paulo: Cia. das Letras.

Anjos, G. dos. 2013. "A Questão 'Cor' ou 'Raça' nos Censos Nacionais." *Indicadores Econômicos FEE* 41 (1): 103-118, Porto Alegre.

Bastos, E. R. 2006. *As Criaturas de Prometeu: Gilberto Freyre e a Formação da Sociedade Brasileira*. São Paulo: Global.

Castelo, C. 2011. *"O Modo Português de Estar no Mundo": O Luso-Tropicalismo e a Ideologia Colonial Portuguesa (1933-1961)*. Porto: Edições Afrontamento.

Costa, R. C. R. da. 2010. "O Pensamento Social Brasileiro e a Questão Racial." *Revista África e Africanidades* 3 (10).

Costa, S. 2001. "A Mestiçagem e seus Contrários: Etnicidade e Nacionalidade no Brasil Contemporâneo." *Tempo Social* 13 (1): 143-158, São Paulo.

Costa, S. 2006a. *Dois Atlânticos*. Belo Horizonte: UFMG.

Costa, S. 2006b. "Prefácio." In *Em Busca da Nação*, de Gabriel Fernandes, 9-11. Florianópolis: Editora da UFSC.

DaMatta, R. 1987. *Relativizando*. Rio de Janeiro: Rocco.

Domingues, P. 2007. "Movimento Negro Brasileiro: Alguns Apontamentos Históricos." *Tempo* 12 (23): 100-122, Niterói.

Eagleton, T. 1997. *Ideologia: Uma Introdução*. São Paulo: Unesp; Boitempo.

Fairclough, N. 2001. *Discurso e Mudança Social*. Brasília: Editora da Universidade de Brasília.

Feres Jr., J. e L. A. Campos. 2013. "O 'Discurso Freyreano' sobre as Cotas Raciais: Origem, Difusão e Decadência." In *Ação Afirmativa em Questão*, organização de Angela Randolpho Paiva. Rio de Janeiro: Pallas.

Feres Jr., J., V. T. Daflon e L. A. Campos. 2012. "Ação Afirmativa, Raça e Racismo: Uma Análise das Ações de Inclusão Racial nos Mandatos de Lula e Dilma." *Revista de Ciências Humanas* 12 (2): 399-414.

Fernandes, F. 2007. "Introdução." In *O Negro no Mundo dos Brancos*, 25-36. São Paulo: Global.

Fernandes, F. 2008. *A Integração do Negro na Sociedade de Classes*. Vol. 1: *Ensaio de Interpretação Sociológica*. São Paulo: Globo.

Fernandes, G. 2006. *Em Busca da Nação*. Florianópolis: Editora da UFSC.

Freyre, G. 2006a. *Casa-Grande e Senzala: Formação da Família Brasileira sob o Regime da Economia Patriarcal*. São Paulo: Global.

Freyre, G. 2006b. *Sobrados e Mucambos: Decadência do Patriarcado Rural e Desenvolvimento do Urbano*. São Paulo: Global.

Freyre, G. 2010a. "Uma cultura moderna: a luso-tropical." In *Um Brasileiro em Terras Portuguesas*, 127-152. São Paulo: É Realizações.

Freyre, G. 2010b. "Em Torno de um Novo Conceito de Tropicalismo." In *Um Brasileiro em Terras Portuguesas*, 167-180. São Paulo: É Realizações.

Goss, K. P. 2008. *Retóricas em Disputa: O Debate entre Intelectuais em Relação às Políticas de Ação Afirmativa para Estudantes Negros no Brasil*. Tese (Doutorado em Sociologia Política). Florianópolis: Centro de Filosofia e Ciências Humanas, Universidade Federal de Santa Catarina.

Guimarães, A. S. 2006. "Depois da Democracia Racial." *Tempo Social, Revista de Sociologia da USP* 18 (2): 269-287.

Guimarães, A. S. 2012. *Classes, Raças e Democracia*. São Paulo: Editora 34.

Hall, S. 1992. "The West and the Rest: Discourse and Power." In *Formations of Modernity*, de Stuart Hall e Bram Gieben, 184-227. Oxford: Blackwell Publishers.

Hall, S. 1996. "The Question of Cultural Identity." In *Modernity: An Introduction to Modern Societies*, edição de Stuart Hall, David Held, Don Hubert e Kenneth Thompson. Oxford: Blackwell Publishers.

Hasenbalg, C. 2005. *Discriminação e Desigualdades Raciais no Brasil*. Belo Horizonte: Editora UFMG.

Jaccoud, L., org. 2009. *A Construção de uma Política de Promoção da Igualdade Racial: Uma Análise dos Últimos 20 Anos*. Brasília: Ipea.

Jesus, R. E. e N. L. A. Gomes. 2014. "'Constituição' da Nação Brasileira em Disputa: O Debate em Torno da (In)Constitucionalidade das Ações Afirmativas." *Tomo* 24: 86-107.

Maggie, Y. e P. Fry. 2002. "O Debate que Não Houve: A Reserva de Vagas para Negros nas Universidades Brasileiras." *Enfoques* 1 (1): 93-117.

McCrone, D.e F. Bechhofer. 2015. *Understanding National Identity*. Londres: Cambrigde University Press.

Moya, T. S. e V. R. Silvério. 2009. "Ação Afirmativa e Raça no Brasil Contemporâneo: Um Debate sobre a Redefinição Simbólica da Nação." *Sociedade e Cultura* 12 (2): 235-250, Goiânia.

Munanga, K. 1999. *Rediscutindo a Mestiçagem no Brasil: Identidade Nacional versus Identidade Negra*. Petrópolis, RJ: Vozes.

Ortiz, R. 2006. *Cultura Brasileira e Identidade Nacional*. São Paulo: Brasiliense.

Pallares-Burke, M. L. 2005. *Gilberto Freyre: Um Vitoriano dos Trópicos*. São Paulo: Editora UNESP.

Pallares-Burke, M. L. e P. Burke. 2009. *Repensando os Trópicos: Um Retrato Intelectual de Gilberto Freyre*. São Paulo: Editora UNESP.

Portela Jr., A. 2018. *Ações Afirmativas com Recorte Racial no Ensino Superior e Disputas de Identidade Nacional no Brasil*. Tese (Doutorado em Sociologia). Recife: Programa de Pós-Graduação em Sociologia, Centro de Filosofia e Ciências Humanas, UFPE.

Ribeiro, M. 2014. *Políticas de Promoção da Igualdade Racial no Brasil (1986-2010)*. Rio de Janeiro: Garamound.

Ruiz Ruiz, J. 2009. "Sociological Discourse Analysis: Methods and Logic." *Forum: Qualitative Social Research* 10 (2): Art. 26, http://nbn-resolving.de/urn:nbn:de:0114-fqs0902263. Acesso em 29 janeiro 2016.

Schwarcz, L. M. 1993. *O Espetáculo das Raças*. São Paulo: Cia. das Letras.

Skidmore, T. 2012. *Preto no Branco: Raça e Nacionalidade no Pensamento Brasileiro (1870-1930)*. São Paulo: Companhia das Letras.

Soares, E. V. 2011. "Literatura e Estruturas de Sentimento: Fluxos entre Brasil e África." *Sociedade e Estado* 26: 95-112, Brasília.

Telles, E. 2003. *Racismo à Brasileira: Uma Nova Perspectiva Sociológica*. Rio de Janeiro: Relume Dumará, Fundação Ford.

Wodak, R., R. De Cillia, M. Reisigl e K. Liebhart. 2009. *The Discursive Construction of National Identity*. Edinburgh University Press, Edinburgh.

ARISTEU PORTELA JÚNIOR é sociólogo e professor da Universidade Federal Rural de Pernambuco (UFRPE). Autor de "A nação em disputa: ações afirmativas com recorte racial no ensino superior e controvérsias em torno da identidade nacional no Brasil" (Recife: Editora UFPE, 2020).

IV. Afrodescendência e a Afro-diáspora: representações e produções culturais

FERNANDO ARENAS

Africanos e Afrodescendentes no Cinema Português Contemporâneo: Imigrantes, Cidadãos, Humanos

RESUMO: O presente ensaio oferece uma panorâmica crítica de longas-metragens e documentários ligados às experiências de africanos e afrodescendentes no Portugal contemporâneo, visando investigar como a dita produção cultural reflete uma nação portuguesa em plena mutação, onde as fronteiras entre o Portugal pós-colonial e as ex-colónias africanas, tal como as noções acerca do que é "ser africano" ou "ser europeu," estão a ser redefinidas. As longa-metragens e documentários que serão objeto de reflexão neste ensaio apresentam uma diversidade de abordagens estéticas e estruturas narrativas, mas, ao mesmo tempo, uma convergência ética visando trazer sujeitos afrodescendentes para o centro da representação e para o âmbito duma cidadania social e cultural.

PALAVRAS-CHAVE: Estudos de longas-metragens/documentários; diaspora português/africano; Portugal pós-colonial

ABSTRACT: This essay offers a critical overview of feature films and documentaries related to the experiences of Africans and Afro-descendants in contemporary Portugal, aiming to investigate how this form of cultural production reflects a Portuguese nation in full mutation, where the borders between post-colonial Portugal and the former African colonies, as well as the notions about what is "being African" or "being European," are being redefined. The feature films and documentaries that will be the object of reflection in this essay present a diversity of aesthetic approaches and narrative structures, but, at the same time, an ethical convergence aiming to bring Afro-descendent subjects to the center of representation and to the sphere of a social and cultural citizenship.

KEYWORDS: Film/documentary study; Portuguese-African diaspora; post-colonial Portugal

Introdução

Os destinos de Portugal e de várias regiões do continente africano têm estado entremeados durante séculos como resultado da expansão marítimo-colonial portuguesa e o comércio transatlântico de escravos, onde o Brasil colonial e independente também desempenhou um papel fundamental, com consequências profundas de ordem histórica, geopolítica, sócio-económica e cultural para todas as partes envolvidas. Assim, a relação entre Portugal e África é absolutamente crucial para o entendimento do imaginário nacional português e a construção da sua identidade.

Apesar de haver uma enorme produção literária nos géneros históriográfico, memorialístico, ficcional, de viagens em torno da experiência portuguesa em África, tem havido uma verdadeira explosão de representações da experiência negra ou afro-descendente em Portugal no âmbito da música popular, com particular ênfase no género do rap, tanto no circuito comercial como fora dele. Em contrapartida, a produção fílmica focalizada na representação de africanos e afro-descendentes em Portugal tem sido mais limitada. Contudo, esta produção cultural constitui uma plataforma fundamental para a representação simbólica e empoderamento de comunidades periféricas africanas e afroportuguesas, assim como um prisma através do qual são projetadas uma multiplicidade de formações identitárias, quer flutuantes, quer sobrepostas, assumidas ou impostas: estrangeiro, nacional, negro, branco, africano, "afro-tuga," europeu. Ao longo do ensaio, focar-nos-emos nas estratégias de ordem estética, narrativa e ética adotadas por vários cineastas: Pedro Costa, Inês Oliveira, Leonel Vieira, Joaquim Leitão, e o coletivo composto por Kiluanje Liberdade, Inês Gonçalves Vasco Pimentel.

*

A presença de africanos e descendentes em Portugal não é um fenómeno exclusivamente moderno, como nos informa a historiadora Isabel Castro Henriques (2009; 2013). Há sinais da presença de africanos negros em Portugal, e na Península Ibérica em geral, desde os períodos romano, mouro e medieval, com base em provas iconográficas, poéticas e esculturais (Henriques 2009, 18–23). Contudo, devido aos empreendimentos comerciais-marítimos portugueses ao longo das costas do norte da África, assim como da África ocidental e central durante os períodos medieval e início do moderno, surgiu um número substancialmente maior de africanos em Portugal na forma de escravos, assim como de mulheres e homens livres (inclusive diplomatas). A população africana e afrodescendente, que compreende negros e mulatos, começou a declinar após a proibição da importação de escravos no século XVIII, ao ponto de quase se diluir na maioria da população branca por volta do início do século XX. Entretanto, atualmente, a população africana e afro-diaspórica em Portugal cresceu a níveis que se aproximam dos números dos períodos anteriores.

A primeira chegada historicamente documentada de negros africanos escravos a Portugal deu-se em 1444, num leilão na cidade de Lagos, no Algarve (Blackmore 27).[1] Desde então, escravos africanos foram importados para uso em trabalho doméstico nas zonas urbanas, e em menor escala para trabalho agrícola em áreas rurais, a fim de substituir antigos escravos mouros (Klein 12). Vitorino Magalhães Godinho, em *Os descobrimentos e a economia mundial* (1963–65), relata que possivelmente até 300.000 escravos negros africanos tenham sido importados para Portugal ao longo do século XVI, com base na documentação histórica da época (539). Baseado nesses cálculos, José Ramos Tinhorão estima que de 10 a 20% da população total de Lisboa fosse africana durante o século XVI (1988, 102–3).[2] Vários viajantes, jornalistas e historiadores europeus, alguns citados por Magalhães Godinho (1963, 542), Tinhorão (1988, 79–110), Jean-Yves Loude (115–16) e Isabel Castro Henriques (37–39; 67–69), descrevem a presença africana em Portugal entre os séculos XV e XIX com palavras que variam entre sarcasmo ou pena e a condescendência, repulsa ou horror.[3] O Marquês de Pombal proibiu a importação de escravos a Portugal em 1761, não necessariamente por razões humanitárias, mas a fim de redirecioná-los às minas de ouro do Brasil e para evitar a sua concorrência com mão-de-obra livre em virtude dos seus esforços para modernizar a economia portuguesa.

Apesar da escravatura não ter desaparecido por completo da paisagem portuguesa, conforme argumentado por Tinhorão (1988, 374–75), tal decisão, em última análise, funcionou como uma estratégia de engenharia social com o objetivo de diluir uma das maiores populações africanas na Europa. Existe abundante evidência imaterial e material da presença de africanos e afrodescendentes, sejam escravos ou homens/mulheres livres, entre os séculos XV e XIX em Portugal (sobretudo nas regiões de Lisboa, Alentejo e Algarve), com base na documentação encontrada em arquivos municipais e jornalísticos, assim como em igrejas e museus. A irmandade católica da Nossa Senhora do Rosário dos Pretos e as festividades em comemoração de reis e rainhas congoleses (ou *congadas*) – ambas bastante difundidas no Brasil – foram algumas das mais duradouras manifestações culturais e institucionais afrocêntricas até ao final do século XIX

(Lahon 57–76). Africanos e afrodescendentes deixaram suas marcas no acervo genético português, nas origens do fado,[4] na literatura oral, nas palavras que foram incorporadas no léxico da língua portuguesa, em topónimos, enquanto imagens de africanos são bastante comuns em antigas representações artísticas portuguesas, tais como pintura, azulejos, desenhos, cerâmica e escultura, assim como no teatro e na poesia (vide Tinhorão, Lahon, Loude e Henriques).

Não obstante a rica evidência indicando uma vigorosa presença africana nos primórdios do Portugal moderno, a sua diluição desde a abolição do comércio negreiro em 1836 e, mais tarde, a abolição da escravatura em 1869, foi acompanhada de preconceitos culturais e raciais profundamente enraizados, além de discursos hegemónicos eurocêntricos e cristãos sobre identidade nacional inseridos no imaginário coletivo português (os quais se consolidaram sob o regime de Salazar no século XX). Estamos perante um estado de "amnésia coletiva," conforme a define Miguel Vale de Almeida (74), que tem prevalecido em torno da presença, não apenas de negros africanos em Portugal, mas também de judeus e mouros.

*

Uma das dinâmicas de maior destaque no Portugal pós-colonial é a questão da imigração. Os fluxos migratórios direcionados a Portugal estão ligados de forma inextrícavel à história colonial, sobretudo em relação à África e ao Brasil. Tais fluxos têm estado a mudar de forma decisiva o quadro demográfico do país, em particular a região da Grande Lisboa, assim como a própria identidade nacional. Como se sabe, ao cabo de mais de 500 anos enquanto exportador de emigrantes para o mundo, Portugal tornou-se, desde a Revolução do 25 de abril, as independências africanas entre 1974-75, e a adesão à União Europeia em 1986, receptor de imigrantes oriundos das ex-colónias e outros pontos do planeta (norte e leste europeu, continente asiático, e alguns países africanos não lusófonos, entre outros).

É ponto assente o facto de que a imigração é uma necessidade sócio-económica em grande parte do norte global. De modo semelhante aos seus parceiros europeus, o crescimento demográfico de Portugal é extremamente baixo. No entanto, tal como no resto da Europa, têm surgido em Portugal atitudes que oscilam entre a ambivalência e resistência à intolerância e ao racismo em relação aos africanos subsaarianos e os seus descendentes. Desde o final da década de 1990, numerosos estudos e sondagens nas ciências sociais e nas humanidades têm-se debruçado sobre questões relacionadas com imigração e racismo em Portugal.[5] Ao mesmo tempo, diversas organizações governamentais, ONGs e associações têm envidado esforços a fim de apoiarem os imigrantes, os seus direitos enquanto cidadãos, a sua integração social, assim como na luta contra o racismo.[6] Simultaneamente, um discurso anti-racista tem-se tornado mais proeminente nos debates públicos e políticos nos *média* portugueses. Ao longo dos últimos 20 anos, tem surgido um léxico no discurso político português, assim como em debates no âmbito da antropologia e sociologia, relativo à interculturalidade, multiculturalismo, minorias étnicas, etnicidade, integração e políticas migratórias.

Desde meados da década de 1990, a legislação portuguesa evoluiu ao ponto de conceder direitos políticos e sociais aos imigrantes, incentivando a sua integração, assim como uma maior apreciação das diferenças culturais. O alto comissário para a imigração e minorias étnicas, Rui Marques, citado por Ana Paula Ferreira, estabelece uma ligação entre aquilo que seria o "modelo intercultural português" a uma identidade de "fusão" supostamente baseada na experiência colonial portuguesa. Esta terceira via "intercultural" adotada oficialmente em Portugal, encontra-se emaranhada a ideologias ligadas ao hibridismo e aos afetos tais como o Lusotropicalismo, em contraste com o "multiculturalismo" britânico e o "assimilacionismo republicano" francês, enfatizando o reconhecimento e a integração dos imigrantes no Estado-nação, onde a identidade cultural tornar-se-ia na única via de "inserção pública." Em última instância, segundo João Oliveira, o modelo intercultural seria um obstáculo às reivindicações de caráter sócio-económico e material. Este impasse deve-se à falta de reconhecimento oficial da categoria de identidade étnica, considerada contraproducente por alguns segmentos da sociedade portuguesa que favorecem uma auto-imagem idealizada do colonialismo português como sendo mais aberta historicamente à miscigenação.

Em 2019, ainda não havia um reconhecimento oficial da distinção entre a categoria de imigrante e a noção de minoria étnica ou racial. Aliás, a questão da etnicidade constitui um tabu no discurso governamental português, assim como em outras nações europeias como a França, tal como nos informa Joana Gorjão Henriques (2012). No caso português, ainda existem impedimentos de ordem legal na coleta de dados baseados na etnicidade ou raça. Esta conjuntura tem resultado num desfasamento da parte das autoridades políticas portuguesas em lidarem com as mudanças demográficas em curso. O relatório das Nações

Unidas de 2012 sobre a questão racial em Portugal aponta para um "racismo subtil" que ainda prevalece no país. O relatório é crítico em relação à lacuna oficial de categorias raciais e étnicas a nível oficial, o que acaba por confinar os afrodescendentes nascidos em Portugal no âmbito da imigração, portanto, dificultando o seu avanço social. O relatório acrescenta que nem os currículos oficiais nem os livros de texto oferecem uma imagem exata do passado colonial português, nem o reconhecimento do contributo positivo de africanos e afrodescendentes para a formação da sociedade portuguesa.

É inquestionável o facto de que Portugal é agora uma sociedade mais multiétnica e multicultural do que no período do auge da expansão marítima dos séculos XV e XVI. Hoje em dia, ser-se português ou europeu já não significa ser exclusivamente branco. Esta realidade reflete os limites das narrativas portuguesas de homogeneidade cultural, ao mesmo tempo em que se coloca em xeque o excecionalismo cultural português. Portanto, os imigrantes e o seus descendentes, e de uma forma particularmente dramática, os africanos e os afrodescendentes "articulam a narrativa da diferença cultural que não permite que a história nacional se enxergue narcissísticamente no olho" (palavras do crítico pós-colonial Homi Bhabha). Contudo, como aponta Inocência Mata, 40 anos após o colapso do império colonial português, a nação ainda textualiza os africanos e os seus descendentes como "os outros." Aliás, apesar do seu estatuto legal, quer como imigrante, quer como cidadão, origem nacional ou classe social, os africanos e os seus descendentes tendem a ser diluídos ou homogeneizados nas categorias de "negros" ou "africanos." Em ambos os casos, eles tendem a ser objetivizados como "o outro" pela população portuguesa de maioria branca.

Segundo vários estudos de âmbito sociológico (Bruno Peixe Dias e Nuno Dias, 2012; João António e Verónica Policarpo, 2011), Portugal, em última instância, não seria tão diferente face a outros países europeus em termos das atitudes racistas ou falta de hospitalidade em relação a imigrantes africanos e os seus descendentes. Essa conclusão contrasta de modo contundente com mitos nacionais de excecionalismo cultural profundamente enraizados, tais como o Lusotropicalismo. Os mitos em questão baseiam-se na perceção ou interpretação da empreitada colonial portuguesa como tendo sido mais benigna e aberta ao convívio intercultural e à mestiçagem racial do que outras experiências coloniais europeias, devido a uma série de fatores interrelacionados de ordem climatológica, geográfica, histórica, cultural, e genética. O conceito de Lusotropicalismo é atribuído ao antropólogo brasileiro Gilberto Freyre, embora as premissas já fizessem parte do campo inteletual português.[7] De qualquer forma, como indica Ana Paula Ferreira, o "Lusotropicalismo genérico" (tal como é chamado pelo antropólogo Miguel Vale de Almeida), tem-se tornado uma forma de "sentido comum cultural" bastante disseminado no Portugal pós-colonial.

*

Expressões culturais tais como cinema, música popular, e literatura ficcional estão a proporcionar uma plataforma-chave para a representação simbólica e o empoderamento sócio-político das periferias africana e afroportuguesa, quer como veículos de auto-expressão, quer como projetos artísticos de cineastas e escritores brancos (e não só) em alinhamento ético com subjetividades periféricas. Os/as cineastas e escritores/as em questão (Pedro Costa, Inês Oliveira, Joaquim Leitão, Leonel Vieira, Lídia Jorge e Antonio Lobo Antunes, entre vários outros) operam, em determinados textos, como mediadores sociais no âmbito da cultura entre sujeitos negros e a sociedade hegemónica branca. No campo do cinema, filmes que oscilam entre longas metragens com influência do *mainstream* hollywoodiano e documentários de caráter etnográfico e social, assim como filmes de caráter autoral, fora do circuito comercial, compartilham uma política de empatia e equanimidade, enquanto oferecem abordagens estéticas e éticas, assim como graus de profundidade contrastantes na representação das vidas de africanos e afrodescendentes em Portugal.[8]

Nesse campo cada vez mais fecundo, o consagrado cineasta Pedro Costa oferece um dos projetos mais instigantes, documentando as vidas de africanos – mais especificamente cabo-verdianos – no Portugal pós-colonial. A filmografia de Pedro Costa complexifica as fronteiras de género ficcional e documentário. Os filmes *Ossos* (1997), *No Quarto de Vanda* (2001), *Juventude em Marcha* (2007), e *Cavalo Dinheiro* (2014) destacam personagens cabo-verdianas que, junto com portugueses ciganos e brancos pobres, dividem vidas difíceis de profunda alienação social nos bairros mais pobres de Lisboa. O olhar empático que predomina nos seus filmes pressupõe também uma ética de representação autoconsciente onde sujeitos subalternos – neste caso, homens e mulheres negros – assumem a fala, ao mesmo tempo em que surgem fisicamente em todo o seu esplendor e dignidade.

Juventude em Marcha (2007) conclui a trilogia das Fontaínhas, onde Pedro Costa documenta o desmantelamento paulatino do bairro degradado na periferia de Lisboa e os seus efeitos sobre os habitantes, assim como as memórias da vida antes da destruição. Estes moradores são representados por personagens da vida real, nomeadamente o cabo-verdiano Ventura e a portuguesa Vanda, na medida em que são transferidos para os novos prédios de habitação social do Casal da Boba. Ventura é a personagem de maior proeminência que perambula através de múltiplos planos temporais entre as ruínas de Fontaínhas e os novos prédios, visitando membros da comunidade, incluindo Vanda, que ele considera como os seus filhos. Ventura tenta juntar os seus fragmentos de vida: as recordações enquanto operário de obras de construção desde 1972, a incerteza e o medo em relação ao destino dos africanos na altura da Revolução do 25 de abril, a euforia em torno da independência cabo-verdiana, e a saudade pelo seu *kretxeu* (o ser amado, em crioulo cabo-verdiano), na medida em que procura um sentimento de pertença e fixação num lar após a destruição física e simbólica da sua comunidade, como resultado de políticas urbanas do Estado-nação moderno.[9]

Juventude em Marcha é um filme exigente do ponto de vista cinematográfico e uma produção estilizada. Parco em termos de diálogo, o filme atinge um alto grau de lirismo nos registos quotidianos e poéticos do crioulo cabo-verdiano, que é, de facto, a língua dominante ao longo do filme. Entretanto, os espaços habitacionais desolados (tanto o interior das barracas em ruínas, como dos prédios novos a brilharem de tão brancos), junto com os habitantes semi-fantasmáticos, são transfigurados em planos que fazem lembrar quadros de pintura barroca. Nos planos em questão, vários tipos de luz e escuridão concedem aos sujeitos representados (principalmente sujeitos negros e pobres) um aura de humanidade, equilíbrio, e graça, que muitas vezes lhes são negados pela sociedade dominante. O crítico James Quandt afirma que "os close-ups emotivos das personagens abjetas aproximam-se do beatífico" (356).

A noção do enquadramento afetivo ou da imagem-afeto (de Gilles Deleuze) é extremamente útil para entendermos as intenções estéticas e éticas de Pedro Costa. A imagem a seguir é um *close-up* intermédio em *contre-plongée* do Ventura com as costas voltadas para os novos prédios de habitação social para os quais ele foi transferido. A sua presença física, simultaneamente majestosa e calorosa, junto com a pose contemplativa, feições escuras e as formas curvilíneas da sua figura humana, contrastam dramaticamente com a luminescência fria e impessoal das estruturas arquitetónicas brancas e modernas com as suas formas retilíneas.

A próxima imagem paradigmática tem lugar no Museu Gulbenkian, que o próprio Ventura ajudou a construir na vida real, segundo Pedro Costa. Trata-se de outra justaposição, desta vez entre Ventura e uma estátua clássica de bronze representando uma figura masculina. Mais uma vez, observamos o protagonista através de um primeiro plano num *close-up* intermédio junto ao perfil da cabeça da estátua. Aqui, Ventura torna-se uma escultura em si próprio. Através desta justaposição, Costa deseja relativizar noções eurocêntricas canonizadas de beleza estética, enquanto traz figuras periféricas negras como Ventura ao centro da grande arte, ao mesmo tempo deitando abaixo figurativamente as paredes físicas da instituição que homens como Ventura ajudaram a construir. Podemos argumentar que a presença física de Ventura no museu representa uma dupla *mise-en-scène*: o museu enquanto instituição em si, produto do imperialismo europeu e arquivo privilegiado por excelência de obras da arte do mundo ocidental e não só, e a presença transgressiva de Ventura no próprio espaço do museu – ele, um imigrante africano de uma ex-colónia portuguesa que é transformado pelo filme de Pedro Costa num objeto de arte a título próprio.

Nos filmes de Pedro Costa, o antigo centro do império português é visto a partir das margens. Ao mesmo tempo, o mundo representado por Costa fica afastado da cultura hegemónica e é, portanto, desconhecido pela maioria dos portugueses. A política de empatia e equanimidade que se impõe em relação ao "outro" nos filmes de Pedro Costa reverbera num efeito duplo junto dos espectadores portugueses: temos o estabelecimento de um pacto de cumplicidade entre o público em relação ao outro representado no ecrã, ao mesmo tempo provocando um sentimento de estranhamento junto com uma sensação de claustrofobia, desorientação espacial, assim como uma desterritorialização cultural e linguística. Esta última dinâmica revela-se de modo particularmente impactante na cena de abertura, que tem lugar no bairro à noite. A *mise-en-scène* altamente teatral inclui um plano estático duma casa dilapidada, através do uso da técnica de vinheta, onde uma luz de estúdio é projetada sobre a casa enquanto os contornos ficam escurecidos. O efeito estético lembra um desenho a carvão de livros ilustrados, que, neste caso, serve como preâmbulo para a história que será imediatamente contada. Simultaneamente, ouvimos barulho diegético de vozes do bairro junto com o estrondo violento de eletrodomésticos e mobília que são atirados a partir da janela, criando uma atmosfera desconfortável.

Logo depois, surge uma figura feminina de uma mulher mais velha cabo-verdiana (Clotilde – a atriz Isabel Cardoso) empunhando uma faca no meio da escuridão, desatando num longo monólogo falado na variante *badia* da língua cabo-verdiana, no qual ela também canta. O seu monólogo de caráter alegórico trata sobre estórias da vida dela em Cabo Verde, onde Clotilde, uma moça forte e independente, costumava nadar no mar como um peixe, a tal ponto que nem rapaz nem tubarão conseguiam trazê-la de volta à praia. Nem as mornas das serenatas dos rapazes a poderiam trazer de volta. Clotilde conta a história das dúvidas sobre ser mãe da sua criança e descreve o terror da criancinha frente à hipótese de ser abandonada pela mãe junto ao mar. Mais uma vez, no fim, de modo desafiante, Clotilde reivindica a sua independência em relação aos rapazes e, por extensão, à ordem patriarcal e às expetativas culturais impostas sobre ela enquanto mulher. Na medida em que ela se afasta para o fundo, aquilo que nós enxergamos é a faca que continua a brilhar na escuridão, como uma metáfora que condensa toda a violência que não será objeto de representação ao longo do filme. Mais tarde, descobrimos que Ventura era o seu marido e que, depois de ter sido esfaqueado por Clotilde, teria sido abandonado por ela. De tal forma, o espectador é testemunha da intimidade das personagens, tanto nas suas dimensões universais como na sua especificidade cultural e linguística cabo-verdiana no coração de Portugal.

Costa destaca uma dinâmica complexa e paradoxal de "proximidade distante," que Derek Pardue define como "íntima e contraditória" (*Cape Verde, Let's Go* 24), entre Portugal e Cabo Verde, no que diz respeito aos laços privilegiados de ordem histórica, cultural e linguística entre ambas as nações como resultado do colonialismo, miscigenação – uma suposta afinidade cultural entre os dois países, um estatuto especial de Cabo Verde no império colonial português em África, para além da migração maciça de cabo-verdianos a Portugal e à dependência económica das Ilhas em relação à antiga metrópole. Costa tenta lidar com essa dinâmica de proximidade distante, tanto existencial como cultural, através de duas estratégias ético-estéticas: um princípio axiográfico (teorizado pelo crítico Bill Nichols 1991, 77 e 93) na construção do espaço fílmico e um princípio dialógico no processo do planeamento de guião (ou roteirização, como se diria no Brasil). No caso do princípio axiográfico, que implica uma determinada configuração espacial duma ética de representação, deparamo-nos com o uso constante de *close-ups* contemplativos, *close-ups* intermédios e *contre-plongées* que incluem formas geométricas, textura, cor, e luz contrastantes. No caso do princípio dialógico, temos uma parceria artística e amizade pessoal que o cineasta cultiva com seus atores na construção coletiva das cenas, incluindo as cenas conversacionais que povoam o filme. Este princípio dialógico aproxima-se daquilo que a teórica pós-colonial Gayatri Spivak descreve numa entrevista como "uma estrutura de responsabilidade em relação ao subalterno com respostas fluindo em ambas as direções" (*The Spivak Reader* 293). No pensamento de Jacques Rancière, Costa oferece uma complexa poética de "trocas, correspondências e deslocações" (*Cem mil cigarros* 55) no que diz respeito ao relacionamento do cineasta com os sujeitos-atores representados, tentando estabelecer uma ponte entre as suas diferenças sócio-económicas, raciais e étnicas.

A longa-metragem *Bobô* (2013), de Inês Oliveira, é justamente baseada em trocas e alianças entre as duas personagens principais: Sofia (Paula Garcia), portuguesa branca, arquiteta, e Mariama (Aissato Indjai), guineense, filha de imigrantes e empregada-a-dias. Sofia sofre um profundo trauma pela perda do seu irmão num acidente 20 anos atrás, cujas sequelas continuam presentes na vida adulta ao ponto de paralisá-la emocionalmente. Aliás, Sofia passa por um processo de catexia devido à morte prematura do irmão, ao ponto de manter um quarto dum filho bebé, como se ela própria fosse a mãe que perdeu o filho. A verdadeira mãe de Sofia, a morar no Brasil, intervém nessa situação, contratando uma empregada-a-dias de confiança, Mariama, não só para os afazeres do espaço doméstico mas para acompanhar a Sofia. No início, Sofia resiste àquilo que ela vê como "uma invasão" do seu espaço íntimo. Contudo, Mariama, uma jovem mulher extrovertida e segura de si mesma, consegue ganhar paulatinamente a confiança da Sofia. Aos poucos, vai surgindo uma curiosidade mútua de uma mulher pela outra, que se manifesta através da exploração do quarto e casa de banho de cada uma e da observação do quotidiano das duas. O relacionamento muda definitivamente com a entrada em cena da irmã caçula (ou kodê) de Mariama, Bobô (Luana Quadé), uma menina de aproximadamente 6-7 anos, no limiar da idade para o ritual da excisão (ou mutilação genital) feminina. Sofia rende-se aos encantos da miúda cuja presença tem efeitos terapêuticos na vida dela. A amizade entre todas elas vai-se solidificar com o convite da Mariama para um típico casamento guineense de etnia fula e a chegada da avó de Mariama, interpretada pela maior atriz guineense, Bia Gomes, num feroz papel da mais velha encarregada de fazer o ritual da excisão.

O ponto climático do filme acontece quando Mariama e Sofia se unem para impedir que a pequena Bobô sofra as mazelas de tal prática. O filme *Bobô* estabelece uma aliança, não só feminina, mas feminista, em defesa dos direitos humanos das meninas e mulheres contra a prática da excisão feminina – prática ainda disseminada em aproximadamente 30 países em África, Médio Oriente e Ásia, mas também em comunidades diaspóricas dos países em questão (como é o caso retratado no filme). Sofia, entretanto, descobre África em Portugal, mais particularmente a Guiné-Bissau e uma das suas principais etnias, fula (ou *Halpulaar*), predominantemente muçulmana, mostrando curiosidade pela cultura, mas, ao mesmo tempo, ultrapassando as diferenças culturais em prol de uma causa humanista e feminista comum.

Há dois filmes do circuito comercial que surgem como a antítese dos filmes da arte do Pedro Costa e da Inês Oliveira em termos narrativos e estéticos: *Zona J* (1998), de Leonel Vieira, que teve amplo sucesso de público, e *A esperança está onde menos se espera* (2009), de Joaquim Leitão. *Zona J* conta a história de filhos de imigrantes angolanos que compartilham uma vida turbulenta com jovens brancos portugueses de baixa renda nas margens da sociedade lisboeta. As tensões de raça, classe, e nacionalidade vêm à tona numa história maniqueísta, onde a exuberância juvenil e a esperança sofrem um embate de cara ao preconceito da cultura hegemónica. Isabel de Sousa Ramos afirma que a representação crua de atitudes e atos racistas neste filme ainda eram raros no cinema português até aquela altura. A maioria das personagens em *Zona J* é levada à tentação do crime devido a estruturas familiares fracas e à falta de oportunidades económicas. No meio desta existência precária, surge um caso de amor interracial do angolano-português Tó (Félix Fontoura) e a portuguesa Carla (Núria Madruga), que é destinado ao fracasso sob a enorme pressão de forças adversas. Um dos elementos mais destacados deste filme pioneiro é a banda sonora, que inclui a melhor música rap comercial do seu tempo em Portugal, interpretada mormente por artistas negros, o que, para a época, ainda constituía uma novidade junto do *mainstream* português. A música da *Zona J*, oriunda da periferia da sociedade portuguesa, deixou marcas sonoras indeléveis na paisagem cultural do país, contribuindo para o processo de assimilação e apropriação do rap, na medida em que foi incorporado ao *mainstream* musical luso.

O filme português *Zona J* participa do zeitgeist de finais do século XX, onde surgem filmes paradigmáticos em vários pontos da diáspora africana a retratar a alienação social e falta de oportunidades que afeta as vidas de jovens negros (e não só), junto com a ameaça da criminalidade e violência por parte de quadrilhas e também da polícia: *Boyz in the Hood* (John Singleton, 1991, USA), *La Haine* (Mathieu Kassovitz, 1995, França), *Cidade de Deus* (Fernando Meirelles e Kátia Lund, 2002, Brasil).

Dez anos mais tarde, no filme *A Esperança Está onde menos se Espera*, do realizador Joaquim Leitão, o universo privilegiado de Cascais encontra-se cara a cara com a Cova da Moura, a comunidade de baixa renda mais conhecida de Lisboa, onde moram maioritariamente cabo-verdianos e os seus descendentes. Conta-se a história da família de um treinador rico e bem amado (Francisco Figueiredo, interpretado por Vergílio Castelo), eticamente contrário à corrupção praticada em jogos de futebol. Ao longo da história, ele perde o seu emprego e a sua fortuna, assim como a sua mulher, que emigra para Angola, enquanto o filho Lourenço (Carlos Nunes) é obrigado a abandonar a sua escola de elite bilíngue para ser transferido a uma escola pública frequentada por muitos alunos negros de baixa renda da Cova da Moura. Ao mesmo tempo que o pai fica paralisado pelo trauma emocional da perda de emprego, fortuna e identidade, o seu filho consegue lutar para eventualmente recuperar um sentido de dignidade e autoestima, ao cultivar uma relação romântica com uma colega de curso cabo-verdiano-portuguesa, Kátia (Alcídia Vaz). Enquanto Lourenço é aceite, em última instância, pela família da moça e pela sua comunidade, ele resgata o seu pai do abismo onde se encontra e trá-lo à Cova da Moura para se tornar um treinador local. O final feliz hollywoodiano do filme *A Esperança Está onde menos se Espera*, no meio da terrível crise económica que assolou Portugal a partir do final de década de 2000, contrasta significativamente com o final trágico de *Zona J*, durante os tempos eufóricos do boom económico português de finais dos anos 1990, que culminaram com a Expo 98.

O documentário *Outros Bairros* (1999), de Kiluanje Liberdade, Inês Gonçalves e Vasco Pimentel, centra o seu olhar etnográfico em jovens afroportugueses, cabo-verdianos ou luso-caboverdianos e as novas formações identitárias que têm estado a surgir em múltiplas comunidades da periferia lisboeta: Arrentela, Santa Filomena, Almada, Pontinha, Porto Salvo – com destaque para Pedreira dos Húngaros, um dos bairros que foram demolidos e cujos habitantes foram transferidos para novos prédios de habitação social. A rodagem do filme coincidiu justamente com o período da demolição do bairro. O documentário, aliás, antecipa-se ao filme de Pedro Costa, *No Quarto de Vanda*, ao documentar a destruição física do bairro e os efeitos psíquicos e emocionais sobre os habitantes. Antes do genérico inicial, desfilam rapazes negros sozinhos e em grupo, na sua maioria olhando diretamente para a câmara, com expressões que denotam altivez, alegria e serenidade, acompanhados por sons extra-diegéticos dum comboio a passar e vozes do bairro. A seguir aparece o título do filme e, mais tarde, "Lisboa" em grandes letras, com os nomes dos bairros retratados debaixo, em letras menores. As imagens iniciais remetem-nos ao género de fotografia sócio--documental (uma estratégia também adotada por Pedro Costa no seu filme mais recente, *Cavalo Dinheiro*).

Imediatamente depois, irrompe uma cena caótica a cores num registo meta-fílmico de *cinéma vérité*, onde o camarógrafo se vê confrontado com a polícia a invadir o bairro, proibindo-o de filmar e querendo confiscar a câmara e o material gravado. O camarógrafo recusa o pedido e o filme corta para o plano seguinte com um rapaz do bairro a rir dizendo, "Que é diferente, é diferente. Disso não tenhas dúvidas, pá." O documentário assume um compromisso ético e uma "militância da imagem em prol de uma política de representação voltada para os excluídos, pobres e oprimidos" (Teixeira 251), sem esconder a dimensão de vida periclitante face ao poder do estado nas suas várias dimensões, tanto política como policial.

A narrativa fílmica é construída principalmente a partir de interlúdios lírico-musicais de rap e reggae em kriolu badiu, português, inglês e francês, cenas conversacionais de rapazes e garotas sobre amor, relacionamentos afetivos e intimidade, assim como depoimentos em português ou kriolu badiu sobre o bairro, o destino do bairro e a impossibilidade de o mundo exterior conhecer verdadeiramente os bairros periféricos. Os rapazes também discorrem sobre a sua identidade pessoal e cultural, o sentimento de pertença ou não, quer em relacão ao bairro, Lisboa, Portugal, Cabo Verde, ou à diáspora cabo-verdiana. Um dos jovens mostra uma galeria de fotos afirmando que o "bairro somos nós"; "Pedreira vai continuar onde quer que estivermos." Outro rapaz salienta que "Esta ilha é nossa. Isto pode ser Portugal, mas a gente aceita este chão como outra ilha, outra ilha de Cabo Verde." Os sujeitos representados neste documentário encontram-se de facto num espaço liminar entre culturas, línguas, espaços geográficos e nações, levando uma vida altamente criativa, pragmática e autónoma, onde estão a forjar uma nova cultura no coração de Portugal e da diáspora cabo-verdiana.

*

O filme de Pedro Costa, *Cavalo Dinheiro* (2014), é descrito pelo crítico James Quandt como uma "visão fantasmagórica de um purgatório psicológico." Este filme, que foi aclamado pela crítica, aprofunda a investigação do trauma sofrido por Ventura ao ter sido espancado por oficiais revolucionários, que visavam bater em africanos em ato de vingança por terem sido derrotados na guerra contra movimentos africanos de libertação nacional. O filme tem lugar principalmente em espaços e temporalidades indefinidos; quase exclusivamente em espaços interiores (incluindo um hospital) que representam simbolicamente o estado

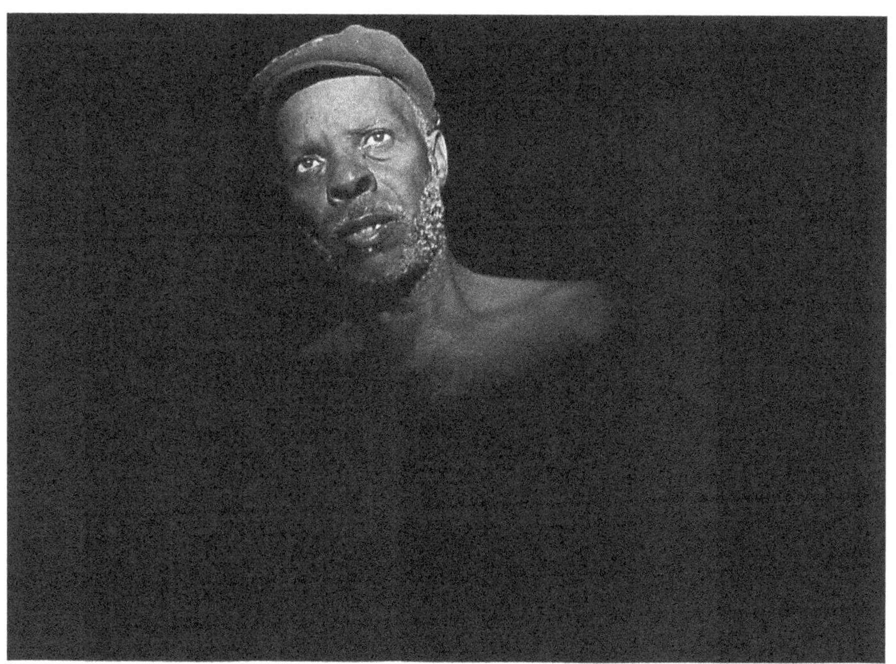

Cavalo Dinheiro (2014)

Cavalo Dinheiro (2014)

físico, mental e emocional do protagonista Ventura (visivelmente envelhecido e mostrando sinais da doença de Parkinson's). Surgem espaços cavernosos que produzem uma sensação de claustrofobia, incluindo escadarias e corredores, que são percorridos pelas personagens Ventura e Vitalina (Vitalina Varela), que acaba de chegar a Portugal a fim de obter a sua pensão de viúva (o marido dela era amigo do Ventura). Um dos momentos climáticos em *Cavalo Dinheiro* tem lugar num elevador preso entre andares, onde Ventura defronta os demónios interiores, representados por um soldado branco em uniforme militar com o rosto coberto de pintura de camuflagem, literalmente estático, numa pose de estátua ao pé de Ventura, falando sem mover os lábios. É uma figura fantasmática ligada ao trauma do protagonista, numa longa e excruciante cena de exorcismo psíquico-emocional.

Cavalo Dinheiro interrompe a narrativa de heroísmo ligada à Revolução do 25 de abril que pôs fim à mais longa ditadura do século XX na Europa ocidental, dando início ao fim do colonialismo português em África e Timor-Leste. Para Ventura e outros trabalhadores africanos das obras residindo em Portugal antes de 1974, a revolução adquiriu conotações sinistras. Paradoxalmente, o evento transformador que conduziu ao renascimento da moderna democracia portuguesa e a uma rutura na história do fascismo-colonialismo, passa por um processo de ressignificação no filme de Pedro Costa por conta do trauma sofrido por Ventura. Em vez de nos depararmos com uma rutura histórica, o trauma de Ventura revela uma continuidade na longa história duma ideologia racista, junto com atitudes de supremacia racial que alicerçaram o colonialismo apesar do seu colapso institucional entre 1974-75. Esta complexa dinâmica é um poderoso exemplo dos vestígios do colonialismo após o seu colapso, amplamente discutido por críticos da teoria pós-colonial, ilustrando em última instância a "colonialidade do poder" que ainda perdura e cujo fundamento reside num eixo racial hierárquico e eurocêntrico (Anibal Quijano).[10]

Outra sequência climática no meio do filme *Cavalo Dinheiro* constitui uma espécie de entre-ato, que inclui uma ponte musical comovente da famosa banda cabo-verdiana Os Tubarões, com a música intitulada "Altu Kutelu," dos anos 1970, cuja letra fala sobre as tribulações dos imigrantes cabo-verdianos em Portugal, num registo de denúncia social ao ritmo do som cubano melancólico. Ao mesmo tempo, surge uma série de retratos em *close-up* de mulheres e homens cabo-verdianos (na sua maioria, idosos) nos seus humildes espaços domésticos, em alguns casos olhando diretamente para a câmara, ou vestindo a sua melhor roupa. A sequência de retratos constitui uma homenagem à experiência individual e coletiva cabo-verdiana na diáspora, celebrando a sua luta e resiliência enquanto o mais antigo grupo de imigrantes na história do Portugal moderno.

O filme *Cavalo Dinheiro* foi em parte inspirado pela obra do fotógrafo dinamarquês-americano Jacob Riis, conhecido como um dos maiores fotógrafos numa vertente sócio-documental de finais do século XIX. Riis centrou a sua obra nas vidas dos imigrantes trabalhadores pobres em Nova Iorque, no auge da grande imigração europeia para o continente americano, mas também a grande migração afro-americana do sul do pós-guerra civil dos EUA para o norte em plena expansão industrial. De facto, o filme *Cavalo Dinheiro* abre com uma sequência de imagens fotográficas de Riis. Temos aqui uma clara convergência ético-estética entre o fotógrafo, Costa e ainda o coletivo de cineastas por trás do documentário, *Outros Bairros*, quanto à solidariedade em relação aos marginalizados nas suas respetivas sociedades e tempos, e o desejo dos artistas de inserirem imigrantes e descendentes, destituídos de direitos, num espaço simbólico de representação na luta pela cidadania social e política.[11]

Considerações Finais

Nos gestos de equanimidade e responsabilidade ética em relação aos "outros" (neste caso, africanos e portugueses negros e mulatos), os cineastas (na sua maioria portugueses brancos) abordados ao longo deste estudo surgem, em última instância, como mediadores culturais entre uma sociedade *mainstream* predominantemente branca e os seus "outros." Ao mesmo tempo, existem outras plataformas de expressão cultural e artística tais como a música popular, a literatura, o teatro e as artes visuais (para além do cinema), onde há uma presença não mediada de vozes africanas e afroportuguesas que têm sido, até agora, relativamente pouco estudadas no meio académico, mas que merecem toda a atenção da crítica.[12]

A produção cultural e artística que destaca as experiências de africanos e afroportugueses desempenha um papel fundamental enquanto suplemento que preenche a lacuna em termos de cidadania política plena, assim como ausência oficial de categorias raciais e étnicas na sociedade portuguesa contemporânea. No presente entudo, privilegiámos os esforços de mediação principalmente de artistas portugueses brancos na sua representação de africanos e afroportugueses, muitos dos quais ocupam um espaço liminar entre imigração e subjetividade portuguesa, afroportuguesa ou "afrotuga" em busca do alargamento do espaço para o exercício duma "cidadania social."

NOTAS

1. O cronista Gomes Eanes de Azurara ou Zurara (1410?–1474?) oferece um dos primeiros relatos sobre a chegada e leilão de escravos africanos em Lagos (Algarve), em 1443 e 1444. Vide os capítulos 24–25 e *Crónica do Descobrimento e Conquista da Guiné*, de 1448. Para o relato mais exaustivo sobre representações portuguesas, da era medieval até o início da modernidade, da figura do "africano" e do "mouro," as quais influenciaram de forma decisiva o imaginário ocidental, vide o estudo incisivo de Josiah Blackmore, *Moorings* (2009).

2. Isabel Castro Henriques discute a história de um bairro predominantemente negro no coração de Lisboa, chamado Mocambo (palavra umbundu que significa "pequeno vilarejo," de acordo com Luís Kandjimbo, citado por Henriques [39]), que existiu entre o final do século XVI e meados do XIX (47–65). De acordo com ela, é mais uma prova da grande população africana e de afro-descendentes durante parte da história de Lisboa no início da era moderna, a qual, em grande parte, foi esquecida.

3. Vide, por exemplo, os relatos da viajante inglesa Marianne Baillie em *Lisbon in the Years 1821,1822, and 1823* (Lisboa nos anos 1821, 1822 e 1823).

4. Os mais respeitados musicólogos modernos de fado, o brasileiro José Ramos Tinhorão e o português Rui Vieira Nery, concordam sobre as raízes africanas/afro-brasileiras do fado, principalmente a nível da estrutura rítmica e harmónica, além da coreografia. Acredita-se que o fado tenha suas origens em vários vieses musicais/coreográficos/poéticos: dois géneros de música afro-brasileiros do século XVIII – fofa e lundum – e o fandango espanhol (também de influência africana, de acordo com Tinhorão [16]). Estes eram todos géneros musicais muito populares, sensuais e transculturais que evoluíram até surgir o fado, ao longo do século XIX, tornando-se um género exclusivamente de canções. Portanto, a teoria das origens mouras do fado foi rejeitada em 1890 por um dos fundadores da musicologia portuguesa, Ernesto Vieira, citado por Ruy Vieira Nery em *Para uma História do Fado* (2004, 2012); ele argumenta que não há documentação, musicológica ou outra, que prove a existência do fado antes do século XIX (53). A influência árabe/moura seria um mito. Amália Rodrigues, a maior cantora de fado de todos os tempos, é considerada a responsável por introduzir elementos melismáticos com influência árabe ao seu estilo vocal, como resultado das músicas da Beira Baixa e da Andaluzia que ela ouvia. O seu estilo vocal tornou-se o padrão dentro desse gênero musical.

5. Vide António, João H.C. e Verónica Policarpo (2011); Batalha, Luís (2004); Dias, Bruno Peixe e Nuno Dias (2012); Fikes, Kesha (2009); Knudson-Vilaseca, Emily (2007); Machado, Fernando Luís (1994); Mata, Inocência (2006); Mendes de Gusmão, Neusa Maria (2004).

6. SOS Racismo; Afrolis; Djass (Associação de Afro-descendentes); FEMAFRO (Associação de Mulheres Negras, Africanas e Afrodescendentes); Observatório do Controlo e Repressão; Casa do Brasil; CAIPE – Coletivo de Ação Imigrante e Periférica; Consciência Negra; Socialismo Revolucionário; SOS Racismo; Plataforma Gueto; Nêga Filmes; Ass.

Cultural Moinho da Juventude; Associação Multicultural do Carregado; Khapaz – Associação Cultural de Jovens Afodescententes; Solidariedade Imigrante – Associação para a defesa dos direitos dos imigrantes (SOLIM); Associação Passa Sabi; Associação dos Filhos e Amigos de Farim (AFAFC); APEB – Ass. de Pesquisadores e Estudantes Brasileiros de Coimbra; Organização dos Estudantes da Guiné-Bissau de Coimbra; Letras Nómadas – Ass. de Investigação e Dinamização das Comunidades Ciganas; Em Luta; Teatro Griot; INMUNE – Instituto da Mulher Negra em Portugal; Associação Nasce e Renasce; Associação Krizo; A Gazua; Coletivo Chá das Pretas; Festival Feminista do Porto; A Coletiva; Núcleo Antifascista de Braga; UMAR – União de Mulheres Alternativa e Resposta (Braga); STCC – Sindicato dos Trabalhadores de Call Center; AIM – Alternative International Movement; Banda Exkurraçados; Hevgeniks; Kalina – Associação dos Imigrantes de Leste; Comunidade Bangladesh do Porto; União Romani Portuguesa; AMEC – Associação de Mediadores Ciganos; CIAP – Centro Incentivar a Partilha; Associação Mais Brasil; Coordenadora Antifascista Portugal; Associação Saber Compreender; GAP – Grupo Acção Palestina; GERA – Grupo Erva Rebelde Anarquista; Existimos e Resistimos; Rede Ex aequo; Porto Inclusive; Disgraça; Nu Sta Djunto; Outros Ângulos; Assembleia Feminista de Coimbra; UMAR – União de Mulheres Alternativa e Resposta (Coimbra); Txiribit; Projeto Aparte; Instituto das Comunidades Educativas (ICE); Ass. Desenvolvimento do Minho Rural (ADMIR); Coletivo Tuía de Artifícios; Associação Cultural e Recreativa Estrela da Lusofonia; Sindicato dos Estudantes; Associação Atividade Motora Adaptada; ILGA – Intervenção Lésbica, Gay, Bissexual, Trans e Intersexo.

7. Ver o estudo de Pedro Schacht Pereira no presente volume, "Henry Koster, Hegel and Humane Colonialism: Unexamined Links in the Genealogies of Lusotropicalism."

8. Devemos acrescentar aqui o documentário de caráter etnográfico do realizador Otávio Raposo sobre a cena rap não comercial da periferia lisboeta, *Nu Bai: O Rap Negro de Lisboa* (2006). Neste filme, onde predomina o enfoque observacional, o realizador dirige o seu olhar sobre os jovens afro-portugueses da cena rap, na sua maioria de origem cabo-verdiana; as suas vidas, os seus pontos de referência culturais-musicais, o seu lugar de enunciação na sociedade portuguesa e as suas reivindicações de caráter político-social e identitário.

9. Na década de 1990, foi instituído na grande Lisboa o Programa de Realojamento Urbano (PER) a fim de demolir bairros peroféricos "favelizados" ou auto-construídos, que, por sua vez, seriam substituídos por prédios modernos de caráter "social." Críticos apontam, segundo Ana Naomi de Sousa no jornal *The Guardian*, que os bairros periféricos foram substituídos por *ghettos*.

10. Ver "Coloniality of Power, Eurocentrism, and Latin America," *Nepantla*, 2000.

11. O documentário *Nu Bai: O Rap Negro de Lisboa*, de Otávio Raposo, tem um papel de destaque no alargamento do espaço de representação no âmbito documental de caráter etnográfico.

12. Em termos de producão literária portuguesa de autoria afro-descendente, vide *Estórias de Amor para Meninos de Cor* (Kalaf Epalanga, 2011), *O Angolano que comprou Lisboa (por Metade do Preço)* (Epalanga, 2014), *Esse Cabelo* (Djaimilia de Almeida Pereira, 2015) e *Também os Brancos Sabem Dançar* (Epalanga, 2017).

OBRAS CITADAS

Almeida, Djaimilia Pereira de. *Esse Cabelo*. Teorema, 2015.

António, João H.C. e Verónica Policarpo, eds. *Os Imigrantes e a Imigração aos Olhos dos Portugueses*. Fundação Gulbenkian, 2011.

Baillie, Marianne. *Lisbon in the Years 1821,1822, and 1823*. John Murray, 1825.

Batalha, Luís. *The Cape Verdean Diaspora in Portugal: Colonial Subjects in a Postcolonial World*. Lexington Books, 2004.

Blackmore, Josiah. *Moorings: Portuguese Expansion and the Writing of Africa*. University of Minnesota Press, 2009.

Costa, Pedro, dir. *Cavalo Dinheiro*. Sociedade Óptica Técnica, 2014.

———. *Juventude em Marcha*. Contracosta Produções, L'Étranger, Unlimited, Ventura Film, RTP, RTSI, Arte France, 2006.

———. *No Quarto de Vanda*. Atalanta Filmes, 2001.

———. *Ossos*. Atalanta Filmes, 1997.

Dias, Bruno Peixe e Nuno Dias, eds. *Imigração e Racismo em Portugal: O Lugar do Outro*. Edições 70 & Le Monde Diplomatique, 2012.

Epalanga, Kalaf. *Histórias de Amor para Meninos de Cor*. Caminho, 2011.

———. *O Angolano que Comprou Lisboa (por Metade do Preço)*. Caminho, 2014.

———. *Também os Brancos Sabem Dançar*. Todavia, 2017.

Fikes, Kesha. *Managing African Portugal: The Citizen-Migrant Distinction*. Duke University Press, 2009.

Godinho, Vitorino Magalhães. *Os Descobrimentos e a Economia Mundial*. Arcádia, 1963-65.

Henriques, Isabel Castro. *A Herança Africana em Portugal*. CTT Correios de Portugal, 2009.

Henriques, Joana Gorjão. "Falar de Etnias É Tabu." *Público Online*. 18 março 2012. http://www.publico.pt.

Kassovitz, Mathieu, dir. *La Haine*. Canal+, 1995.

Klein, Herbert. *The Atlantic Slave Trade*. Cambridge University Press, 2010.

Knudson-Vilaseca, Emily. *Embodying the Un/Home: African Immigration in Portugal and Spain*. 2007. University of Minnesota, Dissertação de Doutoramento.

Lahon, Didier. *O Negro no Coração do Império: Uma Memória a Resgatar – Séculos XV-XIX*. Entreculturas, 1999.

Landry, Donna e Gerald MacLean. *The Spivak Reader: Selected Works of Gayatri Chakravorty Spivak*. Routledge, 1996.

Leitão, Joaquim, dir. *A Esperança Está onde menos se Espera*. MGN Filmes, 2009.

Loude, Jean-Ives. 2005. *Lisboa na cidade negra*. Lisboa: D. Quixote.

Liberdade, Kiluanje, Inês Gonçalves e Vasco Pimentel, dir. *Outros Bairros*. Filmes do Tejo, 1999.

Machado, Fernando Luís. "Luso-Africanos em Portugal: Nas Margens da Etnicidade." *Sociologia - Problemas e Práticas*, vol. 16, 1994, pp. 111-34.

Mata, Inocência. "Estranhos em Permanência: A Negociação da Identidade Portuguesa na Pós-Colonialidade." *"Portugal Não É um País Pequeno": Contar o "Império" na Pós-Colonialidade*, edição de Manuela Ribeiro Sanches, Livros Cotovia, 2006, pp. 285-315.

Meirelles, Fernando e Kátia Lund, dir. *Cidade de Deus*. O2 Filmes, Globo Filmes, Videofilmes, 2002.

Mendes de Gusmão, Neusa Maria. *Os Filhos da África em Portugal: Antropologia, Multiculturalidade e Educação*. Imprensa de Ciências Sociais, 2004.

Nery, Rui Vieira. *Para uma História do Fado*. Público, 2004.

Nichols, Bill. *Representing Reality: Issues and Concepts in Documentary*. Indiana University Press, 1991.

Oliveira, Inês, dir. *Bobô*. David & Golias, 2013.

Pardue, Derek. *Cape Verde Let's Go: Creole Rappers and Citizenship in Portugal*. University of Illinois Press, 2015.

Pereira, Pedro. "Henry Koster, Hegel and Humane Colonialism: Unexamined Links in the Genealogies of Lusotropicalism." *Portuguese Literary and Cultural Studies*, 2019.

Quandt, James. "Still Lives." *Artforum*, 2006, pp. 354-359.

Quijano, Anibal. "Coloniality of Power, Eurocentrism, and Latin America." *Nepantla: Views from South*, edição de Walter Mignolo, Duke University Press, 2000, pp. 531-580.

Ramos, Isabel de Sousa. "A Intersecção das Categorias de Raça e Classe na Representação Cinematográfica de Jovens Afro-Descendentes." Manuscrito não publicado, 2011.

Rancière, Jacques. "Política de Pedro Costa." *Cem Mil Cigarros: Os Filmes de Pedro Costa*, edição de Ricardo Matos Cabo, Orfeu Negro, 2009, pp. 53-63.

Raposo, Otávio, dir. *Nu Bai: O Rap Negro de Lisboa*. Centro Audiovisual do ISCTE, 2006.

Singleton, John, dir. *Boys in the Hood*. Columbia Pictures, 1991.

Sousa, Ana Naomi de. "Lisbon's Bad Week: Police Brutality Reveals Portugal's Urban Reality." *The Guardian*, 31 janeiro 2019. https://www.theguardian.com/cities/2019/jan/31/lisbons-bad-week-police-brutality-reveals-portugals-urban-reality?CMP=share_btn_fb&fbclid=IwAR2YZCYtjAdeZRkGXMycJNwVeGkSKBLutQ2geJ2iqR8f9BfMK1TTKKP5-VE

Teixeira, Francisco Elinaldo. *Cinemas não narrativos*. Alameda, 2013.

Tinhorão, José Ramos. *Fado, Dança do Brasil Cantar de Lisboa: O Fim de um Mito*. Caminho, 1994.

————. *Os Negros em Portugal: Uma Presença Silenciosa*. Caminho, 1988.

Vieira, Leonel, dir. *Zona J*. MGN Filmes/SIC, 1998.

Zurara, Gomes Eanes de. *Crónica do Descobrimento e Conquista da Guiné*. Publicações
    Europa-América, 1989.

FERNANDO ARENAS (1963-2019) foi Professor de Literaturas Lusófonas e Estudos Culturais nos Departamentos de Línguas e Literaturas Românicas e Estudos Afro-Americanos e Africanos da Universidade de Michigan. Foi membro do conselho editorial de *Portuguese Literary & Cultural Studies*. O presente número da revista (PLCS 34/35) é dedicado à sua memória.

ANA CRISTINA PEREIRA

O Peso do Passado em Conversas sobre *Cavalo Dinheiro* (2014), de Pedro Costa: (Re)Formulação e (Re)Produção do Discurso Racista e Colonialista através de "Novas" Estratégias Discursivas

RESUMO: A longa-metragem *Cavalo Dinheiro* (2014) de Pedro Costa mergulha nas lembranças, delírios e pesadelos de Ventura, para falar de uma geração de cabo-verdianos que deixou a sua terra natal e imigrou para Lisboa em perseguição de uma vida melhor, e que perdeu a juventude, a saúde e por vezes morreu, tentando atingir esse sonho. Como dialogam jovens portugueses brancos com as representações identitárias do "Outro" africano propostas pela obra? Qual a relação que se desenvolve com um filme que questiona discursos vigentes sobre a história, as expressões simbólicas e a identidade portuguesa? O filme foi mostrado e discutido em universidades do norte de Portugal, com alunos de licenciatura em Teatro e Comunicação. Apresenta-se uma leitura do filme seguida do resultado dessas conversas, numa análise de caráter crítico discursivo, que desvela a persistência de estereótipos racistas e a reprodução de discurso colonialista.

PALAVRAS-CHAVE: Cavalo Dinheiro; Pedro Costa; Ventura; Análise Crítica do Discurso;

ABSTRACT: Pedro Costa's feature film *Horse Money* (2014) delves into Ventura's memories, delusions and nightmares, to speak about a generation of Cape Verdeans who left their homeland and emigrated to Lisbon in the pursuit of a better life, and lost their youth, their health and sometimes died, trying to achieve that dream. How do young Portuguese dialogue with the identity representations of the African "Other" proposed by the Film? What is the relationship that they develop with a film that questions current discourses about history, symbolic expressions, and Portuguese identity? The film was shown and discussed in central and northern universities in Portugal, with undergraduate students in Theater and Communication. We present a reading of the film and then the result of these conversations, in a critical discursive analysis, that reveals the persistence of racist stereotypes, as well the reproduction of colonialist discourse.

KEYWORDS: Horse Money; Pedro Costa; Ventura; Critical Discourse Analysis

Uma Leitura de *Cavalo Dinheiro* (2014)

Há fotografias de nitidez, estas são obscuras.
São feitas por mim, segundo a minha vontade.
Jaime (1974), de António Reis

Figura 1. Imigrantes em Nova Iorque fotografados por Jacob Riis (1890)

Figura 2. Imigrantes em Nova Iorque fotografados por Jacob Riss (1890)

A abrir *Cavalo Dinheiro*, vemos fotografias de Jacob Riis (1890) onde figuram trabalhadores imigrantes em Nova Iorque, no final do século XIX. As pessoas fotografadas encontram-se consideravelmente próximas, quase amontoadas. Estas imagens retratam ambientes ruidosos que o tempo cobriu de silêncio; talvez por esse motivo, o autor não achou necessário que algum som as acompanhasse. A sequência das fotografias de Riis culmina no plano do retrato de um homem negro e triste, pintado por Géricault. Estas primeiras imagens, sem som, confundem o filme na história do mundo e o passado no presente, ao mesmo tempo que instituem o tom (elevado/sério) com que o filme revelará a obscuridade de uma parte da história da humanidade. Desde os primeiros momentos, é esta a proposta de *Cavalo Dinheiro*: mostrar a obscuridade, que é o contrário de iluminar a obscuridade.

Além de universalizarem a estória que *Cavalo Dinheiro* vai contar, as fotografias que dão início ao filme estabelecem uma conexão informal (van Leeuwen 2008) com os "filhos" que Ventura terá espalhados pelo globo, ligando assim *Cavalo Dinheiro* a *Juventude em Marcha*, o filme que Costa, Ventura e os restantes

Figura 3. Busto de negro de Gericoult em *Cavalo Dinheiro* (2014), de Pedro Costa

companheiros estrearam em 2006. Porque, se é verdade que *Cavalo Dinheiro* conta uma parte da história universal, também é verdade que o filme se alimenta da memória dos filmes feitos por esta mesma equipa e que o precederam, bem como das circunstâncias particulares destes imigrantes, desta comunidade específica e deste país que é Portugal. Mais tarde, sensivelmente a meio do filme, veremos imagens "atualizadas" de imigrantes, já não em grupo, porque agora se vive mais isolado, e já não em silêncio, mas sim acompanhadas do tema *Alto Cutelo*, da banda cabo-verdiana Os Tubarões. Tal como os fantasmas das fotografias iniciais e ligadas a eles por uma espécie de "destino comum" (Lewin 1997, 165), as pessoas que habitam estas imagens não são necessariamente personagens do filme, mas são parte essencial da sua estória que contém história. O poema cantado e escrito por Ildo Lobo descreve a realidade que conduz à emigração, a dureza da vida de emigrante e finalmente revela o sonho que permite prosseguir sem desesperar.

> Na Alto Cutelo cinbrom dja ca ten
> (dja seca)
> Raiz sticado djobe água, q' atcha
> (dja seca)
> Água sta fundo e ni omi ca tral
> (dja seca)
> Mudjer um sumana sê lumi ca cende
> (na casa)
> Sê fidjo, na strada so um ta trabadja
> (pa dozi mirés)
> Marido dja dura q' i bai pa Lisboa (contratado)
> Pa bai pa Lisboa e bende sê tera
> (metadi di preço)

Ali, el ta trabadja na tchuba na bento
(na frio)
Na Cuf, na Lisnave e na Jota Pimenta
Mon d'obra barato, pa mas q'i trabadja (serventi)
Mon d'obra barato, baraca sem luz
(cumida a pressa)
Inda mas nganadu q' i s' irmon branco (splorado)
Mas um dia, que n' volta pa terra
Monte Gordo e Malagueta
Nhos tem q' i da-m água
Cu força na braço, consiencia di mi,
E mi q' i trabadja, tera e poder e pa mi
Cu sinbrom na cutelo
(nos tera)
Midju na tchon
(nos tera)
E barco na porto
(nos tera)

Figura 4. Homem jovem, *Cavalo Dinheiro* (2014), de Pedro Costa

Figura 5 - Mulher sentada, *Cavalo Dinheiro* (2014), de Pedro Costa

Figura 6. Homem sentado, *Cavalo Dinheiro* (2014), de Pedro Costa

Muito antes destas imagens-som, contudo, durante o plano do quadro de Géricault começamos a ouvir passos e, logo depois, um movimento inesperado da câmara para a direita dá lugar à primeira imagem com movimento e som do filme: Ventura desce uma escada estreita que o conduzirá à escuridão de um túnel subterrâneo. Quem o conseguir acompanhar, não poderá sair antes do fim. *Cavalo Dinheiro* é estruturado com uma montagem de cortes aparentemente irracionais, descontínuos, deslocados dos princípios de *raccord* que legitimam o cinema narrativo clássico (Deleuze 2015) e que facilitam a vida ao leitor/espectador. A viagem de Ventura através dos túneis subterrâneos da memória será um *continuum* de imagem "direta no tempo" e culminará na sua salvação, ou na sua morte. Coragem.

Memória e Fantasma

Cavalo Dinheiro pode ser descrito como um manifesto poético que nos confronta com as lembranças, os sonhos, alucinações e os pesadelos do cabo-verdiano Ventura, que imigrou para Portugal no início da década de 1970, onde, desprevenido, se sobressaltou com a Revolução dos Cravos (1974), onde trabalhou até se reformar, ainda bastante jovem na sequência de um acidente de trabalho, e onde vive até hoje. Através da memória de Ventura, o filme fala de uma primeira geração de cabo-verdianos que deixou a sua terra natal para perseguir uma vida melhor em Portugal, e que perdeu a juventude, a saúde e por vezes morreu, tentando atingir esse sonho. Existe, porém, um caso banal que serve de rede aos voos aparentemente desamparados do filme. Uma zanga entre irmãos/companheiros acaba numa briga de facas que conduz à hospitalização de Ventura e ao encarceramento do outro homem. Uma mulher e uma família ficam em Cabo Verde sem ter ninguém para ajudar ao seu sustento. De camisa vermelha e por vezes brincando com uma faca, Tito – esse antigo companheiro – primeiro exigirá a Ventura que se retrate e, mais tarde, aparece a perguntar-lhe quem sustentará a sua família. Ventura não está em paz com este passado, talvez se culpe por não ter feito tudo o que devia.

Figura 7. Ventura, *Cavalo Dinheiro* (2014), de Pedro Costa

O processo de amentar de Ventura procura a redenção. O Pioneiro cabo-verdiano visita o passado, não para o reviver, ou para o corrigir, mas para dele se libertar por doação: *Cavalo Dinheiro* é a epopeia trágica dos cabo-verdianos em Portugal. Deste modo, o tempo histórico dilui-se num tempo messiânico em que cada instante é, ao mesmo tempo, passado, presente e futuro. Através da utilização desse dispositivo que é o exercício de lembrar, o passado e o presente confluem no mesmo momento, e é recorrendo à ideia de que tudo se passa na cabeça de Ventura que Pedro Costa consegue este feito (Guerreiro 2014). A memória e os seus mecanismos de interrupção e suspensão e as imagens que lhe são inerentes – os seus *phantasma* – são tema de *Cavalo Dinheiro* a par com a estória contada.

Na primeira sequência falada do filme, no hospital, Ventura é visitado, ou imagina a visita, dos seus companheiros de infortúnio e diz-lhes:

> A nossa vida continuará a ser dura... continuaremos a cair do terceiro andar. Continuaremos a ser trucidados por máquinas. As nossas cabeças e os nossos pulmões continuarão a doer do mesmo modo... seremos queimados... ficaremos doidos. É por causa do mofo nas paredes de nossas casas. Nós sempre vivemos e morremos assim, essa é a nossa doença. Se não me matares primeiro com a tua faca.

Estas palavras de Ventura surgem no final da visita durante a qual Tito revela as "notas biográficas" de Delgado, Benvindo, Daniel e Lento, acompanhadas pelos retratos individualizados dos rostos destes camaradas de Ventura, proporcionados pela lente expressionista de Costa: Delgado pôs fogo à casa com a família dentro e nunca mais falou; Benvindo e Daniel caíram do terceiro andar de um edifício em construção. O primeiro sofre de epilepsia e Daniel morreu na caixa do elevador; Lento vendia droga para complementar o seu magro vencimento como calceteiro e, quando foi apanhado, os "tratamentos" que recebeu da polícia tiveram como consequência uma injeção diária para os nervos, até hoje. Ventura prevê a continuidade do sofrimento e, deste modo, não só traz para o presente como projeta no futuro, a realidade vivida pelo grupo de imigrantes. Estas personagens são o "Outro" de todas as gerações do passado e do presente, esmagados pelo funcionamento estrutural e institucional do país e do mundo, que os continua a encurralar na base da pirâmide social, base essa cada vez mais larga, por oposição a um vértice cada vez mais estreito.

Cavalo Dinheiro é a história obscura da imigração cabo-verdiana em Portugal e do também obscurecido falhanço político e social do projeto de país iniciado com o 25 de abril de 1974: a história que não foi contada, a que não faz parte dos manuais escolares, nem sequer da retórica de nenhum dos partidos políticos – esta história não é a dos vencedores, nem tão pouco a dos vencidos; é a odisseia dos que não foram tidos como existentes. E porque a parte contém o todo, é também, de algum modo, a história de todos os apagados de todas as revoluções do mundo.

À visita dos seus segue-se a difícil entrevista do médico (que parece visar um diagnóstico de esquizofrenia) em que a câmara parada regista a atuação de Ventura perante as perguntas que lhe são feitas, numa espécie de introito para a cena do elevador que acontecerá mais tarde. O estado de espírito de Ventura, permeado talvez por uma desconfiança em relação ao médico, vai navegando entre a tristeza, o medo e a nostalgia. Inicialmente, está sentado e até algo altivo, mas acaba deitado (tal como mais tarde, no elevador). No final, o médico aproxima-se para o reconfortar e a câmara também. Ventura fica com a esferográfica do médico.

Segue-se o momento prodigioso em que o herói se confronta com uma máscara africana. Ventura, que é tantas vezes (e desde Juventude em Marcha) filmado em contrapicado, agora está sentado e é visto de cima para baixo. Escreve(-se), rescreve(-se) em face desta *persona*. Mais tarde, senta-se de novo para escrever, desta feita numas escadas e na presença de um corpo negro nu, numa pose enroscada de estátua renascentista. Não sabemos o que escreve Ventura, mas parece claro a sua escrita estará contaminada por estas outras formas de representação de uma história que também é a dele.

O filme sugere que talvez tudo se tenha começado a partir, na cabeça de Ventura, daquela noite de abril de 1974. Todos procuram Ventura sem sucesso, inclusivamente crianças e até um motard montado em modelo vermelho ostensivo e um homem com uma cabra aos ombros (depois seguido por outras) – mistura de personagens que indica um encontro entre um mundo urbano e uma certa ruralidade. Um sino toca a rebate. Um homem tenta escalar um pequeno monte ou parede e cai. Zulmira, a mulher de Ventura reza. Na estrada, Ventura aproxima-se envergando apenas cuecas vermelhas e botas. É apanhado pelos militares que circulam de chaimite pelas ruas. Apontam as armas a Ventura, que levanta os braços. Não se percebe se desapareceu de casa ou do hospital, mas ao que parece, não sabe muito bem onde está. Daquela data em diante conheceu bem muitos hospitais.

Encontraremos Ventura pela cidade, em frente às janelinhas iluminadas do Hospital de Santa Maria, na Fonte Luminosa da Alameda, e veremos também estátuas, planos lusco-fusco da cidade, autoestradas e placards publicitários, que evidenciam a desorientação de um herói de outro tempo, num mundo pós-moderno, pós-industrial e também pós-revolucionário. Curiosamente, Ventura parece mais confortável, ou pelo menos mais norteado, em ambientes cavernosos, com escadas, subterrâneos, corredores, portões com grades de ferro, salas mal iluminadas, ruínas de fábricas ou armazéns, onde todos os fantasmas vivem albergados clandestinamente. Os fantasmas de Ventura que por aqui vivem desde os filmes de Tourneur ou de Lang, estão prontos a alimentar a imaginação expressionista de Pedro Costa. Ao longo das ruínas que habita, o cabo-verdiano passará ainda pela fábrica onde trabalhou. Na fábrica encontra-se novamente com Benvindo, um dos seus companheiros de infortúnio, e também com as memórias do tempo em que construiu a sua casa e criou a sua própria família. As narrativas são difíceis de aceitar pela sua dureza e, por vezes, crueldade, mas o testemunho de uma vida difícil é sempre contrabalançado com memórias de prazer e com uma espécie de ternura que atravessa as relações entre todos. Um exemplo do que aqui se diz é a cena em que Benvindo e Ventura – iluminados como se estivessem dentro de um ecrã, criando um efeito de ecrã dentro do ecrã – discutem sobre a memória de uma cantiga popular que tentam entoar:

> *Ei, ei, ei, ei ya*
> *Nta pupa sima kabalu*
> *Nta bera cima limária*
> *Sinhor dotor nhu flam kusé kim n'teni*
> (Cantando juntos)
> *Ei, ei, ei ei ya*
> *N'teni fomi n'ka podi kumi*
> *N'teni sedi n'ka podi bebi*
> *N'teni sono Ká podi durme*
> *Ei, ei, ei, ei ya*
> *N' tem sodadi de Tchada São Francisco*
> *N' tem sodadi Tchada Bela Kusa*
> *N' tem sodadi camarada Pepi Lopi*

> Benvindo: Não, Tio!
> Ventura: *Foi assim que eu aprendi.*
> Benvindo: Não!

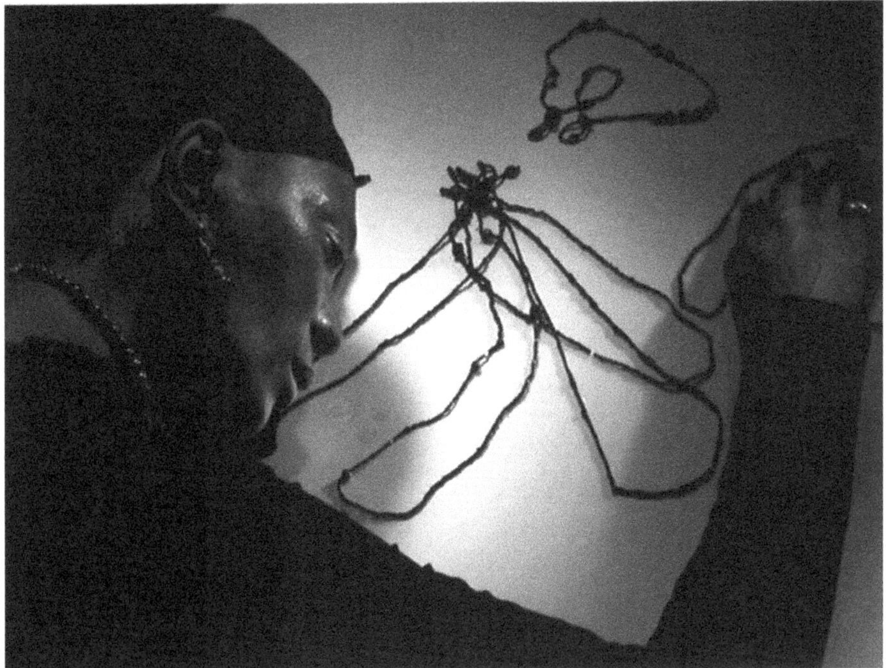

Figura 8. Vitalina, *Cavalo Dinheiro* (2014), de Pedro Costa
Figura 9. Vitalina prostrada, *Cavalo Dinheiro* (2014), de Pedro Costa

Ventura: É assim que as pessoas cantam.
Benvindo: *Pepi Lopi. Achada Pepi Lopi, Tio!*
Ventura: *Errado, Benvindo. É camarada Pepi Lopi!*
Benvindo: *Comarada Pepi Lopi?!* (abana a cabeça) *Tchada Pepi Lopi!*

Antes de cantarem, Benvindo informara Ventura (à semelhança do que acontecera na visita inicial) do paradeiro e também dos acidentes e infelicidades dos vários companheiros. Nada há a discutir sobre a vida de imigrantes explorados. Essas estórias parecem claras – a memória delas permite manter uma conversa e dar, desse modo, continuidade ao presente. Uma memória diferente, contudo, que os liga à terra natal e que os une num mesmo grupo particular, numa mesma diáspora de trabalhadores cabo-verdianos, já não tem a nitidez de outrora e parece estar a perder-se. Benvindo e Ventura parecem querer capturar essa memória, cristalizá-la, mas a única coisa que o filme pode fazer é registar a dúvida e as duas hipóteses do poema. São claras as memórias sobre a realidade diária, datada em acidentes, mais ou menos aparatosos. Menos claros, ou menos fáceis de enunciar, são os sentimentos que elas provocam. Esta ideia parece atravessar todo o filme e é mais forte no caso de Vitalina.

Vitalina Varela

Como convém ao cinema das imagens-tempo (Deleuze 2015), Vitalina é uma personagem numa situação limite e, se ajusta contas com Ventura é para lhe oferecer uma possibilidade de redenção. Em trânsito das Ilhas de Cabo Verde para a periferia de Lisboa, presa nas teias burocráticas que caracterizam as relações entre os dois países, perdida na Lisboa noturna onde aparece quase como uma sombra, Vitalina desloca-se do mundo rural para o urbano. Durante esse percurso, as promessas do patriarcado cristão vão-se desfazendo por via da máquina capitalista e da sua urgência permanente de lucro, mas também do abandono dos seus pares.

Vitalina e Joaquim de Brito Varela casaram em Cabo Verde e, logo depois, o noivo regressou a Portugal para trabalhar. Um dia, Vitalina foi surpreendida pela irmã com a notícia da morte do marido e correu para a embaixada para conseguir os documentos exigidos para ir ao funeral em Lisboa. O processo não foi suficientemente rápido, a viagem não foi fácil e, quando chegou a Lisboa, o enterro já tinha acontecido. Vitalina partilha as suas memórias dolorosas, com Ventura e connosco, e procede à leitura de documentos oficiais, como certidões de nascimento, de casamento e de morte, sempre com uma voz que se projeta mal e com doloroso esforço. O sussurro de Vitalina não surge como uma opção, é uma falta de voz, como uma primeira voz depois de muito tempo de silêncio. A sua dificuldade em fazer-se ouvir indica o silenciamento a que se submetem os subalternizados pela via da naturalização da sua condição; o esforço quase palpável de Vitalina para arrancar ao silêncio estas memórias revela mais sobre a sua dor do que a descrição dos acontecimentos. É certo que a leitura dos documentos lembra os poetas surrealistas e a sua descoberta da poesia intrínseca na prosa oficial (Romney, 2015), mas, aqui, expressa sobretudo o vazio de informação relativamente à vida que está entre as datas registadas legalmente e a incapacidade dos documentos de preencher esse vazio.

Esta mulher condensa na sua estória – quer pelo que conta, quer pela forma como conta – toda a história das mulheres, que ficaram (em/na "terra") sempre que os homens partiram, fosse por força da lei, da ambição, ou da miséria. A estória de Joaquim de Brito Varela é a de Ventura, ou a de Tito e, deste modo, a ausência de Varela (e de Tito) é também a falha de Ventura. Eles são os jovens briguentos que dançavam e bebiam e amavam nos encontros de cabo-verdianos do Jardim da Estrela, nos anos 1970. Além disso, Ventura é o pioneiro de uma diáspora e, juntamente com os seus companheiros, o construtor de novas cidades e de novas possibilidades de vida. Os homens, enganados e explorados, são, ainda assim, o polo positivo desta epopeia, muito ignorada, é certo, mas que se projeta na esperança de um futuro menos sombrio. Eles são bravos guerreiros, heróis de uma elegia trágica a ser lembrada e celebrada. A Vitalina resta o esquecimento, e a quase mudez de sua voz explicita essa quase impossibilidade de se fazer ouvir. Ela é também a mulher que ofereceu a camisa vermelha a Tito, num dia de aniversário. Elas ficaram à espera. Pelas mais variadas razões, eles não regressaram. A vida de Vitalina tabela--se pelos momentos registados em documentos oficiais e tudo o que permeia as datas aí registadas não é referido. Ao contrário de Penélope, que esperava Ulisses, Vitalina é pobre, nada indica que tivesse um filho, nem que soubesse fiar e, também ao contrário de Penélope, o homem por quem esperava não

Figura 10. Sorriso final, enigmático de Vitalina, *Cavalo Dinheiro* (2014), de Pedro Costa

regressou. À espera junta-se agora a tormenta da viagem. Vitalina chega tarde para enterrar Joaquim, mas não para confrontar Ventura, que a guarda na memória. Ventura carrega uma culpa e Vitalina vai assumindo o papel de conterrânea (cúmplice que traz notícias), médica, sacerdotisa, mulher, perante quem ele se revela, confessa e reconstrói.

Ventura recupera visivelmente da sua doença imediatamente depois de falar com Vitalina e, progressivamente, vai-se transformando em seu marido, ao mesmo tempo que se transformam um no outro, num processo de troca identitária conseguida através de uma não realista e às vezes não coincidente troca entre imagens e texto e entre vozes e imagem: Vitalina e Ventura assumem as memórias um do outro como se tivessem ambos vivido ambas as estórias e toda a história dos cabo-verdianos pobres e emigrantes. Como já foi referido, à semelhança do regime de imagens-tempo descrito por Deleuze (2015), *Cavalo Dinheiro* constrói-se sobre ruturas; cortes inesperados e esbatidos que decorrem de ações não ancoradas no jogo estímulo e resposta. A *imagem-tempo* capacita-se para pensar e compreender o mundo, precisamente porque abdica do efeito sensorial de verdade ou de realismo, e o filme revela-se deste modo – acreditamos – um meio favorável à produção de ruturas na ordem simbólica dominante e daí à transformação do conhecimento.

Por fim, Vitalina é chamada a um gabinete onde irá receber a pensão de viúva, ou tratar de questões burocráticas relacionadas. Esta cena permite compreender de outro modo, a importância dos documentos anteriormente mencionados, e o momento atual da vida de Vitalina. Esta mulher, percebemos agora, colige os documentos de uma vida (aliás duas) com o objetivo de tratar da sua permanência em Portugal, ou simplesmente da sua pensão de viúva. Se este novo facto não fosse suficiente, segundos antes, Ventura entregara-lhe finalmente a carta que anda a escrever há muito tempo e o sorriso enigmático de Vitalina, depois de a ler, abre para uma nova possibilidade por contar, quiçá um novo filme.

O Elevador

> *A revolução é a máscara da morte. A morte é a máscara da revolução.*
> Heiner Muller, A Missão (2017, 17)

O já referido deslocamento do tempo e do espaço culmina com a cena do elevador em que Ventura, de mãos tremeluzentes, fala com uma galeria de personagens da sua vida: os que estão vivos, os que estão mortos, e alguns que são apenas

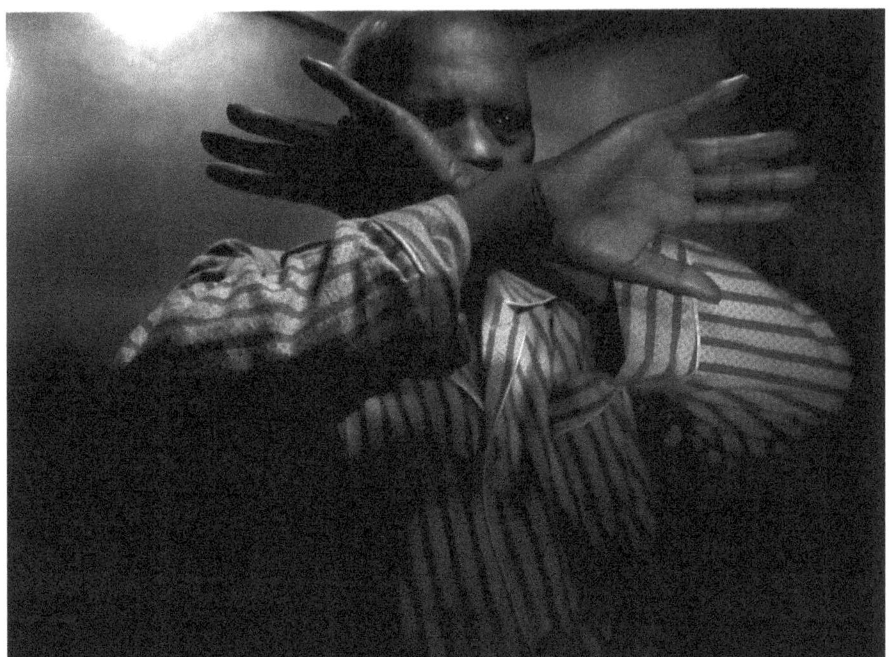

Figura 11. Ventura no elevador, *Cavalo Dinheiro* (2014), de Pedro Costa
Figura 12. O Soldado Estátua, *Cavalo Dinheiro* (2014), de Pedro Costa

símbolos. Esta cena do elevador não traz propriamente informação nova. Ventura repete as memórias que já o ouvimos contar em momentos anteriores e que foram (como já referimos) relatadas quase do mesmo modo e com as mesmas referências na entrevista inicial com o médico – 25 de abril de 1974; doença; hospitais; de quando trabalhava na construção civil; da briga que lhe valeu um internamento e 93 pontos na cabeça; do seu medo dos militares; do medo de perder o contrato de trabalho; de quando se encontrava com outros emigrantes cabo-verdianos no Jardim da Estrela; de quando lhe roubaram a aliança de casamento (quem rouba uma aliança de casamento a um homem caído?); pássaros negros; Spínola; 11 de março; etc. Enfim são poucas as novidades, mas agora o passado e o presente confundem-se brutalmente e, por isso, a cena contém uma grande carga emocional. É uma travessia em que Ventura experimenta o medo, o pânico, a loucura, também alguma nostalgia, e que culmina em prostração. Durante esta viagem, o herói exprime-se de formas diversas e por vezes antagónicas, começando num tom de preocupação com o Soldado Estátua que o acompanha, passando por estados de lamento quase infantil quando se lembra da sua vida de trabalho, que desembocam numa voz zangada e áspera de acusação e num rosto particularmente duro que precede o momento em que canta a sua versão de *Alto Cutelo* dos Tubarões. Na viagem de elevador, Ventura ouve carpir a sua própria morte em crioulo de Cabo Verde e fala com o Soldado Estátua e também com Zulmira, sua esposa.

A câmara de Pedro Costa, que durante a entrevista com o médico estivera parada, posiciona-se agora em lugares diferentes, consoante o momento, sublinhando os estados de espírito da personagem, ou dito de outro modo, provocando em quem vê sentimentos distintos. Como se descêssemos um degrau (ou vários) no estado de espírito de Ventura, agora já não é possível à câmara apenas contemplar e registar; ela dialoga com o herói e toma posição. Através de diferentes alturas e ângulos, Ventura pode parecer frágil ou forte, ingénuo ou maldoso. No fim desta viagem catártica de elevador (que pode ser uma metáfora para a cabeça de Ventura), sentado a um canto, o protagonista vira a cabeça para a câmara e diz: "esta é a história da vida jovem," mas a estátua do soldado que o acompanhou durante a viagem completa:

> *Soldado (ângulo contrapicado)* – E da vida ainda por vir. E de todas as coisas que se seguirão. Fica perto de mim: o tempo vai voar. O dia virá em que seremos capazes de aceitar o nosso sofrimento. Não haverá mais medo nem mistério.
>
> . . .

Soldado (de pé, ângulo contrapicado) – Esta estória ainda não acabou. As nossas dores serão alegria para toda a humanidade futura. Eles vão dizer coisas boas sobre nós. Não tarda muito ficaremos a saber porque vivemos e porque sofremos. Saberemos tudo. Tudo.

As palavras finais do Soldado Estátua revelam uma grande fé no cinema como meio para a transformação da realidade pela sua suspensão e distanciamento, e como meio para a instituição de uma memória do mundo. Liberta da "moldura do significante" a cena do elevador como um todo, recorta a realidade, amplia a sua complexidade e permite-nos desse modo uma outra compreensão da vida de Ventura e dos imigrantes cabo-verdianos e de Portugal.

Restabelecido, depois de sair do elevador, Ventura dá de comer a Tito, apesar da sua tremura, e logo depois deixa o "hospital," conduzido até à porta pelo médico. Do lado de fora, um amanhecer(?) expressionista em que o edifício negro de onde sai Ventura tem como fundo um céu vermelho. Tempo ainda para uma montra com facas, onde se espelham possivelmente as pernas e os pés de Ventura, sugerindo um passado que se faz presente ou um recomeço – uma *Imagem-cristal*, "desdobramento constitutivo em presente que passa e passado que se conserva, a estrita contemporaneidade do presente com o passado que ele será, do passado com o presente que ele foi" (Deleuze 2015, 429).

O Peso do Passado em Conversas sobre *Cavalo Dinheiro* (2014) de Pedro Costa

Cavalo Dinheiro é a quarta longa-metragem que Pedro Costa faz com a comunidade das Fontainhas/Casal da Boba. *Casa de Lava* (1994) foi filmado em Cabo Verde, onde o autor teve contacto com a língua e com a cultura do arquipélago. É através de conhecimentos que fez, nesta altura, que chega ao bairro das Fontainhas, na periferia de Lisboa, onde depois continua a trabalhar.

Fiz um filme em Cabo Verde: *Casa de Lava* . . . . Aproximei-me tanto destas pessoas em Cabo Verde, que no final das filmagens eles deram-me coisas que eu deveria trazer para Lisboa, para os seus parentes. Fui uma espécie de correio, Pai Natal – trouxe tabaco, café (sorriso) cartas, e tinha que encontrar este lugar . . . . Fui lá com o saco e… estamos a falar, claro, de um sítio perigoso, mas eu não tive dificuldade nenhuma em entrar… tinham guardas em 95, era um grande mercado de droga, é pequeno, podíamos dar a volta em 20 minutos, 5 mil pessoas. (Costa a Gorin 2010, *vídeo*)

Desta relação nascem, até à presente data, as seguintes longas metragens: *Ossos* (1997), o *Quarto de Vanda* (2000), *Juventude em Marcha* (2006); *Cavalo Dinheiro* (2014), e *Vitalina Varela* (2019). A câmara de Pedro Costa acompanhou ao longo dos anos primeiro a vida dos jovens nas Fontainhas, depois a demolição do bairro, seguida do realojamento dos seus habitantes nos novos prédios asséticos do Casal da Boba; e, à medida que cresce a intimidade com os moradores desta periferia de Lisboa, cresce também o afastamento do mundo da produção de cinema tradicional. Os filmes fazem-se cada vez com menos pessoas e com menos dinheiro. Quando já não há dinheiro e quando já não há sequer o bairro das Fontainhas onde esta comunidade imigrante se instituiu e onde a relação com o cineasta nasceu, resta a memória. *Cavalo Dinheiro* é o filme da memória de Ventura sobre a história recente de Portugal, que é também a história da construção desta comunidade, da qual foi pioneiro. O filme é proposto pelo realizador como uma autorrepresentação, na medida em que é Ventura quem fala e quem escreve o texto, é a memória dele que serve de mote ao filme. Afirma Costa que:

> Eles não são só atores, são argumentistas, escrevem o texto, escrevem o filme, são um pouco técnicos de tudo. Podem ajudar com a luz, podem ajudar com o som. Ajudam fisicamente a carregar e descarregar o material, portanto fazem parte de uma equipa. Eles não são atores vedetas, estrelas, como nós também não. Nós, parte técnica, também fazemos de tudo, é uma outra relação, não é uma relação de ator/diretor, é uma relação de autor/autor de facto. O Ventura devia estar creditado como autor, e não só o Ventura, todos os outros. (Mulvey, Modi e Costa 2014, *vídeo*)

Herdeiro orgulhoso de uma tradição de cinema de autor, eclética e purista, o projeto cinematográfico de Costa conduz, de forma quase inevitável, a uma reformulação da pergunta de Gayatry Spivak (1988): podem os subalternizados falar através do cinema de Pedro Costa? Serão capazes de se fazer ouvir? Empreendemos um estudo/exercício exploratório de receção, no qual mostrámos o filme em duas universidades do norte de Portugal a alunos dos cursos de Sociologia (Braga) e Teatro (Porto), para perceber como dialogam públicos jovens e não especializados em cinema com as representações (auto e hétero) propostas pela obra. Realizaram-se um total de duas mostras e quatro discussões sobre a obra, em que participaram 49 estudantes, 22 homens e 27 mulheres. À exceção de uma participante brasileira, todos são de nacionalidade portuguesa. Todos os participantes são percebidos socialmente como brancos.

A análise aqui proposta trabalha com o sentido dos textos: apresenta-se uma leitura dos discursos, com enfoque nas posições discursivas dos sujeitos, legitimadas pela junção dos aspetos sociais, da história e da ideologia, produzindo sentidos a partir das imbricações destes fatores. Nesta análise crítica do discurso (van Dijk 1984; 1992; 1993; van Leeuwen 2008), a leitura (repetida) do *corpus empírico* provoca o movimento em que o enunciado conduz ao enunciável e vice-versa, e à exploração de marcas linguísticas.

ESMAE, 3º ano de Teatro, Porto
António – O povo cabo-verdiano… conheço mais ou menos… e eles são muito… é assim é, é, é um clima perfeito… aquilo Cabo Verde é fantástico… quase não chove…
Maria – A seca é maravilhosa… [risos]
António – E todos os povos que têm muito calor… usa-se pouca roupa e… são povos muito quentes, muito…
Mário – Muito quentes… é isso…António – Os cabo-verdes pronto é isso… são muito sexuais pronto…
Mário – É isso…
António – É a ideia que eu tenho, pode estar errada… também não estou aqui… eles não têm… se calhar não têm o peso que nós temos, os complexos… e até é um povo religioso… eles são quase todos católicos.
Mário – Mas não têm se calhar aquele pudor que nós temos…

A personagem Ventura, um homem velho e doente, convoca no imaginário de alguns participantes as ideias de "calor" e de "sexualidade despudorada." Mais, Ventura, nas leituras destes participantes, deixa de ter um nome e passa a ser representante de "os cabo-verdes," que apesar de serem "quase todos católicos" não têm "aquele pudor que nós temos" por causa do "calor" e de usarem "pouca roupa."

Outros estereótipos que associam as pessoas negras, ou os cabo-verdianos em particular, com agressividade são trazidos para a discussão. Os participantes parecem estar conscientes da prevalência de estereótipos sociais e mostram desacordo. Contudo, algumas vezes, ao mesmo tempo que discordam, procuram justificações e mostram partilhar das representações sociais vigentes.

Fausto (UM A, 1º ano Sociologia, Braga) – Só que há sempre aquela parte. Pronto, aqueles problemas que aconteceram aqui há uns anos atrás nos bairros da Damaia e Amadora… os grupos maioritariamente são negros…

associa-se logo a confusão, a rebeldia aos negros, então em Lisboa pior ainda, porque há bairros tipicamente negros… eu acho que é um bocadinho também a frustração deles perante a sociedade… é um bocadinho a forma deles também de demonstrarem que estão revoltados, de certa forma é um problema de integração. Acho eu.

Além da aceitação implícita da ideia de que os negros são agressivos, porque é assim que expressam a sua frustração, o comentário de Fausto revela que a realidade da periferia lisboeta é relativamente longínqua para participantes do norte do país, que a conhecem apenas através dos meios de comunicação social, e que, por esse motivo, podem referir Amadora e Damaia como bairros vizinhos. Notícias como a do falso arrastão de 2006, no qual se teriam envolvido 500 negros, em Carcavelos (Gomes 2006), ou mais recentemente, já em 2018, a notícia de uma violenta rixa de 100 pessoas negras, que se traduziu em zero mortos, zero feridos, zero detidos e zero queixas, e que era afinal uma discussão sobre futebol igual a tantas outras (*Primeiro Jornal* da estação de televisão SIC e *Jornal Expresso*, 04 agosto 2018), deixam na memória coletiva as imagens de corpos negros em "atividade agressiva" e ajudam a sustentar a suspeita de que a comunicação social portuguesa tem sido parte ativa do racismo estrutural (Lawrence e Keleher 2004) em Portugal. Fausto refere diretamente "problemas que aconteceram aqui há uns anos atrás, nos bairros da Damaia e Amadora… os grupos maioritariamente são negros," não podemos saber concretamente a que problemas e a que notícias se refere, mas comentários como o deste participante lembram que nomes como Damaia (entre outros como Cova da Moura, ou Buraca) aparecem nos meios de comunicação social, muitas vezes, precisamente associados a essa ideia de perigo, agressividade e impenetrabilidade. Paradoxalmente, nas discussões sobre *Cavalo Dinheiro*, alguns participantes consideram a comunidade cabo-verdiana mais próxima dos portugueses do que outros africanos.

UM A, *1º ano de Sociologia, Braga*
Ricardo – Há uma situação que se fala… pronto, associar a raça negra a problemas. Dentro da raça negra há nacionalidades, por norma, com culturas diferentes, dão origem a mais problemas… não sei se por acaso fomos buscar a cabo-verdiana que é aquela talvez que mais se assemelha à nossa sociedade: conceito de família, religião, a cultura deles é muito semelhante à nossa, não sei se foi de propósito… arranjarem uma cultura negra, uma sociedade negra parecida com a nossa e mesmo assim nós rejeitamos…

Goreti – Se calhar para mostrar que a única diferença entre nós e eles é mesmo a questão do tom de pele, não é mais nada...

Belarmino – Porque é assim... grandes comunidades cabo-verdianas aqui em Braga... Guimarães aqui na Universidade do Minho, quer dizer e eles, quer dizer só mesmo o tom de pele, porque quer dizer os costumes... tem uma diferenças, mas... é tudo igual a nós...

Moderadora – Muitos nasceram cá...

Belarmino – Sim... em relação à comunidade angolana ou moçambicana já é muito diferente.

Moderadora – Acham que é muito diferente?

Josefina – São um pouco mais diferentes de nós... e creio que como o colega disse, eles foram buscar uma raça negra, os cabo-verdianos, mais parecida com a nossa para mostrar que só mesmo a cor é que é o nosso problema.

Esta noção tem raízes na forma como o colonialismo se desenvolveu no arquipélago (Henriques 2016; Torgal e Paulo 2008), mas também nas diferentes fases de imigração, e diferentes origens socioculturais dos imigrantes de Cabo Verde em Portugal (Batalha 2004). A ideia prevalece mesmo que a comunidade representada no filme não obedeça ao estereótipo "eles são quase como nós": os processos de diferenciação (por exemplo, Silva 2000) entre "nós" e "eles" e de essencialização (Wagner, Holtz e Kashima 2009) fazem com que os participantes comparem e coloquem em pé de igualdade trabalhadores que vivem na zona metropolitana de Lisboa, com estudantes universitários, seus colegas, num todo indivisível constituído por "eles, os cabo-verdianos."

UM A, 1° ano Sociologia, Braga

Vasco – Desorganização total, quer dizer... eu acho que é um bocadinho... que eles não eram... mas no fundo o que querem mostrar é que aos olhos dos brancos era um bocadinho por aí quer dizer, nós eramos muito organizados... muito metódicos e eles não... um bocadinho viver assim mesmo por viver, com objetivo nenhum na vida.

Cristiano – A sociedade portuguesa de certa forma... de certa forma pronto... deve ser dos povos que melhor os aceita, porque teve uma grande ligação com eles, no passado e daí os soldados que estiveram lá, eles sabem no fundo que *aquilo* são pessoas, não são uns animais. E daí os soldados que estão no fundo a retratar alguma ligação próxima que tiveram com os negros, conviveram com eles diretamente. Agora cá, de certa forma são um bocadinho aceites em relação à maioria dos países europeus...

Os participantes tendem a assumir que a exploração de imigrantes está muito difundida na Europa e que os portugueses se distinguem pela positiva, na forma como se relacionam com os outros povos. Este retrato lusotropicalista dos portugueses (e. g. Castelo, 1998; Piçarra, 2015), que foi levado a cabo pelo Estado Novo e largamente difundido pelo cinema, entre outros meios, prevalece no discurso do senso comum em Portugal; além disso, vários autores registam uma tendência universal dos grupos de favorecer as características do endogrupo e desfavorecer as do exogrupo (Tajfel 1982/1983; van Dijk 1992). Poderíamos, neste caso, dizer que a valorização das caraterísticas dos portugueses se produz a dois níveis discursivos – por um lado, não se identificam com africanos porque eles são desleixados, imaturos, preguiçosos e violentos/agressivos, mas, por outro lado, não se consideram intolerantes e frios como os restantes europeus.

UM A, 1º ano de Sociologia, Braga
Gaspar – De certa forma, no subconsciente continua a existir, não é? Os negros são vistos como um ser inferior. As mentalidades estão a mudar, mas continua lá ainda qualquer coisa...
Andreia – Mas há sempre aqueles vestígios...
Gaspar – Exato. Talvez se olhe para um preto de uma maneira diferente da que se olha para um branco. Eu acho que é um bocadinho por aí...

Estratégias de desresponsabilização ou negação, seguidas de uma afirmação racista, estiveram largamente presentes nos debates. Podem aparecer como aparente negação, aparente concessão, transferência ou contraste, e são construídos sobre a representação positiva do *self* e representação negativa do "Outro" (van Dijk 1992). Como exemplo de aparente negação, observou-se a afirmação, quase sempre em termos extremamente enfáticos, "eu não sou racista," que permite acrescentar a injunção "mas," à qual se segue, por via de regra, uma forte afirmação do ponto de vista racial ou racializante.

Alberto (UM B, 1º ano, Sociologia) – Também há muitos imigrantes que trabalham, mas a maioria acaba por viver de esquemas...
Augusto (ESMAE, 3º ano de Teatro, Porto) – Eu gosto muito do povo cabo-verdiano e da música, mas é curioso que hoje em dia estão muito associados à violência e ao crime.

Ideias raciais muito fortes tendencialmente são expressas numa lógica de "sim," mas também "não" (por exemplo, Bonilla-Silva 2006) – incorporar no discurso ideias opostas às que se pretende defender permite sustentar ideias controversas e expressá-las em termos raciais, sem ser socialmente percebido como racista.

> Diana (UM B, 1º ano Sociologia, Braga, *Cavalo Dinheiro*) – Eu acho que também é opção dos próprios indivíduos imigrantes, mas porque lá está, quando eles imigraram para cá havia muito a questão do racismo... e isso claro que ajuda muito a que eles fiquem fechados no grupo... e os próprios portugueses neste caso que eram puramente racistas, faziam isso... vocês vão pra qui, pronto.

Também se registaram exemplos de desresponsabilização por transferência e/ou contraste. Outro recurso usado pelos participantes nas discussões foi o uso do diminutivo, que permite expressar posições que podiam ser consideradas racistas sem o parecer (Bonilla-Silva, 2006). O diminutivo também serve para suavizar o racismo dos portugueses.

> UM B, 1º ano de Sociologia, Braga
> Filomena – A raça negra, eu acho que no fundo está um bocadinho massacrada na sociedade atual, pela raça mais clara. Mas eu acho que em todo o mundo... não é só os brancos europeus...
> Sílvia – Nós todos fazemos isso um bocadinho... fazemos isso, todos uns aos outros...

A projeção tem sido considerada um recurso efetivo e muito comum como instrumento para nos defendermos (por exemplo, Pinto 2014) e é também um dispositivo eficaz para criar identidade corporativa: "nós" versus "eles." O aspeto mais interessante deste dispositivo é que nos ajuda a "escapar da culpa e da responsabilidade e a alocar a culpa noutro lugar" (Bonilla-Silva 2006, 64). *Cavalo Dinheiro* parece dificultar os exercícios discursivos de projeção, mas estes assumem formas e níveis ou graus de refinamento diferentes. No caso acima transcrito, as participantes optaram discursivamente por diluir a culpa num todo humano, deslocando a discussão sobre a imigração de origem africana em Portugal para as relações entre seres humanos na sua globalidade. A projeção, de acordo com van Dijk (1992), alia-se a uma estratégia argumentativa de salvar-a-cara, que dispõe de uma bateria de ações semânticas e uma dessas consiste na inversão: colocar o *focus* na intolerância do "outro" – os negros são os mais racistas. Associada à intolerância do "outro" aparece, claro, e culpabilização das pessoas segregadas pela sua própria condição.

UM B, 1º ano de Sociologia, Braga
Alice – Ele vê o lado negativo da revolução e não o lado positivo...
Luísa – Eu acho que qualquer imigrante sofre o mesmo porque... normalmente eles isolam-se em bairros onde existem pessoas da mesma nacionalidade e muitas vezes esses bairros não têm as condições mínimas... e são explorados... porque como não são do país para onde vão, as pessoas exploram-nos sempre... mas eles isolam-se e ficam só na memória da cultura deles.

Ao encontro de estudos de receção recentes (por exemplo, Macedo 2016), prevalecem nos discursos de jovens portugueses estereótipos racistas, e também a reprodução de ideias que naturalizam as relações de dominação colonialista, mesmo na leitura de uma obra fílmica que pretende questionar esses mesmos discursos e lógicas. De acordo com inúmeros estudos, embora o racismo perdure nas sociedades contemporâneas de forma estrutural, institucional e quotidiana, a assunção de uma postura racista é socialmente malvista (e frequentemente inaceitável) na atualidade. Por conseguinte, quando o debate visa direta ou indiretamente a exposição de pensamento sobre "raça," os indivíduos e os grupos adotam uma série de estratégias discursivas para poderem ser aceites socialmente.

As regras da ideologia, como as da gramática, são criadas e aprendidas socialmente e, portanto, os princípios de "como falar" corretamente não são questionados dentro do contexto em que foram estabelecidos, na medida e que aparecem como "naturais." Deste modo, é quase sem surpresa que se constata a convergência com outros estudos (Cabecinhas 2007; Vala e Pereira 2012) na análise das discussões em grupo: a persistência de estereótipos negativos respeitantes a africanos e afrodescendentes, indicando que o passado colonial influencia significativamente o imaginário e a identidade social das novas gerações. Como em outros estudos portugueses e internacionais (Bonilla-Silva 2006; Howarth 2009; 2011), constata-se a reprodução de códigos comunicativos da ideologia hegemónica sobre "raça," dito de outro modo: usa-se os quadros comunicativos que permitem expressar ideias potencialmente problemáticas sem aparecer socialmente como racista.

Podem os subalternizados fazer-se ouvir através do cinema de Pedro Costa? Segundo este pequeno estudo exploratório de receção, a resposta a esta reformulação da pergunta de Spivak parece continuar a mesma que a autora deu em

1982. A tia de Spivak planeou rigorosamente o seu suicídio de forma a que não fosse possível pensar-se que se matara por estar grávida; no entanto, a estória da sua morte perdurou na memória familiar como a do suicídio de uma mulher solteira grávida. Também a voz de Ventura, coautor, segundo Costa, de *Cavalo Dinheiro*, não é percebida pelos públicos não especialistas escutados, como a voz de um pioneiro fundador de uma comunidade, mas sim como o eco da tragédia de mais um desses "Outros" africanos, vítimas de um mundo que os rejeita, mas sobretudo de si próprios.

REFERÊNCIAS BIBLIOGRÁFICAS

Batalha, Luís. 2004. *The Cape Verdean Diaspora in Portugal: Colonial Subjects in a Postcolonial World*. Lanham, MD: Lexinton Boocks.

Bonilla-Silva, Eduardo. 2006. *Racism without Racists: Colour Blind Racism and the Persistence of Racial Inequality in the United States*. Maryland: Rowman & Littlefield Publishers.

Cabecinhas, Rosa. 2007. *Preto e Branco: A Naturalização da Discriminação Racial*. Porto: Campo de Letras.

Castelo, Cláudia. 1998. *"O Modo Português de Estar no Mundo," o Luso-Tropicalismo e a Ideologia Colonial Portuguesa (1933-1961)*. Porto: Edições Afrontamento.

Deleuze, Gilles. 2015. *A Imagem-Tempo, Cinema 2*. Lisboa: Documenta.

Gomes, Adelino. 2006. "O 'Pseudo-Arrastão' de Carcavelos Considerado Exemplo de Má Cobertura Jornalística." *Público*, 9 de junho, 2006. https://www.publico.pt/2006/06/09/portugal/noticia/o-pseudoarrastao-de-carcavelos-considerado-exemplo-de-ma-cobertura-jornalistica-1260403#gs.F6FzLKdo. Acedido a 20 fevereiro 2019.

Gorin, Jean Pierre. 2010. "*Ossos*, Conversation between Pedro Costa and Jean Pierre Gorin." *Criterion DVD edition of Ossos*. https://www.youtube.com/watch?v=1h2zBBaSfOo. Acedido a 20 fevereiro de 2019.

Guerreiro, António. 2014. "Uma História de Fantasmas." *Público*, 4 de dezembro, 2014. https://www.publico.pt/2014/12/04/culturaipsilon/noticia/uma-historia-de-fantasmas-1678020. Acedido a 10 fevereiro 2019.

Henriques, Joana Gorjão. 2016. *Racismo em Português*. Lisboa: Tinta da China.

Howarth, Caroline. 2009. "'I Hope We Won't Have to Understand Racism One Day': Researching or Reproducing 'Race' in Social Psychological Research?" *British Journal of Social Psychology* 48(3): 407-426, DOI: 10.1348/014466608X360727.

Howarth, Caroline. 2011. "Representations, Identity and Resistance in Communication." In *The Social Psychology of Communication*, edição de Derek Hook, Bradley Franks e M. Bauer, 153-168. Londres: Palgrave, DOI: 10.1057/9780230297616_8.

Lawrence, Keith, e Terry Keleher. 2004. "Chronic Disparity: Strong and Pervasive Evidence of Racial Inequalities Poverty Outcomes – Structural Racism." Artigo apresentado na Race and Public Policy Conference, Berkeley, CA.

Lewin, Kurt. 1997. *Resolving Social Conflits & Field Theory in Social Science*. Washington: APA.

Macedo, Isabel. 2016. "Youth and Portuguese Cinema: The (De)Colonisation of the Imaginary?" *Comunicação e Sociedade* 29: 291-309.

Müller, Heiner. 2017. *A Missão*. Lisboa: Livros Cotovia.

Mulvey, Laura, Mehelli Modi e Pedro Costa. 2014. *Horse Money: Q&A with Pedro Costa hosted by Laura Mulvey*. ICA. https://www.youtube.com/watch?v=ygSIKWpOUBo. Acedido a 15 fevereiro 2019.

Piçarra, Maria do Carmo. 2015. *Azuis Ultramarinos. Propaganda Colonial e Censura no Cinema do Estado Novo.* Lisboa: Edições 70.

Pinto, Elza Rocha. 2014. "Conceitos Fundamentais dos Métodos Projetivos." *Ágora* 17, nº 1 (jan./jun.): 135-53. http://dx.doi.org/10.1590/S1516-14982014000100009. Acedido a 20 fevereiro 2019.

Riss, Jacob. 1890. *How the Other Half Lives: Studies among the Tenements of New York.* Boston: Bedford/St.Martin's.

Romney, Jonathan. 2015. "Film of the Week: *Horse Money*." *Filmcomment*, 16 julho, 2015. http://www.filmcomment.com/blog/film-of-the-week-horse-money. Acedido a 26 janeiro 2019.

Silva, Tomaz Tadeu. 2000. "A Produção Social da Identidade e da Diferença." In *Identidade e Diferença – A Perspectiva dos Estudos Culturais*, edição de Tomaz Tadeu da Silva, Kathryn Woodward e Stuart Hall, 74–101. Petrópolis: Vozes.

Spivak, Gayatri Chakravorty. 1988. "Can the Subaltern Speak?" In *Marxism and the Interpretation of Culture*, edição de Cary Nelson e Lawrence Grossberg, 271-313. Basingstoke: Macmillan Education.

Tajfel, Henry. 1982/1983. *Grupos Humanos e Categorias Sociais.* Lisboa: Livros Horizonte.

Torgal, Luís Reis e Heloísa Paulo, org. 2008. *Estados Autoritários e Totalitários e suas Representações.* Coimbra: Imprensa da Universidade de Coimbra.

Vala, Jorge e **Cícero Pereira**. 2012. "Racism: An Evolving Virus". In *Racism and Ethnic Relations in the Portuguese-Speaking World*, edição de Francisco Bethencourt e Adrian J. Pearce, 49-70. Nova Iorque: Oxford University Press.

van Dijk, Teun A. 1984. *Prejudice in Discourse: An Analysis of Ethnic Prejudice in Cognitio and Conversation.* Amsterdão: Benjamins.

van Dijk, Teun A. 1992. "Text, Talk, Elites and Racism." *Discours Social/Social Discourse* (Montreal): 37-62.

van Dijk, Teun A. 1993. "Analysing Racism through Discourse Analysis: Some Methodological Reflections." In *Race and Ethnicity in Research Methods*, edição de John Stanfield, 92-134. Newbury Park, CA: Sage.

van Leeuwen, Theo. 2008. *Discourse and Practice: New Tools for Critical Discourse Analysis.* Nova Iorque: Oxford University Press.

Wagner, Wolgang, Peter Holtz e Yoshihisa Kashima. 2009. "Construction and Deconstruction of Essence in Representing Social Groups: Identity Projects, Stereotyping, and Racism." *Journal for the Theory of Social Behaviour* 39 (3): 363-93.

FILMOGRAFIA

Costa, Pedro, dir. 1994. *Casa de Lava*. Portugal: Madragoa Filmes. DVD.

Costa, Pedro, dir. 1997. *Ossos*. Portugal: Madragoa Filmes. DVD.

Costa, Pedro, dir. 2000. *O Quarto de Vanda*. Portugal: Contracosta Produções; Pandora Film. DVD.

Costa, Pedro, dir. 2006. *Juventude em Marcha*. Portugal: Optec. DVD.

Costa, Pedro, dir. 2014. *Cavalo Dinheiro*. Portugal: Optec. DVD.

Costa, Pedro, dir. 2019. *Vitalina Varela*. Portugal: Optec. Filme.

Reis, António, dir. 1974. *Jaime*. Portugal: CPC. Filme.

ANA CRISTINA PEREIRA é doutorada em Estudos Culturais, pela Universidade do Minho, com a tese "Alteridade e Identidade na Ficção Cinematográfica em Portugal e em Moçambique." Tem como principais interesses de investigação: racismo, identidade social, representações sociais e memória cultural no cinema, numa perspetiva pós-colonial e interseccional, sobre os quais tem editados vários artigos científicos em publicações nacionais e internacionais. Vem fazendo parte da equipa de projetos científicos sendo, no presente momento, investigadora do projeto (THE)OTHERING. É membro do NARP – Núcleo Antirracista do Porto. Pereira é também investigadora no Centro de Estudos Sociais (CES) da Universidade de Coimbra, membro do projeto (De)Othering. Este trabalho foi financiado por FEDER – Fundo Europeu de Desenvolvimento Regional, através do COMPETE 2020 – Programa Operacional Competitividade e Internacionalização (POCI) e por fundos nacionais através da FCT – Fundação para a Ciência e a Tecnologia, no âmbito do projeto 029997.

Stomach-Thought: Popular Portuguese Imageries of Ethnic Food, Indirect Group Representations, and the Sociocultural Condition of Afrodescendants of Cabo Verdean Origin

ABSTRACT: This study is inspired by an ongoing associational project to discuss issues of intercultural communication and to raise our awareness of existing cultural representations and possible discriminatory practices in Portuguese society. It focuses on representations in popular Portuguese imageries of ethnic food, i.e., "African" food versus "Asian" food. The Asian comparison is mainly used to illustrate, highlight, and make sense of the African case. The objective is to use food as a lens of analysis to present a dynamic picture of contemporary Afro-experiences in the West and more specifically in Portugal. The materials discussed were collected over four years of residence and fieldwork in Portugal and abroad using anthropologically-based methods. The present study politicizes our "stomach-thought," proposing a creative way to understand the challenges and opportunities for Afrodescendants and especially Afrodescendants of Cabo Verdean origin in Portugal, whose experiences form the basis of this article.

KEYWORDS: Cabo Verde, Cultural representations, Food, Ethnic, Fieldwork, Afrodescendants of Cabo Verdean origin

RESUMO: O presente estudo inspira-se num projeto associativo que aborda problemáticas de comunicação intercultural e que nos consciencializa das representações culturais correntes e das possíveis práticas discriminatórias na sociedade portuguesa. O estudo foca as representações no mundo imaginário português acerca da alimentação étnica, ou seja, "africana" versus "asiática". O caso asiático serve sobretudo para ilustrar, frisar e reforçar o caso africano. O objetivo deste estudo é usar a alimentação como uma lente de análise para apresentar um quadro dinâmico das experiências africanas no Ocidente e especialmente em Portugal. Os materiais foram recolhidos durante quatro anos de residência e de trabalho de campo em Portugal e no estrangeiro com métodos de matriz antropológica. Trata-se de uma proposta de politização do "pensamento-estômago" e

compreensão criativa dos desafios e oportunidades para os afrodescendentes, sobretudo afrodescendentes de origem cabo-verdiana em Portugal, cujas experiências constituem a base do presente artigo.

PALAVRAS-CHAVE: Cabo Verde, Representações culturais, Alimentação, Étnico, Trabalho de
campo, Afrodescendentes de origem cabo-verdiana

Introduction

This study is inspired by an ongoing inter-associational project to discuss issues
of intercultural communication and to raise our awareness of differential cultural representations and possible discriminatory practices in Portuguese society. It is a joint project proposed by Associação para a Mudança e Representação
Transcultural[1] and O Graal[2]. Since 2018, these associations have worked to
engage people from all walks of life, including activists and academics, to discuss
issues of immigration, racism, communication, and social and cultural representations. The project is multi-ethnic and multi-cultural. From the beginning,
even when many of the organizers and participants were African immigrants or
Afrodescendants, they displayed a strong willingness to discuss issues beyond
color or racism based on appearances. Past discussions were highly inclusive,
and the implications are applicable to all (see figures 1 and 2). Importantly, this
project does not encourage Black self-victimization but promotes mutual understanding. The organizers and participants try to compare openly the experiences
of ethnic Portuguese, Cabo Verdeans, Guineans, Angolans, Brazilians, Indians,
Chinese, Romani people, etc. In the initial explorative process, we reminded
ourselves how certain greetings, stereotypes, and reactions had taken root in
Portuguese society and how we had struggled to understand ourselves and
understand others at different stages of our lives, and we dared to imagine living
in a global society wherein differences are assets, not liabilities.

Taking inspiration from this project, the present study creates parameters for
a transcontinental triangulation. It investigates popular Portuguese imageries
of food and the indirect representations of certain social groups. For instance,
African feasts are commonly imagined to be musical, festive, celebratory, and
abundant (Murray 2015; Beyala 2000), while Asian food is often associated with
secretive Chinese-run restaurants that evade taxes and charge "laughably low"

Figure 1. Calling people names. Unhos, Loures, January 20, 2018 (Photo by the author)

Figure 2. "*Preto*." Unhos, Loures, January 20, 2018 (Photo by the author)

prices (Bedell 2018; Liu 2016). Most people take these imageries light-heartedly and do not problematize them.

The title of the present article is borrowed from an artistic project called "Stomach-Thought. Musa Paradisiaca" or "*Pensamento-Estômago. Musa Paradisiaca*" in Portuguese, curated by David Santos in March 2015. An introduction to the exhibition at the National Museum of Contemporary Art —Museu do Chiado states:

> Departing from the idea of a stomach-thought, as the core of the plot, the project presented in the context of the RAUM platform introduces a new dimension in this conversational and experimental process, brought by the opening, through the anonymity of its participants, to the discourse of the unknown narrator. Within the system of a non a priori controllable network of participants, dependent as it is on the natural and concrete temporality of the web reality, another stage of collaboration is opened, challenging RAUM's visitors to discuss a "thought" that will not only literally, but also in analogy, pass through the "stomach" and the "digestion" process. These "thoughts" accomplish a sort of dissection, revealed in the truth of those "guts," simultaneously obscure and transparent, especially when observed in the raw analysis of the sediment of a conversation sustained by the statement "if all may be eaten, all may be thought through the stomach." (Santos 2015a)

Then, on the RAUM interactive platform, there were the following open dialogues: "When you say that a stomach thinks, what are you talking about?" "I am talking about a relationship with the world, more sensible, extensible and form-less." (Santos 2015b).

Using a body part to think critically about something is not new. This article also draws on the seminal book *Politics of the Womb* in regard to the contestation of power:

> Through the politics of the womb, competing reproductive concerns and domains of power intersected and, eventually, became entangled. People, things, and ideas moved back and forth, between households and hospitals in rural areas; government offices and medical training centers in Nairobi; the Colonial Office and the House of Commons in London; and, later, between international aid offices and conferences in New York and Beijing. (Thomas 2003: 6)

The womb is not devoid of politics, and we have to attend to matters of the womb (Dossa 2011). We also need to politicize the stomach-thought leading to popular Portuguese imageries of ethnic food, knowing that the ethnic quality of food is relative:

> In America (unlike in some cultural/historical contexts), for instance, what one eats at home is relatively unmarked–even valorized, as an enduring symbol of the melting pot–whereas in the public sphere ethnic food is a particularly palatable form of multiculturalism, in contrast with the conformity expected, demanded, or even legislated in areas such as language and clothing. One might, then, consider what the ubiquity of food in maintaining historically constituted identities owes not only to the properties of food itself, but also to the social and cultural conditions that allow or encourage this to be a space for resilient identities where other arenas are far more stigmatized (Holtzman 2006: 373).

This article serves, therefore, to present a food-centered perspective on contemporary migrant experiences. It explores the ways in which Portugal is stigmatizing or liberating as a space, and how this relates to the social, cultural and political situations of the people involved. While some of the following observations are critical, they are strictly designed to encourage collective reflections and not intended to offend any community or individual. And yet, to address the unspoken, the silenced, and the ambiguous (Furtado 2012), it is important that we discuss what is not to be discussed, that we reveal what is not to be revealed, prior to properly suturing the open veins of the postcolonial (Galeano 1997).

Concepts and Methods

The study of food can be found in all academic disciplines. To start, we know that the history of mankind is also the history of man's food (Chastanet, Chouin, and Lima 2014). Then, anthropology explores food and social change, food insecurity, eating and ritual, eating and identities (Mintz and Du Bois 2002). Moreover, economists and development theorists have come to understand food not as a mere economic question but as a total social fact (Briand 2007). Widely accepted concepts have been used in the studies of food. Classically, foodways are understood as comprising the common ways in which people belonging to the same cultural group feel, think, and behave about food (Simoons 1994); we can also explore the linkages and mutual influences of the city and the country today, namely the global foodscapes (Domingos, Sobral, and West 2014). Food as a lens of analysis is particularly versatile and is adopted innovatively. There are interdisciplinary studies of food conducted around the world. For a Caribbean example, Wilk (1999) described how Belizean food is positioned between Belize and the developed world; the flow of migrants, imported food, media, tourists, and colonial history make their mark on Belizean food and identity. Meneses (2009) gauged people's memories of food and of curries, the relations between the Portuguese, Goans, and Mozambicans, and the exchanges of food products in the Indian Ocean. Reviewing Chinese history, food was of the utmost importance; for this reason, food was incorporated into the Chinese understanding of governance and livelihoods—this noble political attitude supposedly distinguished China from all others (Zhao 2014). In a study of Nauru Island, McLennan (2017) integrated the discussion of obesity and land disputes in the analysis of changing local foodways and accounted for the failure of internationally driven community gardening initiatives to promote food security.

Ethnic food studies have matured in the United States, and they have often approached the food question not only gastronomically but also socially, so that an ethnic food study is also a modern social survey of relationships and power (Liu 2016; Modan 2008). By contrast, in Portugal, research on food traditions and nostalgia maintains a strong influence (Oliveira 2013).

The present study politicizes our "stomach-thought," especially in relation to Africans and African cultures, with special implications for their descendants, acknowledging that what is seemingly harmless, recreational, and ubiquitous among them today can be traced back to a complex European imperial history of rule and control (Akyeampong and Ambler 2002).

The materials used in this study were collected by me over four years (2015–2019) of residence and fieldwork—applying anthropologically-based techniques—in the Lisbon metropolitan area, which involved constant interaction with Cabo Verdeans, Guineans, Saotomeans, Angolans, and their families, African university students and researchers, Africanists, Afro-activists, and associational leaders in diverse settings, including home gatherings, immigrant festivals, conferences, and other academic meetings in several European countries. I also participated and volunteered in some civic associations in order to better understand their work and contribute in small ways. As the ongoing research is focused on the food, culture, and politics of Cabo Verde, I draw heavily on my on-the-ground experiences and self-reflections on the Atlantic islands. Due to my limited exposure to the realities of all African Lusophone countries, the following account may be skewed toward the areas with which I am most familiarized.

The experiences of Afrodescendants of Cabo Verdean origin form the basis of this article. Gibau (2005) presented one of the most elucidating works on the onerous maneuvering of Cabo Verdean identity in the United States, the implications of which are highly relevant for Portugal as well:

> Since Cape Verdeans are of African and Portuguese descent, their experiences have been one of constant negotiation of identity along racially ascribed and culturally defined lines. Other Black immigrants, from the Caribbean and Africa, have undergone similar experiences once confronted with the United States system of racial classification based on physical appearance and the demarcation of identity "boxes." However, Cape Verdeans who are comfortable with asserting multiple identities actively challenge ideas of racial categorization. The Cape Verdean diaspora community of Boston can be accurately described as being in a constant state of transformation, where identities are contingent upon the community's task of defining and redefining itself internally and to outgroup members. The individual and collective identities proffered by Cape Verdeans can be interpreted as identities of resistance in relation to the United States system of racial classification and its attendant ideology of racial hierarchy. (p. 433)

Other authors have also contributed to our understanding of the subtleties of navigating a treacherous sea of possible and plausible identities in the Cabo Verdean case (Challinor 2012).

By presenting this study, I put myself in the position of Afrodescendants of Cabo Verdean origin and become immersed in their struggles as they navigate a bewilderingly diverse global African diaspora with "complex threads of connections, convergences, and commonalities," knowing that the colored, Black and white "American-style regimes of racialization" may not apply to the majority of Africans on the move in contemporary history (Zeleza 2010: 2, 9).

Of the Asian examples, Chinese ones dominate not only because I am Chinese, but also because most Asian-styled eating outlets in Portugal are Chinese or Chinese-run.

Besides information collected first-hand in the form of recordings, photos, and field notes, I also draw on second-hand materials, such as printed cookbooks and old records, internet pages, online sites, and other public information. The analytical process revolved around three elements: food, people, and environment. For coherence, they are presented here in an integrated manner.

Tradition

Asian and African cuisines are generally appreciated for being traditional in Portugal and remain largely unaffected by what may be called fusion food, a seemingly recent concept. However, Macanese food, a unique fusion between Portuguese and Chinese food, which has been recognized by UNESCO as the world's first fusion food with a history that covers more than 450 years, is little known outside the city of Macau, China (Keegan 2019). In Portugal, for the general market, successful cooks tend to be the ones who best preserve traditional cooking. To understand the above, we can think of the cooks as culture-makers, who are involved in a culture-making process to mass-produce food traditions for others in foreign lands (Renne 2007).

This contradicts what we know about Cabo Verdean cuisine, which is a creole cuisine of a creole people whose past and present histories have been a constant struggle to negotiate their social and cultural identity (Rodrigues 2003; Henriques 2016). Creole means mixture. A study of Africa's Gold Coast in the Atlantic Era, for instance, showed how creativity and innovation, integral to fusion foodways, are old and originate in Africa (La Fleur 2012). Cabo Verdeans invented their "national dish" (Cusack 2000) in order to survive in exceedingly harsh conditions, explaining why there are differences and adaptations in dietary habits in Cabo Verde in pre-colonial history as early as the fifteenth century (Torrão 1995). *Cachupa* is the quintessential creole stew of edible, nutritious, locally sourced ingredients. Seen from this perspective, Cabo Verdean food is creativity; it is human ingenuity. In Portugal, on the contrary, in a culture-making process that is market-driven, Cabo Verdeans are encouraged to maintain and re-produce tradition to suit foreign tastes, denying the essence of that very tradition.

From fieldwork, I have observed that the *cachupa* that is consumed on the Cabo Verde islands is often more modern than the *cachupa* that is eaten in Portugal. Cabo Verdeans have explained and demonstrated to me what preparing this stew—the most recognizable dish of the country—means to them in their cultural context. Gathering ingredients, or *juntar ingredientes*, is an active experience that is at once practical and emotional. It is practical because there is no definitive list of ingredients and what goes into the stew depends on the day, season, personal taste and, certainly, purchasing power. It is emotional because foreign ingredients are often used, not only because people can easily buy canned, semi-prepared ingredients in Chinese shops, but also because they often use what others send or bring. The emotional aspect is all the more important as cooking enables an intimate connection to loved ones who pick the ingredients.

For instance, a family preparation of *cachupa* that I enjoyed on a weekend in Tarrafal (northernmost city of Santiago, Cabo Verde) included imported European carrots, deep-frozen Dutch meat, and Brazilian maize that the hosts had bought in Praia (the capital of Cabo Verde and the southernmost city of Santiago), cabbage bought in the small municipal market in front of the house, beans and sweet potatoes that had arrived in a boat and were sent by relatives living and farming on the island of Fogo, and *Chouriço Alentejano* that I had brought with me from Portugal as an *encomenda* (a gift). This rich combination is due to the fact that *a cachupa leva tudo*, meaning everything goes into its making.

Similarly, to most Portuguese, Chinese cuisine means *arroz chau chau* (an old, bizarre name for Yangzhou fried rice) and *massa chinesa* (a monotonous selection of stir-fried noodles, often cooked with pork, shrimp, and other seafood ingredients). Other well-known Chinese pastries in Portugal are also deep-fried. They appeared frequently in imperial-era-styled cookbooks, such as *A Cozinha Descoberta pelos Portuguesas* (Valente 1989), which illustrate Portuguese influences and contacts on different continents. They are so ingrained in Portuguese culture that, being Chinese, when I am in Portugal I am frequently asked if I know how to cook and if I would be so kind as to cook these "typical" Chinese dishes for my friends. In reality, they are not part of my regular diet, and I only eat them if I am in a restaurant, partly because, according to popular Chinse medicinal knowledge, consuming too much stir-fried food will cause "hot air" to rise in the body and make one ill.

The implications of this Portuguese mentality are relevant for Afrodescendants who were born in Portugal or assume a clear Afro-identity as adults and who are constantly compared with first generation immigrants. The latter group tends to be docile, hard-working, and poorly educated. First generation immigrants rarely fight for their rights (for a study of early arriving Cabo Verdeans, the most numerous non-white immigrant community besides Brazilians, see Batalha 2004). Importantly, they are traditional, conservative, family-oriented, and present a resigned attitude. Afrodescendants are burdened with the social expectation that they should preserve the qualities of first-generation immigrants, just as the Portuguese wish to enjoy traditional African food as they first knew it. This can be unsettling and difficult to digest for some.

Post-Colonial Rediscoveries

In Portuguese society, middle-class, white consumers can afford to be omnivorous and enjoy a broad range of food options (Johnston and Baumann 2007). This means that they can choose to eat expensively like the rich and vary their diets with occasional meals for the poor, and they can afford to go to high-end restaurants and visit street stalls once in a while. Ethnic specialties are good for gatherings and for weekend socialization. In the academic circle, conferences and seminars may end gastronomically and at an elegant price, with guest speakers and distinguished participants gathering for quality African cuisines.

Sometimes, these dietary alternatives are dubbed "green," "pure," "natural," or "healthy," not unrelated to the transnational pursuit of exotic African superfood (Said-Moorhouse 2016), which are common African food or drink ingredients rediscovered by Western scientists and health specialists because of their abilities to remove toxins from the body. This may be understandable if we recognize that, per fixed quantity of calorie consumption, West Africa has some of the healthiest diets in the world because of the high intake of lean meats, vegetables, legumes, and staple starches, outperforming the diets of many Western, developed countries (Kuo 2015).

Asian cuisines, meanwhile, have long been viewed by the West as healthy. In fact, to take one example, the Chinese diet has been modernized and drastically Westernized, and China, with rising rates of obesity, now has the largest number of obese children in the world (Zhuang 2017). In another example, I once heard a university professor assure his students during a class that Chinese do not use salt, the excessive use of which is a major health concern in Portugal, because they use soy sauce. This is not possible. Salt is needed to manufacture soy sauce, and humans cannot remain healthy without salt. Moreover, in Chinese history, salt was a major currency of trade as well as an asset.

The above shows that there are many contradictions in our understanding of what comprises good food. The "positive" qualities projected on African food may be said of any other diet.

African cuisines are to no small extent promoted by cookbooks, a major means of promoting a culinary culture (Appadurai 1988). When traveling to African countries, Portuguese tourists like to purchase cookbooks. These recipes are often sold in touristic areas and are in great demand in high seasons. From my experience, however, when visiting the homes of local people, it is rare to find the same cookbooks on their shelves. They almost always have only Portuguese recipes, especially healthy Portuguese recipes, neglected or for mere decoration. When I asked for an explanation as to why local people do not buy their own cookbooks, it was explained to me that Cabo Verdean, Angolan, Mozambican recipes, etc., are very difficult to cook; the ingredients are not readily available, there are too many steps, most recipes are desserts. They suggested to me that there are many simpler, practical Brazilian recipes online for reference, which require only minor adaptation.

Catholicism, the most important religion in Portugal, may account for the insistence on purity, as it is important to stay away from sins. From a cultural anthropological perspective, what is not pure is dangerous and from a young age people learn to rid themselves of impurity and dirt, both personally and socially (Douglas 2003), justifying why food consumption is regulated by taboos in all cultures. Nevertheless, in the Portuguese case, I suggest that Africa is still thought to be closer to Nature, more ecologically friendly, a place where people are more likely to cultivate plants, raise animals, and produce their own food, and that African diets are perceived as less industrialized and as containing fewer chemicals.

Interestingly, a similar mentality was also registered among busy, trans-nationally-styled migrants who live on a different continent and idealize the mass-produced and mass-packaged food from their land of origin (Renne 2007). This begs the question of what tradition has become in modern times as far as food is concerned:

> The raw materials used to produce the canned or packaged item may also be illustrated, as in can labels of Ruker Cream of Palm Fruits, which depict the palm nut fruits themselves (from which palm oil is made) and a large cook pot overflowing with palm nut soup. Yet despite the authenticating imagery of traditional technologies and labor-intensive production process used in the packaging of foodstuffs sold in West African grocery stores, their preparation represents new concerns about time and health. (p. 619)

Accordingly, whether it is to appeal to Westerners or emigrants, tradition is merely exploitative, sentimental marketing that has more to do with industries and commerce, and less to do with culture.

Knowing that about half of the world's population is urbanized, including in Africa, living and feeding have become increasingly challenging, if not dangerous, on the peripheries, i.e., in between the city and the country (Rodrigues 2008). There is little opportunity to go foraging in the open, little space and soil to grow food, and there is the tendency to feed rations to chickens and pigs. In metropolitan cities in Europe, such as Lisbon, Paris, and London, the livelihood of Africans is equally worrying.

With knowledge of the above, an implication for Afrodescendants in Portugal is the perceived difference. As Portuguese food is marked as different from African food, the people are also seen differently. By assuming that African food is more authentic and closer to the source, there is also the sentiment that African people are the guardians of something from the past.

When it comes to food in Portugal, Asian food is much more affordable than African food, even when there are many more people of African origin than of Asian origin in this southern European country.

This is curious if we agree that Western appreciation of African "cuisines" — not just food customs and diets—is rather new. It may be described as a post-colonial rediscovery of the food and culture of the former colonial subjects. The long-time association of Africa with hunger is still strong, due to the quintessential images of starving Ethiopian children transmitted by English-language media (Ramos 2018). As a result, African food is still in the process of gaining recognition from a wider public.

By comparison, there is always a small selection of Asian food in major supermarket chains operating in Portugal. A good example is Koka "Chinese" instant noodles which are in fact Singaporean. In large Pingo Doce or Continente supermarkets, there is ready-to-eat Japanese sushi. It is rare to find African food items on the shelves, except during the celebration of African Week in supermarkets like Lidl. I once bought two bottles of spicy sauce, one labelled "Angolan" and the other "Cabo Verdean," and was disappointed to find out later that they had been produced by a Portuguese company for the Portuguese market. To add to my dismay, I was told by my Cabo Verdean home-cooking friends that these products were made specifically for African Week and were not regular products.

A Portuguese couple who travelled to China once shared their experience with me, confessing that they had not known before the trip that there are so many varieties of Chinese food. Throughout their adult lives, they had eaten Chinese food thinking that it was "mild" in taste and easily suited all people, hence the general popularity of Chinese food in Portugal. Then, during their first trip to China, they visited several cities and provinces and realized that Chinese food can be quite spicy and that people there do not eat the same mild food.

African food undergoes changes abroad much more rapidly than in their respective countries. There are three instances of changes in *cachupa*, the typical Cabo Verdean dish, that deserve our attention. First, the meaty version of *cachupa*, or *cachupa rica*, is said to be a copy of *cozido à portuguesa*. When Cabo Verdeans arrived en masse in Portugal in the last century, they were urged by the Portuguese to prepare typical food from their land. The Cabo Verdeans began to worry that their food was too "poor" and not presentable. So, they enriched the *cachupa*, borrowing ingredients from a popular Portuguese dish, i.e., *cozido à portuguesa*, and the Portuguese were satisfied. This is how *cachupa rica* came about, according to anecdotes. Presently, the *cachupa* eaten in Lisbon is almost always the rich, high animal protein, elaborate version, and so is the *cachupa* eaten on especial occasions and in restaurants on the Cabo Verde islands due to external influences.

Another instance of change is *cachupa* with rice (figure 3) served in Portuguese restaurants. This is becoming more and more frequent in some "traditional" Cabo Verdean cafés and restaurants in Amadora, Portugal. On the islands, this serving style is unknown. Combining *cachupa*, a maize-based stew, with rice is an obvious redundancy. *Cachupa* is a stew complete in itself, a common feature of African food traditions (McCann 2009). A third, curious development is preparing "Muslim" *cachupa* for children whose parents converted to Islam and "vegetarian" *cachupa* for young European tourists who visit Cabo Verdean neighborhoods.

Once, when dining at Cantinho do Aziz in Mouraria, part of the Lisbon historical center, and reading the menu with fellow colleagues, among them Mozambicans and Angolans, I understood what a marketable Mozambican, or "African," menu is expected to look like in Portugal. It is structured like any other European menu, with many options, allowing people to order their preferred portion.

A seminal work about India discusses the menu ("the invoking of the menu idea") in these terms:

> Many recent cookbooks have suggested menus, based on a series of slots . . . which are then filled with items from different regional or ethnic traditions. The interesting thing about this process is that while, in European and some other cuisines, the idea of a menu is associated with a succession of courses, Indian meals do not normally have a significant sequential dimension. Everything arrives more or less at once in most everyday contexts. . . The idea of a menu is clearly a way to organize the proliferation of specialized regional and ethnic traditions and to subordinate them to the counterweight of an Indian culinary idiom. (Appadurai 1988: 20)

In relation to its other restaurant in Leeds, England, Cantinho do Aziz is said to offer "a Portuguese menu with some Mozambican influences" (Cantinho do Aziz 2016). This is exemplary of the success of African cuisine in Europe but also of the necessary compromises.

I have known Angolan mothers who declare that they only prepare Angolan food and Saotomenean women who are adamant that they would never be tempted to eat like the Portuguese. This closure from others explains why immigrants tend to stick to their respective communities and why their food is not sufficiently promoted and commercialized in Portugal. For Afrodescendants, this is not realistic because they necessarily incorporate more than one culture; they eat African, they eat Portuguese, and they eat Chinese as well.

Afrodescendants struggle daily to maintain the right balance between two forces. In Portugal, through education and other institutions of socialization, certain ways of approaching, understanding, experiencing, and preserving the exotic are fossilized. The creation and promotion of categories for the other is not an innocent act. As Edward Said has eloquently explained, it is part of a Western power game with the ultimate goal of fixing positional superiority and championing Western hegemony (Said 1978).

Go Down the Alley and Up the Hill

Portugal has more than 7,000 Chinese commercial establishments (Barra 2017), which is a significant number considering the size of the country. These shops are most common in the historic center and in neighborhoods where there is a high concentration of elderly residents and other ethnic businesses.

It may be difficult to determine the door number for a Chinese restaurant, especially when it is located in a neighborhood that was built haphazardly a long time ago. The restaurant is often where the owners and workers live and sleep, so the bathroom for guests is also residential. It may be in a building waiting to be renovated or to be sold by the Portuguese owner. In fact, many such restaurants operate clandestinely to evade taxes. As a result, the Portuguese clients have learned to be cooperative. They bring friends along, go down the alley, up the noisy wooden stairs, and knock on the door. Even if the employees have a limited Portuguese vocabulary, communication with Portuguese clients is seldom a problem.

The situation is surprisingly similar for African eatery outlets. The locations of African restaurants may be historical. Some have established themselves at a certain location, almost always at the highest elevation of a given locality. Reaching the place is a form of ritual and requires not only willingness but physical aptitude.

The Cabo Verdean case is, again, a good example. Cova da Moura is the best-known, independently formed Cabo Verdean immigrant neighborhood in Portugal, where there are several well-established traditional restaurants. In a highly ritualized act, Portuguese clients have to go up a hill and pass by the many houses and spontaneous barbecue stalls that border the curves leading to their destination. Not rarely, the residents inspect the Portuguese visitors with inquisitive expressions. The journey is often lively because of the creole conversations of neighbors and the popular African music heard along the way.

Whether Chinese or Indian, Asian people have a reputation in Portugal for being hard-working, serious, and frugal. They have earned this by keeping their businesses open for the most hours possible and suppressing their operational costs. These qualities are reflected in the above description of clandestine Chinese restaurants. In comparison, Africans are thought to be group-oriented, laid-back, free-spirited, expressive, and festive. They populate certain parts of the city, color them in their distinct styles.

In either case, eating Asian or eating African food is a ritualized encounter that is inherently imbalanced. Chinese restaurant owners run the risk of paying fines to the Portuguese authorities if denounced by an unsatisfied Portuguese client. They are often not fluent in the Portuguese language and some of the workers may even be undocumented. In the Cabo Verdean example, if serious crimes occur in the neighborhood and the local council imposes restrictions in the name of maintaining law and order, restaurants will lose Portuguese clients who are concerned for their own safety. They may eventually have to close if they lose their spaces to the rightful Portuguese heirs wanting to reclaim their lands in Cova da Moura.

Generally speaking, the Portuguese language is not a problem for Afrodescendants, and they are unlikely to face disadvantage because of an inability to defend themselves verbally, when renewing their residency permits or applying for Portuguese nationality at the Portuguese Foreigners and Borders Service (SEF), being subject to document checks on the street or responding to interrogations in a police station, challenging a schoolteacher's recommendation to choose technical training and not university, etc. All of these encounters are ritualized in the sense that both sides know roughly the socially sanctioned behaviors and probable outcomes. In all of these, the prejudice against Afrodescendants is rampant and well-documented (for experiences of working-class Cabo Verdeans and their families in postcolonial Portugal, see Batalha 2004).

Cooks, not Chefs

The cooking process is gendered in many cultures (Counihan and Kaplan 2005). The cook in a Chinese restaurant is almost always a man, partly because throwing the heavy metal *wok* requires physical force and because cooking for other people has long been established as a business for men. By contrast, in African cultures, "eating out" is not yet widespread, especially beyond the major cities; cooks are women, at home and on the street. Similarly, in Portugal, the simpler the Cabo Verdean restaurant is, the more likely the cook will be a woman. They are cooks, not chefs. Imagine a woman in her fifties or sixties in an apron quietly laboring away in a clean, well-kept kitchen, helped sometimes by an adult daughter or son. Her clients congratulate her on her cooking skills, and she comes out, thanks them humbly in simple but cordial Portuguese, and returns promptly to mind her stoves.

Throughout history, cooking has been classified as a female performance, and anthropologists continue to analyze how it affects women's lives and how gendered notions of household responsibilities persist through generations (Perez 2012). For many women in African countries, cooking is not only a domestic task; it is also their livelihood. They sell home-cooked food on the street in order to feed their children and sometimes even their husbands. Therefore, cooking is also their profession, be it in the formal or informal economies. This may explain why African food is largely prepared by women. When these women emigrate, they continue cooking and, in the case of cafés or restaurants, cooking for non-family members. We know that "women always work. They are not in and out of economic activity, but at various stages of their life cycle they are either paid for their work or not and their work is either recognized as economic activity or not" (Morokvasic 1984, 888). The food prepared has a motherly touch to it; the clients are like the "sons and daughters" of the cook in what feels like a heart-warming moment of food appreciation and enjoyment. There are many life histories of women who proudly claim to be African and who demonstrate a unique relationship with cooking. In the process of my research, I was encouraged to talk to the small but important group of female African chefs who have fought for their place in a white and masculine culinary world. Gender has major implications beyond cooking. In reality, female Afrodescendants are often the most vocal in defending collective interests, which explains why I have constantly seen more female than male participants in workshops and academic meetings that discuss racism, minority rights, and social problems. Female Afrodescendants are highly participative and gather broad support, and their organizations are more democratically run. They act as channels of intercultural communication and of social consensus. Figuratively, their singing makes up the chorus of their shared cultural experience. A self-sacrificing attitude, unfortunately prevalent among first-generation immigrant families, has the potential to be dangerous; mothers constantly deny their rights to rest, to share family and work responsibilities with their husbands, and to receive care from grown children. In these cases, to be a mother is to be the cook for life, the substitute husband, the devoted wife, the unpaid nanny, and the exploited worker. Female Afrodescendants have unique problems that need different solutions.

Conclusions

It is not easy to approach possible instances of discrimination because doing so may offend others. It is doubly difficult to discuss the situation of Afrodescendants because it is an open and flexible category. We take this as encouragement for us to seize present and future opportunities to study generalized categories like "African" and "Afrodescendants" in greater detail.

Mobility is a constant characteristic of human society, and we are plural, hybrid beings. Stuart Hall (1996) and others with multicultural backgrounds who live transnationally would agree that people have bits and pieces of various cultures in them but sometimes do not realize it, and often deny it. Scholars would agree that identity is almost always constructed across differences, and we do not maintain a single, stable identity throughout our lives.

The Afrodescendant consciousness symbolizes a sense of unity and common destiny. This sociocultural study of popular Portuguese imageries of ethnic food and indirect group representations adopted the same spirit. The African-Asian comparisons added perspective to our discussion, showing that there is a unique case to be made for Afrodescendants in Portugal, for its members accumulate personal qualities, familial connections, and social engagements that set their experiences apart.

Afrodescendants may find themselves living in the shadow of first-generation immigrants, feeling the burden to preserve the positive qualities of the latter group. This limits the social, cultural, and political participation of Afrodescendants who desire to form their own groupings, make themselves heard, and manifest their diverse interests in distinctive ways.

African food is perceived to be closer to the source than Portuguese food; there is also the sensation that the people are the guardians of a tradition, of something historical. This lineal, progressive imagination of social relationships is likely to limit Afrodescendants' visions for the future. While the Portuguese can easily access African cultures for all types of experiences, Africans rarely enjoy the same privilege when trying to be part of the Portuguese world.

A barrier to overcome is the shame that some Afrodescendants feel about their food and, more generally, about the culture in which they grew up and know is part of their heritage. In Portuguese society, people have internalized a certain way of appreciating African cultural manifestations. Through education and other forms of socialization, the Portuguese promote their ways of approaching, understanding, experiencing, and preserving the exotic.

Afrodescendants often find themselves in positions with less power, in what can be described as ritualized, inherently unequal encounters. Many battle daily against prejudice. Additionally, even while accepting the common objectives of Afrodescendants, we admit that male and female Afrodescendants do not have completely identical experiences. Female Afrodescendants participate actively in social movements, and they facilitate intercultural communication and social consensus.

We hope this discussion has provided some food for thought on the subject of Afrodescendants and their struggles in postcolonial societies. We should continue to problematize such categories as "Asian" or "African" and unravel the entanglements caused by previous racialization and ethnicization processes.

NOTES

1. Associação para a Mudança e Representação Transcultural is the new name of Associação de Melhoramentos e Recreativo do Talude, or in short, AMRT (https://www.amrtranscultural.org/). It was first created in 1993 to defend the rights of Cape Verdean immigrants who had settled and built houses in the peripherical and administratively challenging neighborhood of Talude in Catujal, Loures. While the Association continues to promote the welfare of grassroots Cape Verdean migrants, it has made increasing efforts to reach out to other communities and interest groups.

2. Graal – Associação de Caráter Social e Cultural characterizes itself as a Christian movement, an international community of women from different backgrounds (http://www.graal.org.pt/). In practice, the association organizes a wide range of activities and serves less privileged social groups, including immigrants and their descendants, on a regular basis.

WORKS CITED

Akyeampong, Emmanuel, and Charles Ambler. 2002. "Leisure in African History: An Introduction." *The International Journal of African Historical Studies* 35, no. 1: 1–16. doi/10.1146/annurev.anthro.32.032702.131011.

Appadurai, Arjun. 1988. "How to Make a National Cuisine: Cookbooks in Contemporary India." *Comparative Studies in Society and History* 30, no. 1: 3–24.

Barra, Luís. 2017. "Viagem ao mundo das lojas chinesas." *Expresso*, December 25, 2017. https://expresso.pt/sociedade/2017-12-25-Viagem-ao-mundo-das-lojas-chinesas.

Batalha, Luís. 2004. *The Cape Verdean Diaspora in Portugal: Colonial Subjects in a Postcolonial World*. Lanham: Lexington Books.

Bedell, Malcolm. 2018. "6 Profitability Secrets Chinese Restaurants Don't Want You to Know." *Food Truck Empire*. https://foodtruckempire.com/restaurant/6-profitability-secrets/.

Beyala, Calixthe. 2000. *Comment cuisiner son mari à l'africaine*. Paris: Albin Michel.

Briand, Virginie. 2007. *Manger au quotidien: La vulnérabilité des familles urbaines en Afrique*. Paris: Karthala.

Cantinho do Aziz. 2016. http://cantinhodoaziz.com/.

Challinor, Elizabeth Pilar. 2012. "Researching Ethnicity, Identity, Subjectivity: Anything but the Four-Lettered Word." *Ethnic and Racial Studies* 35, no. 9: 1558–76. doi.org/10.1080/01419870.2011.593641

Chastanet, Monique, Gérard Chouin, and Dora De Lima. 2014. "Pour une histoire de l'alimentation en Afrique avant le XXe siècle: Introduction au dossier." *Afriques* 5: 1–12.

Counihan, Carole, and Steven Kaplan, eds. 2005. *Food and Gender: Identity and Power.* Amsterdam: Harwood Academic Publishers.

Cusack, Igor. 2002. "African Cuisines: Recipes for Nation-Building?" *Journal of African Cultural Studies* 13, no. 2: 207–25.

Domingos, Nuno, José Sobral, and Harry West, eds. 2014. *Food Between the Country and the City: Ethnographies of a Changing Global Foodscape.* London: Bloomsbury.

Douglas, Mary. 2003. *Purity and Danger: An Analysis of Concepts of Pollution and Taboo.* Oxford: Routledge.

Fleur, James Daniel La. 2012. *Fusion Foodways of Africa's Gold Coast in the Atlantic Era* vol. 26, Leiden: Koninklijke Brill NV.

Furtado, Cláudio Alves. 2012. "Raça, classe e etnia nos estudos sobre e em Cabo Verde: As marcas do silêncio." *Afro-Ásia* 45: 143–71.

Galeano, Eduardo. 1997. *Open Veins of Latin America: Five Centuries of the Pillage of a Continent.* New York: Monthly Review Press.

Gibau, Gina. 2005. "Contested Identities: Narratives of Race and Ethnicity in the Cape Verdean Diaspora." *Identities* 12, no. 3: 405–38. doi.org/10.1080/10702890500203702.

Hall, Stuart. 1996. "New Ethnicities." In *Stuart Hall: Critical Dialogues in Cultural Studies,* edited by David Morley and Kuan-Hsing Chen, 441–49. London: Routledge.

Henriques, Joana Gorjão. 2016. *Racismo em português: O lado esquecido do colonialismo.* Lisbon: Tinta da China.

Holtzman, Jon. 2006. "Food and Memory." *Annual Review of Anthropology* 35, no. 1: 361–78. doi.org/10.1146/annurev.anthro.35.081705.123220.

Johnston, Josée, and Shyon Baumann. 2007. "Democracy versus Distinction: A Study of Omnivorousness in Gourmet Food Writing." *American Journal of Sociology* 113, no. 1: 165–204. doi:10.1086/518923.

Keegan, Matthew. 2019. "Macau's Rare Fusion Food." *BBC,* January 14, 2019. http://www.bbc.com/travel/story/20190113-macaus-rare-fusion-cuisine/.

Kuo, Lily. 2015. "West Africans Have Some of the Healthiest Diets in the World." *QuartzAfrica,* August 6, 2015. https://qz.com/africa/473598/west-africans-have-some-of-the-healthiest-diets-in-the-world/.

Liu, Xiaohui. 2016. *Foodscapes of Chinese America: The Transformation of Chinese Culinary Culture in the U.S. since 1965.* New York: Peter Lang Edition.

McCann, James C. 2009. *Stirring the Pot: A History of African Cuisine.* Athens: Ohio University Press.

McLennan, Amy K. 2017. "Local Food, Imported Food, and the Failures of Community Gardening Initiatives in Nauru." In *Postcolonialism, Indigeneity and Struggles for Food Sovereignty: Alternative Food Networks in Subaltern Spaces*, edited by Marisa Wilson, 127–45. London: Routledge.

Meneses, Maria P. 2009. "Food, Recipes and Commodities of Empires: Mozambique in the Indian Ocean Network." *Oficina do CES* 335: 1–34.

Mintz, Sidney, and Christine Du Bois. 2002. "The Anthropology of Food and Eating." *Annual Review of Anthropology* 31, no. 1: 99–119. doi:10.1146/annurev. anthro.32.032702.131011.

Modan, Gabriella. 2008. "Mango Fufu Kimchi Yucca: The Depoliticization of 'Diversity' in Washington, D.C. Discourse." *City & Society* 20, no. 2: 188–221. doi:10.1111/j.1548-744X.2008.00017.x.

Morokvasic, Mirjana. 1984. "Birds of Passage Are Also Women . . ." *International Migration Review* 18, no. 4: 886–907.

Murray, Edmundo. 2015. *A Symphony of Flavors: Food and Music in Concert*. Newcastle upon Tyne: Cambridge Scholars Publishing.

Oliveira, Tiago Silveiro de. 2013. "Alimentação, identidade e memória: Práticas alimentares cabo-verdianas num contexto migratório." *Habitus* 11, no. 1: 19–35.

Perez, Rosa. 2012. "Alimentação e codificação Social: Mulheres, cozinha e estatuto." *Cadernos Pagu* 39: 227–49. doi:10.1590/S0104-83332012000200008.

Ramos, Manuel João. 2018. *Of Hairy Kings and Saintly Slaves: An Ethiopian Travelogue*. Canon Pyon: Sean Kingston Publishing.

Renne, Elisha. 2007. "Mass Producing Food Traditions for West Africans Abroad." *American Anthropologist* 109, no. 4: 616–625. doi.org/10.1525/AA.2007.109.4.616.Renne.

Rodrigues, Isabel Fêo. 2003. "Islands of Sexuality: Theories and Histories of Creolization in Cape Verde." *International Journal of African Historical Studies* 36, no. 1: 83–104. doi:10.2307/3559320.

———. 2008. "From Silence to Silence: The Hidden Story of a Beef Stew in Cape Verde." *Anthropological Quarterly* 81, no. 2: 343–76. doi:10.1353/anq.0.0001.

Said, Edward. 1978. *Orientalism*. London: Routledge & Kegan Paul Ltd.

Said-Moorhouse, Lauren. 2016. "Cooking up a Storm: The Rise of African Superfoods." *CNN*, April 27, 2016. https://edition.cnn.com/2015/03/12/africa/african-superfoods-gastronomy-cuisine/index.html/.

Santos, David. 2015a. "Stomach-Thought. Musa Paradisiaca." *National Museum of Contemporary Art – Museu do Chiado*. http://www.museuartecontemporanea.gov.pt/pt/programacao/1746.

———. 2015b. "Stomach-Thought. Musa Paradisiaca." *RAUM*. http://raum.pt/en/mnac.

Simoons, Frederick. 1974. "Rejection of Fish as Human Food in Africa: A Problem in History and Ecology." *Ecology of Food and Nutrition* 3, no. 2: 89–105. doi:10.1080/03670 244.1974.9990367.

Thomas, Lynn. 2003. *Politics of the Womb: Women, Reproduction, and the State in Kenya.* Berkeley and Los Angeles: University of California Press.

Torrão, Maria Manuel. 1995. *Dietas alimentares: Transferências e adaptações nas ilhas de Cabo Verde.* Lisbon: Centro de Documentação e Informação do IICT.

Valente, Maria Odette Cortes. 1989. *A cozinha descoberta pelos portugueses.* Lisbon: Círculo de Leitores.

Wilk, Richard. 1999. "'Real Belizean Food': Building Local Identity in the Transnational Caribbean." *American Anthropologist* 101, no. 2: 244–55.

Zeleza, Paul Tiyambe. 2010. "African Diasporas: Toward a Global History." *African Studies Review* 53, no. 1: 1–19. doi.org/10.1353/arw.0.0274.

Zhao, Rongguang. 2014. *Zhongguo yinshi wenhua shi* [A Food and Drink History of China]. Shanghai: Shanghai People Publishing House.

Zhuang, Pinghui. 2017. "China Has Largest Number of Obese Children in World, Study Says." *South China Morning Post*, June 13, 2017. https://www.scmp.com/news/china/ society/article/2098042/china-has-largest-number-obese-children-world-says-study.

KAIAN LAM is Research Fellow at the Center for International Studies of ISCTE University Institute of Lisbon. She holds a Ph.D. in African Studies. From May to July 2021, she was Visiting Post-Doctoral Fellow at the Faculty of Social Sciences of the University of Macau. Her recent articles include "Island-raised but foreign-made: Lived experiences, trans-national relationships, and expressions of womanhood among Cape Verdean migrant women in Greater Lisbon," *Island Studies Journal* 16 (2021), 101–114; "In poverty we will always stay: History of famine and contemporary politics of social in-distinction in Cape Verde," *Food, Culture & Society*, forthcoming.

V. Afrodescendência e enunciação literária

EMERSON INÁCIO

"Língua de Preto" e Dicção Negra:
Do Dialeto Barroco à Veiculação Identitária[1]

RESUMO: Partindo do fato de que a autoria e a dicção negras se vêm insurgindo no concerto da Literatura Portuguesa mais contemporânea – como contradicurso às identidades hegemônicas e como manifestação literária identitariamente marcada –, o presente artigo pretende discutir e analisar o poemário *Açafate de Floremas* (1971), de António Cruz, tomando-o como possível ponto de emergência de uma discusividade literária afroportuguesa.

PALAVRAS-CHAVE: Autoria Afroportuguesa; Poesia Portuguesa contemporânea; Identidades; Relações Étnico-raciais.

ABSTRACT: Based on the fact that black authorship and diction have been insinuating in the concert of the most contemporary Portuguese Literature – as a contradiction to hegemonic identities and as an identitarily marked literary manifestation –, the present article intends to discuss and analyze the poem collection *Açafate de Floremas* (1971), by António Cruz, taking it as a possible point of emergence of an Afro-Portuguese literary discourse.

KEYWORDS: Afroportuguese Author; Contemporary Portuguese Poetry; Identities; Ethnic-racial relations.

> O grande jogo da história será de quem se apoderar das regras, de quem tomar o lugar daqueles que as utilizam, de quem se disfarçar para pervertê-las, utilizá-las ao inverso e voltá-las contra aqueles que as tinham imposto; de quem, se introduzindo no aparelho complexo, o fizer funcionar de tal modo que os dominadores encontrar-se-ão dominados por suas regras.
>
> (Michel Foucault, 1979. P. 25-26)

I. Preâmbulo

Os processos de investigação científica, em particular aqueles vivenciados nas áreas de Ciências Sociais e Humanas, muitas vezes resultam no encontro de elementos inesperados que desviam o pesquisador do curso presumido pela atividade de pesquisa. O artigo que se segue, de certa maneira, nasce de um inesperado encontro, resultando do estágio de pesquisa realizado entre abril e setembro de 2018, em Lisboa. Tendo ido em busca de bibliografia que sustentasse a investigação que venho realizando desde 2017 – "Intersecções: As Literaturas de Língua Portuguesa, Comparativismo e Convergências" –, nomeadamente textos literários que contemplassem o que venho chamando de "textualidades *queer*," acabei por me deparar com uma significativa produção literária de autoria assumidamente negra. Tal *acontecimento* contribui para singularizar a projetada investigação, uma vez que o intento inicial – encontrar manifestações literárias de viés intersemiótico e com marcada deriva entre os gêneros literários e discursivos – resultou num recorte específico que tem priorizado a configuração de um lugar de enunciação estética negra em Portugal, baseada na análise, em curso, das 20 obras encontradas. À semelhança dos trabalhos já realizados no Brasil, por Eduardo de Assis Duarte, Domício Proença Filho e Luíza Lobo – ou seja, a realização de uma cartografia descritiva da autoria negra no Brasil –, o desenho atual da investigação visa, objetivamente, determinar se as obras obtidas reúnem condições de produção discursiva e estética que as delimitem dentro do campo que tenho chamado de "Literatura Afroportuguesa."

Em paralelo, a investigação em curso se assume em seu viés político, muito motivada pelos cada vez mais relevantes movimentos antirracismo e em defesa da cidadania plena das pessoas negras em Portugal. Evidentemente, me parece concreta a hipótese de que, ao lado de manifestações em favor de uma política identitária específica para os afrodescendentes portugueses, devam haver, também, fenômenos de caráter literário que, esteticamente, conformem os mais de 500 anos da presença negra em solo português. A detecção, a descrição e a publicização destes fenômenos literários é parte de uma tarefa emancipatória que visa localizar as pessoas negras, nascidas ou não em Portugal, dentro de um quadro cultural que corresponda à sua relevância histórica e política, bem como a sua contribuição para a existência, seja do falecido "império" seja na conformação político-identitária lusitana atual.

Nessa perspectiva, o reconhecimento das particularidades discursivas de obras como *Açafate de Floremas*, de António Cruz, *Esse Cabelo*, de Djaimilia Pereira de Almeida, e, antes delas, *O Preto do Charleston*, de Mário Domingues, significaria, necessariamente, reconhecer a existência de discursos descontínuos, mas presentes, no conserto aparentemente tão bem arranjado em que se arvora a identidade portuguesa "pós-colónias": as pessoas negras são sempre o Outro-Estrangeiro, a contraface material da memória de uma África onde tudo interessava, menos o seu capital humano. Noutras palavras: é possível que possamos perceber a atual produção literária negra em Portugal como um "local de contestação estratégica" (Hall 2003, 341) capaz de mover, esteticamente, muitos dos sentidos naturalizados na cultura portuguesa, dentre os quais um sentido identitário unicista. E é justamente nesse ponto de fratura, de desnaturalização, em que o (supostamente) dominado incorpora as regras do dominador para derrisoriamente subvertê-las (Foucault 1979, 25) que se situa a escrita literária afroportuguesa e, em forma de discurso descontínuo, a poesia de António Cruz.

A respeito dessas (des)apropriações, Franz Fanon, ainda nos anos de 1950, já apontava para o fato de que "falar é existir de modo absoluto para o outro . . ., assumir uma cultura, suportar o peso de uma civilização" (Fanon 1983, 17). A distância que dele nos separa nos permite, entretanto, passar a entender que essa apropriação da fala e das formas expressivas do outro possa se constituir, também, como prática política estratégica que, sendo o único meio de o negro habitar alguns lugares, passa a ser com isso um procedimento que sempre instauraria a ruptura. Um desses casos seria a carta da escravizada Esperanza Garcia, que, ainda no século XVIII, numa distante província do Brasil, se dirige ao administrador português para reclamar daquele que dela se apossara e que lhe impedia de cuidar de seus filhos, ir ter com seu esposo e de frequentar as missas. No uso da linguagem, no uso rogativo de certo discurso, é que Esperanza rompe com sua condição subalternizada onde o silenciamento parecia, a muitos, naturalizado, dominando a língua e a linguagem do escravizador de forma a apropriar-se simbolicamente de algum poder, ainda que ínfimo, traduzível pela linguagem. A carta de Esperanza, nesse sentido, não só geraria um desequilíbrio nos jogos de dominação próprios do sistema escravocrata, como afirmaria sua integridade como indivíduo e sujeito, fazendo-a "ser" na linguagem, ainda que fosse, em seu cotidiano, peça substituível numa série.

Antecipando algumas possíveis conclusões deste trabalho, o caso da poesia de Cruz – cujo livro é publicado em 1971, num momento de acirramento das lutas por libertação em algumas das colônias e de acentuação das práticas repressivas por parte do governo português – se demarcaria tanto como a apropriação de linguagem num espaço e em condições não previstas – Lisboa –, quanto apontaria para a insurgência de uma dicção negra "metropolitana" e, portanto, desidentificada com a emergência das literaturas nacionais africanas de língua portuguesa. Visto unicamente por este lado, o livro de Cruz – independentemente de sua qualidade estética – se constitui como um fenômeno que determina a existência de uma consciência cultural de matriz negra que se quer manifestar e que tem clareza de sua identidade. Contudo, no panorama cultural português de então, se constitui como "a" diferença em si mesma, inferindo, assim, uma base de "tradição alternativa" e conflitante (Williams 2000, 11) quando vista em relação ao sistema/canône literário português.

II. Língua de Preto e a Paródia Barroca

No artigo "Poemas em *Língua de Preto* dos séculos XVII e XVIII" (2003, 211-38), a poeta e ensaísta Ana Hatherly procura não só palmilhar a presença do negro na cultura portuguesa no período barroco, como se debruça sobre a caracterização e o uso da chamada "língua de preto" pela poesia burlesca e pelo teatro, pelo menos desde Gil Vicente. A despeito dos maneirismos de linguagem, característicos de certa escritura barroca, a que a poeta-crítica denomina poesia *joco-séria*, a "língua de preto" se constitui como um recurso expressivo que, nas mãos da inventividade hiperpotencial dos autores daquele período estético, se constituiu como uma marca obliterada pelo sentido mais moderno que fora atribuído ao Barroco. Falar em "língua de preto," no barroco português em particular, demonstrava para a poeta e ensaísta a apropriação da fala oral das pessoas negras escravizadas, tendo sido utilizada como um recurso estético que atenderia a "muitas e curiosas facetas do gosto pelo extravagante, que dominou todo esse período da arte europeia" (211-12). Cabe destaque ao fato de que – segundo Hatherly, apoiando-se em estudos filológicos e literários anteriores ao seu ensaio – era notável a presença da fala negra nas letras portuguesas, nomeadamente desde o *Cancioneiro Geral* de Garcia de Resende, em poema assinado por Anrique de Mota, texto provavelmente datado de 1455 (212).

Usada inicialmente com fins cômicos, a "língua de preto," segundo a poeta, também servira como forma documental e representativa dos "negros nas sociedades em que foram obrigados a integrar-se" (213). Entretanto, Hatherly, ao assinalar uma "sintaxe e uma morfologia rudimentares . . . havendo ausência de concordâncias" (213), deixa de apontar o uso estereotipado desse falar, como também não problematiza o fato de que, na medida em que o negro é reproduzido e representado e não necessariamente se produz em seu próprio dizer, o elemento então escravizado era tornado duplamente objeto do discurso alheio. Primeiro, porque escravizado e, na sequência, porque silenciado dentro de uma expressão linguística que, certamente, era a forma dialetal maioritária, mas não a única.

Não espero aqui, claro, que Hatherly se dispusesse ao estudo da expressividade negra no período barroco, posto que, de fato, se a houve, ainda não foi detetada ou devidamente descrita ou sistematizada pelo campo dos estudos de literatura e mesmo na cultura, como bem o aponta José Ramos Tinhorão em seu *Negros em Portugal: Uma Presença Silenciosa* (1988). Da assertiva da poeta-ensaísta acerca da "sintaxe rudimentar," nascem questões, já agora relativas tanto à representação do negro, quanto de sua presença e expressão no concerto cultural português, incluindo-se nisto a língua. Evidentemente, não fizera parte do escopo da ensaísta, por exemplo, a abordagem de *Viola de Lereno*, de autoria de Domingos Caldas Barbosa (1944), publicado originalmente em 1798 – um dos primeiros textos de assinatura negra presentes nas literaturas de língua portuguesa –, poemário este muito mais identificado com as letras árcades.

A primeira questão estaria no fato de que, no jogo entre dicção e tematização, a língua tida por "correta" seria – para aqueles negros representados nos poemas que Hatherly analisa – uma impossibilidade sociocultural e, da mesma forma, se constituiria como uma "mimese falhada" (ao meu ver, reapropriada) da língua, tal qual a "língua de preto" de fato o foi.

O segundo argumento é de ordem cultural, visto que poucas das pessoas escravizadas tiveram acesso ao conhecimento formal da Língua Portuguesa escrita, o que impediria sua expressão literária e comprometeria, consequentemente, sua posição como "autoria" e/ou como agente da enunciação, estando tais atores sociais restritos, portanto, ao papel de personagem, de meros coadjuvantes ou de responsáveis pelo teor satírico do poemário barroco. Os poucos negros que o fizeram, como aponta Sílvio Romero (1888), em termos brasileiros, e José Ramos Tinhorão (1988), na cultura portuguesa mais especificamente, o fazem desde as regras do bom funcionamento das séries literárias em que se inserem, portanto, respeitando as normas vigentes da língua sua contemporânea ou incorporando ao seu dizer os "desvios" e variantes aceites pelo contexto cultural.

Isso posto, cabe sempre lembrar dos processos de infatilização do negro, justamente pela linguagem, aludidos por Fanon em "O Negro e a Linguagem": visam sempre a minorização do outro – o negro –, subalternizado, pela produção de hierarquias pautadas na linguagem vista desde sua função como instrumento da colonialidade (Fanon 1983, 25). Parece-me claro, não quero, aqui, atribuir sentidos ao rico trabalho de Hatherly, posto que, considerada a sua história de poeta, a ensaísta o configura e descreve como um recurso utilizado por um procedimento literário de que não compactua. Mas é importante frisar que o recurso à "língua de preto" revela consigo um posicionamento que, visto desde nosso ponto de vista localizado na contemporaneidade, reafirmaria como o outro-negro – menor, infantil, pelo não domínio pleno da linguagem – era social e culturalmente configurado: de sua expressão nasceria o riso jocoso e jamais uma expressão de um sujeito falante que, à sua maneira, se revelaria como um ser de seu tempo.

III. Do Uso (ou do Domínio) Emancipatório da Linguagem Poética

É de se notar, entretanto, que a "língua de preto" aduzida por Ana Hatherly em seu ensaio retorne à poesia portuguesa, posteriormente, no poemário *Açafate de Floremas*, assinado por António Cruz e publicado em Lisboa, em 1971. O conjunto de 35 poemas traz em si uma temática variada, com ênfase no uso do laudatório e panegírico, muitos dos quais dedicados a familiares e amigos. Soma-se a isso um viés lírico-amoroso, de teor corriqueiro e cotidiano, de viés Romântico, claramente conotados com experiências que parecem envolver a instância autoral, ao que se sucede, ainda um certo espírito de época, sobretudo no que se aplica ao excesso metalinguístico e aos confrontos do sujeito na e com a linguagem: a dificuldade de dizer, a busca das formas possíveis, a impotência do autor/enunciador diante da palavra poética e a suspeita acerca do valor estético dos poemas ou de sua pertença ao que se rotula como literário.

As achegas textuais e paratextuais feitas pelo próprio autor – e conotado enunciador – acerca do que escreve e publica servem como uma espécie de alerta aos seus leitores "'SIMPLES-SIMPLES/ como eu,/ simples" (9): se, por um lado, carregam um tom desculposo relativo à qualidade dos poemas contidos na publicação, por outro estabelecem com seus leitores um pacto, trato este que considera que a leitura de *Açafate* deve ser procedida desde outros parâmetros estéticos, já agora estabelecidos por uma autoria insurgente, uma vez que se trata de um "pigmeu poeta" (15).

A par disso, discursivamente, seus leitores são referidos, nos textos que funcionam como introdução aos poemas, como "amigos." Daí decorrem duas hipóteses: a primeira, a de que o livro se dedique a uma comunidade específica de pessoas negras/afrodescendentes capazes de perceberem as intencionalidades do conteúdo, dado o uso da segunda pessoa do singular "tu," pronome pessoal que pressupõe intimidade e depõe, supostamente, as hierarquias sociais e discursivas só possíveis entre os que comungam de fatores sociais, políticos, financeiros e raciais próximos. Se estabelecermos uma correspondência entre os usos linguísticos entre a ex-"metrópole" e as ex-"colônias," levando em consideração os jogos de espelhamento propriamente pragmáticos, pode-se inferir disso que o uso do pronome pessoal "tu" em Cruz carrega consigo o mesmo valor semântico-cultural visto, por exemplo, no caso emblemático do conto "A Menina Vitória," de Arnaldo Santos: a excessiva proximidade somente mantida entre os que supostamente ocupam o mesmo lugar na cadeia discursiva racial, revelada na sequência final do conto Santos – ao ler a sua redação para a Professora Vitória, Gigi é severamente repreendido pela mestra, porque "que tinha carapinha. Ela que era filha de uma negra" (45), e por utilizar o "tu" para se referir ao representante do governo colonial:

> Como é que ele se atrevera a tratá-lo por tu! Como é que ele tivera o arrojo de o nomear por um simples artigo definido?
> – Ouve lá... tu pensas que ele anda sujo e roto como tu, e come funge na tua sanzala? (Santos 1965, 44)

A segunda hipótese, advinda ainda da "intimidade com que te trato" (12), pressupõe a modificação da leitura essencialista da palavra poética por si mesma em favor de outra que se estabelece pelo pacto de afeto e identidade, reiterado nos três "poemas" sem título antepostos à dedicatória e que servem de introito aos outros dezassete que compõem o açafate do poeta. Se considerarmos aqui o contexto cultural e poético português daquele momento – fins dos anos de 1960 –, sobejado pelo experimentalismo, pela ênfase exacerbada no significante, por certo hermetismo e pela economia no uso da linguagem, a poesia de Cruz parecerá a muitos palavrório neo-romântico. Entretanto, quando vista desde sua condição de homem negro que conclama relações de identidade e afeto baseadas na experiência profunda de seu livro, essa poesia pode assumir um outro teor: justamente aquele relativo a demarcar, no quadro poético-discursivo, tanto sua condição identitária étnico-racial, quanto o valor retórico que esta condição assume em seus poemas.

Do título do livro já advém a sua linha criativa, bem como o aspeto despretensioso da obra: *açafate* – do árabe, cesto sem tampa – associado a *floremas*, exercício morfológico que une flor e poemas, ou seja, indicando como vetor aquilo que faz nascer frutos, que se reproduz, portanto. Enquanto signo denotativo/conotativo de beleza, o último elemento do par semântico que forma o título apontaria para o uso cultural da poesia, remetendo-se, assim, aos "jogos florais": certame literário, normalmente envolvendo competição, no qual são apresentados temas de gosto popular, nomeadamente marcado pelo uso das redondilhas, medida poética tradicionalmente portuguesa. Nessa perspectiva, o livro se traduziria como um conjunto de escritos diversos, ligados por seu conteúdo poético e relacionados com uma poesia de caráter mais simples, cotidiana, cujo exercício não é, senão outro, sempre voltado ao metalinguístico e metapoético, já que a prática floral seria, antes de tudo, um exercício de mestria e de domínio da palavra. A escolha do substantivo *florema*, um neologismo, nesse caso, se constituiria como uma estratégia, depois justificada pelo autor nas partes pré-textuais e poéticas do volume que publica, como logo se verá.

Em pesquisa realizada em bases de dados das bibliotecas portuguesas, bem como em motores de busca, constam apenas dois resultados relativos a António Cruz (1925-?) e à sua produção: uma ocorrência na Biblioteca Municipal de Sintra, que registra o tombamento de *Açafate de Floremas*, com a particularidade de incluí-lo como "poesia portuguesa"; e outra, relativa a um manuscrito enviado a Natália Correia, por um nomeado António Oliveira Brito e Cruz, em 1993, onde se lê "Dedicado desde já à mais revolucionária das mulheres. Natália Correia." Esta ocorrência faz parte do acervo do Arquivo Regional de Ponta Delgada, nos Açores, e que relaciona o remetente à extinta Companhia Nacional de Navegação, a mesma empresa pública a que o apenas assinado "António Cruz" declara ter sido funcionário, na orelha do livro. Sobre o autor de *Açafate de Floremas*, mais nenhuma informação, nem sequer notícia do depósito legal da obra na Biblioteca Nacional, o que me leva a supor que tenha apenas circulado entre pessoas íntimas, e de que posso inferir da máxima "todo homem deve fazer um filho, plantar uma árvore e escrever um livro" referida no prefácio de sua autoria.[2]

Daí que *Açafate de Floremas* se trate de um exercício literário único da parte de Cruz, já que do manuscrito referido no arquivo açoriano parece não configurar, de fato, o conteúdo daquilo que fora enviado à poeta. O que importa, acerca do livro publicado por António Cruz, é o seu papel enquanto fenômeno contemporâneo e autorreferido como sendo de autoria afrodescendente ("mulato") e lisboeta, com certa consciência de seu tempo, e não se vinculando a nenhum dos sistemas literários africanos de língua portuguesa que, à altura, 1971, estavam em formação. Nos manuais de peso em termos de estudos de literaturas dos PALOPs, como os de Pires Laranjeira, de Manuel Ferreira ou de Alfredo Margarido, não constam referências a Cruz ou ao seu livro, o que nos permite afirmar que tenha se tratado de um fenômeno estrito e circunscrito à experiência portuguesa do início dos anos setenta do século XX. Outro dado relevante sobre como fazer figurar autor e obra dentro de um sistema literário específico advém, ainda, do fato de que, em não havendo "pistas" seguras a respeito de sua ascendência – uma vez que "mulato" pode se referir a um indivíduo cujos familiares podem ter vivido em Portugal desde, pelo menos, a chegada da primeira pessoa negra àquela terra – e se dizendo lisboeta, optei por seguir, também, o critério de catalogação utilizado pela Biblioteca Municipal de Sintra, associado, pois, ao conteúdo relevante da obra.

A tal "língua de preto," aludida por Hatherly, talvez se atualize como recurso estético-discursivo semelhante no poema "Lotação esgotada!!!," de António Cruz. Obviamente, não se trata nem de um contexto de barroco tardio ou sequer do mesmo daquele uso cartografado pela poeta-ensaísta. Mas, sim, de uma proposição em que o enunciador agora vivencia certo hibridismo miscigenatório, que se traduz em recurso de linguagem, uma vez que no poema, como se verá, são utlizadas formas da língua culta e da língua oral, em medidas correlatas à expressão de seu conteúdo. O uso da primeira pessoa do discurso, maioritária nos poemas que compõem *Açafate de Floremas*, surge agora como uma espécie de "outramento," já que, quando visto em contraste com os demais textos do livro, é o único em que o recurso à reprodução de uma modalidade de língua falada acontece. Aqui, não se trata de empregar apenas o recurso da oralidade, mas de seu uso enquanto forma estrita, o que parece buscar uma reprodução da realidade da língua. Se tomarmos o padrão linguístico mantido nos demais poemas da obra, observa-se que o conotado poeta "cede" lugar a um outro discursivo – algo distanciado dos demais enunciadores poemáticos – que oscila entre a linguagem padrão e uma fala coloquial distensa, mas consciente dos registros cultos da língua portuguesa:

> Não tenho lugá na praia
> está cheia di gente!
>
> Não tenho lugá na cidade
> há genti di mais

Não tenho lugá no cinema
está esgotada a lotação

não tenho lugá em ninhum lado
estou dislocado...

Na praia (quando é verão)
Na cidadi (em todas as estações)
No cinema (nas noites di estreia)

Ó coração
ó ilusões
qui ideia
tão infeliz
para dizer que no meu País
eu só terei lugá
quando soá
a hora di morrê... di descansá
(Cruz 1971, 81)[3]

Hatherly, ao descrever o uso barroco da "língua de preto", fará menção aos abrandamentos finais nas palavras terminadas em "r" (verbos, por exemplo), bem como para um uso particular dos encadeamentos sintáticos. A tentativa barroca de reproduzir a língua falada pelos escravizados resultaria numa notação particular de língua, mimetizada no poema e filtrada pelo ouvido do autor barroco – branco – que a reproduz no poema, ensejando a formulação (ou conformação), a seu modo, de um "dialecto crioulo-português . . ., uma *língua literária parodística*, uma espécie de *idiolecto barroco* cultivado como uma forma exótica para efeito de um divertimento amaneirado, tão caro ao gosto português, adoçado por *lunduns* e *modinhas* e talvez já inundado de *kitsch*" (Hatherly 2003, 212-14).

Começando pelo fim do excerto de Hatherly, o conjunto poético representado disposto em *Açafate de Floremas* carrega consigo certo tom *kitsch*, no sentido em que a maioria de seus poemas traz em si um estilo popularesco e cotidiano, conotado por algumas referências às questões caras da poesia moderna, apenas que pouco ou nada elaboradas. Entretanto, como já expus, o próprio autor se considera um poeta menor e, nessa perspectiva, o "defeito" verter-se-ia em qualidade, no sentido em que não almejaria figurar entre os "grandes" poetas, mas apenas enunciar-se como homem negro/mestiço, dizendo poesia menor numa língua maior (Deleuze 1977). Noutra laçada, recorrendo a um maneirismo poético da matriz popular e cotidiana – um não-sublime ou outro, um sublime das miudezas? –, Cruz se inscreveria numa larga tradição poética sobre o comum e o corriqueiro e na qual se inscrevem Reinaldo Ferreira e António Osório de Castro – ambos, diga-se, cultores de uma poesia de viés popular e simples, legível por quaisquer pessoas e tão "ao gosto português." De uma linguagem tida por "falhada," entremeio entre a poesia pretensamente culta e oralidade e as realidades cotidianas, Cruz faz da falta uma festa para a subjetividade neo-romântica que instaura em seus poemas.

No caso mais contemporâneo da poesia de Cruz, o procedimento apontado por Hatherly se potencializaria, já que o uso de linguagem não se pretende paródístico nem produtor de quaisquer divertimentos, mas pode ser visto desde a instauração de uma forma de abjeção, ou seja, um incômodo estabelecido no interior da linguagem (Kristeva 1980), elemento que a paródia pode trazer e a que muitas vezes recorre. "Lotação esgotada" operaria a abjeção – no sentido linguístico dessa noção, na medida em que recusa a assimilação linguística total da língua do outro, operando na duplicidade de se marcar no discurso/texto e na reclamação de um lugar possível para ser e estar, previsto apenas na morte – por parte de seu enunciador.

Se considerarmos o viés eminentemente linguageiro, vemos sentenças em que o uso formal escrito e o uso oral passam a conviver em certa harmonia, procurando demonstrar no procedimento de linguagem do sujeito que se enuncia uma tentativa de equalizar dois universos, já que, pela lógica da reprodução da língua oral, teríamos "genti" e "ladu," em lugar de "gente" e "lado," como vemos no poema. O confronto entre quem se enuncia e a sua ambiência se repetiria – a língua culta –, ainda, na oscilação entre usos próprios da norma culta escrita e a sua vertente oral, como, por exemplo em "Na cidadi (em todas as estações)," demonstrando aí o duplo desconforto da instância enunciadora, que parece nem estar à vontade nos espaços que a comportam e nem sequer na linguagem que lhe traduz como sujeito.

Visto isoladamente, o poema não passaria de mais um exemplo do clássico embate "eu vs. mundo," tão caro ao romantismo, apenas que lançando mão de recursos estilísticos e estéticos que o vinculariam a uma tentativa de transcrição da linguagem oral. Entretanto, quando olhado em termos de usos de imagens que reportam a espaços sociais notadamente brancos, a suposta tensão neo-romântica se potencializa, apontando para uma tentativa de explicitar situações nas quais aqueles que não dominam a norma culta não têm lugar. O enunciador "dislocado" não se referiria apenas a uma não pertença a estes espaços, mas à impossibilidade de acesso a locais onde, por ser pobre e, possivelmente, negro, não deveria estar. Ainda que o índice racial não compareça ao poema, pode-se dele inferir que o "poetazinho" (como se refere a si na aba/orelha de seu livro) demarca-se como, repito, de "raça mestiça"; portanto, nele subjaz, em alguma medida, uma identificação com as experiências negras de seu tempo, certamente, também elas "deslocadas" dos espaços de vivência social e cultural da maioria branca.

O terceto que medeia o pequeno poema traduz-se como uma entrada para os sentidos possíveis do poema: a tríade semântica praia/cidade/cinema não revelaria senão a questão racial, traduzível, por exemplo, em frases do tipo "porque um preto precisa ir à praia?," donde redunda a inexistência de um lugar para si, posto que, para o senso comum de teor racista, o tom de pele escuro dispensaria as pessoas negras do usufruto do lazer, uma vez que o imaginário social preponderante as circunscreveria ao universo do trabalho subalterno ou subalternizado. No verso seguinte, "Na cidade (em todas as estações)," a sequência enunciativa constrói-se desde o *apartheid* social e da consciência afirmativa do não pertencimento ao tecido humano que comporia a *urbis* Lisboa àquela altura. Inúmeros trabalhos das áreas de Sociologia Urbana, de Urbanismo e Antropologia têm vindo a demonstrar que a capital do então "império colonial português" tem sido objeto de fluxos migratórios árabes, judeus e posteriormente negros – em função da chegada de pessoas escravizadas –, pelo menos desde os séculos XVI e XVII. Em *ritornello*, o verso em discussão anteciparia a ideia expressa em "no meu País/eu só terei lugá/quando soá/a hora di morrê...," na medida em que a "cidadi" (metonímia de país) lhe reservaria apenas um túmulo onde, obviamente, não poderia desfrutar nem de lazer, nem de pertencimento social e político ou sequer do acesso à cultura.

Por questões das mais variadas, tais populações foram se estabelecendo nos arredores da Baixa Lisboeta (zonas da Mouraria/Alfama e Madragoa),[4] àquela altura regiões desocupadas ou com topografia desfavorável, mas próxima a eixos de comércio e trabalho. Mais recentemente, desde meados dos anos de 1960 e sobretudo nos anos subsequentes ao 25 de abril, em razão das guerras (por libertação e, depois, civis) que ocorrem em alguns dos territórios/países africanos (Angola, Guiné e Moçambique), grandes levas de "imigrantes"[5] aportaram em Lisboa. Muitos dos quais, enfrentando dificuldades de ambientação, obtenção de emprego formal, documentação e mesmo de inserção no novo contexto, foram habitar as zonas menos privilegiadas e distantes das cidades, principalmente a Linha de Sintra, a Margem Sul do Tejo e a chamada "Zona J," que compreendia as regiões orientais de Lisboa. Muitos desses imigrados, nomeadamente pessoas negras e afrodescendentes, por razões sociais e económicas as mais diversas, foram habitar as barracas, que se converteram em "bairros de lata" e, posteriormente, em zonas de habitação irregular, como é o caso dos Bairros Cova da Moura e Seis de Maio, no município da Amadora, cidade vizinha a Lisboa. O verso de Cruz materializa aquilo que boa parte da população negra e pobre passou a vivenciar: um não pertencimento ou a não participação na vida cotidiana da cidade de Lisboa, quer por medo de sofrer preconceitos quer por razões de não identificação com o todo maioritário que compõe a cidade e que demarcaria negros, árabes, sul-asiáticos, ciganos e demais pessoas com peles não-brancas como adendos à experiência da cidade.

O último verso do terceto, "No cinema (nas noites di estreia)," por sua vez, parece apontar para a reafirmação, no campo das expressões culturais e de lazer, do espaço que esse cidadão sem "lugá em ninhum lado" deve ocupar. As noites de estreia, destinadas a certa elite intelectual, se constituem como um campo em que sua indigência múltipla se caracteriza, já que, enquanto metonímia que cruza experiências sociais, culturais, estéticas e políticas, o cinema se conformaria como heterotopia, já que o indicativo temporal ("noites di estreia") desenha, utopicamente, uma possibilidade de estar e de se constituir, ainda que numa outra noite, uma subjetividade aderente àquele espaço.

Como futuramente irá ocorrer com grande parte da produção afroportuguesa contemporânea, trata-se aqui de uma edição de autor, com sinais claros de um espírito *owner*, já que em todo o livro se percebe a presença e a interferência, bem como a nítida correspondência entre autoria e enunciação. Se levarmos em conta os elementos paratextuais e pré-textuais, como orelhas, prefácio e apresentação, a figura do Cruz – aquele que escreve – se impõe como uma presença constante, oferecendo linhas de leitura e intervenções autocomiserativas acerca de sua obra, inclusive, pelo recurso a textos de caráter introdutório aos poemas, como é o caso da "Carta do aprendiz de poeta":

Daí a razão porque te aparece nas mãos ou na frente aos teus olhos o paradoxo de um livro vulgar escrito por um sonhador – que por o ser – confunde poesia com espetáculo . . . Julgo, no entanto, que de todo não te enfastiarás com o "espetáculo," apesar dos seus altos, médios e baixos momentos, apesar dos seus momentos baixos serem mais do que os médios e os altos, não passarem de rasos.

. . . Tu que não me conheces, lê o "MEU AÇAFATE DE FLOREMAS" perdoa a intimidade com que te trato e procura compreender as minhas intenções e o meu acordo: a tua simpatia em troca do meu livro. (Cruz 1971, 11-12)

Ora, o excesso "desculposo" da instância autoral não me parece inoportuno, considerado o fato de que Cruz aparenta não ter pertencido a nenhuma tertúlia nem ter-se vinculado a associações culturais ou coisa que o valha, como era prática comum em termos de poesia portuguesa ou mesmo da poesia produzida em Portugal, e que depois passará a compor as literaturas nacionais africanas em Língua Portuguesa, como terá sido o caso de Francisco José Tenreiro e seu *Ilha de Nome Santo* (1942). No caso específico do autor de que ora trato, este fato observa-se em termos de valor estético irregular e uma poesia ainda pouco apurada, muito vincada no derramamento transcrito de episódios de caráter biográfico e confessional. Talvez daí redunde o fato de o autor continuamente pedir vênia e tentar estabelecer com a instância leitora "pactos" de leitura, como o visto acima, que condicionam duplamente sua poesia como uma língua menor:

SE, ENTRE VÓS, UNS E OUTROS ACHARDES QUE
ESSAS FLORES SÃO MURCHAS OU TÊM ALGO DE
"EXÓTICO-RIDÍCULO" E, POR ISSO APENAS
CONSPURCAM A POESIA – então, humildemente
Peço que me perdoem os intelectuais, os poetas e todos –
(Cruz, 9)

Acerca dos pactos, a orelha do volume – provavelmente também de autoria de Cruz, dado o viés ali assumido, presente também em textos do interior do livro – oferece aos leitores uma linha de significação e interpretação valiosa, tanto no que aponta para um pacto de leitura que identifica o autor dentro de certo tecido social, quanto para o que indica uma dicção afroportuguesa ou negroportuguesa, bem como a emergência desse discurso estético naquele concerto cultural:

– onde nasceu? da raça mestiça, em Lisboa
dizem que tem a alma branca... essa é boa!

e até aqui, ei-lo biografado
sobre seu presente e sobre o seu passado...
ah! mas falta ainda responder
que o cidadão em causa é pobre
é plebeu... não descende de gente nobre
(Cruz 1971, 4ª. capa)

A orelha do livro – componente/aba da capa – geralmente tem por função apresentar as credenciais do autor e da obra, e pode, em alguns casos e quando assinadas por outros que não o próprio, oferecer ao leitor linhas gerais sobre autor e obra, funcionando tanto como uma prévia do que será lido, quanto como uma espécie de contexto usual que facilitaria a abordagem do material propriamente textual. Normalmente, seu conteúdo é de caráter referencial, podendo ainda valer-se de fragmentos da obra, descrição de alguma personagem ou apresentar obras anteriores de um mesmo autor. No caso de Cruz, a orelha apresenta-se estruturalmente em estranheza em relação ao usual, já que a mancha impressa não preenche de uma margem a outra a face do papel, somando-se a isso o fato de que todo o texto da orelha apresenta ritmo, rima e cadência invulgar, o que caracterizaria – formalmente – uma poesia[6].

Agregam-se aí, ao "poema-orelha" – "insólita autobiografia/ dita em pretensioso estilo de poesia" (Cruz 1971) – informações de caráter sociopolítico e cultural, relevantes, certamente, para aquela edição: a saber, o fato de ser afrodescendente ("da raça mestiça"), ter nascido em Lisboa e de ser *pobre* e *plebeu*, portanto, previamente alijado de um capital financeiro, de ascendência que lhe inscreva num ordenamento social tido por relevante. A peculiaridade da orelha ainda residiria no fato de induzir à uma nacionalidade possível, recusando, entretanto, sua inclusão num processo assimilatório que, se presume, fosse recorrente: "dizem que tem alma branca... essa é boa!" Ao afirmar-se mestiço e ao rejeitar uma outra pertença que não a relativa a cor de sua pele, instaura discursivamente a emergência de uma autoria que se quer racialmente negra e lisbonense, apontando para aquilo que mais recentemente se convencionou chamar "afroportuguês."

Claro está que aqui não se deseja reclamar para António Cruz uma condição original ou de *grau zero* de uma escrita afroportuguesa, mas sim de observá-lo num sentido de proveniência, na acepção em que Michel Foucault descreve o processo, ou seja: aquele momento em que, na história das lutas brutas

e silenciadas, os discursos poemas-vida se insurgiriam contra os dizeres hegemônicos que interditam e ordenam os demais, garantindo que estes permane-
çam à margem e que a violência estruturante opere. Até porque dimensionar
uma "gênese" da escrita afoportuguesa ensejaria um trabalho de pesquisa cujos
intentos se distanciam dos propósitos desta investigação. Além do que, como se
trata da dobra do autorreconhecimento identitário sobre a matéria propriamente
literária, seria preciso palmilhar séculos de produção e acervos, num exercício
arqueológico de busca de autoras e autores que se referenciassem a si e à sua
obra como pertencentes a certo universo identitário e cuja produção, nesse sentido, pudesse ser assim arrolada enquanto referencial minimamente consciente
de uma posição identitária vinculada à situação étnico-racial. Trata-se, então,
desde condições específicas de produção estético-discursiva – cujas formações
levam em conta aspectos como o colonialismo e a colonialidade; a presença e o
peso cultural das pessoas negras em Portugal; os processos assimilatórios e as
questões que constituem a diferença étnico-racial enquanto fator decisivo –, de
determinar um ponto em que esta "consciência" racial de matriz portuguesa se
insurge enquanto recurso e procedimento possível de ser apontado dentro da
produção literária portuguesa mais contemporânea.

A questão ganha relevos ainda mais acidentados se se considerar o ano de
publicação, 1971, momento de acirrados combates pela libertação nos territórios
africanos ocupados por Portugal, e quando em algumas das então "colônias"
as lutas ganham, também, certos contornos racializados, como fora o caso da
Guiné Bissau segundo bem aludiu Amílcar Cabral (1976). Em meio das guerras
pela independência (1962-1974), onde signos tais como autodeterminação dos
povos, liberdade ou mesmo a indireta e anterior reivindicação de igualdade entre
negros e brancos em espaço "colonial" eram questões de ordem, não me parece
inoportuno um verso da orelha em que o conotado autor se autorreferencie, na
terceira pessoa, como "nosso homem é bípede racional." Talvez consciente da
hierarquia que frontalmente atingia as pessoas não brancas, na "metrópole"
ou fora dela, e dos consequentes processos de reificação e animalização a que
as pessoas negras eram submetidas em solo colonial, Cruz ousasse afirmar-se
homem, bípede e racional. "Ousadia," talvez; dizer possível, com certeza, já que
o livro vem a público num momento em que a empresa censória no Portugal
caetanista seguia a passos largos. Daí que o excessivo investimento no lado poético da orelha de *Açafate de Floremas* resulte numa espécie de burla aos discursos de carater diferenciador e falsamente igualitários, resultante das lógicas

lusotropicalistas e miscigenatórias adotadas pelo discurso colonial português como forma de "apaziguar" e minimizar as diferenças, fosse dentro ou fora do território europeu (Lourenço 2014).

"Onde nasceu? De raça mestiça, em Lisboa" (Cruz 1971, 4ª. Capa) ressoa, certo modo, no que Eduardo Lourenço declarará sobre a produção dos mitos acerca da empreitada colonial portuguesa: "*o ideal da miscigenação (mais a mais invocado pelo colonizador) não é outra coisa que a expressão máxima do Colonialismo traduzida sob o plano do sexo*" (2014, 55 – sublinhado do autor). E Cruz encontra eco no filósofo, justamente porque à consciência mestiça subjaz, evidentemente, a percepção objetiva da diferença, fenotipicamente marcada na pele negra, reproduzida no retrato do poeta encimando a mesma orelha que agora comento. Marcar-se textualmente como *mestiço* – signo à altura ideologicamente positivo – e em imagem mostrar-se *negro* talvez fosse uma estratégia utilizada por Cruz como forma de construção identitária procedida desde uma dialética transversal. Ou seja, visivelmente negro, não podendo afirmar-se como tal, mas incluindo-se na "casta do negro" (31), sobretudo porque era, ele mesmo, resultado de uma política assumida pelo colonialismo português, Cruz lança mão das possibilidades enunciativas vigentes para demonstrar-se identitariamente diverso daquilo que diz.

Acerca dessa minimização de diferenças etnicorraciais – largamente utilizada como estratégia de embranquecimento, diga-se – que no fim só acirrava as diferenças, produzindo ainda mais racismo, ao continuar seu comentário sobre a "mitologia colonial portuguesa," Eduardo Lourenço enfatiza que "uma qualquer forma de superior humanização [a mestiçagem, no caso] é simples 'racismo' às avessas" (Lourenço 2014, 55). Se visto em relação à orelha, o poema "Lotação Esgotada," aqui já referido, talvez nos forneça índices que favoreçam a inclusão do poeta António Cruz dentre a lista prévia que constitui o *corpus* afroportuguês de que aqui trato: consciência de si como pessoa afrodescendente que produz literatura; contextualização (ainda que indireta) de um cenário português no qual esse afroprodutor se inseriria; recorrência ou busca por uma afirmação identitária de recorte étnico-racial no espaço expressivo da literatura portuguesa.

A despeito dos comentários de Lourenço sobre as políticas miscigenatórias portuguesas, ou melhor, sobre sua "mitologia" contraditória, posto que visando integrar, produziria racismo e preconceitos, o poema "Preto: 'ser ou não ser'...", de António Cruz (1971, 31-34), se denota como contraface estética do exercício filosófico posterior. Partindo da clássica frase shakespeariana, o poema, desde seu título, já impõe um campo polissêmico, uma vez que, como se verá no correr do texto, sobretudo nos momentos em que o enunciador explicita as diferenças minimizadoras que as pessoas brancas impõem às pessoas, não se trata apenas de ser ou não ser negro, mas de sugerir uma discussão ontológica em torno do fato de que o negro – quando visto desde as perspectivas racistas e preconceituosas – não é tido como um ser em particular, mas como um objeto animalizado ou subumano. A esse respeito, Franz Fanon, em *Peles Negras, Máscaras Brancas*, nos sugere perguntas e respostas que parecem dialogar com o poema de Cruz: "Que quer o homem? Que quer o homem negro? . . . O negro quer ser branco" (Fanon 1983, 29). Não se trata aqui apenas de referências aos mecanismos assimilatórios do aparato colonial, mas de levar em conta o jogo identitário e de solapamento das identidades, vividos pelas pessoas negras que, obviamente – como o primeiro verso do poema de Cruz indicará –, em algum momento tenham imaginado para si outra condição racial, menos carregada de estigmas, menos violentada, menos minimizada:

> De modo sincero, gostaria que – depois da leitura do desabafo contidas nas páginas que ides ler – aquelas em que falo das pessoas como eu, genérica e discutivelmente designadas por "pessoas de cor" – a seguir, ou mais depressa nascesse em muitos de vós (já que não em todos – o desejo de amardes o "preto próximo" como a vós mesmos.
> – Oxalá!
> (Cruz 1971, 31)[7]

Novamente recorrendo ao princípio do "pacto de leitura" como forma de mobilizar sua recepção/seu leitor, o poeta-autor apresenta uma nota introdutória ao poema, que tanto pode ser vista como epígrafe quanto como o estabelecimento de condições prévias na construção do sentido do texto, uma vez que aparece destacada, abaixo do título e em formatação distinta do resto do poema; além, claro, de tratar-se caracteristicamente de um texto em prosa. O tom rogatório, que parafraseia as orações cristãs, parece querer mobilizar a instância leitora para o reconhecimento de uma alteridade no qual o enunciador, conotado autor, também se inclui metalinguisticamente pelo uso da primeira pessoa.

A sequência enunciativa do poema começa com a referência a uma máxima popular, "Não sei se seria franco/dizendo que não queria ser franco" (31), e, até pelo menos a metade do poema, o enunciador parece oscilar entre assumir-se como "casta do negro" e "querer mudar de cor." Ele conduz o leitor por entre as diversas tensões e conflitos – subjetivos e objetivos – enfrentados pelas pessoas "de cor" (33), inclusive o fato de ver a sua condição humana continuamente questionada, já que "negro – um homem que sê-lo não basta." E ao exercício do "defeito de cor" sucede-se uma construção identitária referenciada por expressões adjetivas tais como "tragicamente morenos," "perpétua escuridão," "destino adverso," dentre outras que se vão construindo como justificativa ao primeiro verso e ao desejo oscilante de mudar a cor de sua pele. A isto se soma a consciência da coisificação e da espetacularização da pessoa negra, particularmente descritas na forma como o enunciador se sente em relação às demais pessoas brancas, "que nos olha de soslaio . . ./ao ver-nos em certos locais sentados..." (33), de quem percebe não estar em condições de igualdade:

> porque ao negro, ao preto, ao mulato
> – se bem que em sentido abstrato –
> não baste ser homem ou mulher,
> para ser idêntico a qualquer;
> não, eles têm algo de mais ou de menos
> são escuros, tragicamente morenos!
> (Cruz 1971, 31)

A hipótese de Eduardo Lourenço (2014), ao chamar *mitológica* toda a política integracionista e assimilacionista posta em prática nos anos do governo Salazar, em particular aquelas cuja matriz foi o pensamento lusotropical/apaziguador de Gilberto Freyre, parece se comprovar: o enunciador do poema enfatiza o estatuto da desigualdade, incluindo neste processo, inclusive, aqueles que podem ser tomados por mais claros – os mulatos –, dando a ver, indiretamente, o fato de que só há um patamar na hierarquia, justamente aquele ocupado pelas pessoas brancas que "me olham com insistência/ não para mim, mas para a minha cor" (33). Se em "Lotação esgotada" o enunciador dava a entender alguma consciência, no poema em tela assume-se a completa desalienação tanto cultural quanto racial, potencializada pelo fato de que se percebe como sujeito marcado pela diferença, seja ao autodeclarar-se negro, rejeitando a assimilação branca, seja pelo branco que o lembra constantemente da cor de sua pele.

A esse respeito, ainda em 1977, Manuel Ferreira, no artigo "Da Dor de Ser Negro ao Orgulho de Ser Preto," ao referir-se à construção da identidade negra na poesia africana de Língua Portuguesa dos séculos XIX e XX, versará a respeito da tensão entre os universos negro e branco que se traduzia naquela poesia. Sobretudo, pontua o fato de que, em boa parte da produção poética da segunda metade do XIX, o embate entre eu e o mundo e de viés romântico se revelará na oposição cromática entre os universos e padrões europeizados que habitavam a imaginação literária daqueles primeiros poetas e uma realidade poética nativista. Os referenciais dessa realidade eram negros e vistos sempre em gradiente menorizado, que dizia respeito tanto às coisas próprias das colônias quanto ao tom da pele, fosse do enunciador fosse da mulher muitas vezes descrita, redundando, obviamente, num sentido de "inferioridade racial" (Ferreira 1977, 21-22).

O *pantone*[8] racial de Cruz, entretanto – e a despeito do título algo interrogativo do poema –, opera em outra escala, ao, por exemplo, reconhecer que é o *outro* quem produz hierarquias, não as pessoas negras, que são inferiorizadas e não inferiores. É também nesse *outro* do discurso onde se localiza o motivo da desigualdade racial, cultural e social que veem no negro "um somatório de defeitos" (Cruz 1971, 33). O "destino adverso" que este poeta relaciona à experiência negra não é, neste diapasão, uma questão para os negros, mas para os brancos, ainda que os primeiros sofram do preconceito "de quem passa lá fora na rua/ e pensa que não sendo minha pele igual a sua / . . . há que afastar o negro da sociedade" (32).

É de se ressaltar que há, nos poemas de Cruz comentados aqui, uma nomenclatura racial indiferenciada: preto e negro referem-se ao mesmo componente identitário, sem a tensão que mais contemporaneamente se observa em relação ao primeiro termo, relacionado ao passado colonial e à forma como os brancos colonos em África se referiam aos nativos.[9] Entretanto, quando se diz respeito ao mulato/mestiço, a laçada relativa à "bivalência racial" (Ferreira 1977, 25) não acontece, já que os estigmas apontados nos poemas são os mesmos, não importando aí a tonalidade da pele, do que se infere que o discurso subjacente ao poema opera-se nos pares dicotômicos (ou antagônicos) branco e negro/ preto. O ponto de interesse nesse quesito reside no fato de que, embora em sua "orelha" o poeta se autorreferencie como pertencente a uma "raça mestiça," no correr do poema "Preto: Ser ou não Ser...," o enunciador se caracterize como "preto," demonstrando com isso que, embora assuma uma deriva em termos das formas de autorreferenciação, se percebe no âmbito da diferença marcada pela cor da pele.

NOTAS

1. Este artigo é parte dos resultados alcançados na investigação "Interseccionalidades e Teoria *Queer*: a produção estética contemporânea, outros sujeitos e novos sentidos," realizada entre abril e setembro de 2018, com financiamento da Fundação de Amparo à Pesquisa do Estado de São Paulo (FAPESP) e do Conselho Nacional de Pesquisa (CNPq).

2. O exemplar de *Açafate de Floremas* foi adquirido da pesquisadora e livreira Raja Litwinoff, figura recorrente em eventos culturais ligados aos afrodescendentes, alfarrabista suíça que também administra as páginas *Literaturas Afrikanas*, tanto na plataforma Blogspot quanto no Facebook. Consta no exemplar, em caligrafia do próprio autor, a seguinte dedicatória: "Ao Armando Duarte – Que mal me parecia ao fim de tantos anos ainda te não dedicasse algumas palavras que mais nos que mais nos emocionam como colegas e amigos. Teu – António Cruz – 22.09.71."

3. Manteve-se a organização espacial do poema, conforme o original.

4. A respeito das zonas de ocupação eminentemente negra, consultar: (a) *A Cidade entre Bairros*, trabalho coordenado por Maria Manuela Mendes, Teresa Sá, José Luís Crespo e Carlos Henriques Ferreira, publicado pelo Centro de Investigação em Arquitetura, Urbanismo e Design, em 2012; e (b) *Os Africanos em Portugal – História e Memória – Séculos XV-XXI* [catálogo de exposição, 2011], de autoria de Isabel Castro Henriques e produzido no âmbito do projeto UNESCO "Rotas da Escravidão."

5. Embora a palavra "imigrante" possa querer reportar à chegada no espaço lisboeta de pessoas não pertencentes às antigas colônias, o termo também as inclui, o que gera uma lógica de não pertença no que diz respeito aos cidadãos portugueses – sobretudo negros – vindos dos antigos territórios africanos.

6. Hendel, Richard, *O Design do Livro* (São Paulo: Ateliê Editorial, 2003).

7. Como a leitura do excerto, atenta ou não, poderá comprovar, o poeta faz uso de recursos gráficos e de pontuação de maneira pouco usual, como por exemplo o travessão dentro de outro travessão ou o uso de um só parênteses aberto, o que interfere na progressão sintática da nota introdutória ao poema, sem no entanto comprometer-lhe o sentido.

8. Sistema de cores referência adotado pelas artes gráficas, pela moda etc.

9. A esse respeito, cabe referência aos *Cadernos de Memórias Coloniais*, de Isabela Figueiredo (2010), onde bem se observa o valor que o termo "preto" revelava em contextos de colonização portuguesa.

REFERÊNCIAS BIBLIOGRÁFICAS

Cruz, António. 1971. *Açafate de Floremas*. Lisboa: Edição do autor.

Deleuze, Gilles e Guatatari. 1977. *Kafka: Por uma Literatura Menor*. Rio de Janeiro: Imago.

Fanon, Franz. 1983. "O Negro e a Linguagem". In *Peles Negras, Máscaras Brancas*, 17-36. Rio de Janeiro: Fator.

Ferreira, Manuel. 1977. "Da Dor de Ser Negro ao Orgulho de Ser Preto." *Colóquio Letras*, 17-29. Lisboa: Fundação Calouste Gulbenkian.

Figueiredo, Isabela. 2009. *Cadernos de Memórias Coloniais*. Coimbra: Angelus Novus.

Foucault, Michel. 1979. "Nietzsche, a Genealogia e a História." In *Microfísica do Poder*, 15-38. Rio de Janeiro: Graal.

Hall, Stuart. 2003. "Que Negro É Esse na Cultura Negra?" In *Da Diáspora: Identidades e Mediações Culturais*, 335-52. Belo Horizonte: Editora UFMG.

Hatherly, Ana. 2003. "Poemas em *Língua de Preto* dos Séculos XVII e XVIII". In *Poesia Incurável*, 211-238. Lisboa: Editorial Estampa.

Lourenço, Eduardo. 2014. "Do Colonialismo como Nosso Impensado." In *Do Colonialismo como Nosso Impensado*. Lisboa: Gradiva.

Vala, Jorge; Rodrigo Brito e Lopes Diniz. 2015. *Expressões dos Racismos em Portugal*. Lisboa: ICS / Imprensa de Ciências Sociais.

Williams, Raymond. 2000. "Com Vistas a uma Sociologia Da Cultura." In *Cultura*, 9-32. São Paulo: Paz e Terra.

EMERSON INÁCIO é Professor Associado da área de Estudos Comparados de Literaturas de Língua Portuguesa da Faculdade de Filosofia, Letras e Ciências Humanas da Universidade de São Paulo (FFLCH/USP) e bolsista de produtividade em pesquisa nível 2 do CNPq.

O Sentimento de um(a) Ocidental Declinado no Feminino[1]

L'héritage n'est jamais un donné, c'est toujours une tâche.
Avant même de vouloir l'héritage ou de le refuser, nous sommes des héritiers endeuillés.
Jacques Derrida

RESUMO: Este artigo aborda o trabalho literário inicial de três mulheres afrodescendentes portuguesas perseguindo as suas buscas identitárias entre Portugal e as histórias familiares antigas que as ligam a Angola e a Cabo Verde. Em análise estão as obras de Djaimilia Pereira de Almeida, *Esse Cabelo* (2015), de Tvon, *Um Preto muito Português* (2017) e de Yara Monteiro, *Essa Dama Bate Bué* (2018).

PALAVRAS- CHAVE: afrodescendência, literatura, mulheres, Portugal.

ABSTRACT: This article discusses the initial literary work of three Portuguese women of African descent, and their pursuit for identity between Portugal and their old family histories that link them to Angola and Cape Verde. Under analysis are the works of Djaimilia Pereira de Almeida, *Esse Cabelo* (2015), Tvon, *Um Preto Português* (2017) and Yara Monteiro, *Essa Dama Bate Bué* (2018).

KEYWORDS: Afro-descent, literature, women, Portugal

A Abrir

O fim dos impérios ultramarinos europeus – com processos de descolonização muitas vezes pautados por conflitos armados e insurreições – foi trazendo para a Europa ao longo das décadas de 1960, 70 e 80 importantes fluxos populacionais, num processo marcado por deslocações, ambiguidades e integração, mas também fraturas, exclusões, segregação, invisibilidade, trauma e novas e complexas identidades: repatriados, *pieds noirs*, retornados, ex-combatentes das guerras coloniais, ex-colonizadores, ex-colonizados, refugiados. Desde então, tem-se vindo a assistir à emergência e afirmação de uma performance artística marcante nas artes visuais, perfomativas, cinema, música, dança e literatura, protagonizada não apenas pela geração que viveu os eventos, e que deu, na maioria dos casos, um testemunho traumatizado deste regresso ou desta desterritorialização, mas também pela geração dos filhos destes antigos impérios. Estes, ao mesmo tempo que reinterrogam a situação de rutura que viveram como crianças ou que já nem viveram, por terem nascido depois, também procuram genuinamente conhecer uma história outra, relativa às origens dos seus pais, e, como eles, do seu país.

Como se deu a transferência de memória intergeracional relativamente ao processo do final do colonialismo europeu? Como é que esta memória se manifesta social e culturalmente hoje na Europa? Qual é o impacto dessa memória, muitas vezes latente, na Europa dos dias de hoje? *Memoirs – Filhos de Império e Pós-memórias Europeias* é um projeto de investigação do Centro de Estudos Sociais da Universidade de Coimbra, financiado pelo Conselho Europeu de Investigação, em que analisamos a presença destas memórias – ou melhor, pós-memórias – de lastro colonial, seja na experiência quotidiana dos cidadãos, seja através das múltiplas e diversas narrativas elaboradas nos campos da literatura, cinema, música, artes performativas e artes visuais, explorando os conceitos de herança, memória e pós-memória. A sua dimensão comparativa entre Portugal, França e Bélgica – onde ecoam memórias de Angola, Moçambique, Guiné Bissau, São Tomé e Príncipe, Cabo Verde, Argélia e Congo – permite-nos olhar as gerações seguintes numa proporção não apenas portuguesa, mas europeia. Ou seja, o âmago do projeto é o campo de batalha mais delicado e incerto do destino europeu.

Situarei a minha reflexão em Portugal na análise da literatura recentemente produzida por mulheres afrodescendentes negras. Numa época em que as associações se manifestam e organizam as suas agendas, os romances sucedem-se, Marlene Freitas Monteiro extravasa completamente as fronteiras de Portugal ou de Cabo Verde para se afirmar como uma estrela da dança europeia (facto confirmado pelo Leão de Prata da Bienal de Veneza), e o Teatro Griot mantém o seu excelente reportório. Nas artes visuais, Francisco Vidal e Délio Jasse, entre outros, afirmam-se como artistas internacionais, e surgem as primeiras longa metragens, como o *Canto do Ossobá* (2017), de Siles Tiny, ou *Djon África* (2017), de João Miller Guerra e Filipa Reis, em que os protagonistas partem, à semelhança do que acontece com algumas personagens da literatura, real ou metaforicamente, para espaços africanos anteriormente colonizados à procura da (sua) história.

Estes são os filhos dos anos 1990, em que Portugal exibia para si e para o mundo a Expo 98, com a sua mitologia universalista baseada na aventura marítima portuguesa, e com um enorme impacto pela dimensão, meios envolvidos, cosmopolitismo e programação, combinada com os vários episódios de comemoração destas mesmas "Descobertas," lideradas pela Comissão Nacional para as Comemorações dos Descobrimentos Portugueses, como fica visível no lema que a lançou: "os oceanos – uma herança para o futuro." Como hoje nos é possível ver, este foi um dos momentos iniciais do pós-colonialismo português, o momento em que nos confrontamos com a surpresa nacional sobre a reação dos países anteriormente colonizados por Portugal a estas propostas comemorativas. O Brasil, Angola, Moçambique, Guiné-Bissau, S. Tomé e Príncipe ou Goa não aderiram entusiasticamente às comemorações dos "Descobrimentos," iniciadas em 1998, com a celebração da descoberta do caminho marítimo para à Índia, desenvolvidas pela Comissão Nacional para as Comemorações dos Descobrimentos Portugueses. Recordemos o momento em que Portugal, e com ele o Ocidente, quis comemorar a chegada dos portugueses à India, celebrada por Luís de Camões em *Os Lusíadas*, e os indianos mostraram outras fontes historiográficas – vejamos, por exemplo, o incómodo que causou o livro de Sanjay Subrahmanyam, *The Career and Legend of Vasco da Gama* (1997) – e as outras visões dessa chegada; em que quis comemorar as aportagens ao longo da costa africana e não havia muito a celebrar; em que quis homenagear Pedro Álvares Cabral e Colombo e os cinco séculos da sua descoberta da América e, como bem viu Eduardo Lourenço, a América quis "matar Colombo," não apenas pela mão daqueles que a chegada de Colombo exterminou, mas também por aqueles que a aventura de Colombo transladou de África para a América, e até da Europa para o Novo Mundo (Lourenço 2014, 337-338). Como advertiu o ensaísta em "A morte de Colombo," não se tratava do fim da História, mas de uma mudança da ordem da História e do fim do Ocidente como mito, ou seja, como a luz do mundo que julgava ser quando chegou às terras de Porto Seguro, no Brasil (Lourenço 2005, 16).[2] Tratava-se da emergência de outras narrativas protagonizadas e vocalizadas por outros sujeitos etno-culturais, senhores de outros arquivos e outras memórias de uma história aparentemente comum. Como claramente disse o líder indígena Ailton Krenak, quando foi convidado para participar nestas comemorações em Portugal: "Essa é uma festa portuguesa, vocês vão celebrar a invasão do meu canto do mundo. Não vou." (Krenak 2019, 9-10).

Foi sobre estes filhos e, em particular, sobre *Os Filhos de África*, que Neuza Gusmão publicou o estudo *Os Filhos da África em Portugal: Antropologia, Multiculturalidade e Educação* (2007), onde abordava a presença da segunda geração de imigrantes africanos em Portugal. Neste grupo é a condição étnica que sobressai como elemento diferenciador, observada pela autora em dois palcos: o bairro e a escola, que seriam os palcos da sociedade seguinte, ou seja, daqueles que são hoje os produtores culturais e os sujeitos politicamente ativos, que acima nomeei. Esta presença ganhou em Portugal uma dimensão cosmopolita, dialógica e formativa, em alguns nichos de reflexão académica e com diferentes intensidades: desde as reflexões matriciais de Eduardo Lourenço sobre Portugal e a Europa[3] aos ensaios de Boaventura de Sousa Santos (1994); desde os ensaios de autores africanos protagonizados pelos estudos das designadas literaturas africanas de língua portuguesa às investigações de caráter histórico, sociológico e político levadas a cabo por uma nova geração de historiadores, iniciada pela publicação, em 1998, dos cinco volumes da *História da Expansão Portuguesa*, organizados por Francisco Bethencourt e Kirti N. Chaudhuri (1998); desde o trabalho de centros de investigação como o Centro de Estudos Sociais da Universidade de Coimbra, o Instituto de História Contemporânea da Universidade Nova de Lisboa, o Instituto de Ciências Sociais, entre outros, à insinuante e muito recente presença nos media destas questões, onde se destacaria o trabalho militante de Joana Gorjão. Surgem ainda, por esta época, os primeiros romances que abordam de forma ficcional as dores e os fantasmas da questão africana para além das memórias da Guerra Colonial – de que poderia destacar *Partes de África*, de Helder Macedo (1991), *O Esplendor de Portugal*, de António Lobo Antunes (1997), e *A Verdade de Chindo Luz*, de Joaquim Arena (2005). Na cena musical, essencialmente lisboeta, começam a ser ouvidas outras vozes e outros ritmos, e Rogério de Carvalho afirma-se como encenador português negro. Mas foi sobretudo na dimensão crítica e criativa trazida pelo programa *Próximo Futuro*, da Fundação Calouste Gulbenkian, com coordenação geral de António Pinto Ribeiro, que o debate sobre o pós-colonial português se alargou para outros públicos e a presença da emergência criativa do Sul ganhou visibilidade. Alguns programas desta Fundação vinham abrindo este caminho e colocando determinados temas na agenda da programação portuguesa, como em *O Estado do Mundo e Distância e Proximidade*. Contudo, é com *Próximo Futuro*[4] que a escala da criação contemporânea dessas outras geografias do Sul, outrora colonizadas, desembarca em Portugal, trazendo o debate sobre o pós-colonial e dando a possibilidade de formação de jovens artistas portugueses e africanos rumo a um futuro europeu e cosmopolita. São eles que hoje compõem, em grande parte, a cena artística portuguesa relacionada com o que podemos designar genericamente, e de forma muito heterogénea, de uma pós-memória colonial de referência africana.

É, portanto, neste tempo que é o nosso, e que é já um tempo de trânsito, como escreveu Roberto Vecchi, entre as testemunhas – aqueles que protagonizaram os acontecimentos que levaram ao fim do colonialismo – e um tempo das gerações seguintes, que se situam as criações artísticas que analisamos no projeto *Memoirs*, acima referido. Este é um "tempo de extrema delicadeza em que as relações privadas são políticas" (Vecchi 2018, 18), em que a intensidade da passagem de testemunho para as gerações seguintes é grande, combinada com uma procura destas mesmas gerações sobre um passado que explique o contemporâneo privado e público. Por isso, podemos considerá-lo já um tempo de herdeiros, "em que as narrações, os documentos, os restos do passado constroem uma dupla monumentalidade: uma pessoal na dimensão privada familiar, uma outra pública a partir de um contrato historiográfico" (Vecchi 2018, 18) e social.

Este é o gesto das três mulheres escritoras que apresento – Djaimilia Pereira de Almeida, com *Esse Cabelo*, sobre o qual muito se escreveu; *Um Preto muito Português*, de Tvon, que é o nome artístico de Telma Escórcio da Silva; e Yara Monteiro, com *Essa Dama Bate Bué*. Três livros de mulheres, de lastro biográfico – ou em que a intensidade da experiência vivida pelas autoras se reflete nas suas criações –, mas sobretudo ficções de identificação de um sujeito num tempo e num espaço, no sentido do que Jennifer A. Gonzaléz cunhou de "autotopografia" (1995), ou seja, a identificação de um sujeito, não apenas a partir de um sentido temporal próprio da biografia, mas também a partir dos espaços reais e simbólicos, que o compõem e fizeram. Neste aspeto, estas ficções articulam-se com um outro conceito importante para a sua leitura – o conceito de pós-memória criado por Marianne Hirsch, no seu livro *Family Frames* (1997), no âmbito dos estudos da memória e, mais especificamente, de segunda geração do Holocausto. Nas palavras de Marianne Hirch, de acordo com a tradução de António Sousa Ribeiro, a pós-memória aponta "para a relação da segunda geração com experiências marcantes, muitas vezes traumáticas, que são anteriores ao seu nascimento, mas que, não obstante, lhes foram transmitidas de modo tão profundo que parecem constituir memórias em si mesmas" (Hirsch 2008, 104).[5] A pós-memória surge, assim, como uma "herança" direta ou indireta de uma experiência traumática que, ainda que vivida por outro, teve reflexo na esfera privada ou familiar e, portanto, pode ser assumida como um legado explícito ou mediado e pode ser reelaborada. Marcada pela distância geracional e pela imaginação exercitada a partir dos rastos deixados, que podem ser narrativas, palavras, fotografias, casas e espaços significativos, e situações temporal e espacialmente distantes, a pós-memória não coincide, portanto, com a memória pessoal – ligada à experiência e à titularidade do testemunho – mas funciona, na sua condição de "não-experimentado," como uma memória do "quase" ou do "como se," como refere Rafaella di Castro falando da memória de terceira geração do Holocausto (Di Castro 2008). É um tipo de memória constitutiva, movida pela necessidade de compreender, e que alimenta o gesto das gerações seguintes, na procura de tomar conhecimento das situações e dos contextos que estiveram na sua origem.

A crítica argentina Beatriz Sarlo, não adotando a formulação de Hirsch e criticando a sua noção de transmissão linear, acaba por densificar o conceito, ao pensá-lo à luz das heranças das ditaduras latino-americanas, sublinhando o investimento que as gerações seguintes optam conscientemente por fazer relativamente à tomada de conhecimento de factos que as precederam (Sarlo 2007, 90-113). A pós-memória enquanto ação afasta-se da operação historiográfica pela dimensão subjetiva e emocional que a enforma, ligada ao ambiente familiar, ao mesmo tempo que questiona a macro-história no quanto ela se interceta com a micro-história. Talvez por isso, os discursos e as práticas artísticas se tornam o terreno particularmente propício para a sua expressão, sobretudo numa época de *selfies* em que o retratado e o fotógrafo coincidem, em que o narrador e protagonista também podem coincidir. Esta é a situação das autoras e das protagonistas das obras que pretendo ler e, por isso, proponho, dentro da linha do referido projeto *Memoirs*, a migração do conceito para a análise de contextos pós--coloniais que estas obras tematizam (Ribeiro e Ribeiro 2018, 277-8).

Leituras

As três obras que proponho para leitura foram publicadas entre 2015 e 2018, escritas por jovens escritoras, e seguem tipologias narrativas diferentes. Mais próximo de um registo autobiográfico, o livro de Djaimilia Pereira de Almeida, *Esse Cabelo*; de transposição para uma personagem masculina das interrogações interiores (e exteriores) dos jovens negros portugueses, no caso de Tvon, em *Um Preto Muito Português*; e de considerável elaboração narrativa e ficcional, no romance de Yara Monteiro, *Essa Dama Bate Bué*. Une-os a referenciação afrodescendente negra portuguesa das personagens, as referências à sua cidadania portuguesa e a outros territórios, anteriormente colonizados e, portanto, a outros tempos em que se iniciaram as histórias das famílias das personagens. Desta combinação entre a temporalidade, espaço e memória ou pós-memória, como acima referi, nasce a operação política que estes livros propõem: ao mesmo tempo que olham para o lado objetivo, público, de histórias atravessadas pelo colonialismo português, vão ao encontro da subjetividade do privado, através da imaginação da vida das famílias permeada pela história recente destes países.

O livro de Djaimilia Pereira de Almeida, *Esse Cabelo*, ensaia um questionamento sobre as heranças, objetivas e subjetivas, do processo colonial português que cruza a história de vários países. Filha de mãe angolana negra e de pai branco filho de colonos, primeiro em Moçambique, depois em Angola, Almeida abandona Luanda com três anos e cresce em Portugal numa família branca,[6] a sua do lado paterno, em que o seu corpo, absolutizado no cabelo da protagonista, é a marca dessa história anterior da família, como acontece com a personagem principal do romance, que procura identificar uma pessoa que vive entre dois mundos, duas cores de pele, duas cidades.

> A verdade é que a história do meu cabelo crespo cruza a história de pelo menos dois países e, paranoicamente, a história indireta da relação entre vários continentes. . . . Cheguei a Portugal em oitenta e cinco, vinda de Angola. O meu pai precedera-me em um ano regressando para um novo emprego. Fora no final de setenta em Luanda, com pouco mais de vinte anos, que conhecera a minha mãe. Quando eu for a última testemunha, e já não me lembrar se foi nos correios, no consulado, na televisão, se na praia, que os meus pais se conheceram, os meus netos consolar-se-ão com o livro deixado. (Almeida 2015, 58)

Ao longo do romance, Mila associa lembranças dos seus "traumáticos" penteados com memórias da sua infância, vivida em Lisboa com os avós, e as visitas à sua mãe em Luanda. Romance-reflexão ou inicial ensaio sobre uma identidade em questionamento centralizado no corpo e, em particular, na "personagem cabelo," esta é uma procura do lugar deste corpo numa sociedade europeia maioritariamente branca. A tentativa de resposta à pergunta "de onde vim?" não vem de fora, como no caso do protagonista de *Um Preto muito Português*, de Tvon, mas do interior de si mesma. *Esse Cabelo* é uma audaciosa desconstrução de clichés, interrogando-os de frente a partir da experiência, mas sem entrar nas esperadas leituras que associariam de forma programática raça, género e exclusão. Almeida vai muito além disso – como aliás confirma no seu segundo romance, *Luanda, Lisboa, Paraíso* (2018) –, sendo que uma leitura crítica interseccional que combine essas categorias seria bem-vinda para os seus livros (Collins, Bilge 2016, 131-35).

A trajectória que Mila realiza, a partir da sua biografia e dos espaços que a compõem, torna-se simultaneamente um percurso de tomada de consciência política da sua história e do seu corpo – um "going b(l)ack," como poderíamos dizer em inglês – que epitomiza o processo central de *Esse Cabelo*, ou seja, o da tomada de consciência e da assunção da sua condição, não apenas do seu cabelo, finalmente assumido, mas da consciência histórica da sua escolha. Yara Monteiro, autora de *Essa Dama Bate Bué*, mostra este propósito explicitamente, numa entrevista recente dada à jornalista Joana Gorjão Henriques, ao jornal *Público*: "Eu sei onde me situar. Onde é que os outros me situam? Isto é mutável de acordo com a localização onde estou. Mas decidi que a minha identidade é negra" (Henriques 2019).

Parafraseando a experiência descrita por Stuart Hall em "Cultural Identity and Diaspora" (1994), que é a sua própria experiência de jamaicano negro no Reino Unido, é neste momento que a protagonista se descobre negra num meio maioritariamente branco e filha de uma história colonial. Descobre-o diretamente através da sua vivência quotidiana, mas sobretudo indiretamente, ou seja, mediada pelo impacto das narrativas privadas e públicas e pelas lutas que conduziram ao tempo pós-colonial que vivemos. Estas são também as linhas que orientam os recentes livros de Yara Monteiro, de considerável elaboração narrativa, e de Tvon, autora de *Um Preto Muito Português*, ambos publicados em 2018. Trata-se de duas propostas narrativas muito diferentes, unidas pela reclamação da história, a partir de uma busca identitária familiar.

> Sou filho de cabo-verdianos que há muito residem em Portugal. Sou neto de cabo-verdianos que nunca conheceram Portugal. Sou bisneto de holandeses que mal conheceram Portugal. Sou bisneto de africanas que muito ouviram falar de Portugal.
>
> E donde sou eu? Eu até sou nascido em Lisboa mas sou tão tido como estrangeiro. Não por minha opção, no princípio mas depois com o tempo, com as pessoas, apercebi-me de que era um dos inúmeros lisboetas não considerados alfacinhas. O meu nome é João mas eu conheço-me como Budjurra, ainda que este não esteja no meu BI Amarelo, esse documento que me foi tão difícil obter. (Tvon 2018, 5)

Ensaiar uma resposta à recorrente pergunta – de onde és? –, tão frequentemente dirigida a portugueses negros, é o que leva Budjurra, a personagem principal de *Um Preto muito Português*, a elaborar a narrativa que compõe este livro. Convocando a sua herança familiar – a história dos seus pais e avós – e um lugar – a periferia de Lisboa, o "ghetto" onde habita (assim designado na visão dos outros) –, Budjurra fornece ao leitor as suas coordenadas e as coordenadas de leitura do seu romance-reflexão. Assim, a partir deste lugar de fala, vai produzir uma primeira auto-identificação a dois níveis: a um primeiro nível, uma auto-identificação com uma dimensão temporal, cronológica, como são todas as "autobiografias"; e uma auto-identificação com uma dimensão espacial – ou uma "autotopografia," recorrendo aqui ao conceito de Jennifer A. González já evocado – traçada entre Portugal e o seu bairro de pertença e espaços das antigas colónias portuguesas africanas com as quais a sua família tem relação, no caso Cabo Verde. A um segundo nível, esta auto-identificação configura-se como relacional, ou seja, é produzida em diálogo explícito ou implícito, com potenciais interlocutores em que o preconceito centraliza o modo de receção. Budjurra elabora os seus pensamentos sobre este olhar, enquadrando-os nas ansiedades e dúvidas de uma adolescência tardia, e numa linguagem que estabelece um diálogo com o leitor, ora numa versão mais introspetiva de monólogo interior, ora mais comunicativa, que procura outras linguagens, entre as quais a poesia e o rap. Assim se estabelecem os protocolos de apresentação destes portugueses "afilhados desta Terra" (Tvon 2018, 45), ou seja, de alguém pertencente a uma minoria, cujo corpo/cor chega antes de si próprio e que, nas interações que traça, vai descobrindo uma história outra que explica os efeitos do ser e estar colonial transmitidos para as gerações seguintes.

Budjurra é um jovem negro português, filho de caboverdianos que emigraram para Portugal. Tem uma irmã revoltada, que adora dar-se com brancos, e um irmão mais velho amante de rap e da vida noturna lisboeta, cujos amigos são negros. Budjurra cresceu nos bairros periféricos, imaginando uma África onde nunca foi como uma "árvore-casa" (Tvon 2018, 137). Foi o único da família que frequentou a universidade e declara-se como um "viciado em pensar e analisar todas estas questões de identidade que nos atormentam, a nós pretos muito portugueses" (Tvon 2018, 122). Apesar de ter um curso superior, trabalha num *call center* e, no seu dia-a-dia, vai lidando com o racismo estrutural dos portugueses, até ser "batizado" com um contacto com *skinheads* e uma passagem pela esquadra da polícia. Este episódio confronta-o com a injustiça e o racismo para além do preconceito (episódio 41, "Os Suspeitos do Costume"), com a realidade de pertença a uma minoria étnica e com a permanência de uma posição de subalternidade que ecoa comportamentos e divisões sociais de matriz colonial. Ao mesmo tempo que sofre a injustiça e discriminação na sua terra, é confrontado com a ideia inerente à geração dos seus pais – o "regresso" a Cabo Verde – e que representa, de facto, a distância geracional. Regressar a onde? Para quê? Quem era ele afinal? De onde era ele afinal?

Um Preto Muito Português mostra-nos um certo mundo de afrodescendentes portugueses vivendo hoje as suas interrogações, os seus confrontos com uma sociedade que discrimina, tanto no dia-a-dia, de forma aparentemente inocente, como de forma ativa, através de grupos específicos de motivação racista e mesmo do Estado. Os temas levantados por estes questionamentos narrativos, aparentemente simples e a partir de personagens relativamente planas, implicam dois aspetos que me parecem muito relevantes: por um lado, o estranhamento, a discriminação ou o racismo manifesto no Portugal contemporâneo experienciado por estes sujeitos cuja cor de pele não é a da maioria da população portuguesa; por outro lado, e de forma mais institucional, constituem claras demandas sobre quem são (quem podem ser) os cidadãos e as cidadãs de Portugal contemporâneo e, num sentido mais lato, da Europa atual. Quem pode fazer parte da nação portuguesa pós-colonial e democrática? Quem pode ser europeu, como visualmente nos interpela o mosaico de fotos de identidade do artista visual Délio Jasse, no seu trabalho de 2010, significativamente intitulado *Schengen*?

A questão já há muito foi equacionada, mas a resposta foi sempre silenciada ou evasiva e adiada e, por isso, hoje, estas escritoras filhas das histórias imperiais alheias escrevem/inscrevem Portugal e África, reclamando uma identidade a partir do questionamento da história: uma história coletiva e uma história familiar que muitas vezes não foi transmitida, mas insinuada. Para estas escritoras, essa história passada numa imaginada "África" (Angola e Cabo Verde, nos casos em análise), de que sempre ouviram falar nas narrativas familiares, são já e apenas representações. Elas não têm a titularidade da experiência, nem são autoras do possível testemunho que configuraria a sua situação como de emigração ou de exílio (Mata 2018). São, contudo, herdeiras simbólicas de uma ferida aberta sobre a qual elaboram uma narrativa construída a partir de fragmentos de relatos da família, de histórias, discursos, retratos, e outros objetos do domínio privado, mas também de fragmentos retirados das narrativas públicas e, sobretudo, de muita imaginação. As imagens assim produzidas, envoltas em sentimentos e relações subjetivas, são a pós-memória.

Délio Jasse, *Schengen*, 2010. Gelatina de prata, 15 x 40 x 50 cm. Cortesia do artista.

A partir destas representações familiares e da imagem de uma mãe que a este universo africano se ligava com narrativas héroicas de guerrilheira da libertação em Angola, Vitória – a protagonista de *Essa Dama Bate Bué*, romance de estreia de Yara Monteiro – vai à procura das suas origens, saindo de Portugal, em fuga de um casamento *a priori* abortado. O tempo tinha chegado com as suas questões colocadas por Vitória sobre uma fotografia – a fotografia da sua mãe – e sobre uma série de fragmentárias narrativas transmitidas por mulheres da sua família que a ela se ligavam, ou que Vitória a ela ligava, e que a conduzem Angola, epicentro da história familiar da protagonista.

Em Luanda, a família que a acolhe, as pessoas e os hábitos são, simultaneamente, familiares e distantes. Só a meio da narrativa temos acesso à história da família ligada à antiga colónia, a partir do que Vitória saberia: o casamento do avô mestiço assimilado com a avó em Angola, o nascimento das suas filhas, a casa no Huambo, uma filha (a mãe de Vitória) que desafia a fidelidade portuguesa dos avós em tempos de libertação e que parte para a guerrilha, voltando para entregar a criança aos avós em fuga para Portugal, para de novo desaparecer nos trilhos da guerra e da utopia. Dela resta um nome, uma fotografia e o sentimento de abandono que perpassa Vitória. Tudo está envolto em silêncio ou numa fantasia própria das histórias de família em terras distantes e em imagens sépia. Vitória segue os rastos e os indícios que lhe vão apresentando uma história incompleta, feita de imagens e referências que se cruzam com a história entrelaçada de Portugal e de Angola, e a partir da qual as gerações seguintes constroem uma genealogia credível para si própria.

> O que acontece é que a memória familiar não é apenas de quem a viveu. Quem nasce a seguir carrega a biografia de quem chegou primeiro. Eu existo naquele passado, e a memória pertence-me. A Angola que conheço é a evocação das lembranças que não foram extintas pelo tempo. É a utopia da felicidade. É dessa Angola que a minha família tem saudades. (Monteiro 2018, 81-82)

A Angola que vai encontrar é outra, ainda que insinue sinais de uma vida oculta dos seus antepassados, a partir dos quais Vitória vai tecendo uma rede, primeiro com a inexperiência dos recém-chegados, até perceber o ritmo das coisas, as ocultações e os não ditos – em suma, os protocolos de apresentação gerados, mas nunca expressos –, num país martirizado pelo colonialismo e pelas suas heranças e pela guerra. Luanda é o lugar dos primeiros encontros, entre festas e velórios, desmesuras e desigualdades; é o lugar da casa de Romena, que a recebe, da consulta dos arquivos, das histórias difusas, do general Zacarias Vindu, de Georgina e de pistas e de rastos que conduzem Vitória ao Huambo, o centro da narrativa da vida da sua família e, provavelmente, onde a sua mãe teria ficado na luta. À medida que vai deambulando pela cidade, Vitória vai atualizando memórias ou pós-memórias – pois, na verdade, são apenas imagens e narrativas alheias que possui – que lhe permitem a identificação com o lugar, traçando uma "autotopografia" pós-memorial que lhe viabiliza respostas temporárias, precárias, mas respostas apesar de tudo, para a demanda que a tinha conduzido a Angola. De entre as ruínas que escondem as vidas que ficaram para trás, engolidas pela guerra, pela natureza, pelo abandono, emerge a voz de Juliana Tijamba, antiga guerrilheira e companheira da mãe de Vitória, um fantasma de um mundo melancólico por um sonho adiado pela guerra.

Pela voz cuidadosa mas total de mamã Ju, Juliana, Vitória vai tendo acesso ao que é a guerra e ao que foi aquela guerra e, com ela, ao início de si própria no mundo: "Conta que nos primeiros combates não se acredita na truculência da guerra. Vive-se a utopia, do sonho. Isso acontece até que se tenha de matar para não ser morto. Na guerra, matar não chega. É massacrar, torturar, mutilar e violar. . . . O propósito de mamã Ju não é chocá-la. É partilhar com ela a sua verdade" (Monteiro 2018, 154). E Juliana continua o seu testemunho, explica as causas, desvenda o sonho, narra o conflito que viveu com os seus pais negros assimilados, e sobretudo fala da guerra a partir da perspetiva feminina das mulheres guerrilheiras, vítimas também do machismo dos seus companheiros, tantas vezes humilhadas e violadas. É deste mundo que emerge a figura da mãe de Vitória – "Camarada Rosa Chitula, 'Dinamite a própria.' Era assim que se apresentava, com voz grossa de comando" (Monteiro 2018, 158), dizia Juliana, mas que, apesar da fama que lhe dava o nome, foi vítima de desrespeito e perseguição. Era uma mulher e uma mulher na guerra:[7]

> Nem todos respeitavam a tua mãe. Como era mulher sabes como é? O Palanca era um deles. Gostava de a humilhar.
> – Mas as mulheres também combatiam – admira-se Vitória com o comentário.
> – Mesmo assim. Achavam que éramos inferiores. (Monteiro 2018, 162)

Percebemos depois que Rosa Chitula estava sob ameaça e um dia disparou matando Palanca, que ambicionava deitar-se com ela. A ordem do comando era para a apanharem e matarem, mas as colegas deixaram-na fugir, até que Juliana a encontraria refugiada numa aldeia, magra, grávida e muito doente. Vitória nasceria apesar de tudo e seria entregue aos avós que vinham para Portugal na sequência da guerra civil em Angola. Mas mais haveria ainda para saber: Juliana tinha traído a sua mãe após a ter entregue ao tão respeitado como temido general Zacarias Vindu, que Vitória tinha encontrado em Luanda, e com quem combinava recitais de poesia. Ao ritmo de declamações poéticas, o poderoso e sinistro general teria torturado a sua mãe. Este é o trabalho de decifração reservado a Vitória, ou às gerações seguintes, desde que inicia a procura objetiva da sua mãe numa terra em que há sempre alguém à procura de um familiar, onde há sempre uma história por trás de outra história. E estas histórias ocultas de mulheres, tão pouco pronunciadas como gloriosas, mudaram Vitória. Pela narrativa de Juliana, a fotografia da mãe torna-se uma prova histórica da existência desta mulher, um elemento objetivo que entra em confronto ou complementaridade com um objeto subjetivo, que era esta fotografia para Vitória, e a partir da qual tinha construído uma narrativa íntima que, ao mesmo tempo que a reconfortava, a assombrava. Que cruzamento poderia Vitória fazer entre a narrativa contruída à volta daquela imagem – uma narrativa necessariamente "mítica," que como diria Hayden White, "pertence à categoria do que podemos chamar "o discurso do imaginário" ou o "discurso do desejo" – e a narrativa de "representação histórica" que "pertence ao discurso do real," (Hayden 1987, 20) e que o discurso de Juliana representaria? Como conciliar o que não se poderia unir sem dor? A partir de agora, ambas alimentavam a sua imaginação, e a sua identidade carregará as marcas desse combate.

Vitória está na encruzilhada do espaço e do tempo de uma história mediada que espalha os seus tentáculos até hoje. O jogo de detetive, a teatrealização da revelação, os indícios que persegue e as vozes que lhe revelam a história implicam uma escolha da parte de Vitória. Não sabe exatamente o que fazer entre a narrativa e o seu referente, ou seja, entre a palavra de Juliana e a fotografia da sua mãe, entre a verdade que tinha construído e as verdades que vai ouvindo. Contudo, perante a notícia da morte do avô, decide não ir a Portugal, decide desembaraçar-se do fantasma europeu; sente que tem de viver a história que lhe estava reservada e que fora interrompida, sente que pertence a Angola, ao Huambo, onde fica à espera que a mãe/camarada Rosa chegue um dia, pelo portão da casa de Juliana, com os fantasmas da guerra, do abandono, da incerteza, das verdades que atormentam Vitória e, com ela, as gerações seguintes.

> Vitória cai de joelhos em frente de Juliana e deita-se no seu colo, abraçando--lhe as pernas. Entre soluços e lágrimas pergunta porque é que não lhe contou a verdade.

– Qual delas meu amor? A da tua mãe, a minha, a da tua família, a que querias ouvir, a verdade do general... Qual delas? – questiona Juliana . . . (Monteiro 2018, 225)

De momento, a casa está ali e é neste espaço que Vitória aguarda: "– O que achares melhor para ti. Pode parecer estranho, mas, aqui, te queremos todos bem. Espera, Vitória. Espera só. És de um povo que ainda está à espera, que espera, sempre" (Monteiro 2018, 226).

Qual é a verdade sobre toda esta história privada que é um fragmento de uma história pública mais vasta? Qual a verdade afinal? E de quem? A reflexão elaborada por Stuart Hall, em "Cultural Identity and Diaspora" (1994), relativa a uma identidade que se descobre diaspórica – e que todas estas escritoras tratam nos seus livros –, é muito pertinente para a interpretação destes romances na literatura portuguesa, na sua articulação com a pós-memória. Como refere o crítico,

a identidade é qualquer coisa, não apenas uma ilusão da imaginação. Tem as suas histórias – e as histórias têm efeitos reais, materiais e simbólicos. O passado continua a falar connosco. Mas não se dirige a nós como um simples e factual passado, uma vez que a nossa relação com ele, tal como a relação de uma criança com a sua mãe, dá-se sempre depois da rutura. É sempre algo construído através da memória, da fantasia, da narrativa e do mito.[8]

Nesta afirmação, o crítico revela-nos a especificidade da importância da relação que as comunidades diaspóricas vão construindo com o seu passado familiar e cultural e com os territórios a ele ligados. Do ponto de vista da intensidade, a imagem utilizada pelo crítico não poderia ser mais íntima e mais forte – a relação que uma criança estabelece com a sua mãe, que tem uma caraterística muito específica, pois só se configura como tal após a rutura, ou seja, após o parto, com a transferência da criança do seu lugar matricial (e útero significa matriz) para um outro espaço em que será autónoma e se desenvolve. A memória dessa rutura não é dela, mas é essa rutura que a estrutura e que inicia a sua biografia, como lhe será sempre contado pelos familiares mais velhos. Trata-se, portanto, de uma relação com um passado matricial alimentado pela memória dos outros, pela fantasia, e geradora de uma mitologia de origem. No entanto, a diáspora não se esgota aqui. Como refere Stuart Hall (1994), não se trata de um movimento ancestral de referenciação, arqueológico no seu modo, a um longínquo e imaginário território, mas sim do resultado da sua transfiguração, cujos efeitos se prolongam até hoje. Isto não significa, portanto, uma rutura cultural e identitária com o passado, pois ele não existiu enquanto tal para estes sujeitos. Para as segundas gerações, esse passado é uma herança, uma representação, sem mais mitologias de retorno – "voltar para onde?" como questiona Budjurra. O seu passado é posterior à rutura e, logo, ele é em si uma reconstrução – como os passos de Vitória por Angola bem documentam –, uma recriação de histórias sobre um processo de desterritorialização dos seus antepassados recentes. Sendo assim, estas são identidades em que o processo de pertença se realiza a partir de um percurso em que o sujeito faz escolhas ou estas lhe são impostas a partir do exterior – por exemplo, de ser português e assumir a sua memória/herança angolana, mas também de ser português e assumir-se como negro. Filhas da diáspora, estas são identidades que, ao se afirmarem em território europeu, pela reclamação da história e dos seus prolongamentos, denunciam as soluções coloniais que a Europa tem vindo a dar para as situações pós-coloniais que elas representam, ao mesmo tempo que colocam sob suspeita o absolutismo das identidades nacionais, revelando-as como perigosas e irreais. Nenhuma identidade é fixa, mas antes o resultado de constantes negociações do passado e do presente, o que passa naturalmente não por uma inversão dos protocolos de narração da história, e sim por uma outra narração de uma história comum, a partir de outros sujeitos. Que verdade, afinal, como questiona Juliana, perante as perguntas de Vitória? Esta é uma narrativa nova no espaço da literatura portuguesa que, ao mesmo tempo que quebra as noções de tempo, espaço e geração, desestabiliza as categorias tradicionais do Estado-nação europeu, denunciando-o como artificial, face ao seu encontro com as dobras da história (e das histórias) que construíram a nação, muito para além dos limites do território europeu e da qual todos somos herdeiros. Essa dobra é a pós-memória.

A Fechar

Nestes primeiros livros de Djaimilia Pereira de Almeida, Tvon e Yara Monteiro, o que desfila diante dos nossos olhos são personagens negras e diaspóricas, herdeiras de vidas dispersas, de famílias fragmentadas, de glórias e de infortúnios, sempre em algum momento pautados por desvalorização, discriminação, preconceito, e que de novo se condensam em torno da história da família dispersa e afastada de uma mítica e mitificada terra natal. Esta memória representa em si os movimentos históricos e intercontinentais de populações, compulsivamente transportadas ou levadas em circuitos de colonizações, descolonizações ou emigração ligados à pobreza, à falta de desenvolvimento, à guerra, e geradores de novas identidades. São histórias a partir das quais as narradoras questionam a herança colonial e abordam a variedade de trânsitos que compõem o Portugal atual a partir desse o passado – e penso também e em particular em *O Retorno*, de Dulce Maria Cardoso, *Caderno de Memórias Coloniais*, de Isabela Figueiredo, ou *País Fantasma*, de Vasco Luís Curado.

Em conjunto, e a partir da evocação de diferentes experiências, estas obras acusam uma viragem essencial na tomada de consciência pós-colonial do espaço antigamente colonial e das vivências aí havidas como essenciais à nossa identidade de portugueses, de europeus e às nossas identidades individuais. Por isso, a viagem de retorno pós-colonial que estes livros encenam – de Portugal para África – inverte o sentido ulissiano da *história de regressos*,[9] sobre o qual se foram construindo e narrando os impérios ultramarinos europeus. A viagem europeia realizada por estes sujeitos e agora empreendida é mais complexa: ela constitui um reconhecimento de que grande parte da história que nos constitui se passou fora de Portugal e da Europa. Para perceber a "fratura colonial" (Blanchard, Bancel e Lemaire 2005) que nos marca a todos, têm de se contadas as narrativas das pertenças e vinculações de muitos sujeitos àquelas outras terras outrora parte do império e desses "outros" sujeitos à história de Portugal.

Trata-se, portanto, de uma linha narrativa de filhos do império, ou seja, de relatos de segunda geração, que tem por cenário, contexto ou prosa uma evocação e uma reflexão sobre o passado africano e colonial do seu país, na maioria das vezes iniciado a partir de um percurso de memória familiar transmitida ou herdada, e certamente reinterrogada nas suas histórias-fábula, nos seus silêncios e nos seus reflexos e prolongamentos contemporâneos. Os seus livros registam os laços e as tensões entre imaginários fantasmáticos europeus e imaginários – não menos fantasmáticos – africanos, reproduzidos em várias reproduções de origens míticas desde a Angola/África colonial dos portugueses à Angola/África da mestiçagem, até às mitologias da luta de libertação e, com ela, da fundação de uma nova nação situada *antes da história* ou *fora da história*, como ambicionam ser todos os inícios. O passado colonial dos seus antepassados marcou-as de diferentes formas ou, pelo menos, diz-lhes respeito enquanto herança e património.

Estas três narrativas escritas por mulheres revelam-nos indícios de um Portugal a desembaraçar-se do passado, a descolonizar-se das suas ex-colónias, a libertar-se das imagens do ex-colonizador e do ex-colonizado, a olhar para os fantasmas dos seus objetos e para as fantasias das suas narrativas cristalizadas e lusotropicais. São, portanto, sinais de um Portugal e de uma Europa que, ao rever as suas narrativas nacionais, equaciona outro futuro. Um futuro que se recusa a colocar um ponto final na história, não para contemplar esterilmente o passado, mas para a partir dele olhar o presente e contruir um futuro em que a pluralidade de histórias recuse as lógicas excludentes do esquecimento ou da desmemória. E essa reivindicação escolhida e ativa da história é a pós-memória.

O título que escolhi para esta reflexão evoca um conhecido poema de Cesário Verde, em que a definição do mundo ocidental convoca cidades de tradição europeia da Península Ibérica até à Rússia. No tempo de Cesário Verde, autor do longo e enigmático poema "O Sentimento de um Ocidental" – de leitura só entendível a partir de Helder Macedo (1975) – este era o mundo e o mundo era o Ocidente. Os livros aqui analisados, que de certa forma inauguram em Portugal uma escrita de mulheres portuguesas de segunda geração de ascendência africana, recordou-me de imediato o poema de Cesário Verde numa reclamação do alargamento desse "ocidente," ou seja, de nos revelar os "outros" desse mesmo ocidente no Ocidente. Não se trata mais de narrativas de perda, como seriam as narrativas da geração dos seus pais a olhar para o passado, envoltas numa mitologia de referência à metrópole como um lugar central, ou numa mitologia do regresso à África ancestral, à África colonial, à África da utopia das lutas de libertação. Trata-se de narrativas de uma segunda geração que olha para o presente e que nele descobre histórias anteriores ligadas a outros espaços e outros registos, que se prolongam ou transfiguram no seu presente. Assim se explicam os contornos da complexa herança que o compõe e os seus prolongamentos atuais, nomeadamente no assombramento que se projeta até hoje das políticas coloniais que associaram raça a uma identidade e a uma homogeneidade nacional e racial. E é nesse presente, informado de várias temporalidades e espacialidades, e sempre em transformação, que estas gerações querem participar, exigindo-nos uma democracia com memória.

NOTAS

1. Este artigo resulta do trabalho desenvolvido pelo *projeto* MEMOIRS – *Filhos de Império e Pós-memórias Europeias*, financiado pelo Conselho Europeu para a Investigação (ERC) no quadro do Horizonte 2020, programa para a investigação e inovação da União Europeia (contrato nº 648624). Sobre o projeto ver: http://memoirs.ces.uc.pt. Agradeço a Délio Jasse a autorização para publicar neste artigo o seu trabalho "Schengen," 2010.

2. É importante aqui assinalar que, em 1992, a Exposição Universal de Sevilha visa comemorar o quinto centenário da viagem de Colombo, sob o tema geral de "Descubrimientos."

3. A reflexão de Eduardo Lourenço é fundamental no "repensar" Portugal e a Europa pós império, logo após o 25 de abril de 1974 até praticamente o seu falecimento, em 2020: 1976; 1978; 1988; 1994; 1999; 1999, 2005, 2014.

4. Para mais informações, ver a página do programa https://proximofuturo.gulbenkian.pt /proximo-futuro e a carta programática do coordenador António Pinto Ribeiro. Ver ainda o artigo de Restivo 2017; Ribeiro 2020.

5. "Postmemory describes the relationship of the second generation to powerful, often traumatic, experiences that preceded their births but that were nevertheless transmitted to them so deeply as to seem to constitute memories in their own right" (Hirsch 2008, 104).

6. Djaimilia Pereira de Almeida em entrevista ao projeto *Memoirs – Filhos de Império e Pós-Memórias Europeias* (ERC Consolidator Grant nº 648624), em 10 de novembro de 2018, realizada por Margarida Calafate Ribeiro e António Pinto Ribeiro.

7. Sobre a condição da mulher na guerra em Angola ver os livro de Kasembe e Chiziane 2008; Paredes 2015. De acordo com Yara Monteiro, o livro de Paredes foi uma referência para o seu romance (Henriques 2019).

8. "It is *something* – not a mere trick of the imagination. It has its histories – and histories have their real, material and symbolic effects. The past continues to speak to us. But it no longer addresses us as a simple, factual 'past,' since our relation to it, like the child's relation to the mother, is always-already 'after the break.' It is always constructed through memory, fantasy, narrative and myth" (Hall 1994).

9. A expressão remete para o título do meu livro *Uma História de Regressos – Império, Guerra Colonial e Pós-Colonialismo* (2004).

REFERÊNCIAS BIBLIOGRÁFICAS

Almeida, Djaimilia Pereira de. 2015. *Esse Cabelo*. Lisboa: Teorema.

Bethencourt, Francisco e Kirti Chaudhuri, dir. 1998. *História da Expansão Portuguesa*. *Lisboa: Círculo de Leitores*.

Blanchard, Pascal *et al*. 2005. *La Fracture Coloniale. La Société Française au Prisme de L'héritage Colonial*. Paris : La Découverte.

Collins, Patricia Hill e Sirma Bilge. 2016. *Intersectionality*. Cambridge: Polity Press.

Di Castro, Raffaella. 2008. *Testimoni del Non-Provato. Ricordare, Pensare, Immaginare la Shoah nella Terza Generazione*. Roma: Carocci.

Gusmão, Neuza. 2007. *Os Filhos da África em Portugal: Antropologia, Multiculturalidade e Educação*. Lisboa: ICS.

Gonzaléz, Jennifer A. 1995. "Autotopographies." In *Prosthetic Territories – Politics and Hypertechnologies*, edição de Gabriel Braham Jr. e Mark Driscoll, 133-150. Boulder, San Francisco, Oxford: Westview Press.

Hall, Stuart. 1994. "Cultural Identity and Diaspora." In *Identity: Community, Culture, Difference*, edição de Jonathan Rutherford, 222-37. London: Lawrence & Wishart.

Henriques, Joana Gorjão. 2019. "Sou Trineta da Escravatura, Bisneta da Mestiçagem, Neta da Independência e Filha da Diáspora." *Público*, 21 de março, 2019 https://www.publico.pt/2019/03/21/culturaipsilon/noticia/trineta-escravatura-bisneta-mesticagem-neta-independencia-filha-diaspora-1865819. Acedido em 14 abril 2019 (Entrevista a Yara Monteiro).

Hirsch, Mariane. 1997. *Family Frames: Photography, Narrative, and Postmemory*. Cambridge, MA: Harvard University Press.

Hirsch, Mariane. 2008. "The Generation of Postmemory," *Poetics Today* 29 (1): 103-28.

Jasse, Délio. 2010. *Schengen*. Gelatina de prata, 15x40x50 cm. Cortesia do artista.

Kasembe, Dya e Paulina Chiziane, org. 2008. *O Livro da Paz da Mulher Angolana*. Luanda: Nzila.

Krenak, Ailton. 2019. *Ideias para Adiar o Fim do Mundo*. São Paulo: Companhia das Letras.

Lourenço, Eduardo. 1976. Situação Africana e Consciência Nacional. Amadora: Publicações Génese.

Lourenço, Eduardo. 1978. *O Labirinto da Saudade – Psicanálise Mítica do Destino Português*. Lisboa: Publicações D. Quixote.

Lourenço, Eduardo. 1988. Nós e a Europa ou as Duas Razões. Lisboa: Imprensa Nacional – Casa da Moeda.

Lourenço, Eduardo. 1994. *A Europa Desencantada – Para uma Mitologia Europeia*. Lisboa: Visão.

Lourenço, Eduardo. 1999a. A Nau de Ícaro seguido de Imagem e Miragem da Lusofonia. Lisboa: Gradiva.

Lourenço, Eduardo. 1999b. Portugal como Destino seguido de Mitologia da Saudade. Lisboa: Gradiva.

Lourenço, Eduardo. 2005. *A Morte de Colombo: Metamorfose e Fim do Ocidente como Mito*. Lisboa: Gradiva.

Lourenço, Eduardo. 2014. "A morte de Colombo." In *Do Colonialismo como o Nosso Impensado*, organização de Margarida Calafate Ribeiro e Roberto Vecchi. Lisboa: Gradiva.

Macedo, Helder. 1975. *Nós – Uma Leitura de Cesário Verde*, 1ª edição. Lisboa: Plátano Editora.

Mata, Inocência. 2018. "Uma Implosiva Literatura Exílica." *Público*, 14 de Dezembro, 2018. https://www.publico.pt/2018/12/14/culturaipsilon/critica/implosiva-geografia-exilica-1854334. Acedido em 20 janeiro 2019.

Monteiro,Yara. 2018. *Essa Dama Bate Bué*. Lisboa: Guerra e Paz.

Paredes, Margarida. 2015. *Combater Duas Vezes – Mulheres na Luta Armada em Angola*. Vila do Conde: Verso da História.

Restivo, Maria Manuela. 2017. "O Pós-Colonialismo e as Instituições Culturais Portuguesas: O Caso do Programa Gulbenkian Próximo Futuro e do Projeto Africa. cont." *Buala*, 17 de junho de 2017. http://www.buala.org/pt/a-ler/o-pos-colonialismo-e-as-instituicoes-culturais-portuguesas-o-caso-do-programa-gulbenkian-proxi. Acedido em 20 janeiro 2019.

Ribeiro, Margarida Calafate. 2004. *Uma História de Regressos – Império, Guerra Colonial e Pós-colonialismo*. Porto: Afrontamento.

Ribeiro, Margarida Calafate. 2020. "Viagens no Contemporâneo – Pós-Colonialismo, Cosmopolitismo e Programação." *Mulemba* 12, nº 22 (jan.-jun.): 127-47. https://revistas.ufrj.br/index.php/mulemba/article/view/39821

Ribeiro, António Sousa e Margarida Calafate Ribeiro. 2018. "A Past that Will not Go Away. The Colonial War in Portuguese Postmemory." Lusotopie 17 (2): 277-300.

Santos, Boaventura de. 1994. *Pela Mão de Alice – O Social e o Político na Pós-Modernidade*. Porto: Afrontamento.

Sarlo, Beatriz. 2007. *Tempo Passado. Cultura da Memória e Guinada Subjetiva*. São Paulo/Belo Horizonte: Companhia das Letras/ Editora da UFMG.

Subrahmanyam, Sanjay. 1997. *The Career and Legend of Vasco da Gama*. Cambridge: Cambridge University Press.

Tvon. 2017. *Um Preto muito Português*. Lisboa: Chiado Editora.

White, Hayden. 1987. *The Content of the Form*. Baltimore: Johns Hopkins University.

Vecchi, Roberto. 2018. "Depois das Testemunhas: Sobrevivências." *Memoirs – Jornal, Público*, 14 setembro, 2018, 18. http://memoirs.ces.uc.pt/index.php?id=22153&id_lingua=1&pag=22637

MARGARIDA CALAFATE RIBEIRO é investigadora-coordenadora do Centro de Estudos Sociais da Universidade de Coimbra e co-responsável pela Cátedra Eduardo Lourenço da Universidade de Bolonha/ Camões (com Roberto Vecchi). Das suas diversas publicações destaca-se Uma História de Regressos: Império, Guerra Colonial e Pós-colonialismo (2004), *África no Feminino – as Mulheres Portuguesas e a Guerra Colonial* (2007), *Memória, Cidade e Literatura – De São Paulo de Assunção de Loanda a Luuanda, de Lourenço Marques a Maputo* (2019) com Francisco Noa e Heranças Pós-Coloniais nas Literaturas de Língua Portuguesa (2019) com Phillip Rothwell.

ERIN MCCOMBE

The Right to Represent, Reproduce, and Refuse: Memory, Photography, and Postcolonial Ekphrasis in the Work of Djaimilia Pereira de Almeida[1]

ABSTRACT: By employing Gabriele Rippl's edited collection *Handbook of Intermediality* (2015), which aims at developing a theoretical framework for Intermedial Studies within the Anglophone context, this article proposes to explore examples of postcolonial ekphrasis and word-image configurations across the works of Djaimilia Pereira de Almeida. This includes her novel *Esse Cabelo* (2015) and the *crónica* "Pérola sem rapariga." The article proposes to establish a dialogue between memory, photography, and postcolonial ekphrasis within the Lusophone context. I argue that Almeida as an Afrodescendant woman writer, employs intermedial references to inscribe new forms of representations of Black women's bodies and attribute agency to Black women, both past and present. By doing so, she counteracts the official historical narrative, which continues to silence the memory of Africans and Afrodescendants in Europe.

KEYWORDS: Postcolonial ekphrasis; memory; photography; Djaimilia Pereira de Almeida; Afrodescendant literature

RESUMO: Partindo da coleção *Handbook of Intermediality* (2015), editada por Gabriele Rippl, que pretende construir um quadro metodológico para os Estudos de intermidialidade, centrando-se no contexto anglófono, este artigo propõe explorar exemplos da écfrase pós-colonial e da combinação imagem-texto nas obras literárias de Djaimilia Pereira de Almeida. Tal inclui o seu romance *Esse Cabelo* (2015) e a crónica "Pérola sem rapariga." O artigo pretende estabelecer um diálogo entre a memória, a fotografia e a écfrase pós-colonial no contexto lusófono, alegando que como uma escritora afrodescendente, Almeida usa referências intermidiais para inscrever novas formas de representação do corpo da mulher negra e para dar visibilidade às mulheres negras, tanto passada como presente. Dessa forma, ela vai contra o discurso histórico oficial que até hoje continua a silenciar a memória dos Africanos e dos Afrodescendentes na Europa.

PALAVRAS-CHAVE: écfrase pós-colonial; memória; fotografia; Djaimilia Pereira de Almeida; literatura afrodescendente

---

Introduction

Afrodescendant writer Djaimilia Pereira de Almeida was born in Luanda, Angola, in 1982, to an Angolan mother and a Portuguese father, both journalists. She migrated to Lisbon, Portugal, at the age of three, where she was raised by her paternal grandparents. Thus, Almeida did not form part of the initial wave of postcolonial migration of Africans and their descendants that characterized the late 1970s following the independence of Lusophone Africa in 1975 (Sanches 122). In fact, she migrated during an interim period, which preceded Portugal's accession to the European Economic Community (ECC) in 1986. As Bernd Reiter underlines, membership in the ECC would be significant both for the way in which Portugal projected itself as a nation, breaking away from its self-identification as an expansive empire and instead presenting itself as a white European nation-state, and for its future migratory patterns (101-102). In Lisbon, Almeida spent most of her childhood and teenage years growing up on the outskirts of the city in the middle-class neighborhood of Oeiras, apart from a few trips to Luanda to visit her mother. It is in this way that her background contrasts with the typical situation of African migrants and their offspring who originated from Portuguese-speaking countries such as Angola, Guinea-Bissau, and Mozambique. These migrants who constituted part of the first wave of postcolonial migration and who, as Manuela Ribeiro Sanches highlights, arrived in Portugal fleeing war and poverty, to continue to live in Lisbon's underprivileged *bairros* on the outskirts of the city (122). Additionally, it also distinguishes her from the wave of economic migrants, which consisted mostly of Eastern Europeans, who arrived following Portugal's entry to the European Union.[2]

In the same vein as Sanches, Portuguese journalist Joana Gorjão Henriques, in her book *Racismo no País dos Brancos Costumes* (2018), underlines the persisting marginalization of Africans and Afrodescendants in Portuguese society; however, she extends the debate beyond housing, and includes their struggle for jobs, education, and even justice and citizenship (14). She aims to disrupt the persisting myth that Portugal is a non-racist country, highlighting the lack of Black subjects in positions of power; this includes areas such as the political sphere, the media, the executive administrations of large business corporations, academia, and, finally, literature (11). Moreover, regardless of the desire of the Portuguese elite to present Portugal as a white European nation-state following decolonization, Henriques indicates that the presence of Africans and Afrodescendants in Portugal dates to the fifteenth century (19). That said, the fact that their presence in Europe is noted in centuries, rather than a specific year (whereas the supposed "discovery" of African states and populations by European explorers is carefully chartered with specific dates), likewise testifies to the persistent marginalization of the historic memory of Black people in Europe in the twenty-first century.[3]

Against this backdrop, it could be argued that Almeida's distinct background (middle-class family upbringing and a PhD in Literary Theory) has to some extent allowed her to overcome the marginalization faced by the majority of Afrodescendants. She became one of the first Afrodescendant women novelists of her generation in Portugal when she published *Esse Cabelo* in 2015.[4] In short, the novel tells the story of narrator-protagonist Mila, who embarks on a journey of self-discovery; Mila's afro hair is employed as a trope to uncover the memories of her childhood and adolescent years and to delve deeper into her family's past which spans across the Portuguese-speaking world (Portugal, Mozambique and Angola). Although *Esse Cabelo* is most often read as a work of autobiographical fiction, literary scholar Bianca Mafra Gonçalves rightly warns us that simply relegating the novel to the genre of autobiographical fiction constitutes a simplistic or superficial reading of the text (44-45).[5] Instead, for Gonçalves the book occupies a supposedly "impossible" space between autobiography and essay (42). Yet, while bearing in mind Gonçalves's criticisms, it is equally futile to ignore the obvious connections between Almeida and narrator-protagonist Mila, which the author herself has acknowledged in interviews (Almeida, "Eu mesma"). For instance, like Almeida, Mila is born in Luanda, Angola, to an Angolan mother and a Portuguese father and moves to Portugal at the age of three in 1985 to live with her paternal grandparents, namely, Manuel and Lúcia. Moreover, most of Mila's childhood is based in the neighborhood Oeiras. Hence, there is no denying that Almeida's life and that of her narrator-protagonist Mila are, to adopt the words of historian Marianne Hirsch, "shaped by exile, emigration and relocation" from the very outset (xi). In fact, this is one of the most prominent parallels between the author and narrator-protagonist. Hirsch, speaking from her own perspective as the child of a Holocaust survivor, states that in families impacted

355

by such upheaval "photographs provide perhaps even more than usual some illusion of continuity over time and space" (xi). This affirmation by Hirsch may help explain the motif of photography that runs through Almeida's debut novel *Esse Cabelo* and online *crónicas*. In the novel this most often takes the form of verbal descriptions of photographs, otherwise known as ekphrasis. In contemporary society, ekphrasis is a literary device typically used to describe a visual image; however, it was traditionally only used in relation to high art.

In this article, I intend to establish a dialogue between memory, photography, and postcolonial ekphrasis within the Portuguese-speaking world. The article will be divided into two parts: the first section deals with the presence of postcolonial ekphrastic passages in *Esse Cabelo* within the context of Mila's personal life, particularly the family photo album; the second section explores the ethics of representation surrounding Black women's bodies through the material reproduction of photos and their associated postcolonial ekphrastic descriptions, also known as word-image configurations. I have specifically chosen to explore the *crónica* "Pérola sem rapariga" (Jan. 2016), published in the online newspaper *Observador*.6 In this *crónica* Almeida physically alters a photograph from the colonial archive of an enslaved Brazilian woman, who appears naked from the waist up.

Although Almeida employs postcolonial ekphrasis and word-image configurations in other *crónicas*, this study has been limited to the aforementioned selection for two reasons.7 First, it allows the reader to understand how the bodies of Black women were depicted in Brazil, a Portuguese colony, from 1500 until the official abolition of slavery in 1888. Second, it enables a comparison with the former colonial metropole in the postcolonial moment, demonstrating how colonial attitudes impact the present and the ways in which contemporary and innovative literary production by Afrodescendants speak back to othering portrayals of Black women's bodies. In addition, this division of the article into two sections, creates a dialogue between the role of photography in the familial setting, which is to construct the past, and in the public space, where images of Black women from past to present are readily available and subjected to a persisting colonial gaze. However, prior to engaging with the selected ekphrastic passages and word-image configurations, I present a theoretical framework, mainly drawing upon Marianne Hirsch's theory of postmemory (including subsequent adaptions of the theory in the Portuguese colonial and postcolonial contexts) and Gabriele Rippl's edited collection *Handbook of Intermediality*, which situates postcolonial ekphrasis within the emerging field of Intermediality Studies.

Intermediality, Intermedial References, and Postcolonial Ekphrasis

According to Gabriele Rippl, the concept of "Intermediality" generally refers to the combining or juxtaposition of different forms of media, and the rise of studies into intermediality is indicative of the digital age (1-2). Notwithstanding the fact that the *Handbook of Intermediality* focuses specifically on the Anglophone context, the collection has two aims that are relevant to the argument of this article. First, the collection endeavors to develop a theoretical basis for intermediality and applies this to examples in Anglophone literatures (Rippl 1). The strong theoretical focus allows the collection to be adapted to other geographical contexts, such as the Portuguese-speaking world. Second, it aspires to develop a link between ekphrasis (as a specific example of intermediality) and postcolonial literatures (Rippl 15).

Reflecting upon Irina O. Rajesky's theory of intermediality, Rippl categorizes the types of intermediality; this article will focus specifically on intermedial references, including the visual descriptions of works of art, i.e., ekphrasis (10-12). In the opening essay of the collection, James Hefferman, who had in the early 1990s expanded the meaning of ekphrasis to go beyond the classical meaning of a literary description of high art, reaffirms that in the twenty-first century ekphrasis is simply "the verbal representation of visual representation," adding that the definition is more dynamic than ever before (48). Rippl highlights how the emergence of ekphrasis was embedded within the Renaissance discussion of the *paragone*, that is, the competitive tension between the medium of visual art and the written word (4). For Birgit Neumann, this *paragone* remains in contemporary intermedial productions and yields a transformative potential in postcolonial literatures, a body of works concerned with the rupturing of hierarchies and the problematization of binary structures and cultural homogeneity (513-14). Similarly, Rippl believes that the future of intermediality lies in the under-researched presence of ekphrasis in postcolonial literatures, identifying the Anglophone world as the source of a wealth of examples (15). Considering this, postcolonial ekphrasis and word-image configurations potentially speak to and counteract what Paul Gilroy identifies as the emergence of new kinds of visual cultures as a result of technological advancements, which he believes "re-incarnate" racial differences in innovative ways and on a global scale (xii). This article intends to add to this debate by focusing on ekphrasis in literature written in Portuguese and specifically those produced by a contemporary Afrodescendant woman writer.

Memory, Photography, and Black Women in the Private and Public Spheres

Although the presence of ekphrasis in postcolonial literatures written in Portuguese has not yet been the focus of scholarly attention, Portuguese historian Filipa Lowndes Vicente published an article in 2018 on the visual representations of bodies of Black women in the Portuguese colonial archive. In her analysis, Vicente highlights that photographs of Black women across the archive, most commonly taken by men, are racialized and sexualized (16). Both hair and breasts are at the center of the erotic lens, and these images are readily accessible for audiences of all ages to see, a fact that continues to expose the bodies of Black women to a colonial gaze (20). Moreover, Vicente expresses uncertainty as to whether the reproduction of such photographs, alongside a critical theoretical discussion in universities or museums, is enough to decolonize the archive (22, 38). Thus, she brings to the fore the question of who holds the right to reproduce these photos and in what context. This places her work in direct dialogue with sociologist Sheila Khan's question: Who is responsible for a postcolonial education? (44). For Khan, it belongs to those who claim the civic responsibility of engaging with a critical, interventional, and open discussion of memory and postmemory (48). Postmemory, originally conceptualized by Hirsch, "characterizes the experience of those who grow up dominated by narratives that preceded their birth, whose own belated stories are evacuated by the stories of the previous generation shaped by traumatic events that can be neither understood nor recreated" (22). Such "traumatic" experiences are not limited to the Holocaust, but also include populations affected by colonization, as has been demonstrated through the development of postmemory in the collection *Geometrias da Memória*, edited by António Sousa Ribeiro and Margarida Calafate Ribeiro.[8] Thus, postmemory is indicative of the experiences of many Afrodescendants and *retornados*, such as Almeida, who were born in the late 1970s and early 1980s, and who currently reside in Portugal. It is in this context that viewing the novel as strictly autobiographical becomes problematic. Almeida, in addition to acknowledging the similar life trajectory that she and Mila have taken, also acknowledges that, despite the novel initially being a product of her own "inquietação," she came to realize that such "inquietações" were not just personal to her (Almeida, "Eu mesma"). Instead, she notes that the book is in fact a culmination of emotions and intuitions that she noticed in people "próximas e afastadas, desconhecidas ou não, com uma história semelhante ou diferente" to her own (Almeida, "Eu mesma"). From this it is possible to extrapolate that Almeida does not just recount elements of her own story in *Esse Cabelo*, but part of the story of a generation.

Despite Vicente's concern with the perpetuation of violence through the reproduction of photographs in the public space, she nevertheless highlights the power of "counter-narrative photographic practices and uses" which problematize the subjugation and sexualization of Black women and work to inscribe new "possibilities of subjectivity and agency" (41-42). She cites examples from the African American context such as Sojourner Truth (1797-1883), who managed to use photography as a tool of power (40). Truth, after freeing herself from her master, became an abolitionist and a gifted orator, selling *cartes-de-visite* of herself to make a living. Nevertheless, Vicente also highlights the fact that images, in which Black women had freely consented to be photographed, faced limited circulation, remaining within the private sphere (40-41). This indicates a dichotomy between the function of photography in the public and private spheres, particularly in a colonial context, and how it has impacted the historical memory of Black women. As we have seen, from Hirsch's perspective, in families dispersed by migration, the family photo album successfully documents the past and is viewed as a positive tool (xi). In contrast, African-American writer bell hooks characterizes photography as a source of oppression in an essay on the role of photography in Black family life; because her father's eye was behind the camera throughout her childhood hooks had always associated photography with patriarchy (391). However, many scholars acknowledge that in the public sphere, photography, which developed in the colonial context of the nineteenth century, as a tool of power to document ethnographies of free and enslaved Africans and Afrodescendants, is complicit in representing Black subjects as inferior and that it reinforced supposedly scientific or biological racial differences.[9] It is this dichotomy between the function of photography in the public and private spheres that will be discussed across the analysis of Almeida's selected works.

The Family Album as a Window to the Past and Present in
Esse Cabelo (2015)

Esse Cabelo is a novel replete with postcolonial ekphrastic passages of photographs of Mila and her family members from family albums. The examples of postcolonial ekphrasis, which appear unaccompanied by images, form part of Mila's journey of self-discovery. The presence of photographs or postcolonial ekphrastic descriptions in *Esse Cabelo* has not previously been discussed by literary scholars. However, Almeida has acknowledged in an interview that she had originally planned to structure the book in the form of a family photo album (Almeida, "Eu mesma"). In a 2015 interview with journalist Marta Lança she states: "Comecei por imaginar escrever um livro com a estrutura de um álbum de fotografias de família: imagens que podem ou não ter sido captadas, que podem ou não ter existido," while also highlighting that she believes that family albums and how they are organized or utilized determines our perception of childhood, particularly our lapses in memory (Almeida, "Eu mesma"). Through Almeida's tactful allusions to the existence or non-existence of photographs, which formed part of the early inception of the novel, the author brings to the fore a debate about the presence of the real and fictional in *Esse Cabelo*. Moreover, by discussing how the family photo album can alter how we view the past, the author may allude to her own uncertainty about which memories exactly are real or fictionalized due to her own inability to fully recall her childhood. However, this interpretation may fall into the trap of being a simplistic autobiographical reading of the novel; the author does not given any direct indication in the interview (for instance, by employing a personal pronoun) that the family album she discusses is in fact her own. In this same interview, Almeida also acknowledges that during the process of writing *Esse Cabelo* the trope of hair became the central focus (Almeida, "Eu mesma"). Nonetheless, I argue that photographs remain a recurrent motif and are employed to understand both the past and present, as is implicit in the following quote:

> Tenho diante de mim fotografias de família antigas que folheio à procura de sentidos, ligações, uma explicação para tudo. As explicações que procuramos são, por vezes, um bando nunca avistado. (Almeida, *Esse Cabelo* 58)

Mila's need to find an answer in the family photo album is reminiscent of Hirsch's search for continuity in photographs. Moreover, the trope of hair and photography are often dealt with simultaneously. In fact, when viewing the photographs of her childhood or models in magazines at the hairdressers, Mila focuses on the subjects' hairstyles. This is exemplified in the following quote:

> Fotografaram-me para um novo passaporte verde, em que surjo com um grande buraco nos dentes da frente. Não me lembro da juba do dia seguinte, mas ostentei-a decerto com orgulho. (Almeida, *Esse Cabelo* 50)

In this short example of ekphrasis, the author emphasizes the mnemonic function of the photograph as Mila is unable to remember the state of her hair the following day. Therefore, although the photograph successfully documents one of the few positive interactions Mila has with her hair, Almeida employs ekphrasis to show how photography merely captures a temporary state. It does not necessarily represent Mila's everyday reality. Moreover, since the focus is on hair, it brings us back to Vicente's comments on Black women's hair being at the center of the erotic gaze in colonial photographs that circulated publicly. For Mila, however, her hair plays a different role in the context of her family album. It signifies racial difference, which sets her apart from her paternal white Portuguese family, who are responsible for most of her upbringing (her mother remains in Angola, and is therefore absent during most of her childhood, except for intermittent visits during the summer). Additionally, this is the second reference to a passport photo in the novel and although the ekphrasis is clearly fixed on Mila's physical appearance, the description of the passport is also noteworthy.[10] The fact that the passport is "novo" could indicate that her previous passport has expired, and she is thus renewing it. However, because this second photo is taken in Portugal, after her departure from Angola, it may suggest that this is her application for Portuguese citizenship. The color "verde" is indicative of the Green Book in America, a travel guide which indicated places that were deemed safe for Africans and Afrodescendants in twentieth century America, during a time of deep racial tension. This brings to the fore some of the issues that Afrodescendant populations face, as identified by Henriques and Reiter, namely, citizenship and highlights their continued marginalization in the twenty-first century.

The focus on the physical attributes or appearance of women continues throughout *Esse Cabelo* and goes beyond Mila's hair. This is evident in the longest and most vivid description of a family photograph (traditionally known as *enargetic* ekphrasis) of Mila's stepmother or "mãe portuguesa," who in contrast to Mila's persistently absent birth mother, is presented with admiration, and as the driving force behind Mila's childhood memories:

A noiva dançou em mini-saia; deixou-se fotografar bebendo um café num baldio com o desprendimento e a propriedade de uma estrela: sabia-se linda e assim a achávamos…Neste balanço, em que a beleza e a liberdade são mutuamente dependentes, a minha mãe portuguesa, o olho por detrás de quase

> de todas as fotografias deste álbum, teve o lugar de zeladora da liberdade necessária para fazer de mim uma pessoa e, enfim, a paciência para a minha entretanto eclodida timidez em deixar-me fotografar...Não existe álbum sem fotógrafo e, mesmo quando não existem nem um nem outro, o que conhecemos da infância são os olhos que nos viram, nos fixaram, nos atuaram, nos amaram. (Almeida, *Esse Cabelo* 118-19)

Mila's declared admiration for her stepmother through positive nouns such as "estrela," "beleza," "liberdade," and "paciência" counteracts the typical Western narrative of the evil stepmother, as represented in the story of Cinderella. The picture depicts a family wedding; in it, a white European woman is confined to the family environment and the subject of the photo is clothed. Notably, Mila feels the need to confirm that the onlookers at the wedding or those who have access to the family photo album agree that the bride was correct in thinking she was "linda," through the plural form of the verb *achar*. This highlights the plurality of gazes directed at the subject in a photograph, which go beyond that of the photographer. Moreover, the repetition of the verb *deixar* with the change of the subject pronoun from "deixou-se fotografar" to "deixar-me fotografar" highlights the fact that the white Portuguese woman has given her consent and Mila has acquired the agency to carry out the physical act of taking the photo. This suggests a level of female companionship in the act of photography and deviates from the photographs in the colonial archive, which Vicente notes are normally taken by and remain in the possession of men (16). By assigning Mila the power of representation, Almeida places her as an active agent rather than a passive subject of the photo. However, the author suggests that much like her ability to mediate the description of a real or imagined photograph in the form of postcolonial ekphrasis (which undoubtedly affects our viewing of an image) childhood memories are also mediated. Although they are lived memories, we do not necessarily remember specific moments; such episodes are normally recounted to us by an adult, transforming them into a form of postmemory. For Mila, it is her stepmother who mediates such memories, as she is the eye behind all the photographs. However, in the form of postmemory, it is Almeida, through Mila's postcolonial ekphrasis of real or imagined photographs, who documents such memories and reproduces them to a wider public in the written form of a novel.

In *Esse Cabelo*, the description of photographs of Mila and her respective family members are never accompanied by the reproduction of those photographs.

Given the similar life trajectories of both author and narrator mentioned previously, coupled with Almeida's interview which creates ambiguity surrounding the existence of photographs, the reader is led to further question whether the descriptions, which are at times described in meticulous detail, are based on photographs of real-life events. Moreover, when compared to examples of Almeida's online *crónicas*, in which ekphrastic descriptions form part of word-image configurations, the reader is left to question the reason for not including photographs in the novel.[11] Almeida's decision to exclude photographs of Mila's family, which seems broadly similar to her own, parallels Hirsch's analysis of Roland Barthes' *Camera Lucida*, in which she argues that Barthes' decision not to reproduce photos of his mother shows that we do not form part of the "familial network"; our gaze as readers is excluded (2). In this way, the power of representation lies with the writer, Almeida. She employs ekphrasis to create tension between what is fact and what is fiction, thus forcing the reader into the *paragone* of visual and textual representations. Our perspective is therefore entirely influenced not only by Mila's description of the photograph, but also by her emotional reaction to it. In the first quotation, regardless of whether these memories are autobiographical or not, the postcolonial ekphrasis reveals the true impact that the open racialization and sexualization of Black women in the public realm has on a young child, as depicted through the relationship Mila has with her afro hair in photographs. In the second photograph, Mila, as a child, carries out the physical act of taking the photo, while her stepmother guides her lapses in memory. This suggests that the documenting of memory and the story behind it is reconstructed in a joint effort. By presenting a consensual relationship of power between photographer and the object/subject of the photo, Almeida subtly counteracts the patriarchal, colonial gaze.

Obstructing the Colonial Gaze of the Nineteenth Century *Carta-de-visite* in "Pérola sem rapariga"

When analyzing the material reproduction of the *carte-de-visite* in Almeida's *crónica* "Pérola sem rapariga," it is important to consider the social constructions of race and gender, as well as class in the representation of Black women's bodies. The *carte-de-visite* was a type of photograph invented and patented by André Disdéri. Beatriz Jaguaribe and Maurício Lissvosky note that it became particularly popular in Brazil among middle-class families during the 1860s due to its low cost (75). According to Jaguaribe and Lissvosky, Disdéri claimed that the *carte-de-visite* was a successful portrait because it was the result of a "photographic pact between the photographer and the person being depicted"; the portrait itself should reveal the "distinct character" of the individual, and the models were able to choose their own material props (75-77).

However, Jaguaribe and Lissvosky also inform us that when the Azorean photographer Christiano Júnior began to take *cartes-de-visite* of enslaved individuals in Rio his photos did not comply with the "photographic pact"; the background was no longer adorned with traditional bourgeoise furnishings, and enslaved people were depicted carrying out activities from their daily lives (77-79). This exemplifies how photography strove to represent reality, and thus entered the debate of the *paragone*, alongside literature (Straub 159-160). The *carte-de-visite* analyzed by Almeida, which she encountered on the online portal *Brasiliana Fotográfica*, depicts an enslaved Brazilian woman, and was taken by the nineteenth century German photographer Alberto Henschel (1826-1882).[12] Sven Schuster and Alejandra Buenaventura argue that Henschel's portraits are different from Júnior's in their depiction of enslaved individuals with backgrounds of exotic fruits or wearing fictitious "African" attire in order to appeal to a European audience interested in exoticism (82). Paradoxically, however, they also argue that Henschel respected the individuality of the models and did not reduce them to mere objects (82). This would suggest that his photographs were closer to the photographic pact envisaged by Disdéri. Nevertheless, Henschel, like Júnior, did not document the names of his models. Jaguaribe and Lissvosky argue that this is because at the time those who were enslaved were not seen as "citizens" but rather "objects" (79). This resonates with the aforementioned work of Henriques, in which the Afrodescendants in Portugal continue to be denied access to full citizenship rights (14). Yet, the word-image configurations that Almeida presents to her reader contest the claims made by Schuster and Buenaventura regarding Henschel's respectful attitude toward his chosen models and support Jaguaribe and Lissvosky's argument by demonstrating how Black women were objectified in colonial photography. The section will first deal with the materially reproduced photograph of the enslaved woman before analyzing the ekphrasis that accompanies it.

In "Pérola sem rapariga," the photo of the enslaved Brazilian woman that Almeida presents to us is surrounded by a black permanent marker, a red pencil, and scissors.[13] On a closer look at the *carte-de-visite*, it becomes apparent that the lips of the model have been colored with the red pencil and that the dress she is wearing has been added with permanent marker, as indicated by the gaps left in the coloring below the woman's breasts. Initially, it was unclear to me who had edited the photo. Then, on reading another *crónica* published by Almeida, in which she makes an 'apelo' for editing photos, it became evident that Almeida is responsible (Almeida, "O apelo da colagem"). The alteration of the photo is confirmed by comparison to the original photograph taken by Henschel in which the woman appears nude from the waist up, wearing only an earring and a bracelet.[14] The original photo was also printed in the then traditional sepia style, whereas the edited version is shown in black and white (apart from the splash of red on the woman's lips). Moreover, the border with Henschel's name and the place the photo was taken have been removed. Through these alterations made by Almeida the photo has been completely displaced from the era in which it was produced. This allows the photo to be removed from the reality it was originally intended to document and opens up the possibility of inscribing the image of the enslaved woman with new stories and subjectivities.

Considering the differences between the two photos, it is important to highlight what Almeida leaves available to the gaze of the reader. Almeida encourages the reader to find the original photo by directly citing the *Brasiliana Fotográfica* online portal. Yet, by not reproducing the original nude photo of the enslaved Brazilian woman, she avoids being complicit in what Vicente labels as the perpetuation of violence and racism and thus prevents the reproduction of the colonial gaze (22). This is particularly relevant given that this *crónica* is published in an online newspaper and can therefore reach a wider audience. It thus has the potential to disrupt the continued marginalization and misrepresentation of Africans and Afrodescendants in the media. The act of editing this photo can be seen as a "counter-narrative photographic practice," as described by Vicente and serves to contest the official discourse of memory, a discourse that continues to marginalize Black subjects in the postcolonial moment (41).

Almeida's edited photograph resonates with the work of South African artist and art historian, Nomusa Makhubu. In her "Self-Portrait" series, Makhubu mixes photographs of herself with historical photographs of other Black subjects in an attempt to obstruct the colonial gaze. In an interview with Claire Counihan, Makhubu states that her editing, which consists of mixing photographs and changing the title of the original photo, questions the supposed truth represented in the photograph (314). Almeida's work mimics this practice not by superimposing historical photographs, but through the physical act of drawing over the photo and by attempting to "legendar" the photograph of the enslaved Brazilian with her own life (Almeida, "Pérola sem rapariga"). In addition to editing the photograph, Almeida, like Makhubu, edits the original caption of the photograph. On the online portal, the caption appears as *Mulher negra da Bahia*, whereas Almeida refers to the enslaved women as "A nua da Bahia" (Henschel; Almeida "Pérola sem rapariga"). Almeida thus focuses on the sexualization of the enslaved women in the photograph, while the portal's title focuses on her race. This, arguably, contradicts her edited photograph, in which the model now appears clothed, again bringing literature and photography into the *paragone* debate, in a fight for the power of representation.

The title of the *crónica* "Pérola sem rapariga" is also noteworthy. It is intrinsically linked to the title of the famous seventeenth-century painting by Johannes Vermeer entitled *Girl with a Pearl Earring*. This painting depicts a white girl in exotic clothing; in addition to the eponymous pearl earring, she wears a bright blue and yellow turban. It is considered unusual in Vermeer's *oeuvre*, which usually depicts women carrying out daily chores and in more traditional attire. In Almeida's *crónica*, however, the title is an inversion of the Dutch painting, altering both subject and agency. From the outset, it places importance on the pearl earring, rather than the Black woman depicted. The focus on jewelry continues in Almeida's short ekphrastic passage, while the enslaved individual is presented as lifeless and vacant: "Ela está longe de estar despida na imagem. Se não a descortino, é talvez porque não está lá. Apenas o brinco e a pulseira (emprestados?) reluzem no retrato" ("Pérola sem rapariga"). In Almeida's reading, the only things that sparkle are the bracelet and the pearl earring. The adjective "sparkling," which can also be used to describe a person's eyes, is in this instance specifically used to focus on material possessions, which Almeida implies are both borrowed. This serves to highlight the social position of the enslaved woman, who would not have had the means to possess such jewelry. In Almeida's ekphrastic representation this woman has been silenced and is devoid of individuality.

Almeida's overall focus in the *crónica*, seems to be on the photographer's motives, which is in direct contrast with the characterization of a consensual relationship between the subject and photographer in *Esse Cabelo*. Instead, a hierarchal power relation has been created, as reflected in the following questions Almeida poses: "Como terá Henschel mandado que se despisse? Quem lhe terá posto os brincos e a pulseira de contas? O que se terá seguido àquele momento?" ("Pérola sem rapariga"). Almeida's carefully selected wording highlights the uneven nature of the relationship and underlines the lack of agency attributed to the enslaved Brazilian women. First, the European colonial photographer is referred to by his surname, which suggests a level of formality and recognizes his importance as a historical figure. On the other hand, the enslaved Brazilian woman is addressed as "ela," which again removes any sense of individuality. Moreover, Almeida underlines the enslaved woman's lack of power in the relationship by implying that Henschel ordered her to get undressed. This eliminates the possibility of the model having chosen to undress for the photo and implies she had been forced into the situation. It is further insinuated that someone else has put the earring and bracelet on for her and that Henschel is likely to have taken advantage of the woman after the photography session. The experience of the enslaved Brazilian woman stands in stark contrast to the "liberdade" which Mila associates with photography in the private sphere (De Almeida, *Esse Cabelo* 118-19). In the imperial project, where photography was used as a colonial tool, the subject's name was unimportant. Rather, subjects were often defined by their ethnographic category (e.g., "negra") and by place of origin (Jaguaribe and Lissvosky 77). The failure to record the slave's name, allows her to be silenced and forgotten, overshadowed by the male professional photographer. It counteracts any claims that Schuster and Buenaventura make regarding Henschel's desire to preserve the individuality of the enslaved models (82). Akin to the way in which the memory of Africans and Afrodescendants in Europe has been historically marginalized from the Eurocentric hegemonic national narratives, given the vague charting of the African presence in Europe, the nameless enslaved woman is invisible in the written word. Almeida employs ekphrasis to denounce what Hirsch would refer to as the "traumatic events" of those that came before her (22). However, in this instance, Almeida's postmemory delves deeper into the past and includes generations of colonized people before her, rather than only those who were impacted by the immediate history of the colonial wars in Africa.

Ultimately, neither the narrator nor the reader of the *crónica* knows exactly what happened on this specific occasion between Henschel and the unnamed enslaved woman. The insinuations made by the narrator regarding the photographer's actions and the focus on the "nua" in the *crónica's* title are representative of the sexual violence that many Black women have faced across the centuries. The "Nua da Bahia," whose name and story we will never know, is a microcosm, representing the many other women who were subjugated and abused at the hands of the colonial enterprise. This kind of artistic response, accompanied by ekphrastic descriptions of the Black enslaved woman, is shocking for the reader. This shock has the power to ignite change, and Almeida uses this potential to produce counter-narratives to the representations of Black women's bodies in the colonial archive (Vicente 41). In this way, she also assumes the role as postcolonial educator, as conceptualized by Khan, by presenting an open and critical dialogue on postmemory and the memory of Black women, which has been marginalized for centuries (48).

Conclusion

This article has analyzed the representations of Black women's bodies in the Portuguese-speaking world through the postcolonial ekphrasis and word-image configurations that are present in the work of the Afrodescendant Djaimilia Pereira de Almeida. In the private sphere, photographs, or the imagining of non-existent family photographs, act as a means of understanding the past and present and of distorting the line between fact and fiction. By returning to these photos later in life, the narrator expresses a desire to find a place of belonging, especially when the national narrative excludes her because of the color of her skin. Photography is presented as a contested medium, and this article has demonstrated its dual ability; it can be employed as a tool to subjugate, sexualize, and racialize women, particularly at the hands of the colonial enterprise, or to empower women. In the public sphere, Almeida tries to break the repetition of the past and the colonial gaze through her ekphrastic passages, word-image configurations, and by the editing of photos from the colonial archive. In the private sphere of the family photo album, photography can be employed to empower Afrodescendants, particularly when they hold the right to represent. A comparison of public and private spaces also reveals the effect that the sexualization and racialization of Black women's bodies in the public space have on a young, Afrodescendant woman growing up in a European nation that presents itself as white. Mila's response to her hair in photos is a direct product of the centuries of negative representations of Black women's bodies.

Ideally Almeida's "counter-narrative photographic practices," as well as those of other Afrodescendants, will reach a level of circulation that gives them the visibility and the power to counteract new visual cultures, which, as Gilroy has highlighted, "re-incarnate" racial differences (Vicente 41, Gilroy xii). To overcome the othering portrayals of Afrodescendants and Africans, the right to represent and reproduce photographs of Black women's bodies must lie with those who engage with a critical, interventional conversation on memory and postmemory, as Almeida has successfully done (Khan 48). The "photographic pact" between photographer and model should be a consensual agreement in which the model holds the right to consent or refuse (Jaguaribe and Lissvosky 75-77). Almeida's intermedial references of postcolonial ekphrasis and word-configurations are complex and layered, which provokes a level of ambiguity for the reader regarding the relationship between photographer and model, as well as fact and fiction. This forces the reader of both image and text to rethink the ethics of representation and the reproduction of colonial photographs, particularly in our increasingly digital world.

NOTES

1. Excerpts of this article originally formed part of my master's thesis entitled *Negotiating Diaspora in Female-Authored Writings of Postcolonial Iberia: A Comparison of Literary Works by Equatoguinean Ángela Nzambi and Angolan Djaimilia Pereira de Almeida* submitted in 2018 to Queen's University Belfast.

2. The situation of economic migrants and their daily life in Lisbon is represented in the documentary film *Lisboetas*, directed by Sérgio Tréfaut. It was awarded the prize for Best Portuguese Feature Film in the first edition of Indie Lisboa in 2004.

3. For instance, Angola was "discovered" in 1483.

4. More recently, Almeida has been joined by other novelists of Angolan descent in Portugal such as Kalaf Epalanga, who published *Os Brancos Também Sabem Dançar* (2017); Telma Tvon, author of *Um Preto Muito Português* (2017); and Yara Monteiro, author of *Essa Dama Bate Bué* (2018).

5. *Many scholars read Esse Cabelo (2015) as a work of autobiographical fiction. The strongest advocate for an autobiographical reading of the novel is Vanessa Gatelli, who makes the claim that all the information she has located in interviews with the author "vão ao encontro da história narrada no livro." (3011-12).* However, Milena Britto takes a more balanced view, claiming that "Em certos momentos, a obra é um ensaio filosófico sobre o encontro das diferenças, em outros é uma ficcionalização do passado de seus avós, e em outros, ainda, suas próprias memórias" (216-17).

6. Between 2015-2018 Almeida regularly published *crónicas through this online newspaper.*

7. At the time of the submission of my master's thesis, Almeida had only published two books: *Esse Cabelo* (2015) and *Ajudar a Cair* (2017). This article does not explore the presence of postcolonial ekphrasis or word-image configurations in *Ajudar a Cair* (2017) or any subsequent book publications.

8. The collection *Geometrias da Memórias* was published as part of a series by the European Council Research Project MEMOIRS – *Filhos de Império e Pós-memórias Europeias*. This is a comparative research project that focuses on the memories of the descendants of those directly impacted by the decolonization of the former colonies of France, Belgium, and Portugal. One of the main aims of the project is to apply the term "postcolonial" not only to the former colonies, but also to Europe. See António Sousa Ribeiro and Margarida Calafate Ribeiro (2016).

9. For a discussion of the negative role of photography in the representation of the Back body in the colonial era, see Straub (2015); Makhubu (2016); and Vicente (2018).

10. The first reference to a passport photograph describes a photo that documents Mila's departure from Angola to Portugal: "Trazia vestida uma camisola de lã amarela hoje reconhecível numa fotografia de passaporte em que impera um sorriso rasgado, própio daquele desentendimento feliz quanto ao significando de se ser fotografado" (Almeida, *Esse Cabelo* 16).

11. For further examples of *crónicas* by Almeida that contain word-image configurations see "O apelo da colagem" (Jun. 2018); "Parto e resgate" (Mar. 2017) and "Uma fotografia com Mariam." (Apr. 2018). However, this is not an exhaustive list.

12. Established in 2015, the portal digitally collates photographic collections related to Brazil from 1800-1930, in order to give visibility to documentary photography. See http://brasilianafotografica.bn.br/.

13. To view the photo edited by Almeida, which she entitles "A nua da Bahia," see "Pérola sem rapariga" observador.pt/opiniao/perola-sem-rapariga/.

14. For direct access to Henschel's original photo, see https://brasilianafotografica.bn.gov.br/brasiliana/handle/20.500.12156.1/4502.

WORKS CITED

Almeida, Djaimilia Pereira de. *Esse Cabelo*. Teorema, 2015.

———. "Eu mesma – entrevista a Djaimilia Pereira de Almeida." Interview by Marta Lança. *Buala*, 16 Sept. 2015.

———. "O apelo da colagem." *Blog da Companhia*, 19 Jun. 2018.

———. "Parto e resgate." *Revista Pessoa*, 8 Mar. 2017.

———. "Pérola sem rapariga." *Observador*, 27 Jan. 2016.

———. "Uma fotografia com Mariam." *Blog da Companhia*, 24 Apr. 2018.

Britto, Milena. "Um mapa diaspórico nas tramas do cabelo."*Afro-Ásia*, no. 57, 2018, pp. 215-20.

Gatelli, Vanessa Hack. "Negociações identitárias em *Esse Cabelo*, de Djaimilia Almeida e *Americanah*, de Chimamanda Adichie." *Anais eletrônicos do XV encontro ABRALIC*, Dialogarts, 2017, pp. 3011-17.

Gilroy, Paul. *Between Camps: Nations, Cultures and the Allure of Race*. 2nd ed., Routledge, 2004.

Gonçalves, Bianca Mafra. "Em torno da filosofia de um cabelo crespo: uma análise de *Esse Cabelo*, de Djaimilia Pereira de Almeida." *Silenciamento e exclusão na literatura*, CPCP, 2019, pp. 39-48.

Hefferman, James A. W. "Ekphrasis: Theory." *Handbook of Intermediality: Literature-Image-Sound-Music*, edited by Gabriele Rippl, De Gruyter, 2015, pp. 35-49.

Henschel, Alberto, *Mulher negra da Bahia*, 1869. *Brasiliana Fotográfica*, http://brasilianafotografica.bn.br/.

Henriques, Joana Gorjão. *Racismo no País dos Brancos Costumes*. Tinta da China, 2018.

Hirsch, Marianne. *Family Frames: Photography, Narrative and Postmemory*. Harvard UP, 1997.

Hooks, bell, "In Our Glory: Photography and Black Life." *The Photography Reader*, edited by Liz Wells, Routledge, 2002, pp. 387-94.

Jaguaribe, Beatriz and Maurício Lissvosky. "The Visible and the Invisibles: Photography and Social Imaginaries in Brazil." *Rio de Janeiro: Urban Life Through the Eyes of the City*, Routledge, 2014, pp. 73-104.

Khan, Sheila. "A educação das cerejeiras: a quem pertence a responsabilidade do pós-colonial?" *Revista Mulemba*, vol. 9, no. 16, Jan.-Jul. 2017, pp. 44-53.

Makhubu, Nomusa, "Interview with Nomusa Makhubu." Interviewed by Clare Counihan, *Comparative Studies of South Asia, Africa and the Middle East*, vol. 36, no. 2, 2016, pp. 307-19.

Neumann, Birgit. "Intermedial Negotiations: Postcolonial Literatures." *Handbook of Intermediality: Literature-Image-Sound-Music*, edited by Gabriele Rippl, De Gruyter, 2015, pp. 512-29.

Reiter, Bernd. *The Dialectics of Citizenship: Exploring Privilege, Exclusion and Racialization*. Michigan State UP, 2013.

Ribeiro, António Sousa and Margarida Calafate Ribeiro. "Introduction." *Geometrias da memória: configurações pós-coloniais*, edited by António Sousa Ribeiro and Margarida Calafate Ribeiro, Edições Afrontamento, 2016, pp. 5-11.

Rippl, Gabriele. "Introduction." *Handbook of Intermediality: Literature-Image-Sound-Music*, edited by Gabriele Rippl, De Gruyter, 2015, pp. 1-31.

Sanches, Manuela Ribeiro. "Where is the Post-colonial? In-Betweenness, Identity and 'Lusophonia' in Trans/National Contexts." *New Hybridities: Societies and Cultures in Transition*, edited by Frank Heidenmann and Alfonso de Toro, Olm, 2006, pp. 115-45.

Schuster, Sven and Alejandra Buenaventura. "Entre *blanqueamiento* y *paraíso racial*: el Imperio de Brasil y la legitimación visual de la esclavitud en las exposiciones universales." *Imaginando América Latina: Historia y cultural visual, siglos XIX-XXI*, edited by Sven Schuster and Óscar Daniel Hernández Quiñones, Editorial Universidad del Rosario, 2017, pp. 59-92.

Straub, Julia. "Nineteenth-century Literature and Photography." *Handbook of Intermediality: Literature-Image-Sound-Music*, edited by Gabriele Rippl, De Gruyter, 2015, pp. 156-72.

Vicente, Filipa Lowndes. "Black Women's Bodies in the Portuguese Colonial Visual Archive (1900-1975)." *Transnational Africa: Visual Material and Sonic Cultures of Lusophone Africa*, edited by Christopher Larkosh et al., Tagus Press, 2018, pp. 16-67

ERIN MCCOMBE is a doctoral candidate based at Queen's University Belfast. Her research project explores contemporary literature by Afrodescendant women writers in Spanish and Portuguese and is funded by the Northern Bridge Consortium.

Literatura Negra Brasileira e os Diálogos com o Cânone: Outros Olhares, Outras Histórias

RESUMO: Este trabalho tem por objetivo refletir sobre aspectos da construção identitá-ria observada em poemas de autoria negra em confronto com a representação desses sujeitos, em uma escrita orientada pelos valores éticos e estéticos fundamentalmente brancos. Busca-se também apontar, nos autores brasileiros escolhidos, uma trajetória de resistência que enseja construir um horizonte utópico em que o negro surge enfim como voz essencial no âmbito do sistema literário nacional. Nesse sentido, problematizar-se-á de que maneira a literatura de autoria negra, muito além de constituir-se na voz dos dominados, ameaça e dissolve a visão hegemônica que simula uma sociedade brasileira homogênea, monocultural e unidimensional.

PALAVRAS- CHAVE: poesia negra brasileira, resistência, utopia.

ABSTRACT: This work aims to reflect on aspects of the identity construction observed in poems of black authorship in confrontation with the representation of these subjects, in a script oriented by fundamentally white ethical and aesthetic values. In the chosen Brazilian authors, I also tried to point out a trajectory of resistance that leads to the construction of a utopian horizon in which the black man emerges as an essential voice within the national literary system. In this sense, I will question how the black authorship literature, much as it constitutes the voice of the dominated, threatens and dissolves the hegemonic vision that simulates a homogeneous, monocultural, and unidimensional Brazilian society.

KEYWORDS: Brazilian black poetry, resistance, utopia.

Questões Iniciais

Este trabalho tem por objetivo refletir sobre aspectos da construção identitária observada em poemas de autoria negra brasileira em confronto com a representação desses sujeitos, numa escrita orientada pelos valores éticos e estéticos fundamentalmente brancos. Busca-se também apontar, nos autores escolhidos, uma trajetória de resistência que enseja construir um horizonte utópico em que o negro surge enfim como voz essencial no âmbito do sistema literário nacional.

Para tanto, alguns poemas foram escolhidos porque representam, segundo entendemos, esse impulso vital que autores negros assinalam como tarefa primordial na elaboração de um texto que espelhe uma espécie de genealogia da experiência negra, tanto literária quando histórico-social, em um país onde o racismo é elemento estruturante em suas relações sociais. Para esses poetas, a escrita é a forma encontrada para se contrapor a um discurso oficial que reiteradamente coloca os sujeitos negros no campo do vulgar, do folclore ou, pior, da invisibilidade e da não existência. É preciso, pois, nessa perspectiva, resistir a tal condição, desvelando literariamente os mecanismos alienadores/alienantes muito vivos e eficazes na manutenção da ideologia colonial escravista que ainda regula as relações sociais e, sobretudo, raciais na sociedade brasileira.

A literatura coloca-se, então, como espaço privilegiado de disputas ideológicas em que o estético se soma ao ético, de modo a projetar um futuro em que se engendrem verdadeiras e definitivas transformações. É possível afirmar, assim, que os escritores aqui referenciados recuperam e atualizam as reflexões de Frantz Fanon sobre a cultura nacional e o papel dos intelectuais sob o jugo colonial: "O homem colonizado que escreve para o seu povo, quando utiliza o passado, deve fazê-lo com a intenção de abrir o futuro, convidar para a ação, fundar a esperança" (Fanon 2005, 266).

Nessa perspectiva de completo engajamento assumem uma voz coletiva, desempenhando uma função que Edward Said, retomando Bourdieu, classifica como insubstituível, pois seu trabalho contribui de maneira efetiva para que se desenvolvam "as condições sociais para a produção coletiva de utopias realistas" (Bourdieu apud Said 2003, 37). Este trabalho artístico tem, portanto, a intenção de intervir ativamente no debate público sobre as opressões concretas e simbólicas sofridas pela população negra e contribuir para os processos de desalienação, levando, consequentemente, a transformações sociais há muito requeridas.

Dessas escritas, pulsam palavras insubmissas que insistem em desvelar e confrontar uma história oficial, expondo as contradições internas do país e os limites do processo de descolonização e modernização de nossa sociedade. Nela, o apagamento da incômoda presença negra resultante do colonialismo, no capitalismo colonial que lhe sucede, para usar a definição de Caio Prado Jr., se coloca como um imperativo a ser efetivado. O negro, a escravidão, a indigência desses indivíduos no pós-abolição e na república constituem-se em entraves constrangedores para a concretização da ideia de nação que se pretendia imaginar pela elite dirigente do país. Mais do que esquecida, a população negra e suas contribuições para a formação da sociedade brasileira vão sendo extirpadas do cenário nacional.

Nesse sentido, esses escritores trazem dentro de si o passado – as marcas e as humilhações das feridas inerentes ao processo colonial e escravista que se torna ainda muito presente. Mais uma vez, Fanon pontua com precisão quando afirma: "O negro, que nunca foi tão negro como depois que foi dominado pelo branco, quando decide provar a sua cultura, fazer obra de cultura, percebe que a história lhe impõe um terreno preciso, que a história lhe indica uma via precisa e que deve manifestar uma cultura negra" (Fanon 2005, 245). Esse passado tornar-se-á vida pelo trajetos da memória acessados e reverberados em cada verso de poema ou cada linha narrativa.

Não se pode esquecer, como aponta Said, que a cultura sempre se colocou como campo de disputa pela mesma história, tanto pelos opressores como pelos oprimidos e que: "Assim como uma cultura pode predispor e preparar ativamente uma sociedade para a dominação ultramarina de outra sociedade ela também pode preparar essa primeira sociedade para renunciar ou modificar a ideia de dominação ultramar" (Said 1995, 255).

Evidentemente, essa postura caminha *pari passu* com o desejo real de transformação e de outras formas de luta e de resistência. O que a literatura de autoria negra faz, muito além de dar voz aos dominados, é ameaçar e dissolver a visão hegemônica que simula uma sociedade brasileira homogênea, monocultural e unidimensional: "A nação não é mais o quadro uniforme em que se encerrava a consciência da coletividade" (Nora 1993, 12). Trata-se de abrir caminhos, desalienar consciências, e o texto literário surge como uma via que leva a imaginar uma nova comunidade nacional, em que se concebam ideias de libertação, de igualdade e de insubmissão aos padrões. São escritas que propõem um profundo reordenamento das relações de poder na estrutura social, contestando sua legitimidade e forjando um lugar capaz de desestabilizá-la. É, em essência e por natureza, um discurso contraideológico.

Em síntese, observa-se no trabalho poético de autores negros aqui selecionados que esse projeto deseja viver o passado pelo rompimento, em que a memória vai projetar-se na descontinuidade (Nora 1993, 19). O trabalho com a memória, no resgate da história não contada, é, como também pontua o sociólogo francês, Maurice Halbwachs (2003), um processo de reconstrução em que, por meio da experiência individual (mas sempre pensada e pautada nas e pelas relações sociais), a memória resgate e reconecte o coletivo a suas origens e a seu passado.

Dessa forma, coloca-se em prática a feliz afirmação do historiador Jacques Le Goff (2003, 471) de que a memória coletiva deve libertar e não escravizar.

O acesso ao passado tem o objetivo de, mais do que puramente lembrá-lo, reescrevê-lo agora sob nova perspectiva, que visa, sobretudo, a reivindicar-se como sujeito de sua história, reabilitar-se, enfim, diante de si e do outro, produzindo, assim, "poesia de revolta, mas poesia analítica," como reivindicava Frantz Fanon (2005, 260).

Leituras em Diálogo

Os autores focalizados neste artigo – Miriam Alves, Cuti, Éle Semog, Jônatas Conceição, Salgado Maranhão e Sacolinha – pertencem a gerações diferentes, mas compartilham projetos cujos procedimentos literários e intelectuais são marcados por posicionamentos políticos e ideológicos categóricos.

O paulista Luís Silva, ou Cuti, como é conhecido, participou do grupo fundador do *Quilombhoje*, responsável pela série *Cadernos Negros*, que, desde 1978, faz circular uma produção de autoria negra em contos e poemas. Além disso, é possível observar que todos têm presença destacada em organizações e movimentos sociais ligados especialmente às periferias e espaços negros de alta vulnerabilidade, trabalhando com sujeitos em áreas em que a literatura tem pouco ou nenhum significado. A título de exemplo, mencione-se Éle Semog, do Rio de Janeiro, que participou de inúmeros grupos da cidade como "Negrícia," "Garra Suburbana" e "Bate-Boca," voltados para o estudo e a produção da poesia afrodescendente; e Jônatas Conceição, baiano, professor de Língua Portuguesa, radialista, que foi coordenador do Projeto de Extensão Pedagógica do Bloco Afro Ilê Aiyê, grupo pioneiro no resgate e valorização da cultura negra de projeção nacional.

Todos os poetas aqui elencados são presenças habituais em antologias, mas já apresentam igualmente uma produção literária individual relevante. Cuti, por exemplo, entre prosa, teatro e poesia, já publicou 17 títulos, desde edições do próprio autor a trabalhos veiculados por editoras comerciais. Possui, na mesma medida, uma produção ensaística que merece distinção, como os livros Literatura Negro-Brasileira, de 2010, e Quem tem Medo da Palavra Negro, de 2012. Salgado Maranhão, por sua vez, também com obra individual bastante sólida, foi premiado com o Jabuti em 1999 (Mural de Ventos) e indicado para o mesmo prêmio em 2016, com a obra Ópera de Nãos. Miriam Alves, a única mulher desta coletânea, além da produção literária em antologias e trabalhos individuais, em que se destaca o livro de contos de 2012, *Mulher Mat(r)iz*, assim como outros autores, apresenta uma reflexão importante sobre o fazer literário e o corpo negro, com o título *BrasilAfro Autorrevelado: Literatura Brasileira Contemporânea* (2010).

Finalmente, é preciso ressaltar que esses autores atuam também em diferentes espaços institucionais. Éle Semog foi presidente do CEAP (Centro de Articulação de Populações Marginalizadas) e Conselheiro Executivo do Instituto Palmares de Direitos Humanos. Sacolinha, da novíssima geração, destaca-se em várias iniciativas artístico-culturais, tendo idealizado o projeto Cultural Literatura no Brasil, levado a termo em rádios comunitárias; foi presidente do Centro de Pesquisas e Desenvolvimento Sócio Cultural Negro Sim e, em 2005, assumiu oficialmente a Coordenadoria Literária da Secretaria Municipal de Cultura de Suzano (estado de São Paulo), além de colaborar com o Ministério da Justiça no projeto "Uma janela para o mundo – Leitura nas Prisões," desenvolvido nas Penitenciárias de Segurança Máxima. À atuação política ativa desses escritores soma-se um trabalho literário vigoroso e expressivo, como pontuo a seguir a partir dos poemas selecionados de cada um dos autores.

A Letra, o Espaço

Passo, Praça

Paissandu a Praça
Passo no Paissandu
   a Praça
   há Pedra
   há
Rosário negro a desfiar...
há estória

Paissandu a Praça
Passo
Ouço
Rosário rezado
     reisado
negro a desfiar...
há estória em gêge
praça pedra a pedra

conta
        a
conta

Conta
das costas que não se curvaram
conta
        ah!
conta
apesar da cruz (cristã cristã) pesar
apesar
conta

Rosário rezado
                Reisado nagô
conta a conta
                        conta
(Alves 1994, 40-41)

Nesse poema de Miriam Alves, "Passo Praça," publicado nos *Cadernos Negros* 17, de 1994, observamos o eu lírico recuperar um espaço fortemente ligado às vidas e paisagens negras na cidade de São Paulo. Essa ligação bem concreta apresenta uma esfera também abstrata que se consolida no imaginário simbólico da cidade, ao capturar a cultura religiosa evocada pela praça onde se cruzam o rosário e o reisado nagô. Todo o poema é, assim, elaborado a partir do desejo de resgatar a presença negra e os significados a ela inerentes.

A praça vai sendo, desse modo, metonimicamente renovada pelo movimento das muitas mãos e costas que não se curvaram e não se curvam ante tantos obstáculos. O reisado que é negro e o rosário que se torna negro são marcas da resistência anunciada. A praça (o espaço), é bom lembrar, alude a uma guerra de caráter duvidoso, para dizer o mínimo, como a Guerra do Paraguai, já que a batalha do Paysandu antecede o grande conflito, e com ele guarda significados históricos da opressão imperial.

O largo do Paissandu, na cidade de São Paulo, abriga a Igreja Nossa Senhora do Rosário, ou Igreja de Nossa Senhora do Rosário dos Homens Pretos, como é mais conhecida, construída por trabalhadores negros, já que eram proibidos de frequentar as igrejas de brancos. Em frente à igreja encontra-se o monumento à Mãe Preta do Largo do Paissandu, formando um conjunto que é referência como marco da resistência negra na cidade. O culto a Nossa Senhora do Rosário é um dos mais antigos e funde-se com a própria gênese da cidade. A igreja ocupou vários espaços, tendo sido sempre desalojada quando comprometia o ímpeto "modernizante" da cidade e de seus mandantes.[1]

Como se pode observar na composição poética da autora paulistana, o espaço mobilizado pelo eu lírico apresenta uma ambivalência, pois traz à tona, por um lado, o projeto urbano modernizante que desconsiderava o patrimônio material e imaterial do homem negro; por outro, a firme e ferrenha resistência ao abuso e à arbitrariedade: escancaram-se, pois, as contradições da lógica do desenvolvimento social pretendido.

Nesse sentido, o Paissandu é entendido como um palco onde se desenvolvem, se organizam e reorganizam radicalmente – "pedra a pedra" (v. 15), "conta a conta" (v. 16-18) – as relações históricas em que sobressaem a dominação e a expropriação: evoca o trabalho escravo, aqui transfigurado em tarefa desejada; as costas que nunca se curvam e que contam esse trabalho utópico de insubmissão são as molas propulsoras para a resistência e a liberdade presente e futura.

Esse olhar – ao mesmo tempo crítico e sensível – à espacialidade e suas construções, não só históricas como geográficas, evidencia que o ser social rememorado está ativamente posicionado no espaço e no tempo. A espacialidade, a temporalidade e o indivíduo, entendidos em conjunto, envolvem todas as dimensões da existência humana, produzindo uma realidade empírica e sendo concomitantemente produzidos por ela.

Assim, no poema analisado, o espaço geográfico que expressa todas as interdições passa, na disputa que se coloca frente aos discursos hegemônicos, a significar a luta e a resistência. Na lógica do mundo branco/dominador/cristão insinuam-se, pelos versos da construção do poema e da própria igreja, as ciências africanas que insistem em não deixar-se elidir. Escolhas lexicais dão contundência ao traçado concebido; o tratamento rítmico baseado nas aliterações e assonâncias vai afirmando e confirmando significações. Reencena-se, no andamento poético, o ritmo das rezas e das ladainhas, em jogos polissêmicos que evocam dialeticamente contrários e contradições e que quebram a circularidade e os sentidos, ali imiscuindo-se, sorrateiras mas com vigor.

David Harvey (2006, 144), ao refletir sobre a questão espacial e sua importância para a compreensão das relações sociais sob o capitalismo, assim pontua:

Nossa tarefa é elaborar uma teoria geral das relações espaciais e do desenvolvimento geográfico sob o capitalismo, que possa, entre outras coisas, explicar a importância e a evolução das funções do Estado (locais, regionais, nacionais e supranacionais), do desenvolvimento geográfico desigual, das desigualdades inter-regionais, do imperialismo, do progresso e das formas de urbanização etc. (Harvey 2006, 144).

Já a literatura, por seu turno, pode contribuir para esse processo e essa análise, como demonstro na leitura dos poemas em tela, os quais confirmam que as contradições inerentes ao desenvolvimento das cidades sob a ação do capital, e que reproduzem as desigualdades socioeconômicas, também se fazem presentes quando focalizamos as questões raciais nesses mesmos espaços.

Os seguintes poemas, de Salgado Maranhão e Jônatas Conceição, reiteram a voz poética de Miriam Alves, estabelecendo, ao mesmo tempo, diálogos com os discursos literários do cânone não apenas brasileiro mas universal:

Terra Minha

> *"Minha terra tem palmeiras*
> *Onde canta o sabiá"*
> Gonçalves Dias

Quando eu te reconheci,
havia um rio entre nós,
desde então sigo cantando
no leito da tua voz.

Quando eu te reencontrei,
já era marcado a ferro,
sem ao menos perceber
o poder do próprio berro.

Passa por mim esse *slide*
como um cinema secreto,
como se dessa paisagem,
fosse meu próprio alfabeto.

Me lanço por entre mares,
por caminhos que nem sei...
para no fim retornar
ao ponto que iniciei.

Mesmo listando ao presente
as memórias do futuro,
acabo por te encontrar,
cada vez que me procuro.
(Maranhão 2009, 180)

À questão do espaço reconfigurado – aspecto fundamental na organização do poema "Terra Minha," de Salgado Maranhão – articula-se o diálogo com a tradição, corporificada na epígrafe, um trecho do clássico poema romântico "Canção do Exílio," do também escritor maranhense Gonçalves Dias (1823-1864), cuja ideia de pátria é fortemente idealizada e acessível a apenas uma pequena parcela da sociedade. O diálogo sugerido pela epígrafe projeta ideologicamente discursos que restringem a presença negra à subserviência social; no entanto, vai subverter esse ideal de pátria na significativa inversão sintagmática do próprio título do poema.

Dessa maneira, na voz do poeta maranhense contemporâneo, a pátria é um espaço bipartido (as partes que são separadas pelo rio, v.2), cuja gênese se explica historicamente. O diálogo com a pátria romântica – no "tu" que surge já no primeiro verso – recupera a história e a trajetória negra que vão sendo reconstruídas, agora sob novas perspectivas, que se concretiza e articula nas escolhas lexicais como "reconheci" (v.1) e "reencontrei" (v.5), em que se propõe uma recuperação articuladora de movimentos de desalienação. A paisagem vai sendo, assim, destrinchada, surgindo ante a aguda perspectiva do eu poético, que explicita de maneira rigorosa a dolorosa consciência/percepção do lugar ocupado pelo negro na lógica do capital em sua essência colonial, persistindo na configuração da sociedade brasileira contemporânea.

O eu lírico, assumindo uma voz coletiva, propõe-se a explorar uma nova geografia, em movimentos que miram o passado com o que alimenta o presente e, sobretudo, projeta o futuro, recuperando e redesenhando a trajetória de tantos para, finalmente, encontrar a sua própria essência: dessa maneira, o particular e o coletivo formam um corpo só. A identidade individual e também a coletiva só se tornam verdadeiramente significativas quando todas essas pontas são (re) conectadas. Como afirma Fanon (2005, 261), o futuro numa cultura de resistência é essencial, mas ele só é possível se o passado for recuperado em novas bases. É exatamente esse impulso vital que irrompe do poema.

A pátria mobilizada ao longo da composição resgata o espaço africano em uma projeção especular: a África recuperada e reconquistada (ecos de "Paradise Lost" e "Paradise Ragained," de John Milton?) concretiza-se pela reversão de valores: o mar, as águas, os rios surgem como espaços privilegiados porque, ao mesmo tempo que dividem, unem; ao mesmo tempo que se constituem no caminho dado, são o espaço reconquistado. O mar assume, nesse processo poético, o valor da morte, mas também da vida. Essa identidade perseguida é, por natureza, contraditória: a de encontrar-se nos espaços e tempos históricos que se deseja apagar e esquecer.

Já em dois poemas do baiano Jônatas Conceição, "Naquele Tempo Tinha Bonde" e "Porto sem Mar," publicados nos *Cadernos Negros 09*, de 1986, e *Cadernos Negros 19*, de 1996, respectivamente, podemos apontar uma simetria com os poemas anteriores: o espaço assume o protagonismo, para que se entenda o lugar ocupado pelo indivíduo negro nesses cenários de interdições e impedimentos.

Porto sem mar

Como um rio que não deságua
o porto desta cidade não me transporta.
As cidades como dois rios
que caminham mas não me encontram.

Cá, nas campinas,
o porto inexiste, não por faltar o mar
mas o amar.
O porto da minha cidade
não me leva a um ponto salvador.
O porto que gostaria que tivesse na minha cidade
carrego comigo, à procura de um mar.

CONCEIÇÃO, Jônatas. "Porto sem mar." In: *Cadernos Negros 19*, 1996, p. 94.

Em "Porto sem mar" (1996), como já se nota em outras produções poéticas do autor baiano, o mar pessoano é evocado no diálogo com a tradição, aqui marcado pelo tom melancólico, pela confirmação das carências – não por acaso, o poema inicia-se pela negativa, por tudo o que não há, sublinhando a "consciência dilacerada" (Candido, 1987) do próprio subdesenvolvimento. A grandeza simbólica do mar português contrasta inapelavelmente com a violência intrínseca que define a nação gestada, agregando nessa equação histórica a tópica racial.

O espaço que rivaliza com a grandeza, sobressaltando-se a aparente insignificância, é o espaço cindido em que se explicita a exclusão e a tensão social daí decorrente. Esses espaços e suas gentes (v. 4) estão lado a lado, mas nunca se tocam ou se relacionam, a não ser para ratificar as estruturas espoliativas. Observa-se uma vez mais o colapso e a desintegração da urbanidade, tudo forjado a partir da antítese – mar/lá, em oposição ao cá –, que estrutura o poema. Assim, a integração social verdadeira e a cidadania pretendida só podem ser alcançadas quando o mar for verdadeiramente igual para todos.

Naquele tempo tinha bonde

Seu passar nos divagava.
Devagar longe nós íamos
para o não sei onde
para o não sei quando.
A cidade era imensa...
O bonde lhe atravessava.
Nós ficávamos partidos
no caminho.

O bonde nos trazia os mistérios
por palavras
que vinham
com a Tarde
sob braços suados.
Era a cidade que se aproximava.
No devagar do bonde.
No divagar de nossa vida
(Conceição 1986, 73)

À questão do espaço apartado soma-se agora a noção do tempo em "Naquele Tempo Tinha Bonde," de 1986. A cisão expressa em "Porto sem Mar" aprofunda-se aqui. A cidade surge em toda sua amplitude e imensidão, que, no entanto, não é compartilhada e usufruída por todos; o diálogo e a interação são limitados entre as partes. O espaço dos trabalhadores é o espaço lateral, marginal: a cidade da ordem só se aproxima abstratamente pelas notícias trazidas pelos trabalhadores, como está explicitado ao longo dos versos 8 a 13. De novo, espaço destinado aos mais pobres, aos trabalhadores – metonimicamente referenciado no suor que embala o ir e vir (vv. 10-13) – está dividido, é o espaço disruptivo por excelência. Na melancólica constatação desse panorama de exclusão, sobressaem as incertezas e os mistérios que cercam/envolvem essas vidas.

Podemos então perceber que, nos poemas examinados até este ponto, cada um à sua maneira, o eu lírico abandona a ideia de pátria que se define pela convivência amena, pela obediência dócil, pela falta de antagonismos de classe, pela despreocupação e por seu cariz exótico: pátria não é mais a personificação de natureza exuberante do ideário romântico. Nos poemas, observamos a violência em estado latente, a desintegração da urbanidade, o inconformismo diante do lugar ocupado pelos pobres e negros, marcando o que Antonio Candido (1987, 160) chama da "passagem da consciência de país novo² à consciência de país subdesenvolvido," com todas as consequências políticas que o segregacionismo social e, sobretudo, racial implicam.

Miriam Alves, Salgado Maranhão e Jônatas Conceição representam liricamente, em cada projeto poético, a desigualdade e a injustiça, descartando o sentimentalismo e a subjetividade inerentes ao gênero. Ainda que a literatura se constitua como meio para o homem negro colocar sua existência particularizadora no mundo, é um movimento que remonta a toda uma coletividade. No texto seminal "Lírica e Sociedade" (1983), Adorno ressalta que, diferentemente da totalidade subjetiva hegeliana, é possível observar no gênero uma concepção de individualidade que será a expressão das opressões de uma sociedade. O filósofo alemão salienta que a poesia lírica acaba por subverter, nesse sentido, a concepção burguesa de indivíduo, ultrapassando seus limites.

Os poemas vão, assim, descrevendo as relações de poder e dominação, explicitando literariamente o que anima as práticas hegemônicas de uma sociedade excludente, mas também as forças de resistência com suas possibilidades de transformação social que se organizam nesse contexto. Se o espaço aparece como dado seminal na confrontação com o espaço projetado em vários textos canônicos, partimos agora para a exploração desses diálogos a partir de outra perspectiva.

Cravos Vitais

escrevo a palavra
escravo
e cravo sem medo
o termo escravizado
em parte do meu passado

criei com meu sangue meus quilombos
crivei de liberdade o bucho da morte
e cravei para sempre em presente
a crença na vida
(Cuti 2007a, 38)

Cuti, com seu "Cravos Vitais," confirma uma vez mais seu trabalho estético significativo, em que urde de maneira precisa o confronto do homem negro na sociedade de classes marcada pela lógica colonial. As escolhas estéticas – prevalência das consonâncias (uso de oclusivas surdas) – colaboram para a construção de uma melodia que não abranda as tensões, ao contrário, aprofunda-as. É um canto de resistência porque, ao dialogar com as forças que atuam hegemonicamente, impõe uma presença que não mais pode ser ignorada. As dicotomias ao redor das quais se organiza o poema (vida-morte, presente-passado, eu-outro) refletem exatamente as contradições da pátria partida invocadas pelos poetas anteriores.

Como se pode observar, as tensões sociais, de classe, de raça estão profundamente implicadas no fazer literário. O tom, no entanto, permite vislumbrar um projeto utópico do devir e da vida que anuncia os caminhos da liberdade, apenas em movimentos de resistência e de luta.

A tradição Reverenciada

Tradição

sob a vasta bigodeira de machado
os lábios da raça escondidos acho
a lâmina do riso e o discreto escracho

em cruz fico muito à vontade
para reunir setas de revolta
angústia e cravos

ensaio o arrombamento de portas
com o pé-de-cabra
que me empresta
com o deboche de sua risada
o gama

com o lima afio as facas
entro na trama

solano eu abraço
no boi-bumbado *socialistado*
num salto *a-rap-iado*
chego junto com os mano
nossa vida
muito tato e tutano
(Cuti 2007b, 14)

Conversa com Cruz e Sousa

a toda hora paredes sobrem, Cruz
a cada passo
a cada sonho
impondo uma queda no desânimo

em seguida
a nossa velha fênix
sacode as cinzas
e vem o sol nascendo pleno

logo novos muros de clara angústia
sobrem com a névoa das derrotas
mas a palavra rota
feito louca
salta
se enfurece
fura o cerco
muda o pelo
e espera
enquanto recupera a força

a toda hora, Cruz
o branco passado encobre
a luta nossa de cada dia
que o desafia
em gestos de libertação
nessa espessa fumaça de moscas
onde a fresta se faz
com o coração

a toda hora, Cruz
reacende a nossa
a tua luz
(Cuti 2000, 34-35)

Nesse percurso literário adotado, o autor paulista agora conclama vozes do cânone nacional, com as quais intenta desenhar uma genealogia a que vai vincular-se, não deixando dúvidas sobre sua filiação artística. No processo, desvela os impasses e contradições da sociedade que, como reiteradamente apontamos, ainda mantém intacto o seu viés colonial.

Cuti resiste frente aos processos impostos de silenciamentos diversos e em várias tonalidades e feições: de cada autor referenciado, cujo pertencimento racial é destacado, extrai um signo com o qual arquiteta e articula um diálogo não apenas com eles, mas, sobretudo, com as forças dominantes. Dessa forma, o tom de confronto não é nunca amenizado, como é traço distintivo em sua produção artística: das referências pulsa uma agonia violenta no mais bruto estado. As sutilezas não são mais possíveis, por isso as escolhas lexicais e a expressiva harmonia rítmica devem traduzir essa condição e circunstância. A violência apresenta-se uma vez mais como a única possibilidade de desafiar a violência sofrida.

O passado histórico-artístico mobilizado, de novo, se faz por princípio estético e ético, para integrar o que, pelas forças que atuam em nossa sociedade, sofreu rupturas, diluição e isolamento. Cuti e os autores com quem dialoga constituem, assim, uma espécie de confraria, cujas vozes insubordinadas desaguam na ferocidade do rap contemporâneo, estabelecendo uma síntese reveladora. Nesse sentido, a tradição aqui evocada revela resistência e luta, mas, sobretudo, revela pertencimento racial.

De Origem Jornalística

> *Ao Manuel Bandeira*
> *e seu personagem "João Gostoso"*

Zé Negão, ajudante de pedreiro,
Andava na madrugada de sábado,
Na saída do baile pela polícia foi abordado
   Revistado
   Interrogado
   Surrado
  Seu corpo foi encontrado
Pelas crianças
  Que brincavam no terreno ao lado

Cheio de mato
Próximo à avenida do Estado,
Num terreno abandonado
(Sacolinha 2006, 22)

Já com Sacolinha, o diálogo estabelecido segue a via do humor corrosivo permitido pela paródia desabrida, e que não faz, em hipótese alguma, concessões, o que possibilita levar a dissonância à ideologia literária. Quando evoca Manuel Bandeira (1886-1968) e seu "Poema Tirado de uma Notícia de Jornal," o autor instaura um contra-discurso, quebrando a harmonia em relação à tradição, com a qual, ao mesmo tempo, parece evocar pertencimento.

Aqui, o lirismo dá lugar à realidade rude experenciada pelo negro pobre brasileiro nas diversas periferias do país, que se assemelham todas nas ausências e carências: de novo, o espírito da ruptura dá o tom. A cidade vivenciada por esses indivíduos é a concretização do colapso do Estado, o império da repressão social, da perda de todos os sentidos. Esses são versos que apontam a impossibilidade de lirismo e ternura, porque aos de baixo, aos oprimidos e aos negros, só sobram a injustiça e a desigualdade.

O gesto crítico em relação à ideologia que emana do poema de Bandeira convoca o leitor a refletir sobre a real correlação de forças nessa cidade bipartida, recuperando a tensão percebida em Miriam Alves, Salgado Maranhão, Cuti e Jônatas Conceição. Em grande medida, o poema causa incômodo, porque desvela a verdadeira natureza do ordenamento social e racial da sociedade brasileira. Recusa-se, assim, a alimentar a falsa e imaginária narrativa de uma nação pacificada, cotidianamente veiculada e que guarda inescapáveis laços com o pensamento lusotropicalista.

Concluindo...

Finalmente, é possível, então, afirmar que os poemas aqui problematizados são formas de resistência que se colocam frente a variados discursos – da literatura à história – e confirmam, assim, a afirmação de Alfredo Bosi:

A poesia resiste à falsa ordem, que é, a rigor, barbárie e caos . . . Resiste ao contínuo "harmonioso" pelo descontínuo gritante; resiste ao descontínuo gritante pelo contínuo harmonioso. Resiste aferrando-se à memória viva do passado; e resiste imaginando uma nova ordem que se recorta no horizonte da utopia. (Bosi 2000, 169)

Nesse sentido, vemos que a poesia de autoria negra pode funcionar – dialeticamente nos diálogos que estabelece com a ideologia dominante – como um plano em que as contradições reais sejam enfrentadas, manifestando-se enquanto voz que evoca um despertar, e em que os sentidos perdidos de integração, de justiça, de igualdade sejam mais do que meras e vazias palavras de ordem.

NOTAS

1. Em 1721, a igreja (então uma pequena capela) é construída na região onde hoje está a Praça João Mendes, constituindo-se em ponto de encontro de escravos. Em 1737, um novo templo é erguido na região da atual rua 15 de Novembro (onde permaneceu por quase 150 anos). No ano de 1872, o governo desapropria imóveis e o cemitério de escravos ali existente para criar o Largo do Rosário; então, em 1903, com mais uma ampliação modernizante, a área da igreja e seus vizinhos são desapropriados. O novo prédio da igreja foi erguido no seu atual endereço, inaugurado apenas em 1908.

2. A consciência de país novo está presente em "Canção do Exílio," por exemplo.

REFERÊNCIAS BIBLIOGRÁFICAS

Adorno, Theodor W. 1983. "Lírica e Sociedade." In *Textos Escolhidos*, edição de Walter Benjamin *et al.* São Paulo: Abril Cultural (Os Pensadores).

Alves, Miriam. 1994. "Passo Praça." *Cadernos Negros* 17: 40-41.

Bosi, Alfredo. 2000. "Poesia-Resistência." In *O Ser e o Tempo na Poesia*. São Paulo: Companhia das Letras.

Candido, Antonio. 1987. "Literatura e Subdesenvolvimento." In *A Educação pela Noite e Outros Ensaios*. São Paulo: Ed. Ática.

Conceição, Jônatas. 1986. "Naquele Tempo Tinha Bonde." *Cadernos Negros* 09: 73.

Conceição, Jônatas. 1996. "Porto sem Mar." *Cadernos Negros* 19: 94.

Cuti. 2000. "Conversa com Cruz e Sousa." *Cadernos Negros* 23: 34-35.

Cuti. 2007a. "Cravos Vitais." In *Negroesia*, 38. Belo Horizonte: Mazza Edições.

Cuti. 2007b. "Tradição." In *Negroesia*, 14. Belo Horizonte: Mazza Edições.

Fanon, Frantz. 2005. "Sobre a Cultura Nacional." In *Os Condenados da Terra*. Juiz de Fora: EdJF.

Halbwachs, Maurice. 2003. "Memória Individual e Memória Coletiva" e "Memória Coletiva e Memória Histórica." In *A Memória Coletiva*. São Paulo: Centauro.

Harvey, David. 2006. *A Produção Capitalista do Espaço*. São Paulo: Annablume.

Le Goff, Jacques. 2003. "Memória." In *História e Memória*. São Paulo: Editora Unicamp.

Maranhão, Salgado. 2009. "Terra Minha." In *A Cor da Palavra*, 180. Rio de Janeiro: Imago e Fundação Biblioteca Nacional.

Nora, Pierre. 1993. "Entre Memória e História – A Problemática dos Lugares," tradução de Yara Aun Khoury. *Projeto História* 10: 7-28.

Sacolinha. 2006. "De Origem Jornalística." In *Cadernos Negros* 29: 22.

Said, Edward W. 1995. "Resistência e Oposição." In *Cultura e Imperialismo*. São Paulo: Companhia das Letras.

Said, Edward W. 2003. "O Papel Público de Escritores e Intelectuais." In *Cultura e Política*. São Paulo: Boitempo Editorial.

ROSANGELA SARTESCHI é professora doutora da área de Estudos Comparados de Literaturas de Língua Portuguesa da Faculdade de Filosofia, Letras e Ciências Humanas da Universidade de São Paulo. Atualmente é também vice-diretora do Centro de Estudos Africanos da mesma Universidade.

Essay

Introduction to "O Rumo da literatura negra"

Agostinho Neto, the first president of Angola and one of the nation's most renowned poets, is not an uncontroversial figure. He headed a liberation movement, the MPLA, that was riven by factions and ideological disagreements during and after the struggle for independence. Some revere him as the father of the nation. They see him as a leader driven by the desire to bring dignity, literacy, education and development to Angolans.[1] Others loathe him, pointing to his autocratic tendencies and intolerance of dissent. They claim his hands were steeped in the blood not just of his fellow countrymen and women but of thousands of members of the movement he led.[2]

Before Neto became the towering figure of Angolan independence, he co-founded in 1950 the short-lived Center for African Studies in Portugal, with one of Portuguese-speaking Africa's most formidable intellectuals, Amílcar Cabral, and Francisco José Tenreiro – the poet from São Tomé e Príncipe whose work is often read to exemplify negritude in the Portuguese language. The other co-founder was Mário Pinto de Andrade, a fellow Angolan with whom Neto had an increasingly fraught relationship that completely broke down shortly after Angolan independence. From the 1950s onwards, Andrade curated anthologies of "black" writing from Portuguese-speaking Africa that repeatedly included work by Neto. "Aspiração", one of Neto's first published poems, appeared in Tenreiro and Andrade's 1953 anthology *Poesia negra de expressão portuguesa*.[3] In it, Neto juxtaposes the Congo, Georgia and Amazonas, as well as the traditional Angolan musical instrument the quissange, the marimba, the viola and the saxophone, following the aesthetic paradigm of negritude that sought to represent a cross-continental solidarity of experience and culture as it affirmed black pride.

In the 1950s and 1960s, Neto became an international cause célèbre. The Salazar regime attempted to silence his calls for an independent Angola and to crush the liberation movement of which he was part. After one of Neto's many detentions by the New State, the writers Doris Lessing and Irish Murdoch were among those who signed a letter to the *Times* calling for his release. They characterized him as Portuguese-speaking Africa's equivalent to Léopold Sédar Senghor.[4]

Like Neto, the Senegalese poet Senghor would go on to become the first president of his liberated country. Alongside the Martinican Aimé Césaire, he is credited with formalizing the concept of negritude. Interestingly, Senghor saw positive parallels between practitioners of his kind of negritude and the Portuguese national self. On a state visit to Portugal in 1975, he claimed among other things that the Portuguese and black Africans shared the same gift of being instinctively and genetically poets.[5] Even more oddly, Senghor's address to the Lisbon Academy of Sciences showed a complete imbibition by the Senegalese president of Gilberto Freyre's lusotropical mythology as it had been distorted by the then-overthrown New State. The supposed conviviality of the Portuguese and their Brazilian scions found a parallel in Senghor's essentialized black Africans.

All this points to the limitations of Lessing and Murdoch's comparison of Neto with Senghor. Politically and personally, the two were far apart. One suspects that in visiting post-revolutionary Portugal and linking lusotropicalism with black affirmation, Senghor knew he would irritate his Angolan rival. Senghor was averse to the revolutionary Marxism that would come to underpin Neto's MPLA. Neto developed misgivings about the affirmation of race as a unifying concept, particularly in post-independence Angola, where he spoke out against what he perceived to be the anti-white racism directed against those in his coterie of Portuguese descent. For him, to be Angolan was a political choice that implied commitment to an MPLA agenda. It was not a blood right or a territorial given.

This is what makes the text that follows so curious. As Alexandra Reza has pointed out, negritude was always an evolving concept. Senghor and Césaire did not hold a monopoly on its definition, even if their names continue to be most closely allied to its theorization as a literary practice. In reality, negritude was often articulated to "racially informed expressions of class politics that retained a more-than-national perspective."[6] Neto's "O rumo da literatura negra" sits more comfortably in that vein than with the racialized essentialism of his Senegalese counterpart. Taken from Mário Pinto de Andrade's archive held at the Mário Soares Foundation, the text was originally written for the Center for African Studies, and attempts to grapple with what counts and does not count towards black literature. The difficulty Neto finds in reaching a pure definition parallels the ease with which he enumerates exclusions from Machado de Assis to Rui de Noronha, who despite his "Surge et ambula" "is "merely" a Portuguese poet. Neto would use a similar tactic when it came to defining who was Angolan, excluding opponents from the framework of national identification, and limiting the concept of Angolanness to a marker of ideological commitment.

Black literature for Neto ultimately seems to be about social commitment. There is no room for introspection. There needs to be a psychological identification with a way of being in the world – something that can only be achieved affectively, by being the committed mirror of the social life of a people. That, one assumes, is what he thought he was doing when he wrote his poetry.

NOTES

1. Roberto de Almeida, *A vida e a obra de Agostinho Neto* (Luanda: MPLA, 1987).

2. See for example, Carlos Pacheco, *Agostinho Neto: O perfil de um ditador* (Lisbon: Vega, 2016).

3. Francisco Tenreiro and Mário Pinto de Andrade, *Poesia negra de expressão portuguesa* (Lisbon: África, 1982) [1953], pp. 59-60.

4. Marga Holness, Introduction to translation of *Sagrada esperança*, reproduced in *A noção de ser*, Pires Laranjeira and Ana T. Rocha (eds) (Luanda: Novo Rumo, 2014), p. 770.

5. Léopold Sédar Senghor, *Lusitanidade e negritude* (Lisbon: Academia das Ciências de Lisboa, 1975), p. 51.

6. Alexandra Reza, *African Literary Journals in French and Portuguese, 1947-1968: Politics, Culture and Form* (Oxford DPhil Thesis, 2018), p. 98.

PHILLIP ROTHWELL is King John II Professor of Portuguese at the University of Oxford.

O Rumo da literatura negra[1]

A literatura, como índice da cultura dum determinado agrupamento humano, só pode ser compreendida na medida em que se torna possível a limitação e isolamento desse grupo, permitindo-se deste modo o conhecimento da sua índole social, das tendências psicológicas e mesmo das suas realizações materiais.

Partindo deste princípio e para compreendermos a literatura negra, devemos conhecer primeiro que indivíduos para ela contribuem, a fim de evitar a confusão de conceitos que actualmente se faz ao referirmo-nos aos negros, grupo aliás difícil de limitar em virtude das divergências de pontos de vista existentes quer sob o aspecto sociológico, quer ao considerar o critério étnico. Incapazes, pois, de encontrar definição adequada para os indivíduos que vamos considerar, encará-los-emos apenas dentro do quadro social-literário em que se desenvolvem ou a que se adaptaram.

Incluir neste grupo todos os indivíduos de cor, negros ou seus descendentes e apenas por este motivo, seria um erro porquanto, embora a sua cor, muitos deles – por qualquer motivo; a educação, por exemplo – não possuem aquele mínimo de cultura *africana* para serem encarados dentro deste sector literário, mesmo quando observamos a multiplicidade da vida actual. Escritores que não traduziram nenhum aspecto *negro* na sua obra, melhor serão enquadrados nas correntes literárias dos países ou povos cuja cultura reflectem. O reticente Machado de Assis é um exemplo. Gonçalves Crespo outro.

Adoptando o mesmo critério consideramos integrados na literatura negra as obras daqueles autores que de alguma forma reflectem a maneira de ser dos povos negros, os seus sentimentos, os seus processos de reacção; sendo este reflexo não apenas uma *tradução*, mas uma verdadeira *identificação*. Assim, não incluímos aqui aquelas obras "bem intencionadas" de escritores que, à caca de pitoresco ou para inspirar piedade enfileiram no negrismo. *A cabana do pai Tomas* ou os poemas de Jorge de Lima não pertencem à literatura negra. Tão pouco a desconcertante *literatura* colonial que por vezes extasia os europeus como crianças num jardim zoológico. Mesmo os negros que encarreiraram pelas puras ideias europeias são excluídos do campo literário que nos ocupa. Rui de Noronha, negro moçambicano é, literariamente, apenas um poeta português, mesmo ao tomarmos conhecimento do seu poema "Surge et Ambula", dos poucos em que ele se apercebe da existência da África.

Não cremos, como W. Somerset Maugham, "que possamos conhecer ninguém a fundo, a não ser os nossos próprios compatriotas. Pois os homens não são somente eles; são também a região onde nasceram, a fazenda ou o apartamento da cidade onde aprenderam a andar, os brinquedos que brincaram em crianças, as lendas que ouviram dos mais velhos, a comida de que se alimentaram, as escolas que frequentaram, os desportos em que se exercitaram, os poetas que leram e o Deus em que acreditaram. [...] E essas coisas [...] só pode conhecê-las quem é parte delas."[2]

Para que a determinada obra literária se atribua nacionalidade é necessário que ela se baseie na vida dos representantes dessa nacionalidade. E para que isso seja possível é necessário que o autor tenha conhecimento da vida dos seus elementos constituintes. Ora, o conhecimento dos negros, actualmente, não está ao alcance de todos os autores rotulados de negros. Conhecer, neste caso, não é apenas coleccionar percepções sensoriais é ainda ter uma noção da parte psíquica dos homens, é ainda assumir certa atitude afectiva. Este conhecimento só o tem quem é capaz de se identificar psicologicamente com a maioria dos indivíduos do seu grupo para poder sentir como eles, os incidentes do dia a dia e as manifestações de carácter cultural ou material.

Não sabemos, por exemplo, até que ponto os indivíduos de cultura puramente europeia podem entender o poema "Sabás", de Nicolás Guillén. Seguindo a nossa maneira de ver, o verso "Porqué Sabás, la mano abierta?" exige, não só a intervenção da inteligência, mas a identificação com Sabás para podermos reprovar em cada negro, com essa ternura insinuante de Guillén, a inconsciência da atitude de "mão aberta". Só um profundo conhecimento, não desligado da experiência, e a aceitação insofismada da realidade do nosso mundo pode ajudar a apreender a latitude daquele verso; a submissão psicológica, aparente ou não, do negro da rua, ou o "arrivismo flagrante do negro beneficiado pelo poder, pela cultura ou pela riqueza"[3] – ou seja: a atitude de "mão aberta".

★

Porém, o *conhecimento* do negro, tem sido prejudicado pelas condições da sua vida desde o século XVI.

O seu contacto com o europeu ficou marcado com um acto violento – a conquista. Depois, outros actos não menos violentos o forçaram a ir exercer um papel essencial na edificação dos países das Américas, como esclarece Gilberto Freyre[4] e a manter-se até hoje na sua situação de inferioridade perante os outros povos, ante a impossibilidade de educação em larga escala e as dificuldades na vida social dos países que habitam, além de outras razões que não importa trazer aqui.

Para R.P. Aupiais[5] é nestes actos violentos que reside a base de preconceitos de cor. Mas nós não desejamos encarar a questão sob este aspecto, para não nos afastarmos do nosso objectivo.

Estas violências determinaram a submissão do negro, que por vezes se traduz em desejo de penetrar com direitos de cidade na cultura europeia e na sua vida social, umas vezes com persistência consciente e outras com franco desespero ante a intransigência branca. E grande parte das obras literárias "verdadeiramente negras" reflecte com maior ou menor evidência este estado de espírito – orgulho ofendido, ambições frustradas, desejos irrealizados, impotência. Literatura de sensibilidade, acima de tudo, por vezes autênticos muros de lamentações sem consequências construtivas.

Os povos negros atravessam o seu período de confusão, por terem abandonado de chofre a sua cultura, modificando totalmente o sistema de vida em uma ou duas gerações, para adquirir uma cultura europeia e estruturada sobre bases frágeis. Esquecendo-se e ao seu povo, para pretender ingressar definitivamente na civilização europeia em que os seus instrumentos lhe são cruelmente sonegados, o negro experimenta, a par da frustração, uma fase ainda mais prejudicial para a sua personalidade, do que as chacinas no campo de batalha ou o chicote da escravidão declarada.

Hoje, negros conscientes já encaram os seus problemas de modo racional. O desejo de reencontrar a sua cultura perdida ou esquecida é dos sintomas mais animadores. Os movimentos culturais de negros que se vão estabelecendo nas Américas e na África, especialmente de cultura francesa, são sinais desejáveis para que estes povos se encontrem e continuem o seu rumo na história da humanidade.

Cremos que destes movimentos sairá a falange de escritores capaz de carrear definitivamente a literatura negra para o seu verdadeiro rumo.

★

A literatura é um reflexo da vida social dos povos e da estrutura histórica que a suporta. Não é este reflexo, porém, que encontramos em muitos escritores negros antigos e em alguns modernos, que se deixam arrastar pelas correntes literárias da Europa. Estes são, para empregar uma expressão corrente, os escritores "apesar de" negros. Assim é Costa Alegre, o negro santomense de quem não conhecemos sobre a sua raça senão algumas frases poéticas que, ao lado da sua importante obra, parecem mais produtos dos momentos de distracção do poeta. Esta característica, de certo modo paradoxal, dever-se-á à falta de consciência de povo ou então a um egoísmo tal que torna impossível a manifestação daquela "personalidade humana" que irradia, por exemplo, do "Batouala", de René Maran.

Conhecemos, das obras de alguns autores europeus que viveram ou vivem em terras de regime colonial, aquele género de livros de exportação em que os homens nos aparecem como brinquedos coloridos para servirem de distracção aos apreciadores de literatura açucarada. Da África e do negro mostram aquilo que para o europeu é exótico, quando não os salpicam de frases mal intencionadas.

Pois esta literatura de fundo mistificado – coisa espantosa! – conta negros entre os seus autores, tal a perversão psicológica causada pelo lirismo doce, nos caminhos do esteticismo puro e... inconsequente. Talvez a esperança duma diluição psicológica na cultura europeia, para esquecer a sua origem cultural os animasse a produzir obras desta qualidade – o que seria uma solução para o seu drama pessoal. Mas caíram na incoerência de se enganarem a si mesmos, o que é inocente e estúpido.

No panorama actual da literatura negra, tende a desaparecer este desencontro entre o escritor e a sua obra. E ainda bem, para todos nós. A realidade dos povos negros deve ser encarada sem a cobertura de remendos convencionais, num contributo para a sua elevação cultural.

Só assim podemos tomar a literatura, no sentido em que J. Paul Sartre[6] vê a poesia negra: "La poésie négre est évangelique, elle annonce la bonne nouvelle: la négritude est retrouvée".

*

Ao consumar-se o acto violento a que atrás nos referimos, os negros viram-se destituídos do bem mais precioso dum povo: a língua. Ainda que seja empregada pela maioria (em África), ela deixou de ser instrumento útil no contacto com a civilização europeia e, praticamente, não é usada nem mesmo conhecida por aqueles que a terminologia colonial rotulou de evoluídos ou assimilados.

Assim, os negros falam e escrevem a língua dos países em cujos territórios vivem, como todos sabem. As suas obras literárias têm sido escritas principalmente em francês e inglês. Notemos a existência de um importante núcleo literário em Dakar, talvez como eco do trabalho de L. Sédor Senghor em Paris e onde se salienta a acção de Diop.

A literatura negra não é conhecida da maioria dos negros, já por virtude da incultura que, para pesar nosso, ainda abarca percentagens elevadíssimas, já pela dificuldade que há nos iniciados na leitura, de entenderem uma língua que não beberam com a leite materno, embora a acessibilidade dos modernos. Cremos que os escritores do futuro criarão novas formas de expressão, ao sofrerem a influência do povo quando trabalharem in loco. Essas formas ainda não apareceram. De resto hoje escreve-se menos para os negros do que para os brancos, como se depreende.

Por outro lado, não existem traduções para as línguas nativas, o que ajudaria a difusão do livro, com consequências benéficas, até mesmo no respeitante à propagação das técnicas e de noções científicas.

Ainda que evidente esta impossibilidade expressional, que afasta o escritor do seu povo, o homem negro vai deixando de figurar na literatura como vítima passiva, no intuito de condenar as organizações sociais que lhe entravam o desenvolvimento – como o vemos ainda em Richard Wright – para tomar já a figura de homem com certeza no olhar para o futuro, como o encontramos em Langston Hughes, em Aimé Césaire e em outros.

Assim se vai precisando cada vez mais a identificação entre o escritor "como" negro e o negro "como" homem.

A influência das modernas tendências literárias é evidentíssima nos autores negros, e não admira que assim seja, pois é em escolas europeias que eles se formam, regra geral; mas essa influência não é o único factor que imprime novas directrizes à nossa literatura. Esse novo ritmo, esse novo humanismo que se vai afastando do tipo de reacção pura e que enternece numa antegozo de melhores dias para a humanidade é o anúncio do renascimento do negro para a alma negra.

Se houver – como é de esperar – um aumento do nível de instrução e se fosse possível traduzir para as línguas Africana as grandes obras literárias, muitas possibilidades haveria de ver os rumos da literatura negra, mais acentuadamente dirigidos para o seu povo onde, inevitavelmente, deve ir buscar os motivos de inspiração e exercer a sua função – que é a de toda a Arte – a consciencialização dos povos ante os seus problemas e os do mundo.

Cremos que o rumo da literatura negra está traçado nesse sentido.

Março de 1951
Agostinho Neto

NOTAS

1. Fundação Mário Soares, Arquivo Mário Pinto de Andrade, 04354.005.003. http://casacomum.org/cc/visualizador?pasta=04354.005.003

Publicado com a autorização da Fundação Agostinho Neto. O texto manuscrito foi transcrito e editado por Mario Pereira. Um agradecimento especial ao Pires Laranjeira e à Diana Simões pela ajuda.

2. *O Fio da Navalha*, Ed. Globo, p. 11.

3. Gilberto Freyre, *Casa Grande e Senzala*, 5º edição, p. 717.

4. Idem.

5. In "L'Homme de couleur"

6. Léopold Sédar Senghor, "Prefácio", *Anthologie de la nouvelle poésie nègre et malgache de langue française*, p. XV.

AGOSTINHO NETO

Translated by Mario Pereira

The Path for Black Literature[1]

Literature as the index of the culture of a certain human grouping can only be understood insofar as the delimitation and isolation of this group becomes possible, thus enabling knowledge of its social nature, its psychological tendencies, and even its material manifestations.

Based on this principle, for us to understand Black literature, we must first know the individuals who contribute to it in order to avoid the confusion of concepts that is currently made when we refer to "Blacks," a group that is, in fact, difficult to define because of the divergence of existing points of view both in sociological terms and when considering ethnic criteria. Incapable, therefore, of finding an adequate definition for the individuals whom we are going to discuss, we will consider them only within the socio-literary context in which they develop or to which they have adapted themselves.

To include in this group all individuals of color, Blacks and their descendants, and to do so only for this reason, would be a mistake since, despite their color, many of them—for whatever reason, education, for example—do not possess that minimum of *African culture* to be considered in this literary group, even when we take into account the rich variety of contemporary life. Writers who do not express any *Black* quality in their work would be better suited to the literary currents of the countries or peoples whose culture they reflect. The reticent Machado de Assis is one example. Gonçalves Crespo, another.

Adopting the same criterion, we consider as belonging to Black literature the works of those authors who in some way reflect the manner of being of Black peoples, their feelings, their processes of reaction, with this reflection being not simply a *translation*, but a true *identification*. Thus, we do not include here those "well-intentioned" works of writers who in pursuit of the picturesque or to inspire compassion align themselves with Blackness. *Uncle Tom's Cabin* and the poems of Jorge de Lima do not belong to Black literature. Neither does the disconcerting colonial "literature" that sometimes enthralls Europeans like children in a zoo. Even Black authors who were guided by pure European ideas are excluded from the literary field that concerns us. Rui Noronha, a Black

Mozambican, is in literary terms merely a Portuguese poet, even when we take into account his poem "Surge et Ambula," one of the few in which he appears aware of the existence of Africa.

We, like W. Somerset Maugham, do not believe that "one can ever really know any but one's own countrymen. For men and women are not only themselves; they are also the region in which they were born, the city apartment or the farm in which they learnt to walk, the games they played as children, the old wives' tales they overheard, the food they ate, the schools they attended, the poets they read, and the God they believed in. [...] And these things [...] you can only know them if you are them."[2]

In order to attribute nationality to a certain literary work, it is necessary that the work be based on the lives of those who represent that nationality. And for this to be possible, it is necessary that the author have knowledge of the life of its constituent elements. However, knowledge of the Black experience is not currently within the reach of all authors who are labeled as Black. Knowing, in this case, is not only the collecting of sensory perceptions, but it is also having a notion of the psychic component of people, it is also assuming a certain affective attitude. This knowledge is possessed only by those who are capable of identifying psychologically with the majority of the individuals of their group in order to be able to feel, as they feel, the incidents of everyday life and the manifestations of a cultural and a material character.

We do not know, for example, the extent to which individuals from a purely European culture can understand the poem "Sabás" by Nicolás Guillén. According to our way of thinking, the verse "Porqué Sabás, la mano abierta?"[3] demands not only the intervention of intelligence, but also the identification with Sabás for us to be able to condemn in each Black person, with Guillén's insinuating tenderness, the lack of awareness of the attitude of the "open hand." Only profound knowledge, not disconnected from experience, and the clear-headed acceptance of the reality of our world can help to comprehend the scope of that verse; the psychological submission, apparent or not, of Black people in the street or the "flagrant arrivisme of the blacks benefiting from power, culture, or wealth"[4]—in other words: the attitude of the "open hand."

★

However, *knowledge* of the Black experience has been hindered by the living conditions of Black people since the sixteenth century.

Their first contact with Europeans was marked by a violent act—conquest. Afterwards, other no less violent acts forced Black people to exercise an essential role in the construction of the countries of the Americas, as Gilberto Freyre clarifies,[5] and to remain to this day in a situation of inferiority in relation to other peoples, due to the impossibility of education on a large scale and the difficulties [encountered] in the social life of the countries in which they live, along with other reasons that are not relevant to mention here.

According to R.P. Aupias,[6] the basis for color prejudices resides in these acts of violence. But we do not wish to approach the question in these terms, so that we do not stray from our objective.

These acts of violence led to the submission of Black people, which translates at times into the desire to penetrate European culture and its social life through the rights of citizenship, sometimes with conscious persistence and other times with outright despair in the face of white intransigence. And most of the "truly Black" literary works more or less clearly reflect this state of mind—offended pride, frustrated ambitions, unrealized desires, impotence. Above all, it is literature of sensibility, on occasion authentic walls of lamentation without constructive consequences.

Black people are passing through their period of confusion for having all of a sudden abandoned their culture, completely changing their system of life in one or two generations in order to acquire a European culture built on fragile foundations. Forgetting themselves and their people, with the intention of definitively entering the European civilization whose instruments are cruelly concealed from them, they experience, along with frustration, a phase even more harmful to their personality than slaughters on the field of battle or the whip of declared slavery.

Today, conscious Black individuals already consider their problems in a rational manner. The desire to rediscover their lost or forgotten culture is one of the most encouraging symptoms. The Black cultural movements that are being established in the Americas and in Africa, especially in culturally French Africa, are desirable signs in order for these peoples to find themselves and continue on their path in the history of humanity.

We believe that it is from these movements that the phalanx of writers will emerge who will be capable of definitively leading Black literature to its true course.

*

Literature is a reflection of the social life of people and the historical structure that supports it. This reflection is not, however, what we find in many old Black writers and in some modern ones who let themselves be dragged along by the literary currents of Europe. They are, to use a current expression, writers "despite" being Black. Such is the case of Costa Alegre, the Black man from São Tomé about whose race we know nothing except for some poetic phrases, which, compared to his important work, seem to be products of the poet's moments of distraction. This somewhat paradoxical characteristic is the result of people's lack of awareness, or rather of such an egoism that renders impossible the manifestation of that "human personality" that radiates, for example, from *Batouala* by René Maran.

From the works of some European authors who lived or presently live in lands under colonial rule, we are familiar with that genre of export books in which men appear to us as colorful toys to serve as distraction for those lovers of sugarcoated literature. What they depict about Africa and Black people is what the European finds exotic; that is, when they are not sprinkling them with malicious phrases.

But this literature of mystification counts—an astonishing fact!—Black authors among its contributors; such is the psychological perversion caused by the sweet lyricism on the paths of an aestheticism that is pure and…inconsequential. Perhaps the hope for a psychological dilution in European culture in order to forget their cultural origins encourages them to produce works of this quality—something that would be a solution for their personal drama. But they fall into the incoherence of deceiving themselves, which is naive and stupid.

In the current Black literature scene, this divergence between the writer and his work tends to disappear. And this is good for all of us. The reality of Black peoples has to be faced without the protection of conventional palliatives to contribute to its cultural elevation.

Only in this way can we consider literature in the sense in which J. Paul Sartre sees Black poetry: "La poésie négre est évangelique, elle annonce la bonne nouvelle: la négritude est retrouvée."[7]

*

Upon the consummation of the violent act to which we made reference above, Black people saw themselves deprived of the most precious asset of a people: their language. Even though it is used by the majority (in Africa), it ceased being a useful instrument in the contact with European civilization, and it is practically neither used nor known by those who colonial terminology has labeled as evolved or assimilated.

Thus, Black people speak and write the languages of the countries in whose territories they live, as we all know. Their literary works have been written principally in French and English. We highlight the existence of an important literary nucleus in Dakar, perhaps as an echo of the work of L. Sédor Senghor in Paris and where Diop's work stands out.

Black literature is unknown to most Black people, by virtue of the lack of culture that, much to our regret, still affects very large numbers, and because of the difficulty that exists for the newly-literate to understand a language that they did not imbibe with their mother's milk, despite the accessibility of the moderns. We believe that the writers of the future will create new forms of expression when they experience the influence of the people by working among them. Those forms have not yet appeared. Moreover, today less is written for Black readers than for white readers, as we can see.

On the other hand, translations into native languages do not exist, something that would help the dissemination of books to positive effect, including even the propagation of technical knowledge and scientific ideas.

Even though this expressional impossibility, which distances the writer from his people, is evident, the Black man ceases to appear in literature as a passive victim in order to condemn the social organizations that hinder his development—as we still see in Richard Wright—and now assumes the figure of the man who looks with confidence to the future, such as we find him in Langston Hughes, Aimé Cesaire, and others.

Thus, the identification between the writer "as" Black and the Black subject "as" a man is increasingly necessary.

The influence of modern literary styles is quite evident in Black authors, and it is not surprising that this is so, because they are, as a general rule, educated in European schools. But this influence is not the only factor that imparts new directives to our literature. This new rhythm, this new humanism that moves away from a type of pure reaction and that excites in anticipation of better days for humanity announces the rebirth of the Black man to the Black soul.

If there will be, as we hope, an increase in the level of education and if it would be possible to translate into African languages the great works of literature, many possibilities for the paths of Black literature would open, paths that are more clearly directed toward its people where inevitably such work must search for its sources of inspiration and exercise its function—which is that of all Art—raising people's awareness of their own problems and those of the world.

We believe that the course of Black literature is drawn in this direction.

March 1951

NOTES

1. Published with the kind permission of the Fundação Agostinho Neto. Special thanks to Grace Holleran.

2. W. Somerset Maugham, *The Razor's Edge (Vintage Books, 1944), p. 3*

3. Trans.— "Why, Sabás, with an open hand?"

4. Gilberto Freyre, *Casa Grande e Senzala* (5th edition), p. 717. Translation mine.

5. Idem.

6. In "L'Homme de couleur."

7. Trans.— "Black poetry is evangelic, it announces good news: blackness has been rediscovered." Jean-Paul Sartre, "Black Orpheus," *The Massachusetts Review*, Vol. 6, No. 1 (Autumn, 1964 – Winter, 1965), pp. 13-52. Originally published as the preface to Léopold Sédar Senghor, *Anthologie de la nouvelle poésie nègre et malgache de langue française* (Paris, 1948), p. XV.

AGOSTINHO NETO (1922-1979) was a poet, physician, and politician. He served as the first president of Angola from 1975 to 1979.

MARIO PEREIRA is Executive Editor of *Portuguese Literary & Cultural Studies*.

Reviews

Nely Nyaka (com Gita Honwana Welch).
Mahanyela: a vida na periferia da grande cidade.
Maputo: Marimbique, 2018.

A visibilidade-invisibilidade das mulheres negras na luta política em Moçambique conhece uma nova faceta com a publicação da história da vida de Nely Nyaka (Vovó Nely) na primeira voz; intitulado *Mahanyela: a vida na periferia da grande cidade*, este livro sai. Publicado com a chancela da editora Marimbique, este livro regista as memórias vividas e críticas de uma mulher que atravessa o longo século XX. O livro abre com o lugar e o tempo onde tudo começou: "Eu nasci em KaTembe, a 2 de Novembro de 1920, um domingo, às 11 horas da manhã. A minha mãe chamava-se Jinita Libombo e o meu pai Jeremia Dick Nyaka. Os meus pais conheceram-se em KaTembe, onde ambos cresceram e frequentavam a mesma Igreja. Foi lá que eles se casaram, e tiveram os primeiros dois filhos: o meu irmão Daniel e eu. Tiveram ao todo sete filhos, quatro rapazes e três meninas." De acordo com estas memórias, o ativismo e a presença política de Nely Nyaka cedo se iniciaram, primeiro na Igreja Metodista Wesleyana e, mais tarde, no Instituto Negrófilo (posteriormente renomeado Centro Associativo dos Negros da Colónia de Moçambique), organização de que o seu pai foi sócio-fundador. Em 1939 casou-se com Raul Bernardo Honwana; o casal foi viver para a Moamba, onde nasceram vários dos seus oito filhos. As referências aos múltiplos episódios que recorda desta vivência estão presentes nos dezasseis capítulos que compõem este livro, o qual integra também uma curta introdução escrita por uma das filhas de Nely Nyaka (por Gita Honwana Welch), assim como um anexo rico em imagens que ajudam a apreciar os vários sujeitos e as várias épocas que o livro abarca. Praticamente metade do livro incide sobre a infância e os primeiros anos da vida de casada da autora, incluindo uma descrição detalhada da sua família e amigos, com enfoque na Lourenço Marques (atual Maputo) dessa altura. Nely Nyaka oferece-nos um retrato da periferia, da "nossa cidade", de como se vivia então, incluindo uma digressão de carácter etnográfico sobre o namoro, o casamento, filhos, etc. O livro continua com um retrato detalhado da vida nas "terras do Sabié", para onde o seu marido havia sido transferido, para depois se centrar nas alterações políticas que aconteceram com a crescente oposição nacionalista em Moçambique. A segunda parte do livro inscreve-se neste ambiente de crescente perseguição política. À prisão do seu marido, um episódio que a marca profundamente, segue-se o regresso a Lourenço Marques e a prisão do seu filho, Luís Bernardo Honwana. Os capítulos que se seguem descrevem já a transição para a independência e as 'coisas da revolução'. Os capítulos finais são como que uma reflexão sobre esta viagem no íntimo vivido de Nely Nyaka, onde se destaca a 'nossa língua e a nossa cultura' e as 'viagens que enriqueceram a minha vida'.

No caso moçambicano, uma das suas especificidades no campo da escrita memorialista é a existência de um acervo já importante de trabalhos, com enfoque sobretudo nas experiências históricas relacionadas com as lutas emancipatórias ao longo das últimas cinco a seis décadas. No entanto, aqui também, menos atenção tem sido dada ao papel indispensável das mulheres nas lutas pela libertação nacional e os seus esforços contínuos, no presente século, pela emancipação da mulher. Este livro vem preencher uma parte deste hiato. O título destas memórias remete para a experiência de vida, para a forma de ser e estar; a prática, a vivência cultural de Nely Nyaka, é expressa através do termo 'Mahanyela', em xironga, sua língua materna, que usou no trato com muitas das pessoas com quem tem convivido. Esta obra dialoga, por exemplo, com vários episódios da economia política das mobilizações das mulheres em Moçambique, incluindo referências à sua presença em múltiplos movimentos sociais que marcam o teatro político nacional, do Centro Associativo dos Negros de Moçambique (de que participam vários familiares e amigos seus) à Organização da Mulher Moçambicana, já após a independência, ou ainda a associação Pfuna, dedicada à luta contra a pobreza e a miséria das crianças órfãs, de que é uma das fundadoras; contém igualmente referência a vários episódios, individuais e coletivos, de resistência e de luta contra o moderno colonialismo. E inclui, sobretudo, duas facetas menos presentes em muita da literatura memorialística: por um lado uma atenção especial é dada às amizades e aos afetos; por outro lado a autora, que dialoga em vários momentos com as *Memórias* de seu marido, Raul Bernardo Honwana (publicadas pela primeira vez em 1985), retoma temas com um cunho distinto, enriquecendo com a sua visão e analise pessoal a descrição do período que o livro cobre, centrado no Sul de Moçambique. Aqui é de destacar uma visão crítica sobre vários dos excessos políticos, sobre a repressão exercida pelo partido-estado da FRELIMO sobre vários sujeitos políticos.

Uma das reflexões em que Nely Nyaka insiste nesta obra é sobre a importância da "língua da terra" e do respeito mútuo pelas culturas em presença, onde "ninguém contestava o princípio que a cultura local era a base da comunidade", associadas ao "respeito de toda a gente".

Mas se estas eram as regras que regiam os espaços e afectos na zona da periferia", nos lugares públicos "o racismo era um facto de todos os dias, mesmo os europeus com quem nos dávamos" faziam questão de deixar claro qual era o lugar dos africanos no contexto colonial. Todavia esta discriminação chocante reforçou o desejo de emancipação, que se ia alargando através de uma leitura política atenta das transformações do mundo.

Desde cedo as mulheres africanas se envolveram na luta contra a presença colonial, ao mesmo tempo que procuravam ocupar um lugar mais central na vida familiar e social. Como o livro destaca, ao longo do século XX, as mulheres resistiram às políticas do domínio colonizador-colonial europeu sob o domínio português. E foram, muitas delas, formando-se politicamente na luta contra o colonialismo, quer através de núcleos religiosos, quer do NESAM, Núcleo de Estudantes Secundários Africanos de Moçambique, ou do Centro Associativo, pilares fundamentais do fermentar da ideia de luta contra o colonialismo. E esta luta trará luto a muitas situações, com a polícia política portuguesa a perseguir, a matar e a fazer desaparecer muitos nacionalistas que Nely Nyaka conheceu. Por isso a dor de ter um filho preso político trespassa parte importante do livro. Foi também uma época de "generosidade e solidariedade", como sublinha.

O precipitar da independência acontece em 1974, associado a varias peripécias políticas que a autora destaca, para referir como a independência, em 1975, significou o regresso de três dos seus filhos a Moçambique, os quais se tinham juntado ao movimento nacionalista, a FRELIMO. Os últimos capítulos do livro refletem já os anos revolucionários, sendo de sublinhar a crítica que a autora faz, com legitimidade argumentativa, da política cega de nacionalização de habitações. Como a autora sublinha, quando se falou da nacionalização dos prédios de rendimento "toda a gente apoiou, porque era a forma de moçambicanizar uma cidade, que por racismo, mantinha de fora todos os que não eram brancos". Mas quando se soube que a nacionalização abrangia, também, as barracas de construção precária, "ninguém compreendeu", pois "as barracas eram o principal recurso de que dispunham as famílias africanas" para completar o parco salário. Este é um dos exemplos citados pela autora de uma política que não teve em conta os anseios e os dilemas que os moçambicanos experimentavam. Muitos foram os percalços que a vida colocou no caminho de Nely Nyaka, que da sua casa em Maputo escreveu estas memórias sobre a sua vida, a sua cultura, a sua luta. Parafraseando Neruda, Nely Nyaka confessa que viveu, nesta obra de cariz autobiográfico, que importa ler.

MARIA PAULA MENESES É investigadora coordenadora do Centro de Estudos Sociais da Universidade de Coimbra.

A Academia Está Na Rua

Manuela Ribeiro Sanches (org.)
Descolonizações. Reler Amílcar Cabral, Césaire e Du Bois no Séc.XXI
Lisboa: Edições 70, 2018.

Chegou um tempo bom para os estudos pós-coloniais. Há muito que não tínhamos uma obra tão próxima de uma língua objetiva e concreta, que nos aproximasse de um mundo humano que nos ligasse às nossas experiências culturais e sociais mais terrenas. Quero com isto dizer que o presente livro *Descolonizações. Reler Amílcar Cabral, Césaire e Du Bois no Séc. XXI*, organizado por Manuela Ribeiro Sanches é, claramente, um livro orientado para um pensamento de um pós-colonialismo do quotidiano, que o leitor menos acostumado a uma escrita e linguagem intricadas e fechadas concetualmente pode absorver, compreender e identificar-se com os temas e leituras que os autores compilados neste livro assumem.

Logo à partida, gostaria de saudar o texto introdutório que merecia a designação de ensaio, porque assume-se como um texto crítico, investindo no leitor desafios que animam e instigam uma reflexão viva sobre, por um lado, uma Europa enfraquecida e a debater-se com problemas internos graves sociais, políticos e culturais; e, por outro lado, sobre uma Europa a quem devemos perguntar: é possível pensar a descolonização sem trazer para o mesmo debate o projeto da modernidade, da narrativa da violência colonial e o nascimento de muitos e diversos hibridismos como o encontro entre culturas, povos, saberes, crenças e identidades? Acrescento, como pensar a descolonização? Manuela Ribeiro Sanches com ponderação responde a estes questionamentos concentrando a atenção do leitor nas seguintes observações: "há que considerar os processos de constituição discursiva desses espaços que nunca estiveram totalmente separados, caracterizando-se, antes, por constantes processos de hibridação – umas vezes tão celebrados, outras, depressa esquecidos, em nome de questões de identidade, ainda e sempre associadas a temas de segurança e vigilância, face a um terrorismo não só, mas também, mais imaginário do que real – que definem o mundo comum que habitamos" (Sanches, 2018:10). Este é o momento pilar e certo da discussão deste livro: discernir e verdadeiramente assumir a factualidade de que a Europa não pode ser mais umbilicalmente entendida sem a reflexão de si mesma com o imaginário e vivência de centro e de periferia, que ela mesma, através de todo o seu projeto de modernidade, de progresso e de civilização, criou e que a ultrapassou pela sua magnitude, pujança e descontrolo da sua realidade e da de outros povos. Esse outro rosto da modernidade é o retorno, a mescla visível e insofismável de que a Europa é também todos os outros mundos humanos e culturais que a fascinaram, atormentaram, que com contra ela lutaram as guerras de poder, que com ela debateram o imperialismo, o colonialismo, o menosprezo identitário e cultural, a recusa frontal dessa perversa e ominosa construção do 'Outro' como ser inferior, subdesenvolvido e castrado de civilização à luz de uma modernidade que, na verdade, só pode pensar-se e descolonizar-se desta maneira e: "dito de outro modo: descolonizar não tem de equivaler a dispensar a «Europa», desde que esta seja entendida em sentido lato, não reduzida a um mero espaço geográfico, o «Ocidente», mas incluindo outros contributos e histórias partilhadas" (Ibidem, 2018:11).

Mas, a outra metade da verdade também importa e exige a sua existência, é que os outros mundos humanos, sociais e culturais não podem rasurar da sua autoridade de memória e da narração da sua História a presença desta Europa, que constantemente dialoga, desafia e marca presença nesse pensamento crítico, reflexivo e histórico das nações que pugnaram pelas suas liberdades políticas, ontológicas e morais. Nesse sentido, este livro mostra muito concretamente ao longo dos seus vários textos que a descolonização não pode passar por ser um exame de consciência de uns com atribuição de privilégios e de dádivas para outros. No mesmo lugar da consciência humana, no trajeto histórico partilhado na construção das nações e sociedades contemporâneas um traço é indelével e incontornável: nada se fez por magia solitária; em torno da grande história do colonialismo, não obstante, os espaços amargos, duros, hediondos desta experiência, temos um dever de memória de pensar que a humanidade se fez e se alimentou de interações humanas, que necessitam no nosso presente de um pensamento aberto à inclusão de diferentes modos de leitura do passado e os legados desse passado; de um pensamento constante, vigilante, arguto e capaz de entender, como bem observa Manuela Ribeiro Sanches, que esta tarefa: "é a tarefa a prosseguir, sempre, porque sempre inacabada" (Sanches, 2018:19).

Por que ler Amílcar Cabral, Césaire e Du Bois no século XXI? Exatamente, porque o passado está sempre ao lado do nosso presente, interfere nos momentos vários das esferas das nossas sociedades contemporâneas. Acima de tudo, porque estes autores foram homens de um tempo de luta, de lutas perante a hegemonia do projeto da modernidade perante um aberrante trabalho de negação e de menosprezo dos seus semelhantes. Porque foram homens, embora em diferentes espaços geográficos e com agendas de trabalho ricamente diferentes mas complementares, que pelo seu compromisso com o seu tempo histórico, social e moral se debateram e recusaram a narrativa da subalternidade, da submissão, da prisão da dignidade humana do 'Outro' imposta por uma crença em que: "o colonialismo baseava-se no pressuposto de uma civilização superior que tinha por missão a sua disseminação para benefício dos colonizados" (Sarr, 2018: 43[1]).

Os textos que albergam os pensamentos de Amílcar Cabral, Césaire e de Du Bois são reflexões de uma profícua partilha, no sentido, em que permitem através da mão que escreve e do pensamento que dita, percorrer os caminhos e os fios da memória histórica, dos desafios encontrados, sentidos, ganhos e perdidos que homens e cidadãos da sua história como Amílcar Cabral, Césaire e Du Bois vivenciaram e expulsaram do seu âmago a partir dos seus textos, dos seus poemas, das suas reflexões e das suas práticas profissionais. Uma grande contribuição deste livro é, claramente, a reunião de autores cujas biografias e percursos de vida marcam o tom e o compromisso com o tema escolhido e que resultam, harmoniosamente, num dever de memória. Aprecio esta riqueza e diversidade cultural dos autores, a idiossincracia marcadamente geracional que traz para esta obra um entendimento salutar sobre a relevância da memória e, também, da pós-memória no que diz respeito a uma revisão, reinterpretação e reaproximação a um passado sempre constante e presente. Relembra-me, por exemplo, as observações de Simone Browne, em *Dark Matters* quando observa que: "the historical, the present, and the historical present – can help social theorists understand our contemporary conditions (...)" (Browne, 2015: 8[2]).

Apenas uma observação ao livro que não é uma crítica, mas antes um detalhe que poderia ter sido acautelado. Os textos não têm o mesmo espaço em termos de ocupação de páginas e, nesse sentido, teria sido mais graciosa uma aritmética igual ou aproximada no que toca a este equilíbrio textual.

Retomo as palavras iniciais. Este é um livro onde se sente a academia e o pensamento académico de mãos dadas com o tempo presente do quotidiano de todos aqueles que direta ou indiretamente viveram o passado colonial e que sentem e experienciam os legados desse passado no tempo da era pós-colonial. Mas, o pós não pode ser só rótulo de revisão e de releitura, tem de ser sinónimo de compromisso cívico e moralmente comprometido com um olhar atento e saudá-vel da História mesclada e partilhada entre 'Nós'|Eles e 'Eles'|Nós. *Descolonizações* manifesta e celebra esta vida e esta presença da academia na rua. Uma academia fora das torres da elite intelectual; uma academia que não escreve em nota de rodapé a sua responsabilidade académica que é civismo e respeito.

NOTAS

1. Sarr, Felwine (2018), "Repensar a economia lendo Césaire". In Sanches, Manuel Ribeiro (org.), *Descolonizações. Reler Amílcar Cabral, Césaire e Du Bois no Séc.XXI*. Lisboa: Edições 70, pp. 37-50.

2. Browne, Simone (2015). *Dark Matters. On the Surveillance of Blackness*. Durham: Duke University Press.

SHEILA KHAN é investigadora de pós-doutoramento no projeto EXCHANGE (2015-2020), financiado pelo European Research Council (Grant agreement 648608) e baseada no Centro de Estudos de Comunicação e Sociedade, Universidade do Minho.

E.F. Souza, I.S. Silva, J.B. Miranda, e C.R. Melo (orgs.)
História e Cultura Afrodescendente.
Teresina: FUESPI, 2018. (Coleção África Brasil, v. 8).

O ÁFRICA BRASIL é um encontro acadêmico bienal organizado pelo Núcleo de Estudos e Pesquisas Afro (NEPA), da Universidade Estadual do Piauí (UESPI), no âmbito dos estudos interdisciplinares das áreas de Literatura, Cultura e História e que, após a realização da sua quinta edição, consolida-se como um dos maiores eventos acadêmicos sobre as produções simbólicas de autorias afro-brasileiras, africanas e indígenas. O evento reúne especialistas nacionais e internacionais de reconhecida atuação acadêmica e produção cultural sobre as temáticas centrais de cada edição.

Homônima ao encontro, a Coleção África Brasil (Editada pela FUESPI) cumpre a relevante função de publicar o conjunto das ideias mais expressivas debatidas durante os eventos, realizados há uma década no Piauí, região nordeste do Brasil. Foi a partir dos contributos do AFRICA BRASIL V, realizado em 2017, sob o tema "Narrativas e Cidadania", que os organizadores fizeram os volumes 8 e 9 da coleção chegarem ao público, em 2018. Não é um livro didático, mas figura como uma oportuna alternativa para contornar a escassez de material sobre o tema e que tem impedido educadores de todo o país de cumprirem integralmente a Lei 10639/03, que inclui no currículo oficial da rede de ensino brasileira, a obrigatoriedade da temática "História e Cultura Afro-brasileira".

O volume 8 da coleção, sob o título *História e Cultura Afrodescendente* é uma contribuição literalmente de peso para ajudar a reverter essa lacuna. As suas mais de 700 páginas, apresentam em 7 capítulos, 47 textos, produzidos por 71 autores. Números eloquentes na demonstração do engajamento da academia com um tema que está no centro do debate sobre as possibilidades de avanço político na construção de novas narrativas sobre as populações afrodescendentes, no Brasil ou em outros territórios. Isto porque, o material fornece subsídios para que outras comunidades de falantes de língua Portuguesa possam se beneficiar, em suas práticas cotidianas, de um percurso já trilhado, dando prosseguimento a uma trajetória ainda por se consolidar na maior parte das realidades institucionais.

Dados do Censo de 2010[1], apontam que 54% da população brasileira se auto-declara não-branca, sendo que de cada 10 brasileiros, 3 são mulheres negras. Já a Pesquisa Nacional por Amostra de Domicílios (Pnad) de 2016[2], aponta que 67% dos negros no Brasil estão incluídos na parcela dos que recebem até 1,5 de salário mínimo, quando entre os brancos, o índice fica em 45%. A mesma pesquisa mostra que a taxa de analfabetismo entre a população não branca é de 10% contra 4,2% entre os brancos e que no trabalho infantil 64% das crianças são pretas ou pardas contra 35% brancas. No desemprego são 15% os não brancos e 9,5% os brancos e entre os desalentados, aqueles que estão sem emprego há mais de 24 meses, dois terços são não brancos contra um terço de brancos.

Esses números se invertem quando se trata de representatividade nas artes, por exemplo. Só 10% dos livros brasileiros publicados entre 1965 e 2014 foram escritos por autores negros, afirma pesquisa[3] coordenada pela professora Regina Dalcastagnè, da Universidade de Brasília (UnB), que também analisou os personagens retratados pela literatura nacional: 60% dos protagonistas são homens e 80% deles, brancos. E, entre 1990 e 2004, o top cinco de ocupações dos personagens negros era: bandido, empregado doméstico, escravo, profissional do sexo e dona de casa[4].

Já a pesquisa "A Cara do Cinema Nacional", da Universidade Estadual do Rio de Janeiro, revelou que homens negros são só 2% dos diretores de filmes nacionais, sendo que 84% são homens brancos. Atrás das câmeras, não foi registrada nenhuma mulher negra. O fosso racial permanece entre os roteiristas: só 4% são negros. O levantamento da Universidade Estadual do Rio de Janeiro (UERJ) considerou as produções brasileiras que alcançaram as maiores bilheterias entre 2002 e 2014. Dentre os filmes analisados, 31% tinham no elenco atores negros, quase sempre interpretando papeis associados à pobreza e criminalidade[5]. E apesar da população não branca ser maioria no Brasil, 80% do elenco dessas produções era de pessoas brancas.

Esses números são uma demonstração eloquente de que a história e a cultura afrodescendentes estão sendo escritas em registros desfavoráveis a uma população que é a maioria no país. Quando se trata de direitos e do bem estar social as taxas de não incidência entre os não brancos são altíssimas e quando se trata de representatividade nas artes são escassas. Uma marca histórica difícil de ser superada pelo último país do mundo a abolir a escravidão, e que o volume *História e Cultura Afrodescendente* tenta, de alguma forma, fazer frente, não apenas problematizando temas que nos fizeram chegar a esse alarmante quadro de desigualdades, mas igualmente apontando algumas possibilidades de contestação e resistência a esse estado de coisas. O livro está estruturado em sete capítulos, onde cada um deles cobre um conjunto de temas relacionados entre si. Em geral, o resultado de pesquisas, por meio das quais o leitor pode ir transitando nos diversos temas, e a partir de várias perspectivas, complementares ou não, de forma que a leitura torna-se interessante, justamente pelas mudanças de prismas em que um mesmo tema pode ser enfocado. São muitas as territorialidades e filiações disciplinares cobertas em cada capítulo.

Especificamente no plano dos conteúdos, o capítulo 1, "O Protagonismo Indígena: História, literatura e cultura brasileira", trata da memória como resistência a uma história incompleta, neste caso, a dos indígenas do território brasileiro; ainda no que diz respeito a memória de uma luta, o capítulo 2, "Territórios Quilombolas: Memória e resistência", reúne um conjunto de textos que exemplifica as tensões do aspecto normativo no reconhecimento de direitos dos quilombolas. As desigualdades como fundamento e a construção da identidade afro-brasileira são a essência dos textos do capítulo 3, "Escravidão no Brasil: Pós-Abolição, trabalho, identidade negra, mulher e resistência". A seção que reúne o maior número de trabalhos é o capítulo 4, "Cultura Afro-Brasileira e Educação: Lei 10.639/2003, capoeira, reggae, relações étnico-raciais e africanismos na Língua Portuguesa", em que a afrodescendência e identidade negra na cultura e na educação brasileiras são referenciados. A tônica do capítulo é a busca por epistemologias afrodescendentes. O capítulo 5, "Imagem do Negro: Charges, política, crônica jornalística e estereótipo racial", cobre as representações do corpo negro na cultura, enquanto o capítulo 6, "Filosofia Africana", reúne quatro textos onde a filosofia africana e afro-brasileira são referenciadas, uma clara demonstração de que algumas disciplinas ainda são essencialmente eurocentradas e que existe todo um *corpus* teórico negligenciado pela academia. O último capítulo, "Religiões De Matriz Africana", apresenta as religiões de matriz africana como um espaço ainda em disputa no reconhecimento do patrimônio cultural brasileiro.

Os organizadores da coletânea em momento nenhum apresentam um esforço de caracterização de quem seria, especificamente, os afrodescendentes cuja história e cultura são apresentadas no volume. Sabe-se que o termo afrodescendente é um conceito polissêmico e que vem sendo apropriado de forma diferente, em diferentes contextos históricos. "Negro" foi o termo que primeiro reuniu o conjunto de estudos dedicados a uma parcela da população mundial comumente associada aos efeitos da escravatura e do colonialismo. É nas Américas, e já no século XX que o prefixo *afro* surge, marcando pela primeira vez a componente territorial da negritude, e associando o conceito a outros fenômenos, tais como cultura e identidade. Afrodescendência sugere, desse modo, uma identidade "entre" referências e operacionalizá-la tem sido um desafio na contemporaneidade.

As identidades são construídas dentro e não fora do discurso, de modo que é necessário compreendê-las como produzidas em locais históricos e institucionais específicos. Além disso, elas emergem no interior do jogo de modalidades específicas de poder, de modo que tão relevante quanto as temáticas apresentadas no volume é revelar as abordagens de uma identidade em disputa, esforço que os organizadores não apresentam. A Organização das Nações Unidas definiu o período compreendido entre 2015 a 2024 como a década dos Afrodescendentes, uma oportunidade ímpar para que acadêmicos e estudiosos do tema apresentem as suas visões sobre os processos de constituição de uma identidade multidimensional. Um debate que o volume acaba por não apresentar e que contudo não diminui o mérito e a qualidade das análises ali reunidas.

Por fim, registramos que, além dos conteúdos em si de cada temática focalizada nos capítulos, o e-book apresenta uma excelente coletânea de investigações, de modo que podem ser observadas as trajetórias e os métodos, bem como os resultados alcançados a partir de cada percurso. Dessa forma, figura como uma interessante fonte de referências para pesquisadores, que podem encontrar nele uma fonte de inspiração para a construção de seus próprios itinerários. É assim, uma relevante contribuição para a academia, de um modo mais amplo.

NOTES

1. Disponível em: https://agenciadenoticias.ibge.gov.br/agencia-noticias/2012-agencia -de-noticias/noticias/21206-ibge-mostra-as-cores-da-desigualdade, acessado em 20/3/2019.

2. Disponível em: https://www.cartacapital.com.br/sociedade/seis-estatisticas-que- -mostram-o-abismo-racial-no-brasil/, acessado em 20/03/2019.

3. Disponível em: https://revistacult.uol.com.br/home/quem-e-e-sobre-o-que-escreve- -o-autor-brasileiro/, acessado em 19/03/2019.

4. Disponível em: https://brasil.elpais.com/brasil/2018/05/21/cultura/1526921273_678 732.html, acessado em 20/03/2019.

5. Disponível em: http://gemaa.iesp.uerj.br/infografico/infografico1/, acessado em 21/03/2019.

SIMONE AMORIM é Doutora em Políticas Públicas pela UERJ – Universidade do Estado do Rio de Janeiro, Investigadora de Pós-doutorado no CEsA – Centro de Estudos sobre África, Ásia e América Latina, da Universidade de Lisboa, onde integra a equipe de pesquisadores do *Projeto AFRO-PORT Afrodescendência em Portugal* (PTDC/SOC-ANT/30651/2017).

A urgência de ler Djamila Ribeiro

Djamila Ribeiro
Quem tem medo do feminismo negro?
São Paulo: Companhia das Letras, 2018.

Em "Sexismo e racismo na cultura brasileira", texto apresentado em 1980 no âmbito do Grupo de Trabalho "Temas e Problemas da População Negra no Brasil" e publicado quatro anos mais tarde, a intelectual e ativista Lélia Gonzalez afirma: "para nós o racismo se constitui como a sintomática que caracteriza a neurose cultural brasileira. Nesse sentido, veremos que sua articulação com o sexismo produz efeitos violentos sobre a mulher negra em particular" (1984, 224). Ao investigar tal neurose cultural, a autora coloca a experiência da escravidão no cerne do debate, e argumenta com ênfase a persistência no Brasil dos paradigmas sobre os quais assentou a exploração escravista dos corpos. À luz dessas persistências, a autora interroga o papel da mulher negra e a ininterrupta reificação do seu corpo numa sociedade cujo imaginário coletivo continua a ser pensado a partir do mito da democracia racial.

A análise de Lélia Gonzalez sobre a condição das mulheres negras no Brasil, além de considerar a escravidão como momento fulcral para compreender relações raciais e de gênero, aponta para a necessidade de pensar tais questões numa perspetiva interseccional, que articule diferentes formas de subordinação, quais, entre outras, o racismo, o sexismo e o patriarcalismo. Gênero, raça e classe passariam então a ser indissociáveis, "a interseccionalidade trataria da forma como ações e políticas específicas geram opressões que fluem ao longo de tais eixos, confluindo e, nessas confluências constituiriam aspectos ativos do desempoderamento" (Piscitelli, 267).

A partir dessa perspetiva interseccional desdobram-se as reflexões de Djamila Ribeiro em *Quem tem medo do feminismo negro?*, coletânea que reúne artigos escritos ao longo de dois anos, de 2014 a 2016, pela intelectual e ativista, então colunista da revista *Carta Capital*. O livro, publicado em 2018 pela Companhia das Letras, é composto por trinta e três artigos nos quais a autora enfrenta assuntos contingentes e questões do cotidiano a partir da perspetiva do feminismo negro, ou seja, de um feminismo que articule questões de gênero, raça e classe:

Ao pensar o debate de raça, classe e gênero de modo indissociável, as feministas negras estão afirmando que não é possível lutar contra uma opressão e alimentar outra, porque a mesma estrutura seria reforçada. Quando discutimos identidades, estamos dizendo que o poder deslegitima umas em detrimento de outras. O debate, portanto, não é meramente identitário, mas envolve pensar como algumas identidades são aviltadas e ressignificar o conceito de humanidade, posto que pessoas negras em geral e mulheres negras especificamente não são tratadas como humanas. (27)

Como no texto de Lélia Gonzalez aqui mencionado, a persistência na contemporaneidade brasileira das dinâmicas de reificação do corpo de mulheres negras, que reproduzem práticas que se impuseram durante a exploração escravista, está no centro do debate e é justamente a partir dessa perspetiva de continuidade que Djamila Ribeiro enfrenta as questões do cotidiano.

Quem tem medo do feminismo negro? abre-se com uma longa introdução-depoimento através da qual a autora relata a sua experiência pessoal no interior de uma sociedade racista e sexista, e a sua aproximação - primeiro enquanto leitora engajada, depois como acadêmica - aos textos de autoras negras de destaque no panorama cultural brasileiro. Nessa introdução, chamada "A máscara do silêncio", a autora relata as tantas violências microfísicas que acompanharam o seu percurso enquanto mulher negra desde a infância, na escola, até à idade adulta, no mundo do trabalho. Às piadas racistas dos colegas, envolvendo a cor de pele e os cabelos, acrescenta-se o desconforto criado pela ausência, em sala de aula, de qualquer protagonismo negro na construção do Brasil, pois a visão dominante, moldada pelos padrões eurocêntricos, retirava do africano e do afrodescendente escravizados qualquer dignidade humana: não tinham um passado na África, não tinham tradições e culturas, não participaram da construção cultural de um país cujas coordenadas identitárias continuam a ser pensadas a partir da perspetiva do colonizador. Ao afirmar que "a vontade de ser aceite nesse mundo de padrões eurocêntricos é tanta que você literalmente se machuca para não ser a neguinha do cabelo duro que ninguém quer" (14) Djamila Ribeiro de fato mostra o funcionamento da máquina do poder – e do racismo intrínseco nela – como sendo uma rede complexa que não se resume apenas à pura repressão, à atuação negativa, mas que se articula com toda uma série de instâncias "positivas", que visam produzir discursos e afetos. Como afirma Michel Foucault em *Microfísica do poder*, "o poder [...] não pesa só como uma força que diz não, mas que de fato ele permeia, produz coisas, induz ao prazer, forma saber, produz discurso. Deve-se considerá-lo como uma rede produtiva que atravessa todo o corpo social" (2018: 45).

Nesse sentido, conhecer outras perspetivas através das leituras de autoras negras representa um momento fulcral na formação da jovem ativista:

Enquanto cuidava do meu pai no hospital, que adoeceu logo depois da minha mãe, conheci a Casa de Cultura da Mulher Negra. Foi lá que tive a primeira oportunidade de um trabalho que valorizava minha formação, oferecida por mulheres negras feministas de fato. Redescobri minha força. Trabalhei quase quatro anos na biblioteca da Casa de Cultura, onde entrei em contato com bell hooks, Carolina Maria de Jesus, Lima Barreto, Sueli Carneiro, Alice Walker, Toni Morrison. Fui aprendendo a falar por outras vozes, a me enxergar através de outras perspetivas. (Ribeiro, 2018, 17)

A partir dessas leituras, retomando uma discussão já presente no seu primeiro livro, *O que é lugar de fala?*, publicado em 2017 pelo Grupo Editorial Letramento, no âmbito da coleção Feminismos Plurais, Djamila Ribeiro volta a sublinhar a necessidade de pensar outras epistemologias para além do modelo único ocidental. Em *O que é lugar de fala?*, tendo como amparo teórico as reflexões de Lélia Gonzalez (1984), a autora traz como exemplo, entre outros, a subalternização sofridas pelos saberes provenientes de religiões de matriz africana, e a urgência de "desestabilizar e transcender a autorização discursiva branca, masculina cis[-gênero] e heteronormativa" (28).

Em *Quem tem medo do feminismo negro?*, por sua vez, Ribeiro retoma tal urgência de descolonizar o pensamento, ao mesmo tempo em que evidencia a relevância operacional do feminismo negro nesse processo:

foi o feminismo negro que me ensinou a reconhecer diferentes saberes, a refutar uma epistemologia mestre, que pretende dar conta de todas as outras. [...] Valorizar o saber das ialorixás e dos babalorixás, das parteiras, dos povos originários é reconhecer outras cosmogonias e geografias da razão. Devemos pensar uma reconfiguração do mundo a partir de outros olhares, questionar o que foi criado a partir de uma linguagem eurocêntrica. (22)

Os trinta e três artigos, todos breves e incisivos, abordam tais questões a partir de acontecimentos do cotidiano. Desta forma, ao discutir um certo tipo de humor na mídia brasileira e em determinadas figuras políticas, ou as postagens nas redes sociais de certas celebridades, a autora aponta para o racismo intrínseco à sociedade brasileira, constituindo-se como uma voz dissidente perante dinâmicas que são, de fato, naturalizadas e cuja violência subjacente acaba sendo ignorada.

Ao lado dessas intervenções pontuais sobre assuntos do cotidiano, em *Quem tem medo do feminismo negro?* a autora aborda também temáticas de atualidade política, como o debate em torno das cotas raciais, no artigo "Ser contra as cotas raciais é concordar com a perpetuação do racismo"(72-76), ou como a discussão sobre o aborto e a chamada "cultura do estupro", que ocupa os textos "Quem se responsabiliza pelo abandono da mãe?" (85-88), "E se tua mãe tivesse te abortado?"(95-98), "O que a miscigenação tem a ver com a cultura do estupro?"(116-119).

Um último grande núcleo de artigos solicita, por sua vez, uma reflexão acerca do próprio feminismo e da luta antirracista. São artigos nos quais a autora percorre de forma singela as etapas que marcaram a formação daquilo que Ribeiro chama de "feminismo acadêmico" e de "feminismo negro", e em que se levantam questões sobre a própria luta contra o racismo. Dentro desse núcleo, destaca-se a entrevista com a teórica e artista portuguesa Grada Kilomba (108-113), no Brasil em 2016 a convite do Instituto Goethe, que tem como temática justamente a descolonização do pensamento.

Em conjunto, os textos publicados na coletânea não abordam os assuntos apresentados de forma acadêmica, deixando aparecer em alguns casos os limites de uma escrita pensada para ter uma ampla e imediata divulgação. No entanto, tais artigos respondem perfeitamente às exigências de uma comunicação direta, engajada, movida pela urgência de trazer para o cotidiano uma discussão que se impõe como necessária perante a atual conjuntura política no Brasil. Publicado em 2018, ano em que as eleições presidenciais determinaram relevantes retrocessos na área dos direitos humanos, ler Djamila Ribeiro torna-se uma tarefa fundamental pois o livro ajuda a detectar e a enfrentar as violências microfísicas e capilares que também participam daquilo que Abdias do Nascimento (2017) chamou de "genocídio do negro brasileiro".

OBRAS CITADAS

Foucault, Michel. *Microfísica do poder*. Paz & Terra, 2018.

Gonzalez, Léila. "Racismo e sexismo na cultura brasileira". *Revista Ciências sociais hoje*, 1984, pp. 223-244.

Nascimento, Abdias. *O genocídio do negro brasileiro: processo de um racismo mascarado*. São Paulo: Editora Perspectiva, 2017.

Piscitelli, Adriana. "Interseccionalidades, categorias de articulação e experiências de migrantes brasileiras". *Sociedade e cultura*, v.11, n.2, jul/dez 2008, pp. 263-274.

Ribeiro, Djamila. *O que é lugar de fala?*. Belo Horizonte: Grupo Editorial Letramento, 2017.

Ribeiro, Djamila. *Quem tem medo do feminismo negro?*. São Paulo: Companhia das Letras, 2018.

LUCA FAZZINI é doutorando em Literatura Cultura e Contemporaneidade na Pontifícia Universidade Católica do Rio de Janeiro (PUC-Rio), onde desenvolve uma pesquisa sobre as persistências dos paradigmas coloniais e escravistas na contemporaneidade urbana, a partir de uma perspetiva literária e cinematográfica.